THE
COMPLETE
COOK

THE AUSTRALIAN
Women's Weekly

THE
COMPLETE
COOK

The new kitchen classic for today's cook

Contents

We are fortunate to have wonderful produce available to us in this country. The size and geography of the country make it possible to grow a wide variety of food, ranging from tropical to cool climate with everything in between. Locally-grown food is plentiful and comparatively inexpensive when it's in season — the best time to buy it. We also have access to good quality imported produce which means we can buy most foods at almost any time, those that would normally be out of season here.

We have enthusiastically embraced the cooking techniques and fabulous flavours of Asian food over the last few decades, what was once an exotic — code for "hard to get" — ingredient, is now mainstream and available in supermarkets all over the country. We've come a long way in a short time.

This is a reference book showcasing the fresh ingredients that are available here. Everything is photographed so that you can see and learn about anything that might be new or unfamiliar to you. There is much information about each ingredient, its availability, seasonality, how to prepare, cook and serve it, storage tips and, of course many Triple Tested® recipes from our famous Australian Women's Weekly Test Kitchen, to help you make the most of our varied and abundant produce.

Pamela Clark

Pamela Clark
Director
The Australian Women's Weekly Test Kitchen

Apples

Apples are full of possibilities. They are the perfect healthy snack for any time of day; add bread and cheese for the best of all lunches to carry in your pocket. At breakfast or brunch, freshly grated apple is the secret of sensational muesli, sautéed apple slices are great companions to bacon or sausage and chopped apple adds flavour and good nutrition to pancakes and muffins.

1 PINK LADY
2 GOLDEN DELICIOUS
3 RED DELICIOUS
4 GRANNY SMITH
5 ROYAL GALA
6 FUJI
7 BRAEBURN

Apple adds a fresh note to spicy soups such as lentil or curried parsnip and crisp sweetness to a salad. In the form of roasted or sautéed pieces or a tangy sauce, it is the perfect foil to rich meats such as pork or duck. Apple jelly is a marvellous old-fashioned treat on bread, toast, scones or pancakes. Finely chopped apple with lemon juice, salt and perhaps a touch of chilli is an excellent sambal to serve with a curry. And all that is before we consider the glorious cavalcade of apple cakes, dumplings, sponges, fools, strudels, charlottes and that most beloved of all desserts, apple pie.

PREPARATION Cut apple gradually goes brown so if you have to peel or cut it ahead of using, brush with lemon juice to destroy the enzyme that causes darkening, or keep it in water with a little lemon juice.

If you want apples to break up in cooking, cook with a little water but no sugar until the end of cooking. If you want the pieces to keep their shape, add sugar at the beginning of cooking — it draws moisture from the fruit so that the pieces hold together. Always cook apples with the minimum of water as they release a lot of their high water content when heated.

CHOOSING Although the apple harvest starts as summer turns toward autumn and ends around mid-winter, today we expect to find good "fresh" apples at the greengrocer all year round. The apple industry meets this demand by growing mainly varieties that will keep well in cool storage, or more correctly in Controlled Atmosphere storage, a precisely controlled condition that puts the fruit "to sleep", so that, theoretically, it emerges as fresh as it went in — though it is obvious to consumers that some out-of-season apples have come through better than others.

Many apples are sprayed with a high-gloss wax before going on sale. This is done simply to make them look good. The wax, which is the same as that used to coat jellybeans, is quite harmless to eat. In an unwaxed apple, a softly gleaming skin is a sign of good condition.

All apples are good to eat raw — the choice depends on your taste, from bramleys and granny smiths at the tart end of the scale, through pink ladies and jonathons with their excellent balance of acidity and sweetness, to red and golden delicious which are aromatic, sweet and juicy but, to some apple-fanciers, a bit insipid because they lack sharpness. If you are buying apples for cooking, select the right type for your purpose: low-sugar apples such as bramley and granny smith will cook to a puree, while higher-sugar varieties will keep their shape better.

7

The best-looking and best-tasting apple sauce is made by cooking the apples, skin, core and all, then sieving. Simply chop the whole apples, cook in a covered saucepan with a little water (about ½ cup for 4 apples) until soft. Rub cooked apple through a sieve then stir in sugar and lemon juice to taste. Add a hint of spice, if you wish, by grating a little nutmeg over the apples or adding a whole clove before cooking.

If your cooking often involves sieving mixtures (as in apple sauce above and the apricot glaze on page 14), a mouli is a good investment. This classic tool has a hand-turned metal plate that forces food quickly and easily through a pierced base. Changeable base plates with different-size holes allow you to sieve coarsely or finely. A mouli is not cheap, but it's worth the price for a lifetime of fast, efficient pureeing.

Since apples do not grow true from seed, new kinds appear constantly. Most will remain nameless and forgotten, but occasionally an "accidental" seedling that appears in an orchard, or one of the thousands raised in breeding programs, will be chosen as a champion. Identical descendants can then be produced by grafting. The following are some of the best known:

PINK LADY One of the great successes of the newer varieties. A late-season apple, with dense, fine, crisp flesh and excellent sweet/tart flavour.

GOLDEN DELICIOUS Mid-to-late season, aromatic, often thought insipid for eating but performs well in cooking (when lemon juice can be added for tartness). Its slices hold their shape well for decorative tarts.

RED DELICIOUS Mid-to-late season, sweet and juicy with the aromatic quality of the delicious family. An immensely popular eating apple though a little flat in flavour for some tastes.

GRANNY SMITH An old, late-season Australian apple now popular world-wide. Excellent for cooking when you want a puree, as for apple sauce. Good eating, with tart, crisp flesh, when fresh, but can be disappointing as an eating apple out of season.

ROYAL GALA An early-season apple developed in New Zealand, with dense, juicy, sweet flesh. Excellent for eating raw and makes good baked or poached apples, but not good for apple puree.

FUJI A juicy, late-season Japanese variety that has become popular internationally. Very dense and juicy, with a distinctive flavour; cooks well.

BRAEBURN A New Zealand variety now grown around the world. A crisp, juicy, early-season dessert apple with outstanding "old-fashioned" apple flavour. At its best when freshly picked but also stores well.

JONATHAN An old early-season variety with outstanding sweet and tangy flavour when eaten fresh and good for cooking and eating. It does not come well through lengthy storage so is in danger of being phased out of production.

BRAMLEY A mid-to-late season heritage English apple with firm, very acid flesh. Prized for cooking when you want the apple to "fluff up".

COX'S ORANGE PIPPIN An old English early-season apple with dense, sharp-sweet flesh, traditionally one of the best eating varieties and also good for cooking, though some apple fanciers think that some of the character has been bred out of them in recent years. Grown mainly in Tasmania, they can be hard to find in shops on the mainland.

STORING
Don't keep apples in the fruit bowl: they will hold their texture and flavour much better if kept in the refrigerator crisper. Don't wash them until you are ready to use them. To store a large quantity of apples, place them, not touching each other, in a cool, dark place where plenty of air can circulate, for example on slatted shelves or in pull-out wire baskets.

❧ **OTHER RECIPES USING APPLES**
Apple cranberry pie, p410
Cranberry and apple fruit mince, p194
Cucumber, celery and apple juice, p146
Ginger, tomato and apple punch, p223
Pork cutlets with fennel apple relish, p443
Roast pork rack with apple sage sauce, p443
Shaved fennel and apple salad, p176
Spiced fig and apple jam, p466
Tamarillo apple chutney, p594
Waldorf salad, p98

Pork with celeriac and apple

PREP + COOK TIME 30 MINUTES **SERVES** 4

50g butter

1 tablespoon olive oil

750g pork fillets

1 small celeriac (550g), peeled, halved, cut into thin wedges

1 small white onion (100g), sliced thinly

2 large red apples (400g), quartered, cored, sliced thinly

1 teaspoon whole yellow mustard seeds

½ cup (125ml) chicken stock

1 tablespoon whole fresh sage leaves

1 Heat half the butter and 2 teaspoons of the oil in large frying pan; cook pork until browned all over. Add celeriac; cook, covered, 10 minutes, turning occasionally, or until celeriac is tender.

2 Meanwhile, heat the remaining butter and oil in medium frying pan; cook onion, apple and mustard seeds, stirring, until onion is soft. Add the stock; cook, uncovered, stirring, for 3 minutes or until the apple is just tender. Remove from heat; stir in sage leaves.

3 Slice the pork thickly and serve with the celeriac and apple mixture.

NUTRITIONAL COUNT PER SERVING 4.4g total fat (2g saturated fat); 393kJ (94 cal); 3.8g carbohydrate; 9.4g protein; 1.2g fibre

---

Baked apples with butterscotch sauce

PREP + COOK TIME 1 HOUR 10 MINUTES **SERVES** 6

6 medium apples (900g)

50g butter, cut into 12 cubes

¼ cup (55g) brown sugar

⅓ cup (40g) finely chopped pecans

1 tablespoon brown sugar, extra

⅓ cup (80ml) cream

1 Preheat oven to 180°C/160°C fan-forced.

2 Core unpeeled apples about three-quarters of the way down from stem end, making hole 4cm in diameter. Use small sharp knife to score around centre of each apple. Stand apples upright in small ovenproof dish.

3 Place one cube of butter and a teaspoon of brown sugar in cavity of each apple; pack nuts firmly into apple cavity. Divide remaining butter and sugar among apples; sprinkle extra sugar around apples.

4 Bake apples 45 minutes. Stir cream into dish; bake about 10 minutes. Transfer apples to serving bowls. Whisk cream in dish briefly; drizzle over apples.

NUTRITIONAL COUNT PER SERVING 17.5g total fat (8.6g saturated fat); 1145kJ (274 cal); 26.7g carbohydrate; 1.3g protein; 3g fibre

The perfect recipe for entertaining when time is limited but you want to serve something special. Garnish with crisp fried sage leaves: heat 2cm olive oil in a frying pan on medium heat until it shimmers. Add a dozen or so perfectly dry sage leaves in batches, fry about 20 seconds, scoop out with a slotted spoon and drain on absorbent paper.

For information on celeriac, see Celeriac, page 96; and for pork, see Pork, pages 440 & 441.

BAKED APPLES WITH BUTTERSCOTCH SAUCE

We used golden delicious apples for this recipe; they are a crisp, almost citrus-yellow apple that keeps well, has excellent flavour and is perhaps the best of all cooking apples. Green-skinned granny smiths, another good cooking apple, can be substituted.

Caramelised apple tea cakes

PREP + COOK TIME 55 MINUTES **MAKES** 12

If it suits you, the apple slices and their caramel sauce can be made and added to the greased muffin pans up to 2 or 3 hours ahead of adding the tea-cake mixture and baking.

125g butter, softened

1 teaspoon vanilla extract

⅔ cup (150g) caster sugar

2 eggs

1 ¼ cups (185g) self-raising flour

½ cup (75g) plain flour

1 teaspoon mixed spice

½ teaspoon ground cinnamon

1 cup (250ml) buttermilk

1 large apple (200g), peeled, grated coarsely

CARAMELISED APPLES

2 small apples (260g)

75g butter

⅓ cup (75g) firmly packed brown sugar

1 Make caramelised apples.

2 Preheat oven to 180°C/160°C fan-forced. Grease two 6-hole (¾-cup/180ml) texas muffin pans with a little butter.

3 Place one slice caramelised apple in each pan hole; spoon caramel sauce over apple.

4 Beat butter, extract and sugar in small bowl with electric mixer until light and fluffy. Beat in eggs, one at a time. Transfer to large bowl; stir in sifted dry ingredients and buttermilk, in two batches. Stir in apple. Divide mixture between pan holes.

5 Bake cakes about 30 minutes. Stand cakes 5 minutes before turning, top-side up, onto wire rack. Serve cakes warm.

CARAMELISED APPLES Slice each unpeeled apple into six 1cm-thick slices. Stir butter and sugar in large frying pan over low heat until sugar dissolves. Add apple slices to caramel sauce; cook, turning occasionally, about 3 minutes or until browned lightly.

NUTRITIONAL COUNT PER CAKE 10.1g total fat (6.2g saturated fat); 974kJ (233 cal); 30.5g carbohydrate; 4.3g protein; 1.1g fibre

Apple pie slice

PREP + COOK TIME 45 MINUTES (PLUS REFRIGERATION TIME) **SERVES** 8

The pastry will be light golden-brown when cooked. It will feel soft in the oven, but will become firm as it cools. Serve warm slice with ice-cream or whipped cream; for extra spice, stir ground cinnamon or nutmeg through either of these.

For more information on pastry, see Pastry, pages 404–406.

1 cup (150g) self-raising flour

½ cup (75g) plain flour

80g cold butter, chopped coarsely

¼ cup (55g) caster sugar

1 egg, beaten lightly

¼ cup (60ml) milk, approximately

1 tablespoon milk, extra

1 tablespoon caster sugar, extra

APPLE FILLING

6 medium apples (900g), peeled, cored, cut into 1cm pieces

¼ cup (55g) caster sugar

¼ cup (60ml) water

¾ cup (120g) sultanas

1 teaspoon mixed spice

2 teaspoons finely grated lemon rind

1 CARAMELISED APPLE TEA CAKES
2 APPLE PIE SLICE

1 Make apple filling.

2 Grease 20cm x 30cm lamington pan; line base with baking paper, extending paper 5cm over long sides.

3 Sift flours into medium bowl, rub in butter. Stir in sugar, egg and enough milk to make a firm dough. Knead on floured surface until smooth. Cover; refrigerate 30 minutes.

4 Preheat oven to 200°C/180°C fan-forced.

5 Divide dough in half. Roll one half large enough to cover base of pan; press firmly into pan. Spread apple filling over dough. Roll remaining dough large enough to cover filling and place over the top. Brush with extra milk; sprinkle with extra sugar.

6 Bake slice about 25 minutes. Stand slice in pan 5 minutes.

APPLE FILLING Cook apple, sugar and the water in large saucepan, uncovered, stirring occasionally, about 10 minutes or until apple softens. Remove from heat; stir in sultanas, spice and rind. Cool.

NUTRITIONAL COUNT PER SERVING 9.7g total fat (5.9g saturated fat); 1463kJ (350 cal); 58.6g carbohydrate; 4.8g protein; 3.4g fibre

Apricots

A perfect tree-ripened apricot, luscious, sweet and aromatic, is food for the gods. Unfortunately, it is difficult to buy such a fruit at the greengrocer as most commercially grown apricots are picked before they are fully ripe, because the ripe fruit is too fragile and perishable to stand up to the handling necessary to get it to market.

To give a professional gloss to fruit tarts or the top of a cake, or to moisture-proof a cooked or uncooked tart shell before adding a moist filling, brush them with apricot glaze, made by boiling 1 cup of apricot jam with ¼ cup of water, stirring often, until the mixture is clear, then rubbing through a sieve. The glaze should just drop from a spoon when hot — adjust the consistency, if necessary, by boiling it down or adding a little boiling water. Keep it in a lidded plastic container and heat it in the microwave before using.

You can ripen apricots by standing them at room temperature, speeding up the process, if you wish, by enclosing them in a paper bag; they will soften and may colour up but they will never have the flavour of tree-ripened fruit. Their season is short, peaking in midsummer when there is the best chance of finding tree-ripened specimens.

If, in spite of careful selection and ripening, they turn out to be disappointing in flavour or woolly in texture, all is not lost. Even mediocre apricots are transformed into something quite delicious when cooked; their sharp-sweet flavour is particularly accommodating and will marry beautifully with pork, chicken, veal, lamb, duck and turkey, as well as other fruits, nuts and spices. Apricots have starred for centuries in Middle Eastern meat cookery and in the finest creations of European pastry chefs.

Aside from the fresh fruit, dried apricots are always available and are one of the best of dried fruits, delicious as a snack, stewed to serve with rice pudding or on breakfast cereal, or for ice-cream, sauces, mousses and jam.

PREPARATION Apricots do not need skinning, but are usually split and the stones removed before cooking. Dried apricots may be soaked before cooking but this is not necessary if they are to be cooked in a liquid.

CHOOSING Choose undamaged, well coloured fruit — though neither colour nor softness are reliable indicators of well-flavoured apricots. The best indicator is a sweet aroma.

When buying dried apricots, choose large, well coloured fruit that is slightly yielding when squeezed. Australian dried

apricots are much better in both taste and texture than the Turkish ones you may find on supermarket shelves. Note that Australian dried apricots are exposed to the gas sulphur dioxide, a preservative, before being sun-dried; this could affect people with chemical sensitivities. Dried apricots which are not treated in this way lose the rich apricot flavour and some of their vitamin content, and become dark.

STORING Keep ripe apricots in a covered container in the refrigerator and use them within a day or two; for fullest flavour, allow them to return to room temperature before eating. Dried apricots will keep well in the cupboard, in their original packaging or a covered container, for months.

Also see Fruit, Dried page 192.

Dried apricots can be reconstituted by just covering them with warm tea and standing overnight with a lid or plate over the bowl. Once plumped and tender, stir in sugar or honey to taste. These are good to serve with cream or on breakfast cereal.

Apricot upside-down cakes

PREP + COOK TIME 40 MINUTES **MAKES** 12

1 tablespoon brown sugar

6 apricots (300g), halved

2 eggs

¾ cup (150g) firmly packed brown sugar, extra

¾ cup (90g) almond meal

1 teaspoon vanilla extract

⅓ cup (50g) wholemeal self-raising flour

½ cup (125ml) no-fat milk

¼ cup (80g) apricot conserve, warmed

You can also use canned apricot halves in this recipe. You will probably have to open a 415g can of apricot halves for the 12 required here — serve the remaining halves with the cakes.

1 Preheat oven to 180°C/160°C fan-forced. Grease 12-hole (⅓-cup/80ml) muffin pan.

2 Sprinkle sugar equally into pan holes; place one apricot half, cut-side down, into each pan hole.

3 Using electric mixer, beat eggs and extra sugar in small bowl until light and fluffy. Stir in almond meal, extract, flour and milk. Divide mixture into pan holes.

4 Bake cakes about 20 minutes. Stand cakes in pan 5 minutes; turn onto wire rack, brush apricot conserve over hot cakes. Serve cakes warm or at room temperature.

NUTRITIONAL COUNT PER CAKE 5.1g total fat (0.6g saturated fat); 439kJ (105 cal); 10.5g carbohydrate; 3.7g protein; 1.6g fibre

**⚘ OTHER RECIPES
USING APRICOTS**
Peach and apricot tarts, p414

For instructions on testing when jam is set and how to sterilise jars, see Preserves, page 465.

Fresh apricot jam

PREP + COOK TIME 1 HOUR **MAKES** ABOUT 1.25 LITRES (5 CUPS)

1kg apricots (about 20)
½ cup (125ml) water
¼ cup (60ml) fresh lemon juice
1kg (4½ cups) sugar

1 Halve apricots; remove and discard stones. Place apricots, the water and juice in large saucepan; bring to the boil. Reduce heat; simmer, covered, about 15 minutes or until apricots are tender.
2 Add sugar to pan; stir over heat, without boiling, until sugar dissolves. Boil, uncovered, stirring occasionally, about 30 minutes or until jam jells when tested. Stand 5 minutes.
3 Pour hot jam into hot sterilised jars; seal while hot.

NUTRITIONAL COUNT PER TABLESPOON 0g total fat (0g saturated fat); 294kJ (70 cal); 17.1g carbohydrate; 0.1g protein; 0.3g fibre

Have heated plates ready to go under the soufflés so that they will stay puffed up as they are taken to the table. A bowl of plain whipped cream, for diners to add as they wish, is the perfect accompaniment.

For information on eggs, see Eggs, page 164.

Apricot and honey soufflés

PREP + COOK TIME 45 MINUTES **SERVES** 6

¼ cup (55g) caster sugar
4 apricots (200g)
¼ cup (60ml) water
2 tablespoons honey
4 egg whites

1 Preheat oven to 180°C/160°C fan-forced. Grease six ¾-cup (180ml) soufflé dishes; sprinkle inside of dishes with a little of the sugar, place on oven tray.
2 Place apricots in small heatproof bowl, cover with boiling water; stand 2 minutes. Drain; cool 5 minutes. Peel and seed apricots; chop flesh finely.
3 Combine apricot in small saucepan with remaining sugar, the water and honey; bring to the boil. Reduce heat; simmer, uncovered, about 10 minutes or until apricots soften to a jam-like consistency.
4 Beat egg whites in small bowl with electric mixer until soft peaks form. With motor operating, gradually add hot apricot mixture, beating until just combined.
5 Divide soufflé mixture among dishes; bake 15 minutes. Dust with icing sugar, if you like.

NUTRITIONAL COUNT PER SERVING 0.1g total fat (0g saturated fat); 372kJ (89 cal); 19g carbohydrate; 2.6g protein; 0.6g fibre

APRICOT AND HONEY SOUFFLES

Artichoke, Globe

The globe artichoke is the fleshy flower-bud of a plant of the thistle family. When very young and tender, the whole slender bud may be eaten, but these are something of a rarity in the shops. What you usually find are handsome, rounded green, purple or bronze heads in various sizes, covered with thick, pointed bracts (leaves that resemble petals). The part you eat is the fleshy base of each leaf, dipped in melted butter or a sauce such as hollandaise, and also the tender heart which is revealed after the leaves are removed.

When serving artichokes, provide each diner with a large napkin and a finger bowl of warm water with a lemon slice. Also, place larger bowls, within easy reach, for the discarded leaves. If serving cold, drop cooked artichokes into a sink of iced water for a minute or two to stop the cooking process, then drain them upside down. Serve cold artichokes with tartare sauce, mayonnaise or a vinaigrette dressing.

Baby artichokes may be eaten raw, braised or fried; larger ones are boiled or braised, and trimmed considerably before cooking.

Devotees of artichokes describe their flavour as "nutty", "smoky" or simply "exquisite". One of their flavour components (cynarin), has the unusual effect of making foods eaten after it taste sweet.

PREPARATION When serving whole, trim the stem so that the artichoke sits flat. Snap off coarse outer leaves until you come to leaves that are yellow-green at the base, then, with kitchen scissors, cut off the thorny tips of these remaining leaves.

When serving as a cup to hold the sauce or a savoury stuffing, trim stem, pull off coarse outer leaves then cut off the top one-third of the artichoke, cut off tips of any lower leaves and use a spoon to scoop out the bristly structure, the choke (actually the flowerets), from the centre.

As the cut surfaces discolour quickly, drop each trimmed artichoke into a bowl of acidulated water (water plus lemon juice) immediately it is prepared. Use a knife with a stainless blade to trim artichokes, and do not cook in aluminium or cast-iron pans or covered with aluminium foil, as these can cause discolouring.

An artichoke is eaten by pulling off each leaf, dipping the base in the sauce, scraping it between the teeth to remove the tender flesh, and discarding the rest. When you come to the centre, cut off the choke (if not removed during trimming), and eat the heart or bottom, the best part.

Prepared artichoke hearts are available canned or bottled in brine or oil. They can be used in salads, antipasto platters, appetisers, pizza toppings and stir-fries.

CHOOSING The classic artichoke season runs from the end of winter to early summer, peaking in early to mid-spring, though some varieties introduced in recent years may appear as early as autumn. Size does not indicate quality. The important thing is that the leaves be tightly closed around the head, the stem firm and rigid and the artichoke plump and heavy for its size. Tiny artichokes may have looser leaves, but they should be firm and springy and when pulled back, make a definite snap.

STORING Artichokes start to deteriorate when they are picked, so eat them as soon as possible after buying. Store in a paper bag, enclosed in a plastic bag, in the refrigerator crisper for up to two days.

Artichokes with lemon herb butter

PREP + COOK TIME 50 MINUTES (PLUS FREEZING TIME) **SERVES** 4

80g butter, softened

2 teaspoons finely grated lemon rind

1 tablespoon finely chopped fresh flat-leaf parsley

2 teaspoons finely chopped fresh basil

4 medium globe artichokes (800g)

1 Combine butter, rind and herbs in small bowl. Place on piece of plastic wrap; shape into log, wrap tightly. Freeze until firm.

2 Meanwhile, remove and discard tough outer leaves from artichokes. Trim stems so that artichoke bases sit flat.

3 Cook artichokes in large saucepan of boiling water 40 minutes or until tender; drain.

4 Serve hot artichokes topped with slices of herb butter, and lemon wedges.

NUTRITIONAL COUNT PER SERVING 16.7g total fat (10.8g saturated fat); 723kJ (173 cal); 1.9g carbohydrate; 3.9g protein; 1.2g fibre

See PREPARATION opposite for details on how to prepare and serve globe artichokes. This delicious butter with its fresh lemon and herb flavour is also good on rich meats such as grilled or pan-fried liver or kidneys.

Artichoke fricassee

PREP + COOK TIME 55 MINUTES **SERVES** 4

1 medium lemon (140g), chopped coarsely

6 medium globe artichokes (1.2kg)

30g butter

2 cloves garlic, crushed

1 medium brown onion (150g), chopped coarsely

1 large leek (500g), sliced thickly

¼ cup (35g) plain flour

½ cup (125ml) vegetable stock

½ cup (125ml) water

1 ½ cups (375ml) skim milk

¾ cup (90g) frozen peas

1 Place lemon in large bowl half-filled with cold water. Discard outer leaves from artichokes; cut tips from remaining leaves, trim then peel stalks. Cut artichokes in half lengthways. Using small knife, remove and discard chokes. Place artichoke in lemon water.

2 Heat butter in large heavy-based saucepan; cook garlic, onion and leek, stirring occasionally, about 5 minutes or until vegetables just soften.

3 Add flour; cook, stirring, 1 minute. Gradually stir in stock, the water and milk, then add drained, rinsed artichokes; bring to the boil. Reduce heat; simmer, covered, about 15 minutes or until artichoke is just tender. Add peas; simmer, uncovered, until peas are heated through.

NUTRITIONAL COUNT PER SERVING 7.4g total fat (4.3g saturated fat); 920kJ (220 cal); 22g carbohydrate; 14.7g protein; 7.1g fibre

This savoury fricassee could be the star of a vegetarian meal, or for non-vegetarians, it would make an impressive companion to grilled, sliced chicken breast.

Asparagus

The young shoot of a plant of the lily family. It comes in green, white and purple varieties — white asparagus is produced by earthing up the asparagus bed to cover the growing shoots to prevent them from greening. It was once a specifically spring vegetable but green asparagus now has a much longer season, though white and purple still have a fleeting spring season only. Green asparagus comes in various thicknesses, purple is fatter and white fatter again. All have a juicy texture and delicate, earthy/woody/grassy aroma and flavour, though purple is the sweetest and white the mildest.

Purple asparagus

✤ OTHER RECIPES
USING ASPARAGUS
*Potato and asparagus salad with
yogurt and mint dressing, p554*

Asparagus can be served with melted butter and lemon, or a sauce such as hollandaise, as a first course or as an accompaniment to meats or seafood. It can go into salads, soups or sauces, or can be used in a quiche filling, savoury custard, frittata, gratin, mousse, stir-fry or many other dishes.

Canned asparagus is available but bears little resemblance to the real thing.

PREPARATION Remove the woody ends of each stalk by bending the stalk near the bottom so it snaps at its natural breaking point — where the woodiness turns to crispness. If the skin towards the broken end still seems tough, it should be trimmed off with a vegetable peeler; white asparagus usually requires peeling almost to the tip.

Asparagus can be boiled, steamed, stir-fried, cooked in the microwave or char-grilled. Whatever the method, cook for only a few minutes (or for seconds in the microwave), just until crisp/tender, still firm and bright-coloured. Because the pigment that gives purple asparagus its colour is soluble, the stalks turn green as they cook — brief cooking will minimise this.

The traditional way of boiling asparagus was in a special tall pot with only the stems in water so that the tender tips would not overcook, but brief steaming or boiling in a wide pan such as a frying pan will give a good result. Cooking it in the microwave is particularly successful: arrange the stems around a plate like the spokes of a wheel, tips to the centre; flick with a few drops of water, cover with plastic wrap and cook on High for 30–45 seconds, depending on quantity and the wattage of the oven. The microwave cooks fastest near the oven walls, so this method works perfectly to cook the tips less than the stems. It won't matter if they overlap. To char-grill, steam thicker stems for 2 minutes or microwave 20–25 seconds, then coat lightly with cooking-oil spray and grill briefly; thin stems are oiled and grilled without pre-steaming.

CHOOSING The cut ends should not look dried out, split or wrinkled, stalks should be smooth with a soft sheen and the tips should be tightly packed with no loose or damaged scales.

STORING Ideally, eat asparagus the day you buy it. Otherwise, stand it upright in about 2cm of water in a glass or mug, drop a plastic bag over, store in the refrigerator and use within a day or two.

1 GREEN ASPARAGUS
2 WHITE ASPARAGUS

1

2

1 ASPARAGUS WITH POACHED
EGG AND HOLLANDAISE
2 ASPARAGUS FRITTATA

Asparagus with poached egg and hollandaise

PREP + COOK TIME 35 MINUTES **SERVES** 4

*The hollandaise sauce can
be made up to 2 days
ahead and refrigerated in
a covered container. When
you want to use it, warm it
by standing the container
in warm, not hot, water.
Hollandaise sauce is
also beautiful on globe
artichokes and steamed or
poached fish.*

*For information on eggs,
see Eggs, page 164.*

1 tablespoon white wine vinegar

2 egg yolks

200g unsalted butter, melted

500g asparagus, trimmed

2 tablespoons white vinegar

4 eggs

¼ cup (20g) shaved parmesan
cheese

1 tablespoon coarsely chopped
fresh dill

1 Blend or process white wine vinegar and egg yolks until smooth. With motor operating, gradually add butter in a thin, steady stream, processing until hollandaise thickens.

2 Meanwhile, boil, steam or microwave asparagus until tender; drain.

3 Add white vinegar to medium deep frying pan of gently simmering water. Break one egg into a cup, then slide into pan; repeat with remaining eggs. Cook eggs, uncovered, about 2 minutes or until white is set and yolk is still runny. Remove with slotted spoon; drain on absorbent paper.

4 Serve asparagus topped with eggs, hollandaise, cheese and dill.

NUTRITIONAL COUNT PER SERVING 51.4g total fat (30.9g saturated fat); 2153kJ (515 cal); 1.7g carbohydrate; 12.6g protein; 1.3g fibre

Asparagus frittata

PREP + COOK TIME 25 MINUTES **SERVES** 2

cooking-oil spray

1 small red onion (100g), sliced thinly

170g asparagus, trimmed, cut into 2cm lengths

2 eggs

2 egg whites

2 tablespoons low-fat cottage cheese

40g baby rocket leaves

2 tablespoons lemon juice

2 teaspoons drained baby capers, rinsed

1 Preheat grill.

2 Spray small frying pan with cooking oil; cook onion over heat, stirring, 1 minute. Add asparagus; cook, stirring, 2 minutes.

3 Meanwhile, combine eggs, egg whites and cheese in medium jug. Pour over asparagus mixture in pan. Cook, uncovered, about 5 minutes or until frittata is browned underneath.

4 Place pan under grill for about 5 minutes or until frittata is set.

5 Combine remaining ingredients in medium bowl; serve frittata with salad.

NUTRITIONAL COUNT PER SERVING 6.3g total fat (1.8g saturated fat); 614kJ (147 cal); 5.4g carbohydrate; 16.3g protein; 1.9g fibre

If the handle of your frying pan is not heatproof, cover it with aluminium foil before placing it under the grill. Frittata is delicious served both warm and cold. If you want to take it to work for lunch, make it the night before, store, covered, in the refrigerator and wrap it in plastic in the morning.

For information on eggs, see Eggs, page 164.

Asparagus with three toppings

PREP + COOK TIME 10 MINUTES **SERVES** 4

600g asparagus, trimmed

ANCHOVY AND GARLIC TOPPING

2 tablespoons extra virgin olive oil

1 clove garlic, sliced thinly

3 drained anchovy fillets, chopped coarsely

PARMESAN BUTTER

20g butter, melted

2 tablespoons flaked parmesan cheese

BALSAMIC DRESSING

2 tablespoons extra virgin olive oil

3 teaspoons balsamic vinegar

1 medium tomato (150g), peeled, seeded, chopped finely

1 tablespoon small basil leaves

1 Cook asparagus on heated, lightly oiled grill plate (or grill on barbecue) about 5 minutes or until tender.

2 Combine ingredients for anchovy and garlic topping in small bowl. Serve a third of the asparagus drizzled with anchovy and garlic topping.

3 Serve another third drizzled with melted butter and sprinkled with parmesan.

4 For balsamic dressing, combine oil, vinegar and tomato in small bowl. Serve remaining asparagus drizzled with balsamic dressing and sprinkled with basil leaves.

NUTRITIONAL COUNT PER SERVING (AVERAGE) 24.6g total fat (6.6g saturated fat); 1037kJ (248 cal); 2.3g carbohydrate; 4.3g protein; 2.1g fibre

Asparagus topped with anchovies and garlic makes a delicious side dish with veal schnitzel. The schnitzels will cook in the same time it takes the asparagus to roast. Serve with lemon wedges. To make parmesan flakes, peel thin strips from a piece of parmesan with a vegetable peeler. Multiply the quantities for the asparagus with balsamic dressing to serve as many as you like, for a lovely vegetable to go with a seafood barbecue.

Avocado

The fruit of a family of large evergreen trees originating in Central and South America. Ripe avocados have soft, buttery flesh and a nutty flavour, and contain a high level of monounsaturated oil (the kind that is good for you). Their season used to be only from autumn to early summer, but with numerous varieties now available, you can buy them all year round with their peak in the traditional season.

Thin-skinned avocados are easy to peel but hard-skinned ones are not. To remove the flesh neatly in one piece from a hard-skinned avocado, cut it in half and remove the stone, then slip the corner of a rubber spatula between flesh and skin at the neck end, slide it right round behind and under the flesh and lift out the flesh.

For avocado slices, leave the fruit whole and unpeeled and use a short, sharp knife to make lengthways cuts through to the stone about 1cm apart all the way round. Use knife to lift out one slice, pulling away the skin at the same time. Repeat with remaining slices; discard stone.

The simplest way to enjoy the buttery richness and nutty flavour of ripe avocado is to squash it lavishly onto bread or toast, season with salt and pepper plus a touch of lemon juice if you wish, and eat it immediately. Avocado is also good served as an accompaniment to chicken, ham or bacon, fish (including canned tuna and salmon) or shellfish, layered in a sandwich with any of these plus tomato and lettuce, or mixed with them in a salad — but be sure to keep the avocado in large enough pieces for its subtle flavour to come through. In its homelands, avocado and corn are a favourite pairing, especially using corn tortillas to scoop up guacamole, the classic combination of chopped or mashed avocado, chilli, onion, lime juice and sometimes chopped coriander or tomato. The natural shape of an avocado half, with its large cavity where the stone was, makes it a perfect case for stuffing with hot or cold mixtures using any of the ingredients mentioned. Avocado does not cook well, as heating spoils both the texture and flavour, but it can take the slight warming imparted by a hot stuffing or hot bacon or chicken in a sandwich.

PREPARATION Cut round the avocado lengthways, going right in to the stone, then pick it up in both hands and twist to separate the two halves. Many cooks remove the stone by placing that half on a board and, while steadying it firmly with one hand, stabbing a small, pointed knife into the stone and twisting to release it; a safer way is to cradle the half with the stone in your hand with the wider end away from you, and use the fingertips of your other hand to pry the stone up and out, starting from the wide end. You can then peel the skin back from the flesh, run a rubber spatula between skin and flesh to scoop it out in one piece, or scoop out flesh in spoonfuls. Cut avocado darkens very quickly, so it is best to prepare it only when you are ready to use it, or if you have to prepare ahead of time, brush exposed surfaces with lemon or lime juice or mix juice through mashed avocado, and cover closely with plastic wrap. Leaving the stone in a half that is not wanted immediately is often said to retard browning, but has only a limited effect.

CHOOSING Unlike most fruit, avocados do not ripen on the tree. Picking starts the ripening process, which takes about a week. They are taken to market while still hard; you will usually find a mixture of hard and fairly ripe ones in the shops. Choose fruit that is undamaged, has no bruises or very soft spots and is heavy for its size. To check ripeness, cradle the avocado in your hand and press very

1 HASS
2 SHEPARD

gently at the neck: it will give slightly if ripe. If it is very soft both at the neck and all over, it is probably overripe and starting to lose flavour, collapse and darken, so choose another one. Many greengrocers ask customers not to handle the avocados but to ask a staff member to check them for ripeness, but in a large supermarket you usually have to check them yourself. Once ripe, they are easily bruised, so it is best to buy them while still hard.

HASS, in season from late winter to early spring, has lusciously creamy flesh, free of fibre and with outstanding flavour. It is the only variety that changes colour as it ripens, its hard, pebbly shell changing from dark green to purple/black. Very occasionally, Hass can be rubbery.

SHEPARD, in season from early autumn to the beginning of winter, is green-skinned, firm and mild-flavoured. It is much more resistant to darkening, once cut, than other varieties. Replace the stone in the remaining fruit and cover the whole tightly with plastic wrap. Some avocado fanciers find Shepard too firm even when fully ripe.

FUERTE, in season from autumn to midwinter, has firmish buttery flesh and rich flavour. Its smooth, thin green skin is easy to peel off. Very occasionally, Fuerte can be watery.

SHARWIL, in season in winter, has knobbly green skin, creamy-textured yellow flesh and a rich smoky flavour.

REED is sometimes called the summer avocado because it is in season from spring to midsummer. It is very large, with thick, rough, dark green skin and yellow flesh of rich, meaty texture and buttery flavour.

COCKTAIL avocados are not a different variety but the unfertilised fruit. They are small and seedless, usually of good flavour though occasionally a little too mild.

STORING Allow avocados to ripen at home in the fruit bowl, hastening the process if necessary by enclosing them with a ripe banana in a paper bag. Once ripe, they can be kept in good condition for a day or two by refrigerating them, but don't refrigerate before they are ripe as this will damage their cellular processes and they will never ripen.

❧ **OTHER RECIPES USING AVOCADO**
Avocado and wasabi rice salad, p642
Grilled corn and zucchini salsa, p140
Ham salad with mustard vinaigrette, p259
Mango and avocado salsa, p309
Mussels with pickled ginger and avocado, p225
Prawn, crab and avocado salad, p536
Sesame tofu salad, p545
Warm balmain bug salad with saffron dressing, p538

Serve guacamole as a dip with corn chips or torn corn tortillas, or as an addition to nachos, burritos and fajitas.

Guacamole

PREP TIME 10 MINUTES **MAKES** 2½ CUPS

2 medium avocados (500g)

½ small red onion (50g), chopped finely

1 medium egg tomato (75g), seeded, chopped finely

1 tablespoon lime juice

¼ cup coarsely chopped fresh coriander

1 Mash avocados in medium bowl; stir in remaining ingredients.

NUTRITIONAL COUNT PER TABLESPOON 2.6g total fat (0.6g saturated fat); 109kJ (26 cal); 0.2g carbohydrate; 0.3g protein; 0.2g fibre

1 GUACAMOLE
2 AVOCADO, COS AND TOMATO SALAD

Avocado, cos and tomato salad

PREP TIME 15 MINUTES **SERVES** 4

1 baby cos lettuce

3 medium tomatoes (450g), chopped finely

2 medium avocados (500g), chopped finely

1 lebanese cucumber (130g), chopped finely

1 small red onion (100g), chopped finely

¼ cup coarsely chopped fresh coriander

¼ cup (60ml) lime juice

2 cloves garlic, crushed

1 Separate lettuce leaves. Reserve several of the larger leaves; shred remaining leaves coarsely.

2 Combine shredded lettuce in medium bowl with remaining ingredients. Serve salad divided among reserved leaves.

NUTRITIONAL COUNT PER SERVING 20.2g total fat (4.3g saturated fat); 970kJ (232 cal); 5.8g carbohydrate; 4.3g protein; 4.8g fibre

This flavoursome, salsa-like salad is great with hot or cold pork or chicken.

For information on cos lettuce, see Greens, Salad, pages 248 & 249; and for tomatoes, see Tomatoes, pages 606 & 607.

Bacon

Meat from the back, sides and belly of a baconer pig, cured (i.e. preserved by salting), and usually smoked as well. A baconer is larger and fatter than pigs bred for ham or fresh pork. Bacon is smoked for extra flavour and to help preserve the meat by drying the surface. Hot-smoking, the usual method, also partially cooks the meat. Unsmoked or "green" bacon is milder in flavour; it is hard to find in Australia as only a few specialist butchers and smallgoods makers produce it. If a recipe calls for it, you can substitute ordinary bacon that has been just covered with cold water, brought to the boil and drained.

To freeze bacon rashers, divide them into pairs and wrap each pair in baking paper, folding in the ends to completely enclose. Freeze in a large resealable plastic bag for up to three months. Remove only as many bundles of rashers as you need. They'll thaw fast. If you are cooking bacon for a crowd, it is easier to bake it than fry it — it requires less attention and doesn't need to be turned. Preheat oven to 200°C/180°C fan-forced. Cut rind from rashers, if preferred, place them in rows on a wire cake rack set over a roasting pan and bake for 10–15 minutes.

The traditional way of making bacon was to dry-cure it by rubbing a mixture of salt, sugar and a little saltpetre (potassium nitrate, a naturally occurring rock salt) into the meat over a period of about two weeks; the saltpetre improved the safety and storage life of the meat, and also gave it the familiar bright pink of cured meats. The meat, still in the large piece, was then smoked and air-dried. Today, most bacon is made much more quickly by soaking it in or injecting it with brine and smoking either naturally or by using a solution of smoke particles in water. Wet-cured bacon is good to eat, but its flavour does not have the depth and complexity of dry-cured, and it tends to give up its moisture while cooking so that it spits, spatters and shrinks in the pan.

BACON is usually sold in rashers (slices) but can also be bought in the piece for baking or boiling from many delicatessens, and at some butchers and growers' markets.

STREAKY BACON, with alternating layers of fat and lean, is cut from the belly.

MIDDLE-CUT RASHERS come from the loin and have a round eye of lean meat at one end and a streaky tail.

SHORT-CUT RASHERS are middle rashers with most of the fatty tail removed.

BACON PIECES are available from some butchers' shops and delicatessens. They are cheaper than rashers and are excellent for any recipe where the bacon is to be chopped or minced.

BACON BONES, available from some butchers and delicatessens, are a good and economical way to give rich bacon flavour to a lentil, pea, cabbage or root-vegetable soup. Any meat on the bones can be stripped off, chopped and added to the soup.

PANCETTA is Italian-style unsmoked belly bacon, cured in salt and spices. It may be a flat piece from which narrow slices are cut, or rolled into a fat sausage shape. It may be mild or chilli-hot. It is usually sold in slices and may be chopped and used in pasta sauces or in meat or vegetable dishes.

SPECK is strongly flavoured, cured and smoked pork belly with a very high proportion of fat. It is sold in slabs and is available from most delicatessens. It can be sliced and fried, chopped and added to stews, or minced for fillings for savoury pastries. Its rendered fat is prized by German, Dutch and Scandinavian cooks for frying potatoes or mushrooms and for browning meat before roasting or casseroling, and the crisp bits left behind from rendering make a delicious garnish for vegetables.

GAMMON is mild-cured bacon, either unsmoked or cold-smoked, which flavours the meat but leaves it raw. It may be sold as a joint for baking or simmering with root vegetables or lentils, or as steaks or rashers for pan-frying. It is not widely available in Australia but may be found in some good butchers' shops or delicatessens.

CHOOSING In general, bacon sold loose at the butcher is a better bet than the packaged kind and may also give you some say in how you like it cut, but there are some good, dedicated producers of fine bacon whose product may be sold in packages. The proof of good bacon is in the cooking, so shop round until you find the one that suits you best.

STORING Large cuts or smaller pieces of bacon can be kept in the refrigerator, wrapped in foil or in a covered container, for two or three weeks. Slices, stored in the same way, can be kept for a week. To keep longer, seal pieces in a freezer bag or plastic container, or lay slices side by side on a plastic-wrap-lined baking tray, and freeze; when frozen, transfer to a freezer bag. Bacon can be frozen for several months.

🍖 **OTHER RECIPES USING BACON**
Bacon-wrapped quail with grape sauce, p240-1
Broccolini with bacon and egg, p77
Cheese gnocchi with fresh tomato sauce
  and pancetta, p109
Chicken with creamy pea and pancetta sauce, p427
Creamy scrambled egg on brioche, p169
Gruyère, leek and bacon tart, p406
Swiss brown mushroom and warm pancetta salad, p326
Tomato, fetta and pancetta frittatas, p166

Streaky bacon

Pancetta

Speck

Gammon

Spinach, speck and poached egg salad

PREP + COOK TIME 30 MINUTES **SERVES** 4

300g speck, sliced thinly
200g baby spinach leaves
¼ cup coarsely chopped
fresh basil
50g pecorino cheese, shaved
4 eggs

GARLIC VINAIGRETTE
2 cloves garlic, crushed
1 teaspoon dijon mustard
⅓ cup (80ml) extra virgin olive oil
¼ cup (60ml) balsamic vinegar

1 Cook speck in large non-stick frying pan, stirring occasionally, until crisp. Drain on absorbent paper; cool.
2 Meanwhile, place ingredients for garlic vinaigrette in screw-top jar; shake well.
3 Place speck in medium bowl with spinach, basil and cheese; toss gently to combine.
4 Half-fill a large frying pan with water; bring to the boil. One at a time, break eggs into cup then slide into pan. When all eggs are in pan, allow water to return to the boil. Cover pan, turn off heat; stand about 4 minutes or until a light film of egg white sets over yolks. Using egg slide, remove eggs, one at a time, and place on absorbent-paper-lined saucer to blot up poaching water.
5 Divide salad among serving plates; top each with an egg then drizzle with vinaigrette.

NUTRITIONAL COUNT PER SERVING 37.6g total fat (10.5g saturated fat); 1898kJ (454 cal); 0.7g carbohydrate; 28.5g protein; 1.7g fibre

Pieces of toasted turkish bread make a great accompaniment to this café-style main-course salad.

For information on eggs, see Eggs, page 164; and for baby spinach leaves, see Spinach, page 568.

Bacon and potato hash

PREP + COOK TIME 35 MINUTES **SERVES** 4

Perfect for breakfast, lunch or dinner, this recipe can easily be doubled to feed a starving army of kids. Add poached or fried eggs on top and a side-serving of toast too, if you like.

For information on potatoes, see Potatoes, pages 448 & 449.

8 rindless bacon rashers (500g)

3 medium potatoes (600g), cut into 1cm pieces

1 large red capsicum (350g), chopped coarsely

5g butter

3 shallots (75g), chopped coarsely

½ teaspoon smoked paprika

LEMON VINAIGRETTE

1 teaspoon dijon mustard

2 tablespoons lemon juice

1 tablespoon olive oil

1 Cook bacon in heated large frying pan, in batches, until beginning to crisp. Coarsely chop half the bacon; keep warm.

2 Meanwhile, boil, steam or microwave potato and capsicum, separately, until almost tender; drain well.

3 Place ingredients for lemon vinaigrette in screw-top jar; shake well.

4 Melt butter in same frying pan, add potato; cook, stirring occasionally, about 10 minutes or until browned lightly. Add shallot, paprika, chopped bacon and capsicum; cook, stirring, until shallot softens. Remove from heat; drizzle with vinaigrette.

5 Serve hash topped with remaining bacon.

NUTRITIONAL COUNT PER SERVING 12.8g total fat (3.8g saturated fat); 1454kJ (348 cal); 24.1g carbohydrate; 31.8g protein; 4g fibre

Bacon, cheese and chilli muffins

PREP + COOK TIME 40 MINUTES **MAKES** 18

A strong vintage cheddar is best to stand up to the other robustly flavoured ingredients. These savoury muffins are a terrific accompaniment to a bowl of soup. They can be made a few hours ahead and warmed in a low oven when required, or you can make them days ahead and freeze them — allow to thaw (for about 2 hours), then warm before serving.

For information on cheddar cheese, see Cheese, pages 103 & 104.

5 rindless bacon rashers (325g), chopped coarsely

2½ cups (375g) self-raising flour

80g butter, chopped

1 teaspoon sweet paprika

½ teaspoon dried chilli flakes

1½ cups (180g) coarsely grated cheddar cheese

310g can corn kernels, drained

1 egg

1 cup (250ml) buttermilk

1 Preheat oven to 200°C/180°C fan-forced. Oil three 6-hole (⅓-cup/180ml) muffin pans.

2 Cook bacon in heated medium frying pan, stirring, until crisp; drain on absorbent paper.

3 Process flour, butter, paprika and chilli until mixture resembles breadcrumbs. Transfer to medium bowl; stir in bacon, cheese, corn and combined egg and buttermilk.

4 Spoon ¼ cup of the mixture into each pan hole; bake about 20 minutes. Turn muffins onto wire rack; serve warm.

NUTRITIONAL COUNT PER MUFFIN 10.3g total fat (5.8g saturated fat); 861kJ (206 cal); 18g carbohydrate; 9.5g protein; 1.2g fibre

Bananas

A banana is a nutritional powerhouse, providing the good kind of carbohydrate that keeps you going for a long time, plus calcium, dietary fibre, Vitamins A and C, iron and potassium. Apart from their role as a healthy and sustaining snack, bananas make an excellent breakfast-on-the-run when blitzed in a blender or food processor with milk, honey, vanilla, yogurt and an egg.

1 CAVENDISH BANANAS
2 SUGAR (LADYFINGER) BANANAS
3 GOLDEN BANANAS
4 PLANTAIN BANANAS
5 BANANA FLOWERS
6 BANANA LEAVES

Don't throw away banana skins — cut off the hard ends, chop roughly and blitz in a food processor with a little water, then pour this phosphorus-rich "soup" round any flowering plants and shrubs (excepting Australian natives). The nutrients in the liquid will encourage flowering and the pieces of skin, which don't look unsightly as they quickly go brown, will add valuable organic matter to the soil. This is a good way to feed potted plants because the nutrients become available gradually. Avoid natives because phosphorus doesn't agree with them.

They also star in muffins, breads and cakes, are essential to a classic fruit salad and make delicious fritters, ice-cream and various spectacular desserts involving baking them with good flavourings, pouring over rum or a liqueur such as Curaçao, lighting and taking in flames to the table. On the savoury side, they can be chopped with Asian herbs, chilli, lime juice and a touch of brown sugar for a salsa, or sliced and sprinkled with lemon juice for a sambal to serve with a curry.

Bananas grow in large bunches on a tropical plant that looks like a palm but is really a large flower stem whose "trunk" is made of tightly furled leaves. After the fruit is harvested, the plant is cut down and a new one grows from suckers. The fruit is always harvested green because it is too fragile to stand up to handling if picked ripe, and because, unlike many fruits, bananas can still ripen to perfection after picking. They start with ample supplies of starch stored in their cream flesh and this gradually converts to sugar, giving full, sweet flavour.

Bananas are available year-round, with peak supplies in summer and autumn. Cut surfaces darken quickly, so prepare only when needed or, if you have to cut them ahead of time, brush with lemon juice to destroy the enzyme that causes discolouration.

CAVENDISH bananas are the predominant variety in Australia: a long, curved fruit with good flavour, called after the family name of a 19th-Century Duke of Devonshire in whose hothouses this banana variety was developed.

SUGAR (LADYFINGER) bananas are short and fat and are tangier and sweeter than cavendish when ripe. They are astringent when unripe so always allow a sugar banana to become fully yellow at the ends before eating. Good for salads or decoration as they brown only very gradually when cut.

GOLDEN bananas are a small Asian variety, sweet and creamy with golden skins, sold in bunches in Asian food shops.

PLANTAIN is a non-sweet banana variety whose astringent, floury flesh is cooked rather than eaten raw. It is popular in Caribbean and Philippine cooking. Available only in some banana-growing areas and in the fresh-vegetable sections of some Asian food stores.

BANANA FLOWER A cone of tightly packed red bracts (leaves that resemble petals), wrapped round thin-stemmed flowers, that grows on the end of the stem holding the bananas. The pale inner leaves can be boiled to remove their bitterness, then sliced and used in meat stews, soups and rice or noodle dishes; the flower stems can be sliced for stir-fries. Available in some Asian food stores or tropical food markets.

BANANA LEAVES are used to wrap food to be baked, and also as decorative "platters" for food. Available in some Asian food stores or tropical food markets.

CHOOSING You can tell how ripe a banana is by looking at it. From bright green when picked, it becomes yellow with green at the ends and the skin has a waxy sheen; at this stage, it is very firm and barely sweet, with noticeable astringency. When bright yellow, still with some sheen and a brown speckle or two, it is quite firm and sweet without astringency. As the skin dulls and brown marks increase, the flesh ripens through sweet and luscious to very soft with a translucent look to very sweet with a strong aroma. It is best to buy bananas while they are still firm as they are hard to get home in good condition when they're fully ripe.

STORING Keep bananas in the fruit bowl until they are as ripe as you like them. You can speed ripening by enclosing them in a paper bag with an apple or an orange. Once ripe, you can stop them from becoming overripe by wrapping them in newspaper and storing them in the refrigerator for up to 5 days. The skins may darken but the flesh will not be affected. Overripe or bruised bananas need not be thrown away but frozen in their skins in a freezer bag, then thawed and mashed for making banana bread, cake or ice-cream, or for breakfast smoothies or a sandwich with peanut butter or hazelnut spread — a snack that children love.

❦ OTHER RECIPES USING BANANAS
Banana-leaf steamed fish, p530
Banana pancakes, p188
Banana passionfruit soy smoothie, p554
Coconut sago pudding with caramelised banana, p234

Banana bread

PREP + COOK TIME 1 HOUR 20 MINUTES **MAKES** 12 SLICES

You need 2 large overripe bananas (460g) for this recipe. Any leftover banana bread can be stored airtight for up to a week and served toasted, or can be sliced and frozen for up to 3 months and, when thawed, will be the same as fresh.

90g unsalted butter, softened
1 teaspoon vanilla extract
1 cup (220g) firmly packed brown sugar
2 eggs
1 cup mashed banana
1 cup (150g) plain flour
1 cup (150g) self-raising flour

1 Preheat oven to 180°C/160°C fan-forced. Grease 14cm x 21cm loaf pan; line base and long sides with baking paper, extending paper 5cm above long sides.
2 Beat butter, extract and sugar in small bowl with electric mixer until light and fluffy. Beat in eggs, one at a time. Transfer mixture to large bowl; stir in banana then sifted flours, in two batches. Spread mixture into pan; cover with a piece of pleated foil.
3 Bake bread 40 minutes; uncover, bake about 30 minutes. Stand 5 minutes; lift onto wire rack to cool. Serve toasted or warm, with butter if you like.

NUTRITIONAL COUNT PER SLICE 9.5g total fat (5.6g saturated fat); 1296kJ (309 cal); 49.7g carbohydrate; 5.1g protein; 1.7g fibre

Sticky banana puddings with butterscotch sauce

PREP + COOK TIME 45 MINUTES **MAKES** 8

You need 2 large overripe bananas (460g) to make 1 cup when mashed. The banana to be sliced for the topping should be fully ripe and slightly soft.

125g butter, softened

⅔ cup (150g) firmly packed brown sugar

2 eggs

1½ cups (225g) self-raising flour

1 teaspoon mixed spice

1 cup mashed banana

¼ cup (60g) sour cream

¼ cup (60ml) milk

2 tablespoons brown sugar, extra

1 large banana (230g), sliced thinly

BUTTERSCOTCH SAUCE

½ cup (110g) firmly packed brown sugar

⅔ cup (160ml) cream

50g butter

1 Preheat oven to 180°C/160°C fan-forced. Grease eight holes of two 6-hole (¾-cup/180ml) texas muffin pans.

2 Beat butter and sugar in small bowl with electric mixer until light and fluffy. Beat in eggs, one at a time; transfer mixture to large bowl. Stir in sifted flour and spice, mashed banana, sour cream and milk in two batches.

3 Sprinkle extra sugar in pan holes; cover bases of pan holes with sliced banana. Divide cake mixture between pan holes. Bake 30 minutes.

4 Meanwhile, make butterscotch sauce.

5 Turn puddings, top-side down, onto serving plates; serve warm with butterscotch sauce.

BUTTERSCOTCH SAUCE Stir ingredients in small saucepan over heat, without boiling, until sugar dissolves. Simmer, stirring, about 3 minutes or until sauce thickens slightly.

NUTRITIONAL COUNT PER PUDDING 31.6g total fat (20.1g saturated fat); 2404kJ (575 cal); 65.5g carbohydrate; 6.3g protein; 2.1g fibre

Banana fritters

PREP + COOK TIME 30 MINUTES **SERVES** 4

Japanese breadcrumbs (panko) come in two sizes: we used the large ones in this recipe. They are crisp and airy but still light in colour so they can be browned without burning. They are available at some supermarkets and good delis. If you can't find them, combine ½ cup of soft white breadcrumbs from day-old bread and ½ cup of packaged breadcrumbs. The taste and texture will be different but still good.

¼ cup (40g) icing sugar

2 teaspoons ground cinnamon

1 egg

¾ cup (50g) japanese breadcrumbs

vegetable oil, for deep-frying

4 large bananas (920g), halved lengthways

1 Combine sugar and cinnamon in shallow medium bowl. Beat egg in shallow medium bowl; place breadcrumbs in another bowl.

2 Heat oil in medium saucepan.

3 Meanwhile, dip bananas in sugar mixture; shake off excess. Dip banana in egg, then in crumbs to coat.

4 Deep-fry bananas, in batches, until browned. Drain on absorbent paper.

NUTRITIONAL COUNT PER SERVING 9.7g total fat (1.5g saturated fat); 1329kJ (318 cal); 49.2g carbohydrate; 6g protein; 3.9g fibre

Upside-down toffee banana and date cake

PREP + COOK TIME 1 HOUR 30 MINUTES **SERVES** 12

1½ cups (330g) caster sugar

1½ cups (375ml) water

3 star anise

2 medium bananas (400g), sliced thinly

1 cup (140g) dried seeded dates

¾ cup (180ml) water, extra

½ cup (125ml) dark rum

1 teaspoon bicarbonate of soda

60g butter, chopped

½ cup (110g) firmly packed brown sugar

2 eggs

2 teaspoons mixed spice

1 cup (150g) self-raising flour

½ cup mashed banana

300ml thickened cream

1 Preheat oven to 180°C/160°C fan-forced. Grease deep 22cm-round cake pan; line base with baking paper.

2 Stir caster sugar, the water and star anise in medium saucepan over low heat, without boiling, until sugar dissolves. Bring to the boil; boil syrup, uncovered, without stirring, about 5 minutes or until thickened slightly. Strain ½ cup of the syrup into small heatproof jug; reserve to flavour cream. Discard star-anise.

3 To make toffee, continue boiling remaining syrup, uncovered, without stirring, about 10 minutes or until toffee is golden brown. Pour hot toffee into cake pan; top with sliced banana.

4 Combine dates, the extra water and rum in small saucepan; bring to the boil then remove from heat. Stir in soda; stand 5 minutes. Blend or process date mixture with butter and brown sugar until almost smooth. Add eggs, spice and flour; blend or process until just combined. Stir in mashed banana. Pour mixture into pan.

5 Bake cake about 40 minutes. Turn cake, in pan, onto serving plate; stand 2 minutes. Remove pan then baking paper.

6 To make star anise cream, beat cream in small bowl with electric mixer until firm peaks form. Stir in reserved syrup.

7 Serve cake warm or at room temperature with star anise cream.

NUTRITIONAL COUNT PER SERVING 14.5g total fat (9.1g saturated fat); 1726kJ (413 cal); 60.3g carbohydrate; 3.7g protein; 2.3g fibre

You need 1 large overripe banana (230g) to make ½ cup when mashed. Make sure the bananas you use for this cake are really soft and overripe, otherwise they won't mash smoothly and can make the cake heavy. For advice on ripening and storing bananas, see STORING, page 34. We use underproof rum in baking because of its more subtle flavour, but you can use overproof rum if you prefer.

For information on dried seeded dates, see Dates, page 156; and for caster and brown sugars, see Sugar, page 576.

Bean Pastes

Pastes of fermented beans have been important flavour bases in Chinese cooking for many centuries. They are available, canned or in jars, in Asian food stores and some supermarkets. They smell very pungent, but are used in only small quantities to deepen and enhance the flavours of a dish or sauce.

Don't limit your use of these flavour bases to Asian cooking. The "savouriness" that bean pastes give to food, also called umami or the "fifth taste" (as well as sweet, sour, salty and bitter), can give depth and savour to a Western-style gravy, soup or casserole just as it can to a stir-fry or Chinese soup. Use black or yellow bean paste according to the colour of the dish, start with a little and add gradually, tasting as you go.

BLACK BEAN PASTE, made from a black variety of soybeans, fermented, flavoured with garlic and spices and heavily salted, is used as a flavouring in beef, chicken, fish, squid and crab dishes, and also in dipping sauces and marinades.

YELLOW BEAN PASTE, similar to black bean paste in saltiness and pungency, is made from fermented yellow soybeans and is used as a flavouring for fish, fowl, vegetables or tofu (bean-curd) dishes where a lighter colour is desired.

CHILLI BEAN PASTE is soybean paste with the addition of chilli. It is very fiery, so use with caution. Used in Szechuan cooking, which is hot and spicy, and with bland ingredients such as noodles and tofu.

RED BEAN PASTE, made from adzuki beans, is sweet and mild. It is used in cakes such as mooncakes, rice balls, steamed buns and sweet dessert soups.

Also see Soya (Miso), pages 552 & 553.

Chicken and yellow bean relish

PREP + COOK TIME 20 MINUTES **MAKES** 1 CUP

3 cloves garlic, quartered

2 purple shallots (50g), chopped coarsely

1 tablespoon vegetable oil

2 tablespoons yellow bean paste

150g chicken mince

⅓ cup (80ml) coconut cream

2 tablespoons chicken stock

¼ teaspoon dried chilli flakes

⅓ cup loosely packed fresh coriander leaves

⅓ cup coarsely chopped fresh mint

8 large trimmed wombok leaves

This relish is quite rich so serve it in small amounts. Spoon a little relish on a wombok leaf and roll it up, or serve as a dip with vegetable sticks.

For information on chicken, see Poultry, pages 456 & 457.

1 Using mortar and pestle, crush garlic and shallot until mixture forms a paste.

2 Heat oil in wok; stir-fry garlic mixture until browned lightly. Add paste; stir-fry until fragrant.

3 Add mince to wok; stir-fry until cooked through. Add coconut cream, stock and chilli; bring to the boil. Reduce heat; simmer, uncovered, about 5 minutes or until thickened. Remove from heat; stir in herbs.

4 Serve relish with wombok leaves, sliced cucumber and carrot sticks, if you like.

NUTRITIONAL COUNT PER TABLESPOON 4.1g total fat (1.7g saturated); 238kJ (57 cal); 1.4g carbohydrate; 3.4g protein; 1g fibre

Beef in black bean sauce

PREP + COOK TIME 35 MINUTES (PLUS REFRIGERATION TIME) **SERVES** 4

500g beef round steak,
sliced thinly

2 cloves garlic, crushed

2 teaspoons grated fresh ginger

2 tablespoons lime juice

½ teaspoon sugar

1 tablespoon peanut oil

1 large brown onion (200g),
sliced thickly

400g broccoli florets

2 large carrots (360g),
sliced thinly

¼ cup (60g) black bean paste

1 tablespoon soy sauce

1 teaspoon cornflour

2 tablespoons water

2 teaspoons finely grated
lime rind

*Brown only a small batch
of beef at a time, over high
heat. It should take only
about 20 seconds as the
slices must still be rare at
this stage so that they
won't be overdone when
they are cooked with the
vegetables.*

*For information on beef,
see Beef, pages 46 & 47.*

1 Combine beef, garlic, ginger, juice and sugar in medium bowl. Cover; refrigerate 4 hours.

2 Heat half of the oil in heated large wok; stir-fry beef mixture, in batches, until browned.

3 Heat remaining oil in wok; stir-fry onion, broccoli and carrot about 2 minutes or until vegetables are tender.

4 Return beef to wok. Add blended paste, sauce, cornflour and the water; cook, stirring, about 2 minutes or until mixture boils and thickens slightly. Serve sprinkled with rind.

NUTRITIONAL COUNT PER SERVING 11.7g total fat (3.7g saturated fat); 1258kJ (301 cal); 11.8g carbohydrate; 33.1g protein; 8.1g fibre

Beans, Fresh

The familiar green bean is the workhorse of green vegetables, available all year round and needing no more preparation than nipping off the stem and end and throwing into boiling water for a few minutes. And no more adornment than a little butter for simple perfection.

Beans are more of an event if they are tossed with butter-fried slivered almonds or chopped onion and bacon gently cooked in a little olive oil. Have the nuts or onion and bacon ready in a pan over low heat, add the beans as soon as they are drained; toss gently and serve immediately.

The rest of the bean family have shorter seasons. All are delicious when cooked plainly in water and used as a hot vegetable or cold in a salad, but are also sensational mixed with fried slivered almonds, fried chopped onion, garlic or bacon, or a mustard and garlic vinaigrette. Indian, Chinese and Italian cooks use them in soups, curries, stir-fries and pasta dishes.

GREEN OR FRENCH BEANS, available all year round, come in several varieties which differ only slightly in shape. Almost all have been bred to be stringless, but always check by nipping off an end with a thumbnail and test whether you can pull down a string; if you can, string each bean on both sides.

BABY BEANS are simply green beans picked very young for their beautifully fresh taste and tenderness.

YELLOW BEANS, also known as wax beans, are delicate yellow in colour with a milder flavour than green beans.

SNAKE BEANS, also known as yard-long beans, are in peak supply in summer and autumn though their season may stretch for longer than this. They have a slightly stronger taste than ordinary green beans but are interchangeable with them in recipes. They are sometimes sold in ordinary greengrocers but are more reliably available in Asian shops.

ROMAN BEANS, also known as continental beans, are in season from later summer into winter. They are flat and a paler green than ordinary green beans, with the seeds giving the edge of the pod a wavy appearance. Their flavour is robust and they usually need stringing.

RUNNER BEANS, also known as flat beans, have their peak season in summer. They are similar to ordinary green beans but are flatter and coarser unless picked young.

BROAD BEANS, in season in from winter through spring, can be cooked whole if

Green beans

Baby beans

Yellow beans

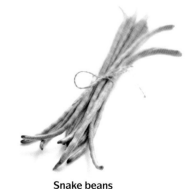
Snake beans

they are very young — only as big as a man's finger — but otherwise they are podded and only the seeds cooked. They are usually popped from their skins after cooking to emerge as tender, bright green kernels that are among the most delicate of vegetables. If they are to be pureed, the leathery skins are usually left on for texture and a stronger beany taste.

BORLOTTI BEANS, whose peak season is autumn, have pink-streaked pods and seeds. They are always podded and only the seeds cooked; they lose their pink streaks in the cooking process. Mealy in texture, they take much longer than green beans to become tender.

PREPARATION
Green beans and yellow beans can be cooked whole or sliced, snake beans need to be cut into shorter lengths and roman beans may need stringing. Borlotti beans are always shelled and only the seeds cooked; mealy in texture, they take about 30 minutes to become tender. Broad beans can be cooked whole if they are very young but otherwise they are podded and only the seeds cooked; it is a matter of choice whether to remove the skins and serve only the tender, bright green kernels, but if you wish to skin them, this is easier after cooking.

Like all green vegetables, beans should be cooked in plenty of lightly salted, boiling water with the lid off so that volatile vegetable acids leached into the water will be driven off, as otherwise they will change the beans' bright colour to a sad brownish green. Beans should be cooked only until they are tender but still quite firm.

CHOOSING
All fresh beans should be taut and bright and have a sheen; damaged, flabby or rusty-looking ones should be rejected. Roman beans and broad beans should not have noticeable swellings where the seeds are, flat beans should have only slight swellings. Small, slender beans are better than large ones.

STORING
Store green beans in the refrigerator crisper in a paper bag enclosed in a plastic bag and eat within a few days.

❧ OTHER RECIPES USING FRESH BEANS
Braised oxtail in peanut sauce, p50–51
Chicken, pea and broad bean risotto, p497
Italian-style bean salad with fresh mozzarella, p108
Lamb leg roast with broad bean mash, p286

Roman beans   **Runner beans**   **Broad beans**   **Borlotti beans**

Orecchiette are pasta shapes like "little ears". Other small shapes such as conchiglie or fusulli (see Pasta, pages 396-98) can be substituted.

For information on ricotta cheese, see Cheese, page 100; and for orecchiette, see Pasta, pages 396-98.

Broad bean and ricotta orecchiette

PREP + COOK TIME 30 MINUTES **SERVES** 4

375g orecchiette pasta

1 tablespoon olive oil

2 cups (300g) fresh shelled broad beans

1 clove garlic, crushed

½ cup (125ml) cream

1 teaspoon finely grated lemon rind

2 tablespoons lemon juice

200g ricotta cheese, crumbled

½ cup coarsely chopped fresh mint

1 Cook pasta in large saucepan of boiling water until tender; drain.

2 Meanwhile, heat oil in large frying pan; cook beans and garlic until beans are just tender. Add cream, rind and juice; simmer, uncovered, until sauce thickens slightly.

3 Combine pasta, sauce and remaining ingredients in large bowl.

NUTRITIONAL COUNT PER SERVING 25.2g total fat (13.4g saturated fat); 2500kJ (598 cal); 67.4g carbohydrate; 21.3g protein; 7.9g fibre

Braised borlotti beans with tomato and garlic

PREP + COOK TIME 1 HOUR 5 MINUTES **SERVES** 4

500g fresh borlotti beans, shelled

⅓ cup (80ml) olive oil

1 cup (250ml) water

1 bulb garlic, cut in half horizontally

3 large ripe tomatoes (450g), chopped coarsely

¼ cup fresh oregano leaves

½ cup coarsely chopped fresh basil

1 Preheat oven to 180°C/160°C fan-forced.

2 Place beans in medium baking dish; drizzle with oil and the water. Add garlic, tomatoes and oregano; cook, covered, in oven, about 50 minutes or until beans are tender.

3 Stir in basil; serve with grilled lamb or beef, if you like.

NUTRITIONAL COUNT PER SERVING 18.4g total fat (2.6g saturated fat); 752kJ (180 cal); 2.3g carbohydrate; 1.2g protein; 1.6g fibre

BROAD BEAN AND RICOTTA ORECCHIETTE

Prosciutto-wrapped bean bundles

PREP + COOK TIME 30 MINUTES **SERVES** 8

200g green beans, trimmed

200g yellow beans, trimmed

8 slices prosciutto (90g)

60g butter

1 tablespoon drained baby capers, rinsed

1 tablespoon lemon juice

⅓ cup coarsely chopped fresh flat-leaf parsley

These wrapped bundles of beans make a stylish presentation with fine steaks or a roast.

For information on prosciutto, see Ham, page 256.

1 Cook beans in medium saucepan of boiling water until just tender. Rinse under cold water; drain. Divide beans into eight equal bundles.

2 Place one slice of prosciutto on board; top with one bundle of beans. Wrap prosciutto over beans; continue rolling to enclose beans tightly. Repeat with remaining prosciutto and beans.

3 Cook bean bundles in heated oiled large frying pan until prosciutto is crisp. Remove from pan; cover to keep warm.

4 Melt butter in same pan; cook capers, stirring, 1 minute. Stir in juice.

5 Serve bean bundles drizzled with caper mixture; sprinkle with parsley.

NUTRITIONAL COUNT PER SERVING 6.9g total fat (4.3g saturated fat); 347kJ (83 cal); 1.5g carbohydrate; 3.3g protein; 1.5g fibre

Chilli beef with snake beans

PREP + COOK TIME 25 MINUTES **SERVES** 4

2 cloves garlic, quartered

2 long green chillies, chopped coarsely

2 fresh small red thai chillies, chopped coarsely

1 tablespoon peanut oil

600g beef mince

150g snake beans, chopped coarsely

1 medium red capsicum (200g), sliced thinly

2 tablespoons kecap asin

¼ cup (60ml) hoisin sauce

4 green onions, sliced thickly

2 tablespoons crushed peanuts

The beef is stir-fried in small batches to ensure that its surface moisture will be driven off quickly so that it browns rather than steams.

For information on beef, see Beef, pages 46–47; and for red thai chillies, see Chillies, page 120.

1 Blend or process garlic and chilli until mixture is finely chopped.

2 Heat half the oil in wok; stir-fry garlic mixture until fragrant. Add beef; stir-fry, in batches, until cooked through.

3 Heat remaining oil in cleaned wok; stir-fry beans and capsicum until tender.

4 Return beef to wok with sauces and onion; stir-fry until hot. Sprinkle over nuts; serve with lime wedges, if you like.

NUTRITIONAL COUNT PER SERVING 18.6g total fat (5.6g saturated fat); 1476kJ (353 cal); 9.6g carbohydrate; 34.8g protein; 4.2g fibre

PROSCIUTTO-WRAPPED BEAN BUNDLES

Beef

Beef can be grass-fed, meaning it was raised entirely on pasture, or grain-fed, meaning it was fattened on a mainly grain diet for at least three months before slaughter. Advocates of grass-fed beef say that it has fuller flavour while those who prefer grain-fed say that it is more tender.

Beef is highly nutritious, providing first-class protein, B vitamins, zinc and iron. As well, up-to-date research shows that, contrary to some earlier opinions, lean beef is not a threat to our cholesterol levels.

All beef is aged before being sold — traditionally by hanging the carcase in a coolroom for a period from about 10 days to a month, but now usually by dividing the carcase into its major parts and enclosing them in cryovac at coolroom temperature. During ageing, naturally occurring enzymes in the meat break down muscle fibre to enhance tenderness. Traditionally hung meat loses weight from dripping so it is usually more expensive, but specialist butchers who prefer this method say that this dry-ageing, as opposed to wet-ageing in cryovac, produces superior flavour.

The most tender meat of any animal comes from the parts that have had the least exercise and so have not developed tough connective tissue — those that lie along the back. This does not mean you should always buy the most tender cut you can afford: braises and stews get their succulence from cuts with plenty of connective tissue, which breaks down in long, slow, moist cooking to give melting tenderness, as well as richness and flavour that an expensive cut would not provide.

BEEF CUTS

ROASTING cuts are fillet, scotch fillet, rump, sirloin and rib, either on the bone (a "standing" roast) or boned and rolled. Fillet is the most tender cut of all and is fatless, so it is perfect for serving with a rich sauce, but rump, sirloin or rib will give more flavour in their own right. You may see cheaper cuts marked "roasting" but these are often tough.

To judge when a roast is done to your taste, use a meat thermometer or run a fine skewer into the centre and check the juice that comes out. Red juice means rare, pink medium and clear well done.

All roasts should be rested in a warm place, loosely covered with foil, 15 minutes before serving to allow the juices to settle and the meat to become more succulent.

GRILLING, CHAR-GRILLING, BARBECUING AND PAN-FRYING cuts are fillet, rump, T-bone and New York cut from the loin, and rib steak on the bone, which is the same cut as a lamb cutlet. These are suitable for grilling under a griller, char-grilling, barbecuing or searing in a pan. Oyster blade from a good butcher can be pan-seared if it is cut thin and cooked only briefly. Nameless cuts marked "grilling" or "barbecuing" may disappoint.

To judge when meat is grilled or pan-fried to your taste, press the surface with a finger or the back of the tongs. Rare meat feels soft and spongy, medium-rare soft but springy, and well-done quite firm.

All grilled meat should be rested in a warm place, loosely covered in foil, for 5 minutes to allow the juices to settle and the meat to become more succulent.

CASSEROLING Cuts for casseroling or stewing with the meat cut into pieces are blade, round, chuck, skirt, brisket, cheeks, oxtail, shin and gravy beef; shin and gravy beef are also used for stock or soup.

POT-ROASTING Cuts for pot-roasting (braising in one piece) are round, topside, silverside and blade.

CORNED BEEF may be silverside for lean meat with fat on top, or rolled brisket for layers of lean meat and fat throughout.

MINCED BEEF Many butchers sell both regular and low-fat or fatless mince. Fat carries a lot of meat's flavour and gives a richer texture while fatless mince can be dry and lack flavour, so for the best eating, choose regular mince for most purposes and fatless mince only for times when it will be mixed with other flavoursome and moistening ingredients, or for when it will be eaten rare (as in a hamburger cooked rare) or raw (for beef tartare). If health reasons dictate fatless meat, try to use it in these ways.

CHOOSING It is hard to judge beef

by looking at it. In general, young meat is lighter and the lean becomes more rich and dark in colour and the fat more creamy-yellow as the age of the animal increases, but the breed and the way it was raised and handled both before and after slaughter are as important as age in determining quality. Price is also a guide but the proof is in the eating so your best bet is a supplier you can trust.

STORING Transfer meat to a container

with the bottom lined with two thicknesses of absorbent paper, cover loosely with foil and refrigerate. The more it has been cut and handled, the less time it will keep. Mince and sausages should be stored for a maximum of 2 days, diced or cubed meat for 3 days, steaks, chops or cutlets for 4 days, roasting joints boned and rolled for 2 to 3 days, roasting joints with the bone in for 3 to 5 days, and corned meat for 1 week. Meat freezes well though it will lose some juices as it thaws. Freeze in a freezer bag enclosed in a second bag; thaw in the refrigerator: small cuts may take 24 hours or more, larger ones may need 36 hours or more.

Corned beef got its name from the covering of large grains or "corns" of salt that used to be rubbed into it during the curing process.

♣ OTHER RECIPES USING BEEF
Beef and barley soup, p231
Beef and beetroot salad with horseradish crème fraîche, p271
Beef and horseradish stew, p270
Beef in black bean sauce, p39
Beef steaks with three-ginger sauce, p223
Chilli beef stir-fry, p122
Chilli beef with snake beans, p45
Chunky beef and vegetable pie, p408
Fettuccine bolognese, p399
Piroshki, p648

Chilli and honey barbecued steak

PREP + COOK TIME 30 MINUTES **SERVES** 4

2 tablespoons barbecue sauce
1 tablespoon worcestershire sauce
1 tablespoon honey
1 fresh long red chilli, chopped finely
1 clove garlic, crushed
4 x 200g new-york cut steaks

1 Combine sauces, honey, chilli, garlic and beef in large bowl; turn beef to coat in mixture.
2 Cook beef on heated oiled grill plate (or grill or barbecue) until browned both sides and cooked as desired.
3 Serve steaks with a creamy coleslaw or warm potato salad, if you like.

NUTRITIONAL COUNT PER SERVING 12.1g total fat (5g saturated fat); 1354kJ (324 cal); 11.7g carbohydrate; 42.4g protein; 0.3g fibre

See opposite for tips on judging when steaks are cooked to your desired degree of doneness.
For a creamy coleslaw, combine 2 tablespoons mayonnaise and 1 tablespoon white wine vinegar in large bowl, add 2 cups finely shredded white cabbage, 1 cup finely shredded red cabbage, 1 coarsely grated medium carrot and 3 sliced green onions. Toss gently.

For information on chillies, see Chillies, pages 118-120.

Barbecued scotch fillet

PREP + COOK TIME 1 HOUR 40 MINUTES (PLUS REFRIGERATION AND STANDING TIME) **SERVES** 6

American mustard is very mild. If you have trouble finding it, use 1 tablespoon of french mustard instead.

¼ cup (60ml) barbecue sauce

2 tablespoons american mustard

4 cloves garlic, crushed

½ cup (125ml) beer

1.4kg piece beef scotch fillet

1 Combine sauce, mustard, garlic and beer in large bowl; add beef, turn to coat in mixture. Cover; refrigerate 3 hours or overnight.

2 Place beef and marinade in lightly oiled disposable aluminium baking dish. Barbecue, covered, using indirect heat, about 1½ hours or until cooked as desired. Cover; stand 15 minutes, slice thinly.

NUTRITIONAL COUNT PER SERVING 14.2g total fat (5.9g saturated fat); 1488kJ (356 cal); 5.9g carbohydrate; 49.7g protein; 0.6g fibre

Tomato mustard beef with baby fennel

PREP + COOK TIME 35 MINUTES **SERVES** 4

Your own home-made soft breadcrumbs are better than any you can buy and should be a staple in your freezer. For details on making and storing them, see Bread, page 67.

For information on fennel, see Fennel, page 174; for wholegrain mustard, see Mustard, pages 328 & 329; and for semi-dried tomatoes, see Tomatoes, page 607.

½ cup (125ml) chicken stock

1 clove garlic, crushed

1kg piece beef eye-fillet, halved horizontally

4 baby fennel (520g), trimmed, halved

⅓ cup (95g) wholegrain mustard

½ cup (75g) semi-dried tomatoes, drained, chopped finely

1 cup (70g) stale breadcrumbs

25g butter, melted

10g butter, softened

1 teaspoon plain flour

1 tablespoon balsamic vinegar

⅓ cup (80ml) water

1 Preheat oven to 240°C/220°C fan-forced.

2 Place stock and garlic in large baking dish; add beef and fennel.

3 Combine mustard, tomatoes, breadcrumbs and melted butter in small bowl; press over beef. Cook beef, uncovered, about 20 minutes or until cooked as desired. Remove beef and fennel from pan; cover to keep warm.

4 Blend softened butter and flour in small bowl. Add to pan juices with vinegar and the water; bring to the boil. Stir until sauce thickens slightly.

5 Serve beef, drizzled with sauce, with fennel.

NUTRITIONAL COUNT PER SERVING 24.7g total fat (11.3g saturated fat); 2378kJ (569 cal); 23.2g carbohydrate; 59.9g protein; 6.7g fibre

BARBECUED SCOTCH FILLET

1 BRAISED OXTAIL IN
PEANUT SAUCE
2 MASSAMAN BEEF CURRY

Braised oxtail in peanut sauce

PREP + COOK TIME 3 HOURS 50 MINUTES **SERVES** 4

*While originally oxtail was
just as it sounds — from the
tail of an ox — these days it
is likely to be from any type
of beef cattle. A flavourful
cut, it is fatty; if you want to
reduce the fat level, make
the recipe to the end of
step 2 then refrigerate the
braising liquid overnight;
remove the solidified fat
from the surface and
continue with the curry.*

*For information on red curry
paste, see Curry Pastes,
page 152; and for peanuts,
see Nuts, page 346.*

2 oxtails (2kg), cut into 5cm pieces

2 tablespoons plain flour

2 tablespoons vegetable oil

1 large brown onion (200g), chopped coarsely

6 cloves garlic, crushed

1 tablespoon ground coriander

1 tablespoon ground cumin

2 star anise

2 fresh long red chillies, halved lengthways

1 litre (4 cups) beef stock

1 litre (4 cups) water

⅔ cup (200g) red curry paste (page 153)

⅔ cup (90g) roasted unsalted peanuts, chopped coarsely

300g green beans, trimmed, chopped coarsely

2 green onions, sliced thinly

1 Coat oxtail in flour; shake off excess. Heat half the oil in large flameproof casserole dish; cook oxtail, in batches, until browned.

2 Heat remaining oil in same dish; cook onion and garlic, stirring, until onion softens. Add spices and chilli; cook, stirring, until fragrant. Return oxtail to dish with stock and the water; simmer, covered, 2 hours. Strain oxtail over large bowl; reserve braising liquid and oxtail, discard remaining solids. Skim fat from braising liquid.

3 Cook curry paste in same cleaned dish, stirring, until fragrant. Add 4 cups of the reserved braising liquid; bring to the boil. Add oxtail; simmer, uncovered, about 45 minutes or until oxtail is tender.

4 Add nuts and beans to dish; cook, uncovered, about 5 minutes or until beans are tender. Serve curry sprinkled with green onion.

NUTRITIONAL COUNT PER SERVING 111.7g total fat (36.8g saturated fat); 5626kJ (1346 cal); 15.6g carbohydrate; 70g protein; 6.7 g fibre

Massaman beef curry

PREP + COOK TIME 2 HOURS 30 MINUTES **SERVES** 4

1kg skirt steak, cut into 3cm pieces

2 cups (500ml) beef stock

5 cardamom pods, bruised

¼ teaspoon ground clove

2 star anise

1 tablespoon grated palm sugar

2 tablespoons fish sauce

2 tablespoons tamarind concentrate

2 x 400ml cans coconut milk

2 tablespoons massaman curry paste (page 155)

8 baby brown onions (200g), halved

1 medium kumara (400g), chopped coarsely

¼ cup (35g) coarsely chopped roasted unsalted peanuts

2 green onions, sliced thinly

Massaman curry is a staple in the Muslim communities in the south of Thailand close to the Malaysian border. It is a fragrant, hot curry with an acid note, showing the influence of traders who came from further west to that coast.

For information on massaman curry paste, see Curry Pastes, page 152.

1 Place beef, 1½ cups of the stock, cardamom, clove, star anise, sugar, sauce, 1 tablespoon of the tamarind and half of the coconut milk in large saucepan; simmer, uncovered, about 1½ hours or until beef is almost tender.

2 Strain beef over large bowl; reserve braising liquid, discard solids. Cover beef to keep warm.

3 Cook curry paste in same pan, stirring, until fragrant. Add remaining coconut milk, tamarind and stock; bring to the boil. Cook, stirring, about 1 minute or until mixture is smooth. Return beef to pan with brown onion, kumara and 1 cup of the reserved braising liquid; simmer, uncovered, about 30 minutes or until beef and vegetables are tender.

4 Stir nuts and green onion into curry off the heat.

NUTRITIONAL COUNT PER SERVING 52.7g total fat (39.5g saturated fat); 3645kJ (872 cal); 29.2g carbohydrate; 67.4g protein; 7.2g fibre

Beef carpaccio with green papaya salad

PREP TIME 30 MINUTES (PLUS FREEZING TIME) **SERVES** 4

600g piece beef eye fillet, trimmed

⅓ cup (35g) coarsely grated fresh coconut

GREEN PAPAYA SALAD

1 small green papaya (650g)

2 purple shallots (50g), sliced thinly

1 fresh long red chilli, chopped finely

¼ cup coarsely chopped fresh coriander leaves

¼ cup coarsely chopped fresh mint

¼ cup (60ml) lime juice

1 tablespoon fish sauce

1 tablespoon grated palm sugar

1 tablespoon peanut oil

1 Wrap beef tightly in plastic wrap; place in freezer about 1 hour or until partially frozen. Unwrap beef; using sharp knife, slice beef as thinly as possible.

2 Make green papaya salad.

3 Arrange carpaccio in single layer on serving plates; top with salad, sprinkle with coconut.

GREEN PAPAYA SALAD Peel papaya, halve lengthways, remove seeds then grate coarsely into large bowl. Add remaining ingredients; toss gently to combine.

NUTRITIONAL COUNT PER SERVING 16.2g total fat (6.7g saturated); 1400kJ (335 cal); 12.2g carbohydrate; 33.2g protein; 3.8g fibre

To open a fresh coconut, pierce one of the eyes then roast coconut briefly in a very hot oven only until cracks appear on the shell. Cool then break the coconut apart and grate or flake the firm white flesh.

For information on green papaya, see Papaya, page 386.

Cantonese beef patties with grilled gai lan

PREP + COOK TIME 45 MINUTES **SERVES** 4

800g beef mince

1 medium brown onion (150g), chopped finely

3 cloves garlic, crushed

2cm piece fresh ginger (10g), grated

1 fresh small red thai chilli, chopped

227g can water chestnuts, drained, rinsed, chopped finely

¼ cup finely chopped fresh chives

1 egg

½ cup (35g) fresh breadcrumbs

1 tablespoon hoisin sauce

1 tablespoon water

2 tablespoons oyster sauce

⅓ cup (80ml) hoisin sauce, extra

2 teaspoons sesame oil

1kg gai lan, chopped coarsely

1 Combine beef, onion, two-thirds of the garlic, ginger, chilli, chestnuts, chives, egg, breadcrumbs and hoisin sauce in large bowl; shape mixture into eight patties.

2 Combine the water, oyster sauce, extra hoisin sauce and remaining garlic in small bowl. Reserve ¼ cup (60ml) hoisin mixture. Brush patties with remaining hoisin mixture; cook patties, both sides, in heated oiled grill pan about 10 minutes or until cooked.

3 Heat oil in same grill pan; cook gai lan until wilted. Serve gai lan with patties, drizzled with reserved hoisin mixture.

NUTRITIONAL COUNT PER SERVING 20.2g total fat (6.8g saturated fat); 2077kJ (497 cal); 26.6g carbohydrate; 48g protein; 8.3g fibre

Gai lan is also called chinese broccoli. If you buy gai lan that is young, with thin stems, it does not need trimming before cooking; if it is older, with some thick stems, it should be peeled first.

For more information on gai lan, see Greens, Asian, page 242.

BEEF CARPACCIO WITH GREEN PAPAYA SALAD

Beetroot

Our grandmothers served beetroot, sliced and well doused in malt vinegar, as a salad vegetable, and otherwise it was seldom seen except for the tradition that a proper Australian hamburger had to include a slice or two of canned beetroot along with the tomato, iceberg lettuce and onion that were stuffed into the bun with the meat.

1 BEETROOT
2 BABY BEETROOT
3 GOLDEN BABY BEETROOT
4 BABY BEETROOT LEAVES

It wasn't until modern chefs discovered its earthy sweetness that it came into its own, served warm or cold as the perfect foil to duck, sausage, pork, hot or cold ham, corned beef, game and rich fish such as tuna and cured herring, and a natural partner to bitter salad leaves, orange rind, sour cream, yogurt, walnuts, chives, horseradish, dill or the merest touch of a mellow vinegar such as balsamic.

BEETROOT is available all year round with its peak season from midwinter to early summer. As well as the familiar red beetroot, golden, white and red-and-white striped varieties have been developed and you may find them in season.

CANNED BEETROOT slices taste harshly of the vinegary liquid in which they are packed, but canned whole baby beets, while they don't have the true flavour and firmness of cooked fresh ones, are among the most successful of canned vegetables and a useful stand-by; rinse them before using.

PREPARATION Trim off leaves, leaving 2–3cm of stem attached. Do not trim the long, tapering root as this would allow the colour to bleed out during cooking. Wash off any dirt.

The leaves can be eaten, so reserve them if you wish, storing in cold water if you intend to cook them that day, or in a paper bag enclosed in a plastic bag in the refrigerator if you want to keep them for a day or two. They can be briefly steamed or boiled, wilted in a little oil in a frying pan or stewed with oil in a covered saucepan and used as a green vegetable or chopped for soups, stuffings, pasta sauces or salads.

The traditional ways to cook beetroot are by boiling, baking or steaming until soft, trimming off the root and slipping off the skin after cooking. Today's chefs also like to char-grill wedges or small halves to retain their slightly crunchy texture. Beetroot can also be grated raw and eaten as a crunchy salad ingredient, or heated in butter and a touch of good vinegar in a covered saucepan and served, still slightly crunchy, as a hot vegetable.

Long-cooked beetroot, for example in a soup, may lose its bright colour and become brownish. To restore the colour, keep back a little raw or more lightly cooked beetroot, grate it and stir in just before serving.

CHOOSING Buy beetroot with smooth skins and no splitting or damage.

STORING Beetroot with the leaves removed can be stored in a paper bag enclosed in a plastic bag in the refrigerator for about a fortnight.

❧ **OTHER RECIPES USING BEETROOT**
Beef and beetroot salad with horseradish crème fraîche, p271
Kangaroo fillet with beetroot relish, p211
Pork steaks with radish and beetroot salad, p489

Zesty beetroot juice

PREP TIME 5 MINUTES   **MAKES** 1 LITRE (4 CUPS)

3 medium beetroots (525g), chopped coarsely

4 medium oranges (960g), peeled, quartered

500g trimmed silver beet

1 cup (250ml) water

1 fresh small red thai chilli, chopped finely

1 Push beetroot, orange and silver beet through juice extractor into glass. Stir in the water.

2 Add chilli; stand 5 minutes. Strain mixture through fine sieve into large jug.

NUTRITIONAL COUNT PER 250ML 0.5g total fat (0g saturated fat); 617kJ (147 cal); 24.5g carbohydrate; 5.8g protein; 10.4g fibre

You need 2kg of silver beet to get the required amount of trimmed leaves here. Don't discard the thick stems left after trimming — string and slice them, then boil until just tender. Serve stems with a cheese sauce for a delicious vegetable with meat or poultry. This super-healthy juice will keep for a week in a covered container in the refrigerator.

Beetroot, merguez and lentil salad

PREP + COOK TIME 1 HOUR 20 MINUTES   **SERVES** 4

2 cups (400g) brown lentils

2 sprigs fresh thyme

20 baby red beetroots (500g)

20 baby golden beetroots (500g)

8 merguez sausages (640g)

1 large brown onion (200g), chopped finely

2 teaspoons yellow mustard seeds

2 teaspoons ground cumin

1 teaspoon ground coriander

½ cup (125ml) chicken stock

300g spinach, trimmed, chopped coarsely

THYME DRESSING

1 teaspoon finely chopped fresh thyme

1 clove garlic, crushed

½ cup (125ml) red wine vinegar

¼ cup (60ml) extra virgin olive oil

1 Place ingredients for thyme dressing in screw-top jar; shake well.

2 Cook lentils with thyme sprigs, uncovered, in large saucepan of boiling water until tender; drain lentils, discard thyme sprigs. Place lentils in large bowl with half of the dressing; toss gently to combine.

3 Meanwhile, discard leaves and most of the stalk of each beetroot. Boil, steam or microwave unpeeled beetroots until just tender; drain. When cool enough to handle, peel beetroots; cut each beetroot in half.

4 Cook sausages in heated large non-stick frying pan until browned and cooked through. Cool 5 minutes; slice thickly.

5 Reheat same pan; cook onion, seeds, cumin and coriander, stirring, until onion softens. Add stock; bring to the boil. Remove from heat; stir in spinach.

6 Add spinach mixture, beetroot, sausage and remaining dressing to lentil mixture; toss gently to combine.

NUTRITIONAL COUNT PER SERVING 55.3g total fat (21.6g saturated fat); 3331kJ (797 cal); 63.2g carbohydrate; 49.9g protein; 27.5g fibre

North African merguez sausages, made from lamb seasoned with garlic and hot spices, are available at many butchers and delicatessens.
Golden beetroot are slightly sweeter than the red variety and make a nice colour contrast. If you can't find them, use all red ones. When trimming them, leave a little of the stalk on so that the colour won't bleed during cooking.

For information on lentils, see Pulses, page 472; and for merguez sausages, see Sausages, page 516.

1 BEETROOT, MERGUEZ AND
LENTIL SALAD
2 TURKISH BEETROOT DIP

Turkish beetroot dip

PREP + COOK TIME 50 MINUTES **MAKES** 2 CUPS

3 medium beetroots (500g), trimmed

1 teaspoon caraway seeds

1 teaspoon ground cumin

¼ teaspoon hot paprika

¾ cup (200g) yogurt

½ cup loosely packed fresh mint leaves

2 cloves garlic, crushed

1 tablespoon lemon juice

Serve thinly sliced fresh, toasted or crisp, twice-baked turkish bread with this fragrant dip.

1 Cook beetroot in medium saucepan of boiling water, uncovered, about 45 minutes or until tender; drain. When cool enough to handle, peel beetroot then chop coarsely.

2 Meanwhile, dry-fry spices in a small frying pan until fragrant; cool.

3 Blend or process beetroot, spices and remaining ingredients until smooth.

NUTRITIONAL COUNT PER TABLESPOON 0.3g total fat (0.2g saturated fat); 67kJ (16 cal); 2g carbohydrate; 0.8g protein; 0.7g fibre

Berries

Because they are fragile and because, except for strawberries, their seasons are fleeting, berries always seem like a treat. Their peak season is summer, except for wild blackberries (a noxious weed in Australia, but still to be found along country roads), which ripen in autumn, but the development of early and late varieties has made it possible to buy one or another kind of berry from late spring until well into autumn.

1 STRAWBERRIES
2 BLUEBERRIES
3 RASPBERRIES
4 BLACKBERRIES
5 TAYBERRIES
6 BOYSENBERRIES
7 YOUNGBERRIES
8 REDCURRANTS

As well as starring in their own right, both raspberries and strawberries make lovely sauces. Puree with a little sugar in a blender or food processor (sieve the raspberries to remove the seeds); add lemon juice or extra sugar to taste. Serve strawberry sauce with a cream-filled sponge cake or lemon ice-cream, or spread on crêpes then roll up and top with whipped cream. Serve raspberry sauce over chocolate ice-cream or poached pears or peaches. Pêche Melba, created in honour of Dame Nellie Melba, is one of the world's most famous desserts — scoop good-quality ice-cream into a stemmed dish, top with a poached peach and drizzle with raspberry sauce.

Strawberries are available year-round in Australia, since those grown in the cooler southern states are in the shops in the warmer months and those from the warm north appear in the colder months. Raspberries have a divided season, with a first flush in early summer to midsummer, then a second flush a couple of months later as summer turns to autumn. Gooseberries have the shortest season of all, just a few weeks in late spring.

All berries are good served simply with cream, ice-cream or both, or served raw in tarts, shortcakes, summer pudding, fools, trifles or gratins where the creamy topping is grilled just long enough to turn it golden without cooking the berries underneath. Most cook well too, starring in puddings and pies, soufflés, cakes, muffins and jams.

STRAWBERRIES can be very good indeed — sweet, juicy and fragrant — but their good looks are sometimes a mask for a disappointing lack of flavour. They do, however, respond particularly well to the sugar and lemon juice treatment described in PREPARATION, page 60. Strawberries are the classic summer berry to eat simply with cream and are also lovely with a sprinkle of brandy or orange-flavoured liqueur, or dropped into a glass of sweet sparkling wine. They are wonderful in a vast array of hot and cold desserts.

BLUEBERRIES are sweet but can be bland and are improved by standing with sugar and lemon juice (see PREPARATION, page 60). They are best either lightly cooked, just until the juice runs, or in cakes and muffins. Dried blueberries are being produced in a small way but are not, as yet, widely available.

RASPBERRIES come in red, the major variety, and also in gold, black and white varieties. They are the most intensely flavoured of all berries, with the perfect blend of sharp, sweet and aromatic flavour notes. They are lovely eaten raw with a dusting of sugar and thick or whipped cream, are the perfect fruit to use, with cream, for filling and topping a sponge cake, and are superb in pastries, ice-creams and sorbets, and puddings of every kind.

BLACKBERRIES Cultivated blackberries, sometimes called dewberries, do not quite capture the distinctive flavour of the wild ones, but they are larger and very good in their own right. Like their wild ancestors they make excellent pies, jams and jellies.

TAYBERRIES are a cross between blackberries and red raspberries.

BOYSENBERRIES, LOGANBERRIES and **YOUNGBERRIES** are all descended from the raspberry and the blackberry. The boysenberry, a cross between a youngberry and a dewberry (cultivated blackberry), tastes much like a raspberry but is much bigger than either of its

ancestors. The loganberry, a raspberry/ blackberry cross, is more acid than a blackberry, less intensely flavoured than a raspberry and seedless. The youngberry is a cross between a dewberry and a raspberry, tastes rather like a loganberry and looks like an elongated blackberry.

CAPE GOOSEBERRIES, a sub-tropical fruit which is no relation to the green gooseberry, are in season from late summer to early autumn. They are enclosed in a light-brown husk which becomes brittle as the berry matures and eventually falls off. Cape gooseberries have shiny yellow skin and a sweet/tart flavour and are fragrant. They a good lightly sugared or macerated in a liqueur such as kirsch, and make excellent jam and jelly.

CRANBERRIES are sharp-flavoured and mainly used in cooking, being particularly good for jams and jellies because of their high pectin content. They are most famously used in cranberry sauce, the traditional relish to serve with roast turkey. Cranberries have rather tough skins so they should be chopped a little before cooking to stop them from popping, and sugar should be added only at the end of cooking to help keep the skins tender. Dried cranberries, marketed under the name, craisins, are used in cakes and muffins.

CURRANTS *Redcurrants and blackcurrants* have nothing to do with the wrinkly black currants that are dried grapes, but belong to a family that also includes gooseberries. *Redcurrants* are sharp/sweet and best known as the basis of redcurrant jelly to serve with meats. They are also a necessary part of a classic summer pudding and, in Australia, may be used instead of the traditional holly to decorate the Christmas pudding. *Blackcurrants* are acid-tasting and high in Vitamin C. They are best when cooked and are used in sauces, jams and jellies, in

the liqueur, crème de cassis, which makes kir royale when mixed with sparkling wine, and in a cordial marketed as being good for children because of its vitamin content.

GOOSEBERRIES are good eaten just as they are when they are ripe and red-flushed, otherwise they benefit from cooking or macerating with sweet wine or liqueur. Lightly cook, mash and fold into thick or whipped cream to make a great fruit fool.

MULBERRIES are sweet and juicy, but when ripe they can be bland so benefit from the addition of sugar and lemon juice as described in PREPARATION. Their juice is notoriously staining. They are good eaten raw, especially mixed with other berries or with lightly cooked apple, and in summer pudding. They make excellent pies, jam and jelly.

PREPARATION
For most purposes, remove the green calyxes from strawberries, though they may be retained as a little "handle" for strawberries that are to be eaten in the fingers, such as those that have been half-coated with chocolate or those to be dipped in a sauce such as sour cream sweetened with brown sugar. Gooseberries need topping and tailing and cape gooseberries may need any remaining husk removed. Other berries need no preparation except to remove any stalks. Do not wash berries until just before using.

The flavour of blueberries and mulberries, which can be a trifle bland, is improved by standing with a sprinkle of sugar and lemon juice for a few hours; the same treatment works for any other berries that are found to lack flavour.

Do not cook berries in aluminum pans, which can affect their colour and flavour, but always use non-reactive pans such as stainless steel, pyrex glass, titanium or enamelled cast-iron.

CHOOSING Choose berries that look bright and fresh — firm, undamaged, shiny or with a soft sheen as appropriate. Also look underneath the container to check that the underneath fruit is not squashed, damaged or oozing juice.

Frozen berries are widely available, some in the form of compressed blocks of fruit, some packed as a box of separate berries. Both are an excellent alternative to the fresh fruit in terms of flavour, but the compressed berries have, of course, entirely lost their shape. The loose ones, though they are much softer, when thawed, than fresh berries, will stay shapely enough to use for a garnish for a short time after coming out of the freezer. Placed in a single layer on a plate in the refrigerator, strawberries will be thawed enough to use but still shapely after about 30 minutes, raspberries after about 20 minutes, and blueberries after about 15 minutes.

STORING As soon as you get berries home, place them gently, not touching each other, in a single layer on a plate or oven tray lined with two layers of absorbent paper, cover with plastic wrap and store in the refrigerator for up to two days. Wash only when you are ready to use them, place on absorbent paper and use the paper to roll the fruit gently to dry it.

❦ **OTHER RECIPES USING BERRIES**
Apple cranberry pie, p410
Balsamic strawberries with mascarpone, p636
Berry and orange cakes, p191
Cranberry and balsamic red onion relish, p468
Mixed berry cake with vanilla bean syrup, p617
Olive oil cake with blueberries, p365
Papaya, strawberry and orange juice, p387
Peach melba, p415
Pomegranate, raspberry and cranberry punch, p437
Raspberry jellies with almond cream, p220
Raspberry mint iced tea, p601
Red wine vinegar and raspberry dressing, p636

Mixed berry punch

PREP TIME 15 MINUTES (PLUS REFRIGERATION TIME) **MAKES** 2 LITRES (8 CUPS)

1 teabag
1 cup (250ml) boiling water
120g raspberries
150g blueberries
125g strawberries, halved
¼ cup loosely packed fresh mint leaves
750ml chilled sparkling apple cider
2½ cups (625ml) chilled lemonade

1 Place teabag in mug, cover with the boiling water; stand 10 minutes. Squeeze teabag over mug, discard teabag; cool tea 10 minutes.
2 Using fork, crush raspberries in punch bowl; add blueberries, strawberries, mint and tea. Stir to combine, cover; refrigerate 1 hour. Stir cider and lemonade into punch just before serving.

NUTRITIONAL COUNT PER 250ML 0.1g total fat (0g saturated fat); 393kJ (94 cal); 21.6g carbohydrate; 0.6g protein; 1.5g fibre

A lovely drink to serve all ages at a family party.

Blueberry crumble

PREP + COOK TIME 55 MINUTES SERVES 4

It's worth making this delicious crumble topping in quantity and stashing it, in batches, in the freezer. It is good with any type of fruit.

¼ cup (55g) brown sugar

¼ cup (55g) caster sugar

¾ cup (110g) plain flour

1 teaspoon ground cinnamon

100g butter, chopped coarsely

¾ cup (65g) rolled oats

½ cup (70g) coarsely chopped roasted macadamias

500g fresh or frozen blueberries

1 tablespoon lemon juice

¼ cup (55g) caster sugar, extra

1 Preheat oven to 200°C/180°C fan-forced.

2 Sift sugars, flour and cinnamon into medium bowl; rub in butter. Stir in oats and nuts.

3 Combine blueberries with juice and extra sugar in medium bowl.

4 Divide blueberry mixture among four 1-cup (250ml) ovenproof dishes; sprinkle with crumble topping. Bake about 40 minutes. Serve with vanilla ice-cream, if you like.

NUTRITIONAL COUNT PER SERVING 35.7g total fat (15.6g saturated fat); 2939kJ (703 cal); 85.9g carbohydrate; 7g protein; 5.5g fibre

---

White chocolate and raspberry bread puddings

PREP + COOK TIME 1 HOUR (PLUS STANDING TIME) MAKES 6

When figs are in season, you can use this recipe to make a wonderful dark chocolate and fig bread pudding: simply replace the white chocolate with dark and the raspberries with 2 large, fresh figs, coarsely chopped.

3 small croissants (150g)

100g white eating chocolate, chopped coarsely

150g fresh or frozen raspberries

1¼ cups (310ml) milk

¾ cup (180ml) cream

2 tablespoons caster sugar

½ teaspoon vanilla extract

3 eggs

1 Preheat oven to 160°C/140°C fan-forced. Grease six-hole (¾-cup/180ml) texas muffin pan; line each pan hole with two criss-crossed 5cm x 20cm strips of baking paper.

2 Split each croissant in half lengthways then tear each half into pieces. Roughly line each pan hole with croissant pieces. Sprinkle with chocolate and berries.

3 Combine milk, cream, sugar and extract in small saucepan; bring to the boil. Whisk eggs in large bowl; gradually whisk in hot milk mixture. Pour custard into pan holes.

4 Place pan in large baking dish; add enough boiling water to come halfway up sides of pan. Bake about 35 minutes or until puddings set. Remove pan from dish; stand puddings 15 minutes. Using baking paper strips, lift puddings from pan holes onto serving plates. Serve dusted with a little sifted icing sugar.

NUTRITIONAL COUNT PER PUDDING 29.2g total fat (17.4g saturated fat); 1760kJ (421 cal); 29.7g carbohydrate; 9.6g protein; 2.1g fibre

BLUEBERRY CRUMBLE

Bread

Today, most of us live within reach of a bakery, health-food shop, delicatessen or specialist food shop selling bread that is a step up from the sliced and packaged supermarket kind. The big bakers do try to give us what we want and their sales say that there is a place for their products, but supermarkets themselves are starting to see that there is a further market for breads that stand out from the crowd, and are moving to get a share of it.

The buzzword is sourdough, but there are plenty of other beautiful breads, many of them beloved specialities brought here by people from distant homelands, others made by local bakers who simply believe that even "ordinary" bread can be a treat if it is made with care and integrity.

WHITE BREAD is sometimes disparaged as boring, but a French baguette or fougasse or a crusty Italian pane da casa or ciabatta are only some of the great breads of the world that are white. Many factors make the difference between boring and beautiful: the way the dough is kneaded and handled, the oven in which it is baked, the quality of the ingredients and the way the dough is raised are some of them.

White bread is made with flour from which the wheat grain's outer casing, the bran, and its kernel, the wheatgerm, have been removed, leaving only the starchy part. White flours can differ considerably in quality. For example, a flour may be unbleached, meaning that no chemicals have been used to whiten it but rather that it has been left, exposed to air, for a month or two after milling, during which time oxidation causes it both to develop better baking qualities and to whiten. The more usual modern practice is to treat the flour chemically to "age" and whiten it in minutes. Another difference is that bread

flour needs a higher-than-average proportion of protein (gluten), which, during mixing, develops into countless fine, elastic strands to provide the structure of the loaf. The best high-gluten flours are made from high-gluten wheat, while lesser flours may simply have gluten added. A further factor that affects the final result is the amount of yeast used to make the dough rise. Commercial bakers tend toward high-yeast loaves because they rise more quickly, but this can give bread that lacks flavour. A slow rise, starting with less yeast, makes for superior texture and more developed, complex flavour (see Yeast, pages 644 & 645).

WHOLEMEAL BREAD True wholemeal bread, which may also be called wholewheat, wholegrain or wheatmeal, is made from flour that still contains all the components of the whole wheat grain. It may be stoneground flour, made by milling the grains into flour by the ancient method of crushing them between two millstones, or it may be made by modern methods which involve shearing the grains, separating out the bran and germ, milling the starchy layer into flour between high-speed steel rollers, then returning some or all of the separated components in bulk — the germ is sometimes left out because it does not keep well. Because of this, plus the heat

To give bread a good crust, bake it at a high heat and have a spray bottle of water beside the oven. As soon as you put the bread into the hot oven, quickly mist both bread and oven sides to make steam, then shut the door immediately. Repeat once or twice during baking.

involved in modern milling which can destroy certain nutrients, and other factors in large-scale manufacturing, wholemeal bread made with stone-ground flour is both more nutritious and better flavoured than most mass-produced loaves.

MULTI-GRAIN BREAD has added grains, mixed into the dough, of whatever cereals and seeds the manufacturer chooses: a typical mixture could be rye, wheat, corn, barley, triticale (a wheat and rye cross), linseed, oats, corn, buckwheat and soybeans. These additions increase the bread's content of dietary fibre, iron and folate (folic acid, important in guarding against anaemia and birth defects).

SOURDOUGH BREAD is made in the ancient way by keeping a piece of dough, called the starter, from each batch and adding it to the new batch to start fermentation — the process by which yeast causes leavening (the production of carbon dioxide which disperses into countless tiny pockets to inflate the dough). It was probably by chance that the ancients discovered that dough left to stand for long would ferment, swelling, changing in texture and smelling strange, but, rather than being spoiled, would make bread that was lighter and better-tasting. If some of this dough were added to the next batch, it fermented in the same way. It was thousands of years before it was realised that the fermenting agent was the yeasts which are everywhere in the air. The characteristic acid tang of sourdough comes from the continued action of the yeast in the starter, past the point where it would normally be killed by the heat of the oven. This sourness was considered a fault in bread, and bakers tried to avoid it by using makeshift leavens such as dried beer froth instead of a starter, until after the 19th-Century American gold rushes, when bread made on the diggings was

always sour as the bakers had no access to other leavens, the miners decided they liked it that way and its popularity spread from there. Today, a baker may initiate the process by exposing a flour-and-water or other food mixture to the air for several days so that airborne yeasts will settle on it, feeding it every day with a little extra mixture to give the yeasts more food and finally incorporating the fermented mixture in a batch of dough, or more simply by using commercial yeast for the first batch of dough and following the sourdough process from there on. Each sourdough has its own character as successive starters continue to be affected by the "wild" yeasts in the air. If a starter is taken to another region, the bread made from it and its successors will change slightly because the airborne yeasts are different there.

RYE BREAD is usually made with a mixture of rye and wheat flour as rye flour does not have enough gluten to produce a strong, open structure in the bread. Rye bread is heavier and more dense than wheat bread, with a pleasant acid tang. Rye breads are popular in northern and eastern Europe and also, thanks to European immigrants, in America and Australia.

PUMPERNICKEL is a dense, moist "black" (actually dark brown) rye bread of German origin, traditionally made by the sourdough method and baked for a long time at a low temperature in long, narrow, lidded pans so that it has little or no crust. It may be made with all rye or with a mixture of rye and wheat flours. In Australia, it is usually sold, sliced, in small packages and keeps for a long time, unopened in its airtight packaging, in the refrigerator.

BARLEY BREAD and **MILLET BREAD** are other traditional European breads but are not commercially made in Australia.

BAGUETTE is the classic long, narrow French loaf, crisp-crusted and featherlight, which is made to be eaten within just hours of baking. A baguette bought early in the morning is starting to stale by evening; French bakers produce two batches a day and many customers buy twice a day. A ficelle ("string") is a smaller and thinner version of a baguette.

BRIOCHE is a small French bread roll shaped like a turban with a topknot (and sometimes, as in our picture page 67, it is made without a topknot), made from a sweet, buttery, egg-rich dough. Brioches are eaten warm with jam for breakfast and may also be hollowed out and filled with a savoury mixture. Square brioche loaves are also available at some bakers.

PANE DI CASA (meaning "the house bread") is the everyday, torpedo-shaped white Italian bread with a heavy, crunchy crust.

CIABATTA is a long, flattish, white Italian bread (the name means "slipper") with a thin, crisp crust and open crumb with large holes.

FOCACCIA is a flattish white Italian bread, rather like a pizza base but thicker and lighter, which is usually dotted with small dents, brushed with olive oil, topped with garlic, herbs or the same kinds of toppings as used for pizza, and baked until the crust is slightly crisped and the topping is cooked as desired.

SODA BREAD is a bread which resembles a scone rather than bread made with yeast. Like scones, it is raised by the action of bicarbonate of soda (baking soda), which reacts with acid in the presence of moisture to give off carbon dioxide. The modern baking powder used now in scones is made from baking soda mixed with a combination of mild acids such as cream of tartar, but the traditional way of making soda bread is to combine a rubbed-in mixture of flour, salt, soda and butter with buttermilk, whose slight sourness provides the acid component. Soda bread was a staple in Ireland and parts of Scotland and is still popular there.

DAMPER, the traditional Australian bush bread, was made from flour, salt, water and some dripping if it was available. It may have derived from soda bread made by Irish convicts or immigrants in the early days of settlement. Damper was baked in a camp oven on the fire, or directly in the ashes, and was usually eaten spread with golden syrup or "cocky's joy", a cocky being a small-farmer.

TURKISH BREAD, also called pide, is a long, flat loaf of white, chewy, holey bread, delicious toasted or untoasted, which can be topped, or split and filled, with a savoury mixture, or split and used as a scoop for meat or vegetable dishes, or sliced and served with dips.

PITTA, also spelt pita, is a small or large, round pocket bread, traditional in Greek, Middle Eastern, Indian and Pakistani cuisines, which may be split and used to wrap round meats such as kebabs or scoop up dips such as hummus or dishes such as curries. Partly split, pita can be stuffed with any hot or cold savoury mixture. Split, oiled, seasoned, cut up and baked until crisp, it makes delicious savoury nibbles.

CHAPATI, which may also be called a **ROTI**, is a griddle-baked Indian flatbread made with atta (wholegrain, durum wheat) flour. Torn-off pieces are used to pick up bites of rice, curry or other cooked dishes.

PURI is an Indian flatbread similar to a chapati, but is deep-fried, which makes it puff up. It is used in the same way as a chapati.

PARATHA is a rich Indian flatbread made by smearing the rolled-out dough with oil, folding it, re-rolling and repeating these steps, in a similar way to making puff

Your own soft breadcrumbs are much better than any you can buy. Refrigerate crusts and odds and ends of bread in a freezer bag and when you have enough, tear them into pieces and whizz in a food processor. Freeze in small freezer bags and use them to give lightness to meatball, hamburger and meat loaf mixtures, in herb and lemon stuffings for poultry and fish, and for crumbed lamb cutlets or chicken fillets to be pan-fried in olive oil and butter and served with lemon wedges.

pastry. It is then cooked on a well-greased griddle. Parathas can be plain or stuffed with vegetables or paneer (Indian cheese). **NAAN** is a teardrop-shaped Indian bread made from leavened dough which is rolled out and slapped on to the inner wall of a tandoori (tall, round clay oven with live coals at the base) to bake. When cooked, naan is bubbly and slightly charred, and pulls into delicate layers when torn.

STORING
To store bread for a day or two, keep it at room temperature in a bread box, bread crock or paper bag, all of which help to prevent it from drying out while not sealing it completely away from air, which could make it go mouldy faster. Keeping it in the refrigerator will ward off mould, but make it go stale much faster. To keep bread for longer periods, freeze it in sealed freezer bags, first slicing unsliced loaves, if you wish, so that you can take out just as much as you want at a time.

Also see Flour, pages 182–185 and Yeast, pages 644 & 645.

⚜ OTHER RECIPES USING BREAD
Creamy scrambled egg on brioche, p169
Prosciutto-wrapped veal and pork meatloaf, p621

Have all the panzanella ingredients prepared but don't mix them together until serving time — that way the bread will take up some of the vegetable juices but won't get soaked enough to collapse.

Panzanella

PREP TIME 20 MINUTES **SERVES** 4

1 litre (4 cups) water

250g stale ciabatta bread, cut into 2cm slices

2 large tomatoes (440g), chopped coarsely

1 small red onion (100g), sliced thinly

2 lebanese cucumbers (260g), chopped coarsely

1 cup firmly packed fresh basil leaves

2 tablespoons olive oil

2 tablespoons red wine vinegar

1 clove garlic, crushed

1 Place the water in large shallow bowl; briefly dip bread slices into water. Pat dry with absorbent paper; tear bread into large chunks.

2 Place bread in large bowl with remaining ingredients; toss gently to combine.

NUTRITIONAL COUNT PER SERVING 11g total fat (1.5g saturated fat); 1104kJ (264 cal); 33.2g carbohydrate; 7.5g protein; 6g fibre

Bruschetta is ideal to hand round at a barbecue or pool party.

For information on tomatoes, see Tomatoes, pages 606 & 607.

Bruschetta

PREP + COOK TIME 15 MINUTES (PLUS STANDING TIME) **MAKES** 12

2 medium tomatoes (300g), seeded, chopped finely

½ small red onion (50g), chopped finely

1 clove garlic, crushed

1 tablespoon red wine vinegar

2 tablespoons olive oil

1 small french bread stick (150g), sliced into 2.5cm slices

cooking-oil spray

2 tablespoons finely shredded fresh basil

1 Preheat oven to 220°C/200°C fan-forced.

2 Combine tomato, onion, garlic, vinegar and oil in small bowl. Stand 20 minutes.

3 Meanwhile, place bread on oiled oven tray; spray with cooking oil. Toast, in oven (or under grill), until browned both sides.

4 Stir basil into tomato mixture, spoon over toast.

NUTRITIONAL COUNT PER BRUSCHETTA 4.3g total fat (0.5g saturated fat); 318kJ (76 cal); 7.4g carbohydrate; 1.5g protein; 0.9g fibre

---

Have all the vegetables prepared and the bread grilled but don't combine them until serving time so that the bread won't soften and the salad will look light, not heavy and settled. Fattoush is a Lebanese dish and goes well with grilled lamb skewers or steaks.

Fattoush

PREP + COOK TIME 20 MINUTES **SERVES** 4

2 large pitta bread (160g)

⅓ cup (80ml) olive oil

2 tablespoons lemon juice

1 clove garlic, crushed

3 red radishes (105g), trimmed, sliced thinly

½ small daikon (200g), grated coarsely

2 medium tomatoes (300g), chopped coarsely

1 lebanese cucumber (130g), chopped coarsely

1 small red onion (100g), sliced thinly

1 small green capsicum (150g), chopped coarsely

1 cup loosely packed fresh mint leaves

1 cup loosely packed fresh flat-leaf parsley leaves

1 Preheat grill to hot.

2 Place bread on oven tray; grill until crisp. Break bread into pieces.

3 Whisk oil, juice and garlic together in large bowl. Add half the bread and remaining ingredients; toss gently to combine.

4 Serve fattoush sprinkled with remaining bread.

NUTRITIONAL COUNT PER SERVING 19.7g total fat (2.7g saturated fat); 1367kJ (327 cal); 28.1g carbohydrate; 6.8g protein; 5.8g fibre

1 FATTOUSH
2 COPPA AND RICOTTA PANINI

Coppa and ricotta panini

PREP + COOK TIME 30 MINUTES **SERVES** 4

⅓ cup (80g) black olive tapenade

¼ cup (60ml) balsamic vinegar

4 focaccia rolls (440g), halved

240g ricotta cheese

½ teaspoon finely grated
lemon rind

1 teaspoon lemon juice

16 slices coppa (240g)

40g baby rocket leaves

A panini is an Italian filled roll. Coppa is a dried, salted, fat-marbled pork sausage which is available in mild and spicy (hot) versions. You can use also prosciutto, if you prefer.

For information on ricotta cheese, see Cheese, page 100; and for prosciutto, see Ham, page 256.

1 Combine tapenade with 2 tablespoons of the vinegar in small bowl; spread over bottom half of each roll.

2 Combine cheese with rind and juice in small bowl; spread over tapenade.

3 Top ricotta with coppa and rocket; drizzle with remaining vinegar then top with roll halves.

4 Cook panini in preheated sandwich press until browned lightly and heated through.

NUTRITIONAL COUNT PER SERVING 18.2g total fat (6.7g saturated fat); 2036kJ (487 cal); 51.3g carbohydrate; 27.6g protein; 3g fibre

Corn and goats cheese quesadillas

PREP + COOK TIME 30 MINUTES **SERVES** 4

2 corn cobs (500g), trimmed

240g soft goats cheese

8 large (20cm) flour tortillas

½ cup (100g) char-grilled capsicum, sliced thinly

40g jalapeño chilli slices, drained

⅓ cup coarsely chopped fresh coriander

20g butter

40g baby spinach leaves

1 lime, cut into wedges

1 Cook cobs on heated oiled grill plate (or grill or barbecue) until kernels are tender and browned lightly; when cool enough to handle, cut kernels from cobs.
2 Spread cheese gently over tortillas. Top 4 of the tortillas with corn, capsicum, chilli and coriander; top with remaining tortillas. Press around edges firmly to seal quesadillas.
3 Heat butter in medium frying pan; cook quesadillas, one at a time, until browned both sides and heated through.
4 Serve quesadillas with salad.

NUTRITIONAL COUNT PER SERVING 21.7g total fat (10g saturated fat); 2169kJ (519 cal); 57g carbohydrate; 19.8g protein; 8.6g fibre

A quesadilla (from queso, Spanish for cheese) is a tortilla "sandwich" which contains cheese and any of a wide choice of spicy ingredients. It is grilled, fried or toasted and often served with salsa.

For information on goats cheese, see Cheese page 104; and for corn cobs, see Corn, page 138.

Chocolate bread and butter pudding

PREP + COOK TIME 1 HOUR 10 MINUTES **SERVES** 6

1½ cups (375ml) milk

2 cups (500ml) cream

⅓ cup (75g) caster sugar

1 vanilla bean

4 eggs

2 small brioche (200g), sliced thickly

100g dark eating chocolate, chopped coarsely

⅓ cup (40g) coarsely chopped roasted pecans

1 Preheat oven to 180°C/160°C fan-forced.
2 Combine milk, cream and sugar in small saucepan. Split vanilla bean in half lengthways; scrape seeds into pan then place pod in pan. Stir over heat until hot; strain into large heatproof jug, discard pod.
3 Whisk eggs in large bowl; whisking constantly, pour hot milk mixture into eggs.
4 Grease shallow 2-litre (8-cup) ovenproof dish; layer brioche, chocolate and nuts, overlapping brioche slightly, in dish. Pour hot milk mixture over brioche.
5 Place dish in large baking dish; add enough boiling water to come halfway up sides of dish. Bake, uncovered, about 45 minutes or until pudding sets. Remove pudding from baking dish; stand 5 minutes before serving.

NUTRITIONAL COUNT PER SERVING 50.1g total fat (27.8g saturated fat); 2796kJ (669 cal); 45g carbohydrate; 12.6g protein; 1.4g fibre

Egg- and butter-rich brioche can be made into a loaf or cylindrical roll, but is usually shaped into a brioche à tête or "roll with a head", formed by topping a round piece of dough with a smaller one. One of France's first regional specialities, brioche originated in Normandy in the 15th Century.

For information on dark eating chocolate, see Chocolate, page 124.

CHOCOLATE BREAD AND BUTTER PUDDING

Broccoli

Broccoli, like its relation cauliflower, belongs to the cabbage family and consists of tiny, tightly clustered flower buds on thick, fleshy stalks, though broccoli has numerous small heads instead of cauliflower's one large one. It comes in green and purple varieties (the purple changes to green as it is cooked). The stalks, which are delicately flavoured and tender once the tough skin has been peeled away, can be used in the same way as the flower heads.

Broccoli is available all year, but its peak season is midwinter into spring. An excellent source of Vitamin C and rich in Vitamins A and B, it should be cooked uncovered to preserve its bright colour, and just until it is tender but still firm to the bite. It can be steamed, boiled or stir-fried and takes as well to Asian flavours as to Western sauces.

CHOOSING Broccoli should have richly coloured, very compact heads with no tinge of yellow or hint of an "off" smell, and firm, undamaged, almost moist-looking stalks.

STORING Store broccoli, enclosed in a paper bag and then in a plastic one, in the refrigerator, and use within four or five days.

Everyday broccoli can be served with melted butter and lemon juice, cheese sauce or plain white sauce. But for an occasion, arrange it in a gratin dish and cover with lush, lemony hollandaise sauce just before serving.

PREPARATION Simply trim off the ends of the stalks and cut up broccoli according to recipe directions, peeling thick stalks and adding them to the florets.

❧ **OTHER RECIPES USING BROCCOLI**
Beef in black bean sauce, p39

Chilli chicken with broccoli and cashews

PREP + COOK TIME 30 MINUTES **SERVES** 4

Kaffir lime leaves are tough, so tear the sides carefully away from the central vein, discard the vein and slice the leaf as finely as possible.

For information on cashews, see Nuts, page 344; and for chicken, see Poultry, pages 456 & 457.

1 tablespoon peanut oil
600g chicken mince
1 clove garlic, crushed
1 small brown onion (80g), sliced thinly
300g broccoli, cut into florets
2 tablespoons fish sauce

1 tablespoon hot chilli sauce
8 green onions, sliced thinly
1¼ cups (100g) bean sprouts
⅓ cup (50g) roasted unsalted cashews
4 kaffir lime leaves, sliced thinly
1 fresh long red chilli, sliced thinly

1 Heat half the oil in wok; stir-fry chicken, in batches, until cooked.
2 Heat remaining oil in wok; stir-fry garlic and brown onion until onion softens. Add broccoli; stir-fry until almost tender.
3 Return chicken to wok with sauces, green onion, sprouts, nuts and leaves; stir-fry just until hot. Remove from heat; sprinkle with chilli.

NUTRITIONAL COUNT PER SERVING 23.4g total fat (5.6g saturated fat); 1643kJ (393 cal); 6.3g carbohydrate; 36.9g protein; 5.8g fibre

1 CHILLI CHICKEN WITH
BROCCOLI AND CASHEWS
2 BROCCOLI AND GARLIC
BREADCRUMB SPAGHETTI

Broccoli and garlic breadcrumb spaghetti

PREP + COOK TIME 25 MINUTES **SERVES** 4

12 slices stale white bread

500g spaghetti

300g broccoli, cut into florets

⅓ cup (80ml) olive oil

50g butter

2 cloves garlic, crushed

¼ cup (20g) shaved parmesan cheese

1 Remove and discard crusts from bread; process bread until fine.

2 Cook pasta in large saucepan of boiling water until tender; drain.

3 Meanwhile, boil, steam or microwave broccoli until tender; drain.

4 Heat oil and butter in large frying pan; cook breadcrumbs and garlic until browned lightly and crisp.

5 Combine pasta, broccoli and breadcrumbs in a large bowl. Serve sprinkled with shaved parmesan.

NUTRITIONAL COUNT PER SERVING 34.2g total fat (11g saturated fat); 4004kJ (958 cal); 129g carbohydrate; 27.7g protein; 10.2g fibre

When crisping and browning the crumbs and garlic, use medium-low heat, stir constantly; watch carefully and tip them out as soon as they are golden — it takes only a few moments too long in a hot pan to darken them and make the garlic bitter.

For information on spaghetti, see Pasta, page 396.

Broccolini

Developed in Japan by crossing regular broccoli with gai lan (see Greens, Asian, page 242) bright green broccolini has small flower-bud heads on slender stalks, and is sold in bunches. It is a little sweeter than broccoli but can be used in the same ways.

PREPARATION The entire vegetable, as sold, is eaten — trim only by cutting off the very ends of the stalks and washing well, just before cooking.

Barbecuing or char-grilling brings out broccolini's sweetness. Microwave it until just changed in colour (or boil or steam about 1 minute), brush with olive oil and barbecue or grill for 1 minute each side.

CHOOSING Broccolini should be richly coloured, firm and unwilted, with more buds and half-opened flowers than fully opened ones.

STORING Store broccolini, enclosed in a paper bag and then in a plastic one, in the refrigerator for up to five days.

🌿 **OTHER RECIPES USING BROCCOLINI**
Lamb teriyaki with broccolini, p512
Mongolian lamb and noodle stir-fry, p285

Pork larb with broccolini

PREP + COOK TIME 25 MINUTES **SERVES** 4

Larb is the national dish of Laos and is also a staple of Thai cuisine. Palm sugar is an unrefined sugar used in Asian and Indian cooking. If you can't get it, use brown sugar.

For more information on palm sugar, see Sugar, page 578. For information on pork, see Pork, pages 440 & 441.

1 tablespoon peanut oil
2 cloves garlic, crushed
600g pork mince
⅓ cup (90g) grated palm sugar
2 tablespoons fish sauce
4 kaffir lime leaves, sliced finely
½ cup (40g) fried shallots
⅓ cup (45g) roasted unsalted peanuts

350g broccolini, trimmed, halved lengthways
1 tablespoon lime juice
1 cup loosely packed fresh coriander leaves
1 fresh long red chilli, sliced thinly
2 tablespoons coarsely chopped roasted unsalted peanuts

1 Heat oil in wok; stir-fry garlic and pork until pork is browned through. Remove from wok with slotted spoon.

2 Add sugar, sauce, lime leaves, shallots and nuts to wok; bring to the boil. Reduce heat; simmer, uncovered, 1 minute. Return pork to wok; cook, uncovered, about 2 minutes or until larb mixture is slightly dry and sticky.

3 Meanwhile, boil, steam or microwave broccolini; drain.

4 Stir juice and three-quarters of the coriander into larb off the heat; serve tossed with broccolini and sprinkled with remaining coriander, chilli and coarsely chopped nuts.

NUTRITIONAL COUNT PER SERVING 23.9g total fat (6g saturated fat); 2006kJ (480 cal); 25g carbohydrate; 39.5g protein; 5.5g fibre

1 PORK LARB WITH
BROCCOLINI
2 BROCCOLINI WITH BACON
AND EGG

Broccolini with bacon and egg

PREP + COOK TIME 25 MINUTES **SERVES** 4

700g broccolini, trimmed

40g butter

2 rindless bacon rashers (130g), chopped coarsely

2 thick slices ciabatta (70g), cut into 1cm pieces

1 clove garlic, crushed

1 tablespoon rinsed drained baby capers

1 tablespoon finely chopped fresh flat-leaf parsley

2 soft-boiled eggs, chopped coarsely

Easy, low-fat, different but not too different — this recipe ticks all the boxes for the centrepiece of a great brunch. Serve fruit to start with and finish with something good from the bakery (or your own kitchen) with tea or coffee.

1 Boil, steam or microwave broccolini until tender; drain.

2 Meanwhile, melt butter in large frying pan; cook bacon until crisp. Add bread and garlic; cook, stirring, until bread is browned lightly. Add capers and parsley; stir until hot.

3 Divide broccolini among serving plates; top with bacon mixture and egg.

NUTRITIONAL COUNT PER SERVING 16.2g total fat (7.9g saturated fat); 1154kJ (276 cal); 9.6g carbohydrate; 19.4g protein; 7.9g fibre

Cabbages

Because cabbage grows well in almost any soil and most climates, poor people have always been able to grow it as a staple of their diet. The result is a legacy of splendid, hearty dishes from generations of peasant cooks who built cabbage into generous soups and nourishing casseroles, pickled it to last through the winter, paired it with the poultry and pork that they had also raised themselves and with the bacon and sausages made from the pig, and even turned leftover cabbage and potatoes into those delicious, homely Irish and British dishes, colcannon and bubble and squeak.

1 WHITE CABBAGE
2 SAVOY CABBAGE
3 RED CABBAGE
4 WOMBOK

The peak season for cabbage is winter, but it is available all year round. The key to cooking any kind of cabbage is to make it brief. White cabbage, savoy cabbage or wombok should be cooked just until it wilts if it is to be served as a separate vegetable; overcooking releases rank aromas and flavours from sulphur compounds in the leaves. All these cabbages also respond well to long, slow cooking with rich meats, herbs and other vegetables. Red cabbage is a special case, see below. Brussels sprouts are cooked when a fine skewer can be pushed, against some resistance, into the centre.

WHITE CABBAGE (really pale green shading to cream or white at the centre) comes in round or long (sugarloaf) varieties. It is good for coleslaw, in stir-fries or steamed in a steamer or a covered saucepan with butter, just until it wilts. Its mild flavour is enhanced by cooking it with butter and a sprinkle of caraway seeds or with chopped streaky bacon which has been lightly fried before adding the cabbage. Cabbage leaves briefly blanched (dropped into boiling water) to soften them can be wrapped round meat and rice stuffings and steamed or casseroled.

SAVOY CABBAGE, crinkly-leafed and rich green shading into cream at the centre, is less compact and more flavoursome than white cabbage. It can be used in the same ways as white.

RED CABBAGE is good raw in salads; otherwise, it repays slow, gentle cooking with a minimum of water plus an acid ingredient such as apple, vinegar or wine. The acid component is needed because plain water may be alkaline, which turns red cabbage a discouraging blue-green with flavour to match.

WOMBOK (also known as chinese cabbage or peking or napa cabbage) is a long, rather loosely packed pale green cabbage with thin, crinkly, delicately flavoured leaves. It can be used in the same ways as white or savoy cabbage and is also used in stir-fries and other Asian cooking.

SAUERKRAUT is shredded white or red cabbage fermented in brine, which makes it pungently sour. It is served with cured and smoked meats.

BRUSSELS SPROUTS are like tiny cabbages. They grow along a thick centre stalk and are at their best in winter. Whole, halved or quartered, they can be briefly boiled or steamed, pan-fried or stir-fried.

❧ OTHER RECIPES USING CABBAGE
Chicken, cabbage and mixed sprout salad, p74
Crisp pork belly with wombok salad, p444

PREPARATION Remove outside leaves from cabbage, trim stem and shred or cut up according to recipe directions. Trim base of brussels sprouts and cut a small, deep cross in the base if cooking them whole so that the heat can penetrate quickly. Taste sauerkraut and, if it is too salty, rinse and drain well.

CHOOSING The cabbage leaves you can see should be undamaged, unwilted and have a slight sheen; the stalk end should be moist and there should be no trace of pungent odours. White cabbage should feel hard and heavy for its size. Brussels sprouts should be bright green with no trace of yellow, and compact with tight leaves.

STORING Store cabbage in a paper bag enclosed in a plastic bag in the refrigerator, where savoy cabbage or wombok will keep for five or six days and more compact cabbages for a week or more. Store brussels sprouts in the same way for a few days if necessary, but use as soon as possible as they quickly lose their sweetness.

Make these rolls ahead on the weekend to serve as a midweek dinner. Reheat the casserole on low heat or in a moderate oven when you get home from work and, by the time you've steamed some rice as an accompaniment, it will be ready.

For information on pork, see Pork, pages 440 & 441.

Pork cabbage rolls

PREP + COOK TIME 2 HOURS 40 MINUTES **SERVES** 6

18 large cabbage leaves

½ cup (100g) uncooked white long-grain rice

250g pork mince

1 medium brown onion (150g), chopped finely

¼ cup finely chopped fresh dill

1 clove garlic, crushed

1 tablespoon tomato paste

2 teaspoons ground cumin

1 teaspoon ground coriander

1 teaspoon ground allspice

4 cloves garlic, quartered

2 medium tomatoes (300g), chopped coarsely

2 x 400g cans crushed tomatoes

¼ cup (60ml) lemon juice

1 Discard thick stems from 15 cabbage leaves; reserve remaining leaves. Boil, steam or microwave trimmed leaves until just pliable; drain. Rinse under cold water; drain. Pat dry with absorbent paper.

2 Using hand, combine rice, pork, onion, dill, crushed garlic, paste and spices in bowl.

3 Place one trimmed leaf, vein-side up, on board; cut leaf in half lengthways. Place 1 rounded teaspoon of the pork mixture at stem end of each half; roll each half firmly to enclose filling. Repeat with remaining trimmed leaves.

4 Place reserved leaves in base of large saucepan. Place only enough rolls, seam-side down, in single layer, to completely cover leaves in base of saucepan. Top with quartered garlic, chopped fresh tomato then remaining rolls.

5 Pour undrained tomatoes and juice over cabbage rolls; bring to the boil. Reduce heat; simmer, covered, 1 hour. Uncover; simmer about 30 minutes or until cabbage rolls are cooked through.

6 Serve with thick greek-style yogurt and a little finely chopped preserved lemon, if you like.

NUTRITIONAL COUNT PER SERVING 3.6g total fat (1.1g saturated fat); 803kJ (192 cal); 24.7g carbohydrate; 14.3g protein; 9.7g fibre

1 PORK CABBAGE ROLLS
2 MIXED CABBAGE COLESLAW

Mixed cabbage coleslaw

PREP TIME 20 MINUTES **SERVES** 4

⅓ cup (80ml) olive oil

2 tablespoons cider vinegar

2 teaspoons dijon mustard

2 cups (160g) finely shredded green cabbage

2 cups (160g) finely shredded red cabbage

2 cups (160g) finely shredded wombok

1 medium carrot (120g), grated coarsely

4 green onions, sliced thinly

1 Whisk oil, vinegar and mustard in large bowl.

2 Add remaining ingredients to bowl; toss gently to combine.

NUTRITIONAL COUNT PER SERVING 18.4g total fat (2.6g saturated fat); 836kJ (200 cal); 4.5g carbohydrate; 2.4g protein; 4.7g fibre

This is a good salad for a barbecue because it will put up with standing for a while and isn't fussy about the temperature at which it is served. Depending on whether the rest of the menu includes a sauce, you may want to make it a creamy coleslaw, easily done by folding mayonnaise through.

Capers & Caperberries

Capers (in vinegar)

Capers (salted)

Baby capers (salted)

Caperberries

For information on oregano, see Herbs, page 264.

CAPERS are the buds of a low bush that grows wild on Mediterranean hillsides and is cultivated in that region and other parts of the world. The smallest and tightest buds, from the tips of the stems, are the most prized; softer, looser ones are less intensely flavoured. They are briefly dried, then pickled in salted vinegar or dry-cured by packing in salt, the form in which connoisseurs prefer them as they are firmer and the tart, piquant caper flavour comes through better. Capers are used in dips such as Provençal tapenade, in hot sauces such as caper sauce to go on boiled mutton or cold, mayonnaise-based sauces such as remoulade, in terrines and pâtés, especially seafood ones, and scattered over smoked or fresh fish, vegetables such as beetroot, and cold or hot meats.

CAPERBERRIES, the fruit of the caper bush, are smooth, olive-green fruits the size of a small olive. They taste like capers, but are less intense. They are pickled in salted vinegar, usually with their stems still on, and eaten like olives or served as part of an antipasto, mezze or tapas spread.

PREPARATION
Vinegar-packed capers need only to be drained on paper towels, salt-packed capers should be well rinsed to remove excess salt, then drained on crumpled paper towels. Either kind of caper can be deep-fried for a few seconds, just until crisp, and drained on paper towels for a delicious garnish. Caperberries need only to be drained, not rinsed.

☙ **OTHER RECIPES USING CAPERS**
Black olive tapenade, p373
Cornichon and dill potato salad, p148
Penne puttanesca, p399
Salsa verde, p267

Creamy caper and oregano dressing

PREP TIME 10 MINUTES **SERVES** 4

2 hard-boiled eggs, quartered

1 tablespoon drained capers

2 tablespoons white wine vinegar

2 tablespoons coarsely chopped fresh oregano

1 clove garlic, quartered

⅓ cup (80ml) olive oil

1 Blend or process egg, capers, vinegar, oregano and garlic until smooth.

2 With motor operating, add oil in a thin, steady stream until dressing thickens.

NUTRITIONAL COUNT PER SERVING 20.9g total fat (3.4g saturated fat); 836kJ (200 cal); 0.5g carbohydrate; 3.4g protein; 0.2g fibre

1 CREAMY CAPER AND
OREGANO DRESSING
2 SALADE NICOISE WITH
CAPERBERRIES

Salade niçoise with caperberries

PREP + COOK TIME 20 MINUTES **SERVES** 4

200g baby green beans, trimmed

2 tablespoons olive oil

1 tablespoon lemon juice

2 tablespoons white wine vinegar

4 medium tomatoes (600g), cut into wedges

4 hard-boiled eggs, quartered

425g can tuna in springwater, drained, flaked

½ cup (80g) drained caperberries

½ cup (60g) seeded small black olives

¼ cup firmly packed fresh flat-leaf parsley leaves

440g can drained whole baby new potatoes, rinsed, halved

1 Boil, steam or microwave beans until tender; drain. Rinse under cold water; drain.

2 Whisk oil, juice and vinegar in large bowl, add beans and remaining ingredients; toss gently to combine.

NUTRITIONAL COUNT PER SERVING 16.9g total fat (3.7g saturated fat); 1522kJ (364 cal); 19.5g carbohydrate; 30.9g protein; 5.2g fibre

This French lunch salad was originally created with the finest local produce from Provence. Its ingredients have varied over time, but green beans, tomatoes, hard-boiled egg, capers or caperberries, black olives and potatoes are always included.

For information on canned fish, see Seafood, page 520; and for fresh tuna, see Seafood, page 523.

Capsicums

Also known as sweet peppers, capsicums are members of the same tropical South American plant family as hot chillies. Their strong colours, crunchy texture and distinctive flavour enliven salads and stir-fries; if cooked for longer, and especially if charred and then skinned, their flesh becomes luxuriously soft and sweet. Their hollow shape ("capsicum" comes from the Latin for case or box) makes them an excellent vegetable for stuffing.

Because most of the capsicums you can buy are quite large, there can often be some left over after the amount needed in a recipe. These are just a few suggestions to use up extra pieces of raw capsicum: add to a stir-fry, a curry or a tomato/onion/ avocado salsa for hot or cold ham or pork; cut into strips and fry in a little olive oil with chopped garlic, serve with steamed rice and barbecued or pan-seared steak or chops; grill and peel capsicum, then marinate in olive oil, garlic and herbs — toss through cooked pasta, place in sandwiches, pizzas, or add to an antipasto platter.

Capsicums are green, with grassy flavour notes, when unripe, and ripen to red, yellow, purple-black or brown, with a sweeter flavour. Their peak season is summer but they are available year-round. Canned red ones are available, often imported under the name pimiento, which is a capsicum variety grown in Spain and Hungary.

PREPARATION Cut capsicum in half lengthways, remove seeds and white ribs and slice or cut up as required. Halves may also be left whole for stuffing. For capsicum rings, slice horizontally and pull away seeds and ribs. If capsicum is to be stuffed whole, cut a lid off the top and pull out the seeds and ribs, then stuff and cook as recipe directs.

To skin a capsicum, spear on a long-handled fork and hold over a gas flame, or char-grill, or place close to a very hot overhead griller, turning until the whole skin is blackened and blistered. Enclose in a plastic or paper bag to steam for about 10 minutes, then rub skin off under cold water. Ripe capsicums are easier to skin than green ones.

CHOOSING Capsicums should be smooth, firm and glossy, and their stems should look fresh. Avoid any with wrinkles or soft spots.

Green capsicum

Red capsicum

STORING Store whole capsicums in the refrigerator crisper, where they will keep in good condition for a few days. Store cut capsicum in a paper bag enclosed in a plastic bag in the refrigerator, where it will keep well for a few days but will gradually soften and collapse if stored for too long.

⚜ OTHER RECIPES USING CAPSICUM
Bacon and potato hash, p30
Chilli beef with snake beans, p45
Chipotle pork ribs with chorizo and smoked paprika, p123
Gazpacho, p610
Mango and avocado salsa, p309
Oven-roasted ratatouille, p658
Roasted vegetable lasagne, p402–3
Sweet and sour pork, p446

Rouille (French for rust), is a thick, rich capsicum, garlic and chilli sauce named for its deep orange-red colour. Best known as the topping for the classic seafood soup/stew bouillabaisse, it is also excellent on any fish stew, grilled white-fish fillets, boiled root vegetables and pan-fried chicken breasts.

If rouille separates, add about 1 tablespoon of boiling water and whisk until smooth.

Rouille

PREP + COOK TIME 20 MINUTES **MAKES** 1 CUP

1 medium red capsicum (200g)
1 cup (70g) stale breadcrumbs
¼ cup (60ml) water
1 fresh small red thai chilli, chopped finely

1 clove garlic, quartered
1 tablespoon lemon juice
½ teaspoon cayenne pepper
¼ cup (60ml) olive oil

1 Quarter capsicum; discard seeds and membrane. Roast under preheated grill or in very hot oven, skin-side up, until skin blisters and blackens. Cover capsicum pieces with plastic or paper 5 minutes; peel away skin then chop coarsely.
2 Combine breadcrumbs and the water in small bowl; stand 2 minutes.
3 Blend or process capsicum and breadcrumbs with chilli, garlic, juice and pepper until smooth. With motor operating, gradually add oil in thin, steady stream; process until rouille thickens.

NUTRITIONAL COUNT PER TABLESPOON 4.8g total fat (0.7g saturated fat); 280kJ (67 cal); 4.6g carbohydrate; 1.1g protein; 0.5g fibre

Yellow capsicum

Orange capsicum

Vine-ripened mini capsicums

Capsicums stuffed with pilaf

PREP + COOK TIME 1 HOUR 10 MINUTES **SERVES** 4

Both the capsicums and the roasted tomato salad are equally good warm or at room temperature; add crusty bread for a perfect, ready-to-serve summer meal for when you come home from the beach or the cricket.

2 teaspoons olive oil

1 medium red onion (170g), chopped finely

1 tablespoon slivered almonds

⅔ cup (130g) white long-grain rice

1 cup (250ml) water

2 tablespoons finely chopped dried apricots

¼ cup (35g) sun-dried tomatoes, chopped finely

¼ cup finely chopped fresh flat-leaf parsley

4 medium red capsicums (800g)

cooking-oil spray

ROASTED TOMATO SALAD

2 medium tomatoes (300g), cut into thick wedges

1 tablespoon cider vinegar

½ teaspoon cracked black pepper

1 teaspoon white sugar

1 cup firmly packed fresh flat-leaf parsley leaves

½ cup firmly packed fresh mint leaves

1 Preheat oven to 200°C/180°C fan-forced.

2 Heat oil in medium saucepan; cook onion and nuts, stirring, until onion softens. Add rice; cook, stirring, 1 minute. Add the water; bring to the boil. Reduce heat; simmer, covered, about 15 minutes or until liquid is absorbed and rice is just tender. Stir in apricot, tomato and parsley.

3 Carefully cut tops off capsicums; discard tops. Discard seeds and membranes, leaving capsicum intact. Divide pilaf among capsicums; place capsicums on oven tray, spray with oil. Roast, uncovered, on oven tray 10 minutes. Cover loosely with foil; cook about 20 minutes or until capsicums are just soft.

4 Meanwhile, make roasted tomato salad.

5 Serve capsicums with roasted tomato salad.

ROASTED TOMATO SALAD Combine tomato, vinegar, pepper and sugar in medium bowl. Drain; reserve liquid. Place tomato on oven tray; roast, uncovered, alongside capsicums about 10 minutes or until tomato just softens. Place tomato and reserved liquid in medium bowl with herbs; toss gently to combine.

NUTRITIONAL COUNT PER SERVING 5.7g total fat (0.6g saturated fat); 1087kJ (260 cal); 43.4g carbohydrate; 8.2g protein; 7.3g fibre

Roasted capsicum and ricotta salad

PREP + COOK TIME 30 MINUTES **SERVES** 4

2 medium orange capsicums (400g)

2 medium red capsicums (400g)

2 medium yellow capsicums (400g)

2 medium green capsicums (400g)

80g baby rocket leaves

1 small red onion (100g), sliced thinly

1 cup (240g) ricotta cheese, crumbled

OREGANO VINAIGRETTE

⅓ cup (80ml) olive oil

2 tablespoons red wine vinegar

1 clove garlic, crushed

1 tablespoon finely chopped fresh oregano

Pair this gorgeous salad with grilled lamb or pork and rice for a perfect dinner, take it on a picnic or serve it at a barbecue.

For information on ricotta cheese, see Cheese, page 100.

1 Preheat oven to 200°C/180°C fan-forced.

2 Quarter capsicums; discard seeds and membranes. Place, skin-side up, on oven tray. Roast, uncovered, about 20 minutes or until skin blisters and blackens. Cover capsicum pieces with plastic or paper for 5 minutes; peel away skin, then slice capsicum thickly.

3 Place ingredients for oregano vinaigrette in screw-top jar; shake well.

4 Combine capsicum with rocket and onion in large bowl; sprinkle with cheese, drizzle with vinaigrette.

NUTRITIONAL COUNT PER SERVING 25.6g total fat (6.9g saturated fat); 1396kJ (334 cal); 12.4g carbohydrate; 12.3g protein; 3.9g fibre

Carrots

Aside from their roles as a cooked vegetable to go with meats or poultry and a raw one to be grated or cut with a vegetable peeler into thin ribbons for salads, carrots are one of the foundation vegetables of good cooking. They are one of the three great aromatic vegetables (the others are celery and onion) that are used constantly in stocks, soups, stews, braises and casseroles.

Carrots don't have to be just boiled. They can be cut into julienne (matchsticks), stir-fried in oil until tender but still with a bit of bite, then tossed with shredded mint; sliced lengthways, brushed with melted butter or oil and barbecued or char-grilled for rich flavour and caramelised charred stripes; cut into halves, then halved or quartered lengthways, brushed with melted butter or oil and roasted on a baking tray at 200°C/180°C fan-forced, turning once or twice, until tender and caramelised; or, for Carrots Vichy, gently cook whole small or baby carrots in a covered saucepan with melted butter, a little sugar, a little lemon juice and a spoonful or two of water until almost tender, uncover, turn up the heat a little and shake the saucepan to roll the carrots until the liquid evaporates and they are glazed; sprinkle with fresh parsley to serve.

The subtle sweetness of a spoonful or two of grated carrot can balance a tomato sauce or any dish that seems too sharp, and grated carrot is the ingredient that gives carrot cake the fresh sweetness and moistness that have made it a star. Carrots also make a delicious juice, and are a rich source of Vitamin A.

Full-size and baby carrots are available. Baby carrots are sold in bunches and may be the thinnings of an ordinary crop or varieties that have been bred to be small when fully grown. They are delicate and tender and look stylish on the plate.

PREPARATION Young carrots need only scraping; larger ones are best peeled with a vegetable peeler as the skin may be slightly bitter. Cut up according to how the carrots are to be used. Baby carrots need no preparation except to remove their leafy tops, and are cooked whole.

CHOOSING Select smooth, bright, undamaged carrots. Avoid very large ones as they may be woody at the centre, and choose well-coloured baby carrots rather than pale ones, as both flavour and nutritional value increase with deeper colour.

STORING Store regular carrots in the refrigerator crisper where they will keep well for a week or so; store baby ones in a paper bag enclosed in a plastic bag in the refrigerator and use within a few days.

Baby carrots

Full-size carrots

Orange and maple-glazed baby carrots with hazelnuts

PREP + COOK TIME 25 MINUTES **SERVES** 4

30g butter

800g baby carrots, trimmed, peeled

2 teaspoons finely grated orange rind

¼ cup (60ml) orange juice

2 tablespoons dry white wine

2 tablespoons maple syrup

½ cup (70g) coarsely chopped roasted hazelnuts

1 Melt butter in large frying pan; cook carrots, turning occasionally, until almost tender.

2 Add rind, juice, wine and syrup; bring to the boil. Reduce heat; simmer, uncovered, until liquid has almost evaporated and carrots are tender and caramelised.

3 Serve carrots sprinkled with nuts.

NUTRITIONAL COUNT PER SERVING 17.2g total fat (4.5g saturated fat); 1145kJ (274 cal); 20.8g carbohydrate; 4.1g protein; 7.7g fibre

A most elegant vegetable to grace roast duck, pork or game birds such as quail or guinea fowl.

For information on oranges, see Oranges, page 380; for hazelnuts, see Nuts, page 346; and for maple syrup, see Sugar, page 579.

Moroccan carrot dip

PREP + COOK TIME 30 MINUTES **MAKES** 2 CUPS

Serve toasted and torn pitta bread or warmed turkish bread, cut into fingers, with this healthy and delicious dip.

4 medium carrots (480g), chopped coarsely

2 cloves garlic, peeled

1 teaspoon ground cumin

1 tablespoon honey

2 tablespoons lemon juice

¼ cup (70g) greek-style yogurt

1 tablespoon coarsely chopped fresh coriander leaves

1 Cover carrots and garlic with water in small saucepan; bring to the boil. Reduce heat; simmer, covered, about 20 minutes or until carrots are soft. Drain.

2 Blend or process carrot mixture with cumin, honey and juice until smooth. Add yogurt; blend until smooth. Sprinkle dip with coriander.

NUTRITIONAL COUNT PER TABLESPOON 0.2g total fat (0.1g saturated fat); 46kJ (11 cal); 1.9g carbohydrate; 0.3g protein; 0.5g fibre

Carrot cupcakes with maple cream cheese frosting

PREP + COOK TIME 1 HOUR (PLUS COOLING TIME) **MAKES** 12

Thanks to the carrot which makes them moist and light, these cakes will keep beautifully for several days in an airtight container.

For information on maple syrup, see Sugar, page 579.

½ cup (125ml) vegetable oil

3 eggs

1½ cups (225g) self-raising flour

1 cup (220g) firmly packed brown sugar

2 teaspoons mixed spice

2 cups (480g) firmly packed coarsely grated carrot

¾ cup (90g) coarsely chopped roasted pecans

6 roasted pecans, halved

MAPLE CREAM CHEESE FROSTING

30g butter, softened

80g cream cheese, softened

2 tablespoons maple syrup

1¼ cups (200g) icing sugar

1 Preheat oven to 180°C/160°C fan-forced. Line 12-hole (⅓-cup/80ml) muffin pan with paper cases.

2 Stir oil, eggs, sifted flour, sugar and spice in medium bowl until combined. Stir in carrot and chopped nuts. Divide mixture among paper cases.

3 Bake cupcakes about 30 minutes. Stand cupcakes 5 minutes before turning, top-side up, onto wire rack to cool.

4 Meanwhile, make maple cream cheese frosting. Spread frosting over cupcakes; top each with a nut.

MAPLE CREAM CHEESE FROSTING Beat butter, cream cheese and syrup in small bowl with electric mixer until light and fluffy; gradually beat in sifted icing sugar until spreadable.

NUTRITIONAL COUNT PER CUPCAKE 22.4g total fat (4.8g saturated fat); 1848kJ (442 cal); 53.4g carbohydrate; 5.4g protein; 2.9g fibre

CARROT CUPCAKES WITH MAPLE CREAM CHEESE FROSTING

Cauliflower

The most delicate member of the cabbage family, cauliflower adapts to many ways of cooking. It is good simply boiled or steamed and served with white sauce, cheese sauce or the classic polonaise garnish of fried breadcrumbs, chopped hard-boiled egg and parsley, or made into fritters, stir-fried or made into a creamy soup.

Although its flavour is delicate, cauliflower contains sulphur compounds similar to those of cabbage, which break down as they cook and release a distinctive odour which gets stronger as long as it is over heat, so have the extractor fan full on and cook cauliflower only until it is tender but still with a little bite. Half-cooking it, then transferring it to an oven dish and covering with cheese sauce to finish cooking in the oven is one way of minimising the problem. Another is to half-cook it and finish by pan-frying in butter with a little lemon juice and good curry powder added.

Indian cooks use cauliflower with other vegetables such as potatoes and peas for vegetable curries. Raw cauliflower florets, with other crudités (raw vegetables) such as carrot sticks, mushrooms, cherry tomatoes and baby beans, can be served with a dip or piquant dipping sauce as healthy appetisers.

Cauliflowers are available all year with their peak season in winter. As well as the familiar white cauliflower with its "curd" of closely-packed, rounded florets, there is a purple variety, a green cultivar (cultivated variety) called broccoflower, and a bright yellow-green variety with pointed florets, called romanesco. There are also baby or miniature cauliflowers. All these can be used in the same way as ordinary cauliflower.

PREPARATION
For a cauliflower to be served whole, use a sharp knife to cut off the heavy main stem and cut a cone-shaped core out of the base to allow heat to penetrate; also make deep incisions in any other thick stems. Trim off large leaves, but young ones may be left on. For miniature cauliflowers, cut off main stems and trim off coarse or damaged leaves, leaving the smaller ones on. Cook as recipe directs.

For cauliflower to be served cut up, break into florets and trim and cook as recipe directs.

Note that cauliflower should be cooked in non-reactive pans as aluminium pans can react with its chemicals and discolour it and create off-flavours.

CHOOSING
Cauliflower should be undamaged, with closely packed, unmarked florets. The leaves should look fresh, without any yellowing. White cauliflower should be white: the curd darkens with age so avoid any with deep-cream, dark-spotted or brownish florets. Coloured cauliflowers should be evenly and brightly coloured, with no suggestion of darkening.

STORING
Heavy main stems and coarse outside leaves may be trimmed off to give a more compact shape for stroring, but do not trim inner leaves or cut cauliflower up until you are ready to use it. Enclose in a paper bag, then in a plastic bag, and store in refrigerator for a few days only: cauliflower readily develops specks of dark mould if it is stored for too long.

❦ OTHER RECIPES USING CAULIFLOWER
Spicy mustard pickles, p469

Everyone's favourite, presented with style. You can, of course, use 750g of regular-sized cauliflower in place of the babies.

Cauliflower gratin

PREP + COOK TIME 30 MINUTES **SERVES** 6

6 baby cauliflowers (750g), trimmed

50g butter

¼ cup (35g) plain flour

1½ cups (375ml) hot milk

½ cup (60g) coarsely grated cheddar cheese

¼ cup (20g) finely grated parmesan cheese

1 tablespoon packaged breadcrumbs

1 Preheat oven to 220°C/200°C fan-forced.

2 Boil, steam or microwave cauliflowers until tender; drain. Place in medium shallow ovenproof dish.

3 Meanwhile, melt butter in medium saucepan, add flour; cook, stirring, until mixture bubbles and thickens. Gradually stir in milk until smooth; cook, stirring, until mixture boils and thickens. Remove from heat, stir in cheeses.

4 Pour cheese sauce over cauliflower in dish; sprinkle with breadcrumbs. Bake about 15 minutes or until browned lightly.

NUTRITIONAL COUNT PER SERVING 14.1g total fat (9g saturated fat); 865kJ (207 cal); 10.2g carbohydrate; 9.1g protein; 2.2g fibre

CAULIFLOWER GRATIN

Roasted cauliflower and garlic soup

PREP + COOK TIME 1 HOUR 25 MINUTES **SERVES** 4

1 medium cauliflower (1.5kg),
cut into small florets

1 medium leek (350g),
sliced thinly

8 cloves garlic, unpeeled

cooking-oil spray

2 teaspoons cumin seeds

1 litre (4 cups) vegetable stock

1 ½ cups (375ml) water

½ cup (125ml) milk

2 tablespoons coarsely chopped
fresh flat-leaf parsley

Roasting the cauliflower, leek and garlic makes them sweet and mellow so that they play perfectly against the spicy rouille.

For information on garlic, see Garlic, pages 214 & 215.

1 Preheat oven to 220°C/200°C fan-forced.

2 Lightly oil two medium baking dishes; divide cauliflower, leek and garlic between dishes. Spray lightly with oil. Roast, uncovered, about 25 minutes or until vegetables are tender.

3 Meanwhile, dry-fry cumin in large saucepan, stirring, until fragrant; reserve 1 teaspoon in small bowl.

4 When cool enough to handle, use fingers to squeeze garlic flesh into pan. Add cauliflower, leek, stock and the water; bring to the boil. Reduce heat; simmer, uncovered, 15 minutes.

5 Blend soup with milk, in batches, until smooth. Reheat soup in same pan; stir in parsley.

6 Serve soup drizzled with sprinkled with reserved cumin seeds and accompany with rouille (see page 85), if you like.

NUTRITIONAL COUNT PER SERVING 4.3g fat (1.4g saturated fat); 656kJ (157 cal); 12.9g carbohydrate; 12.6g protein; 8.6g fibre

---

Cauliflower puree

PREP + COOK TIME 20 MINUTES **SERVES** 4

800g cauliflower, chopped coarsely

30g butter

¼ cup (60ml) cream

1 tablespoon lemon juice

1 Boil, steam or microwave cauliflower until tender; drain.

2 Mash cauliflower with butter, cream and juice in large bowl until smooth.

3 Serve puree with grilled trout, salmon or lamb.

NUTRITIONAL COUNT PER SERVING 13g total fat (8.3g saturated fat); 673kJ (161 cal); 4.8g carbohydrate; 4.8g protein; 3.6g fibre

Celeriac

Also called celery root, celeriac is the corm (solid bulb) of a member of the celery family. When its brownish, knobbly outside is deeply peeled, delicately celery-flavoured white flesh is revealed. It can be cut up, boiled until just tender and served with melted butter or a sauce, baked like parsnip or pumpkin, made into chips, used for soup, or cooked and mashed with or without potato for a luxurious accompaniment to grilled or roasted fish, poultry or meats.

It is also delicious raw: celeriac remoulade, made by mixing crunchy grated celeriac with a parsley lemon/mustard mayonnaise, is a classic French hors d'oeuvre that can be served with prawns, smoked trout or eel as a first course or light lunch.

Celeriac is a good source of dietary fibre and provides moderate amounts of Vitamin C, B vitamins and iron. Its peak season is winter, but it is usually available from autumn to early spring.

PREPARATION Celeriac begins to discolour immediately on contact with air, so it should be dropped into water acidulated with lemon juice or vinegar as soon as it is peeled or cut.

CHOOSING Select celeriac about the size of a tennis ball or a little larger: bigger ones may have a woolly, hollow centre. It is usually sold with the green tops trimmed off, but the remaining stems should look fresh and the celeriac should feel heavy for its size. Smoother skin will mean less waste than a very knobbly one.

STORING Whole, unpeeled celeriac will keep in the refrigerator crisper for up to a week. Once cut, it must be cooked or used immediately, but as cooking destroys the enzymes that cause discolouring, it can be held for later baking or frying by first steaming for 15 minutes or until just tender, then refrigerating in a covered container until wanted.

❦ **OTHER RECIPES USING CELERIAC**
Pork with celeriac and apple, p11

Celeriac puree

PREP + COOK TIME 35 MINUTES **SERVES** 4

2 cups (500ml) chicken stock

1kg celeriac, trimmed, peeled, chopped coarsely

½ cup (125ml) cream

1 tablespoon finely chopped fresh chives

1 Bring stock to the boil in medium saucepan; add celeriac, return to the boil. Reduce heat; simmer, covered, about 30 minutes or until celeriac is tender. Drain.
2 Blend or process celeriac in batches with cream until smooth. Serve sprinkled with chives.

NUTRITIONAL COUNT PER SERVING 14.4g total fat (9.2g saturated fat); 815kJ (195 cal); 7.4g carbohydrate; 5.2g protein; 8.8g fibre

Serve this delicate vegetable with seafood, poultry or game birds such as quail or squab pigeon. For celeriac mash to serve with meats, make this recipe with 500g of celeriac (it will be more liquid) and use a wooden spoon to beat it into 500g of boiled, mashed potato – don't use a food processor as it will turn the potato to glue.

1 CELERIAC PUREE
2 CELERIAC REMOULADE

Celeriac remoulade

PREP TIME 10 MINUTES **SERVES** 4

⅓ cup (100g) mayonnaise

1 clove garlic, crushed

⅓ cup (80g) sour cream

2 tablespoons lemon juice

2 teaspoons dijon mustard

650g celeriac, trimmed, grated coarsely

½ cup coarsely chopped fresh flat-leaf parsley

1 Combine mayonnaise in medium bowl with garlic, sour cream, juice and mustard.

2 Add celeriac and parsley; mix gently.

NUTRITIONAL COUNT PER SERVING 16.3g total fat (6.2g saturated fat); 920kJ (220 cal); 12.3g carbohydrate; 3.1g protein; 6.4g fibre

Generations of diners in grand hotels and top French restaurants have enjoyed celeriac remoulade as part of the hors d'oeuvre selection. To go with it, they might choose a few olives, a little green or tomato salad, artichoke hearts, thinly sliced ham or salami, or perhaps prawns, mussels or smoked trout. You could serve it with any of these as a first course, or add good bread and some cheese for a light lunch.

Celery

We all know celery as a great snack or salad vegetable and as an indispensable aromatic vegetable that goes into stir-fries, underpins hundreds of stocks, soups and casseroles, and flavours corned beef and poached fish or chicken.

Raw celery makes a snack that children love if its channel is filled with peanut butter, cream cheese or, for kids with advanced tastes, mashed creamy blue cheese.

It is less well known as an elegant dish in its own right when braised with butter and chicken stock or sliced, cooked in butter with a little onion then baked with a covering of cream and cheese. Also often overlooked is the celery heart, the base of the bunch, which can be quartered and braised to serve as a tender, delicious vegetable.

PREPARATION Except for the tiny, pale leaves on the inner stalks, cut off the celery tops and trim the base of each stalk. Outer and some inner stalks may need stringing — pull the strings away with a small knife, starting from the top, or run a vegetable peeler down to cut away the strings. It is a matter of choice whether you string celery before eating raw or chopping for a soup or stew, but celery to be served as a separate vegetable should always be well trimmed with a vegetable peeler to ensure that no strings or tough outside will be encountered when eaten.

CHOOSING Celery should have gleaming, uncracked stalks and unwilted leaves. Choose a medium-size rather than a giant bunch which may be over-mature. If buying a half-bunch, look carefully at the edges of the cut and don't buy if they look tired or are discoloured.

STORING Cut off coarse leafy tops a little above the main stalks so that the tiny inner leaves remain intact. Trim root end by taking off a very thin slice so that the base (celery heart) is retained. Cut bunch across into halves and store them in a paper bag enclosed in a plastic bag in the refrigerator. Use within a few days.

✤ **OTHER RECIPES USING CELERY**
Cucumber, celery and apple juice, p146

Waldorf salad is named for New York's Waldorf Astoria hotel, where it was invented. Torn, poached chicken breast may be added to turn it into a main course.

For information on red apples, see Apples, pages 8 - 10.

Waldorf salad

PREP + COOK TIME 20 MINUTES **SERVES** 4

¾ cup (225g) mayonnaise

¼ cup (60ml) lemon juice

5 stalks celery (750g), trimmed, sliced thickly

2 medium red apples (300g), sliced thinly

1 small red onion (100g), sliced thinly

1 cup (100g) roasted walnuts

1 cup loosely packed fresh flat-leaf parsley leaves

1 Combine mayonnaise and juice in large bowl; mix in remaining ingredients.

NUTRITIONAL COUNT PER SERVING 35.7g total fat (3.1g saturated fat); 1852kJ (443 cal); 22.4g carbohydrate; 5.8g protein; 6.3g fibre

Cheese

Cheese means a world of flavour. There are thousands of kinds, each ready to provide splendid eating. They are all made from milk that has been separated into solids (curds) and liquid (whey) by the coagulating action of rennet, an enzyme naturally produced in a calf's stomach and now also produced by modern biotechnology from vegetable sources. Most cheeses are made from the curds but a few, such as ricotta, are made from the whey.

1 EDAM
2 PROVOLONE
3 MOZZARELLA
4 PAESANELLA
5 JARLSBERG
6 STILTON
7 GORGONZOLA
8 PECORNIO
9 PARMESAN
10 MANCHEGO
11 RED WAX CHEDDAR
12 RACLETTE
13 ARLA HAVARTI
14 BOCCONCINI
15 GRUYERE
16 CAMEMBERT
17 FONTINA
18 MASCARPONE
19 COTTAGE CHEESE
20 BRIE
21 MUNSTER
22 GOATS CHEESE (CHEVRE)
23 HALOUMI
24 FETTA

If pasteurised milk is being used, an acidic starter culture is added, too. This live culture, continuing to work throughout the life of the cheese, drives the ripening process. Many cheesemakers say that raw (unpasteurised) milk makes better cheese because it has naturally occurring bacteria which produce this type of culture during cheesemaking, that the natural bacteria make for cheese with more character, and that pasteurisation destroys not only the bacteria but flavour. However, food-safety laws forbid the use of raw milk in some countries including Australia and New Zealand.

Cheeses vary enormously according to the animal from whose milk they were made — cow's, sheep's, goat's or buffalo's — and then by the many ways in which the curds or whey can be worked to produce a particular style of cheese. In addition, the breed of the animal, the region in which it lived, the pasture on which it fed, the time of year and even the time of day it was milked, produce subtle differences. Finally, the length and conditions of the maturation period produce definitive changes between one style of cheese and another. Some cheeses are coated or inoculated with special cultures at this stage to produce the desired characteristics of that style.

FRESH- AND STRETCHED-CURD CHEESES

FRESH CHEESES These delicate, unripened cheeses are perfect to serve with fresh fruit such as figs or grapes and are used for salads and savouries and for cooking, especially sweet pastries and desserts. Often called curd or curd cheese, they may be on sale within days of being made. They are moist and soft as the curd still retains some of the whey — different proportions for different cheeses. One of the best-known fresh cheeses, *ricotta*, is actually made from whey, traditionally that of sheep's milk. *Goat's curd cheeses* are pure white and creamy with a subtle goat tang. *Sheep's curd cheese* has a dense, satiny texture and a subtle sheep aftertaste. Other fresh cheeses are *cottage cheese*, which is low-fat and tangy with a curdy texture; *quark*, which is very low-fat with a finer curd texture than cottage cheese; luscious *mascarpone* which is often thought of as a heavy cream but is actually an unripened triple-cream (65–75% fat) cheese; *fromage blanc* which is delicately sweet; and *fromage frais* which is lightly salted. Fresh *cream cheese*, rich, smooth and tangy, is made from a mixture of cream and milk. Commercial cream cheese, the best-known being Kraft

*When cheese is heated,
it releases fat and, if
overheated, becomes
stringy because moisture
is forced out of the protein.
One way to deal with this
is to grate the cheese
before adding it to a sauce
or dish so that it is well
mixed through and the tiny
amount of fat from each
shred will blend into the
surrounding ingredients,
and the second way is
to keep temperatures
moderate to low when
cooking with cheese. Add
it to sauces off the heat
and at the last minute.
The exception to all this
is when cheese or a cheese-
sauce topping is to be
browned by grilling — in
this case, the heat should
be high and the time
should be short, so that
the top will brown before
the underneath part heats
up too much.*

Philadelphia, is quite a different product, made with cream and milk but also vegetable gum and preservative to give it long life; it is available in regular and reduced-fat forms. **Neufchâtel** is a name that is used commercially for a lower-fat alternative to cream cheese, though it also belongs to a traditional, soft French cheese. **Bocconcini** are small balls of freshly made mozzarella (see Stretched-curd Cheeses). They are soft and white with a delicate, mild flavour. They are packed in brine for sale and should be stored in the brine, in a covered container in the refrigerator, where they will keep for 2 days. **Fetta** is classified as a fresh cheese but is the exception to the usual soft kind. Traditionally made with sheep's milk or a mixture of sheep's and goat's, but now often with cow's milk, it is shaped into large blocks which are salted, sliced and salted again, then packed in whey for about a month before sale. It ends up firm, sharp-flavoured and salty. It is packed in brine or in a moist plastic pack for sale and should be used within a day or so of buying.

STRETCHED-CURD CHEESES are made by dipping the curd in hot whey, then stretching and kneading it to the desired consistency. **Mozzarella**, which is traditionally made from buffalo milk but now also from cow's milk, has a pliant, smooth texture and a complex, nutty flavour; it is the **pizza cheese**, melting smoothly and pulling into stretchy strands when it is cut. **Provolone**, a cow's-milk cheese, is firmer, with a smoky flavour; it may be dolce (mild), which has been aged for 2–3 months, or piccante (strong), which has been aged for 6–12 months.

SOFT SURFACE-RIPENED CHEESES

WHITE-MOULD CHEESES are made by inoculating the lightly drained and shaped curd with a type of mushroom culture which grows, over a period of about a week, into a bloomy rind that covers the cheese and promotes maturation. These cheeses mature from the outside towards the centre. **Brie** and **camembert** types are fully ripe when the centre is as soft as the outside; **triple cream** (65–70% fat) white-mould cheeses will be luscious with the centre just a little firmer.

There are two types of white-mould cheeses, described in the trade as "modern" and "traditional". Modern types are stabilised by partially or completely destroying the live culture that causes ripening, so that the cheeses have a very predictable shelf life of up to 60 days. There is some flavour development over this time, but they are ready to eat almost as soon as they leave the factory; their coating is designed to remain pristine white. Traditional types are not stabilised and ripen naturally: texture and flavour change daily as the cheese matures and, when they reach perfect ripeness, this stage lasts only about 7–10 days, after which they decline, gradually developing a pungent ammonia smell. It is acceptable for the bloom of traditional white-mould cheeses to become slightly wrinkled and discoloured and slightly smelly, though it should never be sticky. The reward for these uncertainties is a cheese of character, with mouth-watering aroma, a luscious, oozing texture and rich, individual flavour.

WASHED-RIND CHEESES are washed repeatedly during maturation with a brine mixture which may contain beer or wine as well as salt. The cheese is matured in cool, dark and damp cellars or maturation rooms where there is a combination of airborne yeasts and flora containing specialised bacteria which migrate naturally to the surface of the cheeses. As the cheeses ripen over a period of 6–12 weeks, the flora contributes a unique dimension to their flavour — and also the characteristic strong smell which makes washed-rind cheese a love-it-or-hate-it proposition. Its devotees point out that it is only the rind that smells and that the cheese itself is beautifully complex in flavour and is often mild and buttery. The most famous washed-rind cheeses are **munster**, made in the Alsace region of France, and **limburger**, which is often described as having the same odour as smelly feet and is the butt of many jokes (Limburger is the only known weakness of Mighty Mouse; the Beverly Hillbillies reserve their wall safe for storing Limburger, etc). It is named for the Belgian city of Limbourg where it was first made, but is now mainly made in Germany and the USA.

When buying washed-rind cheese, check that the rind is not dull, cracked or tacky, which would indicate that it is past its best. The cheese should be served with its rind on but it is preferable to cut it off before eating. Washed-rind cheeses have a longer than average shelf life of 5–6 weeks. They are at their best in autumn because the new grass after summer produces the best milk for making them — and they don't smell as strong in the cooler weather.

BLUE-VEINED CHEESES The characteristic blue-vein aroma and flavour come from blue-mould spores with which the milk is cultured, after which, at the right time in the ripening process, the cheeses are pierced with stainless-steel needles to let air in and allow the blue mould to grow along the needle holes and wander into the crevices of the curd. Blue cheeses can be creamy, firm or crumbly in texture and can be made with any kind of milk: of the three most famous blue cheeses, England's **stilton** and Italy's **gorgonzola** are made from cow's milk and France's **roquefort** is made from sheep's milk. **Danish blue**, also known as danablu, was developed with the intention of making a "Danish roquefort", but has gained worldwide popularity for its rather milder taste with sharp, salty flavour notes. Numerous creamy and gentle blues have been marketed with the aim of attracting people who find the pungent aroma and flavour of traditional blue cheeses off-putting: **blue brie** and Italian **dolcelatte** ("sweet milk"), created especially for the English market, are two successful ones. **Blue castello** is a Danish cheese whose creamy body and mellow flavour place it between the pungent and the very mild blues. The relatively young Australian cheese industry has produced some distinguished blues, including Tasmanian roaring forties, with a moist texture, salty tang and biting flavour with a sweet/acid aftertaste, and Gippsland blue, with a dry, yeasty natural rind, moist, creamy body and mild flavour that becomes stronger with maturity. Blue cheeses go well with dried muscatels and nuts, especially walnuts, and their best wine companions are sweet dessert wines and port — though connoisseurs do not approve of the custom of scooping out the centre of a stilton and pouring in port.

SEMI-HARD CHEESES, firm and sliceable, form the huge cheese group that includes English **cheddar** and **red leicester**, Dutch **edam** and **gouda**, Danish **havarti** and **jarlsberg**, Swiss **tilsit** and **raclette**, Italy's **fontina** and many more. Most of these names are now used to mean a cheese in the style of the original, and cheddars, edams and so on are now made in many

Cheese is highly nutritious, containing in concentrated form most of the protein, much of the mineral content and virtually all the fat and fat-soluble vitamins of the milk from which it was made. In particular, people with lactose intolerance (see Milk, page 316) can usually eat cheese without ill effect as most of the lactose from the milk is left behind in the whey (ricotta and any other cheese made from whey is not, of course, suitable for the lactose-intolerant).

Every cook should have a good cheese grater and a cheese plane. The fastest way to grate a lot of cheese is with a rotary grater — you turn the handle and the cheese falls on to the plate beneath — though a slightly curved Microplane grater, with its rows of razor-sharp blades, which you hold at an angle on a board while running the cheese down it, will also grate fast and more cleanly, and is useful for grating dozens of other foods, from chocolate to zucchini. as well. A cheese plane, which you pull towards you across the surface of the cheese, takes off thinner and more even slices than you can cut by hand and does it faster too.

To slice goats cheese and other cheeses that are too soft or sticky for a knife, use a length of plain dental floss or strong cotton, held taut between your hands, to cut downward into neat slices.

countries. These are the cheese all-rounders, good as snacks or in sandwiches, on the cheese board or grated into sauces, soups, fondues or vegetable dishes. Raclette is famous as a cheese for melting and is also the name of a dish made by melting it over the fire and scraping it on to potatoes or bread. Cheddar and red leicester differ from the other styles in being harder and more open-textured; the others are softer, smoother and more dense. Cheddar styles are, traditionally, cellar-matured for 6–12 months while most other semi-hard cheeses are matured for about 9 months, though vacuum-packing often replaces the traditional ripening conditions (with a consequent lessening of the character and flavour of the cheese). Club cheddar is made by forming milled cheese into a block under pressure. It has a grainy texture and does not hold together well. **Vintage** cheese is a commercial term meaning a well aged and therefore mellow and strong-flavoured cheese. Cheddar, mozzarella and other cheeses are sometimes smoked for a big, new flavour that goes very well with bread and beer.

HARD-COOKED CHEESES are made by cooking the curds at a high temperature so that they contract and squeeze out excess moisture, leaving a drier, more concentrated curd. The cheeses are then formed and placed under heavy pressure to expel more moisture and finally matured for at least six to 12 months, some being kept in the cellars for four or five years. Hard-cooked cheeses may be granular or smooth, depending on how the curd was handled. Granular cheeses are dry and almost brittle; smooth cheeses are slightly more elastic. Italian **parmigiano-reggiano** or **parmesan**, the "king" of hard cheeses, has been copied all over the world but never

equalled. A granular cheese, it can be identified by its name stippled on its rind and also by the crystal-like flake of its texture, indicating its minimum two-year ageing period. Its flavour is huge but mellow. It is often thought of as a cheese for grating, but it is also magnificent on the cheeseboard. **Grana pedano** is a cheese of a similar style but lower in fat, usually less aged, less spectacular in flavour and more reasonable in price. Swiss **gruyère** is very dense with a firm but supple texture and a few small holes from gas given off by bacteria in the ripening culture; **emmenthal**, also Swiss, is medium-hard with larger holes. **Pecorino** is the generic Italian word for cheese made from sheep's milk; **pecorino romano**, the best known outside Italy, has a distinctive, strong, salty flavour and is a favourite cheese to grate over highly-flavoured pasta dishes. All these cheese styles are now made in many other countries than their homelands.

GOAT AND SHEEP MILK CHEESES Goat cheeses, also known as chèvre, range from delicate, fresh curd (see Fresh Cheeses) to full-flavoured, firm, mature styles, often described as affiné (ripened), sometimes shaped into pyramids or logs and coated with ash or herbs, and always with a subtle or earthy goat tang. They have, traditionally, been farmhouse cheeses (see CHOOSING) as many peasant farmers had a few goats. They have gained greatly in popularity in the past decade or two and are now produced on a much larger scale, but small-scale, hand-made cheeses are usually better. Some of the world's best, **kervalla** goat cheeses, come from a small West Australian herd.

Sheep cheeses are milder than goat's; the best known are ricotta (see Fresh Cheeses), roquefort (see Blue-veined Cheeses), and **haloumi**, a salty Greek cheese which is always grilled or fried, when its rubbery texture turns to a firm but tender consistency and its flavour takes on a delicious savoury edge.

Manchego is a famous semi-firm Spanish sheep's cheese which is mild when young, but after ageing for 3 months or longer, becomes a rich golden colour and develops a full, tangy flavour with the characteristic aftertaste of sheep's milk.

PROCESSED CHEESES have been heat-treated to kill the bacterial culture within the cheese so that they will not continue to ripen but will maintain a constant texture and flavour. Some processed cheeses have also had emulsifiers and preservatives added. Though far removed from the complexity and character of natural cheese, these products do have the advantage of melting smoothly without separating, so they behave reliably as ingredients in a variety of dishes and they do not run off if used, say, in a hamburger. Low-fat cheeses have had fat replaced with various proteins and carbohydrates and often include sugar or other flavourings to make up for the loss of the flavour that fat carries; these products do not melt properly but soften and then dry out.

CHOOSING
You can buy respectable, well-made cheeses at the supermarket but they will probably have been heat-treated or otherwise stabilised for long shelf-life so that their full flavour potential has been compromised. For cheese at its best, look to speciality food shops, farmers' markets or a delicatessen with a cheese-enthusiast in charge: it takes trouble and knowledge to look after cheeses and to sell you one that will be in prime condition when you want to eat it. The ideal is to buy cheese that has been freshly cut. If a cheese is marked "*farmhouse cheese*", that means that it has been made using only milk from the herd of the farm where it was made.

STORING
The ideal storage conditions for cheese are to be cloth-wrapped and kept in a damp place such as a cellar at a temperature of 9–12°C. The nearest to this that most of us can provide is the refrigerator. Unprocessed cheese still has the live culture that drives ripening, so it needs air but must be protected from drying. Processed cheese also needs protection from drying but should not be shut off from air either, as that can encourage unwanted mould and off flavours. A reasonable compromise with the ideal is to wrap the cheese loosely in calico or muslin (or the modern equivalent, a new disposable cloth), enclose loosely in a plastic bag and store it in the refrigerator, preferably in the crisper. Cheese should be eaten at room temperature, so should be removed from the refrigerator an hour or two before using.

❦ OTHER RECIPES USING CHEESE

 1
 2

3 4

Quattro formaggio sauce

PREP + COOK TIME 15 MINUTES **MAKES** 1½ CUPS

50g butter

300ml cream

50g gorgonzola cheese, crumbled

1 cup (80g) finely grated pecorino cheese

½ cup (50g) finely grated fontina cheese

1 cup (80g) finely grated parmesan cheese

1 Melt butter in medium frying pan, add cream; bring to the boil then reduce heat. Simmer, uncovered, about 5 minutes or until mixture reduces by half.

2 Remove pan from heat; add cheeses gradually, stirring, until sauce is almost smooth.

3 Serve sauce with gnocchi or pasta, if you like.

NUTRITIONAL COUNT PER TABLESPOON 13.9g total fat (9.1g saturated fat); 598kJ (143 cal); 0.5g carbohydrate; 4.6g protein; 0.0g fibre

Serve this sauce immediately on 500g freshly cooked rigatoni or other short pasta (see Pasta, pages 396-398) to serve 4 as a main course or 6 as a starter. Use other cheeses if the ones here are unavailable. Gruyère, provolone, raclette, vintage cheddar or a mild blue are all great possibilities.

Roquefort and pear salad

PREP + COOK TIME 20 MINUTES **SERVES** 4

1 small french bread stick (150g), sliced thinly

100g roquefort cheese, softened

2 small pears (360g), sliced thinly

1 cup (110g) coarsely chopped roasted walnuts

1 butter lettuce, leaves separated

100g baby spinach leaves

BUTTERMILK DRESSING

¼ cup (60ml) buttermilk

1 tablespoon lemon juice

1 tablespoon olive oil

½ teaspoon caster sugar

1 clove garlic, crushed

Pear and blue cheese is one of the great food partnerships. Any soft blue would work well here.

For information on buttermilk, see Milk, page 317; and for pears, see Pears, pages 416-418.

1 Preheat oven to 200°C/180°C fan-forced.

2 Place bread on oven tray; toast, in oven, until browned both sides.

3 Meanwhile, make buttermilk dressing.

4 Spread toast with cheese.

5 Place remaining ingredients in large serving bowl with dressing; toss gently to combine. Serve salad with cheese toast.

BUTTERMILK DRESSING Whisk ingredients in medium bowl.

NUTRITIONAL COUNT PER SERVING 33.7g total fat (7.4g saturated fat); 2082kJ (498 cal); 31.2g carbohydrate; 14.6g protein; 7.7g fibre

1 QUATTRO FORMAGGIO SAUCE **2** ROQUEFORT AND PEAR SALAD
3 GREEK FETTA SALAD [P 108] **4** ITALIAN-STYLE BEAN SALAD WITH FRESH MOZZARELLA [P 108]

Greek fetta salad

PREP TIME 20 MINUTES **SERVES** 4

Greek fetta salad is a great accompaniment to beef or lamb kebabs — perfect for a summer barbecue or for dinner when you're pressed for time.

¼ cup (60ml) olive oil

1 tablespoon lemon juice

1 tablespoon white wine vinegar

1 tablespoon finely chopped fresh oregano

1 clove garlic, crushed

3 medium tomatoes (450g), cut into wedges

2 lebanese cucumbers (260g), chopped coarsely

1 small red onion (100g), sliced thinly

1 small red capsicum (150g), sliced thinly

½ cup (75g) seeded black olives

200g fetta cheese, chopped coarsely

1 Whisk oil, juice, vinegar, oregano and garlic in large bowl.

2 Add tomato and remaining ingredients to bowl; toss gently to combine.

NUTRITIONAL COUNT PER SERVING 25.8g total fat (9.6g saturated fat); 1359kJ (325 cal); 10.8g carbohydrate; 11.5g protein; 3.2g fibre

Italian-style bean salad with fresh mozzarella

PREP + COOK TIME 20 MINUTES **SERVES** 4

This is a substantial main-course salad, needing only good bread for serving.

For information on green beans, see Beans, Fresh, page 40.

200g green beans, trimmed, halved crossways

2 x 420g cans four-bean mix, rinsed, drained

2 teaspoons finely chopped fresh thyme

2 teaspoons finely chopped fresh oregano

⅓ cup coarsely chopped fresh flat-leaf parsley

100g mozzarella cheese, sliced thickly

¾ cup (110g) drained sun-dried tomatoes, sliced thinly

1 medium brown onion (150g), sliced thinly

1 cup (120g) seeded black olives

ITALIAN DRESSING

1 clove garlic, crushed

2 tablespoons olive oil

2 tablespoons lemon juice

1 Place ingredients for italian dressing in screw-top jar; shake well.

2 Boil, steam or microwave green beans until tender; drain. Rinse under cold water; drain.

3 Place green beans and four-bean mix in medium bowl with remaining ingredients and dressing; toss gently to combine.

NUTRITIONAL COUNT PER SERVING 16.6g total fat (5.1g saturated fat); 1438kJ (344 cal); 28g carbohydrate; 15.6g protein; 10.5g fibre

Gorgonzola fritters

PREP + COOK TIME 30 MINUTES (PLUS STANDING TIME) **MAKES** 36

You can use any other soft blue cheese instead of gorgonzola.

1 cup (200g) ricotta cheese

1 cup (185g) coarsely chopped gorgonzola cheese

2 eggs, beaten lightly

½ cup (75g) plain flour

vegetable oil, for deep-frying

1 cup (80g) finely grated parmesan cheese

1 Combine ricotta, gorgonzola and egg in medium bowl. Whisk in flour; stand 1 hour.

2 Heat oil in large saucepan; deep-fry heaped teaspoons of cheese mixture, turning occasionally, until fritters are browned lightly all over and cooked through. (Do not have oil too hot or fritters will over-brown before cooking through.)

3 Place parmesan in medium bowl; toss hot fritters, in batches, to coat as they are cooked.

NUTRITIONAL COUNT PER FRITTER 3.9g total fat (2.1g saturated fat); 226kJ (54 cal); 1.6g carbohydrate; 3.1g protein; 0.1g fibre

---

Cheese gnocchi with fresh tomato sauce and pancetta

PREP + COOK TIME 35 MINUTES **SERVES** 4

It is best to mix the ingredients for the gnocchi just before cooking them, as they can be heavy if the mixture is left to stand.

For information on pancetta, see Bacon, pages 28 & 29; and for tomatoes, see Tomatoes, pages 606 & 607.

2 cups (480g) ricotta cheese

1 cup (80g) finely grated parmesan cheese

½ cup (75g) plain flour

2 eggs

1 tablespoon olive oil

4 thin slices pancetta (60g), halved

4 medium tomatoes (600g), chopped coarsely

4 green onions, sliced thinly

2 tablespoons coarsely chopped fresh oregano

2 tablespoons balsamic vinegar

1 Preheat grill.

2 Combine cheeses, flour, eggs and oil in large bowl. Drop rounded tablespoons of mixture into large saucepan of boiling water; cook, without stirring, until gnocchi float to surface. Remove from pan with slotted spoon; drain. Keep warm.

3 Grill pancetta until browned and crisp.

4 Meanwhile, combine tomato, onion, oregano and vinegar in medium bowl.

5 Serve gnocchi topped with tomato sauce and pancetta.

NUTRITIONAL COUNT PER SERVING 29.7g total fat (15g saturated fat); 1952kJ (467 cal); 18.4g carbohydrate; 30.1g protein; 2.7g fibre

We used basil, flat-leaf parsley and oregano for the herb mixture here, but you could choose other herbs such as thyme, mint, chives, rosemary or sage.

For information on red chillies, see Chillies, pages 118 – 120.

Parmesan, chilli and herb baked ricotta

PREP + COOK TIME 1 HOUR (PLUS STANDING AND COOLING TIME) **MAKES** 6

½ cup finely chopped mixed fresh herbs

2 fresh long red chillies, chopped finely

1 teaspoon sea salt flakes

½ cup (40g) finely grated parmesan cheese

3⅓ cups (800g) ricotta cheese

2 eggs

1 teaspoon finely grated lemon rind

1 Preheat oven to 120°C/100°C fan-forced. Oil six-hole (¾-cup/180ml) texas muffin pan; line bases with baking paper.

2 Combine herbs, chilli and salt in small bowl; spread evenly onto oven tray. Roast about 20 minutes or until dried; cool. Stir parmesan into herb mixture.

3 Place 1 tablespoon of herb mixture into each pan hole; shake pan to coat bases and sides of holes with mixture. Increase oven to 180°C/160°C fan-forced.

4 Combine ricotta, eggs, rind and remaining herb mixture in medium bowl. Drop spoonfuls of mixture into pan holes; smooth surface with a spatula, pressing down firmly to remove any air bubbles.

5 Bake ricotta about 20 minutes or until firm. Stand in pan 15 minutes. Use palette knife to loosen ricotta from side of pan before turning out, top-side down. Cool.

NUTRITIONAL COUNT PER BAKED RICOTTA 19g total fat (11.5g saturated fat); 1053kJ (252 cal); 1.7g carbohydrate; 18.9g protein; 0.3g fibre

Serve this for lunch with, perhaps, a bowl of soup to follow, or for a substantial snack. Prepare the salad ingredients, make the dressing and slice the cheese ahead of time. Oven-crisped, torn pitta or other flatbread would be a nice accompaniment.

For information on curly endive, see Greens, Salad, pages 248 – 250; and for baby spinach leaves, see Spinach, page 568.

Pan-fried haloumi with green salad

PREP + COOK TIME 20 MINUTES **SERVES** 4

150g curly endive

50g baby spinach leaves

½ cup loosely packed fresh flat-leaf parsley leaves

⅔ cup (125g) drained semi-dried tomatoes, chopped coarsely

250g haloumi cheese

LEMON DIJON DRESSING

¼ cup (60ml) lemon juice

1 clove garlic, crushed

1 tablespoon water

1 teaspoon white sugar

1 teaspoon dijon mustard

¼ teaspoon ground cumin

pinch cayenne pepper

1 Place endive, spinach, parsley and tomato in medium bowl. Cut cheese into eight slices.

2 Heat oiled medium frying pan; cook cheese, in batches, until browned both sides.

3 Meanwhile, place ingredients for lemon dijon dressing in screw-top jar; shake well.

4 Add dressing to salad; toss gently to combine. Serve salad topped with cheese.

NUTRITIONAL COUNT PER SERVING 12g total fat (7g saturated fat); 949kJ (227 cal); 11.8g carbohydrate; 17.3g protein; 5.4g fibre

1 GRUYERE SOUFFLE
2 INDIVIDUAL TIRAMISU

Gruyère soufflé

PREP + COOK TIME 55 MINUTES **SERVES** 4

⅓ cup (50g) plain flour
1⅔ cups (410ml) milk
20g butter, chopped
6 eggs, separated

1⅓ cups (165g) grated gruyère cheese
100g sliced smoked salmon
1½ teaspoons drained baby capers
1 tablespoon fresh chervil leaves

Take the soufflé to the table on a hot plate so that it stays puffed up. To serve it, have two warmed spoons ready, hold vertically and spread the top of the soufflé apart; give each diner some of the crust and some of the creamy centre.

For information on eggs, see Eggs, page 164.

1 Preheat oven to 200°C/180°C fan-forced. Oil 2 litre (8-cup) capacity ovenproof soufflé dish; place on oven tray.
2 Place flour in small saucepan; gradually whisk in milk until smooth. Cook flour mixture over medium heat, whisking constantly, until mixture boils and thickens. Remove from heat; stir in butter. Whisk in egg yolks and cheese. Transfer mixture to large mixing bowl.
3 Beat egg whites in large bowl with electric mixer until soft peaks form. Fold egg whites into cheese mixture, in two batches. Pour mixture into the dish.
4 Bake soufflé about 35 to 40 minutes or until well risen and browned.
5 Arrange salmon on serving platter, top with capers and chervil; serve wtih soufflé.

NUTRITIONAL COUNT PER SERVING 33.8g total fat (18.5g saturated fat); 2048kJ (490 cal); 14.5g carbohydrate; 32.3g protein; 0.5g fibre

Individual tiramisu

PREP + COOK TIME 40 MINUTES (PLUS REFRIGERATION TIME) **MAKES** 6

2 unfilled round sponge cakes (460g)

2 tablespoons instant coffee granules

¼ cup (60ml) boiling water

⅓ cup (80ml) coffee-flavoured liqueur

1 teaspoon gelatine

1 tablespoon boiling water, extra

¾ cup (180ml) thickened cream

¼ cup (40g) icing sugar

1 teaspoon vanilla extract

1½ cups (375g) mascarpone cheese

GANACHE
⅔ cup (160ml) cream

180g dark eating chocolate, chopped coarsely

1 Make ganache.

2 Line each hole of a greased six-hole (¾-cup/180ml) texas muffin pan with plastic wrap. Divide half the ganache over the base of each pan hole. Refrigerate 20 minutes.

3 Meanwhile, cut each sponge cake into three slices horizontally. Cut six 8cm rounds from three sponge slices and six 7cm rounds from remaining three sponge slices.

4 Dissolve coffee in the boiling water in small jug; stir in liqueur.

5 Sprinkle gelatine over the extra boiling water in another small jug; stir until gelatine dissolves. Cool.

6 Beat cream, sifted icing sugar and extract in small bowl with electric mixer until soft peaks form; beat in gelatine mixture. Transfer mixture to large bowl; fold in cheese.

7 Brush both sides of sponge rounds with coffee mixture. Spread half the cheese mixture into the pan holes; top with small sponge rounds. Spread remaining cheese mixture over sponge layers; top with larger sponge rounds.

8 Spread remaining ganache over sponge layers; refrigerate 3 hours or overnight.

9 Remove tiramisu from pan; turn, top-side down, onto serving plates, remove plastic wrap. Serve dusted with a little sifted cocoa powder.

GANACHE Bring cream to the boil in small saucepan; remove from heat. Add chocolate; stir until smooth.

NUTRITIONAL COUNT PER TIRAMISU 70.5g total fat (44.6g saturated fat); 4255kJ (1018 cal); 80.6g carbohydrate; 10.8g protein; 2.1g fibre

After spooning half the ganache into the pan holes, leave the remainder at room temperature so that it will be soft enough to spread on the tiramisu. These are lovely served with fresh blueberries or other seasonal berries.

Cherries

Cherries are among the few truly seasonal fruits still left in our markets. Their first appearance every summer adds a thrill to the food shopping. Most of those that come to market are the dark, fleshy varieties called black cherries, but you will sometimes see bright red or "white" varieties, which are actually cream with a red blush.

Because their season is so fleeting, cherries are one of the best fruits to bottle and enjoy when there are no fresh ones around. They are lovely for all manner of sweet things and also, with their sweetness sharpened by a little lemon juice, to serve as an edible garnish for hot or cold ham, pork or poultry.

♣ **OTHER RECIPES USING CHERRIES**
Brandied cherry jam, p465

They are not only lovely to eat just as they are but also ready to be gently poached or preserved in sugar syrup or wine, starred in pastries and cakes, studded through jelly or ice-cream, or pickled to go with lamb or pork. They can also be packed, intact or stoned, in sugar syrup and frozen (they will be soft when thawed). And if you have the luck to find a sour variety, you have the kind that European pâtissiers choose for their tang in such creations as Black Forest cake. Dried cherries are being produced in a small way but are not, as yet, widely available.

PREPARATION Cherries can be stoned by halving and digging out the stone, or by using a special cherry stoner, available from good kitchen shops or

professional kitchen equipment shops. There are various designs, but they all operate on the principle of placing the cherry in a little cup with a hole and punching out the stone, which falls through the hole.

CHOOSING Select plump, glossy, undamaged cherries with fresh-looking green stems intact; avoid dull or undersized fruit.

STORING Store cherries in a covered container in the refrigerator if you want them to keep as long as possible (about a week), but if you know they'll disappear quickly, give yourself the pleasure of piling them in a pretty dish and enjoying their beauty.

Black cherries

White cherries

Cherries jubilee

PREP + COOK TIME 15 MINUTES **SERVES** 4

250g fresh black cherries, seeded

⅓ cup (75g) caster sugar

1 cinnamon stick

½ cup (125ml) water

2 teaspoons arrowroot

1 tablespoon water, extra

⅓ cup (80ml) brandy

1 Place cherries, sugar, cinnamon and the water in small saucepan; cook, stirring, until mixture boils. Reduce heat; simmer, uncovered, without stirring, 2 minutes. Strain syrup into small heatproof bowl; discard cinnamon.

2 Return cherry mixture to pan; stir in blended arrowroot and the extra water. Cook, stirring, until mixture boils and thickens slightly.

3 Heat brandy in small saucepan; stir into cherry mixture. Serve immediately, with thickened cream and macaroons.

NUTRITIONAL COUNT PER SERVING 0.1g total fat (0g saturated fat); 601kJ (144 cal); 24.3g carbohydrate; 0.5g protein; 0.8g fibre

The great chef Auguste Escoffier invented this dish for one of Queen Victoria's jubilees, though no one is sure whether it was for her golden jubilee in 1887 or her diamond one in 1897. It's fun if you flame the brandy and take the dish in flames to the table. Use a little more brandy as some will be burnt off. With the exhaust fan off, warm it in a small saucepan, set alight with a long match and pour over the cherries.

Cherry chocolate cheesecake

PREP + COOK TIME 1 HOUR 10 MINUTES (PLUS COOLING AND REFRIGERATION TIME) **SERVES** 12

125g plain chocolate biscuits

75g butter, melted

500g cream cheese, softened

⅓ cup (75g) caster sugar

2 eggs

200g dark eating chocolate, melted

3 x 55g Cherry Ripe bars, chopped coarsely

250g fresh black cherries, halved, seeded

1 Grease 24cm springform tin.

2 Process biscuits until fine. Add butter, process until combined. Press mixture over base of tin. Place tin on oven tray; refrigerate 30 minutes.

3 Preheat oven to 180°C/160°C fan-forced.

4 Beat cheese and sugar in medium bowl with electric mixer until smooth; beat in eggs, one at a time. Gradually beat in cooled chocolate; stir in Cherry Ripe and cherries.

5 Spread filling into tin; bake about 50 minutes. Cool in oven with door ajar.

6 Refrigerate cheesecake 3 hours or overnight. Serve topped with dark chocolate curls, if you like.

NUTRITIONAL COUNT PER SERVING 29.9g total fat (18.9g saturated fat); 1738kJ (416 cal); 29.7g carbohydrate; 7g protein; 1.2g fibre

To make chocolate curls, have a bar of plain chocolate at room temperature and use a swivel-bladed vegetable peeler to pare thin curls from the edge. Store the curls on a plate in the refrigerator until needed.

For information on cream cheese, see Cheese, pages 100–102; and for dark eating chocolate, see Chocolate, page 124.

Sweet cherry and almond tarts

PREP + COOK TIME 50 MINUTES (PLUS REFRIGERATION TIME) **MAKES** 8

The best way to divide the pastry accurately into eight equal pieces is by weight. For more information on pastry, see Pastry pages 404–406.

For information on almonds, see Nuts, page 344.

1½ cups (225g) plain flour

150g butter, chopped coarsely

⅓ cup (55g) icing sugar

2 tablespoons iced water, approximately

350g fresh cherries, seeded

2 tablespoons white sugar

ALMOND FILLING

60g butter, softened

⅓ cup (75g) firmly packed brown sugar

1 egg

1 tablespoon plain flour

1 cup (100g) almond meal

1 Process flour, butter and icing sugar until mixture resembles breadcrumbs. Gradually add the water, if required, processing until mixture just comes together. Knead on floured surface until smooth, cover; refrigerate 30 minutes.

2 Preheat oven to 200°C/180°C fan-forced. Grease four oven trays; line with baking paper.

3 Make almond filling.

4 Divide pastry into eight pieces. Roll each piece into a 15cm-round on floured surface; place two rounds on each tray. Divide almond filling among rounds, leaving a 4cm border. Top with cherries; fold over border. Sprinkle with white sugar.

5 Bake about 20 minutes or until pastry is browned lightly.

ALMOND FILLING Beat butter, sugar and egg in small bowl with electric mixer until smooth. Stir in flour and meal.

NUTRITIONAL COUNT PER TART 29.5g total fat (14.9g saturated fat); 1990kJ (476 cal); 44.6g carbohydrate; 7g protein; 2.7g fibre

---

Cherry friand slice

PREP + COOK TIME 55 MINUTES **MAKES** 16

Cut the slice into squares or fingers to serve. Leftovers (if any) will keep for a few days in an airtight container.

For information on almonds, see Nuts, page 344.

4 egg whites

100g butter, melted

1 tablespoon milk

½ teaspoon vanilla extract

1 cup (125g) almond meal

1 cup (160g) icing sugar

⅓ cup (50g) self-raising flour

1 vanilla bean

100g fresh cherries, seeded, chopped coarsely

1 Preheat oven to 160°C/140°C fan-forced. Grease 19cm x 29cm slice pan; line base and two long sides with baking paper, extending paper 5cm over long sides.

2 Whisk egg whites in large bowl with fork until combined. Add butter, milk, extract, meal and sifted icing sugar and flour; stir until just combined. Split vanilla bean in half lengthways; scrape seeds from bean, stir in seeds. Pour mixture into pan; sprinkle with cherries.

3 Bake slice 30 minutes. Stand slice in pan 10 minutes; lift onto wire rack to cool.

NUTRITIONAL COUNT PER PIECE 9.5g total fat (3.7g saturated fat); 631kJ (151 cal); 13.1g carbohydrate; 2.9g protein; 0.9g fibre

Chillies

Chillies are the hot members of the capsicum family. In places where they are a vital part of the food culture, the different varieties are sold by name. Most Australian greengrocers haven't caught up with that and, if asked about the heat of the anonymous chillies on display, may or may not give a reliable answer.

1 JALAPENO
2 GREEN SERRANO
3 PASILLA
4 PIRI PIRI
5 HABANERO
6 SMALL RED THAI (BIRDS-EYE)
7 ANCHO
8 CHIPOTLE
9 CAYENNE
10 LONG GREEN/YELLOW
11 SCOTCH BONNET
12 RED SERRANO

As the ranks of chilli-lovers grow ever greater, however, it is getting easier to find chillies by name at speciality food stores or keen greengrocers. If you know the name, you can get some idea of the heat. If in doubt, you can check for yourself before using a chilli. The burning mouth from eating chilli is caused by a substance called capsicain which also reacts on skin, so cut one end of the chilli open, rub the cut surface on a small patch of the back of your hand and wait 20 minutes. You can judge the fieriness by whether the skin blisters, gets a red mark or merely feels a stimulating buzz. To moderate the heat, you can halve the chilli lengthwise and scrape out the seeds and white membrane, which are the hottest parts; true chilli-lovers leave them in to get the maximum blast. Heat is not, however, the only thing to look for. Fresh chillies vary in their sweet, rich, fresh, mellow, and other flavour flavours, and dried or smoked ones may have savoury or caramel notes. Chillies are available all year.

HANDLING CHILLIES

Even a tiny amount of capsicain left on your hands after cutting chillies can cause trouble hours later if you should happen to touch your eyes or nose. Ideally, wear disposable plastic gloves, available at chemists and supermarkets. Cut on a surface that can be thoroughly washed. Capsicain is oily and hard to wash off, so thoroughly wash everything you have used, including your hands even if you were wearing gloves, in warm soapy water as soon as you have finished cutting. Even the invisible fumes from freshly cut chilli can cause choking and wheezing in some people, so if you have ever had any breathing problem such as asthma or an allergic reaction, get someone else to do the job, or failing that, use some form of prepared chilli such as chilli flakes or powder, chopped freeze-dried chilli or a chilli paste or sauce.

VARIETIES

The colours mentioned below are those of the ripe fruit; some chillies are also used green.

In general, green (unripe) chillies are juicier and stronger-flavoured than ripe ones, while ripe ones are sweeter and more fragrant. The capsicain level increases from pollination until the fruit begins to change from green to the ripe colour: red, yellow, brown, purple, orange or sometimes a deeper green. As ripening continues, the level drops a little. Again in general, the smaller the chilli the hotter it is.
JALAPENO is a medium to hot red chilli with thick, juicy flesh and a complex, slightly sweet flavour.

If you like the flavour of chilli but can't take the heat, there are two commercial preparations you should know about. One is Mexican chilli powder, which has paprika, oregano, cumin, pepper and garlic besides chilli, and is mild in heat but with a good spicy flavour. The other is sweet chilli sauce, a thin, comparatively mild sauce made from red chilli, sugar, garlic and vinegar. It doesn't have enough fire, for most people's taste, to be useful as an ingredient, but is used as a dipping sauce and condiment and in dressings. Both these products are inexpensive and available in most supermarkets.

❧ OTHER RECIPES USING CHILLIES

SERRANO is a round chilli that ripens from green to red to black. It is very hot.

PASILLA is a dried chilaca chilli, the form in which the chilaca is nearly always used. It is dark brown and mild to medium hot, with rich smoky flavour.

PIRI PIRI, also known as peri peri and pil pil, is a red/purple African birds-eye chilli (see above) used in the cooking of the ex-Portuguese colonies of Mozambique and Angola and also widely used in Portugal, especially in piri piri sauce. It is intensely hot.

HABANERO is a short chilli rather like a tiny, pointed red or orange capsicum. It is one of the hottest of all chillies.

SMALL RED THAI, also known as birds-eye, is tiny, bright red and intensely hot.

ANCHO is a poblano chilli dried until it is brownish red. It is mildly hot, with a sweetish full-bodied flavour.

CHIPOTLE is a smoke-dried jalapeño, deep red and very hot, with a smoky flavour.

CAYENNE, the chilli from which cayenne pepper is made, is red and very hot.

SCOTCH BONNET is closely related to habanero and, like it, is one the hottest of all chillies. It is a red chilli but often used at its yellow and orange half-ripe stages. Its name comes from its shape, round and flattish with bumps, suggesting a Scottish tamo'shanter.

CASCABEL, also called bola chilli, is a dried, round, moderately hot brown or red chilli.

KASHMIRI is a large, mild red chilli used for its colour and flavour rather than its heat.

MULATO is, like ancho, a dried poblano chilli, but is dried to a brownish black and is sweeter than ancho.

POBLANO is very dark green, almost black, when unripe and red or brown when ripe. A large, mild, heart-shaped chilli with very thick walls, it is widely used for stuffing.

STORING

Store fresh chillies in a paper bag, enclosed in a plastic bag, in the refrigerator for up to a week or just leave them in an open bowl. They will wrinkle and shrink a bit as they get drier, and their heat will become more concentrated, but they will be fine for up to a week.

Green nam jim

PREP TIME 15 MINUTES **SERVES** 4

3 long green chillies, chopped coarsely

2 cloves garlic, quartered

10cm stick fresh lemon grass (20g), sliced thinly

3 green onions, chopped coarsely

1 coriander root, chopped coarsely

¼ cup (60ml) lime juice

1 tablespoon fish sauce

2 tablespoons grated palm sugar

1 Blend or process ingredients until smooth.

2 Serve nam jim with grilled chicken, beef or fish, if you like.

NUTRITIONAL COUNT PER SERVING 0.1g total fat (0g saturated fat); 146kJ (35 cal); 7.3g carbohydrate; 0.9g protein; 0.6g fibre

1   2

1 GREEN NAM JIM [SERVED
WITH CHICKEN AND SALAD]
2 PIRI PIRI CHICKEN
THIGH FILLETS

Piri piri chicken thigh fillets

PREP + COOK TIME 25 MINUTES **SERVES** 4

4 fresh long red chillies, chopped coarsely

1 teaspoon dried chilli flakes

2 cloves garlic, quartered

1 teaspoon sea salt

2 tablespoons olive oil

1 tablespoon cider vinegar

2 teaspoons brown sugar

8 x 125g chicken thigh fillets

1 Using mortar and pestle, grind fresh chilli, chilli flakes, garlic and salt for piri piri paste.
2 Combine paste with oil, vinegar, sugar and chicken in medium bowl.
3 Cook chicken mixture on heated oiled grill plate (or grill or barbecue) until cooked
through. Serve with lime wedges, if you like.

NUTRITIONAL COUNT PER SERVING 27.2g total fat (6.8g saturated fat); 1822kJ (436 cal); 1.8g carbohydrate;
46.6g protein; 0.3g fibre

*The Afro-Portuguese chilli
paste called piri piri seems
made to enliven grilled
poultry. The name
originally came from the
tiny, hot piri piri chilli which
the Portuguese introduced
to their former colonies of
Angola and Mozambique.*

*For information on
chicken, see Poultry,
pages 456 & 457.*

Chilli beef stir-fry

PREP + COOK TIME 30 MINUTES **SERVES** 4

4 fresh long red chillies, sliced thinly

3cm piece fresh ginger (15g), chopped coarsely

1 small red onion (100g), chopped coarsely

⅓ cup (75g) firmly packed brown sugar

1 tablespoon fish sauce

2 tablespoons vegetable oil

650g beef strips

6 green onions, cut into 5cm lengths

450g gai lan, chopped coarsely

1 tablespoon fish sauce, extra

¼ cup firmly packed thai basil leaves

1 Blend or process chilli, ginger, red onion, sugar, sauce and oil until mixture forms a coarse paste. Stir-fry chilli mixture in heated oiled wok until fragrant.

2 Add beef to wok; stir-fry until browned. Add green onion and gai lan; stir-fry until gai lan wilts. Add extra sauce and basil; stir-fry until hot.

3 Serve stir-fry with steamed rice.

NUTRITIONAL COUNT PER SERVING 20.4g total fat (6g saturated fat); 1818kJ (435 cal); 22.2g carbohydrate; 39.2g protein; 2.5g fibre

Gai lan is also called chinese broccoli. Choi sum or buk choy can be used instead (see Greens, Asian, page 242). The taste and aroma of thai basil are quite different from those of European basil. It is available at some greengrocers and supermarkets and at Asian food stores.

For information on beef, see Beef, pages 46 & 47.

Sambal goreng telor

PREP + COOK TIME 1 HOUR **SERVES** 6

4 fresh long red chillies, chopped coarsely

4 medium brown onions (600g), chopped coarsely

4 cloves garlic, quartered

4cm piece fresh galangal (20g), chopped coarsely

2 teaspoons vegetable oil

2 teaspoons ground coriander

32 fresh curry leaves

1 tablespoon kecap asin

10 medium tomatoes (1.5kg), peeled, seeded, chopped finely

½ cup (140g) tomato paste

1½ cups (375ml) vegetable stock

12 hard-boiled eggs, halved

1 Blend or process chilli, onion, garlic and galangal until smooth.

2 Heat oil in large saucepan; cook chilli mixture with coriander, curry leaves and kecap asin, stirring, about 5 minutes or until fragrant.

3 Stir tomato, tomato paste and stock into mixture; simmer, covered, 30 minutes.

4 Add egg; simmer, covered, until sambal is heated through.

NUTRITIONAL COUNT PER SERVING 13.5g total fat (3.8g saturated fat); 991kJ (237 cal); 9.4g carbohydrate; 17.9g protein; 3.9g fibre

This traditional Indonesian recipe (meaning "eggs in chilli sauce") can accompany meats but it can also be served as a delicious, fragrant curry in its own right with steamed rice and fresh green vegies.

For information on eggs, see Eggs, page 164.

Chipotle pork ribs with chorizo and smoked paprika

PREP + COOK TIME 3 HOURS 10 MINUTES **SERVES** 4

4 chipotle chillies

1 cup (250ml) boiling water

1.5kg pork belly ribs

1 tablespoon olive oil

1 chorizo sausage (170g), sliced thinly

2 medium red onions (340g), chopped coarsely

1 medium red capsicum (200g), chopped coarsely

1 medium green capsicum (200g), chopped coarsely

1 teaspoon smoked paprika

4 cloves garlic, crushed

3 x 400g cans crushed tomatoes

2 medium tomatoes (300g), chopped finely

½ cup finely chopped fresh coriander

2 teaspoons finely grated lime rind

1 clove garlic, crushed, extra

Chipotle chillies are smoked-dried jalapeños (see also page 120). They are available from herb and spice shops, speciality food shops and some delicatessens.

For information on chorizo sausages, see Sausages, page 516; and for paprika, see Spices, page 562.

1   Preheat oven to 160°C/140°C fan-forced.

2   Soak chillies in the boiling water in small heatproof bowl for 10 minutes. Discard stalks from chillies; reserve chillies and liquid.

3   Using heavy knife, separate ribs. Heat oil in large deep flameproof baking dish; cook ribs, in batches, over heat until browned all over.

4   Cook chorizo, onion, capsicums, paprika and garlic in same dish, stirring, until onion softens. Return ribs to dish with undrained crushed tomatoes, chillies and reserved liquid. Cover; cook in oven about 1 hour. Uncover; cook 1½ hours or until ribs are tender.

5   Meanwhile, combine chopped tomato, coriander, rind and extra garlic in small bowl. Cover; refrigerate until required.

6   Top ribs with tomato mixture; serve with flour tortillas.

NUTRITIONAL COUNT PER SERVING 90.8g total fat (30g saturated fat); 4999kJ (1196 cal); 20.1g carbohydrate; 73.2g protein; 7.7g fibre

---

Sweet chilli sauce

PREP + COOK TIME 55 MINUTES (PLUS COOLING TIME) **MAKES** 1 CUP

6 fresh long red chillies, chopped finely

1 cup (250ml) white vinegar

1 cup (220g) caster sugar

2 cloves garlic, crushed

Sweet chilli sauce goes well with salt and pepper squid, grilled chicken tenderloins, Thai fish cakes or Vietnamese rice paper rolls.

1   Combine chilli, vinegar and sugar in small saucepan; stir over heat, without boiling, until sugar dissolves. Simmer, uncovered, 15 minutes.

2   Add garlic; simmer, uncovered, about 15 minutes or until mixture reduces by half. Cool.

NUTRITIONAL COUNT PER TABLESPOON 0.1g total fat (0g saturated fat); 309kJ (74 cal); 18.4g carbohydrate; 0.1g protein; 0.1g fibre

Chocolate

Chocolate is made from the kernels or "nibs" of the cacao bean. The first step is to blend beans from various sources, with various characteristics, to give chocolate of the character that that particular manufacturer requires. After the beans have been fermented, dried, roasted and "winnowed" to remove the hulls, the nibs are ground to make a viscous substance called chocolate liquor, which can be separated under high pressure into cocoa solids and cocoa butter.

When melting chocolate, use a clean, dry, heatproof bowl, preferably a ceramic (pottery) one because it takes up heat slowly and helps protect the chocolate against scorching. Chop the chocolate finely, put it into the bowl and set it over a saucepan with barely simmering water that will come well below the bottom of the bowl — if the bowl touches the water it may become hot enough to scorch the chocolate, making it taste bitter. Leave the chocolate to soften, then stir until smooth, taking care that no water or steam gets into the bowl as any contact with moisture will make the chocolate "seize" that is turn into a lumpy mass that won't melt. For the same reason, don't cover the bowl as the warmth will cause condensation on the

The solids become cocoa powder, and the cocoa butter is mixed with more, unseparated, chocolate liquor in varying proportions according to the kind of chocolate that is being made. The chocolate liquor contributes chocolatiness, the cocoa butter contributes richness and the melt-in-the-mouth effect — it is the only vegetable fat that is solid at room temperature but melts at mouth temperature. For dark eating chocolate, sugars and flavourings such as vanilla are added; if it is to be milk chocolate, milk and milk solids will be part of the blend. Next comes "conching" or kneading/grinding, which in very good brands may last for days, to make the chocolate smooth and the flavour more mellow. Towards the end of conching, a small amount of the natural emulsifier lecithin is added to make the mixture creamily fluid when it melts. The chocolate may also be tempered by cooling and then warming it to precise temperatures to stabilise the fat crystals in the cocoa butter so that the finished product will have a good lustre, be resistant to "blooming" (a dull, whitish appearance on the surface) and break with a snap. All this is a long and skilled process carried out under the supervision of master chocolatiers, and exactly what each one does is a closely guarded secret.

BITTERSWEET CHOCOLATE and **SEMI-SWEET CHOCOLATE** are the chocolates that chefs use. They have a high proportion of chocolate liquor so they are intensely chocolatey. Bittersweet has much less sugar than ordinary dark eating chocolate, so that the bitter edge of the chocolate liquor's flavour comes through; semi-sweet has a somewhat higher proportion of sugar.

BITTER CHOCOLATE, also known as baker's chocolate or cocoa mass, is 95% chocolate liquor and 5% cocoa butter. It is used by professionals when a strong chocolate flavour but not sweetness is required.

COUVERTURE CHOCOLATE is top-quality chocolate with a high proportion of cocoa butter, used for lining moulds and in chocolate work where a thin, even, glossy coating is required. It is also the first choice for general chocolate cooking, for its flavour and richness. It may be bittersweet, semi-sweet or milk chocolate and is sold in blocks or buttons. It is available from speciality chocolate shops, other speciality food shops and some kitchen shops.

DARK (EATING) CHOCOLATE contains chocolate liquor, cocoa butter, sugar, flavouring and lecithin (see above).

MILK (EATING) CHOCOLATE contains smaller amounts of chocolate liquor and cocoa butter, and a larger amount of sugar, than dark chocolate. It also contains milk solids and sometimes liquid milk. It tends to be softer and less snappy when broken than dark chocolate.

WHITE (EATING) CHOCOLATE contains no chocolate liquor; it is a mixture of cocoa butter, milk solids and sugar.

COOKING CHOCOLATE may mean quality bitter, bittersweet or semi-sweet chocolate, or it may mean compound chocolate, which has low amounts of cocoa solids and cocoa butter and added amounts of cheaper fats such as vegetable or coconut oils. It has the advantage of being easier to work with than pure chocolate as it can be easily melted and formed into moulds, and does not need tempering again before use, as pure chocolate does. Compound chocolate comes in varying qualities according to the relative amounts of cocoa solids and cocoa butter to other fats and which other fats are used; quality brands have more cocoa butter and less other fats than cheaper brands and will give better results.

DIFFERING QUALITY

Inexpensive chocolate is made from lesser-quality beans and contains the minimum amount of cocoa solids (present in chocolate liquor) and cocoa butter and the maximum amounts of sugar and, for milk chocolate, milk solids. Fine chocolate is made from top-quality beans selected for their flavour potential and contains far more than the minimum amount of cocoa solids and cocoa butter. Its flavour is stronger and more complex. Expensive chocolate has also cost more to produce, having been conched for much longer and tempered more painstakingly than cheaper kinds. The packaging of premium chocolate is often labelled with the percentage by weight of its cocoa solids and cocoa butter. The higher the percentage, the more intense the chocolate flavour — though this includes the bitterness and astringency of chocolate liquor so that a very high-percentage chocolate, while admired by connoisseurs, may not be to everyone's taste.

STORING
Ideally, chocolate should be stored at a constant 15–18°C; fluctuating temperatures may encourage "blooming" (see opposite), which is caused by some of the fat content having melted, migrated to the surface and hardened again. Painstaking tempering during manufacture should prevent this. Store unopened chocolate in its original packaging; wrap opened chocolate well in foil. Good-quality dark and milk chocolate will keep well at a constant, cool room temperature for many months. White chocolate, which lacks the antioxidants in cocoa solids, will remain in good condition for only a few weeks.

inside of the lid and this will drop moisture into the chocolate. If the chocolate does seize, adding a few drops of vegetable oil and stirring may smooth it out, but otherwise you will have to discard it and start again with more chocolate.

Fudgy chocolate cherry cookies

PREP + COOK TIME 30 MINUTES **MAKES** 36

125g butter, softened

¾ cup (165g) firmly packed brown sugar

1 egg

1 teaspoon vanilla extract

1 cup (150g) plain flour

¼ cup (35g) self-raising flour

⅓ cup (35g) cocoa powder

½ teaspoon bicarbonate of soda

½ cup (125ml) milk

4 x 55g Cherry Ripe chocolate bars, cut into 1cm pieces

100g dark eating chocolate, cut into 1cm pieces

These cookies can be made a week ahead and stored in an airtight container. If you prefer, you can use milk chocolate in place of the dark in this recipe.

1 Preheat oven to 180°C/160°C fan-forced. Grease three oven trays; line with baking paper.

2 Beat butter, sugar, egg and extract in medium bowl with electric mixer until smooth. Stir in sifted flours, cocoa and soda with milk in two batches; stir in cherry ripe and chocolate pieces.

3 Drop level tablespoons of mixture, about 5cm apart, onto trays; press with fork to flatten slightly.

4 Bake cookies about 10 minutes. Stand 5 minutes; transfer to wire rack to cool.

NUTRITIONAL COUNT PER COOKIE 5.5g total fat (3.6g saturated fat); 460kJ (110 cal); 13.5g carbohydrate; 1.5g protein; 0.6g fibre

---

Decadent double-choc slice

PREP + COOK TIME 40 MINUTES **MAKES** 24

250g dark eating chocolate, melted

1¼ cups (135g) coarsely chopped roasted walnuts

150g dark eating chocolate, chopped coarsely

¾ cup (165g) firmly packed brown sugar

3 eggs

Brown sugar adds a rich caramel note to the chocolate flavour.

1 Grease 19cm x 29cm slice pan; line base and sides with foil, extending foil 5cm over long sides.

2 Spread melted chocolate over base of pan; refrigerate until set.

3 Preheat oven to 180°C/160°C fan-forced.

4 Process nuts, chopped chocolate, sugar and eggs until combined. Pour nut mixture over chocolate base.

5 Bake slice about 20 minutes. Cool in pan. Remove from pan; carefully remove foil. Cut into squares.

NUTRITIONAL COUNT PER SQUARE 9.3g total fat (3.3g saturated fat); 686kJ (164 cal); 17.3g carbohydrate; 2.5g protein; 0.6g fibre

These chocolate truffles are sensational served after dinner with coffee.

For information on thyme, see Herbs, page 266; and for lemon, see Lemons, pages 296 & 297.

White chocolate, lemon and thyme truffles

PREP + COOK TIME 40 MINUTES (PLUS REFRIGERATION AND FREEZING TIME) **MAKES** 25

250g white eating chocolate, chopped coarsely

¼ cup (60ml) cream

1 teaspoon finely grated lemon rind

1 tablespoon lemon juice

½ teaspoon finely chopped fresh thyme leaves

250g white eating chocolate, melted

2 teaspoons finely grated lemon rind, extra

1 Stir chopped chocolate, cream, rind and juice in small heatproof bowl over small pan of simmering water until smooth. Remove from heat; stir in thyme. Refrigerate overnight.

2 Working with a quarter of the chocolate mixture at a time (keep remainder refrigerated), roll rounded teaspoons of mixture into balls; place on foil-lined tray. Freeze until firm.

3 Working quickly, using two forks, dip truffles in melted chocolate. Return truffles to tray; sprinkle with extra rind. Refrigerate truffles until firm.

NUTRITIONAL COUNT PER TRUFFLE 7.7g total fat (4.9g saturated fat); 497kJ (119 cal); 11g carbohydrate; 1.5g protein; 0g fibre

A today version of an old favourite that is never out of style.

White chocolate lamingtons

PREP + COOK TIME 1 HOUR **MAKES** 25

6 eggs

⅔ cup (150g) caster sugar

80g white eating chocolate, chopped finely

½ cup (75g) plain flour

⅓ cup (50g) self-raising flour

⅓ cup (50g) cornflour

4 cups (640g) icing sugar

¾ cup (180ml) milk

2 cups (150g) shredded coconut

100g white eating chocolate, grated finely

1 Preheat oven to 180°C/160°C fan-forced. Grease 23cm-square slab cake pan; line base and sides with baking paper, extending paper 5cm over sides.

2 Beat eggs in medium bowl with electric mixer about 10 minutes or until thick and creamy; gradually beat in caster sugar, dissolving between each addition. Fold in chopped chocolate and triple-sifted flours. Spread mixture into pan.

3 Bake cake about 35 minutes. Turn cake immediately onto baking-paper-lined wire rack to cool; refrigerate while preparing the icing.

4 Sift icing sugar into medium heatproof bowl; stir in milk. Place bowl over medium saucepan of simmering water, stir until icing is of a coating consistency.

5 Cut cold cake into 25 squares. Dip each square of cake into icing, drain off excess. Toss squares in combined coconut and grated chocolate. Place lamingtons on wire rack to set.

NUTRITIONAL COUNT PER LAMINGTON 7.9g total fat (5.5g saturated fat); 1062kJ (254 cal); 41.4g carbohydrate; 3.3g protein; 1.1g fibre

Soft-centred chocolate puddings

PREP + COOK TIME 40 MINUTES **MAKES** 6

150g dark eating chocolate, chopped coarsely

125g butter, chopped coarsely

3 teaspoons instant coffee granules

2 eggs

2 egg yolks

⅓ cup (75g) caster sugar

¼ cup (35g) plain flour

2 teaspoons cocoa powder

1 Preheat oven to 200°C/180°C fan-forced. Grease six-hole (¾-cup/180ml) texas muffin pan well with softened butter.

2 Stir chocolate, butter and coffee in small saucepan, over low heat, until smooth; cool 10 minutes. Transfer to large bowl.

3 Beat eggs, egg yolks and sugar in small bowl with electric mixer until thick and creamy. Fold egg mixture and sifted flour into barely warm chocolate mixture.

4 Divide mixture between pan holes; bake, in oven, 12 minutes.

5 Gently turn puddings onto serving plates, top-side down. Serve immediately, dusted with sifted cocoa powder and whipped cream.

NUTRITIONAL COUNT PER PUDDING 28.6g total fat (16.7g saturated fat); 1697kJ (406 cal); 32.9g carbohydrate; 5.7g protein; 0.9g fibre

Use a good-quality dark chocolate with at least 70% cocoa solids. These are available, prominently labelled, in most supermarkets. Serve these luscious puddings with whipped cream and fresh raspberries in season, or with skinless orange or mandarin segments (for details on preparing these, see Oranges, page 382).

Double chocolate mousse

PREP + COOK TIME 45 MINUTES (PLUS REFRIGERATION TIME) **SERVES** 6

100g dark eating chocolate, chopped coarsely

10g unsalted butter, chopped coarsely

1 egg, separated

½ cup (125ml) thickened cream, whipped

1 cup (250ml) thickened cream, whipped, extra

MILK CHOCOLATE MOUSSE

100g milk eating chocolate, chopped coarsely

10g unsalted butter, chopped coarsely

1 egg, separated

½ cup (125ml) thickened cream, whipped

1 Melt chocolate in small heatproof bowl over small saucepan of simmering water. Remove from heat; add butter, stir until smooth. Stir in egg yolk.

2 Beat egg white in small bowl with electric mixer until soft peaks form. Fold egg white and cream into chocolate mixture, in two batches.

3 Make milk chocolate mousse.

4 Divide dark chocolate mousse among six ¾-cup (180ml) serving glasses; top with milk chocolate mousse then extra whipped cream. Cover; refrigerate 3 hours or overnight.

MILK CHOCOLATE MOUSSE Follow steps 1 and 2, using milk chocolate mousse ingredients.

NUTRITIONAL COUNT PER SERVING 43.9g total fat (28.1g saturated fat); 2128kJ (509 cal); 23.5g carbohydrate; 6.1g protein; 0.3g fibre

For an elegant look, serve mousse topped with fresh berries in season or with whipped cream and chocolate curls: for details of how to make these, see recipe for Cherry chocolate cheesecake, page 115.

This cake is super-rich,
so you might like to serve
it as small squares.

Dark chocolate mud cake

PREP + COOK TIME 2 HOURS (PLUS COOLING TIME) **SERVES** 12

250g unsalted butter, chopped

2 cups (440g) caster sugar

½ cup (125ml) milk

½ cup (125ml) strong black coffee

½ cup (125ml) bourbon

1 teaspoon vanilla extract

200g dark eating chocolate, chopped coarsely

1½ cups (225g) plain flour

¼ cup (35g) self-raising flour

¼ cup (25g) cocoa powder

2 eggs

CHOCOLATE GANACHE

½ cup (125ml) cream

200g dark eating chocolate, chopped coarsely

1 Preheat oven to 160°C/140°C fan-forced. Grease deep 23cm-square cake pan; line base with baking paper.

2 Stir butter, sugar, milk, coffee, bourbon, extract and chocolate in medium saucepan over low heat until smooth. Transfer mixture to large bowl; cool 15 minutes. Whisk in sifted flours and cocoa then eggs. Pour mixture into pan.

3 Bake cake about 1½ hours. Stand 5 minutes; turn, top-side up, onto wire rack to cool.

4 Meanwhile, make ganache. Spread cold cake with ganache.

CHOCOLATE GANACHE Bring cream to the boil in small saucepan. Remove from heat, add chocolate; stir until smooth. Stand 10 minutes before using.

NUTRITIONAL COUNT PER SERVING 32.6g total fat (20.4g saturated fat); 2721kJ (651 cal); 78.7g carbohydrate; 6.3g protein; 1.3g fibre

Dark chocolate, fig and muscat brownies

PREP + COOK TIME 50 MINUTES (PLUS COOLING TIME) **MAKES** 36

½ cup (100g) finely chopped dried figs

¼ cup (60ml) muscat

125g butter, chopped coarsely

200g dark eating chocolate, chopped coarsely

⅔ cup (150g) caster sugar

2 eggs, beaten lightly

1¼ cups (185g) plain flour

150g dark eating chocolate, chopped coarsely, extra

1 tablespoon cocoa powder

Cocoa powder is
unsweetened and tastes
slightly bitter. It imparts
a deep chocolate flavour
to baked items such as
brownies, biscuits and
some cakes. When used
with other chocolate, as
in this recipe, the cocoa
powder intensifies the
chocolatiness. For notes
on muscat, see page 180.

For information on dried
figs, see Figs, page 178,
and Fruit, Dried, page 192.

1 Combine figs and muscat in small bowl; stand 20 minutes.

2 Preheat oven to 180°C/160°C fan-forced. Grease deep 19cm-square cake pan; line base and sides with baking paper, extending paper 5cm over sides.

3 Stir butter and chocolate in medium saucepan over low heat until smooth. Cool 10 minutes. Stir in sugar and eggs then sifted flour, extra chocolate and fig mixture; spread into pan.

4 Bake brownies about 30 minutes. Cool in pan. Dust with sifted cocoa; cut into squares.

NUTRITIONAL COUNT PER BROWNIE 6g total fat (3.6g saturated fat); 539kJ (129 cal); 16.2g carbohydrate; 1.6g protein; 0.7g fibre

DARK CHOCOLATE MUD CAKE

Choko

Also called the chayote or cristophine, the choko is a pale green, pear-shaped member of the gourd family. It is native to South America and now grown in Spain, North America, Asia and Australia, where choko vines flourish on many back fences.

To convert choko-haters, cut one or two into pieces the size of small hot potato chips, add to a little oil mixed with a spice blend such as dukkah, berbere, chermoula or good curry powder in a frying pan, and stir gently over medium heat until the "chips" are almost tender but still firm to the bite. Salt lightly and serve in a bowl as a snack, or with chicken, seafood or lamb kebabs.

It is a love-or-hate vegetable whose smooth flesh is described by its enthusiasts as subtle and delicate and its detractors as unpleasant and insipid. Certainly the traditional Anglo way of boiling and covering it with white sauce does little for it; it is better suited to combining with big-flavoured Mediterranean ingredients such as tomatoes, onions, capsicum and garlic, or with Asian ones such as curry spices. Chinese cooks serve it in soup with pork. It can also be treated as a fruit and cooked in a red-wine syrup with cinnamon, like pears, or a white-wine syrup with lemon peel and cloves, like apples. Choko's season is late summer to early winter.

PREPARATION Unless chokoes are young and tender, peel them with a vegetable peeler, working under running water (or, to conserve water, stopping often to dip hands and choko in a bowl of water) because the flesh exudes a sticky liquid which stains the skin. Quarter and remove the central core, or halve and cut out the core if the choko is to be stuffed, then proceed as the recipe directs.

CHOOSING Choose young chokoes, recognisable by their pale green, translucent-looking skin with small, soft spikes. Avoid specimens with yellowish, opaque skin and dry spikes, and any that have the seed protruding from the base, as these will be old and poorly flavoured and possibly tough.

STORING Store chokoes in the refrigerator crisper and use within a few days.

Coffee

Two different but related trees produce coffee berries, whose seeds are coffee beans. One yields superior beans called "arabica" and the other yields beans of lesser quality called "robusta". Arabica beans develop a more complex and balanced flavour; robusta have much less flavour but they have a higher yield and more "body" than arabica, body being the sensation of thickness on the tongue.

Good quality coffee is usually 100% arabica, but some blends include a certain amount of robusta to give flavour plus body. Blending beans of different origins to make the perfect blend is a skilled art. The beans are green at first and are roasted, another skilled art, to reach just the stage that will give the desired aroma and flavour. Generally, a light roast gives lighter flavour and a dark roast gives richer, heavier flavour.

Ideally, the coffee drinker should buy whole roasted beans and grind just the amount required before making the coffee each time, as ground coffee rapidly loses its freshness. However, both convenience and the fact that different methods of making coffee require the beans to be ground to different degrees of fineness, mean that most people buy ready-ground. Both whole beans and ground coffee should be stored in an airtight glass or steel container, away from light, at cool room temperature. Storing in the refrigerator or freezer is often suggested in order to slow staling, but these could cause condensation to form in the container, which would ruin the flavour. The ideal strategy is to buy only enough beans at a time to last a couple of weeks, or enough ground coffee for one week.

BREWING METHODS

There are theoretical objections to most coffee-brewing methods, but each has millions of devotees. A basic rule is that it is better to use too much coffee than not enough. A too-strong brew can be diluted with hot water and retain its good taste, but a too-weak brew can't be fixed.

ESPRESSO For good espresso, the water must be driven through the coffee at just under boiling point and at high pressure, taking only about 30 seconds to brew. Domestic espresso machines that can do this are, inevitably, expensive. Cheaper ones rely on excessively hot steam and take too long to brew, so that undesirable as well as desirable flavour elements are extracted from the coffee and it is harsh.

FILTER OR DRIP MACHINES often deliver the water at too low a temperature and brew for a long time to compensate, so that bitter elements are extracted and aroma is lost.

PLUNGER POTS work well if the water is at just under boiling point, enough coffee is used, brewing time is 1–3 minutes and the coffee is drunk promptly — if left standing, the tiny suspended particles will keep releasing bitterness. It is also important that the pot be pre-heated so that the coffee won't be cold, and that the brew be stirred for a moment after the water is added so that it is well mixed with the coffee.

For a super-easy dessert that is always a hit, serve good vanilla ice-cream topped with instant coffee granules, and liqueur glasses, each with a tablespoon or so of whisky for diners to pour over.

ITALIAN STOVETOP POTS (the kind with two parts that are screwed together) force the water through the coffee at above boiling point, extracting some undesirable flavour elements and producing a strong and flavoursome but somewhat harsh brew.

PERCOLATORS operate at the boil and for too long, tending to extract undesirable flavour elements and produce a flat-tasting yet harsh brew.

THE JUG METHOD of putting the coffee into a jug, pouring near-boiling water over and, after the desired brewing time, serving it through a coffee-strainer, works well as long as the same conditions as mentioned for plunger pots, above, are observed.

INSTANT COFFEE

Instant coffee is available in various styles with such names as "espresso", but is not acceptable as a drink to true coffee enthusiasts. It is, however, a good ingredient in cakes and desserts.

DECAFFEINATED COFFEE

Decaffeinated coffee is made by soaking the beans in water to dissolve out the caffeine or by using a chemical solvent to extract it, then steaming the beans to evaporate off any remaining solvent. A more recent method is to use carbon dioxide at high pressure to extract the caffeine. The method used is usually marked on the container from which the beans are sold or, if pre-packaged, on the package.

Who would believe that this indulgent treat is actually quite healthy, thanks to its low fat content? (The practical reason for the low-fat ice-cream and no-fat milk is that they form a thicker, more lasting foam than fattier products).

For information on cardamom and cinnamon, see Spices, page 556 & 559.

Spiced iced coffee milkshake

PREP + COOK TIME 15 MINUTES **MAKES** 1 LITRE (4 CUPS)

¼ cup (20g) ground espresso coffee

¾ cup (180ml) boiling water

2 cardamom pods, bruised

¼ teaspoon ground cinnamon

1 tablespoon brown sugar

3 scoops (375ml) low-fat vanilla ice-cream

2½ cups (625ml) no-fat milk

1 Place coffee then the water in coffee plunger; stand 2 minutes before plunging. Pour coffee into small heatproof bowl with cardamom, cinnamon and sugar; stir to dissolve sugar then cool 10 minutes.

2 Strain coffee mixture through fine sieve into blender or processor; process with ice-cream and milk until smooth. Serve immediately.

NUTRITIONAL COUNT PER 250ML 1.6g total fat (1.1g saturated fat); 556kJ (133 cal); 20.4g carbohydrate; 8.6g protein; 0.8g fibre

Affogato with frangelico

PREP + COOK TIME 10 MINUTES **SERVES** 6

⅓ cup ground espresso coffee beans

1½ cups (375ml) boiling water

1 litre good-quality vanilla ice-cream

½ cup (125ml) Frangelico

1 Place ground coffee beans in coffee plunger; add the boiling water, stand 4 minutes before plunging.

2 Place 2 small scoops of ice-cream in each of 6 small heatproof glasses or coffee cups; pour 1 tablespoon Frangelico over each. Pour over hot coffee; serve immediately.

NUTRITIONAL COUNT PER SERVING 13.5g total fat (8.6g saturated fat); 1045kJ (250 cal); 23.2g carbohydrate; 3.9g protein; 0g fibre

AFFOGATO WITH FRANGELICO

Affogato is always fun. Use your favourite liqueur to spoon over the ice-cream: orange and/or chocolate flavours work well with the coffee.

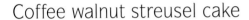

Coffee walnut streusel cake

PREP + COOK TIME 1 HOUR **SERVES** 12

1 tablespoon instant coffee granules

¼ cup (60ml) boiling water

125g butter, softened

1 cup (220g) caster sugar

1 teaspoon vanilla extract

2 eggs

⅔ cup (160g) sour cream

1¼ cups (185g) plain flour

¼ cup (35g) self-raising flour

¼ teaspoon bicarbonate of soda

WALNUT STREUSEL

⅔ cup (100g) self-raising flour

⅔ cup (150g) firmly packed brown sugar

100g cold butter, chopped

1 cup (120g) coarsely chopped walnuts, roasted

1 Preheat the oven to 180°C/160°C fan-forced. Grease 20cm x 30cm lamington pan; line base and two long sides with baking paper.

2 Make walnut streusel.

3 Stir coffee granules and boiling water in small bowl until coffee dissolves. Cool 5 minutes.

4 Beat butter, sugar and extract in small bowl with an electric mixer until light and fluffy. Beat in eggs; transfer to a large bowl. Stir in sour cream and sifted flours and soda, in two batches. Stir in the coffee mixture.

5 Spread mixture into pan; sprinkle with walnut streusel and then remaining walnuts. Bake about 30 minutes. Cool in pan.

WALNUT STREUSEL Combine flour and sugar in medium bowl; rub in butter, using fingertips, until mixture resembles coarse breadcrumbs. Stir in half the walnuts.

NUTRITIONAL COUNT PER SERVING 28.8g total fat (14.4g saturated fat); 2031kJ (486 cal); 50.3g carbohydrate; 5.8g protein; 1.7g fibre

Streusel is German for something sprinkled or scattered, from the verb "streuen" which comes from the same root as the English verb "to strew". A streusel topping is made from flour, sugar and butter, sometimes with a spice flavouring or, as here, chopped nuts.

For details on how to roast the walnuts, see Nuts, page 347.

Coffee almond biscuits

Baking makes the coffee beans brittle so that they are easy to crunch.

For information on almonds, see Nuts, page 344.

PREP + COOK TIME 30 MINUTES **MAKES** 24

1 tablespoon instant coffee granules

3 teaspoons hot water

3 cups (360g) almond meal

1 cup (220g) caster sugar

2 tablespoons coffee-flavoured liqueur

3 egg whites, beaten lightly

24 coffee beans

1 Preheat oven to 180°C/160°C fan-forced. Grease oven trays; line with baking paper.

2 Dissolve coffee in the hot water in large bowl. Stir in almond meal, sugar, liqueur and egg whites until mixture forms a firm paste.

3 Roll level tablespoons of mixture into balls; place on trays 3cm apart; flatten with hand. Press coffee beans into tops of biscuits.

4 Bake biscuits about 15 minutes. Cool on trays.

NUTRITIONAL COUNT PER BISCUIT 8.7g total fat (0.8g saturated fat); 606kJ (145 cal); 11.7g carbohydrate; 3.6g protein; 1.4g fibre

Hot mocha

The definitive winter comfort drink. Use decaffeinated coffee if you are having it as a nightcap.

For information on dark eating chocolate, see Chocolate, page 124.

PREP + COOK TIME 10 MINUTES **MAKES** 1 LITRE (4 CUPS)

1 tablespoon ground espresso beans

1½ cups (375ml) boiling water

2 cups (500ml) milk

100g dark eating chocolate, chopped coarsely

1 teaspoon cocoa powder

1 Place coffee then the water in a coffee plunger; stand 10 minutes before plunging.

2 Heat milk in medium saucepan, without boiling.

3 Meanwhile, divide chocolate among four 1¼-cup (310ml) glasses.

4 Stir coffee into milk then pour mixture into glasses. Dust with sifted cocoa powder before serving.

NUTRITIONAL COUNT PER 250ML 12.1g total fat (7.5g saturated fat); 920kJ (220 cal); 21.9g carbohydrate; 5.7g protein; 0.4g fibre

Corn

Sweetcorn, also known as maize, can be boiled or barbecued to eat as a separate vegetable, or the kernels can be cut off and used in soups and salads or for corn fritters to serve with grilled tomatoes, bacon or sausages. It is available all year round, but its peak season is summer, which fits well with the idea that corn on the cob is best eaten at an outdoor table as it is an enjoyably messy business.

1 SWEETCORN
2 POLKADOT CORN
3 BABY CORN

Its usual colour is sunny yellow but it also comes in a "polka dot" variety with a mixture of white, cream and yellow kernels, and in other colours such as blue, white and red, which you are not likely to see at the greengrocers, though you may see mauve-blue corn chips or packaged tortillas made from blue corn. Baby corn is a miniature form, now grown as several cultivars (cultivated varieties), which was developed in Asia and is now popular with Western cooks for stir-frying or serving as a vegetable accompaniment. It does not have a lot of flavour but is sweet and tender with a pleasant crunchy texture if not overcooked; the entire cob is eaten. Canned corn is available in whole-kernel and creamed (cut-kernel) style. Though lacking the delicacy and crunch of fresh corn, it is satisfactory for using in a soup or for fritters.

PREPARATION To boil corn cobs, remove the green husk and the fine strands of silk. Bring a large saucepan of water to the boil (don't add salt as it would toughen the corn), add the cobs and boil for 4–6 minutes; it doesn't take long as most corn today is almost tender enough to eat even before it is cooked. Overcooking will toughen, not soften, the kernels. Serve the cobs with butter, salt and pepper.

To barbecue, pull back the husk but leave it attached. Remove the silk, fold the husk back over the cob, tie with string and dip into water, then barbecue over hot coals, turning the cobs two or three times, for about 15 minutes. The string will burn off and the husk will be charred; remove it before serving with butter, salt and pepper.

CHOOSING Sweetcorn should be still in its leafy husk, which should be fresh, green, tightly wrapped and almost moist to touch. The silk which protrudes from the husk should be pale and soft. Corn sold without the husk, often in a plastic-wrapped pack of three or four, may have been around too long. Baby corn is usually sold in small packs of six or so, so you see it only through plastic, but check that it doesn't look wilted, damaged or discoloured.

STORING The watchword with sweetcorn is, don't store it but use it the day you buy it: its sugars start to turn into starch as soon as it is picked. If it is going to be a few hours before you cook it, put it in the vegetable crisper of the refrigerator in the meantime. If you must store it longer, leave it in the husk and store in a paper bag enclosed in a plastic bag in the refrigerator.

❦ **OTHER RECIPES USING CORN**
Char siu lamb and noodle stir-fry, p340
Corn and goats cheese quesadillas, p73

Corn fritters with cucumber salad

PREP + COOK TIME 40 MINUTES **SERVES** 6

1 cup (150g) self-raising flour

½ teaspoon bicarbonate of soda

1 teaspoon ground cumin

¾ cup (180ml) milk

2 eggs, separated

2 cups (330g) fresh corn kernels

2 green onions, sliced thinly

2 tablespoons finely chopped fresh coriander

CUCUMBER SALAD

2 lebanese cucumbers (260g), sliced thinly

1 small red onion (100g), sliced thinly

1 fresh long red chilli, sliced thinly

⅓ cup loosely packed fresh coriander leaves

2 tablespoons sweet chilli sauce

1 tablespoon fish sauce

1 tablespoon lime juice

1 Sift flour, soda and cumin into medium bowl. Whisk in milk and egg yolks until smooth.

2 Beat egg whites in small bowl with electric mixer until soft peaks form. Stir corn, onion and coriander into batter; fold in egg whites.

3 Pour 2 tablespoons of the batter into heated oiled large frying pan; using metal spatula, spread batter into round shape. Cook, about 2 minutes each side or until fritter is cooked through. Remove from pan; cover to keep warm. Repeat process, wiping out pan between batches and oiling if necessary, to make a total of 18 fritters.

4 Meanwhile, make cucumber salad. Serve fritters topped with salad.

CUCUMBER SALAD Combine cucumber, onion, chilli and coriander in medium bowl. Place remaining ingredients in screw-top jar; shake well, drizzle over cucumber mixture.

NUTRITIONAL COUNT PER SERVING 4.2g total fat (1.5g saturated fat); 882kJ (211 cal); 31.8g carbohydrate; 9g protein; 4.7g fibre

Grilled corn and zucchini salsa

PREP + COOK TIME 30 MINUTES **MAKES** 7 CUPS

2 corn cobs (800g), trimmed

100g baby zucchini, halved lengthways

2 large avocados (640g), chopped

200g grape tomatoes, halved

1 medium red onion (170g), sliced

¼ cup coarsely chopped fresh coriander

1 tablespoon sweet chilli sauce

⅓ cup (80ml) lime juice

2 fresh small red thai chillies, sliced thinly

1 Cook corn and zucchini on heated oiled grill plate (or grill or barbecue) until tender and browned lightly. Using sharp knife, remove kernels from cobs.

2 Combine corn and zucchini in large bowl with remaining ingredients.

NUTRITIONAL COUNT PER TABLESPOON 1.3g total fat (0.3g saturated fat); 84kJ (20 cal); 1.4g carbohydrate; 0.5g protein; 0.5g fibre

CORN FRITTERS WITH CUCUMBER SALAD

Cream

Cream is the fatty part of whole milk; it rises naturally to the top of unhomogenised milk (see Milk, page 316) if it is left standing, or the milk can be separated by centrifuge to give cream of various grades, classified by their butterfat content.

Recipes in British cookbooks often call for single cream and American ones for half-and-half. Single cream is the same as pouring cream in Australia and contains 33–35% butterfat. Half-and-half is a mixture of half milk and half cream. It has 10–12% butter fat and cannot be whipped.

Cream is used as a luxurious companion to desserts, the essential dollop on hot scones with jam, a cake or pastry filling or decoration, the basis of rich custards and creamy desserts, and an ingredient to add richness and smoothness to soups, sauces and many other dishes.

The names of different types of cream may vary, depending on the brand. The best way to select the kind you want is to look at the fat content displayed on the packaging. Note that all cream should be well chilled for whipping and, if the kitchen is warm, the beaters and bowl should also be chilled.

POURING CREAM is pure cream with a minimum of 35% butterfat. It is the one to use when a recipe calls for cream without any further description. It can be whipped but is easily curdled by overwhipping and does not hold its volume for long.

THICKENED CREAM has a minimum of 35% butterfat and has gelatine or vegetable gums added to thicken and stabilise it. It is faster to whip than pure cream, with less risk of separating from overwhipping, and holds its volume well.

REDUCED-FAT THICKENED CREAM has about 18% butterfat and can be whipped but only to a soft stage.

DOUBLE CREAM is pure cream with a minimum of 48% butterfat. It has a solid consistency.

EXTRA THICK CREAM is double cream that has been homogenised. It falls from the spoon in a dollop that holds its shape.

CLOTTED CREAM is thick, richly coloured cream with a distinctive firm texture and a slightly caramel, cooked flavour. Traditionally, it was made by warming raw, full-cream cow's milk in shallow pans on which the cream had been allowed to rise, holding it at the lowest possible heat until a crust formed, then standing it overnight and scooping off the thick, soft crust. Clotted cream made in factories is produced much more quickly by a technique called direct scalding, and is delicious though not quite the same as the traditional product. It has a legal minimum of 48% butterfat but often has up to 60%, and keeps for much longer than ordinary cream.

SOUR CREAM is cream with a lactic acid culture added to give a slightly tart/tangy flavour. The culture also thickens the cream to a soft spreading or dropping consistency.

LIGHT SOUR CREAM is made in the same way as regular sour cream but has only 18% butterfat so is thinner.

CREME FRAICHE was originally the name the French used in the days before refrigeration for the cream that had ripened, on the 12-hour journey from the dairy region of Normandy to Paris, to a thicker texture with a slightly acidic flavour.

It is now made by adding a lactic acid culture to pure cream. Containing 35–48% butterfat, it is thicker than sour cream and has a different, lighter flavour because of the related but different cultures used. Unlike sour cream, crème fraîche can be boiled without curdling.

LONG LIFE (UHT) CREAM has undergone ultra heat treatment (UHT) by being very briefly heated to a very high temperature to stabilise it so that its shelf life at room temperature is greatly extended. It usually contains 35% butterfat and will whip well if chilled.

CANNED REDUCED CREAM is cream containing 21% butterfat which has been canned and heat-sterilised for an almost indefinite shelf life without refrigeration. The heat coagulates and thickens it. Refrigerate after opening.

🌸 **OTHER RECIPES USING CREAM**
Beef and beetroot salad with horseradish crème fraîche, p271
Broad bean and ricotta orecchiette, p42
Clove panna cotta, p220
Grilled pineapple with coconut ice-cream, p431
Horseradish sauce, p271
Leek and saffron sauce, p290
Lemon sour cream cake, p298
Mustard and basil cream, p330
Poached plums with almond milk ice-cream, p433
Pumpkin and sage ravioli, p483
Raspberry jellies with almond cream, p220
Spiced pumpkin soup with cinnamon cream, p482

Fettuccine alfredo

PREP + COOK TIME 25 MINUTES **SERVES** 4

500g fettuccine
80g butter
300ml cream
½ cup (40g) finely grated parmesan cheese

1 Cook pasta in large saucepan boiling water until just tender; drain.
2 Meanwhile, melt butter in medium frying pan. Add cream; bring to the boil then reduce heat. Simmer, uncovered, about 5 minutes or until sauce reduces by half.
3 Add cheese; stir over low heat about 2 minutes or until cheese melts. Combine pasta and sauce in large bowl; toss gently.

NUTRITIONAL COUNT PER SERVING 53.4g total fat (34.5g saturated fat); 3821kJ (914 cal); 87.5g carbohydrate; 19.4g protein; 4.1g fibre

This sauce is named after the Roman restaurateur Alfredo di Lello who created the dish in the 1920s. Do not reduce the cream mixture too rapidly or by too much as this sauce can burn. Check and stir once or twice and take the pan off the heat when it is reduced correctly. For a lower-fat version, use light thickened cream.

For information on fettuccine, see Pasta, page 396.

Crème fraîche and spinach sauce

PREP + COOK TIME 15 MINUTES **MAKES** 1½ CUPS

30g butter
2 cloves garlic, crushed
6 shallots (150g), chopped finely

2 teaspoons dijon mustard
100g baby spinach leaves
1 cup (240g) crème fraîche

1 Melt butter in large frying pan; cook garlic and shallot, stirring, about 5 minutes or until shallot softens.
2 Add mustard and spinach; cook, stirring, until spinach wilts. Add crème fraîche; cook, stirring, over low heat, until just heated through.
3 Serve sauce with grilled lamb, steak or fish.

NUTRITIONAL COUNT PER TABLESPOON 6.7g total fat (4.4g saturated fat); 272kJ (65 cal); 0.7g carbohydrate; 0.6g protein; 0.3g fibre

This recipe makes enough sauce to serve 6. It is excellent with grilled lamb chops, barbecued beef fillet steaks, grilled chicken breast fillets, or pan-fried crumbed fish cutlets.

For information on baby spinach leaves, see Spinach, page 568.

Vanilla bean ice-cream

PREP + COOK TIME 25 MINUTES (PLUS REFRIGERATION, CHURNING AND FREEZING TIME) **SERVES** 8

2 vanilla beans

1⅔ cups (410ml) milk

600ml thickened cream

8 egg yolks

¾ cup (165g) caster sugar

1 Split vanilla beans lengthways; scrape out seeds into medium saucepan. Add pods, milk and cream; bring to the boil.

2 Meanwhile, whisk egg yolks and sugar in medium bowl until creamy; gradually whisk into hot milk mixture. Stir over low heat, without boiling, until mixture thickens slightly.

3 Strain mixture into medium heatproof bowl; discard pods. Cover surface of custard with plastic wrap; refrigerate about 1 hour or until cold.

4 Pour custard into ice-cream maker, churn according to manufacturer's instructions. Or place custard in shallow container, such as an aluminium slab cake pan, cover with foil; freeze until almost firm. Place ice-cream in large bowl, chop coarsely; beat with electric mixer until smooth. Pour into deep container, cover; freeze until firm. Repeat process two more times.

NUTRITIONAL COUNT PER SERVING 35.5g total fat (21.4g saturated fat); 1856kJ (444 cal); 25.5g carbohydrate; 6.5g protein; 0g fibre

Store the ice-cream, covered, in the freezer for up to 4 weeks.
For passionfruit ice-cream, omit vanilla beans, reduce milk to 1 cup and stir ⅔ cup passionfruit pulp into the custard base before pouring it into the ice-cream maker.
For chocolate ice-cream, omit vanilla beans and add 20g coarsely chopped dark eating chocolate to the milk and cream mixture when heating.

Crème brûlée

PREP + COOK TIME 55 MINUTES (PLUS REFRIGERATION TIME) **SERVES** 6

1 vanilla bean

3 cups (750ml) thickened cream

6 egg yolks

¼ cup (55g) caster sugar

¼ cup (40g) pure icing sugar

1 Preheat oven to 180°C/160°C fan-forced. Grease six ½-cup (125ml) ovenproof dishes.

2 Split vanilla bean in half lengthways; scrape seeds into medium heatproof bowl. Heat pod with cream in small saucepan, without boiling.

3 Add egg yolks and caster sugar to seeds in bowl; gradually whisk in hot cream mixture. Set bowl over medium saucepan of simmering water; stir over heat about 10 minutes or until custard mixture thickens slightly and coats the back of a spoon; discard pod.

4 Place dishes in large baking dish; divide custard among dishes. Add enough boiling water to baking dish to come halfway up sides of ovenproof dishes. Bake, uncovered, in oven about 20 minutes or until custard sets. Remove custards from dish; cool. Cover; refrigerate overnight.

5 Preheat grill. Place custards in shallow flameproof dish filled with ice cubes; sprinkle custards evenly with sifted icing sugar. Using finger, spread sugar over the surface of each custard, pressing in gently; grill until tops of crème brûlée caramelise.

NUTRITIONAL COUNT PER SERVING 52.1g total fat (32.3g saturated fat); 2358kJ (564 cal); 19.8g carbohydrate; 5.8g protein; 0g fibre

The grill must be very hot so that it melts the sugar topping before the heat reaches the crème underneath. If you feel nervous about this, do a practice run for the family to get the timing right.

VANILLA BEAN ICE-CREAM

Cucumbers

Cucumbers are not always "cool as a cucumber", but they are so refreshing that they seem to be: their high water content, fresh flavour and crisp texture make them so. They are available all year but their peak season is summer.

1 TELEGRAPH (CONTINENTAL)
2 GREEN CUCUMBER
3 APPLE CUCUMBER
4 LEBANESE CUCUMBER
5 BABY LEBANESE
CUCUMBERS (QUKES)

Aside from their role as a salad ingredient, they make delicious chilled soups, elegant afternoon-tea sandwiches and an interesting hot vegetable to go with grilled chicken or fish, and can be mixed with yogurt, garlic and lemon for the Greek dip tzatziki or with yogurt and mint for a cooling sambal with curry. And they are all-important for making crunchy pickles for sandwiches, cheese and hot or cold corned beef or other meats.

TELEGRAPH or **CONTINENTAL CUCUMBERS** are long and narrow with thick skin and are less juicy than other varieties.

GREEN or **GREEN RIDGE CUCUMBERS** are long and thick-skinned, with large seeds which can be bitter, so are often removed.

APPLE or **WHITE CUCUMBERS** may be longish or round and have large seeds which may be removed before eating,

if preferred. They are mild and juicy and many people feel they are more digestible than other cucumbers.

LEBANESE CUCUMBERS are small, long, juicy cucumbers with thin, tender skins and small, soft seeds. They can be eaten peeled, partly peeled to give green and white stripes, or unpeeled. Baby lebanese cucumbers, very tender with almost no seeds, are sold as qukes.

GHERKINS or **PICKLING CUCUMBERS** are hard with tough, knobbly skins. Small ones are pickled whole, large ones are cut into chunks for pickling.

❧ **OTHER RECIPES USING CUCUMBER**
Chilled yogurt, cucumber and mint soup, p653
Corn fritters with cucumber salad, p140
Cucumber raita, p654
Onion and spinach pakoras with cucumber raita, p377
Thai cucumber sauce, p511
Tuna cucumber mini-maki, p543

Refrigerate all the ingredients for this juice before blending. It should be served within 30 minutes of making.

For information on green apples, see Apples, pages 8–10; and for celery, see Celery, page 98.

Cucumber, celery and apple juice

PREP TIME 10 MINUTES **MAKES** 1 LITRE (4 CUPS)

1 telegraph cucumber (400g), chopped coarsely

2 stalks celery (300g), trimmed, chopped coarsely

2 large green apples (400g), cored, chopped coarsely

50g baby spinach leaves, stems removed

1 cup (250ml) water

⅓ cup firmly packed fresh mint leaves

1 Blend ingredients, in batches, until pureed; strain through coarse sieve into large jug.

NUTRITIONAL COUNT PER 250ML 0.3g total fat (0g saturated fat); 263kJ (63 cal); 10.8g carbohydrate; 2.2g protein; 4g fibre

Thai cucumber pickle

PREP + COOK TIME 30 MINUTES (PLUS STANDING AND REFRIGERATION TIME) **MAKES** 4 CUPS

6 lebanese cucumbers (780g), halved lengthways, seeded

¼ cup (60g) coarse cooking salt

2 cups (500ml) rice vinegar

½ cup (110g) caster sugar

2 tablespoons fish sauce

2cm piece fresh ginger (10g), grated

2 cloves garlic, crushed

1 fresh long red chilli, sliced thinly

1 small red onion (100g), sliced thinly

1 Place cucumber in colander; sprinkle with salt. Stand 2 hours. Rinse well under cold water; drain. Pat dry with absorbent paper. Slice cucumber into 1cm-thick slices.

2 Stir vinegar, sugar and sauce in medium saucepan over heat until sugar dissolves. Add ginger, garlic and chilli; bring to the boil. Remove from heat.

3 Place cucumber and onion in sterilised jars; pour vinegar mixture over cucumber. Seal jars tightly; cool. Refrigerate overnight.

NUTRITIONAL COUNT PER ¼ CUP 0.1g total fat (0g saturated fat); 205kJ (49 cal); 10.8g carbohydrate; 0.7g protein; 0.8g fibre

This is not a long-keeping pickle: it should be stored in the refrigerator and used within 2 weeks. Enjoy it with chicken skewers, steamed or stir-fried vegetables, deep-fried tofu, curry puffs, Thai fish cakes, cheese or roast-beef sandwiches and hot or cold seafood such as barbecued octopus or prawns, calamari rings or crumbed fish fillets.

Cornichon and dill potato salad

PREP + COOK TIME 30 MINUTES **SERVES** 4

1kg baby new potatoes, unpeeled, halved

2 tablespoons white wine vinegar

½ cup (125ml) olive oil

½ teaspoon sugar

1 teaspoon dijon mustard

⅓ cup (65g) drained baby capers

⅔ cup (140g) drained pickled cocktail onions, halved

1 cup (200g) drained cornichons, halved lengthways

2 tablespoons coarsely chopped fresh dill

1 Boil, steam or microwave potato until just tender; drain.

2 Meanwhile, place vinegar, oil, sugar and mustard in screw-top jar; shake well.

3 Combine potato in large bowl with half of the dressing; cool 10 minutes.

4 Add capers, onion, cornichon, dill and remaining dressing to salad; toss gently to combine.

NUTRITIONAL COUNT PER SERVING 29g total fat (4g saturated fat); 2119kJ (507 cal); 52.2g carbohydrate; 6.5g protein; 6.9g fibre

Cornichon is the French word for gherkin, a very small variety of cucumber. Pickled, they are a traditional accompaniment to pâté; the Swiss always serve them with fondue or raclette.

These flavours are good with fresh or smoked seafood and with cured meats such as corned beef, ham and hot or cold sausages (for suggestions, see Sausages, page 516).

For information on fresh dill, see Herbs, page 264; and for baby new potatoes, see Potatoes, pages 448 & 449.

THAI CUCUMBER PICKLE

Cumquats

Pretty little cumquats look like miniature oranges although they are not really related. They are seldom eaten fresh as they are bitter and tart, but they are delicious as glacé (candied) fruit, pickled with spices or brandied, and they make wonderful marmalade.

CHOOSING If you are buying cumquats, check that they are ripe but firm, with no soft spots or damage, and that the skins are intact. If you have your own tree or access to a friend's tree, pick them when they are ripe but firm and try to pick as close as possible to when you want to use them and when the fruit is dry. If you want to use them whole, snip with scissors rather than pulling, to ensure that the skins remain intact.

STORING Cumquats start to deteriorate from the moment they are picked, so use them straight away. Or, if necessary, store them in a cool place, in a single layer on absorbent paper, disposable cloths or clean old teatowels, for no more than 24 hours.

Drink the flavoured brandy as you would a liqueur or, serve the cumquats with ice-cream and a little of the brandy. Or, use the cumquats in pies, cakes, puddings and crumbles.

Brandied cumquats

PREP TIME 20 MINUTES (PLUS STANDING TIME) **MAKES** 7 CUPS (1.75 LITRES)

750g cumquats
2 cinnamon sticks, halved lengthways
2 vanilla beans, halved lengthways
3 cups (660g) caster sugar
2½ cups (625ml) brandy

1 Place clean jars (and lids) on their sides in a large saucepan; cover jars completely with cold water. Put the lid on the pan, bring to the boil, boil for 20 minutes. Remove the jars carefully from the water; drain upright (to allow the water to evaporate) on the sink until the jars are dry.

2 Meanwhile, wash and dry the cumquats well, then prick each one several times with a fine skewer or a thick needle.

3 Place the cumquats, cinnamon and vanilla in the jars; pour over enough of the combined sugar and brandy to cover the cumquats completely. Seal.

4 Stand the jars in a cool, dark place for at least 2 months before using. Invert the jars every few days to help dissolve the sugar.

NUTRITIONAL COUNT PER 1 CUP 0.2g total fat (0g saturated fat); 2462kJ (589 cal); 97.3g carbohydrate; 0.8g protein; 3.2g fibre

Curry Pastes

Curry pastes are available from speciality food shops, Asian food shops and supermarkets. Neither curry paste nor curry powder is intrinsically better than the other: pastes offer greater convenience because they include both curry spices and "wet" ingredients such as fresh herbs, ginger, lemon grass and garlic, while curry powders allow you to control the texture and flavour of the curry by using more or less of these ingredients and chopping them smaller or larger. Curry pastes are made in different combinations of ingredients for specific types of curry.

Many recipes include directions for making a special curry paste. This usually involves collecting and chopping quite a lot of ingredients, so make a larger quantity while you're about it, divide into one-recipe portions and freeze in small freezer bags for the next time.

THAI RED CURRY PASTE is the most popular and the spiciest of Thai curry pastes, which are classified by colour but all feature such ingredients as galangal, prawn paste and lemon grass. It is a hot blend of flavours to complement the richness of pork, duck and seafood, and also works well in marinades and sauces.

THAI GREEN CURRY PASTE is almost identical with red curry paste except that it uses fresh green chillies instead of red chilli powder. It is the hottest of the traditional pastes but is always used with coconut milk which tempers the fire. It is particularly good for chicken or vegetable curries.

PANANG CURRY PASTE provides the flavours of curries from the island of Penang, off the coast of Malaysia close to Thailand. It is a complex, sweeter and milder version of Thai red curry paste, good with seafood and for adding to soups and salad dressings.

MASSAMAN CURRY PASTE is a South-East Asian paste showing the influence of Muslim and Portuguese traders who brought spices from the Middle East and India to the southern coast of Thailand. The paste is hot and sour and is used for stew-like curries and skewered food. It goes particularly well with beef.

TANDOORI CURRY PASTE is spicy but not hot, being a blend of oil, lemon juice, garlic, onion, ginger and spices such as paprika, cumin and coriander. It is meant to be mixed with yogurt and used to marinate chicken or meat which would, classically, be baked on the wall of a tandoor, a round clay oven with live coals at the bottom, but can be baked in an ordinary hot oven or, better, baked and then finished on a barbecue.

BALTI CURRY PASTE takes its name from the Baltistan region of northern Pakistan, whose cooking has found fame via Pakistani immigrants to Britain. Balti curry paste is an aromatic, medium-hot paste made with coriander, fenugreek and mint, which give it a distinctive mild "green" flavour.

MADRAS CURRY PASTE is a southern Indian paste that is hot to very hot, blended with cumin, coriander and chilli. It is best used with beef but is suitable for pork and chicken too.

VINDALOO PASTE is a Goan paste that illustrates the Portuguese influence on India's west coast. It is made with vinegar, tomatoes, pepper and other spices.

TIKKA PASTE is a mild paste which, in Indian cookery, is made to its maker's choice of spices and oils and sometimes

Mortar and pestle

tomatoes or coconut cream; it is frequently coloured red. The name comes from Persian, the language of the Mughals who once ruled northern India, and meant "small bits and pieces", and tikka, today, usually means small pieces cooked on a skewer. Tikka paste is usually used for marinating or for basting the food as it cooks, rather than as an ingredient. It is most often used with chicken.

☙ **RECIPES USING CURRY PASTES**
Braised oxtail in peanut sauce, p50-1
Chicken green curry, p462-3
Chilli crab laksa, p538-9
Lamb korma, p289
Lemon grass chicken curry, p294-5
Ling and snow pea green curry, p532
Massaman beef curry, p51
Panang seafood curry, p535
Thai coconut scallops, p541

Red curry paste

PREP + COOK TIME 25 MINUTES (PLUS STANDING TIME) **MAKES** 1 CUP

20 dried long red chillies

1 teaspoon ground coriander

2 teaspoons ground cumin

1 teaspoon hot paprika

3 cloves garlic, quartered

2cm piece fresh ginger (10g), chopped finely

1 medium red onion (170g), chopped coarsely

2 x 10cm sticks fresh lemon grass (40g), sliced thinly

2 tablespoons coarsely chopped fresh coriander root and stem mixture

2 teaspoons shrimp paste

1 tablespoon peanut oil

1 Place chillies in small heatproof jug, cover with boiling water; stand 15 minutes, drain.
2 Meanwhile, dry-fry ground spices in small frying pan, stirring until fragrant.
3 Blend or process chillies and spices with garlic, ginger, onion, lemon grass, coriander mixture and paste until mixture forms a paste. Add oil; continue to blend until smooth.

NUTRITIONAL COUNT PER TABLESPOON 1.6g total fat (0.3g saturated fat); 92kJ (22 cal); 1.2g carbohydrate; 0.4g protein; 0.5g fibre

Good-quality curry pastes are available commercially, but creative cooks enjoy making their own, adjusted to their own taste. Make any of the curry paste recipes here just as it is, then fry a spoonful, stir in a little coconut milk or cream, cook a few moments and taste. You may want to add a bit more garlic, lemon grass, galangal, chilli, onion, herbs or spices for the balance that suits you. When it is just right, allow to cool then freeze it in small batches.

Green curry paste

PREP + COOK TIME 20 MINUTES **MAKES** 1 CUP

2 teaspoons ground coriander

2 teaspoons ground cumin

10 long green chillies, chopped coarsely

10 small green chillies, chopped coarsely

1 teaspoon shrimp paste

1 clove garlic, quartered

4 green onions, chopped coarsely

10cm stick fresh lemon grass (20g), chopped finely

1cm piece fresh galangal (5g), chopped finely

¼ cup coarsely chopped fresh coriander root and stem mixture

1 tablespoon peanut oil

1 Dry-fry ground spices in small frying pan over medium heat, stirring until fragrant.
2 Blend or process spices with chillies, paste, garlic, onion, lemon grass, galangal and coriander mixture until mixture forms a paste. Add oil; continue to blend until smooth.

NUTRITIONAL COUNT PER TABLESPOON 1.6g total fat (0.3g saturated fat); 67kJ (16 cal); 0.3g carbohydrate; 0.2g protein; 0.2g fibre

Panang curry paste

PREP + COOK TIME 20 MINUTES (PLUS STANDING TIME) **MAKES** 1 CUP

25 dried long red chillies

1 teaspoon ground coriander

2 teaspoons ground cumin

2 cloves garlic, quartered

8 green onions, chopped coarsely

2 x 10cm sticks fresh lemon grass (40g), sliced thinly

2cm piece fresh galangal (10g), chopped finely

2 teaspoons shrimp paste

½ cup (75g) roasted unsalted peanuts

2 tablespoons peanut oil

1 Place chillies in small heatproof jug, cover with boiling water; stand 15 minutes, drain.

2 Meanwhile, dry-fry spices in small frying pan over medium heat, stirring until fragrant.

3 Blend or process spices with chillies and remaining ingredients until it forms a paste.

NUTRITIONAL COUNT PER TABLESPOON 6.1g total fat (0.9g saturated fat); 288kJ (69 cal); 1.3g carbohydrate; 1.9g protein; 0.9g fibre

Yellow curry paste

PREP + COOK TIME 20 MINUTES (PLUS STANDING TIME) **MAKES** 1 CUP

2 dried long red chillies

1 teaspoon ground coriander

1 teaspoon ground cumin

½ teaspoon ground cinnamon

2 fresh yellow banana chillies (250g), chopped coarsely

1 teaspoon finely chopped fresh turmeric

2 cloves garlic, quartered

1 small brown onion (80g), chopped finely

10cm stick fresh lemon grass (20g), chopped finely

2 teaspoons finely chopped fresh galangal

1 tablespoon coarsely chopped fresh coriander root and stem mixture

1 teaspoon shrimp paste

1 tablespoon peanut oil

1 Place chillies in small heatproof jug, cover with boiling water; stand 15 minutes, drain.

2 Meanwhile, dry-fry ground coriander, cumin and cinnamon in small frying pan, stirring until fragrant.

3 Blend or process spices and chillies with remaining ingredients until mixture is smooth.

NUTRITIONAL COUNT PER TABLESPOON 1.6g total fat (0.3g saturated fat); 84kJ (20 cal); 0.9g carbohydrate; 0.4g protein; 0.5g fibre

Massaman curry paste

PREP + COOK TIME 35 MINUTES (PLUS STANDING TIME) **MAKES** 1 CUP

20 dried long red chillies

1 teaspoon ground coriander

2 teaspoons ground cumin

2 teaspoons ground cinnamon

½ teaspoon ground cardamom

½ teaspoon ground clove

5 cloves garlic, quartered

1 large brown onion (200g), chopped coarsely

2 x 10cm sticks fresh lemon grass (40g), sliced thinly

3 fresh kaffir lime leaves, sliced thinly

4cm piece fresh ginger (20g), chopped coarsely

2 teaspoons shrimp paste

1 tablespoon peanut oil

1 Preheat oven to 180°C/160°C fan-forced.

2 Place chillies in small heatproof jug, cover with boiling water; stand 15 minutes, drain.

3 Meanwhile, dry-fry coriander, cumin, cinnamon, cardamom and clove in small frying pan, stirring until fragrant.

4 Place chillies and spices in small shallow baking dish with remaining ingredients. Roast, uncovered, 15 minutes.

5 Blend or process roasted curry paste mixture, or crush using mortar and pestle, until smooth.

NUTRITIONAL COUNT PER TABLESPOON 1.7g total fat (0.3g saturated fat); 105kJ (25 cal); 1.5g carbohydrate; 0.5g protein; 0.4g fibre

Laksa paste

PREP TIME 20 MINUTES **MAKES** 1 CUP

7 dried small red chillies

1 tablespoon peanut oil

3 cloves garlic, quartered

1 medium brown onion (150g), chopped coarsely

10cm stick fresh lemon grass (20g), chopped finely

4cm piece fresh ginger (20g), grated

1 tablespoon coarsely chopped macadamias

2 tablespoons coarsely chopped fresh coriander root and stem mixture

1 teaspoon ground turmeric

1 teaspoon ground coriander

½ cup loosely packed fresh vietnamese mint leaves

1 Place chillies in small heatproof jug, cover with boiling water; stand 10 minutes; drain.

2 Blend or process chillies with remaining ingredients until mixture is smooth.

NUTRITIONAL COUNT PER TABLESPOON 2.3g total fat (0.4g saturated fat); 109kJ (26 cal); 26.4g carbohydrate; 0.4g protein; 0.5g fibre

Dates

Fresh dates usually come from Israel or California and have been frozen, which keeps them moist, for transporting. Plump and glossy brown, sweet and lush, they are good, unadorned, as a healthy snack or on a cheeseboard, or can be served as a dessert with yoghurt scattered with grated orange or lemon rind or chopped preserved ginger.

Fresh dates

Dried dates

DRIED DATES (actually semi-dried) come in two styles, whole ones which are soft and juicy, and firmer ones pressed into blocks. The whole ones are good as a snack or can be poached with sugar and spices and served with cream or ice-cream, used in couscous, tagines (Moroccan casseroles) or pilafs, or stoned and stuffed with marzipan, chopped glacé fruits or chopped dried fruit and nuts and served in paper cases as petits fours; the pressed ones are usually chopped and used for date scones, slices, cakes and puddings.

PREPARATION Fresh and whole dried dates may be stoned or not, as preferred. Check pressed dried dates for stones and remove these before measuring or weighing. Some recipes call for softened dates, which can be obtained by soaking them for a few minutes in boiling water with a little bicarbonate of soda.

CHOOSING Fresh dates should be plump and undamaged and the skin should not be sticky. Pressed dried dates should be brown and pliable, not black and hard. Check all dates for signs of insect invasion and reject suspect ones.

STORING Dates are so high in sugar that they will keep for months without refrigeration, but they do need to be protected from drying out and insect damage, so store them in glass or metal airtight containers.

❧ **OTHER RECIPES USING DATES**
Date and tamarind chutney, p467
Upside-down toffee banana and date cake, p37

Lemon rind and juice are always good with dates because their fresh taste and aroma balances dates' high sugar content. This slice can be stored in an airtight container for up to 4 days.

Date slice

PREP + COOK TIME 1 HOUR 25 MINUTES (PLUS REFRIGERATION TIME) **MAKES** 24

1½ cups (225g) plain flour
1¼ cups (185g) self-raising flour
150g cold butter, chopped
1 tablespoon honey
1 egg
⅓ cup (80ml) milk, approximately
2 teaspoons milk, extra
1 tablespoon white sugar

DATE FILLING

3½ cups (500g) dried seeded dates, chopped coarsely
¾ cup (180ml) water
2 tablespoons finely grated lemon rind
2 tablespoons lemon juice

1 Grease 20cm x 30cm lamington pan; line base with baking paper, extending paper 5cm over long sides.

2 Sift flours into large bowl; rub in butter until mixture is crumbly. Stir in combined honey and egg and enough milk to make a firm dough. Knead on floured surface until smooth, cover; refrigerate 30 minutes.

3 Meanwhile, make date filling.

4 Preheat oven to 200°C/180°C fan-forced.

5 Divide dough in half. Roll one half large enough to cover base of pan; press into pan, spread filling over dough. Roll remaining dough large enough to cover filling. Brush with extra milk; sprinkle with sugar. Bake about 20 minutes; cool in pan.

DATE FILLING Cook ingredients in medium saucepan, stirring, about 10 minutes or until thick and smooth. Cool to room temperature.

NUTRITIONAL COUNT PER PIECE 5.7g total fat (3.6g saturated fat); 757kJ (181 cal); 28.2g carbohydrate; 2.6g protein; 2.7g fibre

DATE SLICE

Sticky date cheesecake

PREP + COOK TIME 1 HOUR 25 MINUTES (PLUS COOLING AND REFRIGERATION TIME) **SERVES** 12

2 cups (280g) seeded dried dates

¾ cup (180ml) water

½ teaspoon bicarbonate of soda

750g cream cheese, softened

½ cup (110g) firmly packed brown sugar

¼ teaspoon ground cinnamon

¼ teaspoon mixed spice

2 eggs

CARAMEL SAUCE

25g butter

⅓ cup (75g) firmly packed brown sugar

⅓ cup (80ml) cream

The pureed dates make this crustless cheesecake extra rich and fudgy, and the caramel sauce takes it straight to sweet-tooth heaven.

For information on cream cheese, see Cheese, pages 100-102.

1 Preheat oven to 160°C/140°C fan-forced. Grease 24cm springform tin; line base and side with baking paper. Place tin on oven tray.

2 Bring dates, the water and soda to the boil in small saucepan; simmer 5 minutes. Cool mixture 5 minutes; blend or process until almost smooth.

3 Beat cheese and sugar in medium bowl with electric mixer until smooth. Add spices, eggs and date mixture; beat until combined. Pour mixture into tin.

4 Bake cheesecake about 1 hour. Cool in oven with door ajar. Refrigerate cheesecake 3 hours or overnight.

5 Make caramel sauce.

6 Serve cheesecake drizzled with warm or cold sauce.

CARAMEL SAUCE Stir ingredients in small saucepan over low heat until smooth. Bring to the boil; remove from heat.

NUTRITIONAL COUNT PER SERVING 26.2g total fat (16.5g saturated fat); 1655kJ (396 cal); 32.5g carbohydrate; 7.1g protein; 2.3g fibre

Sticky date pudding has been among the top favourite desserts for years and its popularity shows no sign of fading. Ginger gives it new spicy notes.

For information on glacé ginger, see Fruit, Glacé, pages 198 & 199.

Ginger sticky date pudding

PREP + COOK TIME 55 MINUTES **SERVES** 8

1 cup (140g) seeded dried dates

¼ cup (55g) glacé ginger

1 teaspoon bicarbonate of soda

1 cup (250ml) boiling water

50g butter, chopped

½ cup (110g) firmly packed brown sugar

2 eggs

1 cup (150g) self-raising flour

1 teaspoon ground ginger

BUTTERSCOTCH SAUCE

300ml cream

¾ cup (165g) firmly packed brown sugar

75g butter, chopped

1 Preheat oven to 200°C/180°C fan-forced. Grease deep 20cm-round cake pan; line base with baking paper.

2 Combine dates, ginger, soda and the water in food processor; stand 5 minutes then add butter and sugar. Process until mixture is almost smooth. Add eggs, flour and ginger; process until combined. Pour mixture into pan.

3 Bake cake about 45 minutes. Stand 10 minutes before turning onto serving plate.

4 Meanwhile, make butterscotch sauce. Serve pudding warm with sauce.

BUTTERSCOTCH SAUCE Stir ingredients in medium saucepan over low heat until smooth.

NUTRITIONAL COUNT PER SERVING 30.1g total fat (19.6g saturated fat); 2337kJ (559 cal); 65.1g carbohydrate; 4.7g protein; 2.4g fibre

Cream cheese-filled brandied dates

PREP + COOK TIME 40 MINUTES (PLUS STANDING TIME) **MAKES** 24

24 fresh dates (500g)

¼ cup (60ml) brandy

125g cream cheese, softened

1 tablespoon icing sugar

¼ cup (35g) hazelnuts, roasted, chopped finely

½ cup (110g) caster sugar

¼ cup (60ml) water

50g dark chocolate, melted

1 Make a shallow cut lengthways in each date; remove and discard seeds. Place dates in medium bowl with brandy; stand 15 minutes.

2 Meanwhile, combine cheese and icing sugar in small bowl; stir in nuts. Drain brandy from dates; stir into cheese mixture. Spoon or pipe cheese mixture into dates.

3 Stir caster sugar and the water in small saucepan over heat, without boiling, until sugar dissolves; bring to the boil. Reduce heat; simmer, without stirring, until mixture is golden. Remove from heat; stand until bubbles subside.

4 Drizzle 12 dates with toffee and 12 dates with chocolate; stand 20 minutes or until set.

NUTRITIONAL COUNT PER DATE 3.2g total fat (1.5g saturated fat); 351kJ (84 cal); 11.1g carbohydrate; 0.9g protein; 0.8g fibre

GINGER STICKY DATE PUDDING

Eggplant

Eggplant, also called aubergine, is the hero of Middle Eastern cuisine and a major player in the cooking of India and the countries around the Mediterranean, providing bulk, fleshy texture and a world of wonderful flavours for meals that may include little or no meat.

Eggplant soaks up oil like a sponge, especially if it has not been disgorged, thus making the final dish very oily (and kilojoule-laden). If you want to reduce the amount of oil the slices soak up as they fry, first brush them lightly with oil and seal the surface on both sides on a heated char-grill or barbecue. This can be done an hour or two ahead of time, then the eggplant can be fried in just a little oil and the recipe completed when required.

❦ OTHER RECIPES USING EGGPLANT
Chicken green curry, p462–3
Dhal with pumpkin and eggplant, p473
Eggplant chutney, p466
Oven-roasted ratatouille, p658
Roasted vegetable lasagne, p402–3
Tamarind and citrus pork curry, p597

It comes in sizes from pea-size to rockmelon-size, in shapes from the oval that gives them their name to long, smooth round or round with indented segments, and in colours from deep purple to mauve, white, pink-and-white striped, green or orange. The eggplant's great gift is that its soft flesh, delicious in its own right, also marries well with spices, herbs, cheese, yogurt, meats and other vegetables (tomatoes, onions, garlic). Eggplant are available all year; their peak season is summer into autumn.

COMMON EGGPLANT are the oval purple ones in various sizes. Unless otherwise stated in a recipe, these are the ones to use.

BABY EGGPLANT, also known as japanese, oriental and lebanese eggplant, are long and slender. They are thinner-skinned and a little sweeter than common eggplant and do not need to be disgorged.

THAI APPLE EGGPLANT are similar in flavour and texture to common eggplant and can be used in the same ways.

THAI PEA EGGPLANT are seedy and rather bitter but work well in curries where they provide a crisp change of texture.

PREPARATION Common eggplant, unless young and freshly picked, are usually disgorged (salted to draw out the bitter juices) before using; this also reduces the amount of oil the eggplant will soak up when cooking. Cut up the eggplant as required for the recipe, sprinkle generously with salt and leave for 30 minutes or so, then rinse and dry thoroughly. Baby and pea eggplant do not need to be disgorged.

CHOOSING Choose medium-size eggplant that are heavy for their size; large ones may be overmature and seedy. They should be unblemished with smooth, taut, glossy skin, and the fuzzy green calyx and stem should be green and fresh-looking.

STORING Eggplant is highly perishable, especially in extremes of heat or cold, so try to buy on the day you will use it or, if necessary, store for a day or two in a plastic bag in a cool but not cold place.

Common eggplant

Baby eggplant

Thai apple eggplant

Thai pea eggplant

Moussaka timbales

PREP + COOK TIME 1 HOUR 15 MINUTES **MAKES** 6

¼ cup (60ml) olive oil

1 medium brown onion (150g), chopped finely

2 cloves garlic, crushed

500g lamb mince

400g can diced tomatoes

1 tablespoon tomato paste

½ cup (125ml) dry white wine

1 teaspoon ground cinnamon

¼ teaspoon ground nutmeg

¼ cup coarsely chopped fresh flat-leaf parsley

¼ cup (40g) roasted pine nuts

2 small eggplants (460g)

1 Heat 1 tablespoon of the oil in large frying pan; cook onion and garlic, stirring, until onion softens. Add lamb; cook, stirring, until lamb changes colour. Stir in undrained tomatoes, paste, wine and spices; bring to the boil. Reduce heat; simmer, uncovered, about 20 minutes or until liquid has evaporated. Cool; stir in parsley and nuts.

2 Meanwhile, slice eggplant lengthways into 3mm thin slices using sharp knife, mandoline or V-slicer. Mix eggplant slices with remaining oil; cook on heated grill plate until browned lightly. Cool.

3 Preheat oven to 180°C/160°C fan-forced. Grease six-hole (¾-cup/180ml) texas muffin pan. Line each pan hole with eggplant slices, overlapping slightly and extending 4cm above edge of hole. Divide lamb mixture between eggplant cases. Fold eggplant over to enclose filling.

4 Bake timbales about 10 minutes. Stand in pan 5 minutes before serving, top-side down. Sprinkle with a little chopped fresh flat-leaf parsley.

NUTRITIONAL COUNT PER TIMBALE 19.9g total fat (4g saturated fat); 1262kJ (302 cal); 6.3g carbohydrate; 19.8g protein; 3.7g fibre

Moussaka is the national dish of Greece and also popular in other Balkan and Mediterranean countries. Serve it with tzatziki, a Greek dip which is available commercially or can be made by stirring diced cucumber and garlic into natural yogurt. For notes on shopping for pine nuts, see Nuts, page 344.

For information on lamb, see Lamb, pages 282 & 283.

Baba ghanoush

PREP + COOK TIME 55 MINUTES **SERVES** 4

1 small eggplant (230g)

cooking-oil spray

2 teaspoons tahini

1 tablespoon lemon juice

1 tablespoon water

1 clove garlic, crushed

1 Preheat oven to 200°C/180°C fan-forced.

2 Pierce eggplant all over with fork. Place eggplant on oiled oven tray; spray with oil. Roast, uncovered, about 40 minutes or until tender.

3 When cool enough to handle, peel eggplant. Blend or process eggplant flesh with remaining ingredients until smooth.

NUTRITIONAL COUNT PER SERVING 2.5g total fat (0.2g saturated fat); 156kJ (37 cal); 1.7g carbohydrate; 1.2g protein; 1.8g fibre

Tahini is a sesame seed paste available from Middle Eastern food stores, health food stores and in the health food section in some supermarkets. Baba ghanoush is a smoky eggplant puree. It can be made up to a week ahead and stored in the refrigerator until required.

Eggplant parmigiana

PREP + COOK TIME 1 HOUR **SERVES** 6

This is Italian cooking at its rich and gorgeous best. It's worth every kilojoule.

2 large eggplants (1kg)

olive oil, for shallow-frying

½ cup (75g) plain flour

4 eggs, beaten lightly

2 cups (200g) packaged breadcrumbs

750ml bottled tomato pasta sauce

1 cup (100g) coarsely grated mozzarella cheese

¼ cup (20g) finely grated parmesan cheese

⅓ cup loosely packed fresh oregano leaves

1 Using vegetable peeler, peel random strips of skin from eggplants; discard skins. Slice eggplants thinly.
2 Heat oil in large frying pan.
3 Coat eggplant in flour; shake off excess. Dip in egg, then in breadcrumbs. Shallow-fry eggplant, in batches, until browned lightly. Drain on absorbent paper.
4 Preheat oven to 200°C/180°C fan-forced. Oil 2.5-litre (10-cup) ovenproof dish.
5 Spread about one-third of the pasta sauce over base of dish. Top with about one-third of the eggplant, one-third of the cheeses and one-third of the oregano. Repeat layering.
6 Bake parmigiana, covered, 20 minutes. Uncover; bake about 10 minutes or until browned lightly.

NUTRITIONAL COUNT PER SERVING 27.5g total fat (6.8g saturated fat); 2257kJ (540 cal); 49.4g carbohydrate; 19.9g protein; 8.3g fibre

Crispy-fried baby eggplant

PREP + COOK TIME 15 MINUTES **SERVES** 2

You can use besan or polenta instead of the plain flour for a more textured coating. Be careful not to burn the eggplant — you only need to cook it for a few minutes, it should be crunchy on the outside, and creamy in the inside. It's important to add the hot eggplant to the salad at the last minute, it will wilt the leaves ever so gently, but the result is yummy. Eggplant cooked this way is also great served with barbecued steak.

4 baby eggplant (240g), sliced thinly crossways

1 tablespoon plain flour

¼ cup (60ml) olive oil

1 Toss eggplant in flour which has been seasoned with salt and pepper.
2 Heat about one-third of the oil in large frying pan, add about one-third of the eggplant to pan, in single layer, cook over medium heat for about 3 minutes, or until eggplant is browned both sides. Drain on absorbent paper. Repeat with remaining eggplant.
3 Serve eggplant seasoned with sea salt and cracked pepper as a snack or nibble, or tossed into a green salad just before serving.

NUTRITIONAL COUNT PER SERVING 27.7g total fat (3.9g saturated fat); 1204kJ (288 cal); 7.2g carbohydrate; 1.9g protein; 3g fibre

Eggs

The highly nutritious and digestible egg is a favourite food all over the world and indispensable in the kitchen for thickening, binding, aerating, emulsifying, glazing, coating and enriching all manner of food. Besides everyday hen eggs, duck, quail and goose eggs are available at speciality food shops.

1 GOOSE EGG
2 DUCK EGG
3 HEN EGG
4 BANTAM EGG
5 QUAIL EGGS

❦ OTHER RECIPES USING EGGS

HEN EGGS come in various sizes, classified by weight, from about 50g to over 70g. Many recipes use 55g eggs unless otherwise specified; we use 60g eggs in recipes unless otherwise specified. Eggs are also marketed by the conditions in which the hens are kept, though there have been scandals when it was discovered that the purported conditions and the reality were far apart. However, assuming that one can believe the marketing, organic eggs come from hens free to browse outdoors and fed on natural feed free from chemicals or additives; free-range eggs come from hens fed on a varied diet and free to browse outdoors; barn-laid eggs come from hens free to browse in a large barn; other eggs usually come from battery (caged) hens. The colour of the egg-shell varies with the breed of hen and has no bearing on the colour, taste or nutritive value of the egg. Yolk colour and flavour depend on the hen's diet: organic and free-range eggs tend to have richer colour and taste, though some intensively farmed (battery) hens are fed pigments to deepen yolk colour.

BANTAM EGGS, from breeds of hen about half the size of ordinary chickens, weigh 30–40g and are otherwise the same as hen eggs.

DUCK EGGS average about 90g and are richer-tasting than hen eggs. Duck-egg whites do not whisk up well.

QUAIL EGGS taste like hen eggs and are prized for their miniature charm and decorative quality. Their shells are very hard: to shell hard-boiled quail eggs, put them into plenty of cold water immediately after they are cooked, tap the shells all over with a spoon to crack them, leave a minute or two then remove and peel.

GOOSE EGGS weigh 180–200g and have white, very hard shells and a stronger flavour than hen eggs.

CHOOSING

Shop-bought eggs are usually marked with a "best-before" date. If in any doubt about freshness, you can check eggs for freshness before using them: a fresh egg placed in a bowl of water will lie on the bottom, while a stale egg will float big end up.

STORING

Eggs absorb odours through the shell, so store them in their carton or a covered container in the refrigerator. To store leftover egg yolks, cover with water and store in the refrigerator for up to 3 days. To store egg whites, refrigerate them in a covered container for up to a week or so. Egg yolks do not freeze well as they thaw to a pasty consistency, but whites freeze fairly well, though they lose a little of their foaming power. To use them in a recipe, measure 30ml for each white.

To turn out the frittatas, run a small rubber spatula round the sides of each one, then place a greased baking tray or large plate over the muffin pan, hold pan and plate together and reverse so that frittatas drop out. Quickly slide each one on to a heated serving plate.

For information on fetta cheese, see Cheese, page 102; for pancetta, see Bacon, page 28; for roma tomatoes, see Tomatoes, pages 606 & 607.

A luxurious café-style breakfast that is just as good for a casual lunch or Sunday supper.

Tomato, fetta and pancetta frittatas

PREP + COOK TIME 35 MINUTES **MAKES** 6

6 slices (100g) pancetta, chopped coarsely

100g fetta cheese, crumbled

¼ cup (20g) finely grated parmesan cheese

⅓ cup coarsely chopped fresh basil

6 eggs

⅔ cup (160ml) cream

9 mini roma tomatoes (150g), halved lengthways

1 Preheat oven to 180°C/160°C fan-forced. Grease six-hole (¾-cup/180ml) texas muffin pan; line bases with baking paper.

2 Layer pancetta, cheeses and basil in pan holes. Whisk eggs and cream in medium bowl; pour into pan holes. Top each frittata with three tomato halves.

3 Bake frittatas about 25 minutes. Stand in pan 5 minutes before turning out.

NUTRITIONAL COUNT PER FRITTATA 24.1g total fat (13.3g saturated fat); 1170kJ (280 cal); 1.6g carbohydrate; 14.9g protein; 0.4g fibre

Eggs and smoked salmon on blini

PREP + COOK TIME 30 MINUTES **SERVES** 4

8 eggs

200g sliced smoked salmon

2 tablespoons sour cream

1 tablespoon coarsely chopped fresh chives

BLINI

⅓ cup (50g) buckwheat flour

2 tablespoons plain flour

1 teaspoon baking powder

1 egg

½ cup (125ml) buttermilk

30g butter, melted

1 Make blini.

2 Half-fill a large frying pan with water; bring to the boil. Break 1 egg into cup then slide into pan. Working quickly, repeat process with 3 more eggs. When all 4 eggs are in pan, return water to the boil. Cover pan, turn off heat; stand about 4 minutes or until a light film of white sets over each yolk. Using a slotted spoon, remove eggs one at a time; place on absorbent-paper-lined saucer to blot up poaching liquid. Repeat with remaining eggs.

3 Serve blini topped with eggs, salmon, sour cream and chives.

BLINI Sift flours and baking powder into medium bowl; gradually whisk in combined egg and buttermilk until mixture is smooth. Stir in butter. Cook blini, in batches, by dropping 1 tablespoon of the batter into heated oiled large frying pan. Cook blini until browned both sides; you will have 12 blini. Cover to keep warm.

NUTRITIONAL COUNT PER SERVING 25.9g total fat (11.3g saturated fat); 1731kJ (414 cal); 14.1g carbohydrate; 31.5g protein; 1.6g fibre

TOMATO, FETTA AND PANCETTA FRITTATAS

The etiquette of eating omelettes is that each diner begins to eat the moment he/she is served. It is a compliment to the cook to eat his/her masterpiece at its fleeting peak of perfection.

For information on swiss brown mushrooms, see Mushrooms, pages 320 & 321.

Herb omelette with sautéed mushrooms

PREP + COOK TIME 30 MINUTES **SERVES** 4

2 tablespoons finely chopped fresh flat-leaf parsley

2 tablespoons finely chopped fresh chervil

2 tablespoons finely chopped fresh chives

2 tablespoons finely chopped fresh tarragon

50g butter

2 tablespoons olive oil

250g swiss brown mushrooms, halved

½ cup (125ml) water

2 teaspoons finely grated lemon rind

1 tablespoon lemon juice

12 eggs

1 Combine herbs in small bowl.

2 Heat 30g of the butter and 1 tablespoon of the oil in large deep frying pan. Add mushrooms; cook, stirring, 5 minutes. Stir in 2 tablespoons of the water; cook, stirring, until water evaporates and mushrooms are tender. Remove from heat; stir in rind, juice and 2 tablespoons of the herb mixture. Cover to keep warm.

3 Gently whisk eggs and remaining water in a large bowl, whisk in remaining herb mixture.

4 Heat a quarter of the remaining butter and 1 teaspoon of the remaining oil in medium frying pan. When butter mixture bubbles, pour a quarter of the egg mixture into pan; cook over medium heat, tilting pan, until egg is almost set. Tilt pan backwards; fold omelette in half. Cook 30 seconds then slide onto serving plate.

5 Repeat process with remaining butter, oil and egg mixture, wiping out pan before each addition to make a total of 4 omelettes.

6 Serve omelettes topped with sautéed mushrooms.

NUTRITIONAL COUNT PER SERVING 35.3g total fat (12.9g saturated fat); 1714kJ (410 cal); 1g carbohydrate; 22.4g protein; 1.8g fibre

These are nice served with fingers of bruschetta.

For information on fetta and cheddar cheeses, see Cheese, pages 102–104.

Baked eggs with herbs and fetta

PREP + COOK TIME 20 MINUTES **SERVES** 4

1 tablespoon finely chopped fresh flat-leaf parsley

1 tablespoon finely chopped fresh mint

1 green onion, sliced thinly

8 eggs

100g firm fetta cheese, crumbled

⅓ cup (40g) coarsely grated cheddar cheese

1 Preheat oven to 180°C/160°C fan-forced. Grease four ¾-cup (180ml) shallow ovenproof dishes.

2 Divide herbs and onion among dishes; break two eggs into each dish, sprinkle with combined cheeses. Bake, uncovered, about 10 minutes or until eggs are just set.

NUTRITIONAL COUNT PER SERVING 19.7g total fat (9.2g saturated fat); 1083kJ (259 cal); 0.6g carbohydrate; 20.4g protein; 0.2g fibre

Creamy scrambled egg on brioche

PREP + COOK TIME 25 MINUTES **SERVES** 4

250g cherry tomatoes

1 tablespoon olive oil

8 slices thin bacon

8 eggs

½ cup (125ml) cream

2 tablespoons finely chopped fresh chives

30g butter

4 slices brioche, toasted

A great brunch dish, this recipe is best cooked just before serving.

For information on brioche, see Bread, page 67.

1 Preheat grill.

2 Toss tomatoes in oil. Cook bacon and tomato under grill until bacon is crisp and tomato skins start to split. Cover to keep warm.

3 Meanwhile, combine eggs, cream and chives in medium bowl; beat lightly with fork.

4 Heat butter in large non-stick frying pan over medium heat. Add egg mixture, wait a few seconds, then use a wide spatula to gently scrape the set egg mixture along the base of the pan; cook until creamy and just set.

5 Serve brioche topped with egg, bacon and tomatoes.

NUTRITIONAL COUNT PER SERVING 52g total fat (23.9g saturated fat); 3223kJ (771 cal); 40g carbohydrate; 37.6g protein; 2.5g fibre

---

Spanish tortilla

PREP + COOK TIME 45 MINUTES **SERVES** 4

800g russet burbank potatoes, peeled, sliced thinly

1 tablespoon olive oil

1 large brown onion (200g), sliced thinly

200g chorizo sausage, sliced thinly

6 eggs, beaten lightly

300ml cream

4 green onions, sliced thickly

¼ cup (25g) coarsely grated mozzarella cheese

¼ cup (30g) coarsely grated cheddar cheese

Cut tortilla into wedges to serve warm, or allow to cool and serve in small pieces, with other tapas such as olives, cheese and pickled vegetables, to go with drinks.

For information on russet burbank potatoes, see Potatoes, pages 448 & 449.

1 Boil, steam or microwave potato until just tender; drain.

2 Meanwhile, heat oil in medium frying pan; cook brown onion, stirring, until softened. Add chorizo; cook, stirring, until crisp. Drain chorizo mixture on absorbent paper.

3 Whisk eggs in large bowl with cream, green onion and cheeses; stir in potato and chorizo mixture.

4 Pour mixture into heated lightly oiled medium non-stick frying pan; cook, covered, over low heat about 10 minutes or until tortilla is just set. Carefully invert tortilla onto plate, then slide back into pan; cook, uncovered, about 5 minutes or until cooked through.

NUTRITIONAL COUNT PER SERVING 64.1g total fat (32.5g saturated fat); 3390kJ (811 cal); 29.1g carbohydrate; 29.5g protein; 3.8g fibre

Crab, fennel and herb quiche

PREP + COOK TIME 50 MINUTES **MAKES** 12

3 sheets shortcrust pastry

1 tablespoon olive oil

1 medium fennel bulb (300g), sliced thinly

250g crab meat

2 tablespoons finely chopped fennel leaves

2 tablespoons finely chopped fresh flat-leaf parsley

½ cup (60g) coarsely grated cheddar cheese

QUICHE FILLING

300ml cream

¼ cup (60ml) milk

3 eggs

When you trim the fennel for slicing, put the leaves aside to be chopped later. We used lump crab meat from the fish market, but well-drained canned crab meat will work quite well.

For information on fennel, see Fennel, page 174; for shortcrust pastry, see Pastry, page 404; and for crab/crab meat, see Seafood, pages 524 & 527.

1   Preheat oven to 200°C/180°C fan-forced. Grease 12-hole (⅓-cup/80ml) muffin pan.

2   Cut twelve 9cm rounds from pastry; press into pan holes.

3   Heat oil in large frying pan; cook fennel, stirring, 5 minutes or until it softens and browns slightly. Divide fennel between pastry cases; top with combined remaining ingredients.

4   Whisk ingredients for quiche filling in large jug; pour into pastry cases.

5   Bake quiches about 25 minutes. Stand in pan 5 minutes.

NUTRITIONAL COUNT PER QUICHE 27.1g total fat (15g saturated fat); 1509kJ (361 cal); 20.3g carbohydrate; 9g protein; 1.3g fibre

---

Chocolate soufflé

PREP + COOK TIME 35 MINUTES **SERVES** 4

⅓ cup (75g) caster sugar

50g butter

1 tablespoon plain flour

200g dark eating chocolate, melted

2 egg yolks

4 egg whites

The egg whites are beaten to the correct stage when they will stand on the raised beaters in soft peaks with drooping tops.

For information on dark eating chocolate, see Chocolate, page 124.

1   Preheat oven to 180°C/160°C fan-forced. Grease four ¾-cup (180ml) soufflé dishes. Sprinkle inside of dishes with a little of the sugar; shake away excess. Place on oven tray.

2   Melt butter in small saucepan, add flour; cook, stirring, 2 minutes or until it thickens and bubbles. Remove from heat; stir in chocolate and egg yolks. Transfer to large bowl.

3   Beat egg whites in small bowl with electric mixer until soft peaks form. Gradually add remaining sugar, beating until sugar dissolves. Fold egg white mixture into chocolate mixture, in two batches. Divide mixture among dishes.

4   Bake soufflés 15 minutes. Dust with cocoa powder, if you like.

NUTRITIONAL COUNT PER SERVING 27.4g total fat (16.1g saturated fat); 2040kJ (488 cal); 52.3g carbohydrate; 8.1g protein; 0.7g fibre

CRAB, FENNEL AND HERB QUICHE

Baking the pavlova in a
springform tin gives it a
perfect shape with soft
sides and a crisp top that
is easily removed for filling.

Easy pavlova

PREP + COOK TIME 2 HOURS 10 MINUTES (PLUS COOLING TIME) **SERVES** 12

6 egg whites

1½ cups (330g) caster sugar

1 tablespoon cornflour

1 teaspoon vanilla extract

1 teaspoon white vinegar

300ml thickened cream

1 tablespoon icing sugar

1 cup (150g) blueberries

125g strawberries, sliced thinly

1 medium kiwifruit (85g), halved, sliced thinly

¼ cup (60ml) passionfruit pulp

1 Preheat oven to 120°C/100°C fan-forced. Grease 22cm-round springform tin; line base and side with baking paper.

2 Beat egg whites in medium bowl with electric mixer until soft peaks form; gradually add caster sugar, one tablespoon at a time, beating until sugar dissolves between additions. Fold in cornflour, extract and vinegar.

3 Spread mixture into tin; bake about 1¾ hours. Cool pavlova in oven with door ajar.

4 Meanwhile, beat cream and icing sugar in small bowl with electric mixer until firm peaks form.

5 Remove pavlova from tin; peel baking paper from side. Carefully lift top crust from pavlova; set aside. Spread pavlova with half the cream; top with half the berries and half the kiwifruit. Place crust back on top of pavlova; top with remaining cream, berries and kiwifruit. Drizzle with passionfruit.

6 Serve pavlova dusted with extra sifted icing sugar.

NUTRITIONAL COUNT PER SERVING 9.3g total fat (6.1g saturated fat); 957kJ (229 cal); 32.6g carbohydrate; 2.8g protein; 1.4g fibre

Sabayon is the French
version of Italian zabaglione.
This recipe makes enough
sauce for six servings of
either grilled peaches or
nectarines, or poached
pears. It is important to
cook the sabayon slowly
by keeping the water
under the bowl at a gentle
simmer, and to whisk
vigorously all the time.
For a lime sabayon to go
on fresh tropical fruit like
mango, add 1 teaspoon
finely grated lime rind and
2 teaspoons lime juice to
the ingredients before
placing the bowl over
simmering water.
For a coffee sabayon to
serve warm on chocolate
ice-cream or other chocolate
desserts, use 2 teaspoons
of instant coffee dissolved
in ¼ cup of water instead
of the wine.

Sabayon

PREP + COOK TIME 10 MINUTES **MAKES** 2 CUPS

3 egg yolks

¼ cup (55g) caster sugar

¼ cup (60ml) dry white wine

1 Combine ingredients in medium bowl set over medium saucepan of simmering water; do not allow water to touch base of bowl.

2 Whisk vigorously and continually about 5 minutes or until sauce is thick and creamy.

NUTRITIONAL COUNT PER TABLESPOON 0.6g total fat (0.2g saturated fat); 71kJ (17 cal); 2.3g carbohydrate; 0.3g protein; 0g fibre

EASY PAVLOVA

Fennel

Florence or bulb fennel, which Italian greengrocers call finocchio, is a vegetable and herb in one — the feathery leaves can be chopped and used in the same ways as their relation, dill, in salads, sauces and soups and rice dishes, or to go with smoked and fresh salmon and other fish. The tops can be used as a bed on which to steam fish, giving it a delicate aniseed aroma. Similarly, branches of wild fennel that grows along the road can be laid on coals over which fish is grilled to give it a smoky aniseed flavour.

☙ **OTHER RECIPES USING FENNEL**
Crab, fennel and herb quiche, p171
Green salad with fennel and herbs, p252
Pork cutlets with fennel apple relish, p443
Salmon "confit" with fennel and herbs, p365
Tomato and fennel soup, p608
Tomato mustard beef with baby fennel, p48
Vine leaf-wrapped ocean trout, p638

Bulb fennel is crisp and juicy with an aniseed flavour. The bulb consists of overlapping, celery-like stalks, the outer layer coarse and tough but the inner layers pale and tender. It is delicious raw and can be braised, sautéed, stir-fried, grilled or roasted; cooking softens its flavour and brings out its natural sweetness. A large fennel bulb can be as big as a grapefruit, while baby fennel, which are immature bulbs weighing as little as 100g, are especially tender and delicious. Fennel's season is winter into spring.

PREPARATION Remove outer layer(s) until you come to the pale, tender layers.

Trim off the top shoots and trim a thin slice from the base. Cut the bulb in half from top to bottom and use a small, sharp knife to cut out the triangular core of the base.

CHOOSING Try to buy fennel that still has its tops on — they should be fresh and smell delicately of aniseed. Select undamaged, small to medium-size bulbs as large ones may have more wastage before you get to the tender underlying layers.

STORING Refrigerate fennel in a paper bag, in a plastic bag for up to 3 days. It loses its flavour fast so use as soon as possible.

Fennel and pernod sauce

PREP + COOK TIME 30 MINUTES **MAKES** 2 CUPS

1 small fennel bulb (200g)
20g butter
1 tablespoon olive oil
¼ teaspoon fennel seeds
1 teaspoon cumin seeds
¼ cup (60ml) pernod
¾ cup (180g) cream
1 teaspoon lemon juice

1 Using sharp knife, mandoline or V-slicer, slice fennel thinly.
2 Melt butter and oil in medium frying pan; cook fennel and seeds over low heat, uncovered, until fennel softens. Add pernod; bring to the boil. Reduce heat; simmer 1 minute.
3 Add cream and juice; bring to the boil. Reduce heat; simmer 2 minutes or until sauce thickens slightly. Serve with grilled seafood.

NUTRITIONAL COUNT PER TABLESPOON 4.7g total fat (2.7g saturated fat); 230kJ (55 cal); 1.6g carbohydrate; 0.2g protein; 1.1g fibre

Caramelised fennel tarts

PREP + COOK TIME 45 MINUTES **SERVES** 4

These tarts are easy but impressive. They can be served alone or as part of a vegetarian table, or with delicate fillets of whiting or trout. The caramelised fennel can be prepared ahead but place it on the pastry bases only when they are to go in the oven.

For information on puff pastry, see Pastry, page 404.

50g butter

4 baby fennel bulbs (520g), trimmed, halved lengthways

1 teaspoon finely grated orange rind

½ cup (125ml) orange juice

1 sheet puff pastry

2 teaspoons finely chopped fresh thyme

1 Preheat oven to 220°C/200°C fan-forced. Grease and line two oven trays.

2 Melt butter in large frying pan; cook fennel until browned lightly. Add rind and juice; bring to the boil. Reduce heat; simmer, uncovered, about 5 minutes or until fennel is caramelised and tender.

3 Cut pastry sheet into four squares; place on oven trays. Remove fennel from pan, leaving behind the pan juices; divide among pastry squares.

4 Bake tarts about 20 minutes or until pastry is browned.

5 Meanwhile, return pan juices to the boil. Reduce heat; simmer, uncovered, until sauce thickens slightly.

6 Serve tarts drizzled with sauce and sprinkled with thyme.

NUTRITIONAL COUNT PER SERVING 19.8g total fat (11.9 saturated fat); 1145kJ (274 cal); 19.9g carbohydrate; 3.3g protein; 2.7g fibre

Shaved fennel and apple salad

PREP TIME 20 MINUTES **SERVES** 6

This could be a first course, a casual lunch or a partner to hot or cold ham. A mild, creamy blue-vein cheese can be substituted for the brie if you wish.

For information on green apples, see Apples, pages 8–10.

2 baby fennel (260g)

2 medium green apples (300g)

1 cup (120g) roasted pecans

150g brie, sliced thinly

1 red coral lettuce, trimmed, chopped coarsely

MUSTARD VINAIGRETTE

⅓ cup (80ml) olive oil

¼ cup (60ml) lemon juice

1 tablespoon wholegrain mustard

1 Place ingredients for mustard vinaigrette in screw-top jar; shake well.

2 Trim and halve fennel; reserve 2 tablespoons coarsely chopped frond-tips. Halve and core unpeeled apples. Using a very sharp knife, mandoline or V-slicer, slice fennel and apple thinly.

3 Place fennel and apple in large bowl with frond tips, nuts, cheese and dressing; toss gently to combine. Serve salad on top of lettuce.

NUTRITIONAL COUNT PER SERVING 33.3g total fat (6.8g saturated fat); 1496kJ (358 cal); 6.6g carbohydrate; 7.4g protein; 3.5g fibre

CARAMELISED FENNEL TARTS

Figs

Figs can be purple, green, white (actually pale green) or red. In the shops, one colour succeeds another as the different varieties come into season during midsummer to early autumn. Different varieties differ a little in firmness and sweetness. The interior of a fig is a mass of minute, edible flowers and tiny potential fruits that crunch like seeds, embedded in soft flesh; when the fruit is fully ripe, the texture at the centre is moist and luscious.

If you have bought figs that lack flavour or refuse to soften, peel them (or leave the skin on if it is thin), arrange in an oven dish, pour a little water round them and drizzle them with honey. Bake in a 180°C/160°C fan-forced oven for 15–20 minutes, basting the figs several times with the syrup in the dish. Cool in the syrup and serve chilled with cream.

Figs are a great snack to eat as they are, as well as served on a cheeseboard. They are a classic first course with prosciutto or warmed slightly and drizzled with a creamy gorgonzola sauce; raw or grilled, they go well with hot or cold ham, pork or poultry. They can be poached or baked with sugar and a little water plus flavourings such as orangeflower water or spices, then chilled to serve with cream or ice-cream; quartered and soaked for a couple of hours in port, orange juice or an orange liqueur, they make an elegant, simple dessert. Dried figs are available as firm but soft whole fruit, or as glacé (candied) figs, or compressed into blocks for use in cakes and puddings.

PREPARATION Remove the hard bit and any stalk at the stem end of fresh figs. The whole fruit is edible but can be peeled; for presentation, slit the skin downward into quarters, peeling it back like petals. Dried figs may be steamed to soften them before adding to a cake or pudding mixture.

CHOOSING Depending on the variety, a perfectly ripe fig may sag a little, but all varieties will yield when gently pressed. Avoid figs that are hard, damaged, split or mouldy. They should smell sweet — when fully ripe, they are fragile and ferment readily — don't buy if there is a hint of a sour odour.

STORING Fully ripe figs should be eaten the day you buy them. As soon as you get home, arrange them in a single layer on a plate or tray and put them in the refrigerator. Remove the figs an hour or so ahead of serving to bring them back to room temperature as the cold dulls their fragrance and flavour. The Italian custom of placing room-temperature fruit on a bed of ice for serving suits figs perfectly. If you have to hold figs for a day or so, store in a single layer, covered, in the refrigerator crisper. Store dried figs, whole or compressed, in airtight glass or steel containers.

❦ **OTHER RECIPES USING FIGS**
Baby toffee figs, p584
Spiced fig and apple jam, p466

Caramelised spiced fig sauce

PREP + COOK TIME 30 MINUTES **MAKES** 1 CUP

30g butter

6 small fresh figs (210g), quartered

3cm piece fresh ginger (15g), sliced thinly

2 star anise

2 tablespoons brown sugar

¼ cup (60ml) port

½ cup (125ml) chicken stock

½ cup (125ml) water

This sauce is good with pork, game meats and birds, grilled chicken breasts and pan-fried white fish fillets. When fresh figs are out of season, this recipe can be made with dried turkish or greek figs.

1 Melt butter over medium heat in medium frying pan; cook figs, ginger and star anise, stirring, about 5 minutes or until figs are caramelised. Remove figs from pan.

2 Add sugar, port, stock and the water to pan; bring to the boil. Reduce heat; simmer, stirring occasionally, about 10 minutes or until mixture reduces by half.

3 Return figs to pan; simmer, uncovered, 1 minute.

NUTRITIONAL COUNT PER TABLESPOON 2.1g total fat (1.4g saturated fat); 176kJ (42 cal); 4.2g carbohydrate; 0.4g protein; 0.4g fibre

---

Fig, goats cheese and prosciutto salad

PREP + COOK TIME 15 MINUTES **SERVES** 4

6 slices prosciutto (90g)

120g baby rocket leaves, trimmed

4 large fresh figs (320g), quartered

150g soft goats cheese, crumbled

HONEY CIDER DRESSING

¼ cup (60ml) cider vinegar

2 tablespoons olive oil

1 tablespoon wholegrain mustard

1 tablespoon honey

Crumbling the cheese will be easier if you put it in the freezer for 10 minutes first.

For information on goats cheese, see Cheese, pages 100 & 104; and for prosciutto, see Ham, page 256.

1 Preheat grill.

2 Place ingredients for honey cider dressing in screw-top jar; shake well.

3 Crisp prosciutto under grill; drain, chop coarsely.

4 Serve rocket topped with fig, cheese and prosciutto; drizzle with dressing.

NUTRITIONAL COUNT PER SERVING 16.9g total fat (5.7g saturated fat); 1062kJ (254 cal); 13.7g carbohydrate; 11.1g protein; 2.6g fibre

Walnut and ricotta-stuffed figs

PREP + COOK TIME 20 MINUTES **SERVES** 4

8 medium figs (480g)
¼ cup (25g) roasted walnuts, chopped coarsely
½ cup (120g) ricotta cheese
1 tablespoon caster sugar
⅓ cup (80ml) cream
30g butter
⅓ cup (75g) firmly packed brown sugar

1 Preheat oven to 200°C/180°C fan-forced.
2 Cut figs, from the top, into quarters, being careful not to cut all the way through; open slightly. Place on oven tray.
3 Combine nuts, cheese and sugar in small bowl; divide nut mixture among figs. Cook, uncovered, about 10 minutes or until figs are heated through.
4 Meanwhile, combine remaining ingredients in small saucepan; stir over heat until sugar dissolves. Simmer, uncovered, 3 minutes.
5 Place two figs in each serving dish; drizzle with caramel sauce.

NUTRITIONAL COUNT PER SERVING 22.8g total fat (12.2g saturated fat); 1526kJ (365 cal); 32.6g carbohydrate; 6g protein; 3.1g fibre

Barely ripe figs are best for this recipe — if too soft, they are likely to fall apart during cooking. A good way to store fresh figs is in an egg carton, with the lid loosely closed.

For information on ricotta cheese, see Cheese, page 100; and for walnuts, see Nuts, page 344.

Fresh figs with muscat granita

PREP + COOK TIME 25 MINUTES (PLUS COOLING AND FREEZING TIME) **SERVES** 4

1 cup (250ml) water
½ cup (125ml) muscat
½ cup (110g) caster sugar
1 teaspoon black peppercorns
1 teaspoon finely grated lemon rind

1 tablespoon lemon juice
1 tablespoon fennel seeds
½ cup (125ml) water, extra
¼ cup (90g) honey
8 large fresh figs (640g)

1 Bring the water, muscat, sugar, peppercorns, rind and juice to the boil in small saucepan. Cool 10 minutes; strain into 14cm x 21cm loaf pan. Cover with foil; freeze about 4 hours or until firm, scraping granita from bottom and sides of pan with fork every hour.
2 Dry-fry fennel seeds in small saucepan until fragrant. Add the extra water and honey; bring to the boil. Reduce heat; simmer, uncovered, without stirring, 5 minutes or until thickened slightly. Strain through sieve into small jug; discard seeds. Cool syrup 10 minutes.
3 Cut figs lengthways into five slices; divide among serving plates, drizzle with syrup, top with granita.

NUTRITIONAL COUNT PER SERVING 0.5 g total fat (0g saturated fat); 1304kJ (312 cal); 63g carbohydrate; 2.4g protein; 4g fibre

Muscat is a sweet, aromatic, almost musty-tasting dessert wine made from fully ripe muscatel grapes. Tokay, sweet riesling or gewürztraminer can be substituted; drink the rest of the wine with this dessert.

WALNUT AND RICOTTA-STUFFED FIGS

Flour

Now that many of us are cooking recipes from other food cultures as well as our own, we need to know about different kinds of flour beyond the plain, self-raising and wholemeal of the supermarket. Health-food shops, speciality food shops, good delicatessens and some large supermarkets now carry a range of flours made from various grains and from starchy non-grains such as pulses (dried peas, beans and lentils), potatoes and chestnuts, as well as wheat flours of different types and strengths.

1 UNBLEACHED PLAIN FLOUR
2 GLUTEN-FREE PLAIN FLOUR
3 CAKE FLOUR
4 CONTINENTAL FLOUR
5 MAIZE FLOUR
6 BARLEY FLOUR
7 SEMOLINA
8 CHESTNUT FLOUR
9 STRONG (BAKER'S) FLOUR
10 RYE FLOUR
11 BUCKWHEAT FLOUR
12 SOY FLOUR
13 POTATO FLOUR
14 BESAN
15 WHEATEN CORNFLOUR
16 PLAIN FLOUR
17 SELF-RAISING FLOUR
18 WHOLEMEAL FLOUR
19 RICE FLOUR
20 ARROWROOT

To understand how different flours behave, you first need to know about gluten.

Gluten is a protein contained in flour which, when moistened and stirred or beaten, develops into a network of tiny elastic strands throughout a pastry, batter, cake or bread mixture. When heated, these strands set into a firm structure which holds the finished product together. If the mixture includes yeast or baking powder, which produce the gas carbon dioxide within the mixture, then tiny bubbles of the gas become trapped in the gluten network and when the mixture is heated the gas expands, stretching the gluten strands so that the cake or bread rises. The more the mixture is beaten, the more the gluten develops and the more chewy the finished product will be; that is why recipes tell you to mix pastry with a light hand and to fold in the flour for a cake so that the finished products will be tender, but to beat and knead bread dough to give the pleasant chewiness that good bread should have. Wheat has far more gluten than any other grain: hard wheat is high-protein (high-gluten), soft wheat is lower-protein (lower-gluten, but still with more than non-wheat grains).

WHEAT FLOURS

PLAIN FLOUR Formulated as a medium-gluten all-purpose flour, plain flour works well for most cakes, batters, pastries and biscuits. It is available as white, milled from the starchy part of the wheat grain, or wholemeal. When a recipe says "flour" without any further description, it means plain white flour.

UNBLEACHED FLOUR is described in "white bread" under Bread on page 64.

STRONG FLOUR, BAKER'S FLOUR, BREAD FLOUR are names used by manufacturers to denote white flour made from hard wheat or with gluten added so that it has more gluten than ordinary plain flour. Flour marked "gluten flour" usually has a still higher gluten content. These are the flours to use for breads, buns and pizzas.

CONTINENTAL FLOUR is a coarse white flour used for certain European cakes, and also used by some Asians living in Australia for flat breads. Its gluten content varies with different manufacturers.

SELF-RAISING FLOUR contains baking powder to make a mixture rise as it is cooked. If you don't have self-raising flour on hand, you can make your own by mixing 2 teaspoons of baking powder with each cup (150g) of plain flour and sifting together several times. Sometimes a recipe calls for plain flour and baking powder or bicarbonate of soda (baking soda) instead of self-raising flour: the reason for the first is that that particular recipe needs a

If you're not sure whether some flour you have is plain or self-raising, you can check by placing a little on your tongue. If you feel a slight tingle, it is self-raising: the tingle comes from the bicarbonate of soda in baking powder. If still in doubt, mix abut ¼ cup of the flour with water to make a soft, sticky dough and drop it into a saucepan of boiling water. The dough will almost double in size if it's been made with self-raising flour, and won't expand at all if it's been made with plain flour.

Rice flour comes in two grades, a fine one which is sold as rice flour and a coarser one which is sold as ground rice. They can be used interchangeably though ground rice will give a coarser and crunchier texture to the finished product.

different proportion of baking powder from that in self-raising flour, and the reason for the second is that the mixture already has an acid ingredient such as buttermilk, yogurt or honey that takes the place of the chemical acid in baking powder.

CAKE FLOUR, available in some speciality shops, is a low-gluten flour that makes cakes lighter and more crumbly.

WHOLEMEAL OR WHOLEWHEAT FLOUR is milled from whole wheat grains. It may be stone-ground or made by modern methods — these are described in "wholemeal bread" under Bread on pages 64 & 66. Wholemeal flour which still contains the wheat germ (see Bread, page 64) does not keep as well as other wheat flour because the oil in the germ can become rancid.

GLUTEN-FREE FLOUR is made for those who suffer adverse reactions to gluten. It may be made from wheat or other grains, or a mixture, with the gluten removed. Gluten-free flours are available mainly in the form of gluten-free bread mixes, which are usually high in milk powder and contain cellulose and gums that take the place of gluten in the rising process. Even so, gluten-free bread is usually rather crumbly.

CORNFLOUR Confusingly, two different products are sold in Australia as cornflour. One is made from the finely milled starchy part of corn (maize) and the other is wheat starch with the gluten removed. Cornflour has almost twice the thickening power of ordinary wheat flour, and a cornflour-thickened liquid is translucent and glossy.

Maize cornflour has slightly more thickening power than wheaten cornflour and is a better thickener for acid fruits than other flours because others tend to lose their thickening power in the presence of acid.

ATTA is a fine wholemeal flour used for Indian flat breads.

SEMOLINA, SEMOLINA FLOUR Semolina is coarsely milled particles of wheat's starchy part. It comes in degrees of fineness from the large kind used as a breakfast cereal to fine grades which make a granular flour. This flour is not bleached and varies from pale fawn to the prized clear yellow of semolina from durum wheat, the highest grade of hard wheat, which is used to make the finest dried pasta.

NON-WHEAT FLOURS

ARROWROOT is a fine starch from the roots of a family of Caribbean and South American plants. It has about the same thickening power as cornflour but gives even clearer and glossier results.

BARLEY FLOUR is greyish, with little gluten. Bread made from barley flour only is flattish and goes dry quickly, so it is often mixed with wheat flour for bread-making.

BESAN is chickpea flour, creamy yellow and very nutritious. It is used in Indian cooking, especially for pakoras (fritters), dumplings and noodles. The name besan is sometimes used also for lentil flour.

BUCKWHEAT FLOUR is ground from the seed of a cereal-like plant and has a distinctive, almondy flavour. It is used, usually mixed with wheat flour, to make buckwheat pancakes, especially the yeast pancakes called blini.

CHESTNUT FLOUR, made from the sweetish, starchy chestnut, is used for certain European cakes and quickbreads. The flavour becomes tired if the flour is kept for too long.

POTATO FLOUR is very fine and is used as a thickener and in European cakes and biscuits, and is also used for dusting sticky doughs and, made into a paste with water, for glazing rye loaves before and after they are baked.

RICE FLOUR, made from white or brown rice, is fine and slightly gritty. It is used for thickening and the white kind is used to give a short, crisp texture to shortbread. Glutinous rice flour is made from glutinous (sticky) rice and is used for Chinese buns and dumplings.

RYE FLOUR is greyish, with a pleasant sour tang and little gluten, and is usually mixed with wheat flour for breadmaking. Rye bread keeps better than wheat bread.

SOY FLOUR is made from dried soybeans and is very nutritious. Like the other non-wheat flours, it is used in recipes for those who cannot tolerate wheat, and is also used in the manufacture of meat-substitute products.

BUYING Buy flours in quantities that you will use within a few months.

STORING Flour can be stored in its bag if it is kept in a cool, airy place and used within a month or two. Otherwise, store in an airtight container. Don't add new flour to old flour; wait until the old lot is finished, then wash and dry the container before filling with the new flour.

Also see Bread, pages 64–68 and Yeast, pages 644 & 645.

PARATHAS

Parathas

PREP + COOK TIME 1 HOUR 10 MINUTES (PLUS STANDING TIME) **MAKES** 8

1 cup (150g) white plain flour

1 cup (160g) wholemeal plain flour

100g cold butter, chopped

½ cup (125ml) water

300g coliban potatoes, peeled, chopped coarsely

1 tablespoon peanut oil

1 small brown onion (80g), chopped finely

1 clove garlic, crushed

½ teaspoon ground cumin

1 teaspoon coriander seeds, crushed

¼ teaspoon cayenne pepper

1 tablespoon finely chopped fresh coriander

vegetable oil, for shallow-frying

1 Process flours and butter until mixture resembles fine breadcrumbs; add the water, pulse until mixture forms a soft dough. Wrap dough in plastic wrap; stand 1 hour.

2 Meanwhile, boil, steam or microwave potato until tender; drain. Mash in medium bowl.

3 Heat peanut oil in small frying pan; cook onion and garlic, stirring, until onion softens. Add cumin, crushed coriander and cayenne; cook, stirring, until fragrant. Add onion mixture to potato with fresh coriander; mix to combine. Cool filling 10 minutes.

4 Divide dough into 16 pieces. Roll eight pieces on lightly floured surface to form 14cm rounds (use a 14cm plate as a guide). Spread half of the filling over four of the rounds, leaving 1cm border; brush borders with water. Cover with remaining rounds; press edges together to seal. Repeat process with remaining eight dough pieces and filling.

5 Heat vegetable oil in medium frying pan; cook parathas, one at a time, until browned lightly both sides. Drain on absorbent paper; cover to keep warm.

NUTRITIONAL COUNT PER PARATHA 18.8g total fat (8g saturated fat); 1338kJ (320 cal); 30.7g carbohydrate; 5.5g protein; 3.7g fibre

Parathas are best made just before serving. They are traditionally made with ghee and then cooked in ghee, but our version uses butter in the pastry and is cooked in vegetable oil. When you are rolling each paratha, cover the remaining dough with a damp teatowel to stop it from drying out. You can use nicola or sebago potatoes instead of colibans for the filling.

For information on coliban potatoes, see Potatoes, page 448.

BOXTY

Boxty is an old Irish recipe. For a lower-fat version, use low-fat dairy-free spread instead of butter.

For information on potatoes, see Potatoes, page 448.

Boxty

PREP + COOK TIME 1 HOUR 15 MINUTES **SERVES** 4

900g potatoes, peeled

100g butter, softened

1 clove garlic, crushed

3 cups (450g) self-raising flour

1 tablespoon milk

2 teaspoons sesame seeds

1 Boil, steam or microwave half of the potatoes; drain. Mash cooked potatoes in large bowl until smooth. Coarsely grate remaining raw potatoes.

2 Preheat oven to 180°C/160°C fan-forced. Line two oven trays with baking paper.

3 Stir butter, garlic, flour and grated potato into mashed potato until it forms a dough.

4 Knead dough on lightly floured surface; divide into quarters. Using hands, shape each quarter into 20cm round; score a shallow cross into top of each round.

5 Place rounds on trays; brush with milk, sprinkle with sesame seeds. Bake 20 minutes. Cover with foil; bake about 20 minutes or until cooked through.

NUTRITIONAL COUNT PER SERVING 23g total fat (14g saturated fat); 2968kJ (710 cal); 104.9g carbohydrate; 16.3g protein; 7.6g fibre

Rosemary and potato pizza

PREP + COOK TIME 1 HOUR **SERVES** 8

3 medium potatoes (630g), unpeeled

1 teaspoon fresh rosemary leaves

2 tablespoons olive oil

1 cup (150g) self-raising flour

1 cup (150g) plain flour

30g butter

1 egg, beaten lightly

⅓ cup (80ml) milk

½ cup (40g) finely grated parmesan cheese

2 cloves garlic, crushed

For a lower-fat version of this pizza, use low-fat dairy-free spread instead of butter, and no-fat milk.

For information on potatoes, see Potatoes, page 448.

1 Peel and coarsely chop one of the potatoes; boil, steam or microwave until tender, drain. Mash in small bowl; reserve ½ cup (110g) mashed potato. Using sharp knife, mandoline or V-slicer, cut remaining potatoes into 1mm slices. Pat dry with absorbent paper. Combine sliced potato in medium bowl with rosemary and oil.

2 Preheat oven to 200°C/180°C fan-forced. Grease 25cm x 30cm swiss roll pan.

3 Combine flours in large bowl; using fingertips, rub butter into flour. Stir in mashed potato, egg and milk until combined. Turn dough onto floured surface; knead until smooth.

4 Roll dough into 25cm x 30cm rectangle; carefully lift onto pan. Using palm of hand, press dough into corners of pan. Top pizza base with cheese and garlic; layer potato slices, overlapping slightly. Bake about 30 minutes or until potato is tender and pizza is browned.

NUTRITIONAL COUNT PER SERVING 10.8g total fat (4.2g saturated fat); 1216kJ (291 cal); 37.6g carbohydrate; 9g protein; 3.1g fibre

Wholemeal cranberry and cinnamon scones

PREP + COOK TIME 35 MINUTES **MAKES** 12

1 cup (160g) wholemeal
self-raising flour

1 cup (150g) self-raising flour

½ cup (70g) fine oatmeal

1 teaspoon ground cinnamon

½ teaspoon finely grated
lemon rind

30g butter

¾ cup (105g) dried cranberries

1 cup (250ml) milk

2 tablespoons honey

1 tablespoon milk, extra

1 tablespoon oatmeal, extra

1 cup (200g) ricotta cheese

1 Preheat oven to 220°C/200°C fan-forced. Grease and flour deep 19cm-square cake pan.
2 Combine flours, oatmeal, cinnamon and rind in large bowl; rub in butter. Stir in dried
cranberries, milk and honey.
3 Knead dough on floured surface until smooth. Press dough to a 2cm-thickness.
Cut twelve 5.5cm rounds from dough; place in pan. Brush with extra milk then sprinkle
with extra oatmeal.
4 Bake scones about 25 minutes. Serve warm with cheese.

NUTRITIONAL COUNT PER SCONE 6.1g total fat (3.5g saturated fat); 836kJ (200 cal); 27.6g carbohydrate;
7g protein; 3.5g fibre

*Dried cranberries are
labelled commercially as
craisins. They are available
at health food stores
and many supermarkets
(see page 60). These
scones are good, too,
split and buttered for
school lunch boxes.*

*For information on
dried cranberries, see
Fruit, Dried, page 192.*

Buttermilk scones

PREP + COOK TIME 40 MINUTES **MAKES** 15

3 cups (450g) self-raising flour

2 tablespoons caster sugar

40g unsalted butter

2 cups (500ml) buttermilk

2 tablespoons buttermilk, extra

300ml thickened cream

250g strawberries, halved

1 Preheat oven to 240°C/220°C fan-forced. Grease 20cm x 30cm lamington pan.
2 Sift flour and sugar into large bowl; rub in butter with fingertips.
3 Add buttermilk; use knife to "cut" buttermilk through the mixture to form a soft,
sticky dough. Knead dough lightly on floured surface until smooth.
4 Press dough out to an even 2.5cm thickness. Dip 6.5cm cutter into flour; cut as many
rounds as possible from the dough. Place scones side by side, just touching, in pan.
5 Gently knead scraps of dough together; repeat pressing and cutting of dough,
place in pan. Brush tops with extra buttermilk; bake about 20 minutes or until scones
sound hollow when tapped firmly on the top.
6 Meanwhile, beat cream in small bowl with electric mixer until soft peaks form.
Serve scones with whipped cream and strawberries.

NUTRITIONAL COUNT PER SCONE 9.9g total fat (6.3g saturated fat); 869kJ (208 cal); 24.4g carbohydrate;
4.8g protein; 1.4g fibre

*Buttermilk makes
especially light scones.
Serve them with your
favourite jam instead
of the strawberries, or
simply buttered.*

*For information on
buttermilk, see Milk,
page 317.*

Shortbread will keep, stored in an airtight container, for 1 week. For pistachio and white chocolate mounds, roast ½ cup unsalted pistachios, chop two-thirds finely and reserve the remainder. Fold chopped pistachios and 100g finely chopped white eating chocolate into basic shortbread mixture before flours are added. Shape level teaspoons of mixture into mounds, place about 3cm apart on oven trays and press a reserved nut into each mound. Bake biscuits about 20 minutes, stand 5 minutes then transfer to wire racks to cool. Serve dusted with icing sugar. Makes 32.

Traditional shortbread

PREP + COOK TIME 1 HOUR **MAKES** 24

250g butter, softened

⅓ cup (75g) caster sugar

1 tablespoon water

2 cups (300g) plain flour

½ cup (100g) rice flour

2 tablespoons white sugar

1 Preheat oven to 160°C/140°C fan-forced. Grease two oven trays.

2 Beat butter and caster sugar in medium bowl with electric mixer until light and fluffy; stir in the water and sifted flours, in two batches. Knead on floured surface until smooth.

3 Divide mixture in half; shape each, on separate trays, into 20cm rounds. Mark each round into 12 wedges; prick with fork. Pinch edges of rounds with fingers; sprinkle with white sugar.

4 Bake about 40 minutes; stand 5 minutes. Using sharp knife, cut into wedges along marked lines. Cool on trays.

NUTRITIONAL COUNT PER PIECE 8.8g total fat (5.7g saturated fat); 644kJ (154 cal); 17g carbohydrate; 1.7g protein; 0.6g fibre

Banana pancakes

PREP + COOK TIME 20 MINUTES **SERVES** 4

½ cup (75g) self-raising flour

1 tablespoon caster sugar

⅔ cup (160ml) buttermilk

1 egg white

2 tablespoons maple syrup

10g butter, melted

1 medium banana (200g), sliced thinly

¼ cup (60ml) maple syrup, extra

¼ cup (30g) roasted pecans, chopped coarsely

When buying maple syrup, check the label for the words "pure maple syrup". There are many imitations but the real thing is by far the best. For notes on roasting pecans, see Nuts, page 347.

For information on bananas, see Bananas, pages 32–34.

1 Combine flour and sugar in medium bowl; whisk in buttermilk, egg white, syrup and butter until mixture is smooth. Stir in banana.

2 Pour ¼ cup of the batter into heated oiled large frying pan. Cook, uncovered, until bubbles appear on surface. Turn; cook until browned lightly. Remove from pan; cover to keep warm. Repeat process with remaining batter to make a total of eight pancakes.

3 Serve pancakes drizzled with extra syrup then sprinkled with nuts.

NUTRITIONAL COUNT PER SERVING 8.6g total fat (2.3g saturated fat); 1271kJ (304 cal); 49.4g carbohydrate; 5.7g protein; 2.1g fibre

Featherlight sponge cake

PREP + COOK TIME 40 MINUTES **SERVES** 10

Unfilled sponges can be frozen for up to 2 months. Sponges and rolls filled with jam and cream are best eaten on the day they are made.

4 eggs

¾ cup (165g) caster sugar

⅔ cup (100g) wheaten cornflour

¼ cup (30g) custard powder

1 teaspoon cream of tartar

½ teaspoon bicarbonate of soda

⅓ cup (110g) apricot jam

300ml thickened cream, whipped

1 Preheat oven to 180°C/160°C fan-forced. Grease and flour two deep 22cm-round cake pans.

2 Beat eggs and sugar in small bowl with electric mixer until thick, creamy and sugar is dissolved; transfer to large bowl. Fold in triple-sifted dry ingredients; divide between pans.

3 Bake sponges 20 minutes. Turn, top-side up, onto baking-paper-lined wire rack to cool.

4 Sandwich sponges with jam and cream.

NUTRITIONAL COUNT PER SERVING 13.3g total fat (7.8g saturated fat); 1158kJ (277 cal); 35.7g carbohydrate; 3.4g protein; 0.2g fibre

Butterscotch pecan muffins

PREP + COOK TIME 40 MINUTES **MAKES** 12

These muffins will remain fresh, stored in an airtight container, for up to 2 days.

For information on pecans, see Nuts, page 346.

¾ cup (240g) Top 'n' Fill Caramel

2 cups (300g) self-raising flour

¾ cup (165g) firmly packed brown sugar

¾ cup (90g) coarsely chopped roasted pecans

80g butter, melted

1 cup (250ml) buttermilk

1 egg

1 Preheat oven to 200°C/180°C fan-forced. Line 12-hole (⅓-cup/80ml) muffin pan with paper cases.

2 Stir caramel in small saucepan over low heat until smooth. Cool 5 minutes.

3 Meanwhile, sift flour and sugar into large bowl. Stir in nuts and combined butter, buttermilk and egg. Do not over-mix; mixture should be lumpy.

4 Divide half the mixture between paper cases. Spoon half the caramel over muffin mixture; top with remaining mixture then caramel. Using a skewer, gently swirl caramel into muffin mixture.

5 Bake muffins 20 minutes. Stand 5 minutes; turn, top-side up, onto wire rack to cool.

NUTRITIONAL COUNT PER MUFFIN 13.4g total fat (5.4g saturated fat); 1325kJ (317 cal); 33.5g carbohydrate; 6g protein; 1.6g fibre

1 FEATHERLIGHT SPONGE CAKE
2 BUTTERSCOTCH PECAN MUFFINS

Patty cakes

PREP + COOK TIME 45 MINUTES **MAKES** 12

125g butter, softened

½ teaspoon vanilla extract

¾ cup (165g) caster sugar

3 eggs

2 cups (300g) self-raising flour

¼ cup (60ml) milk

1 Preheat oven to 180°C/160°C fan-forced. Line a 12-hole (⅓-cup/80ml) muffin pan with paper cases.

2 Place ingredients in medium bowl; beat with electric mixer on low speed until ingredients are combined. Increase speed to medium; beat about 3 minutes or until mixture is smooth and paler in colour. Divide mixture between paper cases.

3 Bake about 25 minutes. Stand cakes 5 minutes, turn, top-side up, onto wire racks to cool.

4 Serve cakes topped with glacé icing (see page 582).

NUTRITIONAL COUNT PER CAKE 10.4g total fat (6.2g saturated fat); 1003kJ (240 cal); 31.7g carbohydrate; 4.3g protein; 1g fibre

For berry and orange cakes, stir in 1 teaspoon finely grated orange rind and ½ cup dried mixed berries at the end of step 2. For citrus cakes, stir in ½ teaspoon each of finely grated lime, orange and lemon rind at the end of step 2. For passionfruit and white chocolate cakes, stir in ¼ cup passionfruit pulp and ½ cup white Choc Bits at the end of step 2.

FLOUR | **THE COMPLETE COOK** 191

Fruit, Dried

Drying fruit not only preserves it but concentrates its sugars and changes its texture from juicy to chewy or leathery. The vitamin C content of fruits is lost in the drying process but minerals, dietary fibre and other vitamins are retained.

1 FIGS
2 PEAR
3 DRIED CURRANTS
4 MUSCATELS
5 PINEAPPLE
6 SULTANAS
7 PAPAYA
8 MANGO
9 RAISINS
10 PEACH
11 KIWIFRUIT
12 DRIED CRANBERRIES
13 APPLES
14 CITRUS PEEL
15 PRUNES
16 APRICOTS

❧ OTHER RECIPES
USING DRIED FRUIT
Bircher muesli, p234
Dark chocolate, fig and muscat brownies, p130
Date and tamarind chutney, p467
Lamb, apricot and almond tagine, p288
Rainbow silver beet with pine nuts, garlic and raisins, p550
Roasted rhubarb and cranberries, p492
Turkey, cranberry and sprout salad, p573
Upside-down toffee banana and date cake, p37
Wholemeal cranberry and cinnamon scones, p187

RAISINS, SULTANAS and **CURRANTS** are dried grapes, medium-size for raisins, small white ones for sultanas, tiny black ones for currants. Sultanas and currants are seedless, raisins are sold either with seeds or seeded. They are sold separately for use in cakes, biscuits, sauces, puddings and also for savoury stuffings and in dishes such as pilaf or couscous, and are also sold mixed, with the addition of candied orange (citrus) peel and stoned glacé cherries (see Fruit, Glacé, pages 198 & 199) as mixed dried fruit to be used for cakes and puddings.

MUSCATELS are muscatel grapes that have been dried in bunches and are served with soft cheeses, especially blue cheese, or in a pretty dish, along with nuts, chocolates and other sweetmeats, to go with after-dinner coffee. Like fresh grapes, muscatels should be served either snipped into small bunches or with scissors for diners to snip off their own bunches.

PRUNES are dried plums. They make a good snack and can be served on breakfast cereal, brandied or stuffed with marzipan for sweetmeats to serve with coffee, poached for desserts, or used in savoury casseroles or with rich meats such as pork.

APPLES, PEARS, PEACHES and **APRICOTS** make excellent snacks and are chopped to go on breakfast cereal, poached for desserts and used in pies and puddings and also in savoury stuffings and certain meat dishes.

CRANBERRIES, DRIED AND SWEETENED, are available in small packets to snack on in the same way as nuts, and are also used in cakes, muffins and puddings. They are marketed under the name craisins and are available from most supermarkets.

MANGO, KIWIFRUIT, PINEAPPLE and **PAPAYA** are best eaten as gourmet snacks.

MANDARIN PEEL has been used, dried, in Chinese cooking and also as a Chinese medicine for centuries. It is available at Asian food stores and it is easy to make your own by drying fresh peel in the sun or a very low oven.

Also see Dates, page 156 and Figs, page 178.

CHOOSING For top quality, choose Australian dried fruits. They are produced to strict standards and are among the best in the world as they start with quality fruit and have been expertly sun-dried to remain moist and pleasantly chewy. In a variety where an Australian product may not be available, look for even, bright, natural colour and chewy but not dry and leathery texture.

STORING Unopened packets of dried fruit can be stored at room temperature for a month or two. Once opened, the fruit should be transferred to an airtight container and stored away from heat and light.

Cranberry and apple fruit mince

PREP TIME 30 MINUTES (PLUS STANDING TIME) **MAKES** 9½ CUPS (2.5KG)

2⅔ cups (325g) dried cranberries

2½ cups (200g) finely chopped dried apples

2 cups (320g) finely chopped raisins

1 cup (250g) finely chopped dried cherries

¾ cup (150g) finely chopped dried figs

½ cup (85g) mixed peel

½ cup (115g) glacé ginger, chopped finely

3 medium apples (450g), peeled, grated coarsely

1½ cups (330g) firmly packed brown sugar

½ cup (160g) raspberry jam

1 tablespoon finely grated orange rind

¼ cup (60ml) orange juice

2 teaspoons mixed spice

½ teaspoon ground clove

1 cinnamon stick, halved

1⅓ cups (330ml) Grand Marnier

1 Mix ingredients in large bowl until combined. Cover bowl with plastic wrap.

2 Store mixture in a cool dry place for 1 month, stirring every 2 or 3 days, before use.

NUTRITIONAL COUNT PER TABLESPOON 0.1g total fat (0g saturated fat); 268kJ (64 cal); 13.3g carbohydrate; 0.2g protein; 0.7g fibre

Celebration fruit cake

PREP + COOK TIME 3 HOURS 50 MINUTES (PLUS STANDING AND COOLING TIME) **SERVES** 16

3 cups (500g) sultanas

1¾ cups (300g) raisins, halved

1¾ cups (300g) dried dates, chopped finely

1 cup (150g) dried currants

⅔ cup (110g) mixed peel

⅔ cup (150g) glacé cherries, halved

¼ cup (55g) coarsely chopped glacé pineapple

¼ cup (60g) coarsely chopped glacé apricots

½ cup (125ml) dark rum

250g butter, softened

1 cup (220g) brown sugar

5 eggs

1½ cups (225g) plain flour

⅓ cup (50g) self-raising flour

1 teaspoon mixed spice

2 tablespoons dark rum, extra

1 Combine fruit and rum in large bowl; mix well; cover tightly with plastic wrap. Store mixture in cool, dark place overnight or up to a week stirring every day.

2 Preheat oven to 150°C/130°C fan-forced. Line deep 22cm-round cake pan with three thicknesses of baking paper, extending paper 5cm above side.

3 Beat butter and sugar in small bowl with electric mixer until just combined. Add eggs, one at a time, beating only until combined between additions. Add butter mixture to fruit mixture; mix well. Mix in sifted dry ingredients; spread mixture evenly into pan.

4 Bake 3½ hours. Brush hot cake with extra rum; cover, in pan, with foil. Cool overnight.

NUTRITIONAL COUNT PER SERVING 15.1g total fat (9g saturated fat); 2429kJ (581 cal); 96.5g carbohydrate; 6.1g protein; 5.7g fibre

Dried fruit and coconut trail mix

PREP + COOK TIME 25 MINUTES (PLUS COOLING TIME) **MAKES** 3 CUPS

2 tablespoons honey

2 teaspoons olive oil

¼ teaspoon mixed spice

½ cup (70g) pistachios

½ cup (80g) almond kernels

½ cup (65g) dried cranberries

½ cup (75g) coarsely chopped dried apricots

½ cup (70g) coarsely chopped dried dates

½ cup (25g) toasted flaked coconut

1 Preheat oven to 180°C/160°C fan-forced.

2 Combine honey, oil and spice in small bowl.

3 Combine nuts in shallow baking dish; drizzle with honey mixture. Roast, uncovered, about 10 minutes or until browned lightly, stirring halfway through. Cool 15 minutes.

4 Stir in remaining ingredients; cool. Store in an airtight container.

NUTRITIONAL COUNT PER ⅓ CUP 11.8g total fat (2.5g saturated fat); 869kJ (208 cal); 20.7g carbohydrate; 4.2g protein; 3.7g fibre

A sustaining treat for a day outdoors. Divide mix into small resealable plastic bags for each adventurer to carry one in their pocket. Don't use it, though, for small children who might choke on nuts — and remember that most schools now forbid nuts of any kind on the premises because some kinds are dangerous to children with certain allergies.

Boiled raisin chocolate cake

PREP + COOK TIME 1 HOUR 40 MINUTES (PLUS COOLING AND STANDING TIME) **SERVES** 12

2 cups (300g) raisins

2 cups (500ml) water

1 teaspoon bicarbonate of soda

⅓ cup (35g) cocoa powder

2 teaspoons ground cinnamon

½ teaspoon ground clove

1 teaspoon vanilla extract

250g butter, chopped

1½ cups (330g) caster sugar

4 eggs

1½ cups (225g) plain flour

1 cup (150g) self-raising flour

CHOCOLATE GLAZE

200g dark eating chocolate, chopped coarsely

100g butter, chopped

1 Preheat oven to 180°C/160°C fan-forced. Grease 24cm bundt pan well.

2 Combine raisins and the water in medium saucepan; bring to the boil. Reduce heat; simmer, uncovered, 10 minutes. Remove from heat; stir in soda, cocoa, spices and extract. Cool to room temperature.

3 Beat butter and sugar in medium bowl with electric mixer until light and fluffy. Add eggs, one at a time, beating until just combined between additions; stir in combined sifted flours and raisin mixture, in two batches. Spread mixture into pan.

4 Bake cake about 1 hour 10 minutes. Stand cake 5 minutes; turn onto wire rack to cool.

5 Stir ingredients for chocolate glaze in medium heatproof bowl over medium saucepan of simmering water until smooth. Pour glaze over cooled cake; stand 30 minutes before serving.

NUTRITIONAL COUNT PER SERVING 31.4g total fat (19.5g saturated fat); 2658kJ (636 cal); 79.2g carbohydrate; 7.6g protein; 2.7g fibre

A bundt pan is a heavily decorated ring pan. You can buy them from cookware shops. Make sure you grease the pan well, we prefer to use butter. If you don't have a bundt pan, the cake mixture can be made in two 20cm ring or baba pans. Each will take about 40 minutes to cook. Raisins and other dried fruit are usually rehydrated (as described in step 2) before being stirred into a cake mixture otherwise it will be drier and chewier instead of melt-in-your mouth luscious.

For information on dark eating chocolate, see Chocolate, page 124.

You could make this for "Christmas pudding" — a little more suitable for a southern-hemisphere Christmas dessert.

For information on cream cheese and mascarpone, see Cheese, pages 100 & 102; and for oranges, see Oranges, page 380–382.

Spiced fig and orange cheesecake

PREP + COOK TIME 1 HOUR 40 MINUTES (PLUS COOLING AND REFRIGERATION TIME) **SERVES** 12

½ cup (80g) brazil nuts

125g plain sweet biscuits

80g butter, melted

1 cup (250ml) orange juice

1¼ cups (250g) finely chopped dried figs

1 cinnamon stick

pinch ground clove

250g cream cheese, softened

1 tablespoon finely grated orange rind

¾ cup (165g) caster sugar

1 cup (250g) mascarpone cheese

2 eggs, separated

1 Grease 22cm springform tin.

2 Process nuts and biscuits until fine. Add butter; process until combined. Press mixture over base of tin. Place tin on oven tray; refrigerate 30 minutes.

3 Preheat oven to 160°C/140°C fan-forced.

4 Combine juice, figs, cinnamon and cloves in small saucepan; simmer, uncovered, 10 minutes or until most of the juice has been absorbed. Discard cinnamon stick. Spread fig mixture over crumb base in tin.

5 Beat cheese, rind and sugar in medium bowl with electric mixer until smooth. Add mascarpone and yolks; beat only until combined. Beat egg whites in small bowl with electric mixer until soft peaks form; fold into cheese mixture.

6 Pour filling over fig mixture; bake about 1¼ hours. Cool in oven with door ajar. Refrigerate cheesecake 3 hours or overnight. Serve dusted with sifted icing sugar.

NUTRITIONAL COUNT PER SERVING 29.5g total fat (16.9g saturated fat); 1914kJ (438 cal); 35.3g carbohydrate; 6.4g protein; 3.8g fibre

These cakes make fabulous Christmas gifts and you can make them weeks ahead — except for the decoration — and store them airtight. Store the whiskey syrup in a screw-top jar, then stand the jar in hot water to thin it again when glazing muscatels.

For information on dark eating chocolate, see Chocolate, page 124.

Rich chocolate christmas cakes

PREP + COOK TIME 2 HOURS 20 MINUTES (PLUS STANDING AND COOLING TIME) **MAKES** 8

1 cup (170g) seeded prunes

1 cup (140g) seeded dried dates

1 cup (150g) raisins

½ cup (75g) muscatels

1 cup (200g) dried figs

5 (100g) glacé orange slices

1½ cups (375ml) Irish whiskey

1½ cups (330g) firmly packed dark brown sugar

185g butter, softened

3 eggs

½ cup (50g) hazelnut meal

1½ cups (225g) plain flour

2 tablespoons cocoa powder

1 teaspoon mixed spice

½ teaspoon ground nutmeg

½ teaspoon bicarbonate of soda

150g dark eating chocolate, chopped finely

¼ cup (60ml) water

2 tablespoons cocoa powder, extra

1 cup (150g) muscatels, extra

1 SPICED FIG AND ORANGE
CHEESECAKE
2 RICH CHOCOLATE
CHRISTMAS CAKES

1 Chop all fruit finely. Combine fruit and ¾ cup of the whiskey in large bowl, cover with plastic wrap; stand overnight.

2 Preheat oven to 120°C/100°C fan-forced. Line eight deep 8cm-round cake tins with two thicknesses of baking paper, extending paper 5cm above sides of tins.

3 Stir remaining whiskey and ¾ cup of the sugar in small saucepan over heat until sugar dissolves; bring to the boil. Remove from heat; cool syrup 20 minutes.

4 Meanwhile, beat butter and remaining sugar in small bowl with electric mixer until combined; beat in eggs, one at a time. Add butter mixture to fruit mixture; mix well. Mix in meal, sifted dry ingredients, chocolate and ½ cup of the cooled syrup. Spread mixture into tins. Bake cakes about 1¾ hours.

5 Bring remaining syrup and the water to the boil in small saucepan; boil for 3 minutes or until thickened slightly. Brush hot cakes with half of the hot syrup, cover cakes with foil; cool in tins.

6 Divide reserved muscatels into eight small bunches; place bunches in remaining syrup. Stand in syrup until cool, drain. Dust cakes with extra sifted cocoa, top with muscatel bunches.

NUTRITIONAL COUNT PER SERVING 31.5g total fat (16.9g saturated fat); 4076kJ (975 cal); 132g carbohydrate; 10.9g protein; 10.4g fibre

Fruit, Glacé

Glacé or candied fruit is made by simmering choice fruits briefly in water to soften them, then steeping them in hot, successively stronger sugar syrups over a period of weeks. During this time, the sugar gradually replaces the moisture in the fruit. Finally, the fruit is drained and dried slowly over a period of several days. When finished, it has a shiny or "glazed" (glacé) surface.

1 GREEN GLACE CHERRY
2 ANGELICA
3 GLACE APRICOT
4 GLACE ORANGE
5 RED GLACE CHERRY
6 GLACE PEAR
7 GLACE PINEAPPLE
8 CITRUS PEEL
9 CLEMENTINE
10 GLACE PEACH
11 GLACE GINGER

❦ **OTHER RECIPES USING GLACE FRUIT**
Beef steaks with three-ginger sauce, p223
Rhubarb, white chocolate and ginger trifles, p491

Small fruits, such as cherries, apricots, cumquats or small figs or clementines (a cross between a mandarin and a Seville orange) are candied whole, others such as mandarins, oranges or limes may be separated into segments, pineapple is skinned, cored and cut into rings and pears, peaches or plums may be halved or quartered. If glacé fruit is coated with caster sugar, it becomes crystallised fruit. Citrus peel, ginger and angelica, which is the peeled green stem of a fragrant European herb, and ginger which is the rhizome (root-like stem) of a tropical plant, are also candied by similar methods. Glacé and crystallised fruits are served in paper cases as elegant sweetmeats; glacé or crystallised ginger can be served with soft cheeses or as a sweetmeat. Crystallised fruit or ginger may also be used, whole or sliced, as decorations on cakes or desserts, or chopped to use as an ingredient. Angelica is used as a decoration on cakes and such desserts as trifle, often cut to resemble the stalks and leaves of sugar or icing flowers.

To chop or slice glacé or crystallised fruit, ginger etc, put a heavy saucepan or other container (one you can't knock over) of very hot water near the chopping board and dip the knife blade into it often so that it won't stick in the sugary fruit. Kitchen scissors may be more convenient for cutting up some fruits; dip the blade of these, too, in the hot water as you go.

STORING Glacé items will keep indefinitely but must be stored airtight to prevent them from becoming sticky from the moisture in the air. They should be arranged in a single layer, or in carefully separated layers, in an airtight container, if possible with a few of the small desiccant packets often packed in bottles of tablets from the chemist's to keep them dry. Failing this, if they are to be stored for long, they should be kept in their container in the refrigerator, which is drying.

1

2

3

4

5

Glacé ginger and pineapple cheesecake

PREP + COOK TIME 1 HOUR 20 MINUTES (PLUS COOLING AND REFRIGERATION TIME) **SERVES** 12

150g butternut snap biscuits

75g butter, melted

500g cream cheese, softened

½ cup (110g) caster sugar

½ cup (120g) sour cream

2 tablespoons plain flour

3 eggs

¼ cup (60g) finely chopped glacé ginger

½ cup (115g) finely chopped glacé pineapple

1 Grease 24cm springform tin; line base and side with baking paper.

2 Process biscuits until fine. Add butter, process until combined. Press mixture over base of tin. Place tin on oven tray; refrigerate 30 minutes.

3 Preheat oven to 160°C/140°C fan-forced.

4 Beat cheese, sugar, cream and flour in medium bowl with electric mixer until smooth; beat in eggs, one at a time.

5 Combine ginger and pineapple; sprinkle one-third over base. Pour filling over fruit; bake 15 minutes. Sprinkle with remaining fruit; bake about 35 minutes. Cool in oven with door ajar. Refrigerate cheesecake 3 hours or overnight.

NUTRITIONAL COUNT PER SERVING 27.3g total fat (17.2g saturated fat); 1622kJ (388 cal); 29.9g carbohydrate; 6.5g protein; 0.6g fibre

This is the traditional rich baked cheesecake with a flavoursome biscuit-crumb base. Ginger and pineapple go very well with each other and with the tangy flavours of cream cheese and sour cream.

For information on cream cheese, see Cheese, page 100 & 102; and for sour cream, see Cream, page 142.

Jewelled rocky road

PREP + COOK TIME 25 MINUTES (PLUS REFRIGERATION TIME) **MAKES** 35

300g toasted marshmallows with coconut, chopped coarsely

½ cup (40g) flaked almonds, roasted

4 slices glacé pineapple (125g), chopped coarsely

½ cup (125g) coarsely chopped glacé peaches

½ cup (100g) coarsely chopped glacé citron

450g white eating chocolate, melted

1 Grease 19cm x 29cm slice pan; line base and two long sides with baking paper, extending paper 5cm over long sides.

2 Combine marshmallows, nuts and fruit in large bowl. Working quickly, stir in chocolate; spread mixture into pan, push down firmly to flatten. Refrigerate until set; cut into squares.

NUTRITIONAL COUNT PER PIECE 5.5g total fat (3.2g saturated fat); 548kJ (131 cal); 18.5g carbohydrate; 1.6g protein; 0.2g fibre

For information on almonds, see Nuts, page 344 and for details on roasting nuts, see page 347. For details on melting chocolate, see Chocolate, pages 124 & 125.

Glacé fruit cake

PREP + COOK TIME 2 HOURS 50 MINUTES **SERVES** 12

185g butter, softened

½ cup (110g) caster sugar

3 eggs

1 cup (250g) finely chopped glacé apricot

½ cup (80g) finely chopped glacé orange

½ cup (90g) finely chopped glacé ginger

¾ cup (210g) finely chopped glacé fig

1 ½ cups (225g) plain flour

½ cup (75g) self-raising flour

½ cup (125ml) milk

¼ cup (60ml) ginger wine

GINGER SYRUP

¼ cup (60ml) ginger wine

¼ cup (60ml) water

¼ cup (55g) caster sugar

2 teaspoons lemon juice

Any type of glacé fruit can be used in this recipe. Ginger wine has 14% alcohol by volume, but this is driven off when the ginger syrup is boiled. You can use dry (white) vermouth instead if you like.

1 Preheat oven to 150°C/130°C fan-forced. Line the base and both long sides of 14cm x 21cm loaf pan with baking paper, extending paper 5cm above sides.

2 Beat butter and sugar in small bowl with electric mixer until just combined. Add eggs, one at a time, beating until just combined between additions; transfer to large bowl. Stir in fruit then sifted flours, and combined milk and wine, in two batches. Spread mixture into pan; bake about 2½ hours.

3 Meanwhile, make ginger syrup.

4 Pour hot ginger syrup over hot cake in pan. Cover cake with foil; cool in pan.

GINGER SYRUP Stir ingredients in small saucepan over low heat, without boiling, until sugar dissolves; bring to the boil. Boil, uncovered, without stirring, about 2 minutes or until syrup thickens slightly.

NUTRITIONAL COUNT PER SERVING 14.7g total fat (9g saturated fat); 1693kJ (405 cal); 60.1g carbohydrate; 5g protein; 1.5g fibre

Fruit, Tropical

The best rule for using tropical fruits is to do as little as possible to affect their natural appeal. Most are best in their raw state: their textures and aromas do not survive cooking. Some benefit by a sweet-sharp sprinkle of sugar and lime juice to point up the flavour, some can be pureed for mousses and ice-creams and many combine beautifully with other fruits, but when in doubt, simplicity is the way to go.

DURIAN is the famous or infamous "smells like hell, tastes like heaven" fruit, barred from public transport or in many hotels in its native Malaysia and other parts of South-East Asia. It is eaten by splitting open the hard, spiky shell and eating the pulp with a spoon, then sucking the last of it from the large seeds. Commercially, it is made into various kinds of confectionary and ice-cream. Durian is in season in late autumn and winter.

SOURSOP is a relative of the custard apple varying in length from 10cm to 30cm and weighing up to nearly 5kg, and covered in soft spines. Its flesh is like that of custard apples but extremely juicy and more acid, usually needing sugar to make it palatable. It is in season from autumn to spring.

STAR FRUIT OR CARAMBOLA is a gleaming yellow-green or yellow fruit, depending on the variety, formed of five ridges so that, when cut across, it is star-shaped. Its flesh is crisp and juicy with a pleasant but rather bland sweetish flavour that benefits from a little sugar and lime juice. It is available for most of the year, its peak season being early summer to midwinter.

JACKFRUIT is a huge fruit with knobbly skin, firm, banana-flavoured flesh and edible, chestnut-like, starchy seeds. Unripe jackfruit is used as a vegetable, usually in curries; ripeness is indicated by an unpleasant odour, but when the fruit is opened, the flesh has a pleasant pineapple/banana aroma. Jackfruit is available fresh and canned.

RAMBUTAN, also called hairy lychee for the tendrils with which it is covered, is native to Malaysia but cultivated elsewhere including northern Australia. Its thin shell encloses white, translucent, perfumed flesh which resembles that of its close relative, the lychee but is not quite so sweet. Rambutans can be red, greenish cream or yellow and are in season from midsummer into autumn.

CUSTARD APPLE is the name given to two related Central and South American fruits, the cherimoya and the bullock heart (also called the sweetsop). The cherimoya is the sweeter of the two. Custard apples have leathery skin enclosing fragrant, creamy flesh studded with shiny black seeds. Their flavour is sometimes described as a blend of banana, papaya, pineapple and vanilla. They are best cut, chilled and unpeeled, into halves or wedges and eaten with a teaspoon. The flesh can be spooned out and used for ice-cream or creamy desserts. They are in season in autumn and winter.

GUAVA is a round or pear-shape fruit varying from plum to apple size, native to tropical Central and South America but cultivated throughout the tropics. It is thin-skinned with aromatic, sharp-sweet flesh. It comes in several varieties including strawberry guava which is red and tastes of passionfruit and strawberries, and cherry

Custard apple

Guava

guava which is walnut-size. Guavas are eaten fresh and used for creamy desserts, ice-cream, a jelly preserve and a stiff paste to serve with cheese. One variety or another is in season most of the year. Guavas are available fresh and canned.

Also see Lychees, page 303; Mangoes, page 308; and Papaya, page 386.

CHOOSING Once ripe, tropical fruits are very perishable so, in general, it is best to buy them just underripe and ripen at room temperature; don't buy very underripe fruit as it may never ripen. The exception is rambutan which does not continue to ripen after picking, so should be bought ripe, indicated by bright colour, but with its tendrils still firm and almost moist-feeling. Ripeness is indicated in star fruit by bright colour, in custard apple and soursop by dull colour and feeling soft, in guava by feeling soft, in jackfruit by the first suggestion of its unpleasant odour, and in durian by its strong, offensive smell.

STORING Slightly underripe fruit can be enclosed in a paper bag, then in a plastic bag and refrigerated for a day or two before bringing to room temperature to ripen — the exceptions being jackfruit and durian. Ripe fruit should be used promptly, refrigerating only long enough to chill if required.

Christmas tree cupcakes

PREP + COOK TIME 1 HOUR 25 MINUTES (PLUS STANDING TIME) **MAKES** 6

125g butter, softened

1 teaspoon coconut essence

⅔ cup (150g) caster sugar

2 eggs

1 cup (180g) finely chopped dried tropical fruit salad

½ cup (75g) macadamia nuts, chopped coarsely

⅔ cup (100g) plain flour

⅓ cup (50g) self-raising flour

⅓ cup (25g) desiccated coconut

¼ cup (60ml) milk

10 star fruit, approximately

green edible glitter

COCONUT ICE FROSTING

2 egg whites

1 teaspoon coconut essence

1½ cups (240g) icing sugar

1 cup (90g) desiccated coconut

1 Preheat oven to 170°C/150°C fan-forced. Line 6-hole (¾-cup/180ml) texas muffin pan with paper cases.

2 Beat butter, essence, sugar and eggs in small bowl with electric mixer until light and fluffy. Stir in dried fruit and nuts, then sifted flours, coconut and milk. Divide mixture between cases; smooth surface.

3 Bake cakes about 45 minutes. Turn cakes onto wire racks to cool.

4 Make coconut ice frosting; top cakes with frosting.

5 Cut star fruit into 5mm slices. Arrange slices to make Christmas tree shapes. Use toothpicks or trimmed bamboo skewers to hold star fruit in position. Sprinkle with glitter.

COCONUT ICE FROSTING Beat egg whites and essence in small bowl with electric mixer until foamy. Beat in sifted icing sugar in about four batches; stir in coconut.

NUTRITIONAL COUNT PER CAKE 42g total fat (24.4g saturated fat); 3687kJ (882 cal); 111g carbohydrate; 10.7g protein; 9.3g fibre

Galangal

Greater galangal, also called thai, siamese or laos ginger, is the hot, aromatic rhizome (root-like stem) of a member of the ginger family native to Java, and is much used in South-East Asian cooking. There is also a lesser galangal native to southern China, but it is mostly used medicinally rather than in cooking.

Fresh galangal

❦ **OTHER RECIPES USING GALANGAL**
Banana-leaf steamed fish, p530
Fish curry in lime and coconut,
   p530–1
Green curry paste, p153
Panang curry paste, p154
Sambal goreng telor, p122
Yellow curry paste, p154

Greater galangal (sold simply as galangal) is available at Asian food stores and most greengrocers. It is much the same shape as ginger but more assertively coloured, often in stripes. Its taste is clean and biting, like ginger with a touch of citrus, and its aroma is sharp and penetrating. It is used, grated or sliced, in Thai hot and sour soup, curry pastes and seafood dishes. It is also available sliced and dried and as a ground spice, when it is called laos.

CHOOSING Fresh galangal should look plump and lustrous and should not be wizened and dried out where it has been cut. It is more pinkish than brown when fresh, fading to brown as it gets old.

STORING Store fresh galangal in the same way as onions or garlic: away from heat and light, in a place where air can circulate. Dried galangal slices should be stored in an airtight container away from heat and light and will remain in good condition for many months. Ground galangal should be stored airtight, away from heat and light, and will retain its flavour for up to a year.

Bruising the lemon grass by pounding with the side of a heavy knife before slicing, helps to release its flavour. Refrigerate the left over coconut milk from the can for up to a week. It is not recommended to freeze coconut milk as it is likely to curdle when cooked after thawing.

For information on chicken, see Poultry, pages 456 & 457.

Chicken and galangal soup (tom ka gai)

PREP + COOK TIME 50 MINUTES (PLUS STANDING TIME) **SERVES** 4

3 cups (750ml) chicken stock

20g fresh galangal, sliced thickly

2 x 10cm sticks fresh lemon grass (40g), cut into 5cm pieces

4 fresh kaffir lime leaves

2 teaspoons coarsely chopped coriander root and stem mixture

500g chicken thigh fillets, sliced thinly

200g drained canned straw mushrooms, rinsed

1 cup (250ml) coconut milk

1 tablespoon lime juice

1 tablespoon fish sauce

1 teaspoon grated palm sugar

¼ cup loosely packed fresh coriander leaves

2 fresh small red thai chillies, sliced thinly

2 fresh kaffir lime leaves, extra, shredded

10cm stick fresh lemon grass (20g), extra, sliced thinly

1 Place stock, galangal, lemon grass pieces, whole lime leaves and coriander mixture in large saucepan; bring to the boil. Reduce heat; simmer, covered, 5 minutes. Remove from heat; stand 10 minutes. Strain stock through muslin into large heatproof bowl; discard solids.

2 Return stock to same cleaned pan. Add chicken and mushrooms; bring to the boil. Reduce heat; simmer, uncovered, about 5 minutes or until chicken is cooked through. Stir in coconut milk, juice, sauce and sugar; cook, stirring, until just heated through (do not allow to boil). Remove from heat; stir in coriander leaves, chilli, shredded lime leaves and lemon grass slices. Serve hot.

NUTRITIONAL COUNT PER SERVING 19.2g total fat (13.2g saturated fat); 1359kJ (325 cal); 6.3g carbohydrate; 30.8g protein; 2.7g fibre

If you can't get fresh galangal, a good strategy can be to use a mixture of fresh ginger for freshness and aroma and finely chopped or sliced dried galangal, reconstituted by soaking in a little hot water (unless it will be rehydrated by cooking in liquid as in a soup), or else powdered galangal.

Game

Most traditional game birds and animals — those that were hunted for food — are now farmed for the table, but the term is still used for culinary purposes. In Australia, the only game meat that is not farmed is kangaroo. Farmed birds and animals don't have the strong flavours of wild ones, which may be considered an advantage or a disadvantage, but farmed ones are easier to cook as they are more tender. Wild game was always hung to tenderise it, but this is not necessary either for farmed meats or for kangaroo, which is as tender as beef. It is not necessary to marinate farmed game either, although it is good for giving the rich flavours that are associated with game-cooking.

Game meats are naturally lean so they are low-cholesterol and low-kilojoule. Being low-fat, they should be either cooked briefly and served rare so that they will not be dry, or cooked long and gently in a savoury liquid that includes a little oil or fat to make them succulent. Game birds are also lean, so they benefit from being gently browned in a little oil or butter before being quickly roasted or slowly casseroled. Note that, if you are serving birds at all rare, it is important to supply diners with sharp knives so that they don't have to struggle to cut the meat off the bones.

BUFFALO Water buffalo are farmed in Australia for their milk, which is used to make cheese and yogurt, or for their meat. Farmed meat animals are slaughtered young — before they have permanent incisors — so that the meat is tender. Tasting like beef, it is available as steaks, roasts, cuts for casseroling and mince for hamburgers and meat loaves. Because it is leaner than beef, it should be char-grilled, pan-seared or barbecued only until rare to keep it juicy, or if it is required more well-done, it should be soaked in oil for an hour or two before cooking. For roasting, an oven bag is recommended to guard against drying out.

CROCODILE is pale pink meat of very mild flavour, usually supplied frozen to ensure quality and food safety. The best part is the tail, though the legs can also be cooked. High heat toughens crocodile, though tenderness can be improved if it is first tenderised by marinating in kiwifruit or pawpaw puree. Casseroling suits it, and it also works well served as carpaccio (raw and very thinly sliced) with fruits or salad leaves and a well-flavoured dressing.

EMU is a red meat with a beefy flavour. The most popular cut is breast fillet, which is very good briefly char-grilled, then roasted at high heat for 5 minutes and rested 5–10 minutes before serving thinly sliced.

GUINEA FOWL are native to West Africa, but have been exported around the world and farmed for the table for many years. They are prized for their good meat-to-bone ratio and mild, pleasant game flavour. They can be cooked in the same ways as chicken provided that their greater leanness is allowed for by frequent basting or wrapping in fatty bacon or caul fat (the lacy network of fat that surrounds the intestines of cows, sheep and pigs). One guinea fowl serves two people.

KANGAROO meat is like darker red, leaner beef. It can be cooked in the same ways as beef but, if cooked by "dry" methods — char-grilling, pan-searing, barbecuing or roasting — it must be served rare so that it is juicy and its flavour shows through. For steaks, briefly char-grill then rest 5–10 minutes, or, for whole fillets, combine brief char-grilling then brief roasting at high heat, followed by resting for 10–15 minutes before being served, to show it at its best. It is also good for casseroling and for stir-frying, provided that it is removed from the wok while it is still rare.

PIGEON (SQUAB) A squab is a fledgling pigeon just ready to leave the nest. It is very tender with a delicious, almost sweet flavour. A squab makes a luxurious meal for one person and is perfect brushed with oil or butter and roasted in a hot oven for 15–20 minutes. It can be stuffed first with a savoury bread or rice mixture if you wish. Squab can also be char-grilled or barbecued.

QUAIL are small birds: a medium-size quail, weighing 160–200g, will serve one person as a first course and two will make a main course. "Jumbo" quail, weighing from 200g up, are also available. Quail are sold fresh or frozen, whole or boned and opened out, usually in a pack of 4–6. They are best roasted, pan-fried or grilled as long, slow cooking gives the meat an overcooked liver taste.

RABBIT may be farmed or wild; most of those on sale are farmed ones, which are larger and more tender than wild rabbits and have a little fat, while wild ones have none. Rabbits are sold whole or jointed. They can be casseroled or roasted (covered with fatty bacon, pork back fat or caul fat to prevent dryness), and the boned back fillets can be pan-fried. Rabbit's larger relative, hare, is darker and more gamey in flavour. Young ones,

called leverets, can be roasted; larger ones should be casseroled.

VENISON is deer meat. It is lean, dark red and can be cooked in the same ways as beef, though it needs to be protected from dryness by covering with fatty bacon or pork back fat for roasting and by including oil or fat in the liquid for casseroling. Roast venison and venison steaks should be served rare to ensure juiciness. Traditional accompaniments are chestnuts, potatoes, Brussels sprouts, lentils, red-wine gravy and redcurrant jelly.

Any of the traditional venison accompaniments can also be served with the other red game meats — buffalo, emu, kangaroo. Rabbit is excellent served with grilled or fried mushrooms or with small rolls of bacon and prunes poached in red wine. Game birds are good with grilled fruits like peaches or apricots, spiced preserved fruits like quinces, cherries or plums, or with fresh grapes, peeled, pipped and dressed with lemon juice. All game, unless casseroled with rich ingredients for moistness, is complemented by gravies and sauces made with red or white wine and/or flavoursome stock, mustard, redcurrant jelly, herbs, shallots, and butter or cream to give richness and moistness. Home-made or good-quality purchased chutney, relish, onion jam and horseradish cream may also be served.

STORING
Transfer game to a container with the bottom lined with two thicknesses of absorbent paper, cover loosely with foil and refrigerate. Use within 2–3 days.

⚜ **OTHER RECIPES USING GAME**
Bacon-wrapped quail with grape sauce, p240-1

Cumberland sauce is a traditional accompaniment to game. For a simple recipe, cut the rind of an orange into very thin matchsticks and place in boiling water for 3 minutes; drain, and reserve. In a medium heatproof bowl, combine 4 tablespoons red currant jelly, 1 tablespoon dijon mustard, juice of 1 lemon and salt and pepper. Place the bowl over a medium saucepan of simmering water and stir until the jelly melts. Stir in ¼ cup port and the reserved orange rind, then leave to cool.

Rabbit stew

PREP + COOK TIME 2 HOURS 20 MINUTES **SERVES** 4

A fragrant and savoury one-pot meal that gives tender, flavoursome rabbit and couldn't be easier. This recipe is not suitable to freeze.

2 tablespoons oil

1kg rabbit pieces

3 medium brown onions (450g), sliced thickly

4 cloves garlic, crushed

1 cup (250ml) water

1 litre (4 cups) chicken stock

410g can diced tomatoes

5 medium potatoes (1kg), chopped coarsely

2 medium carrots (240g), sliced thickly

1 tablespoon balsamic vinegar

3 bay leaves

1 teaspoon dried chilli flakes

⅓ cup coarsely chopped fresh mint

1 cup (120g) frozen peas

1 Heat half the oil in large saucepan; cook rabbit, in batches, until browned.

2 Heat remaining oil in same pan; cook onion and garlic, stirring, until onion softens.

3 Add the water, stock, undrained tomatoes, potato, carrot, vinegar, bay leaves, chilli and mint to pan. Return rabbit to pan; bring to the boil. Reduce heat; simmer, uncovered, 1¼ hours. Add peas; simmer, uncovered, 5 minutes.

NUTRITIONAL COUNT PER SERVING 19.4g total fat (5.1g saturated fat); 2750kJ (658 cal); 44.4g carbohydrate; 70.7g protein; 10.6g fibre

Kangaroo fillet with beetroot relish

PREP + COOK TIME 1 HOUR 50 MINUTES **SERVES** 4

Kangaroo should remain rare in the centre, and must be well rested before being served (see page 209).

For information on fresh beetroot, see Beetroot page 54; and for green peppercorns, see Spices page 560.

1kg beetroot, trimmed

½ cup (125ml) buttermilk

2 tablespoons finely shredded fresh mint leaves

4 kangaroo fillets (750g)

2 tablespoons green peppercorns, chopped finely

¼ cup (60g) wholegrain mustard

1 Preheat oven to 200°C/180°C fan-forced.

2 Wrap beetroot in foil, place on oven tray; roast about 1½ hours or until tender.

3 Peel beetroot; blend or process until pureed, stir in buttermilk and mint. Cover relish to keep warm.

4 Coat kangaroo in combined peppercorns and mustard. Cook kangaroo on heated oiled grill plate (or grill or barbecue) about 2 minutes each side until seared. Stand 5 minutes before slicing.

5 Serve kangaroo with beetroot relish and mashed or scalloped potatoes.

NUTRITIONAL COUNT PER SERVING 3.8g total fat (1.2g saturated fat); 1354kJ (324 cal); 21.3g carbohydrate; 46.6g protein; 7.8g fibre

RABBIT STEW

Serve the roasted quail
and vegetables with rice
to soak up the delicious
sauce. Freeze the quail
necks and use them the
next time you are making
chicken stock.

For information on
prosciutto, see Ham,
page 256.

Italian roasted quail with braised vegetables

PREP + COOK TIME 1 HOUR **SERVES** 4

8 quails (1.3kg)

8 slices prosciutto (120g)

20g butter

½ cup (125ml) dry white wine

2 baby fennel bulbs (260g), trimmed, sliced thinly

4 cloves garlic, unpeeled

1 large red capsicum (350g), sliced thinly

2 medium zucchini (240g), halved lengthways,
sliced thickly

½ cup (125ml) chicken stock

1 medium lemon (140g), cut into eight wedges

¼ cup (60ml) cream

1 tablespoon fresh oregano leaves

1 Preheat oven to 200°C/180°C fan-forced.

2 Discard necks from quails. Wash quails under cold water; pat dry inside and out with absorbent paper. Tuck legs along body; wrap tightly with prosciutto to hold legs in place.

3 Heat butter in large flameproof baking dish; cook quails, in batches, until browned all over.

4 Place wine in same dish; bring to the boil. Reduce heat; simmer, uncovered, until wine has reduced to 1 tablespoon. Add fennel, garlic, capsicum, zucchini and stock; return to the boil. Place quails on top of vegetables; roast, uncovered, in oven 20 minutes. Add lemon to dish; roast, uncovered, about 10 minutes or until quails are cooked through.

5 Remove quails and garlic from dish. When cool enough to handle, squeeze garlic from skins into dish; stir in cream and oregano.

6 Serve quails on vegetables.

NUTRITIONAL COUNT PER SERVING 30.8g total fat (12.4g saturated fat); 2052kJ (491 cal); 6.9g carbohydrate; 39.1g protein; 4.2g fibre

Garlic

While garlic is botanically classed as a vegetable, being the bulb of one of the onion family, it is most often used, in the same way as a spice or herb, to contribute its flavour to other ingredients. It is used in most of the world's cuisines and is especially associated with Mediterranean and Asian cooking.

It is available fresh, preserved as a textured paste in jars, as dried flakes, granules and powder, as jars or packets of chopped, fried garlic to be sprinkled on Asian food and as jars of pickled garlic in vinegared brine to be used as a condiment on Asian noodle or rice dishes. Hot and pungent when raw, garlic is much milder when cooked, becoming especially mild and sweet when baked as a whole head (bulb) or unpeeled cloves (segments), or gently cooked in liquid, as in a casserole. There are many varieties of garlic differing in pungency, in colour from white to brownish pink, and in size: elephant garlic, which is very mild, can have bulbs weighing nearly 500g. Garlic odour carried on the breath after eating can be reduced by chewing parsley or fennel seeds. Garlic is available all year.

FRESH GARLIC

Truly fresh garlic, meaning freshly harvested, is in season in spring and early summer but is not generally available: the best chance of finding it is at a farmer's market. It is juicy and very mild. The fresh garlic sold in the shops has been dried to prevent it from becoming mouldy, though the flesh inside the dried skin is still juicy and crunchy. The flesh develops its full pungency during the drying process.

Peeling Place a garlic clove on a board and whack it with a mallet or the flat of a heavy knife to smash it and split the skin, then lift the skin away.

Crushing Place a peeled garlic clove on a pinch of salt on a board and, holding it steady with one hand and a round-ended knife with your thumb just behind the tip with the other hand, scrape the flesh downward, working from end to end of the clove and smearing out any lumps as you go. You can also use a pierced metal garlic crusher, but these leave some of the garlic behind and are fiddly to clean.

Chopping Place a peeled garlic clove on a board, sprinkle with salt to prevent pieces from flying off and chop with a heavy knife, holding the tip of the blade on the work surface with one hand and chopping up and down in fine cuts with the other, working across the garlic as you go. When you have chopped in one direction, turn the board at right angles, scrape the garlic together and chop in the other direction.

CHOOSING
When buying fresh garlic, try to buy Australian-grown as it will be less dried out than the imported kinds which make up most of the garlic in supermarkets and most greengrocers. The best chance of finding Australian-grown is at farmers' markets. Wherever you buy, look for garlic heads that are holding together compactly, with cloves that are hard and full, not shrinking away from the skin. All forms of dried garlic are best packed in heavy foil,

Never leave the stove while frying garlic, as it can turn dark brown very quickly and if so, has to be discarded as over-browning makes it bitter. Watch carefully and take the pan off the heat and scoop out the garlic as soon as it begins to colour.

heavy plastic or glass as these exclude air and moisture efficiently and are often resealable.

STORING Keep fresh garlic attached to the head as separate cloves lose flavour faster. Store in the same way as onions: away from heat, light and humidity in a place where air can circulate. Don't store in a closed container as this could encourage mould, nor in the refrigerator as this tends to encourage sprouting. If garlic does sprout during storage, remove the sprout and the green spot in the attached clove before using. As a time-saver when cooking, peeled garlic cloves can be stored in oil in a glass jar in the refrigerator and chopped garlic can be frozen in a little water in ice-cube trays, then transferred to a plastic bag, sealed and returned to the freezer. Store all forms of dried garlic in resealed packs like those mentioned in CHOOSING (see opposite), or in a glass or metal container, away from heat and light, and use within 1 year. Follow any directions on the jar or pack to store it, once opened, in the refrigerator.

❦ OTHER RECIPES
USING GARLIC
Anchovy and garlic tuna with tomato and oregano, p531
Braised borlotti beans with tomato and garlic, p42
Broccoli and garlic breadcrumb spaghetti, p75
Creamy chickpea and garlic soup, p478
Dukkah-crusted lamb cutlets with roasted garlic yogurt, p566
Fennel-flavoured veal chops with garlic mustard butter, p625
Lamb and okra in rich tomato sauce with garlic confit, p369
Rainbow silver beet with pine nuts, garlic and raisins, p550
Roasted cauliflower and garlic soup, p95
Roasted parsnip and garlic soup, p391
Steamed mussels in tomato garlic broth, p535

Roasted chicken with 40 cloves of garlic

PREP + COOK TIME 1 HOUR 40 MINUTES (PLUS STANDING TIME) **SERVES** 4

3 bulbs garlic

60g butter, softened

1.5kg chicken

2 teaspoons salt

2 teaspoons cracked black pepper

1 cup (250ml) water

ROASTED POTATOES

1kg baby new potatoes

cooking-oil spray

1 Preheat oven to 200°C/180°C fan-forced.
2 Separate cloves from garlic bulb, leaving peel intact. Rub butter over outside of chicken and inside cavity; press combined salt and pepper onto skin and inside cavity. Place half of the garlic inside cavity; tie legs together with kitchen string.
3 Place remaining garlic cloves, in single layer, in medium baking dish; place chicken on garlic. Pour the water carefully into dish; roast chicken, uncovered, brushing occasionally with pan juices, about 1 hour 20 minutes or until browned and cooked through.
4 Meanwhile, make roasted potatoes.
5 Stand chicken on platter, covered with foil, 15 minutes before serving with roasted garlic and potatoes.

ROASTED POTATOES Boil steam or microwave potatoes 5 minutes; drain. Pat dry with absorbent paper; cool 10 minutes. Place potatoes, in single layer, in large oiled baking dish; spray with cooking-oil spray. Roast, uncovered, for about the last 30 minutes of chicken cooking time or until potatoes are tender.

NUTRITIONAL COUNT PER SERVING 45g total fat (17.9g saturated fat); 3223kJ (771 cal); 38.8g carbohydrate; 46.9g protein; 13.3g fibre

If you haven't had this before, you may be surprised at how mild and creamy the garlic becomes after its long roasting. Feel free to use as many cloves as you like because any left over can be peeled and used for the lovely garlic mayonnaise called aïoli (for recipe, see page 366).

For information on chicken, see Poultry, pages 456 & 457.

Garlic prawns

PREP + COOK TIME 30 MINUTES **SERVES** 4

Prawns are deveined because the vein, which is the gut, may contain grit as prawns are bottom-feeders. For tips on deveining prawns, see Seafood page 526.

Garlic prawns are often served with nothing else but good bread, but they can be served with rice or on pasta.

For more information on prawns, see Seafood, pages 526 & 527.

1kg uncooked medium king prawns

4 cloves garlic, crushed

2 fresh small red thai chillies, chopped finely

2 tablespoons olive oil

1 medium red capsicum (200g), sliced thinly

1 medium green capsicum (200g), sliced thinly

½ cup (125ml) chicken stock

300ml cream

1 tablespoon lemon juice

1 tablespoon finely chopped fresh flat-leaf parsley

1 Shell and devein prawns, leaving tails intact. Combine prawns, garlic and chilli in medium bowl.

2 Heat half the oil in large frying pan; cook prawns, stirring, until changed in colour. Remove from pan.

3 Heat remaining oil in same pan; cook capsicums, stirring, until tender. Return prawns to pan with stock, cream and juice; bring to the boil. Reduce heat; simmer, uncovered, about 5 minutes or until sauce thickens slightly. Remove from heat; stir in parsley.

NUTRITIONAL COUNT PER SERVING 42.6g total fat (22.9g saturated fat); 2169kJ (519 cal); 5.4g carbohydrate; 28.9g protein; 1.4g fibre

Skordalia

PREP + COOK TIME 20 MINUTES (PLUS COOLING TIME) **MAKES** 1 CUP

Skordalia can be used as a sauce or dip, and can be made with breadcrumbs or potato. This recipe makes enough to serve with lamb kebabs for 4, and it also goes well with battered fish and grilled chicken breasts. If the sauce is too thick, stir in a little hot water, in tiny amounts, until it is as you like it.

1 medium potato (200g), quartered

3 cloves garlic, quartered

2 tablespoons cold water

1 tablespoon lemon juice

1 tablespoon white wine vinegar

⅓ cup (80ml) olive oil

1 Boil, steam or microwave potato until tender; drain. Cool 10 minutes.

2 Blend or process potato, garlic, the water, juice and vinegar until mixture is pureed. With motor operating, gradually add oil in thin, steady stream, processing until it thickens.

3 Serve skordalia with lamb kebabs, roasted beetroot or fried zucchini and eggplant, if you like.

NUTRITIONAL COUNT PER TABLESPOON 6.1g total fat (0.9g saturated fat); 280kJ (67 cal); 2.3g carbohydrate; 0.5g protein; 0.4g fibre

Gelatine

Gelatine is a thickening and setting agent made from either collagen, found in animal connective tissue, or agar agar which comes from a particular kind of algae. Gelatine is available in two forms, a granulated powder or fine sheets called leaves.

Leaf gelatine

Powdered gelatine is packed in 2-teaspoon (7g) envelopes and one envelope is equal in thickening or setting power to about 4 gelatine leaves. The two forms are interchangeable but leaf gelatine is preferred by professionals as it gives a more crystal-clear gel.

POWDERED GELATINE is used by sprinkling the required amount into a cup or small bowl containing a few tablespoons of the liquid used in the recipe: water, milk, fruit juice etc. It is left until the liquid is absorbed, then the container is placed in a pan of barely simmering water until the gelatine dissolves completely and the mixture becomes transparent (translucent in the case of milk). The mixture is then added, through a fine sieve, if preferred, in case of any undissolved bits, to the rest of the liquid and the recipe is completed. Finally, the mixture is refrigerated until set or thickened as required, which may take 4–6 hours or overnight.

LEAF GELATINE is used by soaking the required number of sheets in cold water for a minute or two to soften, then removing them, squeezing to remove excess water, adding them to the liquid used in the recipe and heating gently until the gelatine dissolves. The recipe is then completed and the mixture is refrigerated until set or thickened as required, which may take 4–6 hours or overnight.

Don't let a gelatine mixture boil as it may lose its setting power, and do not freeze products containing gelatine as they may become stringy. The exception is gelatine mixtures with a very high fat content, as in ice-cream.

Some recipes, for instance one for a mousse, call for a gelatine mixture to be whisked when it is half-set. At this stage, the gelatine is strong enough to hold the air bubbles created by whisking so that the mixture will increase in volume and, when fully set, will be soft and airy. Frozen and stirred, the whisked mixture becomes ice-cream in which the gelatine contributes to smoothness by interfering with the formation of large ice crystals.

STORING Both forms of gelatine can be stored in their packages in a dry place away from heat and light, and will keep for a year or more.

🍴 **OTHER RECIPES USING GELATINE**
Individual tiramisu, p113
Palm sugar and lime cheesecakes, p585
Roasted pear and almond cheesecake, p421

Almond praline cheesecake

PREP + COOK TIME 1 HOUR (PLUS COOLING AND REFRIGERATION TIME) **SERVES** 10

100g butter, softened

2 tablespoons caster sugar

2 tablespoons rice flour

½ cup (75g) plain flour

2 teaspoons gelatine

2 tablespoons water

375g cream cheese, softened

½ cup (110g) caster sugar

300ml cream

1 teaspoon vanilla extract

ALMOND PRALINE

½ cup (110g) caster sugar

¼ cup (60ml) water

¼ cup (35g) slivered almonds, roasted

ALMOND PRALINE CHEESECAKE

1   Preheat oven to 150°C/130°C fan-forced. Grease 22cm springform tin.

2   Beat butter and sugar in small bowl with electric mixer until light and fluffy. Stir in sifted flours in two batches; knead on lightly floured surface until smooth.

3   Press mixture evenly over base of tin; bake shortbread about 35 minutes or until browned lightly. Cool in tin.

4   Make almond praline.

5   Remove base and shortbread from tin. Line tin with plastic wrap. Replace base and shortbread; secure tin. Pull plastic wrap firmly up side of tin.

6   Sprinkle gelatine over the water in small heatproof jug; stand jug in small saucepan of simmering water. Stir until gelatine dissolves. Cool 5 minutes.

7   Beat cheese and sugar in medium bowl with electric mixer until smooth; beat in cream and extract. Stir in gelatine mixture. Finely chop praline; stir half into cheese mixture. Pour into tin; refrigerate overnight.

8   Serve cheesecake topped with remaining praline.

ALMOND PRALINE   Combine sugar and the water in small saucepan; stir over low heat until sugar dissolves. Boil about 10 minutes or until mixture turns golden brown. Remove from heat. Place nuts in single layer on greased oven tray. Pour toffee over almonds. Stand at room temperature 10 minutes or until set.

NUTRITIONAL COUNT PER SERVING   35.7g total fat (22.1g saturated fat); 2023kJ (484 cal); 35.2g carbohydrate; 6.1g protein; 0.6g fibre

It is worth making more praline than you need for this recipe and storing the surplus in a screwtop jar, where it will keep for weeks. Use pieces of praline to decorate cakes or crush with a rolling pin and sprinkle thickly on custards and creamy desserts or over ice-cream.

For information on almonds, see Nuts, page 344; and for caster sugar, see Sugar, page 576.

Powdered gelatine

Raspberry jellies with almond cream

PREP + COOK TIME 40 MINUTES (PLUS REFRIGERATION TIME) **SERVES** 8

240g fresh raspberries

¼ cup (60ml) water

3 cups (750ml) cranberry juice

1½ tablespoons gelatine

⅓ cup (75g) caster sugar

2 tablespoons lemon juice

2 tablespoons orange-flavoured liqueur

300ml thickened cream

2 tablespoons icing sugar

¾ cup (115g) vienna almonds, chopped coarsely

1 Wet inside of eight ½-cup (125ml) moulds. Divide half the berries among moulds.

2 Combine the water with ¼ cup of cranberry juice in small heatproof jug; sprinkle over gelatine. Stand jug in small saucepan of simmering water; stir until gelatine dissolves.

3 Combine remaining cranberry juice and caster sugar in small saucepan; stir over low heat until sugar dissolves. Stir in gelatine mixture, lemon juice and liqueur. Spoon two tablespoons of mixture over berries in each mould, cover; refrigerate about 1 hour or until set. (Stand remaining mixture at room temperature.)

4 Pour remaining mixture carefully over set mixture in moulds, cover; refrigerate about 3 hours or overnight.

5 Before serving, beat cream and sifted icing sugar in small bowl with electric mixer until soft peaks form. Fold in ½ cup nuts.

6 Wipe outsides of moulds with a hot cloth; turn jellies out onto serving plates. Serve with almond cream, sprinkled with remaining nuts and berries.

NUTRITIONAL COUNT PER SERVING 19.3g total fat (9.5g saturated fat); 1471kJ (352 cal); 36.4g carbohydrate; 5.6g protein; 2.5g fibre

Vienna almonds are toffee-coated and have wonderful roasted flavour as well as the toffee sweetness. They are available from sweets shops, speciality food shops and some delicatessens and supermarkets.

For information on raspberries, see Berries, page 58; and for almonds, see Nuts, page 344.

Clove panna cotta

PREP + COOK TIME 40 MINUTES (PLUS COOLING AND REFRIGERATION TIME) **SERVES** 4

1 teaspoon whole cloves

300ml thickened cream

⅔ cup (160ml) milk

2 teaspoons gelatine

2 tablespoons caster sugar

½ teaspoon vanilla extract

4 medium fresh figs (240g)

2 tablespoons honey

1 Grease four ½-cup (125ml) moulds.

2 Place cloves, cream and milk in small saucepan; stand 10 minutes. Sprinkle gelatine and sugar over cream mixture; stir over low heat, without boiling, until gelatine and sugar dissolve. Stir in extract. Strain into medium jug; cool to room temperature.

3 Divide mixture among prepared moulds, cover; refrigerate 3 hours or until set.

4 Quarter figs; stir honey in small saucepan until warm.

5 Turn panna cotta onto serving plates; serve with figs drizzled with honey.

NUTRITIONAL COUNT PER SERVING 29.3g total fat (19.2g saturated fat); 1639kJ (392 cal); 29.1g carbohydrate; 5.1g protein; 1.3g fibre

Panna cotta means cooked cream. It is lightly set with gelatine — a good panna cotta should be wobbly. It can be flavoured in various ways; this recipe, without the clove, will make a basic vanilla panna cotta to serve with almost any cooked fruit. The figs for this recipe should be fully ripe as they will not be cooked. For shopping and storage notes, see Figs, page 178.

For information on cloves, see Spices, page 556.

RASPBERRY JELLIES WITH ALMOND CREAM

Ginger

Ginger is the hot, spicy, juicy rhizome (root-like stem) of a tropical plant thought to be originally from eastern Asia. It has been known since remote antiquity and is now grown in warm climates throughout the world.

Fresh ginger

Fresh ginger juice is sometimes called for to season an Asian soup or lend its clear, hot flavour and fragrance to a sauce or marinade. To obtain it, stand a grater on a piece of doubled muslin or a new disposable cloth and grate peeled ginger directly on to the cloth, brushing the residue off the grater with a pastry brush. Gather up the ginger in the cloth and squeeze and wring it over a bowl to collect the juice.

❀ OTHER RECIPES USING GINGER
*Asian greens salad with sesame
  ginger dressing, p245
Ginger miso dressing, p553
Ginger sticky date pudding, p158
Gingernuts, p567
Kaffir lime and ginger perch
  parcels, p276
Mixed oyster mushroom and
  ginger noodles, p327*

It is fundamental to the cooking of India and most other Asian countries, is important in African, Middle Eastern and Latin American cooking, and has grown rapidly in popularity in Western countries as new arrivals, especially those from Asia, introduced their cooking styles and ingredients to Western cooks. Ginger is available all year both fresh and in dried, ground, crystallised and pickled forms.
FRESH GINGER is thick and knobby, and grows underground by adding on joints. Whole rhizomes or large pieces are referred to in the trade as races or hands — an appropriate name as they do resemble a plump, deformed hand. Ginger is harvested twice a year, in late summer and winter. Early-harvested ginger is immature and crisply tender with a sweeter and less pungent flavour than late-harvested, which is both hotter and more fibrous. Fresh ginger to be used in cooking is peeled, then sliced, chopped, ground in a mortar or grated. A small, inexpensive ceramic ginger grater, with rows of rounded teeth instead of sharp edges, is a worthwhile investment for grating ginger efficiently without grating your fingers too.
DRIED GINGER is used in herbal teas; in cooking, it lacks the fragrance and juiciness of fresh ginger but, after reconstituting by soaking, is an acceptable substitute.
GROUND GINGER is used mainly in baking, usually for sweet products such as

gingerbread, and can also be rubbed into fish or meat before cooking. It cannot substitute satisfactorily for fresh ginger.
PICKLED GINGER Japanese pickled ginger, thinly sliced and usually dyed pink, is eaten as a palate cleanser and also as a garnish.
PRESERVED GINGER is boiled and steeped in sugar syrup until the sugar has replaced its natural moisture, and is packed in the syrup in glass or ceramic jars. It is used as a sweetmeat, in steamed puddings and in fruit and creamy desserts, and the syrup can be poured over ice-cream.

CHOOSING
Fresh ginger should be plump and firm with lustrous skin and should not be wizened and dry where it has been cut. All forms of dried ginger are best packed in heavy foil, heavy plastic or glass as these exclude moisture efficiently and are often resealable.

STORING
Store fresh ginger in the same way as onions and garlic, away from heat and light and in a place where air can circulate. To save time in cooking, peeled chunks of ginger can be stored in vodka in a jar in the refrigerator. Store dried sliced or ground ginger in an airtight pack such as those mentioned above or in an airtight jar, away from heat and light; use sliced ginger within 2 years, ground within 1 year.

Also see glacé and crystallised ginger in Fruits, Glacé on pages 198 & 199.

Beef steaks with three-ginger sauce

PREP + COOK TIME 20 MINUTES **SERVES** 4

1 tablespoon olive oil

20g butter

4 beef eye-fillet steaks (600g)

1 small brown onion (80g), chopped coarsely

2cm piece fresh ginger (10g), grated

1 tablespoon finely chopped glacé ginger

½ cup (125ml) green ginger wine

1 tablespoon plain flour

1 cup (250ml) beef stock

1 Heat half of the oil and half of the butter in medium frying pan; cook beef, uncovered, until cooked as desired. Remove from pan; cover to keep warm.

2 Heat remaining oil and butter in same pan; cook onion and both gingers, stirring, until onion softens. Deglaze pan with wine. Add flour; cook, stirring about 2 minutes or until mixture bubbles and thickens.

3 Gradually add stock; bring to the boil then reduce heat. Simmer, uncovered, about 5 minutes or until mixture boils and thickens slightly.

4 Serve sauce over steaks.

NUTRITIONAL COUNT PER SERVING 17.8g total fat (7.2g saturated fat); 1417kJ (339 cal); 5.5g carbohydrate; 33.1g protein; 0.5g fibre

BEEF STEAKS WITH
THREE-GINGER SAUCE

Deglazing is the first step in making a pan sauce. It includes the rich flavours of the good browned bits left behind after frying. Add liquid (in this case the wine) to the pan; simmer over low heat, stirring and scraping up the browned bits and coagulated juices.

Ginger, tomato and apple punch

PREP TIME 15 MINUTES **MAKES** 2 LITRES (8 CUPS)

1 medium red apple (150g)

8cm piece fresh ginger (40g), grated finely

125g strawberries, quartered

2 cups (500ml) apple juice

1½ cups (375ml) tomato juice

3 cups (750ml) dry ginger ale

1 Core and chop apple. Over small bowl, press ginger between two teaspoons to extract juice; discard pulp.

2 Combine apple and strawberries in large jug with ginger juice and remaining juices. Cover; refrigerate until cold.

3 Just before serving, stir cold ginger ale into punch mixture.

NUTRITIONAL COUNT PER 250ML 0.1g total fat (0g saturated fat); 330kJ (79 cal); 27.8g carbohydrate; 0.7g protein; 1g fibre

This punch can be prepared the day before, but don't add the ginger ale until just before serving.

Steamed ginger fish

PREP + COOK TIME 20 MINUTES **SERVES** 4

2 baby buk choy (300g), quartered lengthways

4 snapper cutlets (800g)

10cm piece fresh ginger (50g), cut into long strips

2 green onions, cut into long strips

¼ cup (60ml) light soy sauce

1 teaspoon sesame oil

1 fresh long red chilli, sliced thinly

1 cup loosely packed fresh coriander leaves

1 Place buk choy on large heatproof plate inside bamboo steamer; top with fish. Sprinkle ginger and onion over fish, then drizzle with sauce and oil.
2 Steam fish, covered, over wok of simmering water, about 5 minutes or until cooked through. Serve fish topped with chilli and coriander.

NUTRITIONAL COUNT PER SERVING 3.9g total fat (1.1g saturated fat); 786kJ (188 cal); 2.3g carbohydrate; 347g protein; 1.8g fibre

Serve the steamed ginger fish with steamed plain or jasmine rice (see Rice, pages 494-497).

For information on snapper, see Seafood, page 522.

Mussels with pickled ginger and avocado

PREP + COOK TIME 20 MINUTES (PLUS REFRIGERATION TIME) **MAKES** 12

12 large black mussels (600g)

½ cup (125ml) water

½ firm medium avocado (125g), chopped finely

1 tablespoon drained pickled ginger, chopped finely

1 shallot (25g), chopped finely

1 tablespoon lime juice

1 Scrub mussels; remove beards. Bring the water to the boil in medium saucepan, add mussels; cook, covered, about 5 minutes or until mussels open (discard any that do not). Drain; discard liquid. Break open shells; discard tops. Loosen mussels from bottom shells with a spoon; place mussels in shells, in single layer, on serving platter. Cover; refrigerate until cold.
2 Combine remaining ingredients in small bowl; divide avocado mixture among mussels.

NUTRITIONAL COUNT PER MUSSEL 1.9g total fat (0.4g saturated fat); 105kJ (25 cal); 0.6g carbohydrate; 1.4g protein; 0.2g fibre

For notes on buying and cooking mussels, see Seafood, pages 526-528; and for information on avocado, see Avocado page 24-26.

STEAMED GINGER FISH

Bamboo skewers are good to use as a guide for the knife as you split the cake. If the cake is large, long skewers can be pushed through the cake, from one side to the other. If the cake is small, use toothpicks to mark the layer. Use a sharp serrated knife to split the cake. Cut the cake barely above the bamboo skewers or toothpicks, you should feel the knife touch the skewers as you cut through the cake.

For information on limes, see Limes, page 300.

Ginger cake with lime

PREP + COOK TIME 1 HOUR 40 MINUTES (PLUS COOLING AND REFRIGERATION TIME) **SERVES** 12

250g butter, chopped

½ cup (110g) firmly packed dark brown sugar

⅔ cup (230g) golden syrup

12cm piece fresh ginger (60g), grated

¾ cup (180ml) cream

2 eggs

1 cup (150g) plain flour

1 cup (150g) self-raising flour

½ teaspoon bicarbonate of soda

FILLING

½ teaspoon gelatine

1 tablespoon lime juice

125g cream cheese, softened

1 teaspoon finely grated lime rind

1 tablespoon caster sugar

¼ cup (60ml) cream

LIME SYRUP

½ cup (110g) caster sugar

½ cup (125ml) lime juice

½ cup (125ml) water

2 teaspoons finely grated lime rind

1 Preheat oven to 180°C/160°C fan-forced. Grease deep 22cm-round cake pan; line base and side with baking paper.

2 Stir butter, sugar, golden syrup and ginger in medium saucepan over low heat until sugar dissolves. Remove from heat. Whisk in cream, then eggs and sifted flours and soda. Pour mixture into pan.

3 Bake cake about 1 hour. Stand cake in pan 10 minutes; turn onto wire rack to cool.

4 Make filling.

5 Split cake horizontally a quarter of the way from the top; set aside. Place large piece of cake on serving plate. Using small teaspoon or melon baller, scoop 18 holes (at equal distances apart and not through to bottom) out of cake. Pour filling mixture into holes; replace top of cake. Cover; refrigerate overnight.

6 Make lime syrup.

7 Serve cake drizzled with lime syrup.

FILLING Sprinkle gelatine over juice in small heatproof jug; stand jug in small saucepan of simmering water. Stir until gelatine dissolves. Cool 5 minutes. Beat cheese, rind, sugar and cream in small bowl with electric mixer until smooth. Stir in gelatine mixture.

LIME SYRUP Stir sugar, juice and the water in small saucepan, over heat, until sugar dissolves. Boil, uncovered, 10 minutes or until syrup thickens slightly. Remove from heat; stir in rind. Cool.

NUTRITIONAL COUNT PER SERVING 30.4g total fat (19.5g saturated fat); 2128kJ (509 cal); 53.2g carbohydrate; 5.4g protein; 1.1g fibre

Grains

Grains are not only cheap and good for you, they are part of some of the world's great dishes. In northern Italy, rich winter meat dishes are not complete without soft polenta to eat with them, and the rustic grills of summer go with crisp grilled polenta.

1 TAPIOCA
2 COUSCOUS
3 PEARL BARLEY
4 BUCKWHEAT (WHOLE)
5 OATS
6 POLENTA
7 QUINOA
8 BARLEY FLAKES
9 SAGO
10 CRACKED RYE
11 BURGHUL

Spicy Moroccan tagines need couscous, Scotch broth depends on barley for nourishing substance, and Lebanon's tabbouleh, with its balance of earthy burghul and refreshing herbs, has gone out to conquer the Western world as the perfect salad for a party or a barbecue. Oats and breakfast go together, whether in muesli or comforting porridge. Sago is another good hot breakfast, and old-fashioned lemon sago is a dessert waiting to be rediscovered. Rye and buckwheat are staples in cold northern regions where other grains won't grow. Kasha, a buckwheat porridge served with butter or such embellishments as mushrooms and sour cream, is a well-loved Russian standby, and generations of cooks and bakers in those regions have made a virtue of necessity and created splendid rye breads and buckwheat pancakes. The "newest" grain is quinoa (pronounced keen-wa), which is actually ancient, having been used in South America for thousands of years.

BARLEY The barley usually used in cooking is pearl barley, made by husking, steaming and polishing the grains. It has a mild, nutty flavour. Barley flakes are made by steaming and rolling barley grains or pearl barley to make flakes that are like chewier rolled oats and are used in the same ways.

BUCKWHEAT is not a true grain but the fruit of a plant related to rhubarb. It is white and has a taste reminiscent of almonds. Toasted buckwheat meal, called kasha, is used to make the porridge of the same name. Buckwheat flour, mixed with wheat flour to supply the necessary gluten (see Flour, page 182) makes the yeast pancakes, called blini, that are topped with caviar or smoked salmon and served as appetisers with vodka or Champagne.

BURGHUL is cracked wheat which has been hulled, par-boiled or steamed to make it lighter-textured and milder-flavoured, and then dried. It needs no further cooking before use but is soaked in cold water to soften and swell the grains, then squeezed and spread on a towel to dry.

COUSCOUS, the staple cereal of North Africa, is made from fine semolina (the first, grainy millings of the floury part of wheat grains), combined with flour, salt and water to make tiny pellets. It is cooked by first moistening to allow the grains to swell, then steaming — traditionally, in a steamer set over the pot in which the meat and vegetables for the meal are cooking. Couscous can also be bought pre-cooked. Israeli couscous, also known as mograbieh, lebanese couscous or pearl couscous, has larger grains made from more coarsely milled semolina.

POLENTA is the Italian name for cornmeal, made from dried corn ground to various degrees of fineness. It is boiled with water to make a porridge which is soft polenta. Grilled polenta is made by spreading soft

polenta into an even layer, then chilling, cutting into shapes, oiling and grilling until crisp.

OATS, an especially nutritious grain, is milled into oatmeal of varying degrees of fineness for making oatcakes and porridge, thickening soups and stews, giving bulk to sausages and coating fish to be fried. Rolled oats, made from oatmeal that has been steamed and flattened between large rollers, are made into porridge and used in muesli, biscuits, scones and teabreads. Oats have no gluten (see Flour, pages 182 & 184) so oat flour needs to be mixed with wheat flour for breads or cakes that rise.

RYE is used in making beer, whisky and bourbon, but as a food grain, it is best known for rye breads including pumpernickel (see Bread, page 66) and Scandinavian rye crispbreads. Cracked whole rye grains, soaked overnight, can be made into porridge, and rye flakes, which are like rolled oats, can also be used in muesli or for porridge or in baking, similarly to rolled oats.

QUINOA is an exceptionally nutritious South American cereal-like grain — the quality of its protein is approximately equal to that of milk. Its delicate flavour is rather like that of couscous and its tiny seeds cook to about the same size as a couscous grain. It can be served instead of rice or couscous as an accompaniment, used for pilafs or added to soups and stews, and its flour is good for tortillas, breads and biscuits. Quinoa contains no gluten and is thought to be a safe food for people with coeliac disease.

SAGO is not a grain but is used like one, so it is classified with them for culinary purposes. It is a starchy substance extracted from the stems of certain South-East Asian palms and processed into a flour or into tiny pellets known as pearl sago, which can be cooked to make a breakfast porridge or made into hot or cold desserts.

TAPIOCA Not a grain but a starchy substance extracted from the roots of the cassava plant, which is used like a grain so is classified with it for culinary purposes. It is made into flour which is processed into flake, seed and pearl shapes. Pearl tapioca is used in similar ways to sago (see above).

CHOOSING
Buy grains in small quantities, no more than you will use in a month or so.

STORING
Store grains away from heat or light, in lidded containers to prevent mouse or insect damage.

✿ OTHER RECIPES USING GRAINS
Berry crumble, p62
Burghul-stuffed vine leaves with yogurt dip, p640
Crisp potato and peanut cakes, p454
Eggs and smoked salmon on blini, p166
Irish lamb and barley stew, p288
Mandarin, polenta and macadamia cake, p307
Pomegranate and burghul chicken salad, p438

1 POLENTA
2 COUSCOUS
3 PEARL BARLEY

Beef and barley soup

PREP + COOK TIME 2 HOURS 15 MINUTES **SERVES** 6

1 tablespoon olive oil

500g gravy beef, trimmed, diced into 2cm pieces

2 medium brown onions (300g), chopped finely

2 cloves garlic, crushed

¾ cup (150g) pearl barley

3 cups (750ml) beef stock

1.5 litres (6 cups) water

1 bay leaf

1 sprig fresh rosemary

1 sprig fresh thyme

2 medium potatoes (400g), diced into 1cm pieces

2 medium carrots (240g), diced into 1cm pieces

2 medium zucchini (240g), diced into 1cm pieces

2 medium yellow patty-pan squash (60g), diced into 1cm pieces

100g swiss brown mushrooms, chopped coarsely

½ cup finely chopped fresh flat-leaf parsley

1 Heat half the oil in large saucepan; cook beef, in batches, until browned.

2 Heat remaining oil in same pan; cook onion and garlic, stirring, until onion softens. Return beef to pan with barley, stock, the water, bay leaf, rosemary and thyme, bring to the boil. Reduce heat; simmer, covered, about 1 hour or until beef and barley are tender, skimming fat occasionally.

3 Add potato, carrot, zucchini, squash and mushrooms to soup; simmer, covered, about 25 minutes or until vegetables are softened. Remove and discard bay leaf, rosemary and thyme.

4 Serve bowls of soup sprinkled with parsley.

NUTRITIONAL COUNT PER SERVING 8.8g total fat (2.6g saturated fat); 1350kJ (323 cal); 30g carbohydrate; 26.9g protein; 7.8g fibre

The reason for cooking the beef in batches is that there must be plenty of room for its surface moisture to evaporate, allowing the beef to brown and not steam. Use high heat for this, removing the pieces as they are browned. Turn the heat low to cook the onion and garlic, otherwise the garlic will turn black and become bitter.

For information on beef, see Beef, pages 46 & 47.

Cheesy polenta

PREP + COOK TIME 20 MINUTES **SERVES** 4

2⅓ cups (580ml) water

2⅓ cups (580ml) milk

1 cup (170g) polenta

½ cup (40g) finely grated parmesan cheese

30g butter

1 Combine the water and milk in large saucepan; bring to the boil.

2 Gradually add polenta to liquid, stirring constantly. Reduce heat; simmer, stirring, about 10 minutes or until polenta thickens. Stir in cheese and butter.

NUTRITIONAL COUNT PER SERVING 15.9g total fat (10g saturated fat); 1425kJ (341 cal); 36.4g carbohydrate; 12.2g protein; 1.2g fibre

This goes beautifully with meat casseroles, especially those that include red wine. For plain polenta, omit parmesan and season lightly with salt.

For information on parmesan cheese, see Cheese, page 104.

Tabbouleh

PREP + COOK TIME 30 MINUTES (PLUS REFRIGERATION TIME) **SERVES** 4

¼ cup (40g) burghul

3 medium tomatoes (450g)

3 cups coarsely chopped fresh flat-leaf parsley

3 green onions, chopped finely

½ cup coarsely chopped fresh mint

1 clove garlic, crushed

¼ cup (60ml) lemon juice

¼ cup (60ml) olive oil

1 Place burghul in shallow medium bowl. Halve tomatoes, scoop pulp from tomato over burghul. Chop tomato flesh finely; spread over burghul. Cover; refrigerate 1 hour.
2 Combine burghul mixture in large bowl with remaining ingredients.

NUTRITIONAL COUNT PER SERVING 14.2g total fat (2g saturated fat); 790kJ (189 cal); 9.4g carbohydrate; 3.6g protein; 5.9g fibre

It is important that the chopped parsley should be dry when it is mixed through the burghul — it will make the tabbouleh mushy and heavy if wet. For notes on ensuring you have dry chopped parsley, see Herbs, page 264. Serve tabbouleh with skewered lamb or felafels.

Moroccan couscous salad with preserved lemon dressing

PREP + COOK TIME 20 MINUTES **SERVES** 4

1½ cups (300g) couscous

1½ cups (375ml) boiling water

20g butter

420g can chickpeas, rinsed, drained

⅓ cup (55g) sultanas

⅓ cup (50g) roasted pine nuts

100g baby rocket leaves, chopped coarsely

¾ cup finely chopped fresh flat-leaf parsley

1 cup (120g) seeded green olives

PRESERVED LEMON DRESSING

1 tablespoon finely grated lemon rind

¼ cup (60ml) lemon juice

¼ cup (60ml) olive oil

2 tablespoons rinsed and drained finely chopped preserved lemon

1 Combine couscous with the water in large heatproof bowl, cover; stand 5 minutes or until water is absorbed, fluffing with fork occasionally. Stir in butter. Stand 10 minutes.
2 Place ingredients for preserved lemon dressing in screw-top jar; shake well.
3 Combine couscous in large bowl with remaining ingredients and dressing.

NUTRITIONAL COUNT PER SERVING 29g total fat (5.5g saturated fat); 268kJ (686 cal); 85.6g carbohydrate; 17.2g protein; 6.5g fibre

Preserved lemons are a staple in Moroccan cooking. The lemons are quartered and preserved in salt and lemon juice or oil, so they are very soft and taste quite different from fresh lemon. They are available from Middle Eastern and some other delicatessens, speciality food shops and the food departments of large stores. Only the rind is used and must be rinsed well under cold water before use.

1 TABBOULEH 2 MOROCCAN COUSCOUS SALAD WITH PRESERVED LEMON DRESSING
3 BIRCHER MUESLI [P 234] 4 COCONUT SAGO PUDDING WITH CARAMELISED BANANA [P 234]

Bircher muesli

PREP + COOK TIME 15 MINUTES (PLUS REFRIGERATION TIME) **SERVES** 4

You can leave the skin on the orange segments for more fibre, cutting each into two or three pieces, or you can cut skinless segments which are prettier — see Oranges, page 382.

1½ cups (135g) rolled oats

¼ cup (30g) oat bran

¼ cup (15g) natural bran flakes

¾ cup (180ml) milk

¾ cup (180ml) orange juice

¾ cup (200g) low-fat greek-style yogurt

½ cup (100g) finely chopped dried figs

½ teaspoon ground cinnamon

½ cup (70g) roasted pistachios, chopped coarsely

1 large orange (300g), segmented

1 Combine cereals, milk, juice, yogurt, figs and cinnamon in large bowl. Cover; refrigerate overnight. Stir in half the nuts.

2 Divide muesli among serving bowls; top with orange segments and remaining nuts.

NUTRITIONAL COUNT PER SERVING 14.5g total fat (2.9g saturated fat); 1818kJ (435 cal); 56.1g carbohydrate; 15.1g protein; 10.4g fibre

Coconut sago pudding with caramelised banana

PREP + COOK TIME 35 MINUTES **SERVES** 4

This pudding is also great with fresh mango slices. For neat slices, cut both cheeks off the mango then place on a board with the cut sides down and slice downwards, then take one slice at a time and pull the skin off gently, or lay it flat and cut round to remove skin.

For information on sugar bananas, see Bananas, page 32; and for coconut, see Nuts, page 347.

5cm strip fresh lime rind

1 cup (200g) sago

¼ cup (60ml) water

½ cup (135g) firmly packed grated palm sugar

140ml can coconut cream

4 unpeeled sugar bananas (520g), halved lengthways

1 tablespoon grated palm sugar, extra

½ teaspoon finely grated lime rind

1 Place rind strip in large saucepan of cold water; bring to the boil. Discard rind; add sago. Reduce heat; simmer, uncovered, about 15 minutes or until sago is almost transparent. Drain; rinse under cold water, drain.

2 Meanwhile, stir the water and sugar in small saucepan over heat, without boiling, until sugar dissolves. Bring to the boil; boil, uncovered, without stirring, about 10 minutes or until toffee coloured. Remove from heat; stir in coconut cream. Cool 10 minutes.

3 Sprinkle cut side of banana with extra sugar. Place, cut-side down, on heated greased grill plate (or grill or barbecue). Cook about 5 minutes or until tender.

4 Combine sago in medium bowl with coconut mixture and grated rind. Divide among serving bowls; serve with banana, and extra lime rind.

NUTRITIONAL COUNT PER SERVING 7.5g total fat (6.4g saturated fat); 2065kJ (494 cal); 101.3g carbohydrate; 2.1g protein; 4.1g fibre

Polenta and pistachio cake with blood orange syrup

PREP + COOK TIME 1 HOUR 25 MINUTES **SERVES** 12

300g sour cream

125g butter, softened

1 cup (220g) caster sugar

2 cups (300g) self-raising flour

½ teaspoon bicarbonate of soda

⅔ cup (110g) polenta

1 teaspoon finely grated blood orange rind

¾ cup (180ml) water

⅔ cup (100g) roasted shelled pistachios

BLOOD ORANGE SYRUP

1 cup (250ml) blood orange juice

1 cup (220g) caster sugar

1 cinnamon stick

Polenta gives this cake a pleasant grainy texture. The cake is good served warm or cold.

For information on pistachios and notes on roasting nuts, see Nuts, pages 346 & 347; and for blood oranges, see Oranges, page 380.

1 Preheat oven to 160°C/140°C fan-forced. Grease deep 20cm-round cake pan; line base and side with baking paper.

2 Bring blood orange syrup ingredients to the boil in small saucepan, stirring. Reduce heat; simmer, covered, 15 minutes or until syrup thickens. Cool to room temperature.

3 Place sour cream, butter, sugar, sifted flour and soda, polenta, rind and the water in large bowl; beat on low speed with electric mixer until just combined. Beat on medium speed until mixture changes to a slightly paler colour. Stir in nuts. Spread mixture into pan.

4 Bake cake 1 hour. Stand in pan 10 minutes; cool on wire rack. Serve with strained syrup.

NUTRITIONAL COUNT PER SERVING 15.2g total fat (7.6g saturated fat); 1714kJ (412 cal); 64.3g carbohydrate; 5.6g protein; 2.1g fibre

Semolina slice

PREP + COOK TIME 2 HOURS (PLUS REFRIGERATION TIME) **MAKES** 28

1kg coarsely ground semolina

2½ cups (550g) sugar

1 cup (250ml) milk

125g butter

¼ cup (40g) blanched almonds

SUGAR SYRUP

3 cups (750ml) water

2 teaspoons lemon juice

1½ cups (330g) caster sugar

2 teaspoons orange flower water

Known in Middle Eastern and North African countries as basboosa, namoura or harisi, these sweet pastries are appreciated for their lovely orange perfume. Cover the slice loosely with foil if it starts to over-brown while cooking.

For information on almonds (blanched and blanching), see Nuts, pages 344 & 347.

1 Make sugar syrup.

2 Preheat oven to 160°C/140°C fan-forced. Grease 20cm x 30cm lamington pan.

3 Combine semolina and sugar in large bowl. Stir milk and butter in small saucepan over low heat until butter melts; stir into semolina mixture. Spread mixture into pan; smooth top with a wet hand. Score into 4cm diamond shapes; centre one almond on each diamond.

4 Bake slice about 1 hour 20 minutes or until golden brown and slightly firm to the touch.

5 Cut through diamond shapes; gradually pour cooled syrup over hot slice. Cool in pan.

SUGAR SYRUP Bring the water, juice and sugar in medium saucepan to the boil. Reduce heat; simmer, uncovered, about 20 minutes or until syrup reduces to about 2½ cups. Cool to room temperature. Add orange flower water, cover; refrigerate 3 hours or overnight.

NUTRITIONAL COUNT PER PIECE 5.2g total fat (2.8g saturated fat); 1225kJ (293 cal); 55.6g carbohydrate; 4.4g protein; 1.3g fibre

Grapefruit

Grapefruit, a member of the citrus family that also includes oranges and lemons, can be white (actually yellow-skinned with cream flesh) or ruby red (with red-blushed yellow skin and pink flesh) and seeded or seedless. They are usually eaten for breakfast, halved and with the segments detached for eating with a fork, with or without sugar, grilled or not.

1 RUBY RED GRAPEFRUIT
2 YELLOW GRAPEFRUIT

The best way to detach the segments is to ease round behind and under them with a curved-bladed grapefruit knife, then between them with a straight knife. Grapefruit are also good in fruit salads and whole skinless segments strike a fresh and tangy note in duck, shellfish, pork or tuna salads or in side salads to accompany these meats served hot, especially if bitter leaves such as witlof or peppery ones such as watercress are included. To obtain skinless segments, see Oranges, page 382. Grapefruit juice makes excellent sorbets and granitas and is also bottled commercially in a drink to be used straight or as a mixer with gin or vodka. Grapefruit peel can be candied in the same way as orange and lemon peel (see Fruits, Glacé, page 198). White grapefruit are available all year; ruby red ones are available from the end of winter into summer.

CHOOSING Citrus fruit should be picked ripe because they will not ripen further after picking. A ripe grapefruit feels heavy for its size, smells pleasant and gives slightly when pressed. The skin should be smooth and unblemished with no soft spots.

STORING Grapefruit can be stored at room temperature for a week or so; otherwise, store in the refrigerator crisper.

✿ **OTHER RECIPES USING GRAPEFRUIT**
Mint and lime granita with citrus salad, p268

For informationon on smoked salmon, see Seafood, pages 523 & 524; and for mizuna, see Greens, Salad, pages 248 & 249.

Ruby red grapefruit, smoked salmon and mizuna

PREP + COOK TIME 15 MINUTES **SERVES** 4

300g sliced smoked salmon
2 ruby red grapefruit (700g)
2 tablespoons olive oil
1 teaspoon dijon mustard

150g mizuna
⅓ cup (50g) roasted cashews, chopped coarsely
½ small red onion (50g), sliced thinly

1 Reserve four slices of salmon; cut remaining slices into thick pieces.
2 Segment grapefruit over large bowl; add oil, mustard, mizuna, nuts, onion and fish pieces, mix gently.
3 Divide salad among serving plates; top with reserved salmon slices.

NUTRITIONAL COUNT PER SERVING 19.1g total fat (3g saturated fat); 1229kJ (294 cal); 8.6g carbohydrate; 21.1g protein; 2.4g fibre

Grapes

Now that, thanks to modern agriculture and transport, grapes are to be seen in the supermarket almost year-round, they have lost their traditional air of luxury but not their charm. They are still an irresistible snack to children and others, as demonstrated by the sadly depleted bunch you will find in the refrigerator after it has been there a day or two.

1 FLAME SEEDLESS
2 MENINDI SEEDLESS
3 MAROO SEEDLESS
4 RED GLOBES

Grapes are good with soft cheeses, with a rich terrine, in ham or chicken salad or with other fruits in fruit salad, and they make an excellent jelly preserve. When served on a cheeseboard or as table grapes, they should be served with scissors for diners to cut off what they want, or already cut into small bunches. Grapes come in many varieties, white (pale green) or black, seeded or seedless, and in sizes from tiny to the size of a biggish cherry tomato. They are available almost year-round but their peak season is midsummer into autumn.

Wine-grape jellies, in such flavours as cabernet sauvignon, riesling or semillon combined with herbs and aromatics, are among the add-on products being produced by wineries and speciality shops in wine districts. They make intriguing condiments to serve with meats and other savoury foods.

CHOOSING Once picked, grapes do not ripen so, ideally, taste one or at least feel gently to check that they are soft for the variety. All varieties should be plump and stems should not be withered though they should be starting to turn brown in places. Buy only as many as you will use in a couple of days.

STORING Wash only the grapes you intend to use that day and store these on a plate or in an open container in the refrigerator; take them out about half an hour ahead of serving as they have more flavour if not too chilled. Store any remaining grapes in a covered container in the refrigerator.

Also see Vine Leaves, page 638, and Verjuice, page 631.

The grape juice can be stored in the refrigerator for up to 3 days. Add lime juice, soda water and mint just before serving. Have all the ingredients and the glasses well chilled, or pour the spritzer over a few ice cubes in each glass.

Red grape spritzer

PREP TIME 5 MINUTES **MAKES** 1 LITRE (4 CUPS)

1kg seedless red grapes
2½ cups (625ml) soda water
1 tablespoon lime juice
8 fresh mint leaves, shredded

1 Push grapes through juice extractor into glass; stir in soda water, juice and mint.

NUTRITIONAL COUNT PER 250ML 0.3g total fat (0g saturated fat); 715kJ (171 cal); 37.4g carbohydrate; 3.1g protein; 2.3g fibre

Black grape, chicken and wild rice salad

PREP + COOK TIME 45 MINUTES **SERVES** 4

1 litre (4 cups) water

800g chicken breast fillets

1½ cups (300g) wild rice blend

⅔ cup (110g) roasted blanched almonds

1 cup (190g) black grapes

¼ cup loosely packed fresh tarragon leaves

2 green onions, sliced finely

2 teaspoons finely grated lemon rind

1 tablespoon lemon juice

TARRAGON DRESSING

½ cup (120g) sour cream

1 tablespoon dijon mustard

1 tablespoon finely chopped fresh tarragon

1 tablespoon water

2 teaspoons lemon juice

1 Bring the water to the boil in large frying pan; add chicken. Simmer, covered, about 10 minutes or until chicken is cooked. Cool chicken in poaching liquid 10 minutes; drain, slice thickly.

2 Cook rice in large saucepan of boiling water, uncovered, until tender; drain. Cool 10 minutes.

3 Combine ingredients for tarragon dressing in small bowl.

4 Place rice in large bowl with nuts, grapes, tarragon, onion, rind and juice; toss gently to combine. Serve rice salad topped with chicken, accompanied with dressing.

NUTRITIONAL COUNT PER SERVING 32.1g total fat (10g saturated fat); 2575kJ (616 cal); 24.4g carbohydrate; 55.3g protein; 4.5g fibre

Use any black grape for this salad. If you want to remove the pips, you can do this by halving them and flicking out the pips with the point of a small knife, or by pushing a bobbypin into the whole grape from the stem end, hooking it round the pips and drawing them out.

For information on chicken, see Poultry, pages 456 & 457; and for wild rice blend, see Rice, page 496.

Bacon-wrapped quail with grape sauce

PREP + COOK TIME 45 MINUTES **SERVES** 4

4 quails (780g)

1 lemon

20g butter

4 rindless bacon rashers (260g)

⅓ cup (80ml) muscat

250g green beans

½ cup (125ml) chicken stock

150g fresh muscatel grapes, halved

This recipe will serve 4 as a starter or, with the addition of steamed rice, for a light lunch. For notes on muscat, see page 180.

For information on quails, see Game, page 209; and for bacon rashers, see Bacon, page 28.

1 BLACK GRAPE, CHICKEN AND
WILD RICE SALAD
2 BACON-WRAPPED QUAIL
WITH GRAPE SAUCE

1   Preheat oven to 200°C/180°C fan-forced.

2   Discard necks from quails. Wash quails under cold water; pat dry with absorbent paper.

3   Halve lemon; cut one lemon half into four wedges. Place one lemon wedge and a quarter of the butter inside each quail. Tuck legs along body, wrapping tightly with bacon rasher to hold legs in place.

4   Place quails in medium flameproof casserole dish; drizzle with one tablespoon of the muscat and juice of remaining lemon half. Roast, uncovered, about 25 minutes or until quails are browned and cooked through. Remove quails from dish; cover to keep warm.

5   Meanwhile, boil, steam or microwave beans until tender; drain. Cover to keep warm.

6   Return dish with pan liquid to heat, add remaining muscat and stock; stir until sauce boils and reduces to about ½ cup. Add grapes; stir until heated though. Serve quail on beans topped with grape sauce.

NUTRITIONAL COUNT PER SERVING   23.8g total fat (8.8g saturated fat); 1676kJ (401 cal); 9.4g carbohydrate; 33g protein; 2.6g fibre

Greens, Asian

Asian greens are at their best if steamed just until they wilt, or stir-fried in a little oil over high heat, again only until they wilt and change colour. If you are stir-frying a variety of vegetables, greens like these go into the wok last and by the time you have tossed the ingredients two or three times, they will be cooked. If used in a soup, they should again be the last ingredient added, no more than a few minutes before serving.

1 BUK CHOY
2 BABY BUK CHOY
3 CHOY SUM
4 BABY CHOY SUM
5 GAI LAN
6 TAT SOI
7 BABY TAT SOI LEAVES
8 KANG KONG
9 GAI CHOY

❦ **OTHER RECIPES USING ASIAN GREENS**
Cantonese beef patties with grilled gai lan, p52
Chilli beef stir-fry, p122
Prawn and scallop chilli jam stir-fry, p573
Steamed ginger fish, p225
Stir-fried pork, water chestnuts and buk choy, p630
Vegetable dumplings in asian broth, p336

BUK CHOY, also called bok choy or pak choy, usually sold in bundles of three or four plants, is a member of the cabbage family with crisp white stems and dark green leaves that taste mildly cabbagy with a slight mustard tang. Both leaf and stem are used in soups and stir-fries or cooked as a separate vegetable by steaming and serving with oyster sauce or stir-frying with garlic and ginger, or with a drizzle of soy sauce and a tablespoon or two of chicken stock added for the last minute or so.

CHOY SUM, also called chinese flowering cabbage, flowering buk choy or buk choi sum, has small yellow flowers which are eaten with the slightly mustard-tasting leaves and the green stems. It is delicious stir-fried with other vegetables, or stir-fried alone with garlic and oyster sauce.

GAI LAN, also called chinese broccoli or chinese kale, has deep olive green leaves, tiny broccoli-like heads and sometimes small white flowers. The entire vegetable — stems, leaves, heads, flowers — can be eaten though the leaves may be discarded if very coarse. Young, thin stems need only to be cut into the desired lengths, but older, thick stems should be peeled and cut lengthwise in half. Gai lan can be steamed whole and served with oyster sauce, or cut into serving pieces and stir-fried with ginger and sesame oil or with garlic and hoisin sauce.

TAT SOI is also called flat, spoon or rosette cabbage because of its spoon-shaped leaves and rosette shape. Young tat soi is eaten raw in salads, and tat soi of any size is used in soups, steamed or stir-fried.

KANG KONG or **WATER SPINACH** is a delicate vegetable with hollow stems. Use the leaves and top half of the stems, cut into 5cm lengths. Stir-fry, dip in batter and deep-fry, or serve steamed with kecap manis (see Sauces, Asian, page 508).

GAI CHOY, also called oriental or swatow mustard cabbage, has a strong, hot cabbage/mustard taste; some people find it indigestible. The stems, which are less pungent than the leaves, are often pickled as sichuan pickle. Stems and leaves are used in stir-fries, especially if there are other strong-flavoured ingredients. Baby gai choy leaves can be used in salads, to which they will add a hot, mustardy bite.

CHOOSING

All asian greens should be fresh, bright and unwilted, with firm stems that are moist where they have been cut. Choi sum and gai lan should have more buds and half-open flowers than fully open ones.

STORING

Kang kong should be used the day it is bought. Other greens should be enclosed in a paper bag then in a plastic bag and stored in the fridge for up to 2 days.

Serve this with rice or noodles. Buk choy and gai lan can also be cooked this way.

Stir-fried choy sum

PREP + COOK TIME 15 MINUTES **SERVES** 4

1 tablespoon peanut oil

1 fresh long red chilli, sliced thinly

2 cloves garlic, crushed

2cm piece fresh ginger (10g), grated

1kg choy sum, trimmed, cut into 5cm lengths

2 tablespoons fish sauce

2 tablespoons lime juice

1 cup (150g) roasted unsalted cashews

1 Heat oil in wok; stir-fry chilli, garlic and ginger 1 minute.

2 Add choy sum; stir-fry until almost tender. Add sauce and juice; stir-fry until hot.

3 Serve stir-fry sprinkled with nuts.

NUTRITIONAL COUNT PER SERVING 23.6g total fat (4.1g saturated fat); 1271kJ (304 cal); 10g carbohydrate; 10.4g protein; 6.1g fibre

Stir-fried asian greens in black bean sauce

PREP + COOK TIME 25 MINUTES **SERVES** 4

2 cups (400g) jasmine rice

1 tablespoon peanut oil

150g sugar snap peas, trimmed

400g gai lan, chopped coarsely

200g snake beans, trimmed,
cut into 5cm lengths

2 cloves garlic, sliced thinly

1 fresh small red thai chilli,
chopped finely

2 medium zucchini (240g),
sliced thickly

2 tablespoons black bean sauce

1 tablespoon kecap manis

1 teaspoon sesame oil

⅓ cup (50g) roasted unsalted
cashews, chopped coarsely

This dish is good by itself with rice, or an impressive accompaniment to grilled pork chops or beef fillet steaks.

To recreate the way gai lan is served for yum cha, chop a bunch in half crossways, parboil only long enough to soften the stems, drain and splash with a little sesame oil and oyster sauce to serve (note that there is a vegetarian "oyster sauce" which is made from mushrooms and soy).

1 Cook rice in large saucepan of boiling water, uncovered, until just tender; drain.

2 Meanwhile, heat peanut oil in wok; stir-fry peas, gai lan stems, beans, garlic, chilli and zucchini until stems are just tender.

3 Add sauces, sesame oil, gai lan leaves and nuts; stir-fry until leaves are just wilted.

4 Serve stir-fry with rice.

NUTRITIONAL COUNT PER SERVING 13.3g total fat (2.6g saturated fat); 2274kJ (544 cal); 89.5g carbohydrate; 15.4g protein; 8.8g fibre

Asian greens salad with sesame ginger dressing

PREP TIME 20 MINUTES **SERVES** 10

1 small wombok (700g),
sliced thinly

1 red oak leaf lettuce (380g),
torn

100g mizuna

100g snow pea sprouts, trimmed

100g snow peas, trimmed,
sliced thinly

½ small daikon (200g),
sliced thinly

4 green onions, sliced thinly

SESAME GINGER DRESSING

⅓ cup (80ml) salt-reduced
soy sauce

2 tablespoons white vinegar

2 teaspoons sesame oil

1cm piece fresh ginger (5g),
grated

1 clove garlic, crushed

Discard the coarse outer leaves of the wombok and lettuce.

For information on daikon, see Radishes, pages 488 & 489.

1 Place ingredients for sesame ginger dressing in screw-top jar; shake well.

2 Place wombok in large bowl with remaining ingredients and dressing; toss gently to combine.

NUTRITIONAL COUNT PER SERVING 1.4g total fat (0.2g saturated fat); 192kJ (46 cals); 4.8g carbohydrate; 3.2g protein; 3.1g fibre

Roasted duck and stir-fried greens salad

Barbecued ducks are available from Asian barbecue takeaway shops.

For information on duck, see Poultry, page 457.

PREP + COOK TIME 45 MINUTES **SERVES** 4

1kg chinese barbecued duck

1 tablespoon sesame oil

6 green onions, sliced thinly

500g choy sum, trimmed, chopped coarsely

500g tat soi, trimmed

200g fresh shiitake mushrooms, quartered

¼ cup (60ml) water

150g snow peas

2 cups (160g) bean sprouts

2 tablespoons toasted sesame seeds

HOISIN DRESSING

2cm piece fresh ginger (10g), grated

2 tablespoons soy sauce

1 tablespoon sesame oil

1 clove garlic, crushed

1 fresh small red thai chilli, chopped finely

¼ cup (60ml) hoisin sauce

1 Preheat oven to 240°C/220°C fan-forced.

2 Quarter duck; discard all bones. Slice duck meat thickly, keeping skin intact; place on oven tray. Roast, uncovered, about 10 minutes or until skin crisps; discard duck fat.

3 Meanwhile, make hoisin dressing.

4 Heat oil in wok or large frying pan; stir-fry onion, choy sum and tat soi, in batches, until greens just wilt. Place mushrooms in same wok; stir-fry 2 minutes. Add the water; bring to the boil. Reduce heat; simmer, uncovered, about 2 minutes or until mushrooms soften.

5 Place duck, vegetable mixture and mushrooms in large bowl with dressing and snow peas; toss gently to combine. Divide sprouts among serving plates; top with salad, sprinkle with sesame seeds.

HOISIN DRESSING Bring ingredients to the boil in small saucepan. Reduce heat; simmer, uncovered, 2 minutes. Cool 10 minutes.

NUTRITIONAL COUNT PER SERVING 51g total fat (13g saturated fat); 2805kJ (671 cal); 13.4g carbohydrate; 36.4g protein; 9.2g fibre

Greens, Salad

Fresh leaves can stand alone as the perfect green salad or supply the light, bouffant element that sets off other salad ingredients to perfection. They go in sandwich fillings, do duty as cups or wraps to hold other foods, decorate cheeseboards and serving platters, and some have another life in delicate braises or soups or as stylish barbecue items.

A leafy salad should look "bouffant", not heavy and settled. The way to achieve this is to dress the salad at the last moment and use only enough dressing to make every leaf glisten. Add half the dressing to start with, then toss the salad, adding more dressing as you go, but never enough to run off into a puddle at the bottom of the dish.

ICEBERG LETTUCE has stiff, crunchy, pale leaves that are good for shredding, serving in wedges with a creamy dressing, using as cups for fillings such as prawns or chicken salad and for sang choy bow, the delightful Asian dish of savoury minced pork in a lettuce-leaf cup. Iceberg is available all year.

COS LETTUCE is a robust, strong-flavoured long lettuce that stands up well to heavy dressings and other substantial ingredients such as eggs, fish or bacon. Regular cos have a lot of wastage because the outside leaves are coarse, but baby cos have little wastage. Both regular and baby cos are available all year.

MESCLUN is a mixture of baby greens which may include any of those listed here and also baby spinach (see Spinach, page 568). Mesclun is available all year.

BUTTER LETTUCE is a soft-leaf lettuce that forms a loose heart. Its mild-tasting light-green leaves are an attractive background in both looks and flavour for fresh herbs. Butter lettuces are available all year.

MIGNONETTE is a type of butter lettuce but with green and reddish/bronze leaves.

OAKLEAF LETTUCE has loose, soft, ruffled green or red-flushed leaves that look lovely with other leaves in a tossed salad. It is often described as a cut-and-come-again lettuce because, if you grow your own, you can take leaves as you need them without affecting the plant. It is available all year.

CORAL LETTUCE is named for its tightly crinkled leaves. It comes in green or red-flushed varieties. It is a soft-leafed lettuce but its frizzy mouth-feel makes it seem less tender than other soft lettuce. Coral lettuce is available all year.

ROCKET is available both wild and cultivated and also as very young or baby rocket. Its flavour has been described as roast beef with a peppery tang. Wild rocket is the hottest, cultivated rocket is less peppery because it was grown more quickly and baby rocket is the mildest. Rocket is available all year.

RADICCHIO is a sturdy chicory which comes in numerous varieties, some with red and green and some with red and white leaves. The different kinds are often called after their places of origin, such as round-headed Verona and elongated Treviso. Radicchio has robust, bitter leaves that can be torn or shredded for salads, or wedges can be cut for braising or barbecuing. It is available all year but is at its best in winter.

MIZUNA, also called mitsuba, is a leafy Japanese herb with a crisp, aromatic flavour, used in salads, sandwiches, clear and fish soups and savoury custards, and also as a garnish. Its peak season is summer but it is available most of the year.

CURLY ENDIVE, also called frisée for its loose tangle of frizzy leaves, is available in

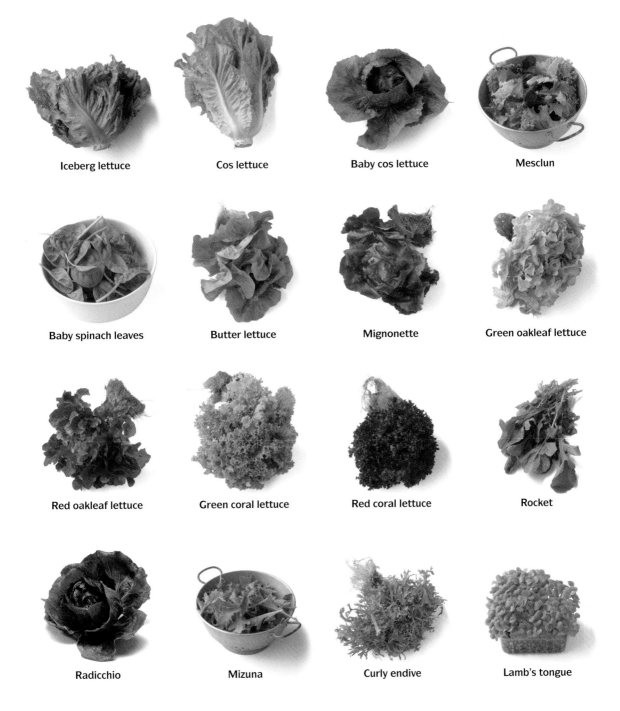

Iceberg lettuce

Cos lettuce

Baby cos lettuce

Mesclun

Baby spinach leaves

Butter lettuce

Mignonette

Green oakleaf lettuce

Red oakleaf lettuce

Green coral lettuce

Red coral lettuce

Rocket

Radicchio

Mizuna

Curly endive

Lamb's tongue

full-size and baby form. It is a bitter green, though only mildly so in the tender baby leaves, which are usually sold as part of the baby-leaf mixture called mesclun. Curly endive is available most of the year but is at its best in winter.

LAMB'S TONGUE, also called lamb's lettuce, mâche and corn salad, has small, tender, velvety leaves. It is sold in punnets and is available from autumn into spring.

CHICORY is a family of bitter-leafed plants including two closely related plant groups of culinary interest whose common names, chicory and endive, have come to be so much interchanged that the same plant may be known as chicory in one country and as endive in another. Three plants, radicchio, witlof and curly endive, are all members of the chicory family but only curly endive belongs to the endivia branch of the family and is therefore botanically classed as an endive. Its flat-leafed variety is called endive in Britain, chicory in Australia, escarole in America and chicorée scarole in France.

WITLOF, also called belgian endive, is a long, slender plant with crunchy, tightly furled leaves. It tastes mild and fresh with a touch of the characteristic bitterness of the chicory family, stronger in the red-tipped variety than in the pale green. It is grown in the dark to keep it white and minimise bitterness. It is used in salads and also made into delicate hot dishes, usually braised in butter and chicken stock to serve with veal, chicken or ham, or blanched, wrapped in ham and baked under a blanket of cheese sauce to be served as a first course or lunch dish. Witlof is available all year.

CRESS The tiny cress seedlings that are sold mixed with mustard seedlings in punnets are a cultivated variety known to growers as garden cress. Both kinds of seedlings, which are related, belong to hot-

flavoured families, but the effect is minimal in these baby plants. Mustard and cress is snipped over salads, used as a garnish and goes into egg and cress sandwiches, which rate with cucumber sandwiches as a classic offering at a proper English afternoon tea (which the English never call afternoon tea, but simply tea).

WATERCRESS grows in clear water. It is a member of the same family as mustard and has the hot flavour characteristic of the family, though watercress tastes fresh and peppery rather than mustardy. The watercress sold in shops is cultivated and is less hot than wild watercress because it has been grown more quickly. Watercress is available all year.

CHOOSING All greens should be undamaged and very fresh with no sign of wilting, and the stem ends or bases should be moist where they were cut. Look carefully at mesclun as greengrocers tend to replenish it without discarding the older layer underneath. If necessary, buy a bit more than you want and throw away the tired bits.

STORING Watercress and mizuna should be stored in the refrigerator, standing up in water with a plastic bag dropped loosely over, and used within a few days. A punnet of mustard and cress should be placed in the shade and used within a few days, moistening it as needed to keep it just damp. Lamb's tongue should be emptied from its punnet into a paper bag, then enclosed in a plastic bag and stored in the refrigerator for no more than a day or two. All other salad greens, untrimmed and unwashed, should be enclosed in a paper bag, then in a plastic bag, and stored in the refrigerator. Radicchio and iceberg lettuce will keep well for a week or so, cos lettuce for 4–5 days;

Witlof (red)

Watercress

Salad spinner

soft lettuces should be used within 2 days. As you remove outside leaves from lettuces when preparing them for use, reserve those that are not too coarse for lettuce soup or the delicious French dish of lettuce, peas and spring onions braised in butter and their own juices, called petits pois à la française.

✤ **OTHER RECIPES USING SALAD GREENS**
Avocado, cos and tomato salad, p27
Five-spice pork and nashi salad, p419
Pear, walnut and fetta salad with walnut dressing, p418
Pork sang choy bow, p442
Prawn, crab and avocado salad, p436
Pumpkin, radicchio and haloumi salad, p482
Roasted capsicum and ricotta salad, p87
Roquefort and pear salad, p107
Sesame tofu salad, p545
Shaved fennel and apple salad, p176

Rocket, parmesan and semi-dried tomato salad

PREP + COOK TIME 10 MINUTES **SERVES** 4

1 tablespoon balsamic vinegar

1 tablespoon olive oil

100g baby rocket leaves

2 tablespoons roasted pine nuts

40g drained semi-dried tomatoes, chopped coarsely

⅓ cup (25g) flaked parmesan cheese

1 Combine ingredients in large bowl; toss gently to combine.

NUTRITIONAL COUNT PER SERVING 12.3g total fat (2.3g saturated fat); 635kJ (152 cal); 4.4g carbohydrate; 5.1g protein; 2.2g fibre

Serve this Italian-style salad with lamb chops and a lemon wedge on the side to squeeze over the meat.

For information on semi-dried tomatoes, see Tomatoes, page 607; and for parmesan cheese, see Cheese, page 104.

Char-grilled radicchio parcels

PREP + COOK TIME 25 MINUTES **SERVES** 4

3 cloves garlic, crushed

1 cup (150g) drained semi-dried tomatoes, chopped coarsely

420g bocconcini cheese

1 cup coarsely chopped fresh basil

2 x 420g cans white beans, rinsed, drained

24 large radicchio leaves

1 tablespoon balsamic vinegar

1 Combine garlic, tomato, cheese, basil and beans in large bowl.
2 Plunge radicchio into large saucepan of boiling water then drain immediately; submerge in iced water to halt cooking process. When cool, drain; pat dry with absorbent paper.
3 Slightly overlap 2 leaves; centre about a quarter cup of bean mixture on leaves then roll, folding in edges to enclose filling. Repeat with remaining bean mixture and leaves.
4 Cook parcels, seam-side down, on heated oiled grill plate (or grill or barbecue) until filling is hot. Serve parcels drizzled with vinegar.

NUTRITIONAL COUNT PER SERVING 20g total fat (11g saturated fat); 1659kJ (397 cal); 18.9g carbohydrate; 28.7g protein; 13.8g fibre

These parcels could be the stars of a vegetarian lunch or barbecue. If cooking them indoors, use a ridged char-grill pan. Get the grill or barbecue really hot and cook the parcels first on the seam sides, then turn carefully and grill the presentation (top) sides for long enough to give them attractive charred stripes.

Any kind of hot or cold seafood is superb with this salad.

For information on fennel, see Fennel, page 174; and for dill and mint, see Herbs, page 264.

Green salad with fennel and herbs

PREP + COOK TIME 15 MINUTES **SERVES** 8

1 baby cos lettuce (180g), shredded finely

200g rocket, trimmed

100g watercress, trimmed

5 green onions, chopped finely

1 small fennel (200g), sliced thinly

¼ cup coarsely chopped fresh dill

½ cup loosely packed fresh mint leaves

½ cup (80g) roasted pine nuts

RED WINE VINAIGRETTE

¼ cup (60ml) olive oil

¼ cup (60ml) red wine vinegar

1 Place ingredients for red wine vinaigrette in screw-top jar; shake well.

2 Place salad ingredients in large bowl with vinaigrette; toss gently to combine.

NUTRITIONAL COUNT PER SERVING 14.2g total fat (1.4g saturated fat); 635kJ (152 cal); 2.4g carbohydrate; 3g protein; 2.6g fibre

Baby cos lettuce have less wastage than the full-sizes ones. If you can't find babies, use one large one but be sure to discard the coarse outer leaves.

Baby cos caesar salad

PREP + COOK TIME 30 MINUTES **SERVES** 4

1 small french bread stick (150g), sliced thinly

¼ cup (60ml) olive oil

4 slices prosciutto (60g)

4 eggs

2 baby cos lettuce (360g), leaves separated

1 cup (80g) flaked parmesan cheese

CAESAR DRESSING

2 egg yolks

1 clove garlic, quartered

4 drained anchovy fillets

2 tablespoons lemon juice

2 teaspoons dijon mustard

½ cup (125ml) olive oil

1 tablespoon warm water, approximately

1 Preheat oven to 180°C/160°C fan-forced. Make caesar dressing.

2 Toss bread and oil in medium bowl; toast bread on oven tray until browned lightly.

3 Meanwhile, cook prosciutto in heated large frying pan until crisp; drain on absorbent paper, chop coarsely.

4 Poach eggs until the whites are set but the yolks are still runny.

5 Place lettuce, cheese, croûtons, prosciutto and dressing in large bowl; toss gently to combine. Divide salad among serving bowls; serve topped with poached eggs.

CAESAR DRESSING Blend or process egg yolks, garlic, anchovies, juice and mustard until smooth. With motor operating, gradually add oil, in a thin steady stream; blend until dressing thickens. Add as much of the warm water as required to thin dressing.

NUTRITIONAL COUNT PER SERVING 54.2g total fat (11.5g saturated fat); 2809kJ (672 cal); 22.2g carbohydrate; 23.6g protein; 3.5g fibre

1 ROCKET, PARMESAN AND SEMI-DRIED TOMATO SALAD [P 251] **2** CHAR-GRILLED RADICCHIO PARCELS [P 251] **3** GREEN SALAD WITH FENNEL AND HERBS **4** BABY COS CAESAR SALAD

*This soup is also beautiful
served chilled.*

Creamy watercress soup

PREP + COOK TIME 1 HOUR **SERVES** 4

1 tablespoon olive oil

1 small brown onion (80g), chopped finely

1 small leek (200g), sliced thinly

3 medium potatoes (600g), chopped coarsely

1 litre (4 cups) chicken stock

350g watercress, trimmed

⅓ cup (80g) sour cream

1 Heat oil in large saucepan; cook onion and leek, stirring over low heat, until vegetables soften. Add potato and stock; bring to the boil. Reduce heat; simmer, covered, about 20 minutes or until potato is almost tender.

2 Reserve four watercress sprigs; stir remaining watercress into pan. Simmer soup, uncovered, about 5 minutes or until potato is tender.

3 Blend or process soup, in batches, until smooth. Reheat soup in same pan then divide among serving bowls; top each with 1 tablespoon of the sour cream then a reserved watercress sprig.

NUTRITIONAL COUNT PER SERVING 14.1g total fat (6.4g saturated fat); 1089kJ (260 cal); 21g carbohydrate; 9.6g protein; 6.4g fibre

---

*Pear, cheese and bitter
leaves balance each other
so well that they have
become a classic
combination. This recipe
makes an excellent first
course, or could be served
with ham or chicken for a
complete light lunch.*

*For information on
blue cheese, see Cheese,
page 103.*

Witlof, pear and blue cheese salad

PREP + COOK TIME 20 MINUTES **SERVES** 4

2 red witlof (250g), trimmed, leaves separated

2 yellow witlof (250g), trimmed, leaves separated

1 medium pear (230g), sliced thinly

¾ cup (90g) roasted pecans, chopped coarsely

BLUE CHEESE DRESSING

⅓ cup (80ml) buttermilk

100g blue cheese, crumbled

1 tablespoon lemon juice

1 Make blue cheese dressing.

2 Place witlof, pear and nuts in large bowl; toss gently to combine.

3 Serve salad drizzled with dressing.

BLUE CHEESE DRESSING Whisk ingredients in small jug until smooth.

NUTRITIONAL COUNT PER SERVING 24.9g total fat (6.5g saturated fat); 1295kJ (309 cal); 9.9g carbohydrate; 9.5g protein; 5.3g fibre

CREAMY WATERCRESS SOUP

Ham

A ham is the salt-cured (-preserved) hind leg of a pig. It may be dry-cured, meaning that salt is repeatedly rubbed into it, or wet-cured, meaning that it is soaked in or injected with brine. The curing recipe may include sugar or molasses for a sweeter, milder ham. Wet-curing is faster than dry-curing, so is the method that most manufacturers use today.

1 SOCCERBALL HAM
2 HAM HOCK
3 PROSCIUTTO
4 SMOKED HAM
5 JAMON
6 SANDWICH HAM

Some hams are smoked, some are not, and some are cooked while others are designed to be eaten raw. All ham is ready to eat when you buy it, though many people like to glaze and bake a whole or half ham for occasions such as Christmas. The name "ham" is now given to legs of mutton or venison that have been cured in the same way as leg of pork and for forequarter pork that has been cured like the leg.

SOCCERBALL HAM, GYPSY HAM These re-shaped ham products vary from manufacturer to manufacturer but are made of individual ham cuts fitted together into compact shapes. The meat may be injected with water and is usually tumbled to loosen and soften the fibres, then filled into a net or casing, or sometimes tied, to form the desired shape. These products may include soy protein and vegetable gums.

HAM HOCK is the shank of the leg, which does not form part of the ham but is salted and smoked in the same way. It is cooked in a soup or dried-bean dish or with vegetables such as kale or mustard greens, to add a deep, smoky flavour. Its small amount of lean meat may also be separated from the bone and gristle from which it is mainly composed, and added back into the dish.

PROSCIUTTO OR PROSCIUTTO CRUDO, meaning raw ham, is a leg that has been dry-salted for up to 2 months, periodically rubbed with more salt and turned, and then hung without smoking in a cool, breezy place to continue curing and to wind-dry for at least several months and up to 2 years. During this time it becomes completely dry and develops rich, complex flavour. The most famous prosciutto is prosciutto di parma or parma ham, which must be made in the Parma district of northern Italy, from pigs fed on the whey left over from making parmesan cheese. Prosciutto is also made in other parts of Italy and in other countries, including Australia. It is cut in paper-thin slices to serve, often with figs or melon, and can be chopped to add to a pasta sauce or other dishes, or grilled until crisp for a garnish or in salads. Other prosciutto-like hams, with their own character, include Spanish jamon serrano and jamon iberico.

SMOKED HAM Hams may be unsmoked or smoked lightly or heavily. Traditionally, smoking means the hams are hung in the smoke from a wood fire, which adds its own flavour to the meat and concentrates the flavour to some degree because the ham loses moisture in the process. Traditionally smoked ham is therefore stronger-tasting than unsmoked; modern manufacturers may use liquid smoke, which adds to the flavour but does not concentrate it. The term "double-smoked" implies extended or repeated smoking for a stronger flavour.

SANDWICH HAM is usually made with shoulder ham that has been re-shaped into

♣ **OTHER RECIPES
USING HAM**
*Cuban black bean soup, p476
Fig, goats cheese and
   prosciutto salad, p179
Italian roasted quail with
   braised vegetables, p212
Prosciutto-wrapped bean
   bundles, p45
Prosciutto-wrapped veal and
   pork meatloaf, p621
Veal saltimbocca, p622*

a rectangular loaf by the same process as described under Soccerball ham, for slices that will fit neatly on sliced bread.

LEG HAM Bone-in leg ham or ham off the bone means meat carved from a whole or half ham. Boneless leg ham may mean meat carved from a whole or half leg that has been boned and trimmed of excess fat, often called an easy-carve leg. Sometimes, however, ham marked "boneless leg" is in a smooth, round shape; this usually means that it consists of pieces of leg ham pressed together, rather than a solid piece of meat.

DANISH HAM, VIRGINIAN HAM are trade terms whose meaning varies from manufacturer to manufacturer to indicate a style of re-shaped ham (see Soccerball ham) with such qualities as mild or strong flavour, sweetness or smokiness. Danish ham is often canned.

CHOOSING It is a matter of personal preference and budget whether one buys ham carved from the leg or one of the numerous forms of re-shaped ham. The best thing is to try several kinds and go with the one that suits you best. Sliced ham of any kind is very perishable, so buy only what you will use within a day or so.

STORING Remove sliced ham from its packaging, layering between slices with greaseproof paper, then wrap the stack in greaseproof paper, enclose in a plastic bag and store in the coldest part of the fridge. Use within 48 hours; if any smells "off" or is sticky, discard it. Wrap a whole ham or large piece in a pillowcase or calico bag rinsed in 1 part vinegar to 5 parts water; store in the coldest part of the refrigerator, re-rinse the wrapping every 2 days. It should stay in good condition for up to 2 weeks.

Cook this sustaining soup for when you come home from the football or sailing. It can be made a day or two ahead, only holding out the silver beet and adding it in the last few minutes of heating.

For information on black-eyed beans, see Pulses, page 472.

Ham and black-eyed bean soup

PREP + COOK TIME 2 HOURS 50 MINUTES (PLUS STANDING TIME) **SERVES** 6

1 cup (200g) black-eyed beans

1 tablespoon olive oil

1 stalk celery (150g), trimmed, chopped coarsely

1 small brown onion (80g), chopped coarsely

1 medium carrot (120g), chopped coarsely

1 bay leaf

2 cloves garlic

1.2kg ham hock

1 litre (4 cups) chicken stock

2 litres (8 cups) water

½ bunch trimmed silver beet (125g), shredded finely

2 tablespoons cider vinegar

1 Place beans in medium bowl, cover with water; stand overnight, rinse, drain.

2 Heat oil in large saucepan, add celery, onion and carrot; cook until vegetables are soft. Add bay leaf, garlic, ham hock, stock and the water; bring to the boil. Reduce heat; simmer, uncovered, 1 hour.

3 Add beans to soup; simmer, uncovered, about 1 hour or until beans are tender.

4 Remove hock from soup. When cool enough to handle, remove meat from hock. Discard bone; shred meat coarsely, return to soup.

5 Add silver beet to soup; cook, stirring, until wilted. Remove from heat; stir in vinegar.

NUTRITIONAL COUNT PER SERVING 7.2g total fat (1.8g saturated fat); 945kJ (226 cal); 16.1g carbohydrate; 21.2g protein; 6.3g fibre

Ham salad with mustard vinaigrette

PREP + COOK TIME 25 MINUTES **SERVES** 4

300g snow peas, trimmed

2 medium avocados (500g), sliced thickly

1⅓ cups (200g) drained semi-dried tomatoes, chopped coarsely

150g baby spinach leaves

350g shaved leg ham, torn into large pieces

MUSTARD VINAIGRETTE

2 cloves garlic, crushed

2 tablespoons white wine vinegar

2 tablespoons finely chopped fresh flat-leaf parsley

1cm piece fresh ginger (5g), grated

1 tablespoon wholegrain mustard

1 tablespoon warm water

¼ cup (60ml) extra light olive oil

1 Boil, steam or microwave snow peas until tender; drain. Rinse under cold water; drain.

2 Meanwhile, place ingredients for mustard vinaigrette in screw-top; shake well.

3 Place snow peas in large bowl with remaining ingredients; toss gently to combine. Divide salad among serving plates; drizzle with vinaigrette.

NUTRITIONAL COUNT PER SERVING 40.9g total fat (7.8g saturated fat); 2445kJ (585 cal); 22.1g carbohydrate; 27.4g protein; 12g fibre

---

Ham and zucchini quiche

PREP + COOK TIME 1 HOUR **SERVES** 4

⅓ cup (50g) plain flour

1½ cups (375ml) milk

3 eggs

3 slices ham (60g), chopped coarsely

3 green onions, chopped finely

1 cup (125g) coarsely grated cheddar cheese

1 medium zucchini (120g), grated coarsely

2 tablespoons finely chopped fresh flat-leaf parsley

1 Preheat oven to 160°C/140°C fan-forced. Oil 20cm round quiche dish.

2 Whisk flour and milk in medium bowl until smooth; whisk in eggs. Stir in remaining ingredients; pour mixture into dish.

3 Bake quiche, uncovered, about 45 minutes or until filling is set.

4 Sprinkle with extra chopped parsley and serve with salad and bread, if you like.

NUTRITIONAL COUNT PER SERVING 19g total fat (10.6g saturated fat); 1313kJ (314 cal); 14.5g carbohydrate; 20.8g protein; 1.2g fibre

Always use full-cream rather than light or skim milk for a quiche as it gives it a creamier texture. You could also use chopped speck instead of ham and a nutty, good-melting swiss cheese like raclette or appenzeller instead of cheddar to make this simple quiche really special.

If you like, or if your oven is full, you can bake the ham in a covered barbecue, using indirect heat, following manufacturer's instructions.

For information on oranges, see Oranges, pages 380–382.

Orange-glazed ham

PREP + COOK TIME 3 HOURS 25 MINUTES **SERVES** 12

6kg smoked leg of ham

2 small oranges (360g), halved, sliced thinly

1 tablespoon (6g) whole cloves

ORANGE GLAZE

½ cup (170g) orange marmalade

¾ cup (180ml) orange juice

¼ cup (50g) firmly packed brown sugar

2 teaspoons dijon mustard

2 tablespoons Cointreau or Grand Marnier

1 Cut through ham rind about 10cm from the shank end of leg. Remove rind from ham by sliding your hand between the rind and the fat layer. Discard rind.

2 Preheat oven to 180°C/160°C fan-forced.

3 Make orange glaze.

4 Secure orange slices with cloves in decorative pattern on ham.

5 Wrap shank in foil; brush ham with some of the orange glaze. Roast ham, covered, brushing occasionally with more glaze, about 2 hours or until orange is lightly caramelised and ham is heated through.

ORANGE GLAZE Stir ingredients in small saucepan over low heat until warm.

NUTRITIONAL COUNT PER SERVING 16.9g total fat (6.2g saturated fat); 1806kJ (432 cal); 14g carbohydrate; 54.4g protein; 0.5g fibre

These little wraps are best made close to serving time. Serve them as appetisers.

For information on bocconcini cheese, see Cheese, page 102.

Marinated baby bocconcini with prosciutto

PREP TIME 20 MINUTES (PLUS STANDING TIME) **MAKES** 40

2 cloves garlic, crushed

1 fresh long green chilli, seeded, chopped

⅓ cup (80ml) olive oil

440g baby bocconcini (milk cherries)

10 slices (150g) thin prosciutto

1 bunch fresh basil

1 Combine the garlic, chilli and oil in medium bowl, add bocconcini; toss to combine. Stand 30 minutes.

2 Halve prosciutto slices crossways, then halve again lengthways.

3 Drain bocconcini from marinade; reserve marinade. Wrap a piece of prosciutto and a basil leaf around each bocconcini; secure with a toothpick.

4 Serve drizzled with reserved marinade.

NUTRITIONAL COUNT PER TOOTHPICK 3.8g total fat (1.4g saturated fat); 192kJ (46 cal); 0.1g carbohydrate; 2.8g protein; 0.3g fibre

ORANGE-GLAZED HAM

Herbs

For cooks, herbs are plants whose green parts, usually leaves and sometimes stalks, are used for their flavours and aromas. Other plant parts such as seeds, bark, fruits and roots are also used in the kitchen, but these are classified as spices. Herbs may be used fresh or dried; many are better fresh but some, including oregano, marjoram, thyme and bay, flavour food better when dried.

1 SAGE
2 OREGANO
3 LEMON THYME
4 VIETNAMESE MINT
5 CHERVIL
6 CURRY LEAVES
7 GARLIC CHIVES
8 MINT
9 THYME
10 CURLY PARSLEY
11 TARRAGON
12 BASIL
13 THAI BASIL
14 CHIVES
15 MARJORAM
16 CORIANDER
17 SORREL
18 FLAT-LEAF PARSLEY
19 DILL
20 ROSEMARY
21 BAY LEAVES

Coriander is called cilantro in America; in American recipes, cilantro means the fresh herb, while coriander means the whole or ground seeds.

BASIL comes in green or purple varieties; it is wonderful with tomatoes in any form and also with eggplant; its clean clove/anise flavour is magic with liver and onions and it is the soul of pesto, the garlicky Italian basil sauce that goes on pasta or a bowl of minestrone. Basil's season is summer, but it can be enjoyed in winter too if you wash and dry leaves and stack in a shallow container, sprinkling a little salt on each as you go, then pour in olive oil to cover, put the lid on and store in the refrigerator for up to 3 months. Dried basil is pleasant but has quite a different flavour from fresh.

BAY LEAVES, alone or as part of a bouquet garni (bay, parsley, thyme and celery), are the essential underpinning to the flavours of hundreds of soups, casseroles and stocks. Their pungent taste can be overwhelming, so one is usually enough unless you are making a large quantity. Dried leaves are better than fresh for cooking, but they should still be green, not yellow. Bay is an all-year evergreen tree.

CHERVIL is a delicate, lacy herb with a fresh, slightly anise flavour. It is one the four fines herbes (the others are parsley, tarragon and chives) that flavour a classic omelette aux fines herbes, and is good used as a garnish or sprinkled on salads, fish, cream soups or cooked vegetables. Chervil is available for much of the year but is at its best in spring.

CHIVES come in two varieties, onion chives which have long, thin, tubular leaves, and garlic chives which have long, thin flat leaves. Their flavours are fresh and subtle; either or both can be snipped over buttered carrots or potatoes, omelettes or scrambled eggs and cream soups. Chives are in season from spring to autumn and die away in winter, but return the next spring.

CORIANDER leaves are essential to hundreds of Asian, Latin American and Middle Eastern dishes; add stems to dishes during cooking to contribute their warm sage/lemon/anise flavour, and the roots are used in cooking chicken and in soups. Coriander is available all year. Try to buy it with the roots on as it will keep fresh longer.

CELERY SEED is the dried seed of a plant closely related to the celery whose stalks we eat, but cultivated specifically for its seeds, which taste like celery with a hint of spice. It is used in breads, scones, soups and dressings and is an ingredient in many spice mixes. It is also ground for celery salt.

CURRY LEAVES are the leaves of a small tree and are used fresh and dried; fresh are preferable as they have more aroma and flavour. Curry leaves don't taste of curry but add another warm, slightly pungent dimension to the flavour and fragrance of a curry or soup. They are especially good in mild, spicy dishes such as mulligatawny and dhal, and can be

Don't wash parsley before chopping because it will stick to the knife or food processor, but chop it, wash in a sieve, turn out on to a cloth, gather up with one hand, squeeze out excess water with the other, then shake up and down to fluff it up.

added to marinades or coatings for seafood or chicken. Fresh curry leaves are available all year, though the supply drops in winter.

DILL The sweet anise flavour of dill seems made for fresh, smoked and cured fish and shellfish, and is also good with cucumber, whether fresh or in dill pickles. Snipped dill is excellent sprinkled on beetroot, potatoes or rice or folded into yoghurt, sour cream or mayonnaise, and whole stems make a simple, beautiful garnish for a serving platter.

LEMON MYRTLE is an Australian native tree which is now also cultivated. Its sharply lemon-flavoured leaves are used either fresh or dried, the dried being more intensely flavoured. Their flavour fades in long cooking but they are excellent, used whole and lightly crushed, for adding to rice as it cooks, flavouring ice-cream or infusing in the liquid ingredient for a cake. Add it finely chopped or crumbled to a stuffing or marinade, sprinkle over fish before steaming or fold into mayonnaise. Dried leaves are available at spice shops and speciality food shops; fresh are not widely available but may be found at some greengrocers.

MARJORAM is one of the herbs whose flavour is stronger and more developed when dried. Fresh, it is mildly savoury and works well, usually with thyme, in stuffings, soups, sandwiches, dumplings, savoury breads and scones. Dried, it lends its warm flavour to tomato sauces and is crumbled and rubbed on lamb chops to be grilled. It mixes well with other herbs.

MINT is a huge family of plants with scents from eau de cologne to peppermint, apple, liquorice and lemon. Only one mint, spearmint-scented pennyroyal, should be avoided as its oil can be toxic to people and animals. The mints that interest cooks are spearmint and common mint. *Spearmint*, with long, smooth leaves, is the one that greengrocers sell while common mint, with rounded, pebbly

leaves, is the one that most people grow. Spearmint has the stronger flavour. *Common mint* goes in mint sauce for roast lamb, combines with bourbon, sugar and ice for mint juleps, lifts a tomato sandwich to another level and is wonderful with yogurt, cream cheese, melon, pineapple, and most vegetables, especially peas, cucumber and new potatoes. *Vietnamese mint* is not a mint at all but a South-East Asian herb with leaves that are more or less spearmint-shaped and taste like a coarser, more assertive coriander. It is used in salads and curries and served with spring rolls and a dipping sauce, and is also used as a garnish. *Japanese peppermint* is a true mint that is not grown for culinary purposes but for the peppermint oil extracted from it.

OREGANO is closely related to marjoram but is more assertive. Like marjoram, it reaches its full flavour when dried. It grows wild in Greece and other Mediterranean countries and its fragrance and flavour are built into the cooking of that region, especially for vegetables such as tomato, eggplant and zucchini, and lamb.

PARSLEY is used by the handful both for cooking and for the "sprinkle of chopped parsley" that adds charm to soups and salads, vegetables, scrambled eggs and omelettes, rice, buttered potatoes and many fish, meat and chicken dishes. Parsley stalks are more strongly flavoured than the leaves and go into stocks and the cooking liquid for corned beef and are used to infuse the milk for béchamel sauce. Parsley is available in curly-leaf or flat-leaf (also called italian or continental) varieties; flat-leaf has a more concentrated flavour.

ROSEMARY is a woody, evergreen Mediterranean herb with strong, resinous fragrance and flavour. Its traditional partner is lamb: a branch can be used to brush chops as they are grilling or sprigs

can be tucked into slits in roast lamb. It also goes well with pork and pairs with tomato for pasta sauces and with eggplant as well as baked and fried potato.

SAGE, with its full, dry, balsamic scent and flavour, needs to be used sparingly as it can easily be too dominant. It is splendid with pork and, with onion, is the traditional stuffing for duck and goose. Italians pair it with veal and prosciutto for saltimbocca. Sage leaves fried in butter or oil just until crisp make an attractive garnish for veal and liver. Sage comes in the well known silver-grey variety and in a smaller variety with purplish leaves. The family also includes pineapple sage, whose pineapple-scented leaves can be chopped for fruit salad.

SORREL The refreshing acid tang of sorrel is magic with fish, veal and chicken and gives a lift to green salads. It is especially good in creamy chicken soup and cream sauce for fish, veal, pork, potatoes or carrots. It can also be cooked like spinach and served as a vegetable in its own right. Cook sorrel in non-reactive pans as aluminium ones can discolour it.

TARRAGON French tarragon is the desirable, subtly flavoured one; Russian has a coarser taste. Soft, slender tarragon leaves have an affinity with chicken, eggs and sauces for fish, and chopped tarragon combines with fine vinegar, egg yolks and butter for béarnaise sauce that is served on roast beef. A good way to have tarragon on hand is to mix chopped leaves with soft butter, shape into a roll with plastic wrap and place in the refrigerator, ready to be sliced on chicken, fish or vegetables.

THYME The savoury warmth of thyme is good with most meats and many vegetables from roast potatoes to sautéed eggplant and grilled tomatoes. It goes into bread and onion stuffings for poultry and rabbit or bread and lemon ones for fish; it pairs wonderfully with red wine in marinades and sauces. There are two well-known varieties, the "common" one with tiny, pointed grey-green leaves and the lemon one with larger green leaves. Common thyme is the stronger and the better to use in cooking, while lemon thyme's fresh flavour works best if added at the end of cooking or scattered over the finished dish. Except when you want the charm of the fresh leaves, dried thyme is a better ingredient because it is stronger.

CHOOSING

Fresh herbs must be bright and firm with no sign of wilting or discolouring. It can be hard to find a delicate herb such as dill or chervil that isn't drooping a little — if so, when home, immerse the whole bunch in a container of water, put it in the refrigerator and use it as soon as you can. Dried herbs should be bought packaged in airtight thick plastic or foil packs or in bottles, preferably with metal, not plastic caps. Herbs packed in cellophane or cardboard, which allow aromas to escape, have already been deteriorating before they are purchased.

STORING

Fresh herbs sold in a lidded plastic box can be stored in the refrigerator as is for a day or two. Bunches can go into a glass of water, away from heat, overnight. If they are to be kept longer, wrap a piece of folded absorbent paper round the end of the stems, wet it, enclose loosely in a plastic bag and refrigerate. Dried herbs should be stored away from heat or light in airtight packages or containers. They should not be stored in the refrigerator because being removed from the cold to a warm kitchen to be used, and then returned to the cold, may cause condensation to form in the pack and spoil the contents. All dried herbs deteriorate over time so they should be checked at least once a year — throw away those that are past their use-by dates.

Chermoulla

PREP TIME 15 MINUTES **MAKES** 1 CUP

½ cup (125ml) olive oil

⅓ cup (80ml) lemon juice

6 shallots (150g), sliced thinly

4 cloves garlic, crushed

1 teaspoon ground cumin

1 fresh long red chilli, sliced thinly

¼ cup finely chopped
fresh coriander

¼ cup finely chopped fresh
mint leaves

¼ cup finely chopped fresh
flat-leaf parsley

1 Combine ingredients in small bowl; use as a marinade or sauce.

NUTRITIONAL COUNT PER TABLESPOON 9.6g total fat (1.3g saturated fat); 376kJ (90 cal); 0.7g carbohydrate;
0.3g protein, 0.4g fibre

*Chermoulla is a Moroccan
blend of herbs and spices,
traditionally used for
preserving or seasoning
fish or meat. We use it as
a quick sauce for fried
fish and barbecued squid
or octopus, but you can
also use it as a baste
or marinade.*

Mint sauce

PREP + COOK TIME 10 MINUTES (PLUS STANDING TIME) **MAKES** 1 CUP

2 cups firmly packed fresh mint leaves

¼ cup (60ml) water

¾ cup (180ml) white wine vinegar

2 tablespoons caster sugar

1 Chop half of the mint coarsely; place in small heatproof bowl.

2 Combine the water, vinegar and sugar in small saucepan; stir over heat, without boiling,
until sugar dissolves. Pour liquid over chopped mint in bowl, cover; stand 3 hours.

3 Strain liquid into bowl; discard mint. Chop remaining mint coarsely; stir into liquid.
Blend or process until chopped finely. Serve with roast lamb.

NUTRITIONAL COUNT PER TABLESPOON 0.3g total fat (0.1g saturated fat); 234kJ (56 cal); 10.1g carbohydrate;
0.9g protein; 1.9g fibre

*Mint sauce is the
traditional accompaniment
to roast lamb. It also goes
well with falafel or mixed-
bean or rice salad. It is
important to let the mint,
vinegar, water and sugar
mixture stand so that the
mint flavour will be fully
extracted.*

Salsa verde

PREP TIME 20 MINUTES **MAKES** 1 CUP

½ cup finely chopped fresh
flat-leaf parsley

¼ cup finely chopped fresh dill

¼ cup finely chopped fresh chives

1 tablespoon wholegrain mustard

2 tablespoons lemon juice

2 tablespoons drained, rinsed
baby capers, chopped finely

1 clove garlic, crushed

⅓ cup (80ml) olive oil

1 Combine ingredients in small bowl. Serve with steaks, lamb cutlets or fish fillets.

NUTRITIONAL COUNT PER TABLESPOON 6.1g total fat (0.9g saturated fat); 242kJ (58 cal); 0.4g carbohydrate;
0.2g protein; 0.3g fibre

*Salsa verde ("green sauce")
is an Italian classic, a zesty
fresh herb sauce that
adds tang to hot or cold
poached or steamed fish
and is a traditional part of
bollito misto, the famous
Piedmontese version of the
boiled dinner. It also goes
well with corned beef,
grilled lamb cutlets and
poached salmon fillets.*

Pesto is the famous Genoese sauce served with all kinds of pasta and gnocchi and the traditional garnish for minestrone. It is also good as a dip for potato wedges, spooned on to grilled tomatoes and as a topping for potatoes baked in their skins: mix 1/3 cup pesto with 2/3 cup spreadable cream cheese to make enough topping for 8 potatoes.

For information on spaghetti, see Pasta, page 396.

Spaghetti with pesto

PREP + COOK TIME 25 MINUTES **SERVES** 4

2 cloves garlic, chopped coarsely

1/3 cup (50g) roasted pine nuts

1/2 cup (40g) finely grated parmesan cheese

2 cups firmly packed fresh basil leaves

1/2 cup (125ml) olive oil

500g spaghetti

1/2 cup (40g) flaked parmesan cheese

1 Blend or process garlic, nuts, grated cheese and basil until almost smooth. Gradually add oil in a thin, steady stream, processing until thick.

2 Cook pasta in large saucepan of boiling water, until just tender; drain, reserve 1/4 cup of the cooking liquid.

3 Combine pasta, pesto and reserved cooking liquid in large bowl. Serve with flaked cheese.

NUTRITIONAL COUNT PER SERVING 45.2g total fat (8.9g saturated fat); 3578kJ (859 cal); 86.2g carbohydrate; 23.6g protein; 5.6g fibre

---

An orange version of gremolata, the classic lemon-rind/parsley/garlic garnish for osso buco, is a brilliantly fresh and pungent garnish for a rich casserole.

Orange gremolata

PREP TIME 15 MINUTES **SERVES** 4

1/4 cup finely chopped fresh flat-leaf parsley

1 tablespoon finely grated orange rind

1 clove garlic, crushed

1 Combine ingredients in small bowl. Serve sprinkled over soups or stews.

NUTRITIONAL COUNT PER SERVING 0g total fat (0g saturated fat); 13kJ (3 cal); 0.4g carbohydrate; 0.1g protein; 0.4g fibre

---

Mint and lime granita with citrus salad

PREP + COOK TIME 15 MINUTES **SERVES** 4

2 medium oranges (480g)

2 small ruby red grapefruit (700g)

1/3 cup finely chopped fresh mint

2 tablespoons icing sugar

1 tablespoon lime juice

2 cups ice cubes

1 Segment orange and grapefruit into medium bowl.

2 Blend or process mint, sugar, juice and ice until ice is crushed; serve with fruit.

NUTRITIONAL COUNT PER SERVING 0.4g total fat (0g saturated fat); 385kJ (92 cal); 18.1g carbohydrate; 2.1g protein; 2.7g fibre

Horseradish

Horseradish is the grated root of a member of the mustard family. Its mustardy aroma and flavour are hot and penetrating: its enthusiasts love it on corned or roast beef, steak, pork, sausage, kidneys and pickled beetroot.

It is sometimes served in the form of a sauce, made with cream, mustard, vinegar and horseradish, or a thicker cream using whipped cream, or as horseradish butter. It is available in jars, with or without vinegar and flavourings such as salt and sugar.

Dried horseradish flakes are also available; these are reconstituted by keeping them covered with water, replenishing it as needed, until they soften, which can take up to 24 hours.

Beef and horseradish stew

PREP + COOK TIME 4 HOURS 10 MINUTES **SERVES** 6

2 tablespoons olive oil

1.5kg beef chuck steak, cut into 5cm cubes

3 medium brown onions (450g), sliced into wedges

3 cloves garlic, crushed

8cm piece fresh ginger (40g), grated

2 teaspoons curry powder

¼ cup (35g) plain flour

3 cups (750ml) beef stock

1 tablespoon worcestershire sauce

50g fresh horseradish, grated

¼ cup coarsely chopped fresh flat-leaf parsley

1 Preheat oven to 150°C/130°C fan-forced.

2 Heat oil in large flameproof casserole dish; cook beef, in batches, until browned. Cook onion, garlic and ginger in same dish, stirring, about 5 minutes or until onion softens. Add curry powder and flour; cook, stirring, 5 minutes.

3 Return beef to dish with stock, sauce and horseradish; stir over heat until mixture boils and thickens. Cover dish tightly; cook in oven for 3 hours, stirring occasionally.

4 Stir parsley through beef mixture off the heat just before serving.

NUTRITIONAL COUNT PER SERVING 18.5g total fat (6.2g saturated fat); 1810kJ (433 cal); 11.2g carbohydrate; 54.1g protein; 1.9g fibre

To preserve fresh horseradish, wash, peel and grate the roots, then fill screw-top jars about two-thirds full. Add ½ teaspoon salt and ¼ teaspoon sugar to each jar and fill with enough distilled white vinegar to cover generously. Add a piece of fresh chilli to the horseradish if you like. Place a round of white paper over the jar and screw down tightly.

For information on beef, see Beef, pages 46 & 47.

Horseradish sauce

PREP + COOK TIME 15 MINUTES **MAKES** 1½ CUPS

2 teaspoons olive oil

2 green onions, chopped finely

¼ cup (60ml) dry white wine

¼ cup (70g) prepared horseradish

300g sour cream

2 tablespoons lemon juice

1 teaspoon dijon mustard

2 teaspoons finely chopped fresh dill

2 tablespoons hot water

Serve this pungent sauce with corned or roast beef, rump steaks and grilled chicken breasts, and as a dip for potato wedges.

1 Heat oil in medium frying pan; cook onion, stirring, until soft. Add wine; bring to the boil then reduce heat. Simmer, uncovered, until liquid has almost evaporated.

2 Add horseradish, sour cream, juice and mustard; cook, stirring, until sauce is heated through. Stir in dill and the hot water off the heat.

NUTRITIONAL COUNT PER TABLESPOON 7.2g total fat (4.2g saturated fat); 305kJ (73 cal); 1g carbohydrate; 0.6g protein; 0.3g fibre

---

Beef and beetroot salad with horseradish crème fraîche

PREP + COOK TIME 45 MINUTES (PLUS STANDING TIME) **SERVES** 4

500g piece beef eye fillet, trimmed

2 tablespoons wholegrain mustard

1 tablespoon horseradish cream

2 tablespoons olive oil

1kg baby beetroot, trimmed

150g baby rocket leaves

2 lebanese cucumbers (260g), sliced thinly

1 cup loosely packed fresh flat-leaf parsley leaves

PARMESAN CROUTONS

1 small french bread stick (150g)

1 tablespoon olive oil

½ cup (40g) finely grated parmesan cheese

HORSERADISH CREME FRAICHE

¼ cup (60g) crème fraîche

2 tablespoons horseradish cream

1 tablespoon lemon juice

Parmesan croûtons are also delicious served with creamy soups such as celery, asparagus or cauliflower.

For information on beef, see Beef, pages 46 & 47; for fresh beetroot, see Beetroot, page 54; and for crème fraîche, see Cream, pages 142 & 143.

1 Preheat oven to 220°C/200°C fan-forced. Oil medium baking dish.

2 Tie beef with kitchen string at 3cm intervals. Combine mustard, horseradish and oil in small jug; brush all over beef. Place beef in dish with beetroot; roast, uncovered, 10 minutes.

3 Reduce oven to 200°C/180°C fan-forced; roast 20 minutes or until beef and beetroot are cooked. Cover beef; stand 15 minutes then slice thinly. Peel and halve beetroot.

4 Make parmesan croûtons. Combine ingredients for horseradish crème fraîche in bowl.

5 Combine rocket, cucumber, parsley and beetroot in large bowl. Serve salad topped with croûtons and beef, drizzled with crème fraîche.

PARMESAN CROUTONS Slice bread thinly; brush slices with oil, place on oven tray. Brown, in oven, towards end of beef cooking time; sprinkle with cheese, return to oven until it melts.

NUTRITIONAL COUNT PER SERVING 33.8g total fat (12.2g saturated fat); 2704kJ (647 cal); 40.7g carbohydrate; 40.2g protein; 10.5g fibre

Jerusalem Artichoke

This knobbly tuber is neither from Jerusalem nor an artichoke. It is native to the Americas and belongs to the sunflower family: the word Jerusalem is supposed to be a corruption of girasole, Italian for sunflower, while the artichoke part came from a fancied likeness to the taste of globe artichokes.

Its flavour is, in fact, delicately earthy/nutty/sweet and its texture when cooked is tender. It is often paired with leeks for a delicious soup, oiled and roasted like potato or pureed with cream and a touch of nutmeg as a vegetable accompaniment. It can also be used raw, cut into crunchy slices for a salad, but needs to be kept in a bowl of water acidulated with lemon juice until serving time as its cut surfaces will discolour otherwise. Jerusalem artichokes are in season from autumn to spring.

PREPARATION Trim off any roots, cut off knobbly bits and peel, dropping each one into acidulated water as you go.

CHOOSING Choose hard tubers with undamaged and slightly lustrous skin. Avoid any that are sprouting.

STORING Keep in a dry place away from heat or light for up to a week.

Like most dense root vegetables, jerusalem artichokes can be made into crisps. Preheat the oven to 200°C/180°C fan-forced; cut 1kg unpeeled jerusalem artichokes into very thin slices, place in a bowl with 2 tablespoons olive oil, 1 teaspoon salt and ½ teaspoon cracked black pepper and mix well. Place slices in a single layer on a wire rack set over a large baking dish and roast for 20 minutes until crisp. Cool and store in screw-top glass jars.

Jerusalem artichoke soup

PREP + COOK TIME 1 HOUR 20 MINUTES (PLUS COOLING TIME) **SERVES** 4

1 tablespoon lemon juice

1 litre (4 cups) water

10 medium jerusalem artichokes (600g)

1 tablespoon olive oil

1 large brown onion (200g), chopped coarsely

4 cloves garlic, crushed

2 medium potatoes (400g), chopped coarsely

1 litre (4 cups) chicken stock

1 Combine juice and the water in large bowl. Peel and coarsely chop artichokes; place in acidulated water.

2 Heat oil in large saucepan; cook onion and garlic, stirring, until onion softens. Add drained artichokes, potato and stock; bring to the boil. Reduce heat; simmer, covered, about 20 minutes or until potato is tender. Cool 15 minutes.

3 Blend or process soup, in batches, until smooth. Reheat soup in same pan. Bowls of soup can be served topped with jerusalem artichoke crisps (see side note for recipe).

NUTRITIONAL COUNT PER SERVING 5.5g total fat (0.9g saturated fat); 744kJ (178 cal); 20.8g carbohydrate; 7.7g protein; 7.2g fibre

Jicama

Also called the mexican turnip, mexican potato and yam bean, jicama doesn't taste like a turnip, potato or yam, but more like a sweeter water chestnut.

As with many foods, the use of jicama in various cuisines can be traced through history: the Spanish conquerors of Central America took it to the Philippines, which they had also conquered, in the 17th Century and from there it spread into Asia and the Pacific.

It is the juicy tuber of a vine native to Central America and is popular in Mexico and also used in Chinese and South-East Asian cooking. Like water chestnuts, jicama stays crisp through cooking. It is mainly eaten raw in Mexico, where its crisp, white flesh stars in both savoury salads and sweet fruit salads, and is eaten as a snack seasoned with chilli, salt and lime juice. It is also used in stews or boiled and served with butter or a creamy sauce. In Asia, it is used for stir-fries and added to soups.

PREPARATION Peel jicama thickly, removing the fibrous layer under the skin as well as the skin itself.

CHOOSING Jicama comes in weights from about 500g to several kilos. Look for firm, heavy tubers free of cracks and bruises.

STORING Store jicama in a cool, dry, airy place, where the tubers will remain in good condition for weeks. Like potatoes, jicamas will convert their starch to sugar if refrigerated and will deteriorate in flavour and texture.

Kaffir Lime Leaves

The kaffir lime tree is grown for its distinctive double leaves rather than its fruit. Kaffir lime leaves are quite different in scent and flavour from ordinary lime leaves.

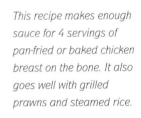

They are used in Asian cooking to give a heady citrus freshness to curries and sambals (relishes served with curry), laksa and other soups and fish and poultry dishes, especially those made with coconut cream. They are rather tough so they are shredded very finely before adding to a dish, or, if they used whole, they are removed before serving. To shred, first tear the leaves away on both sides from the hard central spine, discard the spine, stack two or three leaves together and cut into the finest possible strips. Kaffir lime leaves are available fresh and dried; fresh are better. The fruit of the tree is small, rough-skinned and rather dry, so it has no culinary use but its juice is used in traditional Indonesian medicine and its rind is used for its strong insecticidal properties.

CHOOSING Kaffir lime leaves should be undamaged, glossy and a rich dark green.

STORING The leaves will keep for a week or so in a paper bag enclosed in a plastic bag in the refrigerator, or they can be frozen in the bag, which helps retain their flavour, and used straight from the freezer.

Coconut and kaffir lime leaf sauce

PREP + COOK TIME 20 MINUTES **MAKES** 1 CUP

1 teaspoon peanut oil

1 clove garlic, crushed

2cm piece fresh ginger (10g), grated

1 teaspoon finely chopped coriander root and stem mixture

1 tablespoon finely chopped fresh lemon grass

4 fresh kaffir lime leaves, sliced thinly

140ml can coconut milk

½ cup (125ml) chicken stock

2 teaspoons fish sauce

1 tablespoon lime juice

1 teaspoon caster sugar

2 tablespoons finely chopped fresh coriander

This recipe makes enough sauce for 4 servings of pan-fried or baked chicken breast on the bone. It also goes well with grilled prawns and steamed rice.

1 Heat oil in medium frying pan; cook garlic, ginger, coriander root and stem mixture, lemon grass and half of the lime leaves, stirring, until fragrant.

2 Add coconut milk, stock, sauce, juice and sugar; bring to the boil. Reduce heat; simmer, uncovered, 3 minutes or until sauce thickens slightly. Strain into small jug; stir in remaining lime leaves and chopped coriander.

NUTRITIONAL COUNT PER ¼ CUP 2.9g total fat (2.2g saturated fat); 134kJ (32 cal); 1g carbohydrate; 0.5g protein; 0.3g fibre

Remember this recipe for serving to people who don't like their fish too fishy.

For information on perch, see Seafood, page 523; and for fresh ginger, see Ginger, page 222.

Kaffir lime and ginger perch parcels

PREP + COOK TIME 20 MINUTES **SERVES** 4

4 x 180g ocean perch fillets

3 green onions, sliced thinly

5cm piece fresh ginger (25g), sliced thinly

4 fresh kaffir lime leaves, shredded finely

2 teaspoons sesame oil

1 Preheat oven to 180°C/160°C fan-forced.

2 Place each fillet on large square of oiled foil; top each with onion, ginger and lime leaves, drizzle with oil. Gather corners together; fold to enclose. Place on oven trays.

3 Cook parcels 15 minutes or until fish is cooked through. Remove fish from foil, discard topping; serve with steamed rice and lime wedges.

NUTRITIONAL COUNT PER SERVING 3.4g total fat (0.5g saturated fat); 648kJ (155 cal); 6.3g carbohydrate; 30.4g protein; 0.2g fibre

This recipe is best made close to serving, but you can prepare all the ingredients and complete the recipe to the end of step 3 an hour or so ahead of time. You can spoon portions of pork on to spinach leaves to make individual servings on a large platter, or, if guests are seated, serve spinach and pork separately so that they can assemble their own.

For information on pork, see Pork, pages 440 & 441.

Sticky pork with kaffir lime leaves

PREP + COOK TIME 40 MINUTES **SERVES** 8

2 tablespoons peanut oil

300g pork mince

¾ cup (195g) grated palm sugar

⅓ cup (80ml) fish sauce

4 fresh kaffir lime leaves, shredded thinly

½ cup (40g) deep-fried shallots

½ cup (50g) deep-fried garlic

½ cup (70g) coarsely chopped roasted peanuts

1½ cups lightly packed fresh coriander leaves

4 fresh kaffir lime leaves, shredded thinly, extra

1 fresh long red chilli, sliced thinly

600g spinach, trimmed

1 lime (60g), cut into wedges

CORIANDER PASTE

4 coriander roots

5 cloves garlic, chopped

12 white peppercorns

1 Heat half of the oil in large frying pan; cook pork, stirring, 5 minutes or until browned lightly. Drain on absorbent paper; cool.

2 Meanwhile, make coriander paste.

3 Heat remaining oil in large frying pan; cook paste 1 minute or until fragrant. Add sugar, sauce and lime leaves; simmer, uncovered, 7 minutes or until thick. Add pork with half the shallots, half the garlic and half the peanuts; cook, uncovered, 5 minutes or until sticky. Add remaining shallots, garlic and peanuts. Stir in 1 cup of coriander leaves and extra lime leaves.

4 Top pork mixture with remaining coriander and chilli; serve with spinach and lime wedges.

CORIANDER PASTE Wash coriander roots thoroughly; chop coarsely. Using a mortar and pestle or food mill, crush the roots, garlic and peppercorns to form a smooth paste.

NUTRITIONAL COUNT PER SERVING 12.3g total fat (2.5g saturated fat); 1078kJ (258 cal); 26.1g carbohydrate; 12g protein; 2.8g fibre

Kale

Kale is a coarser, stronger-flavoured relative of cabbage. It comes in many varieties including ornamental ones which are grown for their frilly, brilliantly coloured leaves forming rosettes of white, red, pink, lavender, blue or violet.

The kale that interests cooks comes in smooth or curly varieties and in purple, green, called collard greens in the southern USA, or black, called cavalo nero in Italian cooking. Kale is highly nutritious, being strongly antioxidant and anti-inflammatory and high in beta carotene, vitamins K and C and reasonably rich in calcium. It is cooked in the same ways as cabbage and is especially good for soups and casseroles and for braising with such ingredients as onion, garlic, pork, bacon and sausage. Different varieties of kale are in season for most of the year. Summer kale is paler and thinner than winter kale, but many kale-lovers say that winter kale is best because frosts make it sweeter.

PREPARATION Remove very coarse outside leaves, cut off the other leaves, wash them and cut off their stalks and also their heavy central veins. Stack two or three leaves and cut them across into wide or narrow strips.

CHOOSING Kale should be undamaged, crisp and well coloured with a slight sheen.

STORING Store kale in a paper bag enclosed in a plastic bag in the refrigerator, where it will keep for 5 or 6 days.

Kale is easy to grow, insect-resistant and frost-tolerant — it will grow where even cabbages will not — so it is a staple green vegetable in inhospitable climates such as those of Scotland, Scandinavia and northern Germany. It was one of the most common vegetables grown in World War II Britain when there were food shortages and everyone was urged to "dig for victory", because it is so nutritious and even novice gardeners could grow it.

Kiwifruit

The name comes from the fact that this fruit was first grown commercially in New Zealand; before that, it was called chinese gooseberry, being native to eastern Asia and not much seen in the West (the gooseberry part of that name came from a fancied resemblance in shape to the european gooseberry).

1 GOLDEN KIWIFRUIT
2 KIWIFRUIT

Kiwifruit contains an enzyme which is a natural tenderiser. It is particularly useful for those often tough seafoods, octopus and calamari. Mix these with pureed kiwifruit, cover and refrigerate for 2-3 hours, then rinse, dry and cook. Also try adding a slice to a casserole or stew.

For a healthy "wake up" drink, blend 3 quartered medium kiwifruit, 70g seedless green grapes and ¼ cup water until smooth; pour into a glass.

The first shipment from New Zealand was to England in 1953, but it was the nouvelle cuisine fashion of the 1970s and 80s (a style of cooking that emphasised, among other things, decorative presentation) that made kiwifruit hugely popular for its designer looks in peeled cross-section, with black seeds in a circle enclosing white flesh surrounded by sunray-patterned, bright green flesh. That aspect of its appeal has lessened with the passing of nouvelle cuisine; kiwifruit slices are still used to decorate pavlova and some other desserts but are now at the stage of the fashion cycle where yesterday's fashion has become somewhat out of fashion. The important thing today is that kiwifruit is a luscious and particularly nutritious fruit, being high in vitamins, minerals and antioxidants, believed to be helpful in fighting heart disease, repairing DNA and protecting against cancer. It now comes in gold varieties as well as green and is used as a snack, as a dessert with ice-cream or in fruit salads, on cereal or with yogurt for breakfast or pureed for milkshakes or flavouring a creamy dessert. Kiwifruit is picked unripe and will keep well, refrigerated in that state, for weeks. Tart-flavoured when unripe, it will ripen in a paper bag at room temperature in a few days to a week. It is usually peeled before eating or scooped from the skin with a teaspoon as the thin brown skin is hairy, but the entire fruit can be eaten if the hairs are rubbed off with a paper towel and rinsed away. To enjoy kiwifruit at its best, when tartness and sweetness are in balance and the texture is luscious but firm, takes judgment or luck, as it quickly becomes over-soft and blandly sweet; however, a touch of lemon or, better, lime juice will restore the flavour balance and mashing the fruit or spooning it from the skin can make the softness feel right. Kiwifruit is in season in autumn and winter, but because the unripe fruit can be held in atmosphere-controlled storage for a long time, it is available all year.

CHOOSING Select large, undamaged fruit. For eating immediately, choose fruit that feels yielding but not soft when pressed. For fruit to be stored and ripened later, choose fruit that feels firm but not hard.

STORING Ripe kiwifruit can be stored in the refrigerator crisper for a day or two. Unripe kiwifruit can be stored in a covered container in the refrigerator for several weeks.

KIWIFRUIT AND
PINEAPPLE SALAD WITH
BASIL LEMON SYRUP

Kiwifruit and pineapple salad with basil lemon syrup

PREP + COOK TIME 40 MINUTES (PLUS REFRIGERATION TIME) **SERVES** 4

*A touch of the unexpected
— the basil gives an
intriguing, almost peppery
note to this tangy fruit
salad. You need 4 large
passionfruit for this recipe.*

*For information on fresh
pineapple, see Pineapple,
pages 429 & 430.*

1 ½ cups (375ml) water

2 x 5cm strips lemon rind

½ cup (125ml) lemon juice

1 tablespoon caster sugar

¼ cup firmly packed fresh basil leaves

6 medium kiwifruit (510g), sliced thinly

1 small pineapple (900g), quartered, sliced thinly

⅓ cup (80ml) passionfruit pulp

1 tablespoon finely shredded fresh basil

1 Bring the water, rind, juice, sugar and basil leaves to the boil in medium frying pan.
Reduce heat; simmer, uncovered, 20 minutes.

2 Strain syrup into medium jug; discard rind and basil. Cool 10 minutes; refrigerate.

3 Just before serving, combine syrup in large bowl with remaining ingredients.

NUTRITIONAL COUNT PER SERVING 0.5g total fat (0g saturated fat); 627kJ (150 cal); 26.6g carbohydrate;
3.6g protein; 9g fibre

Kohlrabi

The name comes from the German, meaning cabbage-turnip, but kohlrabi is simply a member of the cabbage family which develops a bulbous stem just above the ground which is the part of most interest to cooks.

The round purple or green globe, with smaller, leafy stems sprouting from the top, does look rather like a root vegetable and is solid like one, but is crisper in texture with a delicate cauliflower/turnip flavour. It can be used in soups or casseroles, peeled, boiled and either mashed with butter or sliced and sauteed in oil or butter, or it can be baked or microwaved whole and unpeeled, then the top can be cut off and the centre scooped out, mixed with other ingredients such as butter, cooked onion or bacon and herbs and filled back into the shell, and baked until browned on top. It is also excellent raw, coarsely shredded or cut in matchsticks for a salad. Kohlrabi is available in winter.

PREPARATION Trim the base and cut off the stalks (the leaves can be cooked like spinach). Peel or leave whole according to the recipe.

CHOOSING Select firm bulbs, large apple-size or smaller, for the best, sweetest flavour.

STORING Kohlrabi will keep in the refrigerator crisper for up to a week.

Kohlrabi cut into matchsticks, mixed with enough cream or sour cream to moisten, a touch of french or german mustard and a small spoonful of caraway seeds and chilled, is a lovely vegetable to eat with a pork chop, corned beef or hot boiled sausages such as kransky.

Lamb

Lamb is a young meat — it must be from animals younger than 1 year old with no permanent teeth to qualify for the name — so it is basically tender. As with all meat, the most tender and expensive cuts, suitable for "dry" cooking methods — grilling, frying and roasting — are those that lie along the back, because these parts have had the least exercise so they haven't developed tough connective tissue.

Lamb cutlets, racks, crown roasts and shanks may be "frenched", that is, cut and trimmed in the French way, with the bone completely cleaned and, in the case of cutlets, racks and crown roasts, all the fat trimmed off to leave a neat round of lean meat. Frenched shanks, sometimes called lamb drumsticks, have the bone trimmed shorter and completely cleaned, and the meat trimmed of excess fat, membrane and sinew. Frenched cuts are a little more expensive, and not everyone wants their lamb to be always fatless, but they are elegant for a lunch or dinner party. Some good butchers prepare their lamb like this and others will do it for you if you give them a few days' notice.

Cuts suitable for "wet" cooking methods — casseroling, stewing and soups — are the best for these methods precisely because they do have plenty of connective tissue, which is needed because long, slow, moist cooking breaks it down to give not only succulent tenderness but richness and flavour that an expensive cut would not provide. Lamb is usually hung by the butcher for several days to enhance flavour and tenderness before it is butchered into separate cuts

SPRING LAMB, usually 3–5 months old though the legal definition is 3–10 months, is available from late winter into summer. It is not only especially tender but especially sweet because it has fed on spring grass.

MILK-FED LAMB is unweaned lamb, usually under 8 weeks old. It is pale, very tender and sweet but so delicate in flavour that it needs flavoursome herbs, vegetables or sauces to set it off. It is available only in spring and usually needs to be ordered ahead. Milk-fed lamb is usually cooked whole or cut into quarters. A leg will provide 2 servings.

HOGGET AND MUTTON are not usually stocked by butchers and need to be ordered ahead. Hogget is a two-tooth animal 13–15 months old; mutton is at least 2 years old. These meats are seldom suitable for grilling but can be slow-roasted, casseroled, minced and

curried, and a carefully "boiled" (actually gently simmered) leg, cooked with herbs and served with onion or caper sauce, is delicious. Hogget and mutton may also be corned (salt-cured) and are cooked in the same way as corned beef.

LAMB CUTS

ROASTING cuts are leg, which may be bone-in or partly boned (called easy-carve); trimmed roasts, which are usually individual leg muscles seamed out for small, fatless roasts; loin on the bone or boned and rolled; saddle, which is two loins still joined; chump, a choice, small, compact roast with some bone; rack, which consists of 8 cutlets still joined or can be ordered by the number of cutlets required (usually 3 or 4 per person, depending on size); shoulder, either on the bone, which is tricky to carve, or boned and rolled; for slow-roasting only, forequarter roast, which consists of forequarter chops still joined but is usually sold boned and rolled; for slow-roasting only, rolled breast, a fatty cut.

Slow-roasting cuts will be tough if roasted at high heat. You may see cheaper cuts marked "roasting" but these are often tough.

When buying loin on the bone, saddle or rack of lamb, ask the butcher to chine it, which means chopping between the vertebrae of the backbone, or removing it altogether, to make carving easy. For a spectacular presentation, two racks of lamb can be sewn together with the fat side out and the bones alternating, like swords at a military wedding, to make a guard of honour, or two racks can be sewn together with all the bones outward to make a crown roast. The butcher will do these if you ask him ahead.

To judge when a roast is done to your taste, use a meat thermometer or run a fine skewer into the centre and check the juice that comes out. Red juice means rare, pink medium and clear well done.

All roasts should be rested in a warm place, loosely covered with foil, for 15 minutes before serving to allow the juices to settle and the meat to become more succulent.

GRILLING, CHAR-GRILLING AND BARBECUING cuts are butterflied leg (boned and opened out — order ahead of time and ask the butcher to do this); chump and loin chops, preferably cut double-thick if they are to be barbecued; cutlets, provided they are cut double-thick if they are to be barbecued or grilled under an overhead grill — single ones can be char-grilled; for char-grilling only, fillet or backstrap, which is from the boned-out loin.

To judge when meat is grilled or pan-fried to your taste, press the surface with a finger or the back of the tongs. Rare meat feels soft and spongy, medium-rare soft but springy, and well-done quite firm.

All grilled meat should be rested in a warm place, loosely covered in foil, for 5 minutes to allow the juices to settle and the meat to become more succulent.

PAN-FRYING cuts are cutlets, plain or crumbed; fillet; backstrap; leg, topside or round steaks; trimmed steaks, which are any of these steaks trimmed of all visible fat.

CASSEROLING Cuts for casseroling are forequarter chops; neck chops (rosettes); shank; cubed meat from the forequarter or breast.

POTROASTING Cuts for potroasting (braising in one piece) are rolled shoulder; forequarter roast; trimmed roasts.

MINCED LAMB is used in pies, in Middle Eastern recipes for meatballs and stuffed savoury pastries and in Greek moussaka.

CHOOSING
As always, a supplier you can trust is your best bet for buying good meat. In general, lamb should be rosy red and fine-grained with white fat. Coarse meat or discoloured fat usually mean the animal was in poor condition.

STORING
Transfer meat to a container with the bottom lined with 2 thicknesses of absorbent paper towels, and cover loosely with foil. The more it has been cut and handled, the less time it will keep. Minced lamb or lamb sausages should be stored for no longer than 2 days, diced or cubed meat 3 days, steaks, chops or cutlets 4 days, boned and rolled roasts 2–3 days, roasts on the bone 3–5 days, and corned meat 1 week. Lamb freezes well though it will lose some juice as it thaws. Freeze in a freezer bag enclosed in a second bag; thaw in the refrigerator: small cuts may take 12 hours or more, larger ones may need 24 hours or more.

🐑 **OTHER RECIPES USING LAMB**
Char siu lamb and noodle stir-fry, p340
Dukkah-crusted lamb cutlets with
  roasted garlic yogurt, p566
Grilled lamb with spicy peach salsa, p414
Lamb and okra in rich tomato sauce
  with garlic confit, p369
Lamb biryani, p500–1
Lamb teriyaki with broccolini, p512
Maple syrup-glazed lamb shanks, p581
Moussaka timbales, p161
Persian lamb and rhubarb stew, p491
Za'atar-crumbed lamb backstrap, p566

Tomato braised lamb shanks

PREP + COOK TIME 3 HOURS 20 MINUTES **SERVES** 8

2 tablespoons olive oil

16 french-trimmed lamb shanks (4kg)

1 large red onion (300g), sliced thinly

1 clove garlic, crushed

2 tablespoons tomato paste

1 cup (250ml) dry red wine

2 cups (500ml) chicken stock

1 cup (250ml) water

400g can diced tomatoes

2 tablespoons coarsely chopped fresh rosemary

Lamb shanks are one of the great comfort foods, and, like most casseroles, they will cook with very little attention. Soft polenta is the "mashed potato" of northern Italy, another comfort food that is good with any meat in a sauce or gravy.

1 Preheat oven to 200°C/180°C fan-forced.

2 Heat half the oil in large baking dish; brown lamb, in batches.

3 Heat remaining oil in same dish; cook onion and garlic, stirring, until onion softens. Add paste; cook, stirring, 2 minutes. Add wine; bring to the boil. Boil, uncovered, until liquid reduces by about half. Return lamb to dish with stock, the water, undrained tomatoes and rosemary; cover, cook in oven, turning lamb occasionally, about 3 hours.

4 Remove lamb from dish; cover to keep warm. Reserve pan juices.

5 Serve lamb drizzled with juices and accompanied with soft polenta.

NUTRITIONAL COUNT PER SERVING 9.7g total fat (3g saturated fat); 1580kJ (378 cal); 4.6g carbohydrate; 61.6g protein; 1.4g fibre

Mongolian lamb and noodle stir-fry

PREP + COOK TIME 40 MINUTES **SERVES** 4

600g lamb backstrap, sliced thinly

⅓ cup (80ml) sweet sherry

2 tablespoons dark soy sauce

2 tablespoons sweet chilli sauce

2 tablespoons peanut oil

1 large brown onion (200g), sliced thinly

2 cloves garlic, crushed

1 medium green capsicum (200g), sliced thinly

175g broccolini, cut into 3cm lengths

1 tablespoon brown sugar

1 teaspoon sesame oil

⅓ cup (80ml) chicken stock

400g hokkien noodles

You can substitute any asian green, such as buk choy or gai lan, for the broccolini, if you prefer. Thick, yellow hokkien noodles are available in the refrigerated section at most supermarkets. They are sold ready to eat.

For more information on hokkien noodles, see Noodles, pages 334 & 335.

1 Combine lamb with half the sherry, half the soy sauce and half the sweet chilli sauce in medium bowl.

2 Heat half the oil in wok; stir-fry lamb, in batches, until browned.

3 Heat remaining oil in wok; stir-fry onion and garlic until onion softens. Add capsicum and broccolini; stir-fry until vegetables are tender. Return lamb to wok with remaining ingredients; stir-fry until hot.

NUTRITIONAL COUNT PER SERVING 17.4g total fat (4.5g saturated fat); 2600kJ (622 cal); 63.6g carbohydrate; 44.5g protein; 5.4g fibre

TOMATO BRAISED LAMB SHANKS

Fresh broad beans are seasonal, but frozen ones are available all year round. If you can't find them, use frozen peas instead.

For more information on fresh broad beans, see Beans, Fresh, pages 40–41.

Lamb leg roast with broad bean mash

PREP + COOK TIME 1 HOUR 50 MINUTES (PLUS REFRIGERATION TIME) **SERVES** 6

2kg lamb leg

2 tablespoons olive oil

2 cloves garlic, crushed

1 tablespoon wholegrain mustard

2 teaspoons finely grated lemon rind

1 tablespoon lemon juice

1.5kg potatoes, chopped coarsely

2 cups (240g) peeled broad beans

40g butter

¾ cup (180ml) hot milk

MINT SAUCE

2 cups firmly packed fresh mint leaves

2 cloves garlic, quartered

½ cup (125ml) olive oil

¼ cup (60ml) white wine vinegar

1 tablespoon caster sugar

1 Using sharp knife, score lamb skin at 2cm intervals. Combine lamb, oil, garlic, mustard, rind and juice in large bowl. Cover; refrigerate 3 hours or overnight.

2 Preheat oven to 200°C/180°C fan-forced.

3 Place lamb on oiled wire rack over large baking dish; roast about 45 minutes. Cover lamb; stand 10 minutes, slice thinly.

4 Meanwhile, boil, steam or microwave potato and beans, separately, until tender; drain. Push potato through fine sieve into large bowl; stir in butter and milk until smooth. Place beans in small bowl; crush coarsely with fork. Fold beans into potato mixture.

5 Make mint sauce.

6 Serve lamb with mint sauce and broad bean mash.

MINT SAUCE Blend or process mint and garlic until smooth; with motor operating, gradually add oil, in a thin steady stream, until mixture is smooth. Stir in vinegar and sugar.

NUTRITIONAL COUNT PER SERVING 45.7g total fat (13.9g saturated fat); 3373kJ (807 cal); 32.6g carbohydrate; 63.6g protein; 6.4g fibre

Meal-in-a-pot stews like this, bulked up with inexpensive barley and potatoes, were once considered "poor people's food", but now everyone enjoys their savoury, sustaining goodness.

For information on pearl barley, see Grains, page 228.

Irish lamb and barley stew

PREP + COOK TIME 1 HOUR 50 MINUTES **SERVES** 6

2 tablespoons olive oil

1kg diced lamb shoulder

1 large brown onion (200g), chopped coarsely

2 medium carrots (240g), chopped coarsely

2 stalks celery (300g), trimmed, chopped coarsely

2 cloves garlic, crushed

1 litre (4 cups) chicken stock

2 cups (500ml) water

1 cup (200g) pearl barley

4 sprigs fresh thyme

3 medium potatoes (600g), chopped coarsely

2 cups (160g) finely shredded cabbage

⅓ cup finely chopped fresh flat-leaf parsley

1 Heat half the oil in large saucepan; cook lamb, in batches, until browned.

2 Heat remaining oil in same pan; cook onion, carrot, celery and garlic, stirring, until vegetables soften. Return lamb to pan with stock, the water, barley and thyme; bring to the boil. Reduce heat; simmer, covered, 1 hour, skimming fat from surface occasionally.

3 Add potato; simmer, uncovered, 20 minutes or until potato is tender. Add cabbage; simmer, uncovered, until cabbage is just tender. Discard thyme. Serve sprinkled with parsley.

NUTRITIONAL COUNT PER SERVING 22.6g total fat (8.2g saturated fat); 2224kJ (532 cal); 37.4g carbohydrate; 40.4g protein; 8.6g fibre

---

Like the word casserole, the word tagine means both the food and the pot in which it is cooked, an attractive pottery vessel with a shallow circular base and a tall, conical lid which collects and condenses the steam so that it drips or slides back into the food in a continuous cycle.

For information on dried apricots, see Apricots, pages 14 & 15 (see also Fruit, Dried, page 192); for preserved lemons, see Lemons, pages 296 & 297; and for almonds, see Nuts, page 344.

Lamb, apricot and almond tagine

PREP + COOK TIME 1 HOUR 50 MINUTES **SERVES** 4

2 tablespoons olive oil

1kg diced lamb

12 shallots (300g), halved

1 medium red capsicum (200g), chopped coarsely

2 cloves garlic, crushed

2cm piece fresh ginger (10g), grated

1 teaspoon ground cumin

1½ cups (375ml) water

1½ cups (375ml) chicken stock

½ teaspoon saffron threads

1 cup (150g) dried apricot halves

1 tablespoon finely chopped preserved lemon

200g green beans, trimmed, chopped coarsely

½ cup (70g) slivered almonds

1 Heat half the oil in large saucepan; cook lamb, in batches, until browned.

2 Heat remaining oil in same pan; cook shallot, capsicum, garlic, ginger and cumin, stirring, until fragrant.

3 Return lamb to pan; add the water, stock and saffron, bring to the boil. Reduce heat; simmer, covered, about 1 hour or until lamb is tender. Add apricots, lemon and beans; simmer, uncovered, 15 minutes. Serve tagine sprinkled with nuts.

NUTRITIONAL COUNT PER SERVING 41.7g total fat (12.1g saturated fat); 3018kJ (722 cal); 22.1g carbohydrate; 61.3g protein; 7.8g fibre

Lamb korma

PREP + COOK TIME 1 HOUR 10 MINUTES (PLUS REFRIGERATION TIME) **SERVES** 4

A korma is a fairly mild, rich curry with a creamy sauce. This recipe uses a ready-made paste, which is easily found in supermarkets.

⅓ cup (55g) blanched almonds

3 tablespoons ghee

800g lamb strips

1 large brown onion (200g), sliced thinly

4cm piece fresh ginger (20g), grated

2 cloves garlic, crushed

2 teaspoons poppy seeds

½ cup (150g) korma paste

½ cup (125ml) chicken stock

300ml cream

⅓ cup (95g) yogurt

1 Blend or process nuts until finely ground.

2 Heat 2 tablespoons of the ghee in large saucepan; cook lamb, in batches, until browned.

3 Heat remaining ghee in same pan; cook onion, ginger and garlic, stirring, until onion softens. Add ground nuts, seeds and paste; cook, stirring, until fragrant.

4 Return lamb to pan with stock and cream; simmer, uncovered, about 15 minutes or until sauce thickens slightly. Serve korma with yogurt.

NUTRITIONAL COUNT PER SERVING 84.1g total fat (40.3g saturated fat); 4172kJ (998 cal); 9.2g carbohydrate; 50.6g protein; 6.4g fibre

Lamb racks with mustard maple glaze

PREP + COOK TIME 30 MINUTES **SERVES** 4

A plain green vegetable such as beans or sugar snap peas provides great contrasting texture and colour with this luxurious meat and vegetable combination.

For information on maple syrup, see Sugar, page 579; and for wholegrain mustard, see Mustard, pages 328 & 329.

4 x 4 french-trimmed lamb cutlet racks (720g)

2 cloves garlic, sliced thinly

2 medium parsnips (500g), cut into 2cm cubes

2 small kumara (500g), cut into 2cm cubes

½ cup loosely packed fresh flat-leaf parsley leaves

MUSTARD MAPLE GLAZE

50g butter

⅓ cup (80ml) maple syrup

2 tablespoons wholegrain mustard

1 Preheat oven to 200°C/180°C fan-forced.

2 Make mustard maple glaze.

3 Meanwhile, using sharp knife, make cuts in lamb; press garlic slices into cuts. Place lamb in large oiled baking dish; brush with 2 tablespoons of the glaze.

4 Combine remaining glaze, parsnip and kumara in medium bowl.

5 Place vegetables in baking dish with lamb; roast, uncovered, about 15 minutes or until vegetables are tender and lamb is cooked as desired. Stir parsley into vegetables; serve with lamb.

MUSTARD MAPLE GLAZE Cook ingredients in small saucepan, stirring, until thickened slightly.

NUTRITIONAL COUNT PER SERVING 26.2g total fat (13.8g saturated fat); 2153kJ (515 cal); 44.4g carbohydrate; 22.8g protein; 5.5g fibre

Leeks

Leeks are the mild members of the onion family. Thin young ones, braised whole, are an elegant vegetable to serve with a sauce as a course in their own right or with meats, fish or poultry.

A soft and golden mass of butter-cooked leek is such a kitchen treasure that it is worth multiplying the quantity you need for a recipe and freezing the rest in batches, ready for instant duty, via the microwave, for any of the uses mentioned in this entry.

❧ **OTHER RECIPES USING LEEKS**
Artichoke fricassee, p19
Green pea soup with
  mint pistou, p427
Gruyère, leek and bacon tart, p406
Potato and leek soup, p450
Roasted cauliflower and
  garlic soup, p95

This recipe makes enough sauce for 6 servings of grilled ocean trout fillets or chicken breasts, pan-fried pork cutlets or grilled white fish fillets.

Diners may need sharp, unserrated knives to cut even young, tender leeks without struggling. Larger ones, sliced and cooked slowly in butter or oil, melt to a luscious mass that can be used in the filling for a savoury tart, a pizza topping, a risotto, a frittata, a soup or a sauce for pasta, chicken or fish. Leeks are available all year, with their peak season from spring to autumn.

PREPARATION The part that is eaten is the thick white stem and the first, pale part of the green top. Because leeks are planted deep to keep them white, they harbour soil between the leaves and have to be washed to remove it. Trim off the green top within a centimetre or two of the white part, cutting to a point so that you remove more of the coarse outside leaves than the tender inner ones. Remove coarse outside leaves and trim off the roots, leaving layers attached at the base. Split the remaining green part and the first few centimetres of the white part down into halves or quarters, and immerse upside-down in water, plunging it up and down to dislodge the dirt.

CHOOSING Buy undamaged leeks, not too large and coarse as they will have more wastage than smaller ones. Leeks to be served whole must be fresh and slim, not much more than a centimetre thick.

STORING Chop off the dark-green tops, enclose the leeks in a paper bag, then in a plastic one, and refrigerate for up to a week.

Leek and saffron sauce

PREP + COOK TIME 20 MINUTES **MAKES** 1½ CUPS

1 tablespoon olive oil
1 small leek (200g), halved lengthways, sliced thinly
2 cloves garlic, crushed
1 teaspoon plain flour

¼ cup (60ml) dry white wine
300ml cream
pinch saffron
1 tablespoon finely chopped fresh flat-leaf parsley

1 Heat oil in medium frying pan; cook leek and garlic, stirring, about 5 minutes or until leek softens. Add flour; cook, stirring, 1 minute or until mixture bubbles and thickens. Add wine; cook, stirring, until sauce boils and reduces by half.
2 Add cream and saffron; bring to the boil. Redue heat; simmer, uncovered, 5 minutes or until sauce thickens slightly. Stir in parsley off the heat.

NUTRITIONAL COUNT PER TABLESPOON 8.3g total fat (4.9g saturated fat); 339kJ (81 cal); 0.9g carbohydrate; 0.5g protein; 0.3g fibre

1 BABY PENCIL LEEKS
2 MATURE LEEKS

Serve the oysters on a bed of rock salt to keep them steady. Any salmon roe (eggs) that is left makes a wonderful hors d'oeuvre on squares of rye bread spread with sour cream, with a few drops of lemon juice squeezed over.

Oysters with leek confit

PREP + COOK TIME 1 HOUR 15 MINUTES (PLUS STANDING TIME) **SERVES** 4

3 small leeks (600g), sliced thinly

2 teaspoons salt

24 oysters, on the half shell (600g)

50g butter

¼ cup (60ml) water

2 tablespoons salmon roe

1 Combine leek and salt in sieve over medium bowl; stand 1 hour.

2 Meanwhile, remove oysters from shells; wash shells, dry thoroughly, reserve. Refrigerate oysters until required.

3 Rinse leek well under cold water; drain. Pat dry with absorbent paper.

4 Melt butter in medium frying pan; cook leek with the water, uncovered, stirring occasionally, over low heat about 45 minutes or until leek breaks down and is almost pulpy. Cool 10 minutes.

5 Divide shells among serving plates; divide leek confit among shells. Place one oyster on leek mixture; top with roe.

NUTRITIONAL COUNT PER SERVING 12.8g total fat (7.5g saturated fat); 748kJ (179 cal); 4g carbohydrate; 11g protein; 2.7g fibre

---

You could serve these alone as a first course, or as an impressive accompaniment to veal or fish. Be sure to supply diners with sharp knives, as even baby leeks can be hard to cut with blunt ones.

Braised baby leeks

PREP + COOK TIME 40 MINUTES **SERVES** 4

16 baby pencil leeks (1.3kg)

30g butter

⅔ cup (160ml) chicken stock

2 tablespoons dry white wine

1 teaspoon finely grated lemon rind

2 tablespoons lemon juice

¼ cup (20g) flaked parmesan cheese

¼ cup coarsely chopped fresh flat-leaf parsley

1 Carefully trim root end from leeks, leaving each leek in one piece. Trim leeks into 15cm lengths; halve lengthways. Rinse well under cold water; drain.

2 Melt butter in large frying pan; cook leeks 1 minute. Add stock, wine, rind and juice; bring to the boil. Reduce heat; simmer, covered, 15 minutes or until leeks are tender. Uncover; simmer about 5 minutes or until liquid has reduced by half.

3 Serve leeks drizzled with cooking liquid then sprinkled with cheese and parsley.

NUTRITIONAL COUNT PER SERVING 8.7g total fat (5.2g saturated fat); 644kJ (154 cal); 8.3g carbohydrate; 6.5g protein; 6g fibre

Lemon Grass

Lemon grass is basic to South-East Asian cooking. Its stems are rich in citral, the substance that also gives lemon rind its fragrance and flavour, so that it not only gives fresh, sharp lemon flavour to a dish but perfumes it too.

Fresh lemon grass

Chopped lemon grass is quite tedious to prepare but freezes well — an hour stripping, slicing and food-processing a sizeable quantity, then bagging it in batches and freezing it, will make your Asian cooking much more relaxed.

The pale lower and inner part of the lemon grass stem, revealed when the leaves and tough outer layers are stripped away, is the part used in cooking. It is still rather hard and fibrous and should be sliced very thinly crossways to break the fibres before chopping or grinding as the recipe directs. Lemon grass is an ingredient in curry pastes and marinades, and is used fresh in many dishes, especially seafood and chicken ones and in salads. Complete stems can be lightly pounded to bruise them, tied in a knot and used as a bed on which fish or chicken is steamed or barbecued in foil, or added to soups or sauces during cooking; remove before serving. Lemon grass is also used in Caribbean cooking and for teas in Latin America and West Africa. It is available fresh all year, and also in dried and powdered form.

CHOOSING Pick fresh-looking lemon grass with firm, white stems.

STORING Store lemon grass as whole stems or pieces in a freezer bag in the freezer for up to 6 months.

Lemon grass chicken curry

PREP + COOK TIME 1 HOUR 10 MINUTES **SERVES** 4

Curry pastes vary in flavour and chilli heat from brand to brand, but in general those called korma, tikka, penang or yellow are milder, while balti, tandoori, rogan josh , leang or red are medium-hot and hot ones are called vindaloo, madras, extra hot, green or crying tiger.

For information on chicken, see Poultry, pages 456 & 457.

1 tablespoon vegetable oil

24 chicken drumettes (1.7kg)

1 medium brown onion (150g), sliced thinly

3 cloves garlic, crushed

½ teaspoon cracked black pepper

3 x 10cm sticks fresh lemon grass (60g), chopped finely

1 long green chilli, chopped finely

¼ cup (75g) mild curry paste

1 tablespoon grated palm sugar

½ cup (125ml) chicken stock

½ cup (125ml) water

1 medium red capsicum (200g), sliced thinly

1 medium carrot (120g), cut into matchsticks

4 green onions, sliced thinly

1 Heat oil in large flameproof casserole dish; cook chicken, in batches, until browned. Drain and discard cooking juices.

2 Cook brown onion, garlic, pepper, lemon grass and chilli in same dish, stirring, until onion softens. Add paste; cook, stirring, until fragrant. Return chicken to dish; cook, stirring, 5 minutes.

3 Add sugar, stock and the water; cook, covered, 10 minutes. Uncover; simmer about 10 minutes or until chicken is cooked through. Remove chicken from dish; cover to keep warm. Add capsicum and carrot; cook, uncovered, about 5 minutes or until curry sauce thickens and vegetables are just tender. Stir green onion into curry off the heat.

4 Serve chicken topped with curried vegetable mixture.

NUTRITIONAL COUNT PER SERVING 36.3g total fat (9g saturated fat); 2286kJ (547 cal); 9.9g carbohydrate; 43.8g protein; 4.3g fibre

LEMON GRASS CHICKEN CURRY

Ocean trout with lemon grass and lime hollandaise

PREP + COOK TIME 30 MINUTES **SERVES** 4

10cm stick fresh lemon grass (20g), chopped finely

3 fresh kaffir lime leaves, shredded thinly

1 tablespoon finely grated lime rind

⅓ cup (80ml) lime juice

3 egg yolks

200g unsalted butter, melted

3 fresh kaffir lime leaves, chopped finely

4 x 200g ocean trout fillets

The egg-yolk and juice mixture is thick enough when it starts to cling to the whisk and you start to see the bottom of the bowl with each stroke. For notes on preparing kaffir lime leaves, see Kaffir Lime Leaves, page 275.

For information on ocean trout, see Seafood, page 523.

1 To make lemon grass and lime hollandaise, combine lemon grass, shredded lime leaves, rind and juice in small saucepan; bring to the boil. Reduce heat; simmer, uncovered, until liquid reduces to 1 tablespoon. Strain through fine sieve into medium heatproof bowl; cool 10 minutes. Discard solids in sieve.

2 Add egg yolks to juice mixture in bowl; set bowl over medium saucepan of simmering water, do not allow water to touch base of bowl. Whisk mixture over heat until thickened.

3 Remove bowl from heat; gradually add melted butter in thin, steady stream, whisking constantly until sauce has thickened. (If sauce is too thick, a tablespoon of hot water can be added.) Stir in finely chopped lime leaves.

4 Meanwhile, cook fish in heated oiled large frying pan until cooked as desired. Serve with hollandaise.

NUTRITIONAL COUNT PER SERVING 52.9g total fat (30.1g saturated fat); 2675kJ (640 cal); 0.7g carbohydrate; 41.6g protein; 0.1g fibre

Lemons

Lemons provide two kitchen treasures: their acid juice, important as an ingredient in hundreds of dishes both sweet and savoury and as an essential seasoning, and their rind, which provides intense lemon fragrance and flavour with little acidity. Most cooks rank lemons second only to salt and pepper as a kitchen staple to keep always on hand. Lemon season is winter, with a second, lesser crop in summer, but lemons are available all year round.

A lemon will give more juice if it is first warmed in hot water or the oven (180°C for 2 minutes), or rolled firmly over a hard surface. A medium lemon yields about 2 tablespoons of juice, so that is the amount to use when recipes say "the juice of 1 lemon".

Microplane

LEMON WEDGES are a standard garnish to hot or cold seafood and crumbed, fried foods such as lamb cutlets, veal schnitzel or chicken breast, and are frequently offered with grilled, char-grilled or barbecued lamb, pork or veal chops as well as curries, spicy rice and lentil dishes. For wedges to be served to diners, remove any seeds and cut off the strip of white core.

LEMON SLICES may be dropped into fruit drinks or hot or iced tea, or may be slit from edge to centre to sit on the rim of the glass. Thin slices brushed with oil may be placed on chicken, pork or veal as it grills under the grill, or char-grilled or barbecued separately to place on the meat for serving.

LEMON JUICE is used for its flavour and to prevent browning of apples, pears, peaches, bananas, potatoes, artichokes, celeriac, and avocados after they are peeled or cut. A squeeze of lemon juice will sour milk or cream as a substitute for commercial buttermilk or sour cream in a recipe. A little lemon juice and sugar adds zing to any fruit salad, and adds flavour to a tasteless crop of fruit like peaches or strawberries; sprinkle sugar and juice over the cut fruit and stand at room temperature for an hour or more, gently mixing once or twice.

LEMON RIND may be grated to go in cakes, biscuits and desserts, as well as meatballs, meat loaves and stuffings. Rind matchsticks may be added to a fruit, vegetable, chicken or seafood salad. Add a strip to poaching liquid for fruit or a spiral into a cocktail. Lemon rind is also important in jam-making as its underlying white pith is rich in pectin, the substance that causes jam to set.

PRESERVED LEMONS are salt-cured, quartered lemons, are available at many delicatessens and are easy to make at home. They have quite a different flavour from fresh lemon. Only the skin is used; it is good sliced and served with seafood or

roast lamb or chicken, added to lamb or chicken casseroles, mixed with couscous or rice or used in dressings, salsas and salads, especially ones to go with seafood.

PREPARATION
Lemons are sometimes waxed to prevent drying out, so if you are using the rind, wash the fruit in warm water, rubbing with a cloth, before using. To obtain rind, grate it off with an ordinary grater, a microplane or a special zester, or peel with a vegetable peeler, being careful to take only the coloured layer and not the underlying white pith. Use a pastry brush to dislodge any rind that sticks to the grater.

CHOOSING
Lemons should be brightly coloured and heavy for their size. Once picked, they do not ripen further so greenish ones will not give as much juice nor be as full-flavoured as ripe fruit. If there is a choice, choose thin-skinned rather than thick-skinned ones as they'll have more juice for their weight. Avoid any with soft spots.

STORING
Lemons will keep in good condition at mild room temperature for a week or more; keep an eye on them and remove any that show mould, and also wash and thoroughly dry the fruit they were touching. For longer storage, store in the refrigerator crisper for up to 4 weeks.

❧ OTHER RECIPES USING LEMONS
Artichokes with lemon herb butter, p19
Lemon aioli, p366
Lemon and macadamia dressing, p367
Lemon and ricotta-filled zucchini flowers, p659
Moroccan couscous salad with preserved lemon dressing, p232
Rigatoni with zucchini, lemon and mint, p398
White chocolate, lemon and thyme truffles, p128

Lemon delicious pudding

PREP + COOK TIME 1 HOUR **SERVES** 6

Serve this old favourite with unsweetened pouring cream.

125g butter, melted
2 teaspoons finely grated lemon rind
1 ½ cups (330g) caster sugar

3 eggs, separated
½ cup (75g) self-raising flour
⅓ cup (80ml) lemon juice
1 ⅓ cups (330ml) milk

1 Preheat oven to 180°C/160°C fan-forced. Grease six 1-cup (250ml) ovenproof dishes.
2 Combine butter, rind, sugar and yolks in large bowl. Stir in sifted flour then juice. Gradually stir in milk; mixture should be smooth and runny.
3 Beat egg whites in small bowl with electric mixer until soft peaks form; fold into lemon mixture, in two batches.
4 Place ovenproof dishes in large baking dish; divide lemon mixture among dishes. Add enough boiling water to baking dish to come halfway up sides of ovenproof dishes. Bake, uncovered, about 45 minutes.

NUTRITIONAL COUNT PER SERVING 22g total fat (13.5g saturated fat); 2069kJ (495 cal); 67.1g carbohydrate; 6.7g protein; 0.5g fibre

Demerara sugar is a large-crystal, light brown type (see Sugar, pages 576 & 578). If you can't find it by that name, look for coffee sugar.

For information on sour cream, see Cream, page 142; and for pine nuts, see Nuts, page 344.

Lemon sour cream cake

PREP + COOK TIME 1 HOUR 15 MINUTES (PLUS COOLING TIME) **SERVES** 16

250g butter, softened

1 tablespoon finely grated lemon rind

2 cups (440g) caster sugar

6 eggs

¾ cup (180g) sour cream

2 cups (300g) plain flour

¼ cup (35g) self-raising flour

½ cup (80g) pine nuts

1 tablespoon demerara sugar

¼ cup (90g) honey

1 Preheat oven to 170°C/150°C fan-forced. Grease deep 23cm-square cake pan; line base and two opposite sides with baking paper, extending paper 5cm over sides.
2 Beat butter, rind and caster sugar in medium bowl with electric mixer until light and fluffy. Add eggs, one at a time, beating until just combined between additions (mixture might separate at this stage, but will come together later). Stir in sour cream and sifted flours, in two batches. Spread mixture into pan; bake 15 minutes.
3 Meanwhile, combine pine nuts and demerara sugar in small bowl.
4 Carefully remove cake from oven; working quickly, sprinkle evenly with nut mixture, press gently into cake. Return cake to oven; bake further 45 minutes. Stand cake 5 minutes; turn, top-side up, onto wire rack.
5 Meanwhile, heat honey in small saucepan. Drizzle hot cake evenly with hot honey; cool before serving.

NUTRITIONAL COUNT PER SERVING 23g total fat (12.2g saturated fat); 1785kJ (427 cal); 48.9g carbohydrate; 5.8g protein; 1.1g fibre

No shop-bought lemonade is as fresh and delicious as this.

Homemade lemonade

PREP + COOK TIME 25 MINUTES (PLUS REFRIGERATION TIME) **MAKES** 6.25 LITRES (25 CUPS) DILUTED

4 medium lemons (560g)

4 cups (880g) caster sugar

2 cups (500ml) water

5 litres (20 cups) mineral water

1 Remove rind from lemons using a vegetable peeler, avoiding white pith; reserve lemons.
2 Stir rind, sugar and the water in large saucepan over low heat, without boiling, until sugar dissolves; bring to the boil. Simmer, uncovered, without stirring, about 10 minutes or until syrup is thickened slightly; cool.
3 Squeeze juice from lemons — you need 1 cup (250ml) juice. Stir juice into syrup, strain into jug. Cover; keep refrigerated.
4 Just before serving, add four parts mineral water to one part lemonade, or to taste.

NUTRITIONAL COUNT PER 1 CUP (250ML) DILUTED 0g total fat (0g saturated fat); 606kJ (145 cal); 35.4g carbohydrate; 0.1g protein; 0.3g fibre

Limes

Limes are native to Asia and are the basic citrus fruit of tropical regions, where they are used for cooling drinks and marinades and as a sharp, refreshing seasoning for seafood, meats, vegetables and some tropical fruits whose flavour lacks acid and is much improved by a touch of lime juice.

If you need lime slices for drinks or decoration, cut the fruit in half and cut slices from both sides, then put the ends away in a refrigerator box for the next time you need some squeezed juice for an Asian dressing.

❧ OTHER RECIPES USING LIMES
Fish curry in lime and coconut, p530-1
Ginger cake with lime, p226
Lime and poppy seed syrup cake, p546
Oysters with two dressings, p541
Palm sugar and lime cheesecakes, p585
Salt and pepper tofu with chilli lime dressing, p604
Thai-style green mango salad with seared tuna, p309
Wasabi and lime mayonnaise, p643

There are two main families of limes, the west indian or key lime (named for the Florida Keys, where it was once cultivated), and the tahitian lime, which is the one to be found at Australian greengrocers. The west indian lime is the same as the original Asian species, is the more acid of the two and is a seeded lime, while the tahitian lime, which is nearly always seedless, is believed to have originated as a hybrid between the original asian lime and the citron, an ancient member of the citrus family. Both kinds, having arrived in Europe via the Middle East, were carried to America and the Pacific by European traders or colonisers. Ceviche, the South American and Pacific Island dish of "cooked" raw fish, is made by marinating fish fillets or other seafood such as scallops or prawns in lime juice until they become opaque, white (or pink for prawns) and tender as if cooked, but still with a pure,

fresh flavour. Fresh lime juice is used widely in both tropical and non-tropical countries for cocktails such as daiquiris, caipiroska, margaritas and cuba libres. Limes are also used to flavour sweet dishes such as sorbets, ice-creams, mousses and lime meringue pie. They are related to lemons but their juice is more piercingly acidic and their rind has a different but equally intense fragrance. As with lemons, they will yield more juice if warmed or firmly rolled before using. They are harvested mature but green, when their flavour is strongest, and are available all year with their peak season in autumn.

CHOOSING Limes should be glossy, bright green and heavy for their size. Avoid any with soft spots.

STORING Limes should be stored in the same way as lemons (see page 297).

Lime curd tart

PREP + COOK TIME 45 MINUTES (PLUS REFRIGERATION TIME) **SERVES** 10

3 eggs

4 egg yolks

2 teaspoons finely grated
lime rind

½ cup (125ml) lime juice

1 cup (220g) caster sugar

200g unsalted butter, chopped

1 cup (50g) flaked coconut

SWEET PASTRY

1 ¼ cups (185g) plain flour

½ cup (80g) icing sugar

¼ cup (20g) desiccated coconut

125g cold unsalted butter

¼ cup (60ml) iced water,
approximately

LIME CURD TART

1 Make sweet pastry.

2 Grease 24cm-round loose-based flan tin. Roll pastry between sheets of baking paper until large enough to line tin. Ease pastry into tin, press into base and side; trim edge, prick base with fork. Cover; refrigerate 30 minutes.

3 Preheat oven to 200°C/180°C fan-forced. Place tin on oven tray; cover pastry with baking paper, fill with dried beans or uncooked rice. Bake 15 minutes; remove paper and beans carefully from pastry case. Bake 10 minutes; cool.

4 Meanwhile, stir eggs, yolks, rind, juice, sugar and butter in medium saucepan over medium heat, without boiling, about 15 minutes or until mixture coats the back of a spoon. Strain lime curd through sieve into medium bowl; stand 10 minutes then pour into pastry case. Refrigerate 2 hours before serving sprinkled with coconut.

SWEET PASTRY Process flour, sugar, coconut and butter until crumbly; add enough of the water to make ingredients come together. Knead dough gently on floured surface until smooth. Wrap in plastic; refrigerate 30 minutes.

NUTRITIONAL COUNT PER SERVING 35.4g total fat (22.9g saturated fat); 2178kJ (521 cal); 44.2g carbohydrate; 6g protein; 1.8g fibre

Resting the pastry before and after rolling it out allows the gluten in the flour (see Flour, page 182) to relax so that the pastry will not shrink or be tough.

For information on sweet shortcrust pastry, see Pastry, page 404.

Lime and mint spritzer

PREP + COOK TIME 10 MINUTES (PLUS REFRIGERATION TIME) **SERVES** 8

1 cup (250ml) lime juice

1.25 litres (5 cups) chilled
mineral water

¼ cup coarsely chopped fresh mint

SUGAR SYRUP

½ cup (125ml) water

½ cup (110g) caster sugar

Chop the mint just before serving time as the edges will go black if left to stand.

For information on mint, see Herbs, page 264.

1 Make sugar syrup.

2 Combine syrup in large jug with juice, mineral water and mint. Serve over ice.

SUGAR SYRUP Sitr ingredients in small saucepan over heat until sugar dissolves. Bring to the boil, remove from heat; refrigerate until cold.

NUTRITIONAL COUNT PER SERVING 0.1g total fat (0g saturated fat); 268kJ (64 cal); 15.1g carbohydrate; 0.3g protein; 0.2g fibre

Loquats

Loquats are related to apples, pears and quinces, but they are quite unlike these cousins and more like another one, the european medlar, being about the size of a plum with refreshing, juicy yellow, orange or cream flesh which is rather like a plum in texture.

Loquats are used in Chinese medicine to make a syrup for soothing sore throats and the digestive and respiratory systems. The fruit is also said to be mildly sedative.

Their distinctive taste is both acid and sweet; some varieties are a little bland and are helped by a touch of lemon. They have never been widely grown commercially as their season is brief — early summer — and they must be picked at the right moment of ripeness for full flavour and they don't travel well. Growers who are prepared to take trouble with picking and transport supply some to good greengrocers, but otherwise loquat eating is confined to those with access to a backyard tree. They are usually eaten fresh but can be poached in spiced, lemon-flavoured or wine syrup for desserts, or used in stuffings for poultry or pork, or made into excellent jam or jelly.

PREPARATION Peel and halve loquats and remove the large seeds, then use as the recipe directs.

CHOOSING Select well-coloured, tender loquats. Brown speckles and slight bruises are acceptable as they indicate ripeness and good flavour.

STORING Refrigerate immediately if loquats feel soft, or keep at room temperature until they soften, then store in the refrigerator crisper for up to 2 days.

Lychees

The pebbly red shell of the lychee encloses one of the most exquisite fruits in the world, a little globe of perfumed, juicy white flesh with a flavour reminiscent of the muscatel grape but richer and more subtle, around a shiny black seed.

Lychees have been cultivated in China for many centuries and are now grown in other countries including Australia. They are used in Chinese cooking for some savoury dishes such as chicken with lychees, but are usually eaten alone as a superbly refreshing way to end a meal. The easiest way to peel them is to slit round the equator of the shell without cutting the fruit, twist the two halves in opposite directions and lift off the shells, or you may wish to lift off only the shell at the stem end and serve the lychees in their scarlet cups. The seed is not eaten but slips easily from the flesh. Canned lychees are available and are good with ice-cream but a far cry from the fresh fruit. Lychees are available in summer.

CHOOSING Lychees should have fresh-feeling, bright red shells. Greenness means that they are not ripe and will not improve as they don't ripen after picking, and browning and dryness indicate that their freshness is gone. Fruit with some stem attached will keep longer than fruit without stems.

STORING Store lychees in a closed container or a paper bag enclosed in a plastic bag in the refrigerator and use within 5–6 days.

❦ **OTHER RECIPES USING LYCHEES**
Green tea ice-cream with fruit salsa, p601

Lychees have always been a prized fruit. In the 1st century AD, China's imperial capital was in the north but lychees could be grown only in the warm south, so a special courier service with swift horses was set up to bring fresh lychees from Canton north to the imperial court.

In the absence of a muddler or a cocktail shaker, whiz the caipiroska ingredients and a few ice cubes in a food processor until the ice is chopped.

Lychee caipiroska

PREP TIME 5 MINUTES **SERVES** 1

2 fresh lychees (50g), seeded
2 teaspoons caster sugar
45ml vodka
10ml lime juice
½ cup crushed ice

1 Using muddler, crush lychees with sugar in cocktail shaker.
2 Add vodka, juice and ice; shake vigorously. Pour into 180ml old-fashioned glass.

NUTRITIONAL COUNT PER SERVING 0g total fat (0g saturated fat); 656kJ (157 cal); 15.3g carbohydrate; 0.5g protein; 0.5g fibre

Pork and lychee salad

PREP + COOK TIME 30 MINUTES (PLUS STANDING TIME) **SERVES** 4

If fresh lychees are available, use 300g of these, halved and peeled. You can use rambutans or longans instead.

Fried shallots are available in packets at Asian food stores. Once opened, they keep for months in an airtight container.

Pickled garlic is the young green bulb, pickled whole and unpeeled in vinegared brine and packed in jars. Eaten as a snack in Thailand, it is used as a condiment to sprinkle over salads or noodle dishes, or using in a dressing as here.

1 tablespoon peanut oil

300g pork fillet

565g can lychees, rinsed, drained, halved

1 medium red capsicum (200g), sliced thinly

10cm stick fresh lemon grass (20g), sliced thinly

2 fresh kaffir lime leaves, shredded finely

100g watercress

2 tablespoons coarsely chopped fresh vietnamese mint

2 tablespoons drained thinly sliced pickled ginger

2 tablespoons fried shallot

PICKLED GARLIC DRESSING

1 tablespoon drained finely chopped pickled garlic

2 fresh small red thai chillies, seeded, sliced thinly

1 tablespoon rice vinegar

1 tablespoon lime juice

1 tablespoon fish sauce

1 tablespoon palm sugar

1 Heat oil in wok; cook pork, turning, until browned all over and cooked as desired. Cover, stand 10 minutes; slice thinly.

2 Place ingredients for pickled ginger dressing in screw-top jar; shake well.

3 Place pork in medium bowl with dressing; toss to coat pork all over. Stand 10 minutes.

4 Meanwhile, combine lychees, capsicum, lemon grass, lime leaves, watercress and mint in large bowl.

5 Add pork mixture to lychee mixture; toss gently to combine. Serve sprinkled with pickled ginger and fried shallots.

NUTRITIONAL COUNT PER SERVING 6.9g total fat (1.5g saturated fat); 911kJ (218 cal); 18.1g carbohydrate; 19.1g protein; 3.3g fibre

Fresh lychees

Mandarins

Mandarins, a citrus fruit looking like smaller, flattened oranges, are nearly always eaten fresh, partly because they are so conveniently designed for it, having easy-to-peel skin and easily separated segments, and partly because their sweet flavour, lacking the acid edge of oranges, does not come through well in cooking, though it can be successful if the rind is used too.

Being more loosely structured than oranges, mandarins can be harder to cut into neat skinless segments as described on page 382. Choose the tightest-skinned mandarins possible, put them in the freezer until they are very firm (not frozen), then remove the skins and outer membranes as described. If the inside flesh is not quite firm, freeze it a little longer and it will then be easy to cut down beside the dividing membranes to obtain clean-cut pieces.

Skinless mandarin segments are a delicious addition to a fruit salad and their bright colour and pretty shape make them attractive decorations for desserts and cakes (see Oranges, page 382). Mandarin peel, being thin and more tangy than the fruit itself, can be dried and combined with herbs to flavour beef, lamb, duck or pork casseroles, and fresh rind can be cut into fine strips and used in a pork or chicken stir-fry, or grated into biscuits and breads to give them fresh fragrance and taste. The main Australian mandarin varieties are **imperial**, an early-season mandarin available from autumn to midwinter, **ellendale**, a mid-season mandarin available from midwinter into spring, and **honey murcott**, a late-season mandarin available from late winter into spring. Ellendale is actually a hybrid (cross) between a mandarin and an orange, and honey murcott is a naturally occurring hybrid of the mandarin, but they are both considered mandarins horticulturally and commercially. Tangerine and clementine are names given by some authorities to certain mandarin hybrids (a honey murcott is, under this system, a tangerine, while a mandarin/seville orange hybrid is a clementine) but a rival system of naming includes tangerine and clementine as simply varieties of mandarin. Mandarins are sometimes waxed to prevent drying out, so if you are using the skin, wash the fruit in warm water, rubbing with a cloth, before using. Skinless mandarin segments are available canned.

CHOOSING Mandarins should be brightly coloured and glossy. While some varieties are naturally loose-skinned, avoid any that are puffy or have soft spots.

STORING Mandarins will keep in good condition in a bowl at room temperature for up to a week, but keep an eye on them and remove any that show mould — wash and thoroughly dry the fruit they were touching. For longer storage, store in the refrigerator crisper for up to 2 weeks.

Also see Fruit, Dried, page 192 for dried mandarin peel.

Mandarin, polenta and macadamia cake

PREP + COOK TIME 2 HOURS 20 MINUTES (PLUS COOLING AND STANDING TIME) **SERVES** 12

4 small mandarins (400g), unpeeled

2 cups (280g) macadamias

250g butter, softened

1 teaspoon vanilla extract

1 cup (220g) caster sugar

3 eggs

1 cup (170g) polenta

1 teaspoon baking powder

1 tablespoon icing sugar

1 Cover whole mandarins in medium saucepan with cold water; bring to the boil. Drain then repeat process two more times. Cool mandarins to room temperature.

2 Preheat oven to 170°C/150°C fan-forced. Grease deep 22cm-round cake pan; line base with baking paper.

3 Blend or process nuts until they form a coarse meal. Halve mandarins; discard seeds. Blend or process mandarins until pulpy.

4 Beat butter, extract and caster sugar in small bowl with electric mixer until light and fluffy. Add eggs, one at a time, beating until just combined between additions; transfer to large bowl. Stir in polenta, baking powder, nut meal and mandarin pulp.

5 Spread mixture into pan; bake about 1 hour. Stand cake 15 minutes; turn, top-side up, onto wire rack to cool. Serve cake dusted with sifted icing sugar.

NUTRITIONAL COUNT PER SERVING 36.5g total fat (14.1g saturated fat); 2015kJ (482 cal); 33g carbohydrate; 5g protein; 2.5g fibre

You can use other nuts such as pecans, almonds or walnuts instead of macadamias, and other citrus fruit such as grapefruit, blood oranges, tangelos etc instead of mandarins.

For information on macadamias, see Nuts, pages 344–346; and for polenta, see Grains, pages 228–230.

Mangoes

The beautiful mango is loved for its paradise perfume and flavour, which have been described as a blend of melon, peach and apricot. It is native to eastern Asia and is cultivated in tropical and sub-tropical regions around the world.

The mango is said to be the most greatly consumed fruit in the world, beating both the tomato and the banana.

Its many varieties range from green through yellow to rich red when ripe and its flesh from yellow to deep orange. It is used both ripe and unripe: the luscious ripe flesh is made into sorbets, ice-creams mousses and frothy drinks or served alone as a perfect start to breakfast; firm-ripe slices are served in salads or with prawns, pork or spicy chicken; and the tart flesh of green mango is used for cooked or fresh chutneys to go with curry, as an ingredient in curries themselves, and in aromatic salads with Asian-style dressings.

PREPARATION The usual approach to a ripe mango is to place it stem-end towards you and narrow side against the cutting board, then cut down beside the flattish central stone on each side to remove each cheek in one piece. Peel the skin from the remaining central section and slice off as much as possible of the flesh round the stone (the cook's reward is to suck the last delicious flesh off the stone).

The cheeks can be peeled and sliced, or placed cut side down on the board and cut into skin-on slices which can then be peeled or served skin-on as you wish, or you can turn each cheek flesh side up and slice, at intervals in both directions, down to but not through the skin, then press the underside and the flesh will open up like a flower, ready for eating.

CHOOSING A ripe mango is fragrant and will yield when you cup it in your two hands and press gently. However, mangoes can ripen properly after picking, so unless you want one to eat that day, it is better to buy a firmer one and allow it to ripen at room temperature.

STORING Once ripe, mangoes are very perishable, so refrigerate them, double-wrapped in plastic or in a closed container so that they won't perfume other foods, for up to 2 days.

Green mangoes

Ripe mangoes

Thai-style green mango salad with seared tuna

PREP + COOK TIME 30 MINUTES **SERVES** 4

1 green mango (350g)

2 teaspoons sesame oil

800g tuna steaks,
cut into 3cm pieces

½ teaspoon dried chilli flakes

2 tablespoons toasted
sesame seeds

2 cups (100g) snow pea sprouts

½ cup firmly packed fresh
coriander leaves

½ cup firmly packed fresh
mint leaves

½ small red onion (50g),
sliced thinly

LIME AND GINGER DRESSING

¼ cup (60ml) lime juice

3cm piece fresh ginger (15g),
grated

1 tablespoon fish sauce

THAI-STYLE GREEN MANGO
SALAD WITH SEARED TUNA

1 Place ingredients for lime and ginger dressing in screw-top jar; shake well.

2 Using vegetable peeler, slice mango into thin ribbons.

3 Combine oil and fish in medium bowl. Cook fish on heated oiled grill plate (or grill
or barbecue).

4 Return fish to same cleaned bowl with chilli and seeds; mix gently.

5 Place mango in medium bowl with remaining ingredients and dressing; toss gently
to combine. Serve salad topped with fish.

NUTRITIONAL COUNT PER SERVING 17.8g total fat (5.4g saturated fat); 1894kJ (453 cal);15.5g carbohydrate;
55.5g protein; 3.7g fibre

*Ensure the grill plate or
barbecue is very hot when
cooking the tuna. Oil well,
then add tuna pieces in
batches, searing for only
about 10 seconds on each
side so they remain juicy.*

*For more information
on tuna, see Seafood,
page 523.*

Mango and avocado salsa

PREP TIME 15 MINUTES **MAKES** 2½ CUPS

1 medium mango (430g), chopped coarsely

1 large avocado (320g), chopped coarsely

1 small red onion (100g), chopped finely

1 small red capsicum (150g), chopped finely

1 fresh small red thai chilli, chopped finely

2 tablespoons lime juice

1 Combine ingredients in medium bowl.

2 Serve salsa with grilled salmon, chicken or pork.

NUTRITIONAL COUNT PER TABLESPOON 1.7g total fat (0.4g saturated fat); 100kJ (24 cal); 1.7g carbohydrate;
0.4g protein; 0.4g fibre

*This salsa also goes well
with roasted sweet corn,
crisped prosciutto and
corn tortillas, or red onion
and black bean salad.*

*For information on
avocado, see Avocado,
pages 24–26.*

For neat mango slices, cut both cheeks from fruit, place, cut-side down, on work surface and cut downward into slices, then separate slices and carefully pull skin off, or lay slice flat and cut skin off.

For information on puff pastry, see Pastry, page 404; and for coconut, see Nuts, page 347.

Mango galettes with coconut cream

PREP + COOK TIME 25 MINUTES **SERVES** 4

1 sheet puff pastry, quartered

20g butter, melted

2 firm medium mangoes (860g), halved, sliced thinly

1 tablespoon brown sugar

⅔ cup (160ml) thickened cream, whipped

2 teaspoons coconut-flavoured liqueur

⅓ cup (15g) flaked coconut, toasted

1 Preheat oven to 200°C/180°C fan-forced. Grease oven tray; line with baking paper.

2 Place pastry squares on oven tray, prick with fork; brush with half the melted butter. Divide mango among pastry squares, leaving 2cm border. Sprinkle sugar over galettes; drizzle with remaining butter. Bake, uncovered, about 15 minutes.

3 Combine remaining ingredients in small bowl. Serve galettes with coconut cream.

NUTRITIONAL COUNT PER SERVING 31.2g total fat (19.7g saturated fat); 1969kJ (471 cal); 40.1g carbohydrate; 5g protein; 3.4g fibre

---

About 1 hour before you want to serve the parfait, put a cutting board into the freezer and the serving plates for the dessert into the refrigerator. About 20 minutes before serving time, use the foil to lift the parfait out of its pan and place it on the chilled board, then peel the foil from the sides and put board and dessert into the refrigerator for 15–20 minutes to allow it to soften enough to cut. Remove from refrigerator, cut into 12 slices, place on the chilled plates and top each with a spoonful of salsa.

Frozen mango parfait

PREP + COOK TIME 20 MINUTES (PLUS FREEZING TIME) **SERVES** 12

1 medium mango (430g), chopped coarsely

2 cups (440g) low-fat ricotta cheese

¾ cup (165g) caster sugar

300ml light thickened cream

TROPICAL FRUIT SALSA

¼ cup (55g) caster sugar

¼ cup (60ml) water

2 medium kiwifruit (170g), chopped coarsely

1 medium mango (430g), chopped coarsely

2 kaffir lime leaves, sliced thinly

1 Line base of 14cm x 21cm loaf pan with foil, extending 5cm over edges.

2 Blend or process mango until smooth.

3 Beat ricotta and sugar in small bowl with electric mixer until smooth; transfer to large bowl. Beat cream in small bowl with electric mixer until soft peaks form; fold into ricotta mixture.

4 Drop alternate spoonfuls of ricotta mixture and mango pulp into pan. Pull skewer through mixture several times for marbled effect; smooth surface. Cover with foil; freeze overnight.

5 Make tropical fruit salsa 1 hour before serving. Cover; refrigerate until cold. Serve parfait topped with salsa.

TROPICAL FRUIT SALSA Bring sugar and the water to the boil in small saucepan. Reduce heat; simmer, uncovered, without stirring, 5 minutes; cool. Combine sugar syrup with remaining ingredients in medium bowl.

NUTRITIONAL COUNT PER SERVING 12.3g total fat (8g saturated fat); 986kJ (236 cal); 27.4g carbohydrate; 4.7g protein; 1.2g fibre

MANGO GALETTES WITH COCONUT CREAM

Melons

Melons and summer go together, and one or more of the melon family are in season throughout the warmer months.

A generation or two ago, every hostess had a melon-baller and the smart way to serve melon was in marble-size balls cut out with this nifty little gadget. Ideas change and most melon-ballers haven't left the kitchen drawers for years, but melon balls, used much more casually, are ready for a comeback. Think of them scattered, with mint leaves, across a platter of ham or, with coriander leaves, on an Asian chicken, pork or seafood salad.

WATERMELON is not, botanically, a melon, but is always regarded as one. Its bright pink flesh, studded with hard black seeds, is mildly sweet, crisp, translucent and very juicy. The main variety is a large fruit, commonly weighing over 10kg, so it is usually sold as halves or quarters. Cultivars include a "mini" variety about the size of a small child's head, and a seedless variety which does have a few seeds, but they are soft, white and edible. There is also a relatively recent cultivar with dark-green markings on a pale skin and very sweet golden flesh, which has been given the name "champagne melon".

ROCKMELON is a netted or musk melon, with a raised netted pattern on the skin and smooth, sweet, richly scented flesh. In Australia and America, it is often, incorrectly, called a cantaloupe. It is available for much of the year but its season is from early summer into autumn.

HONEYDEW is classified as a winter melon but it is at its best from late summer into autumn, though it remains available into winter. It has hard, smooth skin and pale, juicy, slightly crisp flesh which is fragrant and delicately delicious when fully ripe but can be rather tasteless otherwise. The main variety is the white (actually greenish white, ripening to cream) honeydew, but there is also a golden variety, the yellow honeydew.

Rockmelon and honeydew can be served with ice-cream or creamy desserts and used as an ingredient in ice-creams, mousses and sorbets.

CANTALOUPE is a group of small, round melons with rib lines marking the skin into segments. They include some of the best flavoured and most fragrant melons, but they are not well known in Australia as attempts to grow them in commercial quantities have not, as yet, been successful.

JAM MELONS have little flavour when raw, but make good jam when combined with a sharp-flavoured ingredient such as lemon, pineapple or ginger.

CHOOSING
Honeydew is the only melon that will ripen properly after picking. Others may soften and become more juicy, but they will never reach their fully ripe flavour. All melons should feel heavy for their size and be free of soft spots. When ripe, they will give a little when pressed at the stem end. Rockmelon should smell sweet and should have a smooth stem scar, showing that the melon detached readily from the stem because it was fully mature. If it has a jagged scar or some stem still attached, it was not mature so its flavour was not fully developed. A brown mark on the skin does not matter in an otherwise good melon — melon vines lie on the ground and the mark probably shows where the fruit was lifted on to an upturned flowerpot or other support so that it would get good air circulation as it

For a quick juice, blend 450g coarsely chopped watermelon with 4 fresh mint leaves until smooth and serve within 30 minutes. Refrigerate the watermelon and mint before making the juice.

matured. Honeydew melon shows a slight yellowing of the skin when fully ripe. As mentioned above, it will ripen properly if bought unripe, but that does not mean immature — it should have cream, not greenish skin when you buy it and will then ripen fully if left at room temperature for a few days. A whole watermelon should sound hollow if tapped and the mark from where it rested on the ground should be yellowish, not white or green; cut

watermelon should have strongly coloured flesh and black, not white, seeds.

STORING Jam melons will store at room temperature for months. Other melons, once ripe, should be stored in the refrigerator and eaten within a few days. Scented melons should be double-wrapped in plastic or stored in a lidded container, especially if they have been cut, to prevent them from perfuming other food.

Don't chop the mint until just before making this salad, as the edges get black if left to stand. We used a fairly bland fetta so that its flavour didn't overpower the melon.

For information on fetta cheese, see Cheese, page 102; and for mint leaves, see Herbs, page 264.

Watermelon, mint and fetta salad

PREP TIME 10 MINUTES **SERVES** 4

2 teaspoons white sugar

¼ cup (60ml) lime juice

½ cup (100g) crumbled fetta cheese

½ small red onion (50g), sliced thinly

½ cup fresh mint leaves

850g seedless watermelon, cut into wedges

1 Place sugar and juice in small jug; stir until sugar dissolves.

2 Combine juice mixture in large bowl with cheese, onion and mint; spoon over watermelon.

NUTRITIONAL COUNT PER SERVING 6.2g total fat (3.8g saturated fat); 506kJ (121 cal); 10.1g carbohydrate; 5.4g protein; 1.5g fibre

This recipe is easy to multiply to feed a crowd. It is perfect for a picnic, pool party or barbecue.

For information on lime, see Limes, page 300.

Mixed melon salad with lime syrup

PREP + COOK TIME 20 MINUTES **SERVES** 4

⅓ cup (75g) firmly packed brown sugar

2 teaspoons finely grated lime rind

¼ cup (60ml) lime juice

⅓ cup (80ml) water

¼ medium watermelon (1.5kg)

½ large rockmelon (1.3kg)

½ large honeydew melon (900g)

1 Stir sugar, rind, juice and the water in small saucepan over low heat, without boiling, until sugar dissolves; cool.

2 Remove skin and seeds from melons; cut into chunks.

3 Combine melon pieces in large bowl with lime syrup.

NUTRITIONAL COUNT PER SERVING 1.2g total fat (0g saturated fat); 1012kJ (242 cal); 51.3g carbohydrate; 3.1g protein; 5.4g fibre

WATERMELON, MINT AND FETTA SALAD

Milk

The nutritional value of milk is shown in the fact that it can provide complete nourishment for baby humans and animals. After weaning, cow's milk is the one most of us drink or eat in the form of cheese and other milk products, with goat milk coming second. Sheep and buffalo milk have a place, too, in the cheese industry, and processed milks of various kinds are also part of the average diet.

Human beings are the only mammals who continue to drink milk after they have started eating solid food, and like all other mammals their level of the milk-digesting enzyme lactase, high in infancy, declines to a steady minimum level by the age of about five. Most people in regions where milk is an important part of the diet have adapted genetically to maintain enough lactase to cope with milk throughout life, but some people in those regions, and a majority of the human race — cannot digest milk properly after early childhood, giving them symptoms like stomach pain and diarrhoea. The problem is with the milk sugar (lactose), and the condition is called lactose intolerance. It applies to all animal milks because all have lactose.

COW'S MILK is usually pasteurised and homogenised (see TREATED AND PROCESSED MILKS) for human consumption. It is much richer in protein than human milk and can trigger allergic reactions in infants. Baby food formulas are carefully balanced to be more like breast milk. Cow's milk varies from one breed to another but, over all, is a creamy colour. We are accustomed to thinking of rich colour as an indication of rich creaminess, but goat milk, which is white, is actually as rich as cow's milk, while sheep and buffalo milk, also white, are much richer. The colour difference comes from the way the different animals convert the carotene (yellow/orange pigment) in green feed into colourless Vitamin A — cows convert little so more is left to give their milk richer colour, and goats, sheep and buffalo convert nearly all their carotene so their milk is nutritious but white.

GOAT MILK is comparable with cow's milk in fat and protein levels but is claimed to be more digestible and less likely to cause allergic reactions in humans. It has a distinctive, earthy flavour which is carried into goats cheese.

SHEEP MILK has much higher fat and protein levels than cow's milk. It has a distinctive after-taste, also in its cheese.

BUFFALO MILK is white and is the traditional milk used in making mozzarella cheese. It is much richer in fat than cow's milk and has a mild mushroom/freshly cut grass/barnyard flavour, and these differences are reflected in buffalo milk mozzarella compared with cow's milk mozzarella.

TREATED AND PROCESSED MILKS

Cow's milk is almost invariably treated by pasteurisation for human consumption, and usually homogenised as well, and milk can be processed into several other forms to provide flavour, health or convenience benefits.

PASTEURISED MILK has been heat-treated to destroy potentially dangerous bacteria that may be present in raw milk. Pasteurisation also extends the shelf life of milk so that it will keep, refrigerated, for 10 days or more.

HOMOGENISED MILK has had the milk fat divided into smaller globules and dispersed evenly through the liquid so that it will not rise to the surface. This makes the milk feel creamier in the mouth and also makes it more liable to boiling over and curdling.

SKIM MILK AND LOW-FAT MILK are made by spinning milk in a centrifuge so that the fat collects in the centre and the milk can be run off. Some or all of the fat can be removed, as required for the particular product.

UHT MILK (ULTRA HIGH TEMPERATURE MILK), also called long-life milk, has been heated to a very high temperature for 1 to 3 seconds to stabilise it so that it will keep for months without refrigeration. Once opened, it should be refrigerated and used like ordinary milk (though it cannot be used for making junket as the high heat has destroyed the enzymes needed for this). UHT milk has a slightly cooked flavour, but UHT cream (see Cream, page 143) is less affected.

BUTTERMILK originally meant the low-fat liquid that was left after cream had been churned into butter, which would ferment so that it thickened and developed acid flavour. Today, it means skim milk to which a culture has been added to ferment it and produce similar thickness and flavour.

EVAPORATED MILK is milk that has been heated until it has lost about half its water by evaporation and has then been homogenised, canned and sterilised. The heat and concentration produce a slightly cooked taste with a caramel note.

Evaporated milk keeps for many months, but changes very slowly during storage so that milk from a very old can may be dark and taste tired.

SWEETENED CONDENSED MILK has been concentrated by evaporation, then had sugar added to give a total concentration, including the milk sugar, of about 55%. It is available in cans or tubes, will keep for many months on the shelf and, as the sugar acts as a preservative, it will keep after opening for about 1 week without refrigeration and up to 3 weeks if refrigerated. Sweetened condensed skim or low-fat milk is made in the same way, but from skim or low-fat milk.

POWDERED MILK is made by pasteurising, then evaporating milk until only the solids are left. It may be powdered full-cream milk or powdered skim or low-fat milk, depending on the fat content of the milk used. It will keep for months in cool, dry conditions.

Also see Soya, pages 552 & 553.

❧ OTHER RECIPES USING MILK

Bacon, cheese and chilli muffins, p30
Banana pancakes, p188
Buttermilk scones, p187
Butterscotch pecan muffins, p190
Caramelised apple tea cake, p12
Cauliflower gratin, p94
Chocolate bread and butter pudding, p73
Creamed rice, p503
Eggs and smoked salmon on blini, p166
Ham and zucchini quiche, p259
Hot mocha, p136
Orange caramels, p584
Plum clafoutis, p434
Rhubarb and custard mufins, p492
Roasted vegetable lasagne, p402-3
Spiced iced coffee milkshake, p134
Vanilla bean ice-cream, p144
White chocolate and raspberry bread puddings, p62

Béchamel sauce

PREP + COOK TIME 20 MINUTES **MAKES** 1 CUP

30g butter
2 tablespoons plain flour
1¼ cups (310ml) hot milk
pinch nutmeg

1 Melt butter in medium saucepan, add flour; cook, stirring, until mixture bubbles and thickens.

2 Gradually add milk, stirring, until mixture boils and thickens. Stir nutmeg into sauce.

NUTRITIONAL COUNT PER TABLESPOON 3.1g total fat (2.1g saturated fat); 176kJ (42 cal); 2.6g carbohydrate; 1.1g protein; 0.1g fibre

If the béchamel is too thick, gently whisk in up to ¼ cup warm milk until the sauce reaches the desired consistency. If the sauce is lumpy, rub through a sieve into a small bowl.
To reheat, place in a small, heavy-based saucepan over very low heat and stir until just heated through.

Pistachio, honey and cardamom kulfi

PREP + COOK TIME 25 MINUTES (PLUS COOLING AND FREEZING TIME) **SERVES** 4

2 x 375ml cans evaporated milk

¾ cup (180ml) cream

3 cardamom pods, bruised

2 tablespoons honey

⅓ cup (45g) finely chopped roasted pistachios

2 tablespoons coarsely chopped roasted pistachios

1 Bring milk, cream and cardamom to the boil in large heavy-based saucepan. Reduce heat; simmer, uncovered, stirring occasionally, about 10 minutes or until reduced to about 3 cups. Stir in honey, remove from heat; cool 15 minutes.

2 Strain mixture into large bowl; discard cardamom. Divide kulfi mixture among four ¾-cup (180ml) moulds; sprinkle with finely chopped nuts. Cover with foil; freeze 3 hours or overnight.

3 Turn kulfi onto serving plates; sprinkle with coarsely chopped nuts to serve.

NUTRITIONAL COUNT PER SERVING 45.1g total fat (25.6g saturated fat); 2621kJ (627 cal); 36.3g carbohydrate; 19.3g protein; 1.7g fibre

---

Kulfi is a popular Indian dessert. It freezes very solid and is slow-melting, so transfer from freezer to refrigerator 15 minutes before serving time to allow it to soften slightly. To turn out, wipe moulds with a hot cloth, place a plate over each one and reverse, banging plate on kitchen bench to make the dessert drop out, then immediately turn the dessert over on to a serving plate.

For information on honey, see Sugar, page 578; and for pistachios, see Nuts, page 346.

Crème anglaise

PREP + COOK TIME 30 MINUTES (PLUS REFRIGERATION TIME) **MAKES** 1½ CUPS

1 vanilla bean

1½ cups (375ml) milk

⅓ cup (75g) caster sugar

4 egg yolks

1 Split vanilla bean in half lengthways; scrape seeds into medium saucepan, add pod, milk and one tablespoon of the sugar. Bring to the boil then strain into large jug. Discard pod.

2 Meanwhile, combine egg yolks and remaining sugar in medium heatproof bowl set over medium saucepan of simmering water; do not allow water to touch base of bowl. Whisk until thick and creamy; gradually whisk in hot milk mixture.

3 Return custard mixture to pan; stir, over low heat, until mixture is just thick enough to coat the back of a spoon.

4 Return custard to bowl; refrigerate about 1 hour or until cold. Serve with poached fruit or apple pie, if you like.

NUTRITIONAL COUNT PER TABLESPOON 2.1g total fat (0.9g saturated fat); 184kJ (44 cal); 5.2g carbohydrate; 1.4g protein; 0g fibre

Crème anglaise ("english cream") is a more egg-rich French version of a simple custard. It can be made with half cream and half milk or all cream. The custard must be cooked slowly or the eggs may separate and the custard curdle. Ensure the bowl does not touch the water and keep the water at a slow simmer.

For orange crème anglaise, stir 2 teaspoons finely grated orange rind into warm custard; cover and refrigerate.

For passionfruit crème anglaise, stir 2 tablespoons passionfruit pulp into warm custard; cover and refrigerate.

PISTACHIO, HONEY AND CARDAMOM KULFI

Mushrooms

Thanks to the enterprising mushroom-growing and mushroom-gathering industries, we can buy a dozen or more kinds of fresh mushrooms, the cultivated ones, as year-round staples and wild ones in their seasons. Even the precious truffle is being grown in Tasmania. Renowned european varieties such as chanterelles, morels or ceps (French cèpes, Italian porcini and usually sold as porcini), are available in dried form, which intensifies the flavour, and are reconstituted by soaking. If you live within reach of an enthusiastic speciality greengrocer or food shop, you may sometimes see an imported box of fresh european mushrooms — the price per kilogram is fearsome, but mushrooms are light so 50–100g is probably all you need for a food adventure.

CULTIVATED FRESH MUSHROOMS

WHITE MUSHROOMS are sold in three forms. **Buttons**, also called champignons, are small, completely closed and mild in flavour. They remain pale when cooked so they are ideal for pale sauces, fish and chicken dishes; they are also good raw in salads. **Cups** have the velum (veil) just breaking to reveal the pink gills and are good for stuffing and general cooking; brush with lemon juice if you want to keep them pale. To use as a garnish, trim the stems even with the cap and cut downward into umbrella shapes. **Flats** are fully open, dark and more robust in flavour than buttons or cups; these are the mushrooms to use for grilling, serving on toast or using in hearty soups and casseroles, but they can turn pale dishes grey. Large flats are often marked "field mushrooms" in shops, but that is a name that should be reserved for the mushrooms that appear in many paddocks in autumn, which are closely related to but not the same as the cultivated white ones. See Field Mushrooms, opposite.

SWISS BROWN MUSHROOMS, also called roman mushrooms, are cultivated button mushrooms of the same species as cultivated white mushrooms, but are the older form while the white kind are a

Button mushrooms

Cup mushrooms

Flat mushrooms

Swiss brown mushrooms

mutation. The flavour of swiss browns is stronger and fuller than that of white ones.

PORTOBELLO MUSHROOMS are mature, fully opened swiss browns; they are larger and bigger in flavour.

OYSTER MUSHROOMS, also called abalone mushrooms when large, are cultivated. They are prized for their smooth texture and subtle flavour and work well with veal, seafood and poultry. They become unpleasantly slippery if cooked too long so they should added near the end of cooking.

SHIITAKE MUSHROOMS, also called chinese black mushrooms though they are really native to Japan, are cultivated. Their dense, substantial texture and meaty flavour make them a perfect mushroom to be braised, fried or eaten on their own. They are also good raw. Shiitake stems are woody so should be removed before using.

SHIMEJI MUSHROOMS, cultivated mushrooms also called beech mushrooms, grow and are sold in clumps. They are nutty-flavoured and slightly crunchy.

ENOKI MUSHROOMS, cultivated mushrooms also called enokitake, are tiny, long-stemmed, pale mushrooms that grow and are sold in clusters, and can be used that way or separated by slicing off the base. They have a mild fruity flavour and are slightly crisp in texture.

WHITE FUNGUS AND BLACK FUNGUS, also known as wood ear or cloud ear fungus, are thin, frilly cultivated mushrooms which are used sliced and added to stir-fries and Asian soups.

CHESTNUT MUSHROOMS are cultivated mushrooms with a firm texture and strong flavour. They are available only irregularly.

WILD-PICKED FRESH MUSHROOMS

FIELD MUSHROOMS Wild-picked field mushrooms are seldom found in shops, though you may see mushrooms so labelled (see White Mushrooms, opposite). True field mushrooms are the ones that can be gathered from paddocks and forest floors in autumn. They are not the same species as cultivated white mushrooms but a related, more strongly and richly flavoured kind. They may be found in button, cap or flat form and can be treated in the same ways as the cultivated ones.

PINE MUSHROOMS, also called orange flycaps, saffron milkcaps and blood mushrooms, are wild-picked in forests of introduced pine species in late summer and autumn. Their flesh is orange and savoury-tasting. Specimens up to about 8cm across are best; larger ones can be coarse-textured. They should be sliced and immediately fried, stir-fried or used for pasta or risotto, or stuffed whole and baked or grilled.

Portobello mushrooms

Oyster mushrooms

Pink oyster mushrooms

Shiitake mushrooms

When you want mushrooms cooked rich and soft to serve on toast or on top of a steak, slice them, toss with butter on high heat, then cover and cook at medium heat for 4–5 minutes. When you want them firm, shapely and golden brown, trim the stems level with the caps and cook briskly, turning once, in enough sizzling butter and olive oil to cover the bottom of a frying pan generously. Shake the pan gently once or twice; do not crowd the pan or the mushrooms will steam — cook in batches if necessary, then when all are done, return them all to the pan and toss on high heat for moments only before serving.

PINE BOLETUS, also called the australian cep, are wild-picked in forests of introduced pine species in autumn and early winter. They are related to but not the same as the true european cep, but their fruity scent and deep, earthy flavour explain the common name. They are best served very simply: fried quickly or added in the last few minutes of cooking to a soup, sauce or casserole so that their aroma is not lost.

DRIED AND CANNED MUSHROOMS

Various Asian mushrooms including the chinese wood ear and the Japanese shiitake are available dried as well as fresh. European mushrooms such as **PORCINI** (ceps, king bolete), **CHANTERELLES** (girolles, pfifferlinge) and **MORELS** (morille) are available dried. **STRAW MUSHROOMS**, named for the straw on which they are grown, are small and globe-shaped with internal stems. They are cultivated but are so fragile and deteriorate so quickly after harvesting that they are not a commercial proposition fresh, so they are usually canned. Cultivated white button mushrooms are also canned, sometimes under the name of champignons.

PREPARATION Cultivated mushrooms are grown on sterilised mediums and cleaned before they are sent to market. They should be neither washed nor peeled but simply wiped over with damp absorbent paper. Washing could make them water-logged as they mop up moisture very readily, and peeling would remove nutrients and flavour. Wild mushrooms that you buy have usually been cleaned, too, so should be treated in the same way. If mushrooms you picked yourself really need washing, do it quickly under running water, not by immersing them, just before using and dry them well. Peel only if the skins are tough. Soak dried mushrooms in warm water for 30 minutes to an hour, then use in sauces, soups and casseroles or as directed by recipes. Remove the woody stems of shiitake before using.

CHOOSING All mushrooms should be undamaged, free of insect holes, firm and dry. Avoid wizened or discoloured ones.

STORING Enclose white mushrooms, swiss browns, portobellos, pine mushrooms and pine boletus loosely in a paper bag and store in the refrigerator crisper for up to 3 days. Store fresh shiitake, oyster and chestnut mushrooms in a single layer, loosely covered with a barely damp cloth, and use within 3 days. Store shimeji and enoki in their original wrapping and use within 4 days.

Shimeji mushrooms

Enoki mushrooms

Chestnut mushrooms

TRUFFLES

Truffles are among the world's most prized and expensive foods. They are an edible fungus, as mushrooms are, but belong to a different family and, unlike mushrooms, do not appear above ground. They are traditionally a wild treasure that grows under several kinds of trees, mainly oak and hazelnut, and is found by digging after being detected by its scent by trained pigs or dogs. There are two kinds, the black or Périgord truffle named for the south-eastern region of France where they are in greatest supply, and the white or Alba truffle, named for the city of Alba in the Piedmont region of northern Italy where the greatest number and the most aromatic ones are found. Both kinds are typically a dense, knobbly mass ranging from walnut to fist size or larger. Both have strong and pervasive but different aromas: black truffles taste and smell subtle, warm and earthy, while white truffles are stronger and more pungent in aroma and flavour. Cultivation of truffles by planting suitable trees and inoculating their roots with truffle spores has been attempted with some success in Europe and also in New Zealand and Australia, which both now have tiny but improving truffle industries. Canned truffles are available but do not approach the qualities of fresh ones. Store fresh truffles in a covered container with some rice to absorb any moisture (or in a jar of rice which will be deliciously scented by the truffle aroma).

WARNING

Never eat a mushroom unless you are certain that it is edible. It is advisable to get a field guide to mushrooms and take it with you when you go mushrooming. Most toxic mushrooms will only make you sick, but the deathcap is deadly and is known to be in Australia. Before you go mushrooming, go to www.anbg.gov.au/fungi/deathcap.html. It has large, clear colour pictures of the deathcap with detailed descriptions, pictures of safe mushrooms that could be confused with the deathcap, the frightening information that a single mushroom can kill a man and less than that a child, and an emergency phone number.

❧ **OTHER RECIPES USING MUSHROOMS**
Chicken and galangal soup (tom ka gai), p206
Herb omelette with sautéed mushrooms, p168
Veal shin on mushroom ragoût, p624
Veal sweetbreads with duxelles, p359
Vegetable dumplings in asian broth, p336

Pine mushrooms

Porcini mushrooms

Chanterelle mushrooms

Porcini, marsala and rosemary sauce

PREP + COOK TIME 10 MINUTES (PLUS STANDING TIME) **MAKES** 1 CUP

This recipe makes enough sauce for four servings of pan-fried veal cutlets, pan-fried beef eye fillet steaks, roasted lamb backstraps or grilled chicken thigh cutlets. Porcini are superbly flavoured european mushrooms, available here only in their dried form. Save their soaking water to add to a soup, stock or casserole. If you can't find them, use fresh, thinly sliced swiss brown mushrooms.

5g dried porcini mushrooms
20g butter
1 shallot (25g), chopped finely
1 tablespoon fresh rosemary leaves
¼ cup (60ml) marsala
½ cup (125ml) cream

1 Place mushrooms in small heatproof bowl, cover with boiling water, stand 20 minutes; drain. Discard stems; slice caps thinly.
2 Melt butter in small frying pan; cook shallot, stirring, until soft. Add mushrooms, rosemary and marsala; bring to the boil then reduce heat. Simmer, uncovered, 3 minutes.
3 Add cream; bring to the boil then reduce heat. Simmer, uncovered, about 3 minutes or until sauce reduces by half. Serve with grilled veal, beef or lamb, if desired.

NUTRITIONAL COUNT PER TABLESPOON 5.9g total fat (3.9g saturated fat); 259kJ (62 cal); 1g carbohydrate; 0.3g protein; 0g fibre

Mushroom and duck broth

PREP + COOK TIME 40 MINUTES (PLUS STANDING TIME) **SERVES** 6

Chinese barbecued duck is traditionally cooked in special ovens in China; dipped into and brushed during roasting with a sticky sweet coating made from soy sauce, sherry, ginger, five-spice, star anise and hoisin sauce. It's available from Asian food shops as well as dedicated chinese barbecued meat shops. This luxurious soup is a meal in itself — lovely for a winter lunch.

20g dried shiitake mushrooms
15g dried black fungus
1kg chinese barbecued duck
1 litre (4 cups) water
1 litre (4 cups) chicken stock
2 teaspoons grated palm sugar
1 tablespoon mushroom soy sauce

230g can bamboo shoots, rinsed, drained
100g swiss brown mushrooms, sliced thinly
1 tablespoon cornflour
1 tablespoon water, extra
4 green onions, sliced thinly

1 Cover dried mushrooms in small bowl with cold water; stand 1 hour. Drain; slice thinly.
2 Meanwhile, remove bones from duck; reserve skin, slice meat thinly.
3 Preheat grill.
4 Combine the water and stock in large saucepan; bring to the boil. Add duck, dried mushrooms, sugar, sauce, bamboo shoots and swiss browns; return to the boil.
5 Place duck skin, in single layer, on oven tray; grill about 5 minutes or until crisp. Discard excess fat; chop skin coarsely.
6 Meanwhile, add blended cornflour and extra water to soup; stir until mixture thickens slightly. Serve soup sprinkled with duck skin and onion.

NUTRITIONAL COUNT PER SERVING 22.4g total fat (6.8g saturated fat); 1246kJ (298 cal); 4.7g carbohydrate; 19.5g protein; 1.1g fibre

1 PORCINI, MARSALA AND MUSHROOM SAUCE **2** MUSHROOM AND DUCK BROTH **3** SWISS BROWN MUSHROOM AND WARM PANCETTA SALAD [P 326] **4** WILD MUSHROOM RISOTTO [P 326]

1

2

3

4

Serve this salad as a
first course for 6 or a
main course for 4.

For information on
pancetta, see Bacon,
page 28.

Swiss brown mushroom and warm pancetta salad

PREP + COOK TIME 20 MINUTES **SERVES** 6

200g swiss brown mushrooms,
quartered

¼ cup (60ml) balsamic vinegar

8 slices pancetta (120g)

100g baby spinach leaves,
trimmed

2 tablespoons drained
baby capers, rinsed

2 green onions, chopped finely

1 tablespoon olive oil

1 clove garlic, crushed

1 Combine mushrooms with 2 tablespoons of the vinegar in small bowl.

2 Cook pancetta in medium oiled frying pan until crisp; chop coarsely.

3 Drain mushrooms; discard vinegar. Cook mushrooms in same pan until tender.

4 Place pancetta and mushrooms in large bowl with remaining ingredients and remaining
vinegar; toss gently to combine.

NUTRITIONAL COUNT PER SERVING 6g total fat (1.5g saturated fat); 360kJ (86 cal); 1.3g carbohydrate;
5.6g protein; 1.6g fibre

Wild mushroom risotto

PREP + COOK TIME 40 MINUTES **SERVES** 4

Italians say that the rice
should be "thirsty" before
each cup of stock is added
— that is, the liquid must
be completely absorbed
so that the risotto will be
creamy but not liquid.
Only in Venice and the
Veneto region is a little
liquid allowed to remain
after the last addition so
that the risotto will be a
little looser and moister —
all'onda, or like a wave.
It is imperative to use
risotto rice varieties for
making risotto.

For information on arborio
and other risotto rices, see
Rice, pages 494 & 496.

10g dried chanterelle mushrooms

10g dried porcini mushrooms

1 litre (4 cups) chicken or
vegetable stock

2 cups (500ml) water

50g butter

100g chestnut mushrooms,
trimmed

100g button mushrooms,
sliced thickly

2 flat mushrooms (160g),
halved, sliced thickly

4 shallots (100g), chopped finely

2 cloves garlic, crushed

2 cups (400g) arborio rice

½ cup (125ml) dry white wine

½ cup (40g) finely grated
parmesan cheese

2 tablespoons finely chopped
fresh chives

1 Bring dried mushrooms, stock and the water to the boil in medium saucepan. Reduce
heat; simmer, covered.

2 Meanwhile, melt 30g of the butter in large saucepan; cook fresh mushrooms, stirring,
until mushrooms are tender and liquid evaporates. Remove from pan.

3 Melt remaining butter in same pan; cook shallots and garlic, stirring, until shallots soften.
Add rice; stir to coat rice in butter mixture. Return mushrooms cooked in butter to pan with
wine; bring to the boil. Reduce heat; simmer, uncovered, until liquid has almost evaporated.
Add 1 cup simmering stock mixture; cook, stirring, over low heat, until stock is absorbed.
Continue adding stock mixture, in 1 cup batches, stirring, until absorbed between additions.
Total cooking time should be 25 minutes or until rice is tender. Stir in cheese and chives.

NUTRITIONAL COUNT PER SERVING 15.4g total fat (9.4g saturated fat); 2391kJ (572 cal); 82.2g carbohydrate;
17.9g protein; 4.4g fibre

Mixed oyster mushroom and ginger noodles

PREP + COOK TIME 25 MINUTES **SERVES** 4

1 tablespoon peanut oil

2 cloves garlic, crushed

2cm piece fresh ginger (10g), grated

150g oyster mushrooms, chopped coarsely

150g pink oyster mushrooms, chopped coarsely

150g yellow oyster mushrooms, chopped coarsely

450g fresh thin rice noodles

⅓ cup (80ml) vegetarian mushroom oyster sauce

2 tablespoons lime juice

4 green onions, sliced thinly

1 Heat oil in wok; stir-fry garlic, ginger and mushrooms until mushrooms are almost tender.
2 Add noodles, sauce and juice; stir-fry until hot.
3 Divide noodles among bowls; serve sprinkled with onion.

NUTRITIONAL COUNT PER SERVING 5.6g total fat (0.9g saturated fat); 903kJ (216 cal); 0.9g carbohydrate; 7g protein; 6.1g fibre

If you can't get the oyster mushrooms in different colours, use all plain ones — the stir-fry won't have quite the same gorgeous looks, but it will taste just as good.

For information on fresh rice noodles, see Noodles, page 334 & 335.

Baked mushrooms with tomato and basil

PREP + COOK TIME 45 MINUTES **SERVES** 4

8 flat mushrooms (640g)

100g enoki mushrooms, chopped coarsely

3 green onions, chopped finely

125g grape tomatoes, halved

125g cream cheese, softened

½ cup coarsely chopped fresh basil

1 cup (70g) stale breadcrumbs

2 cups (500g) bottled tomato pasta sauce

⅓ cup (25g) finely grated parmesan cheese

1 Preheat oven to 200°C/180°C fan forced.
2 Remove stems from flat mushrooms; chop stems finely. Cook stems in medium heated oiled frying pan, stirring, until tender. Stir in enoki, onion and tomato. Cool 10 minutes.
3 Combine mushroom mixture in medium bowl with cream cheese, basil and breadcrumbs; divide mixture among mushroom caps.
4 Place pasta sauce in medium baking dish; top with mushroom caps, sprinkle mushrooms with parmesan. Bake, uncovered, about 20 minutes or until mushroom caps are tender.

NUTRITIONAL COUNT PER SERVING 14.5g total fat (8.2g saturated fat); 1275kJ (305 cal); 27.9g carbohydrate; 16.2g protein; 8.4g fibre

While we've used flat and enoki mushrooms here, feel free to use whatever types you prefer or are in great supply — swiss brown, portobello, oyster, shiitake or button would all be deliciously suitable.

For information on grape tomatoes, see Tomatoes, page 607.

Mustard

Mustards come from the seeds of three members of the cabbage family: black mustard (*Brassica nigra*), brown mustard (*Brassica juncea*) and white mustard (*Sinapsis alba*).

Used as an ingredient, mustard adds not only its characteristic flavour but depth to the dish. It is essential in vinaigrette and mayonnaise and strangely delicious with spicy fruits — the most famous example being the Italian fruit relish to serve with ham, mostarda di cremona.

A touch of mustard has such an affinity with cheese that some cooks believe in adding a little to every dish with cheese in it.

MUSTARD SEEDS The hottest are ***black mustard seeds***, and were once the main ones used for manufacturing condiment mustards, but they have fallen out of favour because they are not suitable for mechanical harvesting as the seeds scatter too much from the plant, so now ***brown mustard seeds*** are mainly used; the seed is larger and milder than black and can be efficiently harvested by machine. ***White mustard seeds*** range in colour from pale yellow-brown to white, and are large and mild. Mustard seed is not hot in itself but it contains glucosides (bitter substances chemically related to sugar) which, through the action of an enzyme also present in the seed, react with water to form hot, biting oils. To make mustard, the seeds are crushed or ground, water is added and the mixture is left to stand for 10–15 minutes to allow the reaction to take place and the flavour to develop. Once it is completed, vinegar, salt and other flavourings are added. There is no one "best" mustard, though the top-name dijon blends are acknowledged as aristocrats for their subtle complexity. Manufacturers in different countries make mustards that suit their local market: the British like their mustard hot, so that is how British manufacturers make it, but the mark of the true British mustard-lover is to buy powdered mustard and mix it fresh every time it is needed, so that the full effect of the glucoside-and-water reaction will be felt. Americans like

their mustard sweet and mild enough to be slathered on hot dogs and hamburgers. The Germans like it dark and aromatic to go with their sausages, the French like it subtle, and the Japanese like something that blows your head off. You can make your own mustards by soaking seeds then flavouring and grinding it, or by moistening mustard powder with water and adding flavourings of your choice. It is, however, harder than it looks to achieve a flavour balance that rivals the classics.

FRENCH MUSTARD The city of Dijon in Burgundy has been famous for its mustard for some 600 years and is considered the mustard capital of the world. A mustard labelled "dijon" has to be made to a strict set of rules. It must be made with black or brown mustard seeds only; after soaking with water for the glucosides to produce hot oils, it must be ground, sieved, mixed with vinegar, wine or verjuice (the juice of unripe grapes) plus salt and spices, and finally matured for about a week before being bottled. All dijon mustard is hot when it is first made, but brief heating at a later stage of manufacture, which removes some of the heat, allows mild as well as strong styles to be made. Dijon mustard is pale brown and subtly flavoured, having a clean mustard taste with a delicate acid edge. Most, but not all, is still manufactured in Dijon and its environs. If a recipe calls for mustard without specifying the kind, it is safest to use dijon. ***Bordeaux and Meaux***

mustards are wholegrain or seeded mustards, made from a mixture of ground and whole seeds giving a speckled appearance and grainy texture. Bordeaux mustard uses must (the juice of wine grapes before fermentation is complete), and sometimes tarragon or other herbs and spices, for blending; it is mild, sharp/sweet and aromatic. Meaux mustard is fairly strong, with a blend of pleasantly musty, hot and sharp flavours.

ENGLISH MUSTARD English ready-mixed mustard is usually labelled "hot" and provides straightforward, sinus-clearing bite. **English mustard powder** is made from a blend of brown and white mustard with a little wheat flour and turmeric. For freshly-mixed mustard, a few teaspoons of mustard powder are blended with enough cold water to make a smooth, creamy paste, left to stand for 10–15 minutes to let the flavour develop, and used as soon as possible. Ready-mixed mustard not used immediately gradually loses its pungency. There are some local variations on the straightforward hot blast: tewkesbury mustard, famed for its strength, includes horseradish and welsh mustard may be mixed with honey.

GERMAN MUSTARD Germans eat various styles of mustard with their many kinds of sausage, but the local style of Dusseldorf,

the centre of German mustard-making, is usually thought of as typically German. It is dark, aromatic and sharp/sweet and is the one to expect if you buy a jar that is simply labelled German Mustard.

AMERICAN MUSTARD America, with its huge, mixed population, has every kind of mustard, but the classic national one is made from white seeds and is bright yellow and mild. The long-established manufacturer French's is credited with making the Americans into mustard enthusiasts by adding cream to mixed mustard, giving it a cool character that proved to be popular.

ORIENTAL MUSTARDS *Japanese mustard*, made from mustard powder and horseradish and very fiery, is eaten as a condiment with winter dishes. Mustard as a spice turns up occasionally in Chinese sauces, and chinese mixed mustard, very hot and prepared with water or flat beer, is traditionally served with egg rolls; hot english mustard can be substituted. Chinese cooks, on the whole, are more interested in mustard greens, the tops of the brown mustard plant, than in ground mustard.

STORING Mustard powder will remain fresh and potent for about a year in an airtight container in a cool place. Mixed mustards keep best in the refrigerator; use within a few months.

⚜ **OTHER RECIPES USING MUSTARD**
Lamb racks with mustard maple glaze, p289
Spicy mustard pickles, p469

Dijon mustard

Wholegrain mustard

English mustard powder

This makes enough sauce for 4 servings of pan-fried pork cutlets, deep-fried chicken drumsticks, roasted lamb backstraps or roasted pork loins.

Mustard and basil cream

PREP + COOK TIME 15 MINUTES **MAKES** 1 CUP

2 teaspoons olive oil

1 clove garlic, crushed

¼ cup (60ml) dry white wine

300ml cream

1 tablespoon dijon mustard

¼ cup finely chopped fresh basil

1 Heat oil in small frying pan; cook garlic, stirring, until fragrant. Add wine; bring to the boil then reduce heat. Simmer, uncovered, until liquid reduces by half.

2 Add cream and mustard; cook, stirring, until sauce thickens and reduces to about a cup. Remove from heat; stir basil into sauce. Serve with pan-fried pork cutlets or chicken breasts or drumsticks.

NUTRITIONAL COUNT PER TABLESPOON 11.6g total fat (7.3g saturated fat); 468kJ (112 cal); 0.8g carbohydrate; 0.6g protein; 0.1g fibre

Use this dressing for a salad to go with ham, pork or salami.

Honey mustard dressing

PREP TIME 5 MINUTES **MAKES** 1 CUP

½ cup (150g) mayonnaise

¼ cup (60ml) cider vinegar

1 tablespoon honey

2 teaspoons wholegrain mustard

1 Whisk ingredients in small jug until combined.

NUTRITIONAL COUNT PER TABLESPOON 4.1g total fat (0.5g saturated fat); 230kJ (55 cal); 4.5g carbohydrate; 0.2g protein; 0.1g fibre

1 BLACK MUSTARD SEEDS
2 YELLOW MUSTARD SEEDS
3 BROWN MUSTARD SEEDS

Nectarines

Like peaches, luscious nectarines are one of the joys of summer. They are, in fact, a variety of peach, not a cross between a peach and a plum as is often believed. They can be either clingstone (when cut, the flesh clings to the stone) or freestone (when cut, the flesh will fall or twist cleanly away from the stone), and white- or yellow-fleshed.

White nectarines are more fragile than yellow but worth it for their lusciousness and marvellous perfume with flavour to match. Nectarines' thin, smooth skin doesn't need peeling if they are to be eaten out of hand, halved and grilled, or sliced and either drizzled with passionfruit pulp or piled on buttered and sugared brioche for an ambrosial breakfast. For poaching and for peeling raw for a tart filling, cake, crumble, trifle, ice-cream or other summer treat, see Peaches, page 412. As the flesh discolours very quickly after peeling or cutting, it should be brushed with lemon juice if not to be cooked or served immediately. For information on choosing and storing nectarines, see Peaches, page 412. Nectarines are available from early summer into autumn, their peak season being from midsummer into autumn.

White nectarines

Yellow nectarines

Nectarines with sangiovese granita

PREP + COOK TIME 30 MINUTES (PLUS FREEZING TIME) **SERVES** 6

1 cup (220g) white sugar
1 cup (250ml) sangiovese wine
1 cup (250ml) water
2 tablespoons orange liqueur
1 teaspoon lemon juice
6 medium nectarines (1kg), halved, stone removed

1 Stir sugar, wine, the water, liqueur and juice in medium saucepan over low heat until sugar dissolves. Add nectarines; simmer, uncovered, without stirring, 5 minutes. Remove from heat; cool.
2 Using slotted spoon, transfer nectarines to bowl, cover tightly; refrigerate 1 hour.
3 Meanwhile, pour cooled syrup into 14cm x 21cm loaf pan. Cover with foil; freeze 4 hours or until firm, scraping granita from bottom and sides of pan with fork every hour.
4 Divide nectarines among serving bowls; flake granita with fork, spoon over nectarines.

NUTRITIONAL COUNT PER SERVING 0.2g total fat (0g saturated fat); 1074kJ (257 cal); 51.7g carbohydrate; 1.7g protein; 3.5g fibre

Nectarines are easily stewed in the microwave. Simply slice and place nectarines in a covered microwave dish with no water or sugar — don't fill it too full or turn your back during cooking as it can boil up and overflow. Serve on breakfast cereal or with ice-cream.
Full-bodied and fruity, sangiovese is well suited to the nectarines in this recipe.

Poached nectarines with orange almond bread

PREP + COOK TIME 1 HOUR 40 MINUTES (PLUS REFRIGERATION AND COOLING TIME) **SERVES** 4

3 cups (750g) water

1 cup (220g) caster sugar

1 star anise

10cm strip orange rind

8 small white nectarines (800g)

⅔ cup (190g) greek-style yogurt

ORANGE ALMOND BREAD

2 egg whites

⅓ cup (75g) caster sugar

¾ cup (110g) plain flour

1 teaspoon finely grated orange rind

¾ cup (120g) blanched almonds

1 Make orange almond bread.

2 Combine the water, sugar, star anise and rind in medium saucepan, stir over medium heat until sugar dissolves; bring to the boil. Boil, uncovered, 2 minutes. Add nectarines, reduce heat; simmer, uncovered, 20 minutes. Cool nectarines 10 minutes in poaching liquid.

3 Using slotted spoon, transfer nectarines to serving dishes; bring liquid in pan to the boil. Boil, uncovered, about 5 minutes or until syrup reduces to 1 cup; strain into small bowl.

4 Cool syrup to room temperature; pour ¼ cup of the syrup over nectarines in each dish. Serve nectarines with yogurt and almond bread.

ORANGE ALMOND BREAD Preheat oven to 180°C/160°C fan-forced. Grease and line 8cm x 25cm bar cake pan. Beat egg whites in small bowl with electric mixer until soft peaks form. Gradually add sugar, 1 tablespoon at a time, beating until sugar dissolves between additions; transfer to medium bowl. Gently fold in flour, rind and nuts; spread into pan. Bake 30 minutes or until browned lightly; cool in pan. Wrap in foil; refrigerate 3 hours or overnight. Preheat oven to 150°C/130°C fan-forced. Using serrated knife, cut bread into 3mm slices; place slices on baking-paper-lined oven trays. Bake 15 minutes or until crisp.

NUTRITIONAL COUNT PER SERVING 20.6g total fat (3.3g saturated fat); 2867kJ (686 cal); 112.6g carbohydrate; 15.5g protein; 7.9g fibre

Grilled nectarines with passionfruit yogurt

PREP + COOK TIME 20 MINUTES **SERVES** 4

8 nectarines (1.5kg), halved, stone removed

¼ cup (55g) brown sugar

2 tablespoons orange juice

1 cup (280g) yogurt

2 tablespoons icing sugar

2 tablespoons passionfruit pulp

1 Place nectarines, cut-side up, on oven tray; sprinkle with brown sugar and juice. Place under preheated grill until browned lightly.

2 Combine yogurt and sifted icing sugar in medium bowl, swirl in pulp; serve with nectarines.

NUTRITIONAL COUNT PER SERVING 2.7g total fat (1.5g saturated fat); 1124kJ (269 cal); 48.8g carbohydrate; 7.3g protein; 9.2g fibre

POACHED NECTARINES WITH ORANGE ALMOND BREAD

Noodles

Noodles are important in the food of many Asian countries but it is in Chinese and Japanese cuisine that they come into their own for rich variety. Only Italy can compare for the range and interest of its noodles and other pastas, and those are considered in a later entry (see Pasta on pages 396–398). Asian noodles differ from european ones in that they are made not only from wheat but from rice, buckwheat and vegetable starches such as mung bean.

The reason that dried chinese egg noodles are often packed as nests or tight skeins is that they are not meant to be dropped straight into boiling water as you do with Italian pasta. The right way to handle them is to soak them in hot water for about 10 minutes, which will separate the strands, then drain, loosen strands gently and add to a large pot of briskly boiling water with a spoonful of peanut oil added. One nest or skein is supposed to serve one person, but this is up to you and what you know of the diners' appetites.

WHEAT NOODLES

EGG NOODLES, also called yellow noodles or ba mee, are made from wheat flour and hen or duck eggs. They are available fresh or dried and may be sold in skeins or nest-like swirls or packed flat. They range from very fine strands to spaghetti-like lengths as thick as a bootlace.

FRIED NOODLES, also called crispy noodles, are deep-fried egg noodles, often packaged in 100g cellophane packets.

GOW GEE WRAPPERS, also called gow gee skins, are thin, round white noodles used to enclose a filling in a small "money-bag" shape, then steamed.

HOKKIEN NOODLES, also called stir-fry noodles, are thick and soft, having been parboiled before packing. They do not need cooking, just reheating — cover in boiling water, separating with a fork and draining.

RAMEN was traditionally a Japanese soup with noodles, but now the name is given to "instant" wavy, fried noodles sold with a sachet of soup base that can be cooked in a few minutes. It is popular in Japan.

SOMEN are fine, vermicelli-like Japanese noodles.

SHANGHAI NOODLES are plain white noodles, available fresh or dried.

UDON NOODLES are broad white Japanese noodles, available fresh or dried.

WONTON WRAPPERS, also known as wonton skins, are thin, square egg noodles used to enclose a filling in a small fluted package to be steamed. Wonton are used in soups or served with a dipping sauce.

RICE NOODLES

FRESH RICE NOODLES are white, flat noodles prized for their chewy, satiny texture and mild flavour which lets stronger flavours shine. They can be bought in various widths or in sheets to be cut as desired. They do not need cooking or soaking.

RICE PAPER SHEETS are round and translucent. They are used by softening in water then wrapping round fresh ingredients such as vegetables, herbs and chicken or seafood and serving with a dipping sauce.

RICE STICKS, also called sen lek, ho fun or kway teow, are dried noodles in various widths — thin for soups, wide for stir-fries. Soak in hot water until soft before use to prevent them from sticking together.

RICE VERMICELLI, also known as sen mee or mei fun, are fine dried noodles that can be softened in hot water for 15 minutes, then boiled for 3 minutes and rinsed with hot water. They can also be deep-fried, puffing them up into crisp threads; use in coleslaw, as a garnish or as a bed for sauces. One of the most popular Asian dishes, and best-known to the West, is singapore noodles, a lightly curried melange of rice vermicelli, vegetables, chicken and prawns.

BUCKWHEAT NOODLES

SOBA are fresh or dried Japanese noodles made from buckwheat and wheat flour, sometimes with egg yolks; called matcha soba when Japanese green tea is added. Serve cold with a dipping sauce and side dishes of tempura, or in a hot broth, plain or with clams, chicken, mushroon or other meats or vegetables, and various garnishes. They are a popular fast food.

MUNG BEAN NOODLES

BEAN THREAD NOODLES, also known as cellophane or glass noodles for their transparency when cooked, are made from extruded mung bean paste. They are sold in bundles of various sizes. They are soaked to soften them before use, or can be deep-fried like rice vermicelli.

STORING Dried noodles can be stored in their unopened packages and, after opening, in airtight jars or boxes. Soft noodles such as hokkien should be stored in the refrigerator, where they will keep for weeks unopened or opened and rewrapped in plastic wrap and then enclosed in a plastic bag.

❧ **OTHER RECIPES USING NOODLES**
*Mixed oyster mushroom and ginger noodles, p327
Mongolian lamb and noodle stir-fry, p285*

Bean thread noodles

Egg noodles

Fresh rice noodles

Fried noodles

Gow gee wrappers

Hokkien noodles

Ramen noodles

Rice vermicelli noodles

Rice stick noodles

Soba noodles

Somen noodles

Udon noodles

Vegetable dumplings in asian broth

PREP + COOK TIME 1 HOUR 40 MINUTES **SERVES** 4

There can sometimes be a little confusion between sichuan peppercorns and star anise — for information on both, see Spices, pages 560 & 562.

Chinese cooking wine is made from fermented rice. The best is the shao hsing variety, from eastern China; it is also used for drinking. Dry sherry can be substituted.

100g fresh shiitake mushrooms

2 green onions

1 medium brown onion (150g), chopped coarsely

1 medium carrot (120g), chopped coarsely

2 cloves garlic, chopped coarsely

2cm piece fresh ginger (10g), chopped coarsely

1 star anise

1 teaspoon sichuan peppercorns

¼ cup (60ml) soy sauce

2 tablespoons chinese cooking wine

4 coriander roots

1 teaspoon white sugar

1.5 litres (6 cups) water

800g buk choy

1cm piece fresh ginger (5g), extra, grated

1 clove garlic, extra, crushed

227g can water chestnuts, drained, chopped finely

1 egg white, beaten lightly

¼ cup (15g) stale breadcrumbs

2 tablespoons finely chopped fresh coriander leaves

1 tablespoon vegetarian mushroom oyster sauce

20 wonton wrappers

100g enoki mushrooms, trimmed

1 Separate stems from caps of the shiitake mushrooms; reserve stems. Finely chop a quarter of the shiitake caps; slice remaining shiitake caps thinly. Coarsely chop white section of green onion. Thinly slice green section; reserve green section in small bowl.

2 Combine shiitake mushroom stems, white section of green onion, brown onion, carrot, garlic, ginger, star anise, peppercorns, soy sauce, wine, coriander roots, sugar and the water in large saucepan; bring to the boil. Reduce heat; simmer, uncovered, 45 minutes. Strain stock through muslin-lined sieve or colander into large bowl; discard solids. Return stock to same cleaned pan; bring to the boil. Reduce heat; simmer, covered.

3 Meanwhile, separate bases and leaves of buk choy. Finely chop half of the bases; discard remaining bases. Combine chopped bases with finely chopped shiitake mushrooms, extra ginger, extra garlic, water chestnuts, egg white, breadcrumbs, coriander leaves and oyster sauce in large bowl. Make dumplings by placing 1 heaped teaspoon of the mushroom mixture in centre of a wonton wrapper; brush around edges with a little water. Fold wrapper in half diagonally; pinch edges together to seal. Repeat with remaining mushroom mixture and wrappers.

4 Add sliced shiitake and enoki mushrooms to simmering stock; cook, uncovered, 5 minutes. Add dumplings; cook, uncovered, about 5 minutes or until dumplings are cooked through. Stir in buk choy leaves.

5 Divide soup among serving bowls; top with reserved sliced green onion.

NUTRITIONAL COUNT PER SERVING 1.6g total fat (0.2g saturated fat); 978kJ (234 cal); 40g carbohydrate; 11.6g protein; 6.8g fibre

1 ASIAN CRISPY NOODLE
SALAD
2 SOBA AND DAIKON SALAD

Asian crispy noodle salad

PREP TIME 15 MINUTES **SERVES** 4

Sold in cellophane bags or cans, deep-fried wheat noodles can be eaten straight from the pack as a snack or served instead of rice with stir-fries. You can make your own fried noodles by deep-frying bean thread, dried wheat or fresh, thin rice noodles in small batches; use them as a bed for a vegetarian larb or tofu sang choy bow.

½ medium wombok (500g), shredded finely

227g can water chestnuts, drained, sliced thinly

150g snow peas, trimmed, sliced thinly

1 large red capsicum (350g), sliced thinly

100g packet fried noodles

⅓ cup (50g) roasted unsalted cashews, chopped coarsely

1 cup loosely packed fresh coriander leaves

SESAME SOY DRESSING

1 teaspoon sesame oil

¼ cup (60ml) soy sauce

1 tablespoon sweet chilli sauce

2 tablespoons lime juice

1 Place ingredients for sesame soy dressing in screw-top jar; shake well.
2 Place wombok, water chestnuts, snow peas, capsicum and fried noodles in medium bowl; toss gently to combine.
3 Divide salad among serving bowls; sprinkle with nuts and coriander leaves, drizzle with dressing.

NUTRITIONAL COUNT PER SERVING 10.8g fat (2.2g saturated fat); 869kJ (208 cal); 19.1g carbohydrate; 8.3g protein; 6.4g fibre

Soba and daikon salad

PREP + COOK TIME 35 MINUTES **SERVES** 4

300g dried soba noodles

1 small daikon (400g),
cut into matchsticks

4 green onions, sliced thinly

1 teaspoon sesame oil

100g enoki mushrooms

2 tablespoons thinly sliced
pickled ginger

1 toasted seaweed sheet
(yaki-nori), sliced thinly

MIRIN DRESSING

¼ cup (60ml) mirin

2 tablespoons kecap manis

1 tablespoon sake

1 clove garlic, crushed

1cm piece fresh ginger (5g),
grated

1 teaspoon white sugar

*Mirin is a Japanese sweet
rice wine used only for
cooking. Sake is also a
rice wine but is made for
drinking, though it is also
used as an ingredient in
certain dishes. If sake is
unavailable, dry sherry,
vermouth or brandy can
be used as a substitute.*

*For information on daikon,
see Radishes, page 488.*

1 Cook soba in large saucepan of boiling water, uncovered, until just tender; drain.
Rinse under cold water; drain.

2 Place ingredients for mirin dressing in screw-top jar; shake well.

3 Place soba in large bowl with daikon, onion and half of the dressing; toss gently.

4 Heat oil in small frying pan; cook mushrooms, stirring, 2 minutes.

5 Divide soba salad among serving plates; top with combined mushrooms, ginger and
seaweed. Drizzle with remaining dressing.

NUTRITIONAL COUNT PER SERVING 2.4g total fat (0.3g saturated fat); 1292kJ (309 cal); 56.6g carbohydrate;
10.9g protein; 5.3g fibre

Singapore noodles

PREP + COOK TIME 25 MINUTES **SERVES** 4

450g fresh singapore noodles

2 teaspoons sesame oil

2 cloves garlic, crushed

2cm piece fresh ginger (10g),
grated

1 medium carrot (120g),
cut into matchsticks

250g cooked shelled small
prawns

1 tablespoon malaysian
curry powder

3 green onions, sliced thinly

1½ cups bean sprouts (120g)

2 tablespoons soy sauce

¼ cup (60ml) kecap manis

3 cups (480g) shredded
barbecued chicken

*This recipe is perhaps the
most famous of Singapore
street foods. You will need
a large barbecued chicken
(about 900g) to get the
amount of shredded
meat needed.*

1 Place noodles in large heatproof bowl; cover with boiling water. Separate noodles
with fork; drain.

2 Meanwhile, heat oil in wok; stir-fry garlic, ginger and carrot until carrot is just tender.
Add prawns and curry powder; stir-fry until prawns change colour.

3 Add noodles and remaining ingredients; stir-fry until hot.

NUTRITIONAL COUNT PER SERVING 19.1g total fat (6.4g saturated fat); 2057kJ (492 cal); 27.3g carbohydrate;
49.1g protein; 5.8g fibre

Char siu lamb and noodle stir-fry

PREP + COOK TIME 35 MINUTES **SERVES** 4

Char siu sauce, salty and flavoured with the spice blend called chinese five-spice (star anise, fennel seed, cassia, sichuan pepper and cloves), has a dominant anise flavour. It turns the surface of meat red.

For information on lamb, see Lamb, pages 282 & 283.

2 cloves garlic, crushed

2cm piece fresh ginger (10g), grated

1 tablespoon finely grated orange rind

1 teaspoon sesame oil

750g lamb strips

450g hokkien noodles

2 tablespoons peanut oil

200g sugar snap peas

115g baby corn, halved lengthways

2 fresh long red chillies, sliced thinly

⅓ cup (120g) char siu sauce

2 tablespoons water

1 tablespoon rice wine vinegar

1 Combine garlic, ginger, rind, sesame oil and lamb in medium bowl.

2 Place noodles in large heatproof bowl, cover with boiling water; separate with fork, drain.

3 Heat half the peanut oil in wok; stir-fry peas and corn until just tender. Remove from wok.

4 Heat remaining peanut oil in wok; stir-fry lamb, in batches, until browned all over and cooked as desired. Return peas, corn and lamb to wok with noodles, chilli and combined sauce, water and vinegar; stir-fry until heated through.

NUTRITIONAL COUNT PER SERVING 29.2g total fat (9.6g saturated fat); 2725kJ (652 cal); 46.6g carbohydrate; 47.1g protein; 8g fibre

Hot and sour prawn vermicelli salad

PREP TIME 30 MINUTES (PLUS REFRIGERATION TIME) **SERVES** 4

Refrigerating the salad for an hour before serving not only allows it to chill lightly but lets the flavours mingle and balance.

For information on prawns, including tips on deveining, see Seafood, page 526.

1kg cooked medium king prawns

250g rice vermicelli noodles

1 lime

1 lemon

1 medium red capsicum (200g), sliced thinly

1 medium yellow capsicum (200g), sliced thinly

1 medium red onion (170g), sliced thinly

¼ cup (60ml) olive oil

¼ cup (60ml) rice vinegar

1 tablespoon sambal oelek

1 tablespoon fish sauce

2 tablespoons grated palm sugar

1 cup firmly packed fresh coriander leaves

1 Shell and devein prawns, leaving tails intact. Place vermicelli in large heatproof bowl of boiling water, stand until just tender; drain. Rinse under cold water; drain.

2 Meanwhile, halve lime and lemon lengthways; slice 1 unpeeled half of each thinly, place in large bowl. Squeeze remaining halves over bowl; add prawns, vermicelli and remaining ingredients, toss gently to combine. Cover; refrigerate 1 hour before serving.

NUTRITIONAL COUNT PER SERVING 15.4g total fat (2.1g saturated fat); 2057kJ (492 cal); 53.5g carbohydrate; 32.3g protein; 3.5g fibre

CHAR SIU LAMB AND NOODLE STIR-FRY

VIETNAMESE PRAWN
RICE PAPER ROLLS

Vietnamese prawn rice paper rolls

PREP TIME 20 MINUTES **MAKES** 12

For tips on deveining prawns, see Seafood, page 526.

50g rice vermicelli, soaked, drained

¼ small wombok (175g), shredded finely

½ cup loosely packed fresh mint leaves, torn

2 teaspoons brown sugar

2 tablespoons lime juice

500g cooked medium king prawns

12 x 21cm rice paper rounds

HOISIN DIPPING SAUCE

½ cup (125ml) hoisin sauce

2 tablespoons rice vinegar

1 Combine chopped vermicelli in medium bowl with wombok, mint, sugar and juice.

2 Shell and devein prawns; chop meat finely.

3 Meanwhile, combine ingredients for hoisin dipping sauce in small bowl.

4 Dip 1 rice paper round into bowl of warm water until soft; place on board covered with tea towel. Top with a little of the prawn meat and noodle filling. Fold and roll to enclose filling. Repeat with remaining rounds, prawn meat and noodle filling.

5 Serve prawn rolls with dipping sauce.

NUTRITIONAL COUNT PER ROLL 0.9g total fat (0.1g saturated fat); 326kJ (78 cal); 10.8g carbohydrate; 5.5g protein; 1.7g fibre

Rice paper rounds

Peanut and chicken gow gees

PREP + COOK TIME 50 MINUTES (PLUS STANDING TIME) **MAKES** 40

3 dried shiitake mushrooms

1 stalk celery (150g), trimmed, chopped finely

1 tablespoon finely chopped, unsalted, roasted peanuts

1 clove garlic, crushed

1 green onion, chopped finely

2 teaspoons hoisin sauce

200g chicken mince

40 gow gee wrappers

DIPPING SAUCE

¼ cup (60ml) kecap manis

2 teaspoons red wine vinegar

1 Place mushrooms in small heatproof bowl, cover with boiling water; stand 20 minutes, drain. Discard stems; chop caps finely.

2 Combine mushrooms in medium bowl with celery, nuts, garlic, onion, sauce and chicken.

3 Place one heaped teaspoon of the chicken mixture in centre of one wrapper; brush around half of the wrapper's edge with a little water. Pleat damp side of wrapper only; pinch both sides together to seal. Repeat with remaining chicken mixture and wrappers.

4 Poach gow gees, in batches, in large saucepan of boiling water about 5 minutes or until cooked through.

5 Combine ingredients for dipping sauce in small bowl; serve with hot gow gees.

NUTRITIONAL COUNT PER GOW GEE 0.6g total fat (0.2g saturated fat); 54kJ (13 cal); 0.4g carbohydrate; 1.2g protein; 0.2g fibre

Gow gees can be prepared to the end of step 3 up to 4 hours ahead of cooking. Cover and refrigerate until required. They are great to hand around at a party and also go well with stir-fried vegetables.

For information on peanuts, see Nuts, page 346; and for chicken, see Poultry, pages 456 & 457.

Pork kway teow

PREP + COOK TIME 30 MINUTES **SERVES** 4

400g fresh wide rice noodles

1 tablespoon peanut oil

600g pork mince

1 medium brown onion (150g), sliced thinly

1 medium red capsicum (200g), sliced thinly

10cm stick fresh lemon grass (20g), chopped finely

2 tablespoons light soy sauce

¼ cup (60ml) lemon juice

1 tablespoon grated palm sugar

2 fresh small red thai chillies, chopped finely

1 cup coarsely chopped fresh coriander leaves

1 Place noodles in large heatproof bowl, cover with boiling water; separate noodles with fork, drain.

2 Heat half the oil in wok; stir-fry pork until cooked through. Remove from wok.

3 Heat remaining oil in same wok; stir-fry onion, capsicum and lemon grass until onion softens. Return pork to wok with noodles and combined sauce, juice and sugar; stir-fry until heated through. Stir in chilli and coriander off the heat.

NUTRITIONAL COUNT PER SERVING 15.6g total fat (4.7g saturated fat); 1660kJ (397 cal); 29g carbohydrate; 33.9g protein; 1.5g fibre

This wok-cooked noodle dish is a popular hawker food in Singapore.

For information on pork, see Pork, pages 440 & 441.

Nuts

Nuts have been a well-loved food for thousands of years. One of the most popular of all, the peanut, is not a true nut but a legume, but is accorded the name nut on the "looks like, smells like, tastes like" principle.

Nuts make nutritious snacks, providing healthy oils, dietary fibre, vitamins, minerals and protein, and serve us as great ingredients for both flavour and texture in hundreds of dishes. Nut oils are among the finest for salad dressings and cooking, and nut meals (ground nuts) are especially prized for making recklessly rich cakes. Freshness is vital and roasting brings out wonderful new flavour in many nuts (see PREPARATION, CHOOSING and STORING).

WALNUTS are magnificent with cheeses, especially blue ones, and in salads, cakes and desserts. They are usually sold shelled but because they stale quickly, are better bought in shell and can also be found in many supermarkets in cylindrical vacuum packs which are unfortunately not local but imported from America, but they are excellent. Walnut oil is a fine salad and cooking oil.

ALMONDS come in sweet and bitter varieties. Sweet almonds are the most useful of all nuts for the cook, while bitter almonds are used for a flavouring essence and in such products as amaretti biscuits and amaretto liqueur. Sweet almonds are mild-flavoured when raw, but roasting brings out warm, embracing flavour that goes with spicy pilaf, chicken salad, browned butter for fish, Chinese and Indian cooking, almond bread, Christmas cake, nougat and a host of other preparations both sweet and savoury. They are available in shell or as whole kernels either raw or roasted, blanched kernels (brown skins removed), flaked (paper-thin slices) slivered (small pieces cut lengthwise) or ground.

PINE NUTS come from several varieties of pine trees but the best are from the stone pine which is native to the Mediterranean region. There are also cheaper asian pine nuts but the stone-pine nut has superior, buttery flavour, so it is a good idea to check the packet before buying. Pine nuts are usually roasted or fried to bring out their warm savour. They are used in Mediterranean cooking and as both an ingredient and a decoration in Middle Eastern meat and rice dishes, and are an essential ingredient in the famous pasta sauce, pesto. They are always sold shelled and usually packaged.

CASHEWS are second only to peanuts as a popular salted snack. Their full, sweetish flavour works especially well with spices and strong, savoury tastes so they are often used in Chinese and Indian cooking. They are always sold shelled as their shells contain caustic oils which makes removing them a difficult task.

MACADAMIAS, native to Australia, are crisp-textured with warm, buttery flavour. They are roasted and sometimes salted as a luxurious snack and used in biscuits, brownies and chocolate confectionery, and also in savoury contexts such as browned butter to dress brussels sprouts, beans or

freshwater fish. They are notorious for the hardness of their shells so are usually sold shelled, raw, roasted, or roasted and salted.

PECANS are like walnuts but sweeter and milder. Best known in pecan pie, which originated in the American South, they are good in cakes, biscuits and breads, in salads and with cream cheese, celery or apple. They are usually available shelled.

HAZELNUTS The crispness and sweet, aromatic flavour of toasted hazelnuts are wonderful with watercress, orange and rich meats such as duck, and also in meringues, biscuits, cakes and any form of chocolate. Two varieties of hazelnut are called cobs and filberts and these names are also often used confusingly to mean cultivated or wild hazelnuts. Hazelnut oil is a fine and delicate salad and cooking oil. Hazelnuts are available in shell and shelled.

PISTACHIOS are usually sold in their half-opened shells but are also available shelled, either salted to use as a snack or unsalted to use in cooking. Their flavour is mild and slightly resinous. Decoratively bright green, they are used to stud pâtés and terrines, in biscuits, cakes and confectionery, and for a delicate green ice-cream.

CANDLENUTS are native to the Malaysian region but are now grown in India, East Asia, the Philippines and the Pacific islands. They are very oily and their name comes from that fact that they were once used to make candles. The raw nuts are slightly toxic so they are always roasted. They are usually crushed and added to soups, used as a thickener or mixed with such ingredients as garlic, chilli and shrimp paste as a fried flavour base for many dishes. Whole or broken candlenuts are available in Indian and Asian supermarkets. They can be substituted with macadamias.

PEANUTS, also called groundnuts, are the Western world's favourite nut for snacking and are also used by Western cooks in biscuits and toffees and by confectionery manufacturers in many kinds of chocolate bars, and peanut butter is a well-loved spread. For Eastern cooks, they are important for savoury sauces, the most famous of which is satay, and salads, and also as the source of peanut oil which is a favourite cooking oil that can be heated to high temperatures without breaking down. Peanuts are available in shell and as skin-on or skinned raw, roasted or roasted and salted kernels.

WARNING It is important to note that peanuts can cause life-endangering allergic reactions in some people and that for this reason, peanuts or anything containing them should not be offered to children unless one is sure that they do not have this problem. Many schools now forbid any nuts anywhere on the premises.

BRAZIL NUTS are still gathered in their native Amazonian forests as they are difficult to cultivate. Their sweet, rich taste makes an interesting change from other nuts in sweets and biscuits and they are especially delicious dipped in butterscotch toffee as a sweetmeat. Because of their high oil content, they turn rancid quickly. They are available shelled and in the shell; their hard shells are easier to crack if they are frozen.

CHESTNUTS have a sweetish, starchy kernel that is used more like a vegetable than a nut. It can be boiled and puréed to serve with meat and game or used in stuffings and soups. Hot roast chestnuts are sold on the streets of many European towns as a winter snack. The kernels are also used in sweet preparations such as cakes and puddings and are candied (see Fruit, Glacé, page 198) for the elegant sweetmeats marrons glacés. Chestnut meal is used in Italy as a thickener and for flat cakes baked on hot stones. Chestnut flour is also produced (see Flour, page 184).

COCONUTS The fruit of the coconut palm provides cooks with sweet, aromatic grated and shredded flesh for cakes, pastries, biscuits and confectionery and with coconut milk, indispensable for Asian cooking. Whole coconuts are sold as mature nuts with sweet, hard, moist flesh and usually a little juice in the hollow centre. Opening one and extracting the flesh is a business only for the seriously keen, involving a screwdriver or ice pick, a hammer, a small strong knife to prise the flesh off the shell, and a lot of patience. As easier options, desiccated coconut (unsweetened, dried, finely shredded flesh), flaked or shredded coconut, coconut milk and coconut cream, made by blending the flesh with water and straining, are readily available. Coconut oil is not used for cooking except in the form of copha (see Oils & Fats, page 363).

PREPARATION
Roasting nuts enhances their flavour and makes them crunchier. Roast small amounts in a small, dry frying pan over medium heat, stirring until fragrant and just changed in colour. Larger amounts can be roasted in a single layer on an oven tray in a moderate oven for about 5 minutes, checking and stirring once or twice.

Blanching, chopping or grinding are best carried out just before using nuts, as their exposed surfaces rapidly lose flavour when exposed to air.

CHOOSING
Shelled nuts on sale are often stale, so it is best to buy nuts in the shell, which protects them from rancidity, unless you can get them from a trusted retailer with a high turnover, or find vacuum-packed ones. Avoid any nuts in the shell that rattle or are light for their size as these may mean the nuts are wizened.

STORING
Store nuts in the shell in an airtight container away from heat, light and moisture. Store loose shelled nuts under the same conditions for a short period or in an airtight container in the refrigerator for up to 3 months or in the freezer for 6 months. Store shelled nuts in unopened packets in airtight containers (only one kind to a container); once opened, store as described for shelled nuts.

1 RAW PISTACHIOS
2 PISTACHIOS IN SHELL
3 MACADAMIAS IN SHELL

Peanut sambal

PREP + COOK TIME 25 MINUTES **MAKES** 2 CUPS

6 green onions

2 fresh small red thai chillies, chopped coarsely

2 tablespoons lime juice

1 tablespoon peanut oil

1 cup (140g) roasted salted peanuts

¼ teaspoon shrimp paste

410ml can coconut milk

1 tablespoon tamarind concentrate

2 teaspoons brown sugar

1 Finely chop two of the onions.

2 Quarter remaining four onions then blend or process with chilli, juice and half of the oil until chopped coarsely; add nuts, blend or process until mixture is chopped finely.

3 Heat remaining oil in medium frying pan; cook shrimp paste, stirring, 1 minute or until fragrant. Add coconut milk, tamarind, sugar and onion chilli mixture; bring to the boil. Reduce heat; simmer, uncovered, stirring occasionally, 4 minutes or until sauce thickens slightly.

4 Stir in finely chopped onion off the heat. Serve with fried hokkien noodles, spring rolls or raw vegetable sticks, if you like.

NUTRITIONAL COUNT PER TABLESPOON 7.1g total fat (3.6g saturated fat); 330kJ (79 cal); 1.7g carbohydrate; 1.9g protein; 0.9g fibre

This fragrant sauce was originally developed for tossing through stir-fried hokkien noodles as a delicious vegetarian dish. It also goes well with stir-fried rice noodles and makes a good dipping sauce for skewered chicken or pork or raw vegetables.

Cashew-crumbed pork schnitzel

PREP + COOK TIME 35 MINUTES **SERVES** 4

4 x 150g pork medallions

1 cup (150g) roasted unsalted cashews

½ cup (35g) stale breadcrumbs

2 teaspoons finely grated lemon rind

2 teaspoons finely chopped fresh thyme

1 egg

vegetable oil, for shallow-frying

1 medium lemon (140g), quartered

1 Using meat mallet, gently pound pork, one piece at a time, between sheets of plastic wrap, until about 5mm in thickness.

2 Blend or process nuts until coarsely chopped; combine in shallow medium bowl with breadcrumbs, rind and thyme. Whisk egg lightly in another shallow medium bowl. Dip pork in egg then coat in cashew mixture.

3 Heat oil in large frying pan; cook pork, in batches. Drain on absorbent paper. Serve pork with lemon.

NUTRITIONAL COUNT PER SERVING 38.5g total fat (6.8g saturated); 2391kJ (572 cal); 13g carbohydrate; 42.5g protein; 3.3g fibre

Plain pasta such as tagliatelle (see Pasta, page 396) and a simple salad would be best with this rich meat dish.

For information on pork, see Pork, pages 440 & 441.

Caramel cashew tarts

PREP + COOK TIME 45 MINUTES (PLUS REFRIGERATION AND COOLING TIME) **MAKES** 24

1 cup (150g) roasted unsalted cashews

1 tablespoon cornflour

¾ cup (165g) firmly packed brown sugar

2 tablespoons golden syrup

50g butter, melted

2 eggs

2 tablespoons cream

1 teaspoon vanilla extract

PASTRY

1¼ cups (185g) plain flour

¼ cup (55g) caster sugar

125g cold butter, chopped coarsely

1 egg yolk

2 teaspoons water

CINNAMON CREAM

300ml thickened cream

1 tablespoon icing sugar

1 teaspoon ground cinnamon

1 Make pastry.

2 Grease two 12-hole (⅓-cup/80ml) muffin pans. Roll pastry between sheets of baking paper to 3mm thickness; cut out twenty-four 8cm rounds. Press rounds into pan holes; prick bases all over with fork. Refrigerate 20 minutes.

3 Preheat oven to 200°C/180°C fan-forced.

4 Bake pastry cases 10 minutes. Cool. Reduce oven to 160°C/140°C fan-forced.

5 Combine nuts and cornflour in medium bowl; stir in sugar, syrup, butter, egg, cream and extract. Divide filling among pastry cases. Bake about 15 minutes; cool. Refrigerate 30 minutes.

6 Meanwhile, beat ingredients for cinnamon cream in small bowl with electric mixer until soft peaks form. Serve tarts with cinnamon cream.

PASTRY Process flour, sugar and butter until coarse. Add egg yolk and the water; process until combined. Knead on floured surface until smooth. Cover; refrigerate 30 minutes.

NUTRITIONAL COUNT PER TART 15.2g total fat (8.2g saturated fat); 932kJ (223 cal); 18.6g carbohydrate; 29g protein; 0.7g fibre

If the pastry does not come together properly after you add the egg yolk, add 2 teaspoons of water. These luscious treats will keep for 3 days in an airtight container.

For more information on pastry, see Pastry, pages 404–406.

When buying maple syrup, check the label to ensure that it says pure maple syrup, as there are many imitations but they don't have the true maple flavour.

For more information on pastry, see Pastry, pages 404–406.

Pistachio orange pie

PREP + COOK TIME 1 HOUR 20 MINUTES (PLUS REFRIGERATION TIME) **SERVES** 10

1⅓ cups (185g) coarsely chopped unsalted pistachios

1 tablespoon plain flour

2 tablespoons brown sugar

40g butter, melted

2 eggs

¾ cup (180ml) maple syrup

2 teaspoons finely grated orange rind

1 tablespoon orange juice

2 tablespoons orange marmalade, warmed, sieved

PASTRY

1¼ cups (185g) plain flour

⅓ cup (55g) icing sugar

125g cold butter, chopped coarsely

1 egg yolk

1 teaspoon iced water, approximately

1 Make pastry.

2 Grease 24cm-round loose-based flan tin. Roll pastry between sheets of baking paper until large enough to line tin. Ease pastry into tin, press into base and side; trim edge. Cover; refrigerate 30 minutes.

3 Preheat oven to 180°C/160°C fan-forced.

4 Place tin on oven tray. Line pastry case with baking paper; fill with dried beans or rice. Bake 10 minutes; remove paper and beans carefully from pie shell. Bake 5 minutes; cool.

5 Reduce oven to 160°C/140°C fan-forced.

6 Combine nuts, flour, sugar, butter, eggs, syrup, rind and juice in medium bowl. Pour mixture into pastry case. Bake about 45 minutes. Cool. Brush pie with marmalade.

PASTRY Process flour, icing sugar and butter until crumbly. Add egg yolk and enough of the water to process until ingredients come together. Knead dough on floured surface until smooth. Cover; refrigerate 30 minutes.

NUTRITIONAL COUNT PER SERVING 23.7g total fat (10.2g saturated fat); 1785kJ (427 cal); 44.9g carbohydrate; 7.4g protein; 2.5g fibre

These are best eaten the
day they are made but
can be stored airtight
for up to 2 days.

For information on pears,
see Pears, pages 416–418.

Pear and almond friands

PREP + COOK TIME 35 MINUTES **MAKES** 12

6 egg whites
185g butter, melted
1 cup (120g) almond meal
1 ½ cups (240g) icing sugar
¾ cup (110g) plain flour
1 small pear (180g), peeled, cored, chopped finely
¼ cup (20g) flaked almonds

1 Preheat oven to 200°C/180°C fan-forced. Grease 12-hole (⅓-cup/80ml) muffin pan.
2 Whisk egg whites in medium bowl until frothy. Add butter, meal, sifted icing sugar
and flour, then pear; stir until combined.
3 Place ¼-cups of mixture into pan holes; sprinkle with nuts.
4 Bake about 20 minutes. Stand 5 minutes; turn, top-side up, onto wire rack to cool.

NUTRITIONAL COUNT PER FRIAND 19.2g total fat (8.8g saturated fat); 1300kJ (311 cal); 28.8g carbohydrate;
5.3g protein; 1.6g fibre

Macaroons can be stored
in an airtight container for
up to 2 days.

For coconut macaroons,
replace almond meal with
¾ cup desiccated coconut
and ¾ cup shredded
coconut; replace almond
essence with vanilla extract;
omit blanched almonds.

For strawberry coconut
macaroons, replace
almond meal with
1 ½ cups shredded
coconut; replace almond
essence with vanilla
extract; omit blanched
almonds; fold ⅓ cup finely
chopped dried strawberries
into the basic mixture.

Almond macaroons

PREP + COOK TIME 35 MINUTES **MAKES** 22

2 egg whites
½ cup (110g) caster sugar
1 ¼ cups (150g) almond meal
½ teaspoon almond essence
2 tablespoons plain flour
¼ cup (40g) blanched almonds

1 Preheat oven to 150°C/130°C fan-forced. Grease oven trays.
2 Beat egg whites in small bowl with electric mixer until soft peaks form; gradually
add sugar, beating until dissolved between additions. Gently fold in meal, essence and
sifted flour, in two batches.
3 Drop level tablespoons of mixture about 5cm apart on trays; press one nut onto
each macaroon. Bake about 20 minutes or until firm and dry; cool on trays.

NUTRITIONAL COUNT PER MACAROON 4.8g total fat (0.3g saturated fat); 318kJ (76 cal); 6.1g carbohydrate;
2.2g protein; 0.8g fibre

1 PEAR AND ALMOND FRIANDS
2 ALMOND MACAROONS

Orange and honey nut mix

PREP + COOK TIME 30 MINUTES **MAKES** 3 CUPS

1 cup (150g) raw unsalted cashews
1 cup (140g) raw unsalted peanuts
1 cup (160g) raw almond kernels
1 tablespoon finely grated orange rind
¼ cup (90g) honey

Make this nut mix for delectable snacking; store in a screw-top jar.

For information on honey, see Sugar, page 578.

1 Preheat oven to 180°C/160°C fan-forced.
2 Combine nuts, rind and honey in large bowl. Spread mixture onto baking-paper-lined oven tray; cook, stirring occasionally, about 20 minutes or until crunchy.
3 Cool mixture, stirring occasionally to prevent clumping.

NUTRITIONAL COUNT PER ½ CUP 35g total fat (4.5g saturated fat); 1885kJ (451 cal); 18.9g carbohydrate; 14.3g protein; 5.3g fibre

Offal

Offal is defined as the parts of an animal left over from a carcass when it is butchered. Some kinds, such as liver, kidneys, heart and tripe, are internal while others such as trotters, cheek and tail are external. Most kinds have highly distinctive flavours and textures which are adored by many people and detested by many others.

In many cities in the Western world there are tripe clubs whose members are people who adore tripe but can't get it at home because the rest of the family can't stand it, or even the smell of it cooking. The clubs hold tripe dinners and lunches for which at least the main course and often the first course too are tripe dishes. The meetings usually rotate round restaurants or members' other clubs whose chefs enjoy the challenge of preparing such a meal. Most tripe club members are men but many clubs have some women members too.

Some of the world's great and classic recipes are for offal, for example fegato alla veneziana (calf's liver Venetian style) for which thin, sautéed liver slices are smothered in onion cooked slowly until golden, or tripes à la mode de caen (tripe as they cook it in Caen), for which small squares of tripe are casseroled with garlic, aromatic vegetables, wine and apple brandy.

LIVER is very nutritious, being especially high in iron. It goes particularly well with bacon, fried onion, red wine, sharp herbs such as sage, rosemary and basil, grilled polenta and mashed or fried potato. Liver is rich in flavour and many cooks add a touch of balsamic or wine vinegar to cut the richness or serve it with lemon wedges and/or mustard. Calf's liver is tender and delicately flavoured and is usually fried or grilled; beef or ox liver is less tender and more strongly flavoured and is usually casseroled. Lamb's liver, also called lamb's fry, has its own "lamby" flavour and is tender, so it is usually grilled or fried, often with bacon for breakfast. Pork liver is strong-tasting and dark; it may be braised with other flavoursome ingredients but otherwise, in Western cuisine, is used for pâtés. It is, however, the first choice of Chinese cooks.

KIDNEYS are best known in steak and kidney pie or pudding and as the classic British breakfast dish of devilled kidneys and toast, to which may be added grilled bacon, mushrooms or tomatoes. Lamb's kidneys and calf's kidneys, being tender and milder in flavour than other kinds, are the ones usually chosen for frying or grilling, while ox kidney, which is stronger-tasting, goes into soups or long-cooked dishes such as steak and kidney. Pig's kidneys are strong-tasting and are usually used, in Western cuisine, for pâtés and terrines, though they are the first choice of Chinese cooks for soups and stir-fries.

HEART is lean and close-textured with a taste reminiscent of liver but milder. Lamb's and calf's hearts are the most tender and pig's heart is tender if it comes from a young animal; any of these can be stuffed and baked or cut into strips and fried. Ox heart is best slowly braised or stewed.

BRAINS Lamb's and calf's brains are prized for their delicate flavour and creamy texture when cooked. They are first soaked, trimmed and poached in acidulated water until firm, then cut up and served in fritters, or served whole in "black" (actually browned) butter flavoured with parsley, capers and a touch of vinegar.

TONGUE is sold fresh, salted (corned or pickled) or salted and smoked. Ox, calf's and lamb's tongues are used, and also pig's tongue in Asia and some European countries, though in others it is left with the head. Tongue is first poached with herbs, spices and aromatic vegetables until tender, then it may be served cold, sometimes being pressed first into a round cake tin to set in some of its jellied cooking liquid. Alternatively, it may be sliced, crumbed and fried or served hot with a sauce. Lamb's tongues are available canned.

SWEETBREADS are the thymus gland and pancreas of a young animal; in practice they usually come from a calf as these have the most delicate flavour. When cooked, they are white and very tender with a subtle, savoury flavour. They are first soaked and poached until firm and may then be served with a sauce or sliced and sautéed or crumbed and fried.

TRIPE is the stomach of cud-chewing animals — in practice, virtually always calf, cow or ox stomach. It is available as smooth or honeycomb tripe, which is the more tender kind and is so named because of its appearance. It is usually sold blanched (whitened) and partly cooked, but still requires long, slow cooking. It can be plainly simmered and served with a sauce, casseroled, braised or served in a soup.

PIG'S TROTTERS are gristly and bony, so they are cooked long and slowly in stock, which makes the gristle rich, soft and gelatinous. After cooling, they may be crumbed and baked bone-in or boned and rolled, or cooked in other ways such as scoring and brushing with honey for baking. A raw trotter, added to a casserole, will give it richness and flavour. Trotters are also used in Chinese cooking, for which they are usually first chopped into pieces.

CHEEKS, usually beef or pork, are the cheek muscles, which are tough but exceptionally rich and savoury after long cooking. They are usually used in pies and sausages but, casseroled with red wine and aromatics, can be an outstanding dish.

CHICKEN FEET, long-simmered in a stock, make it richly gelatinous. Chinese cooks also serve them, after simmering, with sauces such as black bean. They can be found, declawed and skinned, at some Asian butchers.

PREPARATION
In general, internal offal must be cleared of surrounding tissue such as membranes or fat. It may then need to be trimmed, for example kidneys are cored and heart trimmed of "pipes" (arteries), and may also be soaked before cooking. Details of preparing the particular kind of offal is included in recipes.

CHOOSING
Offal should be undamaged and evenly coloured, smell fresh and look moist but not wet.

STORING
Offal deteriorates quickly so it should be stored in a glass or pottery bowl covered with plastic wrap, in the refrigerator, and used as soon as possible. Items that are simmered to firm or tenderise them before final cooking, such as brains, sweetbreads and pig's trotters, may then be refrigerated, on a plate and covered with plastic film, for 1–2 days before further cooking.

Herb-crumbed lambs brains

PREP + COOK TIME 50 MINUTES (PLUS REFRIGERATION AND COOLING TIME) **SERVES** 4

6 sets lamb brains (600g)

1 litre (4 cups) water

1 tablespoon lemon juice

1 teaspoon salt

1 cup (70g) stale breadcrumbs

2 green onions, chopped finely

1 tablespoon finely chopped
fresh flat-leaf parsley

2 tablespoons finely chopped
fresh tarragon

½ teaspoon cracked black pepper

¼ cup (35g) plain flour

1 egg, beaten lightly

2 tablespoons milk

vegetable oil, for deep-frying

Steps 1 and 2 can be completed up to a day ahead of time, but instead of draining the brains after simmering, they should be cooled in the liquid and refrigerated until needed. Drain them well and pat dry on paper towels before proceeding with crumbing and frying.

1 Remove brain stem by pulling away gently with fingers; divide each set of brains into two lobes. Place in large bowl, cover with cold water; refrigerate, covered, 2 hours. Drain.

2 Place brains in medium saucepan with the water, juice and salt; bring to the boil. Reduce heat; simmer, uncovered, 5 minutes. Drain; cool 10 minutes.

3 Combine breadcrumbs, onion, herbs and pepper in large bowl. Coat brains in flour; shake away excess. Dip brains in combined egg and milk, then coat in breadcrumb mixture.

4 Heat oil in large saucepan; deep-fry brains, in batches, until browned lightly. Drain on absorbent paper. Serve brains hot with celeriac remoulade (see page 97).

NUTRITIONAL COUNT PER SERVING 22.1g total fat (5.1g saturated fat); 1563kJ (374 cal); 19.2g carbohydrate; 24.1g protein; 1.4g fibre

---

Seared calves liver with persillade

PREP + COOK TIME 35 MINUTES **SERVES** 4

400g piece calves liver,
sliced thinly

40g butter

1 shallot (25g), chopped finely

1 clove garlic, crushed

½ cup (125ml) chicken stock

1 tablespoon lemon juice

⅓ cup finely chopped fresh
flat-leaf parsley

The secret of tender liver is to have it sliced thinly and cook it briefly over high heat, in small batches, searing each slice quickly on both sides, then removing it from the pan. If it is cooked further, it will be dry and tough. Persillade is a mixture of chopped garlic and parsley traditionally used either as a garnish or to flavour a sauce, as we have done here.

1 Pat liver dry with absorbent paper. Melt half of the butter in large frying pan; cook liver quickly, in batches, over high heat until browned both sides and cooked as desired (do not overcook). Cover to keep warm.

2 To make persillade, heat remaining butter in same pan; cook shallot and garlic, stirring, until shallot softens. Add stock and juice; bring to the boil, stirring. Remove from heat; stir in parsley.

3 Serve sliced liver topped with persillade, accompany with parsnip mash.

NUTRITIONAL COUNT PER SERVING 16g total fat (7.8g saturated fat); 1012kJ (242 cal); 3.1g carbohydrate; 21.6g protein; 0.4g fibre

HERB-CRUMBED LAMBS BRAINS

Duck liver parfait with red onion jam

PREP + COOK TIME 55 MINUTES (PLUS REFRIGERATION TIME) **SERVES** 8

30g butter

6 shallots (150g), chopped finely

2 cloves garlic, crushed

½ teaspoon ground allspice

1 tablespoon finely chopped fresh thyme

1 teaspoon cracked black pepper

⅔ cup (160ml) brandy

400g duck livers, trimmed

¾ cup (180ml) cream

4 eggs

150g butter, melted, cooled

2 bay leaves, halved

2 sprigs thyme, halved

100g butter, extra

RED ONION JAM

50g butter

4 medium red onions (680g), sliced thinly

¼ cup (55g) sugar

¾ cup (180ml) dry red wine

¼ cup (60ml) port

¼ cup (60ml) red wine vinegar

If brioche is not available, you can serve the parfait with baguette toasts, made by cutting a day-old baguette or other French bread stick into 1cm-thick slices, placing on baking trays and baking in a pre-heated 160°C/140°C fan-forced oven for about 20 minutes or until light golden-brown and crisp.

For information on duck, see Poultry, pages 456 & 457; and for red onions, see Onions, page 375.

1 Preheat oven to 150°C/130°C fan-forced. Oil 1.5-litre (6-cup) ovenproof terrine dish.

2 Melt butter in small frying pan; cook shallot and garlic, stirring, until shallot softens. Add allspice, thyme, pepper and brandy; bring to the boil. Reduce heat; simmer, uncovered, about 2 minutes or until liquid is reduced to about 1 tablespoon.

3 Blend or process shallot mixture with livers, cream, eggs and melted butter until mixture is smooth. Push parfait mixture through fine sieve into medium bowl; repeat process through same cleaned sieve.

4 Pour parfait mixture into terrine dish; place terrine in baking dish. Pour enough boiling water into baking dish to come halfway up sides of terrine dish; cover with foil. Cook in oven about 40 minutes or until liver parfait is just set. Remove terrine from baking dish; cool parfait 10 minutes.

5 Meanwhile, make red onion jam.

6 Decorate parfait with bay leaves and thyme. Melt extra butter in small pan; cool 2 minutes then carefully pour butter fat over parfait, leaving milk solids in pan. Cover parfait in terrine; refrigerate 3 hours or overnight.

7 Turn parfait onto board. Using hot, wet knife, cut parfait into eight slices; serve with red onion jam and toasted brioche.

RED ONION JAM Melt butter in large frying pan; cook onion and sugar, stirring occasionally, over medium heat, about 20 minutes or until onion starts to caramelise. Add wine, port and vinegar; bring to the boil. Reduce heat; simmer, uncovered, about 30 minutes or until jam thickens.

NUTRITIONAL COUNT PER SERVING 50.1g total fat (30.7g saturated fat); 2658kJ (636 cal); 15.3g carbohydrate; 16g protein; 1.4g fibre

Terrine de campagne

PREP + COOK TIME 2 HOURS 20 MINUTES (PLUS REFRIGERATION TIME) **SERVES** 6

350g chicken thigh fillets, chopped coarsely

400g boned pork belly, rind removed, chopped coarsely

300g piece calves liver, trimmed, chopped coarsely

3 bacon rashers (210g), rind removed, chopped coarsely

3 cloves garlic, crushed

2 teaspoons finely chopped fresh thyme

10 juniper berries, crushed

2 tablespoons port

¼ cup (60ml) dry white wine

1 egg

¼ cup (35g) roasted, shelled pistachios

1 Preheat oven to 150°C/130°C fan-forced. Oil 1.5-litre (6-cup) ovenproof terrine dish.

2 Blend or process meats, separately, until coarsely minced; combine in large bowl with remaining ingredients. Press meat mixture into terrine dish; cover with foil. Place terrine in baking dish; pour enough boiling water into baking dish to come halfway up sides of terrine. Cook in oven 1 hour. Uncover; cook further 1 hour or until cooked through.

3 Remove terrine from baking dish; cover terrine with baking paper. Weight with another dish filled with heavy cans; cool, refrigerate overnight. Serve sliced, at room temperature.

NUTRITIONAL COUNT PER SERVING 31.9g total fat (10.1g saturated fat); 2011kJ (481 cal); 3.4g carbohydrate; 42.1g protein; 0.8g fibre

Campagne or country-style terrine, is chunky and rustic compared to the smooth texture of a parfait as in the Duck liver parfait with red onion jam, opposite. Slices of terrine are perfect served with slices of french bread and cornichons (see page 148).

For information on juniper berries, see Spices, page 558.

Veal sweetbreads with duxelles

PREP + COOK TIME 1 HOUR (PLUS REFRIGERATION AND COOLING TIME) **SERVES** 4

500g veal sweetbreads

¼ cup (35g) plain flour

1 teaspoon salt

½ teaspoon ground black pepper

¼ cup (60ml) olive oil

DUXELLES

40g butter

8 shallots (200g), chopped finely

400g swiss brown mushrooms, chopped finely

¼ cup (60ml) port

⅓ cup (80ml) beef stock

2 tablespoons finely chopped fresh flat-leaf parsley

1 Place sweetbreads in medium bowl, cover with cold water; refrigerate 4 hours, changing water every hour, until whitened and water is clear. Cook sweetbreads in saucepan of boiling water 5 minutes; drain. Cool 10 minutes. Remove outer membranes, slice sweetbreads thickly.

2 Meanwhile, make duxelles.

3 Coat sweetbreads in combined flour, salt and pepper; shake off excess. Heat oil in frying pan; cook sweetbreads, in batches, 5 minutes or until cooked as desired; serve with duxelles.

DUXELLES Heat butter in frying pan; cook shallot and mushrooms until shallot softens. Add port and stock; bring to the boil. Reduce heat; simmer, uncovered, 15 minutes or until liquid evaporates. Remove from heat; stir in parsley.

NUTRITIONAL COUNT PER SERVING 43.9g total fat (17.1g saturated fat); 2529kJ (605 cal); 10.1g carbohydrate; 38.1g protein; 3.4g fibre

Duxelles is a classic French ingredient consisting of finely chopped mushrooms and herbs sautéed in butter with shallot or green onion. Used here as a flavourful accompaniment to punctuate the mild creaminess of the sweetbreads, it may also be mixed with sour cream for an omelette filling, with cooked rice or buttered breadcrumbs for a meat stuffing, or slipped under the skin of chicken breasts and baked.
Serve this dish with a herb salad.

Oils & Fats

Oils and fats are not differentiated chemically but by their consistency at room temperature: fats that are liquid at room temperature are called oils, those that are solid are called fats.

1 PEANUT OIL
2 LIGHT OLIVE OIL
3 PURE OLIVE OIL
4 VIRGIN OLIVE OIL
5 EXTRA VIRGIN OLIVE OIL
6 MARGARINE
7 SUET
8 GHEE
9 SESAME OIL
10 BUTTER

Both may be eaten as foods in their own right, for example butter used as a spread or olive oil into which bread is dipped, or used as an ingredient, for example the oil in a salad dressing or the butter in a cake, or used as a medium for cooking other foods, for example any of the many oils and fats used for frying, basting foods as they cook or brushing on to food to be grilled or baked. All pure oils and fats have the same kilojoule content (approximately 190 per 5ml teaspoon); oils labelled "light" are light in flavour, not in kilojoules.

SMOKE POINT AND FLASH POINT

Every oil or fat has a smoke point, the temperature at which it will begin to smoke, showing that it is breaking down, and a flash point, the higher temperature at which it will burst into flames. Oils and fats with high smoke points are the most efficient for frying, though other considerations such as flavour or health implications also come into play when choosing a cooking oil. Note that every kitchen should have a fire blanket, available inexpensively at hardware shops, convenient to the stove. Placed over a fire, it will extinguish it immediately.

FATS

BUTTER is made by beating or churning cream until it separates into a solid fat which is butter and a thin liquid which is the traditional form of buttermilk (see Milk, page 317). Butter may be salted, low-salt or reduced-salt or unsalted. Salt improves its keeping quality. Which kind to use is a matter of preference, except that if a recipe specifies unsalted butter it is important to use that as some foods may stick if fried in salted butter, and the flavour of sauces such as hollandaise and béarnaise, and of some continental cakes and biscuits, will be spoilt if salted butter is used. A good rule in cooking is, when in doubt, used unsalted butter. Butter may also be cultured, meaning that a lactic culture has been added to give it a tangy flavour; cultured butter is unsalted and has a shorter shelf life than salted. "Easy-spread" butters usually have vegetable oils added or are whipped to introduce air; it is a matter of preference whether to use them as spreads and they may be used for frying but they should not be used for baking because their various compositions may not produce the desired results.

Butter gives good flavour to foods fried in it but has a low smoke point, so it is often combined with an oil with a higher smoke point. The oil is heated slowly until it begins to give off a haze, then the butter is added and gently stirred to distribute it evenly. Just as foaming subsides and the mixture starts to change colour, the food is added. The heat is then adjusted as needed, according to the appearance of the food. This works only for shallow-frying;

If you have forgotten to take the butter out of the refrigerator so that it can soften before creaming for a cake, don't try warming it — it only makes it oily. Instead, coarsely grate butter into the mixing bowl and let it stand for about 5 minutes or until it softens.

American recipes often call for a stick of butter, which means 125g.

To prepare butcher's suet for use, chill it first to make it firm, then remove any membrane and grate or chop it finely. If chopping, sprinkle a little of the flour from the recipe on the suet to prevent it from sticking to the knife.

butter is not suitable for deep-frying. Clarified butter can be heated to a higher temperature than regular butter without burning (see Ghee).

GHEE is the name for clarified butter in Indian and other Asian cooking, where it is used both as an ingredient and as a cooking oil. It is available canned, under the name ghee. Clarified butter can be made by gently heating salted or unsalted butter without browning, standing off the heat for a few minutes and gently pouring off the clear yellow liquid which has separated from the milky residue at the bottom. The yellow liquid is clarified butter, which will solidify at room temperature; the residue can be added to soups or sauces to enrich them. Clarified butter has a much higher smoke point than regular butter because it is the milk solids in regular butter that first start to brown and then burn. Ghee is a little different from western-style clarified butter in that the basic butter is heated to the point where the milk solids brown, flavouring the ghee and generating antioxidants that make it keep much longer without going rancid.

MARGARINE is manufactured in two general types, table and cooking margarine. Table margarine is made in various formulations which are designed as healthier and/or more convenient alternatives to butter. They are usually intended to provide health benefits in limiting or lowering the intake of harmful dietary cholesterol, which is implicated in the risk of heart disease, and they are more convenient than butter for using as a spread because they are softer and so are easier to spread straight from the refrigerator. Table margarines are usually made from vegetable oils with some milk solids and sometimes added vitamins, plus other ingredients such as emulsifiers, flavourings and colourings. They may be

labelled "canola spread" or "olive oil spread" if they are predominantly made from these oils, which are particularly beneficial in being high in mono-unsaturated fats, which reduce levels of harmful cholesterol while raising levels of beneficial cholesterol, and are also high in anti-oxidants, which are believed to delay the development of cancer and heart disease. Table margarines can be used for frying and as ingredients in some cakes, but are too soft for use in pastry-making.

Cooking margarines are cheaper than butter and of much the same degree of hardness. They do not provide butter's good flavour in baking but perform well, sometimes better than butter in making tender biscuits and pastry. They are usually made from a mixture of animal fats and vegetable oils plus such ingredients as whey powder and skim milk powder.

LARD is rendered pig fat. Once used extensively as an ingredient, cooking fat and spread, it has fallen out of favour in much of the developed world because of the ready availability of oils and of health concerns over lard's high level of saturated fat. It is still used, often in conjunction with butter, for pastry-making, as it is particularly effective for ensuring crisp and tender texture.

The name lard is also used for unrendered sheets of pork back fat, which is used for larding (threading strips of fat through) lean meat, wrapping pâtés and making confits (preparations of meat stewed in and then preserved in their fat).

SUET is the firm fat surrounding beef, mutton and lamb kidneys. It is used in suet puddings, pastry and mincemeat. It can be bought from butchers, though it will probably have to be pre-ordered, and is available, granulated, coated with flour and commercially packaged, in supermarkets. Fresh suet has to be grated before use.

COPHA is a mainly saturated fat derived from coconut. It is used for certain confections including chocolate crackles and coconut ice.

OILS

Oils are extracted from many seeds, nuts and fruits, sometimes by simply crushing, pressing and filtering, which retains their full natural flavour: these are called cold-pressed oils or, if they were extracted at the first rather than subsequent pressings, virgin oils. Lesser oils are extracted using heat or chemicals, and these are usually refined to make them relatively colourless and odourless and to keep well. Cold-pressed oils are usually expensive and are best when fresh, so it is best to buy them only in quantities that will last for a few months. They are used for salad dressings, as ingredients in some cakes or breads, for lightly frying vegetables or fish where their flavour will contribute to the final effect, or for drizzling on bread, cooked vegetables or finished hot dishes. Refined oils are used as ingredients for cakes, breads and sauces where neutral flavour is required and for frying and cooking generally. There are also "solid oils" which have been processed to make them solid at room temperature, a process which makes them more saturated and therefore less "healthy" than before, but makes them more stable. They are recommended for deep-frying and perform very well, lasting through more times of using than other oils before they begin to break down and have to be changed.

OLIVE OIL is available in several grades. The highest is "extra-virgin" which is virgin oil of the highest quality with an acidity level of no more than 1% and the finest flavour as judged by expert inspectors. The flavours of extra-virgin oils vary considerably from strong and fruity to delicate, and may have a pungent, bitter or peppery flavour — all desirable qualities so long as they are present in moderation and in balance with other flavour components. Just below extra-virgin comes "virgin" oil, described above, and then "pure olive oil" (or simply "olive oil"), which is usually a mixture of virgin and refined oil. Extra-virgin and virgin olive oils are unsurpassed as salad oils and for gentle frying of delicate seafood and meats, and pure olive oil is an excellent general frying oil. Olive oils labelled "light" are not lower in kilojoules than other oils, but are light in flavour — that is, they have been processed to remove most of the flavour.

MUSTARD-SEED OIL may be mild, which is a pleasantly flavoured but not hot oil suitable for using in baking or frying fish, chicken or vegetables where its flavour will come through, or "piquant" oil with mustard heat for dressings or frying where its bite will be appreciated.

HAZELNUT, WALNUT, MACADAMIA and **AVOCADO OIL** are fine cold-pressed oils tasting delicately of their origins. They bring a subtle difference to a salad dressing, especially if some of the appropriate nuts or fruit are included in the salad.

GRAPESEED OIL is a by-product of the wine industry. It is pale gold and slightly aromatic and is a popular choice in France and Italy as a light and mild-tasting alternative to olive oil. It has a high smoke point so it is good for deep-frying.

SESAME OIL is available as a light yellow, light-flavoured cooking oil but is best known as a dark oil with the strong, warm flavour and aroma of toasted sesame seeds, used in Asian cooking as a final dressing for stir-fries or in dipping sauces.

PEANUT OIL is highly regarded by the chefs of many countries because it performs well at high temperatures and

is almost invariably refined to have no distinct smell or taste, so that it does not interfere with the flavour balance of dishes.

CANOLA OIL was developed in Canada as a new, healthy oil developed from rapeseed oil. It is now one of the most popular all-purpose oils suitable for any kind of cooking as it performs well at high temperatures.

PALM OIL comes from an oil palm native to Africa but now cultivated in large plantations in South-East Asia and Papua New Guinea. Unlike most vegetable oils, it is high in saturated fat and is semi-solid at room temperature. It is widely used in Asia as a cooking oil and is also used in the manufacture of soaps and washing powders. The palm oil industry is the subject of controversy because the plantations are replacing natural forests.

SUNFLOWER and **BLENDED VEGETABLE OILS** vary from manufacturer to manufacturer, but in general are refined all-purpose cooking oils high in polyunsaturated and monounsaturated fats and low in saturated fats.

STORING
Cold-pressed oils should be kept in the refrigerator or a dark, cool, dry place and used within a year or less. Some oils will congeal when chilled; pour or spoon out what is required, which will soon melt, and return the rest quickly to the refrigerator. Refined oils will keep for a year or more in a tightly capped bottle away from heat or light.

1 SALMON "CONFIT" WITH FENNEL AND HERBS
2 OLIVE OIL CAKE WITH BLUEBERRIES

Salmon "confit" with fennel and herbs

PREP + COOK TIME 30 MINUTES **SERVES** 4

4 x 200g salmon fillets

sea salt flakes and freshly ground black pepper

2 cloves garlic, sliced thinly

3 cups (750ml) extra virgin olive oil, approximately

2 small bulbs fennel (600g), sliced thinly

½ cup (125ml) dry white wine

1 tablespoon grated lemon rind

2 tablespoons chopped fresh fennel tops

2 tablespoons chopped fresh chervil

1 Preheat oven to 120°C/100°C fan-forced.
2 Place salmon in small ovenproof dish, just large enough to fit. Sprinkle with salt, pepper and garlic; add enough oil to cover salmon completely. Cook salmon, uncovered, in oven, 15 minutes or until cooked as desired. (Salmon doesn't change colour after cooking time as it is at a low temperature). Remove salmon from the oil and drain on absorbent paper.
3 Heat 2 tablespoons of the salmon cooking oil in medium frying pan; cook fennel bulbs, stirring, about 5 minutes or until softened. Add wine and lemon rind; cook 5 minutes or until wine is reduced by half. Stir in herbs.
4 Divide fennel mixture among serving plates, top with salmon.

NUTRITIONAL COUNT PER SERVING 45g total fat (7.5g saturated fat); 2508kJ (600 cal); 3.4g carbohydrate; 40.1g protein; 3g fibre

Confit, from the French verb "confire" meaning to preserve, means both a food item that has been slow-cooked in fat to cover, and also the cooking technique. The method was originally used as a way to preserve foods such as duck, goose or pork for the winter by cooking them in their own fat and sealing them under it. Confit foods are exquisitely soft and delicately flavoured, so the technique is sometimes used, as in this recipe, simply to achieve this luxurious effect.

Olive oil cake with blueberries

PREP + COOK TIME 1 HOUR 25 MINUTES **SERVES** 16

3 eggs

1¼ cups (275g) caster sugar

2 tablespoons finely grated orange rind

½ cup (125ml) olive oil

⅓ cup (80ml) milk

1 cup (150g) plain flour

1 cup (150g) self-raising flour

100g frozen blueberries

¼ cup (80g) apricot jam, warmed, strained

1 Preheat oven to 180°C/160°C fan-forced. Grease deep 19cm-square cake pan.
2 Beat eggs, sugar and rind in small bowl with electric mixer until sugar is dissolved; transfer to large bowl. Fold in combined oil and milk, and sifted flours, in two batches.
3 Pour mixture into pan; bake 20 minutes. Carefully remove cake from oven; sprinkle surface evenly with blueberries. Return cake to oven; bake about 40 minutes. Stand cake 10 minutes; turn, top-side up, onto wire rack to cool.
4 Brush warm cake with jam.

NUTRITIONAL COUNT PER SERVING 8.5g total fat (1.5g saturated fat); 974kJ (233 cal); 35g carbohydrate; 3.4g protein; 0.9g fibre

Don't thaw the frozen berries as they might bleed colour into the cake. In season, fresh ones may be used instead of frozen. The surface of the cake should be flat and just set before the blueberries are sprinkled over it, so that they won't sink in.
This cake is best served warm, with crème fraîche.

For information on blueberries, see Berries, page 58.

Mayonnaise

PREP TIME 15 MINUTES **MAKES** 1 CUP

2 egg yolks

½ teaspoon salt

¾ teaspoon mustard powder

⅔ cup (160ml) extra light olive oil

⅓ cup (80ml) olive oil

1 tablespoon white vinegar

1 Whisk egg yolks, salt and mustard in medium bowl. Gradually add oils, in thin, steady stream, whisking constantly until mixture thickens. Stir vinegar into mayonnaise.

NUTRITIONAL COUNT PER TABLESPOON 19.1g total fat (2.8g saturated fat); 715kJ (171 cal); 0g carbohydrate; 0.5g protein; 0g fibre

While good-quality store-bought mayonnaise is useful for many purposes, it doesn't compare with the fresh, subtle flavour and sumptuous texture of home-made. For best results, whisk ingredients in a glass or ceramic bowl with a balloon whisk. It can also be made in a blender or food processor: process the yolks, salt and mustard until smooth, then, while the motor is operating, gradually add oil in a thin stream, then the vinegar. The oil must be added slowly to prevent the mixture from separating. If it should separate, whisk in 1 tablespoon of hot water.

Lemon aïoli

PREP TIME 15 MINUTES **MAKES** 1 CUP

2 egg yolks

1 teaspoon dijon mustard

⅔ cup (160ml) extra light olive oil

⅓ cup (80ml) olive oil

2 tablespoons lemon juice

2 cloves garlic, crushed

1 Whisk egg yolks and mustard in medium bowl.
2 Gradually whisk in combined oils, in a thin, steady stream until mixture thickens. Stir in juice and garlic.
3 Serve aïoli with salt and pepper squid or fried crumbed chicken drumsticks.

NUTRITIONAL COUNT PER TEASPOON 4.8g total fat (0.7g saturated fat); 178kJ (43 cal); 0g carbohydrate; 0.1g protein; 0g fibre

Aïoli, or garlic mayonnaise, made with lemon juice instead of vinegar has a light, fresh flavour. It goes especially well with fish, shellfish, veal, chicken, asparagus and other cooked vegetables.

Italian dressing

PREP TIME 5 MINUTES **MAKES** 1 CUP

⅔ cup (160ml) olive oil

⅓ cup (80ml) white wine vinegar

1 clove garlic, crushed

1 teaspoon caster sugar

2 teaspoons finely chopped fresh oregano

2 teaspoons finely chopped fresh basil

1 fresh long red chilli, chopped finely

1 Place ingredients in screw-top jar; shake well.

NUTRITIONAL COUNT PER TABLESPOON 12.2g total fat (1.7g saturated fat); 464kJ (111 cal); 0.4g carbohydrate; 0.1g protein; 0.2g fibre

Flavoursome Italian dressing goes with almost any salad, especially those with tomatoes and those to be served with pasta. For a creamy version, beat in ½ cup of mayonnaise.

Lemon and macadamia dressing

PREP TIME 10 MINUTES **MAKES** 1 CUP

½ cup (125ml) macadamia oil

⅓ cup (45g) finely chopped roasted macadamia nuts

2 teaspoons finely grated lemon rind

2 tablespoons lemon juice

1 teaspoon caster sugar

1 Whisk ingredients in small jug until combined.

NUTRITIONAL COUNT PER TABLESPOON 12.4g total fat (1.8g saturated fat); 477kJ (114 cal); 0.6g carbohydrate; 0.3g protein; 0.2g fibre

Drizzle this dressing on grilled or fried fish or chicken or use it to dress a green or seafood salad.

Beurre blanc

PREP + COOK TIME 20 MINUTES **MAKES** 1 CUP

¼ cup (60ml) dry white wine

1 tablespoon lemon juice

¼ cup (60ml) cream

125g cold butter, chopped

1 Combine wine and juice in small saucepan; bring to the boil. Boil, without stirring, until reduced by two-thirds. Add cream; return to the boil, then reduce heat to low.
2 Whisk in cold butter, piece by piece, whisking between additions, until sauce is smooth and thickened slightly.

NUTRITIONAL COUNT PER TABLESPOON 10.4g total fat (6.8g saturated fat); 406kJ (97 cal); 0.3g carbohydrate; 0.2g protein, 0g fibre

When making this delicate sauce, it is important to keep the heat low while adding the butter so that the sauce stays well below boiling point. Add each piece of butter only when the last addition has been absorbed. Beurre blanc is exquisite with poached or steamed salmon, white fish fillets, steamed vegetables and poached or grilled chicken breast fillets.

Brandy butter

PREP TIME 10 MINUTES (PLUS REFRIGERATION TIME) **MAKES** 2 CUPS

250g unsalted butter, softened

⅓ cup (75g) firmly packed brown sugar

1 teaspoon vanilla extract

¼ cup (60ml) brandy

1 Beat ingredients in small bowl with electric mixer until light and fluffy. Cover; refrigerate 1 hour. Serve with Christmas pudding, pancakes or raisin toast.

NUTRITIONAL COUNT PER TABLESPOON 8.5g total fat (5.6g saturated fat); 393kJ (94 cal); 3.1g carbohydrate; 0.1g protein; 0g fibre

Brandy butter, also called hard sauce, is a traditional accompaniment to Christmas pudding and mince pies. It is also good with other steamed puddings.

Okra

The slender green pods of okra, also called ladies' fingers or gumbo, are believed to be native to Africa and are important in the food of the Middle East, India, East Asia and the Americas, especially in the Creole cookery of the Mississippi delta.

Okra belongs to the mallow family of plants, all of whose members have sticky juices. The juice of one member, the marshmallow, was once used to make the sweets of the same name, but they now get their fluffy texture from gelatine beaten with sugar syrup.

They taste rather like eggplant and contain many small seeds and a gummy substance which, when the pods are sliced and cooked, is released as juice described as satin-smooth by those who like it, slimy by those who don't. It is this juice that thickens and gives its essential character to the famous Creole dish, gumbo, which is a highly flavoured soup/stew of pork, ham, seafood, or a mixture of these, and tomatoes. Okra can be sliced and quickly fried to minimise the sticky juices, or cooked whole to prevent them from being released, and is also eaten raw. In India, okra is used in curries and fried with spices, while Middle Eastern cooks add it to flavoursome stews, usually near the end of cooking so that it will retain some crispness. Okra is available in summer and autumn.

PREPARATION Wash the pods, gently scrubbing with a paper towel or vegetable brush, then rinse and drain. Carefully remove the tip and the cap where the pod meets the stem; do not cut the pod and expose the seeds and sticky juices inside. Leave whole or cut up as the recipe directs. Cook okra in non-reactive pans as aluminium ones will turn it grey.

CHOOSING Choose crisp, green pods no more than 10cm long. The pods should snap easily and the seeds feel firm but not hard. Avoid any pods that are shrivelled, limp, bruised or damaged.

STORING Enclose okra in a paper bag, then in a plastic bag and store in the refrigerator for up to 3 days.

Okra and tomato in coconut sauce

PREP + COOK TIME 45 MINUTES **SERVES** 4

5 cloves garlic, quartered

3 shallots (75g), chopped coarsely

2 fresh long red chillies, chopped coarsely

2 green onions, chopped finely

⅓ cup (100g) tamarind concentrate

1 tablespoon vegetable oil

400g can coconut milk

2 tablespoons lime juice

10 fresh curry leaves

500g fresh okra, halved lengthways

400g can crushed tomatoes

OKRA AND TOMATO IN COCONUT SAUCE

Serve this flavoursome vegetarian casserole with rice. For non-vegetarians, add grilled lamb sausages.

For information on coconut, see Nuts, page 347.

1 Blend or process garlic, shallot, chilli, onion and tamarind until smooth.

2 Heat oil in large saucepan; add tamarind mixture. Cook, stirring, 2 minutes. Add coconut milk, juice and curry leaves; simmer, uncovered 5 minutes.

3 Add okra and undrained tomatoes; simmer, uncovered, 20 minutes or until okra is tender.

NUTRITIONAL COUNT PER SERVING 29.5g total fat (18.8g saturated fat); 1384kJ (331 cal); 13.4g carbohydrate; 7.6g protein; 8.9g fibre

---

Lamb and okra in rich tomato sauce with garlic confit

PREP + COOK TIME 2 HOURS 30 MINUTES **SERVES** 4

1 tablespoon olive oil

1kg boned lamb shoulder, trimmed, chopped coarsely

2 medium brown onions (300g), chopped coarsely

7 medium tomatoes (1kg), chopped coarsely

1 litre (4 cups) water

200g okra

½ cup loosely packed fresh mint leaves

GARLIC CONFIT

1 teaspoon coriander seeds

½ teaspoon cardamom seeds

30g butter

5 cloves garlic, sliced thinly

1 teaspoon dried chilli flakes

1 teaspoon salt

For notes on confit cooking, see page 365. In this recipe, the garlic is cooked by the confit method to make it melting-soft; it would also be good with lamb or pork chops.

For information on lamb, see Lamb, pages 282 & 283; for tomatoes, see Tomatoes, pages 606 & 607; and for garlic, see Garlic, pages 214 & 215.

1 Heat oil in large deep saucepan; cook lamb, in batches, until browned all over.

2 Cook onion in same pan, stirring, until soft. Add tomato and the water; bring to the boil. Return lamb to pan, reduce heat; simmer, uncovered, stirring occasionally, about 1 ¾ hours or until lamb is tender.

3 Add okra to lamb mixture; simmer, uncovered, about 15 minutes or until okra is tender.

4 Meanwhile, make garlic confit.

5 Serve casserole with garlic confit, mint and steamed long-grain white rice.

GARLIC CONFIT Using mortar and pestle, crush seeds. Melt butter in small saucepan; cook seeds, garlic, chilli and salt over low heat, stirring, 10 minutes or until garlic softens.

NUTRITIONAL COUNT PER SERVING 33.5g total fat (15g saturated fat); 2286kJ (547 cal); 8g carbohydrate; 53.4g protein; 6.4g fibre

Olives

The fruit of the olive tree has been eaten for thousands of years. It is native to the Mediterranean and, with its oil, is still the foundation of Mediterranean cooking.

Olives are eaten both green (unripe) and black (ripe). Both types are inedibly bitter when picked and must be leached of their bitter juices, traditionally by either dry salt-curing or brining, which take months, but now, in commercial curing, often done with lye, a caustic alkali, which is quick but removes some of the flavour and makes the texture soft instead of firm. Lye-curing is done with green olives and the curing solution may be oxygenated to turn them black, but they lack the flavour of a ripe olive. Most canned and many commercially bottled olives have been lye-cured; clues to identifying them are that they are often sold sliced and that they are a flat, uniform black without the purple nuances of natural black olives.

GREEN OLIVES are firm and tangy. They are available stone-in or stoned and stuffed, usually with pimiento (capsicum), almond or anchovy. They come in sizes from fingernail to cherry tomato; the biggest, sold as spanish or queen olives, are the best size if you want to stuff them yourself with something interesting such as tuna or preserved lemon. They are difficult to stone by hand, so if stoned ones are called for in a recipe, you need a gadget sold as a cherry-stoner or olive-pitter, which punches out the stone leaving a neat hole. Green olives or mixed green and black olives are good to serve with drinks or as part of an antipasto tray, and a green olive is a classic addition to a martini.

BLACK OLIVES have a richer and more mellow flavour than green ones and are softer in texture. They are available plain, not usually identified by variety except for pointed kalamatas or small, wrinkled ligurians, and are also sold in many kinds of marinade from garlic or herbs to lemon and chilli. Black olives are a favourite snack, garnish or addition to a cheese board, are used in cooking from pizzas and breads to pâtés, salads, pasta, risotto and hearty meat dishes, and star in their own right as the soul of the famous Provençal relish, tapenade, which is piled on to sliced baguette or turkish bread, scooped up with torn lebanese bread or crudités (raw vegetables), spooned on to bowls of soup, used for pasta sauces or served as a condiment with grilled meats and fish.

STORING
Green olives should be stored in an airtight jar, black ones in a jar of olive oil, with additions such as sliced garlic if you wish. Olives don't need refrigerating because they are salted, but if green ones are to be kept a long while, they may do better if refrigerated with a little of the brine they came in or freshly-made brine, and turned over from time to time to keep them moist.

❧ **OTHER RECIPES USING OLIVES**
Greek fetta salad, p108
Penne puttanesca, p399
Salade niçoise with caperberries, p83
Spicy sardines with orange and olive salad, p534

1 CHEESE AND OLIVE LOAF
2 BLACK OLIVE TAPENADE

Cheese and olive loaf

PREP + COOK TIME 50 MINUTES **SERVES** 6

This recipe can be made a day ahead and the loaf kept, covered, in the refrigerator. It can also be frozen whole or sliced.

For information on parmesan cheese, see Cheese, page 104.

1 cup (150g) self-raising flour

⅔ cup (50g) coarsely grated parmesan cheese

2 tablespoons coarsely chopped fresh mint leaves

½ teaspoon ground black pepper

1 cup (120g) seeded black olives, chopped coarsely

75g mortadella, chopped coarsely

4 eggs, beaten lightly

80g butter, melted

1 Preheat oven to 200°C/180°C fan-forced. Grease 8cm x 26cm bar cake pan.

2 Sift flour into medium bowl, add cheese, mint, pepper, olives and mortadella.

3 Add egg and butter; stir until well combined. Spread mixture into pan.

4 Bake loaf about 35 minutes or until browned lightly. Turn onto wire rack to cool.

NUTRITIONAL COUNT PER SERVING 21.3g total fat (11.2g saturated fat); 1371kJ (328 cal); 22.5g carbohydrate; 12.1g protein; 1.5g fibre

Black olive tapenade

PREP TIME 5 MINUTES **MAKES** 1 CUP

2 cups (240g) seeded black olives

1 drained anchovy fillet, rinsed

1 tablespoon drained capers, rinsed

2 teaspoons dijon mustard

2 tablespoons olive oil

1 Rinse and drain olives on absorbent paper. Blend or process olives with anchovy, capers and mustard until smooth.

2 With motor operating, add oil in a thin steady stream, processing until tapenade is smooth. Serve with toasted crusty bread.

NUTRITIONAL COUNT PER TABLESPOON 3.3g total fat (0.5g saturated fat); 213kJ (51 cal); 4.6g carbohydrate; 0.6g protein; 0.3g fibre

Sometimes nicknamed "yuppie Vegemite", this classic Provençal preparation is used as a dip for raw vegetables, spread on bread and pizza, and served with fish and meats.

Warm marinated olives

PREP + COOK TIME 10 MINUTES **SERVES** 8

¾ cup (180ml) extra virgin olive oil

1 fresh long red chilli, sliced thinly

1 clove garlic, sliced thinly

¼ cup coarsely chopped fresh oregano leaves

500g black and green olives

1 Gently heat olive oil in large frying pan over low heat with the chilli, garlic and oregano until warm and fragrant.

2 Add olives; shake the pan until warmed through. Serve olives with grissini.

NUTRITIONAL COUNT PER SERVING 10.6g total fat (1.5g saturated fat); 518kJ (124 cal); 7g carbohydrate; 0.3g protein; 0.5g fibre

Store any leftover olives in their flavoured cooking oil in an airtight container to use on pizza or in a green or tomato salad with fetta cheese.

Green olive salsa

PREP TIME 15 MINUTES **SERVES** 4

1½ cups (180g) seeded green olives, chopped coarsely

⅓ cup (80ml) olive oil

1 tablespoon cider vinegar

1 shallot (25g), chopped finely

1 fresh long red chilli, chopped finely

¼ cup coarsely chopped fresh flat-leaf parsley

¼ cup coarsely chopped fresh mint leaves

1 Combine ingredients in small bowl.

2 Serve salsa with grilled tomatoes or roasted chicken, if you like.

NUTRITIONAL COUNT PER SERVING 18.7g total fat (2.7g saturated fat); 886kJ (212 cal); 10.4g carbohydrate; 0.6g protein; 1g fibre

Onions

The indispensable onion family gives depth and savour to hundreds of dishes and stars in its own right in scores of others. Each member has its own character.

The first step in many recipes is to fry chopped onion slowly to a soft, golden mass, which takes about 20 minutes and requires frequent checking and stirring. A quicker way is to warm the butter or oil, add the onion and stir until the pieces are well coated, then barely cover with warm water and cook over high heat until the water has evaporated, and finally stir the now softened onion on medium to low heat for a few minutes until it is golden, adding a little more butter or oil if needed.

BROWN ONIONS are the workhorses of the family, used for everything from a well-charred slice for a hamburger to a softly gold and luscious mass as the start of French onion soup. If a recipe calls for onion without further description, brown onion is the one intended, though white onion will also do. They vary in size and in degree of pungency and sweetness. Brown onions store well and develop more pungency as they age. Some varieties, usually large and light-skinned, are mild, sweet and softer than others; they are usually sold separately.

WHITE ONIONS are thinner-skinned than brown and are often believed to be milder, but they are, on average, more pungent. They come in sizes from large to tiny, which are often sold separately as pickling onions. The very tiny pickled pearl onions sold in bottles, often dyed violent green or red, are not sold fresh in Australia. White onion is preferred to brown if used raw, for example as fine rings in a salad, simply on the grounds of its colour. In cooking, it can be used in the same ways as brown.

GREEN ONIONS, spring onions or shallots are, confusingly, the names usually given to bulbless onions (white onions picked before they develop bulbs, or bunching onions which grow in clumps and never develop bulbs). The term "scallion", which dates back in English to at least 1500 as a name for a long-necked, bulbless onion, is needed but remains in general use only in America. These onions are usually sliced and eaten raw or only lightly cooked. They are mild in flavour and pungency; the white stems and the first few centimetres of the green tops are eaten.

SPRING ONIONS or salad onions are the names usually given to young white onions whose bulbs have only developed to sizes between cherry tomato and ping-pong ball. They are sold with their green tops still on and are used for salads or for cooking whole.

Brown onions

White onions

Pickling onions

Green onions

SHALLOTS or eschalots grow in clusters in the same way as garlic. European shallots may be golden-brown or pinky grey, Asian ones are pink/purple. They are mild, sweet and intense in flavour. Chopped, they can be used in a delicate sauce or savoury butter, but are usually cooked whole — roasted or caramelised. Asian shallots are eaten raw, or sliced and deep-fried then tossed in a stir-fry or used as a condiment; these are available in packets in Asian food shops.

RED ONIONS and purple onions are often called spanish onions. They are usually used raw in salads and for garnishes, for their decorative effect. They are milder and sweeter than white or brown onions; to reduce their mild pungency even further, pour boiling water over onion slices then drop into ice water, then drain and dry.

PREPARATION Remove the skin (or, in the case of green onions, the coarse outside layers) and trim the root end without cutting it off. In green and spring onions, trim the green tops to a few centimetre or remove altogether, according to the recipe.

Shallots are tedious to peel but are easier if separate cloves are first dropped into boiling water for about 10 seconds to loosen the skins. If a large quantity of brown or white onions is to be chopped, large ones are the best to choose because there are fewer to peel. Many ways have

been tried to reduce the stinging fumes that make you cry when chopping onions; the best way is to use a razor-sharp knife that minimises squashing the onion tissues that releases the fumes; the best of the rest seems to be to chill them well before chopping or even semi-freeze them after peeling. The food processor chops onion quickly and easily and is good for chopping coarsely, but not for finely chopped as it releases too much liquid and they will steam in the pan rather than frying.

CHOOSING Select onions and shallots individually rather than buying a bag. Press each one as you pick it up and avoid any that are discoloured, damaged, damp or soft as this indicates breaking down. Spring and green onions should have firm, shiny white parts and crisp green tops.

STORING Store brown, white, red and purple onions in a single layer, not touching, in a cool, dark, dry place where air can circulate round them — sliding wire baskets are ideal. Store shallots in the same way, on newspaper if necessary so that they won't fall through. Use sweet, soft onion varieties within a week or so; use shallots and others within a few weeks.

Store green and spring onions in a paper bag enclosed in a paper bag in the refrigerator and use within 10 days.

🌿 **OTHER RECIPES USING ONIONS**
Cranberry and balsamic red onion relish, p468
Crème fraîche and spinach sauce, p143
Duck liver parfait with red onion jam, p358

Spring onions

Shallots

Red onions

1 CARAMELISED RED ONION
2 ONION AND SPINACH
PAKORAS WITH CUCUMBER
RAITA

Caramelised red onion

PREP + COOK TIME 50 MINUTES **MAKES** 1½ CUPS

This recipe makes enough
caramelised onion to go
with 6 servings of grilled
steak, but it is worth
making double the quantity
or more because it is so
useful to have on hand for
a pizza topping, a quiche,
omelette, hamburger or
sandwich filling, or a
garnish for grilled chicken
or barbecued swordfish.
Caramelised onion will
keep for weeks in a lidded
container in the refrigerator.
You can also use brown
onions instead.

50g butter

4 medium red onions (680g), sliced thinly

1 tablespoon brown sugar

⅓ cup (80ml) dry red wine

¼ cup (60ml) beef stock

1 tablespoon balsamic vinegar

1 Melt butter in large frying pan; cook onion over low heat, stirring occasionally, about 30 minutes.

2 Add sugar; cook, stirring, about 5 minutes or until onion has caramelised. Add wine, stock and vinegar; bring to the boil then remove from heat. Serve with grilled steak.

NUTRITIONAL COUNT PER TABLESPOON 2.3g total fat (1.5g saturated fat); 159kJ (38 cal); 2.8g carbohydrate; 0.6g protein; 0.5g fibre

Onion and spinach pakoras with cucumber raita

PREP + COOK TIME 50 MINUTES **SERVES** 4 (MAKES 16 PAKORAS)

2 cups (300g) besan

2 large uncooked potatoes (600g), grated coarsely

2 large brown onions (400g), sliced thinly

100g baby spinach leaves, chopped coarsely

4 cloves garlic, crushed

1 teaspoon chilli powder

½ teaspoon ground cumin

1 teaspoon salt

¼ teaspoon ground turmeric

1 teaspoon garam masala

¼ teaspoon baking powder

¼ cup coarsely chopped fresh mint

¼ cup (60ml) water

2 tablespoons olive oil

CUCUMBER RAITA

1 lebanese cucumber (130g), grated coarsely

200g low-fat yogurt

¼ cup (60ml) lemon juice

¼ cup coarsely chopped fresh mint

1 Using hand, combine all ingredients except the oil, in medium bowl.

2 Shape ¼ cups of the potato mixture into patties. Heat oil in large frying pan; cook pakoras, in batches, about 10 minutes or until browned lightly both sides.

3 Meanwhile, combine ingredients for cucumber raita in small bowl.

4 Serve pakoras with raita.

NUTRITIONAL COUNT PER SERVING 2.8g total fat (0.4g saturated fat); 489kJ (117 cal); 17.9g carbohydrate; 4.4g protein; 3.4g fibre

Besan, also called chickpea flour, is available in some health food shops and in Indian food shops.
A raita is a yogurt-based dip or accompaniment. There are many kinds with different vegetable, nut, herb or spice flavourings. The cucumber one in this recipe is also lovely on fish.

For information on baby spinach leaves, see Spinach, page 568.

Roasted balsamic onions

PREP + COOK TIME 1 HOUR **SERVES** 4

2 medium red onions (340g), quartered

2 medium brown onions (300g), quartered

2 bulbs garlic, halved horizontally

2 tablespoons olive oil

1 tablespoon balsamic vinegar

1 tablespoon brown sugar

1 Preheat oven to 220°C/200°C fan-forced.

2 Combine ingredients in medium baking dish.

3 Roast, brushing occasionally with pan juices, about 40 minutes or until onions and garlic are tender and caramelised.

NUTRITIONAL COUNT PER SERVING 9.8g total fat (1.4g saturated fat); 702kJ (168 cal); 13.9g carbohydrate; 3.5g protein; 5.6g fibre

These onions can be made ahead and served hot with steak, pan-fried veal, liver and bacon or roast beef, or cold with any cold meat or poultry.

A tablespoon of Cognac, stirred into the soup at the last minute, is an excellent addition.

To make gruyère croûtons, preheat the grill. Finely grate 60g gruyère cheese. Cut 1 small french stick into 1.5cm slices; discard end pieces. Toast slices one side then turn and sprinkle equal amounts of cheese over untoasted sides; grill until cheese browns lightly.

For information on gruyère cheese, see Cheese, page 104.

French onion soup

PREP + COOK TIME 1 HOUR 20 MINUTES **SERVES** 4

50g butter

4 large brown onions (800g), halved, sliced thinly

¾ cup (180ml) dry white wine

3 cups (750ml) water

1 litre (4 cups) beef stock

1 bay leaf

1 tablespoon plain flour

1 teaspoon fresh thyme leaves

1 Melt butter in large saucepan; cook onion, stirring, 30 minutes or until caramelised.

2 Meanwhile, bring wine to the boil in large saucepan; boil 1 minute. Stir in the water, stock and bay leaf; return to the boil. Remove from heat.

3 Stir flour into onions; cook, stirring, 2 minutes. Gradually add hot broth, stirring, until mixture boils and thickens slightly. Reduce heat; simmer, uncovered, stirring occasionally, 20 minutes. Discard bay leaf; stir in thyme. Serve topped with gruyère croûtons.

NUTRITIONAL COUNT PER SERVING 1.1g total fat (0.7g saturated fat); 96kJ (23 cal); 1.4g carbohydrate; 1g protein; 0.3g fibre

You can make the filling and the pastry dough, separately, several days ahead and store them in the refrigerator until required. Store the filling in a lidded container and wrap the dough in plastic wrap, then enclose it in a plastic bag shaped closely round it to exclude air.

For information on pastry, see Pastry, pages 404–406; and for anchovies, see Seafood, pages 520–523.

Onion and anchovy tartlets

PREP + COOK TIME 1 HOUR 15 MINUTES **SERVES** 6

1 tablespoon olive oil

60g butter

3 medium brown onions (450g), halved, sliced thinly

2 cloves garlic, crushed

1 bay leaf

3 sprigs fresh thyme

⅓ cup coarsely chopped fresh flat-leaf parsley

8 drained anchovy fillets, chopped finely

2 tablespoons coarsely chopped seeded kalamata olives

¾ cup (110g) self-raising flour

¾ cup (110g) plain flour

¾ cup (180ml) buttermilk

1 Heat oil and half of the butter in large frying pan; cook onion, garlic, bay leaf and thyme, stirring occasionally, 20 minutes or until onion caramelises. Discard bay leaf and thyme; stir in parsley, anchovy and olives.

2 Meanwhile, blend or process flours and remaining butter until mixture resembles fine breadcrumbs. Add buttermilk; process until ingredients just come together. Knead dough on floured surface until smooth.

3 Preheat oven to 200°C/180°C fan-forced. Oil two oven trays.

4 Divide dough into six pieces; roll each piece on floured surface into 14cm square. Fold edges over to form 1cm border. Place squares on trays; place rounded tablespoons of the onion mixture on each square. Bake about 15 minutes or until pastry browns lightly.

NUTRITIONAL COUNT PER SERVING 12.9g total fat (6.4g saturated fat); 1170kJ (280 cal); 31.8g carbohydrate; 7.7g protein; 2.7g fibre

FRENCH ONION SOUP

Oranges

Oranges are the most popular citrus fruits, a commonplace that is available all year round, but no less well-loved for that. They are a part of daily life for the multitudes who start the day with orange juice or marmalade on the breakfast toast and for those whose afternoon cup of Earl Grey tea owes its fragrance to the bergamot orange.

Two special hand-tools are designed for obtaining fine shreds or julienne (matchsticks) of citrus rind: the zester and the canelle knife. The zester has a flat blade with tiny, sharp holes across its slanting end so that, when you press it on to the rind and draw it towards you, it cuts fine shreds from the rind without removing any of the white pith underneath. The canelle knife has a flat blade with a sharp, v-shaped indent on the end which, as you press it on the rind and draw it towards you, cuts julienne.

For a refreshing juice, push 1 peeled, coarsely chopped large orange, 1 small carrot halved lengthways, and 2cm piece fresh ginger through a juice extractor. Stir juice to combine. Refrigerate all the ingredients before making the juice, or serve it over ice. Drink this juice within 30 minutes.

Oranges flavour cakes and tea breads, make some of the easiest and most refreshing desserts and have a marked affinity with turkey, chicken, duck, lamb and pork. There are two main kinds of orange, the sweet and the bitter. Bitter seville oranges are necessary for making a proper British marmalade — their flesh gives the desired bitter edge behind the sweetness and their rind gives the right aroma. Sweet oranges come in many varieties but the main commercial ones in Australia are navels and valencias, with blood oranges appearing in their season. The relatively new tangelo is not a true orange but an "honorary" one and a welcome addition to the family.

NAVEL ORANGES The washington navel is a winter orange, available from autumn through to spring. Its richly coloured, pebbly skin is easy to remove and it is juicy, well flavoured and all-but seedless. The lane late navel, an Australian variety and also seedless, is a spring orange, available from mid-spring to midsummer. It is lighter in colour than the washington but just as flavoursome.

VALENCIA ORANGES, an Australian variety, are a summer orange, available from early spring into autumn. Valencias don't have the bold good looks of navels: they are smaller, smooth-skinned and often green-tinged because they ripen in warm weather, not the cold weather that gives the bright orange colour, and they do have seeds. Their flesh is sweet, richly coloured and very juicy, so knowledgeable shoppers buy them rather than the showy but paler-fleshed and less flavourful imported navels that are around in late summer when the Australian navels have finished.

SEVILLE ORANGES have thick skin, tough membranes, many seeds and sour flesh with a strongly bitter edge so their use is confined to cooking, especially marmalade-making. They are in season from midwinter into spring, but are not generally available in ordinary greengrocers though they can sometimes be found in large specialist ones.

BLOOD ORANGES taste like other oranges, differing only in having crimson flesh and pink juice and being especially sweet. The skin of some varieties is pink-flushed as well, but most look like any smallish orange from the outside. Slices and segments look spectacular in salads, dessert and garnishes and their juice makes sunset-coloured sorbets, jellies and other desserts; the rind is not as bitter as that of an ordinary orange: grated or thinly peeled, it can be strewn over salads, puddings or cakes. Blood oranges are available from about midwinter into spring.

TANGELOS are a cross between the tangerine (see Mandarins, page 306) and the grapefruit, but resemble oranges more

1 NAVEL
2 VALENCIA

☙ OTHER RECIPES USING ORANGES

than either of these. They look like an especially richly coloured, smallish orange with a slight neck at the stem end, and taste like a tangy orange. Their thick skin peels very easily and they are easy to separate into segments and are available from about midwinter to the beginning of summer.

PREPARATION
Oranges are sometimes waxed to prevent drying out, so if you are using the rind, first wash the fruit in warm water, rubbing with a cloth, and dry well.

SEGMENTING ORANGES

All citrus fruits can be separated into skin-on segments simply by pulling them apart, but segments used for a salad or to decorate a cake or dessert need to be skinless. To obtain them, cut both ends off the fruit, deep enough to expose the flesh, then stand it upright and cut down, following the curved shape, to take off a section of skin with the underlying membrane so that the flesh is exposed. Repeat all the way round, then hold the fruit and cut from the outside to the centre on each side of the dividing membrane to release skinless segments.

CHOOSING
Citrus fruit will not ripen any further after picking, so choose undamaged, well coloured fruit that is heavy for its size. Avoid any that look dried out or wizened and any with soft spots.

STORING
Oranges will keep well for a few days at room temperature; for longer storage, store in the refrigerator crisper.

1 STEAMED SALMON WITH
BURNT ORANGE SAUCE
2 CREPES SUZETTE

1   2

Steamed salmon with burnt orange sauce

PREP + COOK TIME 35 MINUTES **SERVES** 4

½ cup (110g) caster sugar

⅓ cup (80ml) water

1 teaspoon finely grated orange rind

¼ cup (60ml) orange juice

1 tablespoon olive oil

1 tablespoon rice wine vinegar

4 x 200g salmon fillets

350g watercress, trimmed

1 Stir sugar and the water in small saucepan, without boiling, until sugar dissolves; bring to the boil. Reduce heat; simmer, uncovered, without stirring, until light caramel in colour.

2 Remove pan from heat; allow bubbles to subside. Stir in rind and juice; return pan to low heat. Stir until any pieces of caramel melt. Remove pan from heat; stir in oil and vinegar.

3 Meanwhile, place fish in large bamboo steamer set over large saucepan of simmering water; steam, covered, 15 minutes. Serve fish with watercress, drizzled with sauce.

NUTRITIONAL COUNT PER SERVING 19.1g total fat (3.8g saturated fat); 1940kJ (464 cal); 29.4g carbohydrate; 41.6g protein; 3.4g fibre

Steaming is an excellent, moist way to cook salmon. The sauce is not really burnt but caramelised for deep flavour which balances with the vinegar to produce a tangy sweet/ sour effect.

For information on salmon, see Seafood, page 523.

Crêpes suzette

PREP + COOK TIME 40 MINUTES (PLUS STANDING TIME) **SERVES** 4

¾ cup (110g) plain flour

3 eggs

2 tablespoons vegetable oil

¾ cup (180ml) milk

ORANGE SAUCE

125g butter

½ cup (110g) caster sugar

1 ½ cups (375ml) orange juice, strained

2 tablespoons lemon juice

⅓ cup (80ml) orange-flavoured liqueur

1 Sift flour into medium bowl, make well in centre; add eggs and oil, gradually whisk in milk until smooth. Pour batter into large jug, cover; stand 1 hour.

2 Heat greased heavy-based crêpe pan or small frying pan; pour ¼ cup of batter into pan, tilting pan to coat base. Cook over low heat until browned lightly, loosening around edge with spatula. Turn crêpe; brown other side. Remove crêpe from pan; cover to keep warm. Repeat with remaining batter to make a total of 8 crêpes.

3 Make orange sauce.

4 Fold crêpes in half then in half again, place in sauce; warm over low heat. Divide crêpes among serving plates; pour hot sauce over crêpes. Serve with orange segments, if you like.

ORANGE SAUCE Melt butter in large frying pan, add sugar; cook, stirring, until mixture begins to brown. Add juices; bring to the boil. Reduce heat; simmer, uncovered, 3 minutes or until light golden. Add liqueur; remove from heat, ignite.

NUTRITIONAL COUNT PER SERVING 41g total fat (20.4g saturated fat); 3039kJ (727 cal); 66.7g carbohydrate; 10.3g protein; 1.3g fibre

Crêpes suzette are one of the great show-off desserts. In restaurants, they are flamed at the table in a theatrical performance with leaping flames and the waiter chosen for his expertise and showmanship. However, we suggest that you use a long match to ignite them in the kitchen (with the exhaust fan turned off) and carry them flaming to the table.

These are a beautiful variation on the classic favourite, lemon meringue pie. To make the recipe into one for lemon meringue pie, increase the sugar in the filling to ⅔ cup, replace orange rind with lemon rind and replace orange juice with lemon juice.

For information on pastry, see Pastry, pages 404–406.

Blood orange meringue pies

PREP + COOK TIME 50 MINUTES (PLUS REFRIGERATION AND COOLING TIME) **MAKES** 12

½ cup (110g) caster sugar

2 tablespoons cornflour

⅔ cup (160ml) blood orange juice

2 tablespoons water

2 teaspoons finely grated blood orange rind

75g unsalted butter, chopped coarsely

2 eggs, separated

½ cup (110g) caster sugar, extra

PASTRY

1¼ cups (185g) plain flour

¼ cup (55g) caster sugar

125g cold butter, chopped coarsely

1 egg yolk

1 Make pastry.

2 Grease 12-hole (⅓-cup/80ml) muffin pan. Roll pastry between sheets of baking paper to 4mm thickness; cut out twelve 8cm rounds. Press rounds into pan holes; prick bases all over with fork. Refrigerate 30 minutes.

3 Preheat oven to 200°C/180°C fan-forced.

4 Bake pastry cases 10 minutes. Cool.

5 Meanwhile, combine sugar and cornflour in small saucepan; gradually stir in juice and the water until smooth. Cook, stirring, until mixture boils and thickens. Reduce heat; simmer, stirring, 1 minute. Remove pan from heat; stir in rind, butter and egg yolks. Cool 10 minutes.

6 Divide filling between pastry cases. Refrigerate 1 hour.

7 Increase oven to 240°C/220°C fan-forced.

8 Beat egg whites in small bowl with electric mixer until soft peaks form; gradually add extra sugar, beating until sugar dissolves.

9 Roughen surface of filling with fork; using star nozzle, pipe meringue over filling. Bake about 3 minutes or until browned lightly.

PASTRY Process flour, sugar and butter until coarse. Add egg yolk; process until combined. Knead on lightly floured surface until smooth. Cover; refrigerate 30 minutes.

Blood oranges

NUTRITIONAL COUNT PER PIE 15.3g total fat (9.5g saturated fat); 1250kJ (299 cal); 36.7 carbohydrate; 3.2g protein; 0.6g fibre

Papaya

Also known as pawpaw, papaya is a large, thin-skinned tropical fruit with smooth flesh which may be yellow, pink or orange depending on variety, and a hollow centre filled with large, black seeds which, though usually discarded, are edible, being crunchy and mildly peppery- tasting.

In Australia the pink-fleshed fruit is always called papaya; the bigger, orange-fleshed fruit is called pawpaw. In America, both varieties are called papaya.

❧ **OTHER RECIPES USING PAPAYA**
Beef carpaccio with green papaya salad, p52
Green tea ice-cream with fruit salsa, p601

There are considerable differences in flavour among the different varieties, some yellow-fleshed ones being rather sickly and deficient in sweetness, and pink-fleshed ones usually the best. When ripe, papaya is mildly sweet and delicately aromatic but its flavour lacks acid so, if being eaten alone, it is nearly always served with a wedge of lime to squeeze over — a wonderful start to a summer breakfast. It is also superb with passionfruit or a citrus-flavoured liqueur such as Cointreau. Green papaya is used in Asian chutneys and curries. Papaya leaves and fruits, especially unripe ones, contain an enzyme

called papain, which tenderises meat by breaking down the fibres: commercial meat tenderisers, available in powder form, are made from papaya. The enzyme also acts to break down dissolved gelatine so papaya cannot be used for jellied desserts.

PREPARATION At its simplest, which many people consider its best, papaya needs only halving, the seeds removing, peeling and cutting into wedges or cubes.

CHOOSING Choose medium-size papaya, up to about 500g in weight. Papaya is best eaten at the fully ripe but not overripe stage, when it is sweet and tender but still firm enough to cut cleanly. Yellow or mostly yellow skin usually indicates ripeness though some varieties stay green even when ripe. Ripeness can be best judged by smell, which should be mildly aromatic, and by yielding when it is held in two hands and gently pressed. Papaya continues to ripen after picking, so it is best to buy it a little underripe, if possible, and allow it to ripen at room temperature.

STORING Once ripe, a papaya should be refrigerated, double-wrapped in plastic or in a covered container so that it will not perfume other food, for up to 3 days. Cut papaya should be stored in the same way for up to 2 days.

Papaya, strawberry and orange juice

PREP TIME 10 MINUTES **MAKES** 1 LITRE (4 CUPS)

1 large papaya (1.2kg), chopped coarsely

250g strawberries

¾ cup (180ml) fresh orange juice

1 Blend papaya, strawberries and orange juice until smooth.

NUTRITIONAL COUNT PER 250ML 0.4g total fat (0g saturated fat); 502kJ (120 cal); 23g carbohydrate; 2.3g protein; 7.4g fibre

Pickled green papaya salad

PREP + COOK TIME 25 MINUTES (PLUS STANDING TIME) **SERVES** 4

1 cup (250ml) water

½ cup (125ml) rice vinegar

½ cup (110g) white sugar

1 teaspoon salt

1 fresh long red chilli, halved lengthways

1 small green papaya (650g)

150g sugar snap peas

100g bean thread noodles

½ small pineapple (450g), quartered, sliced thinly

1 small red onion (100g), sliced thinly

1 cup firmly packed fresh mint leaves

1 fresh long red chilli, sliced thinly

PALM SUGAR DRESSING

¼ cup (60ml) lime juice

2 tablespoons grated palm sugar

1 Combine the water, vinegar, sugar, salt and halved chilli in small saucepan; bring to the boil. Reduce heat; simmer, uncovered, 5 minutes. Strain into small jug; discard solids. Cool 10 minutes.

2 Meanwhile, peel papaya. Quarter lengthways, discard seeds. Grate papaya coarsely.

3 Place papaya in medium bowl with vinegar mixture, cover; stand 1 hour.

4 Meanwhile, boil, steam or microwave peas until just tender; drain. Place noodles in medium heatproof bowl, cover with boiling water; stand until just tender, drain. Rinse under cold water; drain. Using kitchen scissors, cut noodles into random lengths.

5 Place ingredients for palm sugar dressing in screw-top jar; shake well.

6 Place drained papaya, peas and noodles in medium bowl with pineapple, onion, mint and dressing; toss gently to combine.

7 Divide salad among serving bowls; top with sliced chilli.

NUTRITIONAL COUNT PER SERVING 0.4g total fat (0g saturated fat); 577kJ (138 cal); 29g carbohydrate; 3.1g protein; 6.4g fibre

PAPAYA, STRAWBERRY AND ORANGE JUICE

This juice is beautiful by itself or laced with white rum, gin or vodka. Refrigerate all ingredients before making or pour it over ice. Serve within 30 minutes of making.

For information on strawberrries, see Berries, page 58; and for orange, see Oranges, pages 380-382.

This salad is wonderful with chilli crab, a seafood barbecue, or barbecued pork or chinese barbecued duck from an Asian takeaway.

Parsnips

Parsnips are one of the sweetest root vegetables, excellent for cooking with a roast, mashing with butter, shallow-frying or slicing very thin, deep-frying and salting for savoury chips to serve with drinks or beside a mixed grill.

The best parsnips are grown in cold places as frosts make them sweeter by causing them to convert their starch into sugar.

Their nutty sweetness is especially good with garlic and with curry spices, for example as boiled or steamed parsnip dressed with a garlic and cream sauce or as curried parsnip soup. Parsnips are available all year but their season is winter, when they are at their best as cold weather develops their flavour.

PREPARATION Trim off the root and thin tip, peel thinly with a vegetable peeler and, unless the parsnip is very young and slender, halve lengthwise and check whether there is a woody core. If so, remove it before cooking — most easily, by halving again and cutting it off, or, if parsnip is too thin for that, slicing out the core with a slanting cut on each side of it.

Unless parsnips are used immediately, leave in acidulated water (water with lemon juice or vinegar added) as cut surfaces darken in contact with air.

CHOOSING Parsnips should be evenly cream-coloured, firm and undamaged with no soft spots. Avoid large ones as they are more likely to have a woody centre.

STORING Store parsnips in a paper bag enclosed in a plastic bag in the refrigerator for up to 10 days.

🌿 **OTHER RECIPES USING PARSNIPS**
Lamb racks with mustard maple glaze, p289

Roasted caramelised parsnips

PREP + COOK TIME 1 HOUR 10 MINUTES **SERVES** 4

Caramelising deepens a parsnip's natural sweetness but doesn't make it oversweet because the more sugar is cooked, the more its sweetness is transformed into deep, roasted flavours.

1kg parsnips, halved lengthways
2 tablespoons olive oil
¼ cup (55g) brown sugar
1 teaspoon ground nutmeg
1 tablespoon finely chopped fresh flat-leaf parsley

1 Preheat oven to 220°C/200°C fan-forced.
2 Combine parsnip, oil, sugar and nutmeg in large baking dish; roast about 1 hour or until parsnip is browned and tender. Serve parsnip sprinkled with parsley.

NUTRITIONAL COUNT PER SERVING 9.6g total fat (1.3g saturated fat); 1074kJ (257 cal); 35.8g carbohydrate; 4.1g protein; 5.7g fibre

Roasted parsnip and garlic soup

PREP + COOK TIME 1 HOUR 45 MINUTES **SERVES** 4

1 garlic bulb

2 tablespoons olive oil

1kg parsnips, chopped coarsely

1 tablespoon olive oil, extra

1 small brown onion (80g), chopped finely

1 medium potato (200g), chopped coarsely

1 litre (4 cups) chicken stock

300ml cream

¾ cup (180ml) milk

2 tablespoons finely chopped fresh garlic chives

ANCHOVY TOASTS

6 anchovy fillets, drained, chopped finely

2 tablespoons finely chopped fresh garlic chives

50g butter, softened

1 small french bread stick (150g)

Roasting makes both the parsnip and garlic wonderfully sweet and mellow. When preparing the parsnips, be sure to peel thickly enough to remove all the bitter outer layer, and also to cut off any woody core.

For information on garlic, see Garlic, pages 214 & 215.

1 Preheat oven to 200°C/180°C fan-forced.

2 Place whole unpeeled garlic bulb in large shallow baking dish; roast, uncovered, 10 minutes. Add combined oil and parsnip; roast about 30 minutes or until garlic and parsnip are tender. When garlic is cool enough to handle, halve garlic bulb crossways; use fingers to squeeze garlic puree into small bowl. Reserve.

3 Heat extra oil in large saucepan; cook onion, stirring, until softened. Add parsnip with potato and stock; bring to the boil. Reduce heat; simmer, uncovered, stirring occasionally, about 20 minutes or until potato is softened.

4 Meanwhile, make anchovy toasts.

5 Blend or process soup with reserved garlic, in batches, until smooth. Reheat soup in same pan, stir in cream and milk; bring to the boil. Top soup with chives; serve with anchovy toasts.

ANCHOVY TOASTS Combine anchovy, chives and butter in small bowl. Cut bread into 1.5cm slices; discard end pieces. Toast slices on one side under preheated grill. Turn slices, spread each with anchovy mixture; grill until anchovy mixture bubbles.

NUTRITIONAL COUNT PER SERVING 61.8g total fat (32.2g saturated fat); 3545kJ (848 cal); 52.9g carbohydrate; 16.6g protein; 10.7g fibre

---

Parsnip mash

PREP + COOK TIME 25 MINUTES **SERVES** 4

1kg parsnips, peeled, chopped coarsely

¾ cup (180ml) hot milk

2 cloves garlic, crushed

40g butter, chopped

For parsnip and potato mash, cook equal quantities of potato and parsnip instead of all parsnip and mash as directed in recipe.

1 Boil, steam or microwave parsnip until tender; drain.

2 Mash parsnip in medium bowl with milk until smooth; stir in garlic and butter.

NUTRITIONAL COUNT PER SERVING 10.5g total fat (6.6g saturated fat); 953kJ (228 cal); 24.9g carbohydrate; 5.7g protein; 5.9g fibre

ROASTED PARSNIP AND GARLIC SOUP

Passionfruit

The passionfruit is not only a delicacy in itself but has the quality of bringing out the flavours of other fruits. Although native to tropical America, it grows well in temperate zones, as attested by the thousands of Australian back fences on which it flourishes.

1 PANAMA PASSIONFRUIT
2 COMMON PASSIONFRUIT

Its tough shell encloses magnificently perfumed, intensely-flavoured tangy-sweet pulp with embedded black seeds which are usually eaten. The common variety, which is also the most fragrant and best-flavoured, is small, round and purple-skinned; panama passionfruit, a large, round, light purple/red-skinned cultivar, is almost as good, and there are also banana passionfruit, a long yellow variety somewhat less intense and tangy in flavour, and a round yellow-skinned variety which is less perfumed than the common one. Passionfruit makes an excellent fruit "cheese" or curd and takes beautifully to creamy flavours: its tang comes through strongly in mousses, ice-creams and, most famously, against the meringue-and-cream richness of the favourite Australian dessert, pavlova. The passionfruit season in temperate zones runs from about midsummer to early autumn; in the tropics, the peak seasons are late summer and late winter but vines may bear some fruit all year round.

PREPARATION
The simplest way to eat passionfruit, known to many children with a passionfruit vine on the fence, is to cut one in half and suck out the pulp. A sharp teaspoon is best for scooping it out as it tends to cling to the shell. To obtain seedless juice, process pulp for about 30 seconds in a food processor, then sieve.

CHOOSING
Slightly wrinkled skin and rich skin colour with no tinge of green indicate ripeness, but some cultivars do not wrinkle. The best test is skin colour combined with heaviness for size, which varies considerably as some passionfruit are filled with flesh and some are half-empty. Very wrinkled skin combined with lightness indicates an overripe fruit which will have an unpleasant fermented taste.

STORING
Passionfruit keep well at room temperature for a week or more. For longer storage, they will keep in the refrigerator crisper for 2 or 3 weeks but will gradually shrivel and become mouldy if kept much longer. They can be frozen whole or the pulp can be mixed with about half its volume in sugar to preserve it, and frozen in ice-cube trays then collected into a freezer bag where it will keep for months.

❧ OTHER RECIPES USING PASSIONFRUIT
Banana passionfruit soy smoothie, p554
Grilled nectarines with passionfruit yogurt, p332
Kiwifruit and pineapple salad with basil lemon syrup, p280

You need 3 passionfruit to obtain the amount of pulp needed for this recipe.

It is best to put the custard dishes into the baking dish and pile ice-cubes around them so that the custard will stay cold when the sugar topping is grilled.

For information on coconut, see Nuts, page 347.

Passionfruit and coconut crème brûlée

PREP + COOK TIME 1 HOUR (PLUS REFRIGERATION TIME) **SERVES** 4

1 egg

2 egg yolks

2 tablespoons caster sugar

¼ cup (60ml) passionfruit pulp

280ml can coconut cream

½ cup (125ml) cream

1 tablespoon brown sugar

1 Preheat oven to 180°C/160°C fan-forced.

2 Combine egg, egg yolks, caster sugar and passionfruit in medium heatproof bowl.

3 Combine coconut cream and cream in small saucepan; bring to the boil. Gradually whisk hot cream mixture into egg mixture. Place bowl over medium saucepan of simmering water; stir over heat about 10 minutes or until custard thickens slightly.

4 Divide custard among four deep ½-cup (125ml) heatproof dishes. Place dishes in large baking dish; pour enough boiling water into baking dish to come halfway up sides of dishes. Bake, uncovered, about 30 minutes or until custards set. Remove custards from water; cool. Cover; refrigerate 3 hours or overnight.

5 Preheat grill.

6 Place custards in shallow flameproof dish filled with ice cubes. Sprinkle each custard with 1 teaspoon brown sugar; using finger, gently smooth sugar over the surface of each custard. Place baking dish under grill until tops of crème brûlée caramelise.

NUTRITIONAL COUNT PER SERVING 30.3g total fat (21.6g saturated fat); 1526kJ (365 cal); 16.7g carbohydrate; 5.7g protein; 3.3g fibre

Passionfruit curd sponge cakes

PREP + COOK TIME 30 MINUTES (PLUS REFRIGERATION AND COOLING TIME) **MAKES** 12

3 eggs

½ cup (110g) caster sugar

¾ cup (110g) self-raising flour

20g butter

¼ cup (60ml) boiling water

PASSIONFRUIT CURD

⅓ cup (80ml) passionfruit pulp

½ cup (110g) caster sugar

2 eggs, beaten lightly

125g unsalted butter, chopped coarsely

1 PASSIONFRUIT AND COCONUT CREME BRULEE
2 PASSIONFRUIT CURD SPONGE CAKES

1 Make passionfruit curd.

2 Preheat oven to 180°C/160°C fan-forced. Grease 12-hole (½-cup/125ml) oval friand pan with softened butter; dust lightly with flour.

3 Beat eggs in small bowl with electric mixer until thick and creamy. Gradually add sugar, beating until dissolved between additions. Transfer mixture to large bowl. Fold in sifted flour then combined butter and the boiling water.

4 Divide mixture among pan holes. Bake about 12 minutes. Working quickly, loosen edges of cakes from pan using a small knife; turn immediately onto baking-paper-covered wire racks to cool.

5 Split cooled cakes in half. Spread cut-sides with curd; replace tops. Serve dusted with sifted icing sugar.

PASSIONFRUIT CURD Combine ingredients in medium heatproof bowl; stir over pan of simmering water about 10 minutes or until mixture coats the back of a wooden spoon. Cover; refrigerate 3 hours.

NUTRITIONAL COUNT PER CAKE 12.2g total fat (7.2g saturated fat); 957kJ (229 cal); 25.3g carbohydrate; 3.9g protein; 1.2g fibre

You need 4 passionfruit to obtain the amount of pulp needed for this recipe. You can fill the cakes up to 20 minutes before serving, but not earlier as the moisture in the filling may make the cakes soggy if left to stand much longer.

Pasta

Pasta is Italy's gift to the world and is now "naturalised" in dozens of countries as a satisfying dish that suits the needs of today's busy cooks and appeals to both adults and children. It can be a simple dough of flour and water or enriched with eggs, made into hundreds of different shapes, left plain or coloured and flavoured with such ingredients as spinach, beetroot, tomato, chilli or squid ink, and is available fresh or dried.

1 FETTUCCINE
2 VERMICELLI
3 SPAGHETTINI
4 BUCATINI
5 SPAGHETTI
6 LINGUINE
7 RISONI
8 PENNE
9 FUSILLI
10 ORECCHIETTE
11 FARFALLE
12 CONCHIGLIETTE
13 RIGATONI
14 TORTELLINI
15 MACARONI
16 FRESH RAVIOLI
17 FRESH GNOCCHI
18 FRESH TORTELLINI
19 FRESH SPAGHETTI
20 CANNELONI TUBES
21 TAGLIATELLE
22 ANGEL HAIR
23 LASAGNE SHEETS
24 PAPPARDELLE

As a general rule, 500g of raw pasta is usually enough for 4 people as a main course or 6 as a first course or accompaniment.

KINDS OF PASTA

FRESH PASTA is available commercially or can be made at home, using a small hand-operated or electric machine with rollers and cutters. It is made with ordinary, medium-soft flour (see Flour, pages 182–185) and eggs. Fresh pasta is not superior to dried pasta — both have the same consistency when properly cooked.

DRIED PASTA is the mass-produced kind in boxes and packets on the supermarket shelves. It is made with strong flour made from hard wheat — good-quality dried pasta uses semolina flour made from durum wheat (see Flour, page 184) and will have that fact marked on the package, either as "100% durum wheat" or "pasta di semola di grano duro", or something similar. Mass-produced does not necessarily mean lesser quality — some of the best pasta comes from big manufacturers.

EGG PASTA is available fresh or dried.

WHOLEMEAL PASTA is made with part wholemeal and part white flour.

REFRIGERATED OR FROZEN PASTA
Packets of filled pasta shapes such as ravioli, agnolotti and tortellini, and gnocchi, are available refrigerated or frozen from supermarkets, delicatessens and speciality food stores.

PASTA SHAPES

LONG STRANDS, ROUND IN SECTION spaghetti, spaghettoni (thicker), spagettini (thinner), vermicelli (thinner again), capellini (very thin) and capelli d'angelo or angel hair (fine and delicate, usually shaped into a nest).

TUBULAR macaroni (short and thick), elbow macaroni (with a bend in the middle), rigatoni (short and wide with a ridged surface), bucatini (long and thin) and cannelloni (thin pasta rolled round upon itself to form a wide tube for stuffing).

FLAT RIBBONS fettuccine, plain or verde (green, spinach-flavoured), tagliatelle (wider), tagliolini (narrower), linguine (narrower still) and pappardelle (short and wide).

LARGE SHEETS lasagne, flat or ripple-edged, plain or verde (green, spinach-flavoured), and instant lasagne, which is pre-boiled and needs no cooking before being layered with sauce and cheese and baked.

PASTA FOR SOUP tiny shapes such as stelline (stars) and orzo or risoni (rice-grain shapes).

STUFFED PASTA ravioli (square or round), agnolotti (turnovers), tortellini (turnovers twisted into a ring), capelletti (twisted into a three-corner-hat shape) and capellacci (larger).

SMALL SHAPES WITH HOLES OR CREVICES TO HOLD CHUNKY SAUCES penne (quill or pen-shape), conchiglie (shells), conchiglioni (larger), conchigliette (smaller), fusilli (corkscrews), orecchiette (little ears) and farfalle (butterflies, but often described as bow-ties), farfalloni (bigger), farfaletti, or stricchetti in Bologna (smaller), rotelle (wheels) and fricelli (furled thin pasta).

DUMPLINGS gnocchi, which are not made from the same dough as other pasta but from softer dough based on semolina, polenta, potato or ricotta. They are cooked in water and may be served with a simple sauce such as browned butter with fried sage leaves, or may be topped with cheese or a sauce and baked. Spätzle or spaetzle are tiny dumplings, not of Italian but of German origin, which are made from dough similar to that for fresh pasta, which is spread on a board and then small pieces are scraped off into boiling water, a procedure requiring skill to scrape off even-sized pieces. Alternatively, a thick batter rather than a dough is made and this is

pushed through the holes in a colander held above the pot of boiling water.

Spätzle are served in clear soup or other dishes, or may be tossed with or fried in butter to serve with meat dishes, sometimes with a sauce or gravy, much as potato or rice might be served.

STORING Dried pasta will keep indefinitely in a cool, dry place in its unopened packaging, or after opening, in an airtight jar or box. Fresh pasta will keep for a few days in the refrigerator but tends to stick together if kept longer. Freezing is not very successful as it tends to glue together when it thaws.

❦ OTHER RECIPES USING PASTA
Angel hair pasta with mixed peas, p425
Broad bean and ricotta orecchiette, p42
Broccoli and garlic breadcrumb spaghetti, p75
Cheese gnocchi with fresh tomato sauce and pancetta, p109
Fettuccine alfredo, p143
Pumpkin and sage ravioli, p483
Salami, bocconcini and pasta salad, p517
Spaghetti with pesto, p268
Vongole and chorizo linguine, p539

Rigatoni is a short, tubular pasta; other short shapes such as macaroni can be used instead.

For information on zucchini, see Zucchini, page 656.

Rigatoni with zucchini, lemon and mint

PREP + COOK TIME 20 MINUTES **SERVES** 4

500g rigatoni pasta

¼ cup (60ml) olive oil

2 cloves garlic, crushed

3 medium zucchini (360g), grated coarsely

¾ cup (180g) ricotta cheese

1 cup coarsely chopped fresh mint

½ cup (70g) roasted slivered almonds

2 tablespoons lemon juice

1 Cook pasta in large saucepan of boiling water until just tender; drain.

2 Meanwhile, heat oil in large frying pan; cook garlic and zucchini, stirring, 2 minutes. Add cheese; cook, stirring, until just heated through.

3 Combine zucchini mixture and pasta in serving bowl with remaining ingredients.

NUTRITIONAL COUNT PER SERVING 30.3g total fat (6g saturated fat); 3110kJ (744 cal); 88.9g carbohydrate; 23.9g protein; 8.3g fibre

Fettuccine bolognese

PREP + COOK TIME 1 HOUR **SERVES** 4

1 tablespoon olive oil

1 large brown onion (200g), chopped finely

2 cloves garlic, crushed

600g beef mince

¼ cup (70g) tomato paste

1 cup (125ml) beef stock

2 x 400g cans diced tomatoes

⅓ cup finely chopped fresh flat-leaf parsley

1 tablespoon finely chopped fresh oregano

375g fettuccine

½ cup flaked parmesan cheese

1 Heat oil in large frying pan; cook onion and garlic, stirring, until onion softens.

2 Add mince; cook, stirring, until browned. Add paste, stock and undrained tomatoes; bring to the boil. Reduce heat; simmer, covered, 20 minutes. Uncover; simmer about 10 minutes or until thickened slightly. Remove from heat; stir in herbs.

3 Meanwhile, cook pasta in large saucepan of boiling water until tender; drain.

4 Serve fettuccine topped with bolognese and cheese.

NUTRITIONAL COUNT PER SERVING 20g total fat (7.4g saturated fat); 2893kJ (692 cal); 75g carbohydrate; 48.4g protein; 7.3g fibre

Other pasta shapes such as spaghetti or macaroni can be used instead of fettuccine. Bolognese is the most famous pasta sauce of all. It can be frozen in an airtight container for up to 3 months and can also be adapted as a base for other savoury dishes such as chilli con carne and cottage pie.

Penne puttanesca

PREP + COOK TIME 1 HOUR 15 MINUTES **SERVES** 6

⅓ cup (80ml) olive oil

1 medium brown onion (150g), chopped finely

3 cloves garlic, crushed

¼ cup loosely packed fresh basil leaves

1 teaspoon sea salt

2 tablespoons tomato paste

1.5kg ripe tomatoes, chopped coarsely

500g penne pasta

4 whole drained anchovy fillets

1 fresh long red chilli, sliced thinly

1 cup (120g) seeded black olives

2 tablespoons drained, rinsed baby capers, chopped coarsely

1 Heat half of the oil in large saucepan; cook onion, garlic, basil and salt, stirring, until onion softens. Add paste; cook, stirring, 1 minute.

2 Add tomato; bring to the boil then reduce heat. Simmer, uncovered, stirring occasionally, about 45 minutes or until sauce thickens

3 Cook pasta in large saucepan of boiling water until just tender; drain.

4 Meanwhile, finely chop anchovy fillets. Using side of heavy knife, press down firmly on anchovy to crush.

5 Heat remaining oil in large saucepan; cook anchovy and chilli, stirring, 2 minutes. Add tomato sauce; bring to the boil. Stir in olives and capers, reduce heat; simmer, uncovered, about 5 minutes or until heated through. Add pasta; toss to combine.

NUTRITIONAL COUNT PER SERVING 13.9g total fat (2g saturated fat); 1965kJ (470 cal); 68.8g carbohydrate; 13.4g protein; 7g fibre

This recipe makes enough sauce for 500g pasta, to serve as a great first course for 6. Serve with crusty bread to mop up the last of the sauce.

For information on prawns, see Seafood, pages 526 & 527; and for chillies, see Chillies, pages 118–120.

Chilli prawn linguine

PREP + COOK TIME 25 MINUTES **SERVES** 6

1.5kg uncooked small king prawns

500g linguine pasta

¼ cup (60ml) olive oil

3 cloves garlic, sliced thinly

2 fresh long red chillies, sliced thinly

⅓ cup coarsely chopped fresh flat-leaf parsley

50g baby rocket leaves

1 Shell and devein prawns, leaving tails intact.

2 Cook pasta in large saucepan of boiling water, uncovered, until just tender.

3 Meanwhile, heat half the oil in large frying pan; cook prawns, in batches, until just changed in colour. Remove from pan; cover to keep warm.

4 Heat remaining oil in same frying pan; cook garlic and chilli, stirring, until fragrant.

5 Reserve ½ cup of the pasta cooking liquid then drain pasta. Return pasta to pan with prawns, reserved cooking liquid, chilli mixture, parsley and rocket; toss to combine.

NUTRITIONAL COUNT PER SERVING 10.9g total fat (1.6g saturated fat); 2002kJ (479 cal); 57.2g carbohydrate; 35.3g protein; 3.3g fibre

If you can't find orecchiette, use penne instead. Pasta salad is great for picnics and lunchboxes and as a side salad for grilled chops.

Pasta salad

PREP + COOK TIME 25 MINUTES **SERVES** 4

250g orecchiette

2 tablespoons drained sun-dried tomatoes, chopped coarsely

1 small red onion (100g), sliced thinly

1 small green capsicum (150g), sliced thinly

½ cup coarsely chopped fresh flat-leaf parsley

SUN-DRIED TOMATO DRESSING

1 tablespoon sun-dried tomato pesto

1 tablespoon white wine vinegar

2 tablespoons olive oil

1 Cook pasta in large saucepan of boiling water, uncovered, until just tender; drain. Rinse under cold water; drain.

2 Place ingredients for sun-dried tomato dressing in screw-top jar; shake well.

3 Place pasta in large bowl with remaining ingredients and dressing; toss gently to combine.

NUTRITIONAL COUNT PER SERVING 12g total fat (1.9g saturated fat); 1405kJ (336 cal); 46g carbohydrate; 8.8g protein; 3.6g fibre

CHILLI PRAWN LINGUINE

If you can't get russet burbank potatoes, use any baking or all-rounder variety (see Potatoes, page 448). Potato should be mashed while hot but can be cooled slightly before being mixed with remaining ingredients.

For information on basil, see Herbs, page 262.

Gnocchi with pesto

PREP + COOK TIME 55 MINUTES (PLUS REFRIGERATION TIME) **SERVES 8**

1kg potatoes, unpeeled

2 eggs, beaten lightly

30g butter, melted

¼ cup (20g) finely grated parmesan cheese

2 cups (300g) plain flour, approximately

PESTO

2 cloves garlic, quartered

¼ cup (40g) roasted pine nuts

¼ cup (20g) finely grated parmesan cheese

1 cup firmly packed fresh basil leaves

⅓ cup (80ml) olive oil

½ cup (125ml) cream

1 Boil or steam whole potatoes until tender; drain. Peel when cool enough to handle. Mash, using ricer, food mill (mouli), or sieve and wooden spoon, into large bowl; stir in eggs, butter, parmesan and enough of the flour to make a firm dough.

2 Divide dough into eight equal parts; roll each part on lightly floured surface into 2cm-thick sausage-shape. Cut each sausage-shape into 2cm pieces; roll pieces into balls.

3 Roll each ball along the inside tines of a fork, pressing lightly on top of ball with index finger to form classic gnocchi shape, grooved on one side and dimpled on the other. Place gnocchi, in single layer, on floured tray, cover; refrigerate 1 hour.

4 Meanwhile, make pesto.

5 Cook gnocchi in large saucepan of boiling salted water about 3 minutes or until gnocchi float to the surface. Remove from pan with slotted spoon; drain.

6 Combine gnocchi and pesto in large bowl. Serve with flaked parmesan cheese, if you like.

PESTO Blend or process garlic, pine nuts, cheese and basil until finely chopped. With motor operating, gradually add oil until pesto is thick. Stir pesto and cream in small saucepan over low heat until heated through.

NUTRITIONAL COUNT PER SERVING 26g total fat (9.5g saturated fat); 1944kJ (465 cal); 44.2g carbohydrate; 11.7g protein; 4.5g fibre

Even non-vegetarians will love to share this vegetarian dish. Use scissors to trim lasagne sheets to fit into your baking dish; you may need only 3 sheets in total.

Roasted vegetable lasagne

PREP + COOK TIME 1 HOUR 40 MINUTES (PLUS STANDING TIME) **SERVES 6**

3 medium red capsicums (600g)

2 medium eggplants (600g), sliced thinly

2 tablespoons coarse cooking salt

2 medium zucchini (240g), sliced thinly

600g kumara, sliced thinly

cooking-oil spray

700g bottled tomato pasta sauce

4 fresh lasagne sheets

150g ricotta cheese, crumbled

1 tablespoon finely grated parmesan cheese

WHITE SAUCE

40g low-fat dairy-free spread

¼ cup (35g) plain flour

1½ cups (375ml) skim milk

2 tablespoons coarsely grated parmesan cheese

ROASTED VEGETABLE LASAGNE

1 Preheat oven to 240°C/220°C fan-forced.

2 Quarter capsicums; discard seeds and membranes. Roast, uncovered, skin-side up, about 5 minutes or until skin blisters and blackens. Cover capsicum pieces in plastic or paper for 5 minutes; peel away skin.

3 Reduce oven to 200°C/180°C. Place eggplant in colander, sprinkle with salt; stand 20 minutes. Rinse eggplant under cold water; pat dry with absorbent paper.

4 Place eggplant, zucchini and kumara, in single layer, on oven trays; spray with oil. Roast about 15 minutes or until tender.

5 Meanwhile, make white sauce.

6 Oil deep rectangular 2.5-litre (10-cup) ovenproof dish. Spread 1 cup pasta sauce over base of dish; top with half of the eggplant and half of the capsicum. Layer with lasagne sheet; top with ½ cup of the pasta sauce, ricotta, kumara and zucchini. Layer with another lasagne sheet; top with remaining pasta sauce, remaining eggplant and remaining capsicum. Layer remaining lasagne sheet over vegetables; top with white sauce, sprinkle with parmesan. Bake about 45 minutes or until browned lightly. Stand 5 minutes before serving with rocket salad, if you like.

WHITE SAUCE Melt spread in small saucepan, add flour; cook, stirring, until mixture thickens and bubbles. Remove from heat, gradually stir in milk; cook, stirring, until sauce boils and thickens. Remove from heat; stir in cheese.

NUTRITIONAL COUNT PER SERVING 9g fat (3.2g saturated fat); 1300kJ (311 cal); 44.1g carbohydrate; 14.2g protein; 8.1g fibre

Pastry

The three main types of pastry for home cooks are shortcrust (also called short) pastry, choux pastry and puff pastry or one of its easier relatives, flaky and rough puff pastry. Also of interest are hot-water pastry, which is the traditional pastry for cold pork, veal and ham or game pies, and the yeast pastry used for Danish pastries.

There is a special way of rolling puff, rough puff and flaky pastries. First beat lightly and evenly with the rolling pin from front to back of the pastry to flatten the fat, then bring the rolling pin down firmly just inside the front edge of the pastry; give a short, sharp back-and-forth roll, lift the pin and repeat just behind the first area, working your way from the front to the back of the pastry. The idea is to roll the pastry thinner without pushing the fat about so that it breaks through the surface. Stop rolling just before you get to the back edge so that the pastry is not pushed out of shape. If fat does break through, sprinkle it with pastry and put the board with the pastry on it into the refrigerator for 10 minutes before continuing.

SHORTCRUST PASTRY is crunchy, firm and tender. It is made by mixing flour and butter (or other fat, as the recipe specifies) so that they coat one another in small particles with the butter still firm, then moistening with water (or egg yolk) and mixing to make the particles cohere into a dough, while not working the flour enough to develop its gluten (see Flour, page 182), which would make the pastry tough. The first is done by having the fat chopped and chilled and rubbing fat and flour together between fingertips and thumb, not the warm palms. The second is done by adding the liquid nearly all at once and using a round-ended table knife to cut, rather than stir, it through the flour. The dough is also rested before and after rolling and shaping, to allow the gluten to relax so as to insure against toughness. When the pastry is baked, the fat melts, leaving innumerable tiny air pockets which give the pastry its tender, crumbly texture. Shortcrust pastry may be plain or sweet, for which sugar is added to the flour, and is used for small and large tarts, pies, turnovers and pastries.

PUFF PASTRY is used where the most airy delicacy is required. Its French name is mille-feuille, meaning a thousand leaves. It consists of hundreds of tissue-paper-thin layers of crisp pastry, made by enclosing a flat block of butter in pastry then continually turning, rolling in a different direction,

folding and chilling to keep the butter firm, then repeating this sequence to a total of six, in order to multiply the layers of pastry separated by layers of butter. When baked, they separate and puff up to make a crisp, fragile pastry. It takes some skill to make puff pastry as the butter will break through the ever-thinner pastry layers unless the rolling and handling techniques are correct. The name mille-feuille is also given to the confection made from layers of puff or flaky pastry and crème pâtissière (pastry cream) — also called a napoleon or, more prosaically, a vanilla slice.

ROUGH PUFF PASTRY is made by mixing firm diced fat with flour, adding liquid to make a dough as in making shortcrust pastry, then rolling, folding and turning four times for a pastry that is crisply layered and tender but does not rise as high as puff or flaky pastry. Rough puff is perfect for sausage rolls, turnovers or jam tarts.

FLAKY PASTRY is made by repeatedly folding, rolling, turning and chilling as with puff pastry, but the fat is dotted on to the pastry for each turn, so it is easier to manage than a single block which has to be progressively thinned. In addition, flaky pastry calls for only four turns, one to enclose each addition of fat. The result is a finely layered, crisp pastry which is perfect for pie crusts, vol au vents and any use except the most delicate creations.

CHOUX PASTRY is crisp on the outside and soft within. It is made by melting butter in hot water, adding flour and cooking the mixture until it coheres into a dough, then beating in eggs. The resulting dough is soft enough to spoon or pipe into small mounds on a baking tray for round choux puffs or buns, or pipe into other shapes such as short lengths for éclairs or a ring for a paris-brest gâteau. When these are baked, they puff up into the desired shapes leaving a hollow in the centre. The pastries are filled with a sweet cream or custard or with savoury mixtures such as creamed mushrooms or prawns. Alternatively, the pastry may be made with cheese as well as butter and the puffs served without a filling as a hot appetiser.

HOT-WATER PASTRY is made by combining a mixture of lard and boiling water with flour so that, unlike short or flaky pastries, the flour and fat are not kept as separate substances but melded into a thin, relatively tough crust. The pastry is used while still warm and pliable, traditionally by moulding it round an upturned jar or other mould, then slipping it off when it has cooled enough to be firm and strong enough to stand without support, hence the name "raised" for the end product. For convenience and speed when making a number of pies, or for a special effect such as an oval, ribbed crust, hot-water pastry is often shaped, instead, by lining a mould as with other pastries, but its strength is still an asset because raised pies are high, so the weight of the filling would break weaker pastry. Raised pies always have a top crust, often elaborately decorated.

DANISH PASTRY is a sweet, egg-rich yeast pastry which is made by rolling the dough thin, spreading it with butter and folding, rolling, buttering, turning and chilling and repeating this sequence in the same way as for flaky pastry. The result is a flaky pastry that is crisp on the outside but rich and soft within. It is usually shaped into a closed crescent with a fruit, custard or sweet soft-cheese topping.

FILLO AND KATAIFI PASTRY are two Greek specialities which are in the province of the highly skilled pastrycook rather than the home cook to make from scratch. But both are available ready-made uncooked so it is easy for home cooks to add these to their repertoire.

Fillo pastry, also known as phyllo, is used in the cuisines of Greece and other parts of the former Ottoman empire. It consists of paper-thin sheets of raw pastry which are used by brushing with oil or melted butter and stacking one on another, then cutting or folding as the recipe directs. It makes a distinctly layered, crackling-crisp, airy crust or wrapping for small pastries such as spanakopita (spinach and cheese triangles). Fillo is available in the refrigerated cabinets of supermarkets and delicatessens. It is also available frozen but this form is not recommended as the sheets tend to stick together as it thaws.

Kataifi pastry, also known as konafa pastry, looks like tangled vermicelli. It is made by pouring a batter through a sieve on to a revolving hot copper plate and removed while still pliable. It is used in Greek, Middle Eastern and Armenian cuisine by shaping into sheets of the required size, brushing with melted butter and layering with or rolling around sweet fillings such as nuts with spices and sugar or honey; sugar syrup is often drizzled over the finished pastries. It can also be used with savoury fillings. When baked, kataifi is crunchy on the outside and tender within. It is not widely available but may be found in some speciality food shops and Greek or Middle Eastern delicatessens.

SUET PASTRY is made with suet (see Oils & Fats, page 362), flour and water in much the same way as short pastry except that the fat and flour are not rubbed together, simply mixed. It is used to line the basin for steamed savoury puddings such as steak and kidney or sweet ones such as sussex pond pudding, which is filled with butter and sugar with a lemon in the centre.

CHOOSING
Frozen puff pastry is available in blocks and ready-rolled sheets. It does not rise as high as good home-made puff pastry will. Butter puff is the best. Frozen shortcrust pastry is available in blocks and ready-rolled sheets.

STORING
All types of uncooked pastry except hot-water pastry, which must be used immediately, can be stored in the refrigerator, tightly wrapped in plastic wrap and enclosed in a plastic bag, for up to a week. Pastry to be rolled out should be removed half an hour ahead of time so that it will be pliable but still cool. Kataifi pastry should be removed 2 hours ahead of using. All types of home-made pastry except hot-water pastry can be frozen for up to a month. Kataifi pastry can be frozen for up to 6 months. Fillo should not be frozen. For ready-made commercial puff and shortcrust pastry, follow instructions on package.

Use the pastry trimmings to make fleurons — small leaf shapes, ovals, diamonds or crescents — which are used to garnish dishes made with a rich sauce or served with elegant soups. To make them, roll the pastry thinner, brush with beaten egg and cut out shapes 6–8cm in length. Bake in a 230°C/210°C fan-forced oven about 7 minutes or until light golden brown; when cold, store in an airtight container.

For information on leeks, see Leeks, page 290; for bacon rashers, see Bacon, page 28; and for gruyère cheese, see Cheese, page 104.

Gruyère, leek and bacon tart

PREP + COOK TIME 1 HOUR 10 MINUTES **SERVES** 6

50g butter
2 medium leeks (700g), sliced thinly
2 rindless bacon rashers (130g), chopped finely
2 sheets puff pastry
2 eggs
½ cup (125ml) cream
1 teaspoon fresh thyme leaves
½ cup (60g) finely grated gruyère cheese

1 Preheat oven to 220°C/200°C fan-forced. Oil 24cm-round loose-based flan tin; place tin on oven tray.

2 Melt butter in medium frying pan; cook leek, stirring occasionally, 15 minutes or until soft. Remove from pan. Cook bacon in same pan, stirring, until crisp; drain on absorbent paper.

3 Meanwhile, place one pastry sheet in flan tin; overlap with second sheet to form cross shape, trim away overlapping pastry. Prick pastry base with fork, cover with baking paper; fill with dried beans or uncooked rice. Bake 20 minutes. Remove paper and beans; cool pastry case. Reduce oven to 200°C/180°C fan-forced.

4 Whisk eggs, cream and thyme in small bowl. Spread leek into pastry case; top with bacon. Pour in egg mixture; sprinkle with cheese.

5 Bake tart about 20 minutes or until filling sets. Cool 10 minutes before serving. Serve with a baby rocket and parmesan salad, if you like.

NUTRITIONAL COUNT PER SERVING 34.8g total fat (20.2g saturated fat); 1948kJ (466 cal); 24.5g carbohydrate; 14.4g protein; 2.8g fibre

If you only need to serve four, you can either halve the recipe or freeze the second pie, cooked or uncooked, for up to 3 months.

For information on beef, see Beef, pages 46 & 47.

Chunky beef and vegetable pie

PREP + COOK TIME 2 HOURS 40 MINUTES **SERVES** 8

1 tablespoon olive oil

1.5kg gravy beef, cut into 2cm pieces

60g butter

1 medium brown onion (150g), chopped finely

1 clove garlic, crushed

¼ cup (35g) plain flour

1 cup (250ml) dry white wine

3 cups (750ml) hot beef stock

2 tablespoons tomato paste

2 stalks celery (300g), trimmed, cut into 2cm pieces

2 medium potatoes (400g), cut into 2cm pieces

1 large carrot (180g), cut into 2cm pieces

1 large zucchini (150g), cut into 2cm pieces

150g mushrooms, quartered

1 cup (120g) frozen peas

½ cup finely chopped fresh flat-leaf parsley

2 sheets puff pastry

1 egg, beaten lightly

1 Heat oil in large saucepan; cook beef, in batches, until browned all over.

2 Melt butter in same pan; cook onion and garlic, stirring, until onion softens. Add flour; cook, stirring, until mixture thickens and bubbles. Gradually stir in wine and stock; stir until mixture boils and thickens slightly.

3 Return beef to pan with paste, celery, potato and carrot; bring to the boil. Reduce heat; simmer, covered, 1 hour.

4 Add zucchini and mushrooms; simmer, uncovered, about 30 minutes or until beef is tender. Add peas; stir until heated through. Remove from heat; stir in parsley.

5 Preheat oven to 220°C/200°C fan-forced.

6 Divide warm beef mixture between two deep 25cm pie dishes; brush outside edge of dishes with a little egg. Top each pie with a pastry sheet; pressing edges to seal. Trim pastry; brush pastry with egg.

7 Bake pies about 20 minutes or until browned.

NUTRITIONAL COUNT PER SERVING 27.6g total fat (13.3g saturated fat); 2412kJ (577 cal); 28.6g carbohydrate; 46.4g protein; 4.9g fibre

Portuguese custard tarts

PREP + COOK TIME 55 MINUTES **MAKES** 12

½ cup (110g) caster sugar

2 tablespoons cornflour

4 egg yolks

300ml cream

⅓ cup (80ml) water

3cm strip lemon rind

1 teaspoon vanilla extract

1 sheet sweet puff pastry

These popular little treats can sometimes be over-sweet, but infusing the filling mixture with a strip of lemon rind gives a subtle fresh note to balance the sweetness.

1 Preheat oven to 220°C/200°C fan-forced. Grease 12-hole (⅓-cup/80ml) muffin pan.

2 Combine sugar and cornflour in medium saucepan; whisk in egg yolks, cream and the water. Add rind; stir over medium heat until mixture comes to the boil. Remove from heat; discard rind. Stir extract into custard.

3 Cut pastry sheet in half; place halves on top of each other. Roll pastry tightly (like a swiss roll) from one short side; cut roll into twelve 1cm rounds.

4 Place pastry rounds, cut-sides up, on lightly floured surface; roll each into a 10cm round. Push rounds into pan holes; spoon in custard.

5 Bake tarts about 20 minutes. Stand 5 minutes, before lifting onto wire rack to cool.

NUTRITIONAL COUNT PER TART 14.3g total fat (8.3g saturated fat); 849kJ (203 cal); 16.5g carbohydrate; 2.4g protein; 0.2g fibre

Both granny smith and golden delicious apples are suitable for this recipe.

For information on fresh cranberries, see Berries, page 60; and for apples, see Apples, pages 8–10.

Apple cranberry pie

PREP + COOK TIME 1 HOUR 50 MINUTES (PLUS REFRIGERATION TIME) **SERVES** 8

2 cups (300g) plain flour

150g cold unsalted butter, chopped coarsely

½ cup (125ml) iced water

1 egg

1 tablespoon milk

1 tablespoon caster sugar

CRANBERRY FILLING

½ cup (110g) caster sugar

2 tablespoons water

300g frozen cranberries

APPLE FILLING

10 medium apples (1.5kg)

½ cup (125ml) water

⅓ cup (75g) caster sugar

1 Process flour and butter until crumbly; add enough of the water to bring ingredients together. Press dough into a ball. Cover; refrigerate 1 hour.

2 Make cranberry filling. Make apple filling.

3 Preheat oven to 220°C/200°C fan-forced.

4 Divide pastry in half. Roll half between sheets of baking paper until large enough to line deep 25cm pie dish; lift pastry into dish. Spoon cranberry filling into pastry case; top with apple filling. Bring edge of pastry case up over filling; brush pastry edge with combined egg and milk.

5 Roll remaining pastry until large enough to cover top of pie; press edges together with fork to seal. Brush with egg mixture; sprinkle with sugar.

6 Bake pie 15 minutes. Reduce oven to 180°C/160°C fan-forced; bake 30 minutes.

CRANBERRY FILLING Combine sugar, the water and cranberries in medium saucepan; simmer, stirring, about 10 minutes or until syrupy. Remove from heat; cool.

APPLE FILLING Peel, quarter, core and slice apples thinly; combine in large saucepan with the water. Simmer, stirring occasionally, about 10 minutes or until apple is tender. Drain apple; discard liquid. Stir sugar into apple; cool.

NUTRITIONAL COUNT PER SERVING 16.8g total fat (10.5g saturated fat); 1981 kJ (474 cal); 72.2g carbohydrate; 5.7g protein; 4.9g fibre

Peaches

Although nothing can surpass the pleasure of eating an unadorned, perfectly ripe peach on a summer day, these beautiful fruit respond so well to poaching or grilling, combining with other fruits, baking with a rich stuffing or in a creamy tart or butter cake, layering with cream and meringue or serving in the old-fashioned way with home-made custard, that it is a shame not to enjoy them in those ways too.

1 YELLOW-FLESHED PEACHES
2 WHITE-FLESHED PEACHES

Slices of ripe peach, served instead of the usual figs or melon with prosciutto make an ambrosial first course for a summer lunch, or, for an informal light meal, can be followed simply by a soft cheese and crusty bread. A rosé or light, fruity red wine would match the mood.

Yet it can be quite difficult to buy a truly excellent peach. Their true season is from mid to late summer: much earlier and they can disappoint because they are not properly ripe, much later and they may be dry and mealy because they have been cold-stored. Even in season, they are often picked before they are truly ripe because retailers want firm fruit, and as peaches do not ripen further after picking, they will soften but never attain full, ripe sweetness. Luckily, even a not-quite-wonderful peach can be lovely treated in the ways mentioned above or simply quartered or sliced, sprinkled with a little sugar and lemon juice and the pieces turned over to coat them, then left to stand for an hour or so, turning the pieces over again about halfway through.

Peaches come in yellow and white varieties, both of which can be either clingstone or freestone, defined by whether the flesh separates cleanly from the stone. White peaches are scented and luscious. They are too fragile for some cooking methods but can be poached in their skins as described below. Uncooked, they are the right peaches for Bellinis, the famous Italian summer drink that combines fresh peach flesh and sparkling wine. Yellow peaches, especially freestones which are easier to peel as well as to stone, are the better kind to use in cooking.

PREPARATION To eat a peach out of hand, first rub the downy skin smooth under cold running water. To peel, pour boiling water over, leave up to 30 seconds, depending on ripeness, then drain and pull skin off. As the cut or peeled flesh darkens very quickly, brush with lemon juice if not to be used or served immediately. Peaches are best poached in their skins as the skin gives a pretty rosy flush to the flesh and the cooking softens it so that it is easy to pull off, leaving a perfect, glossy surface behind.

CHOOSING Rich colour and softness are not reliable guides to maturity. The best guide is that a truly ripe peach (or nectarine) has a definite, sweet fragrance.

STORING Buy only enough peaches for a few days at a time. Keep them at room temperature until they are soft; this can be hastened by enclosing them in a paper bag. Once soft, store in the refrigerator crisper for a day or two.

🌿 **OTHER RECIPES USING PEACHES**
Peach and cardamom chutney, p468

Grilled lamb with spicy peach salsa

PREP + COOK TIME 25 MINUTES **SERVES** 4

800g lamb backstraps

SPICY PEACH SALSA
1 small red onion (100g), chopped finely
2 large peaches (440g), chopped finely
2 tablespoons finely chopped fresh flat-leaf parsley
1 fresh long red chilli, chopped finely
1 tablespoon malt vinegar

1 Cook lamb on heated oiled grill plate (or grill or barbecue) until cooked as desired. Stand, covered, 10 minutes then slice thinly.

2 Meanwhile, make spicy peach salsa.

3 Serve lamb with salsa and spinach salad or barbecued kipflers, if you like.

SPICY PEACH SALSA Combine ingredients in medium bowl.

NUTRITIONAL COUNT PER SERVING 17.7g total fat (8g saturated fat); 1530kJ (366 cal); 7.4g carbohydrate; 43.1g protein; 1.8g fibre

A refreshing sweet-sharp spinach salad would pull the salsa and lamb flavours together nicely: put into a bowl 80g trimmed baby spinach leaves, 1 tablespoon malt vinegar, 2 teaspoons olive oil, ½ teaspoon white sugar, 2 tablespoons roasted pine nut and 1 tablespoon dried currants, and toss to combine.

For information on lamb, see Lamb, pages 282 & 283.

Peach and apricot tarts

PREP + COOK TIME 45 MINUTES **SERVES** 8

60g butter, softened
⅓ cup (75g) caster sugar
1 egg
¾ cup (75g) ground hazelnuts
2 tablespoons plain flour
2 sheets butter puff pastry
3 medium peaches (450g)
4 large apricots (320g)
¼ cup (80g) apricot jam, warmed, sieved

1 Beat butter and sugar in small bowl with an electric mixer until creamy. Beat in egg; stir in nuts and flour.

2 Preheat oven to 220°C/200°C fan-forced. Cut the pastry sheets in half; place on two greased oven trays. Spread nut mixture thinly over pastry pieces, leaving a 2cm border.

3 Halve fruit and remove the seeds; slice thinly. Arrange fruit, overlapping slightly, on nut mixture. Bake about 20 minutes.

4 Brush the fruit with jam. Serve warm or cooled with cream or ice-cream.

NUTRITIONAL COUNT PER SERVING 22.2g total fat (9.6g saturated fat); 1597kJ (382 cal); 38.8g carbohydrate; 5.6g protein; 3.1g fibre

For information on butter puff pastry, see Pastry, page 404; and for apricots, see Apricots, pages 14 & 15.

1 PEACH AND APRICOT TARTS
2 PEACH MELBA

Peach melba

PREP + COOK TIME 10 MINUTES (PLUS COOLING TIME) **SERVES** 4

1 litre (4 cups) water

4 medium peaches (600g)

500ml vanilla ice-cream

RASPBERRY SAUCE

200g fresh or thawed frozen raspberries

1 tablespoon icing sugar, approximately

1 Bring the water to the boil in medium saucepan. Add peaches; simmer, uncovered, 5 minutes. Remove peaches; place in bowl of cold water. When peaches are cold, peel off the skin.

2 Meanwhile, make raspberry sauce.

3 Serve peach halves topped with ice-cream, sauce and extra raspberries.

RASPBERRY SAUCE Push raspberries through fine sieve into small bowl; sweeten pulp with sifted sugar to taste.

NUTRITIONAL COUNT PER SERVING 7.7g total fat (4.8g saturated fat); 861 kJ (206 cal); 27.5g carbohydrate; 4.2g protein; 4.5g fibre

The peaches are poached in their skins because this gives them a pretty blush and a perfectly smooth, glossy surface when the skin is removed. If they are especially fine and ripe, you can use them uncooked: run a knife down its natural indentation to only just cut the skin, place in a heatproof bowl then cover with boiling water and stand for 20–30 seconds. Transfer fruit to a bowl of cold water then remove the skins. Unless you're serving them immediately, brush the surface with lemon juice to prevent them browning.

Pears

A fine pear is equally at home with savoury companions or with sweet ones, as good poached in a red-wine syrup and served with ice-cream as it is with a glass of red wine and some bread and freshly cut parmesan, or with blue cheese, walnuts and a sweet dessert wine.

1 BUERRE BOSC
2 PACKHAM'S TRIUMPH
3 CORELLA
4 RED ANJOU
5 WINTER NELIS
6 LEMON BERGAMOT

There are legends of pear-fanciers who were so determined to eat their william pears at their fleeting point of perfect ripeness that, having inspected them in the evening and found some almost ready, they would, if necessary, get up at 3 or 4am to savour the experience of absolute perfection.

Pears are good in salads, especially those with bitter leaves such as witlof or peppery ones such as watercress, and quartered firm pears are excellent baked beside rich meats such as duck or pork as they roast, or grilled with pork chops or ham steaks. On the sweet side, they can be used for a tart filling, a crumble or fruit salad, or poached and served with zabaglione or a drizzle of Poire William (pear eau-de-vie or fruit brandy) and cream, or, most famously, with vanilla ice-cream and hot chocolate sauce for Poires Belle Hélène, named for Offenbach's opera about Helen of Troy. Different varieties of pear have textures ranging, when ripe, from luscious and almost melting to firm and slightly grainy to crisp and crunchy for the Asian pear, the nashi. All pears are unusual in that they ripen from the inside out and should not be allowed to ripen on the tree as they quickly become woolly and their core breaks down if picked ripe. They are best picked mature but still hard and ripened in a cool place over a few days.

BEURRE BOSC is a large pear with russet skin. When ripe, it is soft and juicy with a slightly and pleasantly grainy texture. It is good raw and also suitable for long cooking. It is available from early autumn through to early summer.

PACKHAM'S TRIUMPH, also known as packham, is a large, often bumpy pear which is slow to ripen but, when it does

so, is very juicy with sweet, subtle flavour. The skin may remain green when ripe or may change to light yellow. Used firm, it is a good cooking pear. It is available from autumn through to summer.

CORELLA is a small pear with richly coloured green/red/golden skin and rich flavour, which keeps well. It is available from autumn through to spring.

RED ANJOU is a medium-sized pear, available from mid summer to autumn. Its white, fine-textured flesh makes this variety perfect for salads.

WINTER NELIS, also know as honey pear, are small, rough-skinned, long-keeping pears with spicy, juicy flesh, available in winter.

LEMON BERGAMOT is small to medium in size and is available from autumn to spring. They are ideal to use in desserts and cooking.

WILLIAM, also known as bartlett, is an aromatic, buttery pear with pale yellow skin, sometimes red-blushed, when ripe. Used firm, it is a good cooking pear. Once ripe, it is excellent raw but will not last long in good condition. It is available from summer into autumn.

RED SENSATION is a sport (spontaneous mutation) of the william pear which has bright red skin when ripe. It is like the regular william in cooking, eating and storing quality. It is available from late summer to late autumn.

NASHI is a true pear of Asian origin. It is sweet, juicy and crisp when ripe. Unlike European pears, it is ripened on the tree and keeps well after picking. Nashi are easily bruised so are usually sold in protective netted sleeves. They are available from late summer to late winter and at their peak in late summer-early autumn.

COCKTAIL PEARS are miniature green/gold pears with a crunchy texture, which may be eaten fresh or pickled. They are available in summer.

PREPARATION
As cut or peeled pear discolours quickly, it should be brushed with lemon juice unless it is to be used or served immediately.

CHOOSING
Pears should be undamaged and free of dark or soft spots. Ripeness is indicated by yielding if pressed gently near the stem.

STORING
Pears should be stored at room temperature until ripe; the process can be hastened by enclosing them in a paper bag with a banana or apple. Once ripe, they will keep for a day or so at room temperature or a little longer in the refrigerator; some will keep for longer, as noted above, but pears should be kept under observation as their period of perfect ripeness before they start to break down is brief. They need oxygen around them so should not be stored on top of each other or enclosed in a plastic bag at any stage.

❧ OTHER RECIPES USING PEARS
Pear and almond friands, p352
Pork with maple syrup, bourbon and pear sauce, p581
Roquefort and pear salad, p107
Witlof, pear and blue cheese salad, p254

Pear, walnut and fetta salad with walnut dressing

PREP + COOK TIME 20 MINUTES **SERVES** 4

A firm pear that will hold its shape when cut is best for this salad; refer to the varieties on pages 416-418 for information.

For information on walnuts, see Nuts, page 344; and for fetta and parmesan cheeses, see Cheese, pages 102 & 104.

1 butter lettuce
1 medium pear (230g), cored
⅓ cup (35g) roasted walnuts, chopped coarsely
40g snow pea sprouts, trimmed
50g fetta cheese, crumbled
35g shaved parmesan cheese

WALNUT DRESSING
1 tablespoon walnut oil
2 teaspoons wholegrain mustard
2 tablespoons white wine vinegar
1 tablespoon finely chopped fresh chives

1 Place ingredients for walnut dressing in screw-top jar; shake well.
2 Separate lettuce leaves; tear leaves roughly.
3 Slice unpeeled pear into thin wedges.
4 Place lettuce, pear and dressing in large bowl with remaining ingredients; toss gently to combine.

NUTRITIONAL COUNT PER SERVING 16.6g total fat (5g saturated fat); 957kJ (229 cal); 10.4g carbohydrate; 8.4g protein; 3.3g fibre

1 PEAR, WALNUT AND FETTA
SALAD WITH WALNUT DRESSING
2 FIVE-SPICE PORK AND
NASHI SALAD

Five-spice pork and nashi salad

PREP + COOK TIME 30 MINUTES (PLUS REFRIGERATION TIME) **SERVES** 4

600g pork fillets, trimmed

2 teaspoons vegetable oil

1 teaspoon five-spice powder

300g mizuna

2 green onions, sliced thinly

2 medium nashi (400g),
sliced thinly

CHILLI PLUM DRESSING

¼ cup (60ml) plum sauce

1 tablespoon water

1 tablespoon lemon juice

1 fresh long red chilli, sliced thinly

*Mizuna is an aromatic
Japanese salad herb (see
Greens, Salad, page 248).
If it is hard to find, use
watercress or any crisp
salad green.*

*For information on pork,
see Pork, pages 440 & 441.*

1 Combine pork, oil and five-spice in large bowl; refrigerate 3 hours or overnight.

2 Place ingredients for chilli plum dressing in screw-top jar; shake well.

3 Cook pork on heated oiled grill plate (or grill or barbecue) about 20 minutes.
Cover; stand 10 minutes then slice thickly.

4 Combine mizuna, onion and nashi in large bowl with two-thirds of the dressing.
Serve salad topped with pork, drizzled with remaining dressing.

NUTRITIONAL COUNT PER SERVING 14.8g total fat (4.3g saturated fat); 1522kJ (364 cal); 22.5g carbohydrate;
33.3g protein; 3.1g fibre

Roasted pear and almond cheesecake

PREP + COOK TIME 50 MINUTES (PLUS REFRIGERATION TIME) **SERVES** 8

250g butternut snap biscuits

50g flaked almonds

125g butter, melted

2 teaspoons gelatine

2 tablespoons water

250g cream cheese, softened

⅓ cup (75g) caster sugar

¼ cup (90g) golden syrup

300ml thickened cream, whipped

ROASTED PEARS

5 corella pears (500g), peeled, halved lengthways

⅓ cup (115g) golden syrup

30g butter

You can use low-fat cream cheese in this recipe if you prefer.

For information on cream cheese, see Cheese, pages 100–102.

1 Grease 11cm x 34cm rectangular loose-based flan tin or 22cm springform tin.

2 Process biscuits and almonds until fine. Add butter; process until combined. Press mixture over base and side of tin. Refrigerate 30 minutes.

3 Make filling by sprinkling gelatine over the water in small heatproof jug; stand jug in small saucepan of simmering water. Stir until gelatine dissolves. Cool 5 minutes.

4 Beat cheese, sugar and golden syrup in small bowl with electric mixer until smooth. Stir in gelatine mixture; fold in cream. Pour filling into tin; refrigerate overnight.

5 Make roasted pears. Top cheesecake with pears and syrup.

ROASTED PEARS Preheat oven to 200°C/180°C fan-forced. Place pears in single layer, in large shallow baking dish; drizzle with golden syrup, dot with butter. Roast, uncovered, about 30 minutes, turning occasionally or until pears are soft. Cool to room temperature.

NUTRITIONAL COUNT PER SERVING 51.2g total fat (31.3g saturated fat); 2989kJ (715 cal); 55.6g carbohydrate; 7.7g protein; 2.6g fibre

---

Red wine poached pears

PREP + COOK TIME 1 HOUR 20 MINUTES **SERVES** 6

6 medium pears (1.4kg)

2 cups (500ml) water

2 cups (500ml) dry red wine

2 tablespoons orange-flavoured liqueur

¾ cup (165g) caster sugar

1 teaspoon vanilla bean paste

4 x 5cm strips orange rind

⅓ cup (80ml) orange juice

Vanilla bean paste is a sweetened vanilla concentrate with seeds (see Vanilla, page 616) — 1 teaspoon equals 1 vanilla bean.

1 Peel pears, leaving stems intact.

2 Stir remaining ingredients in large saucepan over heat, without boiling, until sugar dissolves. Add pears; bring to the boil. Reduce heat; simmer, covered, about 1 hour or until pears are tender.

3 Transfer pears to serving bowls. Bring syrup in pan to the boil. Boil, uncovered, about 10 minutes or until syrup thickens slightly. Serve pears drizzled with warm syrup.

NUTRITIONAL COUNT PER SERVING 0.2g total fat (0g saturated fat); 1317kJ (315 cal); 57.1g carbohydrate; 0.8g protein; 3.5g fibre

ROASTED PEAR AND ALMOND CHEESECAKE

Peas

The pea family is represented at the greengrocers by green or "garden" peas, whose pods are not eaten, sugar snap and snowpeas, which are both eaten pod and all, snowpea sprouts or shoots, which are the small-leafed, growing tips of the plant, and pea (usually snowpea) tendrils, which are the thin, curly bits with a few leaves that peas use for climbing, though the name is often given to shoots.

1 SNOW PEA TENDRILS
2 SNOW PEA SPROUTS
3 SNOW PEAS
4 SUGAR SNAP PEAS
5 GREEN PEAS

The only ones missing, except in an enthusiastic or specialised greengrocers, are petit-pois or baby peas, which are simply ordinary green peas picked very young and small; they are necessarily expensive but an exquisite luxury. Green peas are also available frozen.

GREEN PEAS deteriorate rapidly after picking as their sugars immediately begin to turn to starch, to the detriment of both their flavour and tenderness. They are often tough when cooked; the chances of avoiding this lie in selecting carefully and using promptly (see CHOOSING and STORING). Green peas can be boiled with or without mint and served with any meat or fish dish, pureed with potato and cream, mixed with other vegetables such as mushrooms or artichokes, braised with shallots and lettuce if they are reasonably young, or used for soups or in pie or pasty fillings, risottos and creamy pasta sauces. Peas in the pod will yield just under half their weight of shelled peas; 1 kg will serve 4. Green peas are available all year but are best in spring and early summer.

PEA PODS are lined with a tough membrane which makes them too fibrous to eat, but they can be cooked with green peas to sweeten them or cooked in a dried- or fresh-pea soup to add fresh, sweet flavour; remove before serving.

SUGAR SNAP PEAS look like small green peas but their pods do not have the tough membrane of ordinary peas, so are eaten whole. They can be briefly boiled, used raw in salads, added raw to stir-fries and noodle dishes or added at the last minute to clear soups. Small ones can be used in risottos or pasta sauces. They are available all year.

SNOW PEAS have flat, edible pods enclosing tiny peas that do not mature. They are eaten whole or sliced. They can be very briefly boiled and served alone or with other vegetables such as mushrooms to accompany meats or fish or for a vegetable tart filling, used raw in salads, added raw to stir-fries, noodle dishes and spring-roll fillings, added at the last minute to clear soups or used in risottos or pasta sauces. They are available all year.

PEA SHOOTS AND PEA TENDRILS can be used as a garnish or in salads, used in stir-fries, noodle dishes and spring-roll fillings or added at the last minute to a clear soup. They are available, irregularly, all year but mostly in spring.

BABY PEAS are best boiled and served plainly with a little butter or cream so that their delicate flavour and tenderness can be appreciated, or in the classic dish Petits-pois à la Française or peas braised with shallots and lettuce, mentioned above as a way to prepare ordinary green peas but better with babies.

FROZEN PEAS vary from full-size to "baby peas". Theoretically, they are the answer to the tough-pea problem as they are marketed as being picked at their optimum point of development and frozen within hours. They are indeed tender, brightly coloured and quite good-tasting, but don't match truly young and fresh peas for the finer shades of flavour and texture. They are, however, a great convenience and a good product provided they have been correctly handled between the freezing plant and the frozen-food cabinet in the supermarket. They are at their best served with a little help such as braising with shallots and lettuce as mentioned previously.

PREPARATION Green peas should be podded only just before using. Sugar snap and snowpeas need to be stringed: pinch off the stem end and, with a thumbnail, pull down the strings on both sides. Pea shoots and tendrils need picking over to remove any tough stems or ends.

CHOOSING Pea shoots and tendrils should look almost moist and be undamaged, brightly coloured, firm and crisp. The best way to get good green peas, sugar snaps and snowpeas is to take a few minutes to pick them out one by one as there is usually considerable variance in quality in the pile at the greengrocers or supermarket. Look for the smallest and brightest sugar snaps, the smallest, brightest and firmest snowpeas and the smallest and most lustrous green pea pods that are rounded but not bulging. Avoid damaged, dry-looking or dull-coloured specimens. Don't buy ready-shelled peas: they may be days old and tough past redemption. Check frozen pea packages and avoid any that are frozen into a block or feel soft. Take an insulated bag with an ice-pack when you are planning to buy frozen vegetables; take them home as quickly as possible in this and transfer immediately to the freezer.

STORING Refrigerate all peas, shoots or tendrils as soon as you get them home. Shoots and tendrils can stay in their boxes if sold that way. Otherwise, enclose all kinds of pea in paper bags enclosed in plastic bags. Green peas should be used the day they are bought; sugar snaps and snowpeas can be refrigerated for a day or two. Shoots and tendrils are best used the day they are bought but can be refrigerated for a day or two if necessary.

You need about 1kg of peas in the pod to get the amount of shelled peas needed for this recipe.

Peas with mint butter

PREP + COOK TIME 10 MINUTES **SERVES** 4

2¼ cups (350g) fresh shelled peas
40g butter, softened
1 tablespoon finely chopped fresh mint
1 teaspoon finely grated lemon rind

1 Boil, steam or microwave peas until tender; drain.
2 Meanwhile, combine remaining ingredients in small bowl.
3 Serve peas topped with butter mixture.

NUTRITIONAL COUNT PER SERVING 8.6g total fat (5.4g saturated fat); 589kJ (141 cal); 8.6g carbohydrate; 5.2g protein; 5g fibre

1 PEAS WITH MINT BUTTER
2 ANGEL HAIR PASTA
WITH MIXED PEAS

Angel hair pasta with mixed peas

PREP + COOK TIME 30 MINUTES **SERVES** 4

375g angel hair pasta

150g sugar snap peas, trimmed

150g snow peas, trimmed

½ cup (60g) frozen peas

1 tablespoon olive oil

1 medium red onion (170g), sliced thinly

2 cloves garlic, crushed

2 tablespoons drained baby capers, rinsed

½ cup (125ml) lemon juice

½ cup coarsely chopped fresh mint

½ cup coarsely chopped fresh flat-leaf parsley

200g low-fat ricotta cheese, crumbled

For a three-pea salad, cook the same amounts of the three peas in this recipe, refresh immediately under cold water and drain. Mix them with the juice of a lemon and ¼ cup each of finely chopped fresh mint and chives for a tangy-sweet salad that is perfect with anything cheesy.

For information on angel hair pasta, see Pasta, page 396.

1 Cook pasta in large saucepan of boiling water, uncovered, until just tender; drain.

2 Meanwhile, boil, steam or microwave peas until just tender; drain. Rinse under cold water; drain.

3 Heat oil in large saucepan; cook onion, garlic and capers, stirring, 2 minutes. Add pasta; cook, stirring, 3 minutes.

4 Combine pasta mixture, peas, juice and herbs in large bowl. Serve topped with cheese.

NUTRITIONAL COUNT PER SERVING 10.4g total fat (3.7g saturated fat); 1990kJ (476 cal); 73.9g carbohydrate; 20.1g protein; 7.5g fibre

PEAS | **THE COMPLETE COOK** 425

You need approximately 750g of peas in the pod to get the amount of shelled peas needed for this recipe. You can use a 500g packet of frozen broad beans instead of fresh ones: cook and then peel them as instructed in the recipe, but they will not take as long as fresh ones to become tender, so be careful not to overcook them or they will become mushy. Risoni is small, rice-shaped pasta. If it is hard to find, use any other small soup pasta you like.

For information on turkey, see Poultry, pages 456 & 457; and for risoni, see Pasta, page 396.

Mixed pea and turkey salad

PREP + COOK TIME 2 HOUR 5 MINUTES **SERVES** 6

1.2kg single turkey breast

1 tablespoon olive oil

1 tablespoon sea salt

½ teaspoon freshly ground black pepper

2 teaspoons finely grated lemon rind

1½ cups (330g) risoni

750g fresh broad beans

1¾ cups (280g) shelled fresh peas

300g sugar snap peas, trimmed

200g snow peas, trimmed

¼ cup coarsely chopped fresh mint

200g snow pea tendrils

50g baby rocket

LEMON MUSTARD DRESSING

2 tablespoons lemon juice

2 teaspoons wholegrain mustard

2 tablespoons white wine vinegar

1 teaspoon sugar

⅓ cup (80ml) olive oil

1 Preheat oven to 200°C/180°C fan-forced.

2 Tie turkey breast at 6cm intervals with kitchen string. Place on oiled oven tray; rub with combined oil, salt, pepper and rind. Cover with foil; bake 40 minutes. Remove foil; bake about 10 minutes or until cooked through.

3 Meanwhile, make lemon mustard dressing.

4 Cook risoni in large saucepan of boiling water, uncovered, until just tender; drain. Rinse under cold water; drain.

5 Shell broad beans; discard pods. Boil, steam or microwave beans until just tender; drain. Rinse under cold water; drain. Peel away grey-coloured outer shells.

6 Meanwhile, boil, steam or microwave all peas, together, until just tender; drain. Rinse under cold water; drain.

7 Place risoni, beans and pea mixture in large bowl with mint, tendrils, rocket and dressing; toss gently to combine. Slice turkey thinly; top salad with turkey.

LEMON MUSTARD DRESSING Place ingredients in screw-top jar; shake well.

NUTRITIONAL COUNT PER SERVING 23.4g total fat (4g saturated fat); 2947kJ (705 cal); 54.6g carbohydrate; 62.2g protein; 12.2g fibre

Chicken with creamy pea and pancetta sauce

PREP + COOK TIME 35 MINUTES **SERVES** 4

2 tablespoons olive oil

4 x 350g chicken marylands

2 shallots (50g), chopped finely

1 clove garlic, crushed

100g sliced pancetta, shredded finely

½ cup (125ml) dry white wine

300ml cream

½ cup (60g) frozen peas

1 tablespoon coarsely chopped fresh tarragon

1 Heat half of the oil in large frying pan; cook chicken, turning occasionally, 20 minutes or until cooked through. Remove chicken from pan; cover to keep warm.

2 Heat remaining oil in same pan; cook shallot, garlic and pancetta, stirring, over medium heat until pancetta browns. Add wine; bring to the boil. Reduce heat; simmer, uncovered, about 2 minutes or until mixture reduces by half.

3 Add cream and peas; bring to the boil. Reduce heat; simmer, uncovered, 4 minutes, stirring occasionally. Add tarragon; simmer, uncovered, 2 minutes.

4 Serve chicken drizzled with sauce.

NUTRITIONAL COUNT PER SERVING 77.6g total fat (34.5g saturated fat); 3858kJ (923 cal); 3.6g carbohydrate; 49.6g protein; 1.1g fibre

CHICKEN WITH CREAMY PEA AND PANCETTA SAUCE

This creamy sauce should be used immediately after cooking. It also goes well with poached eggs, ham steaks or baked ham.

For information on pancetta, see Bacon, page 28.

Green pea soup with mint pistou

PREP + COOK TIME 30 MINUTES (PLUS COOLING TIME) **SERVES** 4

1 tablespoon olive oil

1 small leek (200g), sliced thinly

1 clove garlic, crushed

2 large potatoes (600g), chopped coarsely

3 cups (360g) frozen peas

3 cups (750ml) water

2 cups (500ml) vegetable stock

MINT PISTOU

2 cups loosely packed fresh mint leaves

¼ cup (20g) finely grated parmesan cheese

1 tablespoon lemon juice

1 clove garlic, quartered

¼ cup (60ml) olive oil

1 Heat oil in large saucepan; cook leek and garlic, stirring, until leek softens. Add potato, peas, the water and stock; bring to the boil. Reduce heat; simmer, covered, about 10 minutes or until potato is tender. Cool 15 minutes.

2 Meanwhile, make mint pistou.

3 Blend or process soup, in batches, until smooth. Return soup to same cleaned pan; stir over medium heat until hot. Serve bowls of soup topped with pistou.

MINT PISTOU Blend or process ingredients until smooth.

NUTRITIONAL COUNT PER SERVING 20.9g total fat (3.7g saturated fat); 1634kJ (391 cal); 32.2g carbohydrate; 12.9g protein; 12g fibre

Persimmons

Persimmons have been admired for centuries for their glowing red-gold beauty and known as the fruit that is inedibly astringent until it reaches full ripeness, when it is as soft as an overripe tomato and its translucent skin is filled with sweet, richly flavoured, pulpy flesh that is most easily eaten with a spoon.

Modern growers have developed another kind of persimmon, which is non-astringent at the firm-ripe stage when it turns from green to yellow or red according to the variety. At this stage it is as crisp as an apple and mildly sweet, but is at its best and sweetest when ripened a little further and just yielding when cupped in two hands and gently pressed; the best-known varieties are the sharon fruit and the fuyu fruit. The skin of all persimmons is edible but the seeds are not. Firm persimmons can be eaten out of hand, sliced or cut into wedges and used in salads, especially those with duck or chicken, or served with soft cheese or with prosciutto in the same way as melon. The flesh of soft persimmons can be spooned from the skin by first cutting around the centre stalk and removing it, or can be used for ice-cream or made into a fruit fool by folding it through sweetened thick cream, or beating a little custard into the fruit and folding this purée through cream. Persimmons are available from late autumn into early winter.

CHOOSING AND STORING

Buy firm persimmon varieties when they are turning from green to their ripe colour or have reached their ripe colour. They can be stored for a week or more at room temperature until ripened to the preferred stage. Buy soft persimmon varieties fully developed and coloured, ripen at room temperature until they are very soft and fragile, then eat lightly chilled.

Pineapple

The simplest, and many people would say the best, ways to enjoy ripe pineapple are to eat it unadorned or sprinkled with rum, kirsch or mint, for all of which it has a marked affinity. It is also splendid with other tropical fruits, contributing the fresh acid note that some of them lack, goes beautifully with sweet, creamy flavours and anything with brown sugar, and is also endlessly useful in Chinese cooking and as an accompaniment to hot or cold pork or ham, in fruity drinks and smoothies and in salsas to go with barbecued meat or seafood.

It can be quite difficult to get a good pineapple as they are often harvested a little unripe for transporting to market and, no matter what the greengrocer says, a pineapple will not ripen further after you buy it. It may soften and change colour, but it will never be any sweeter or more developed in flavour than it was at the moment of picking. If you do buy a disappointing one, it can be improved because the flesh, being open in structure, readily takes up flavours. Peel and slice it, dose the slices with a little brown sugar or honey and let it stand for an hour or two. Pineapple contains an enzyme which breaks down protein, so it should be added to meat, poultry or seafood salads or mixed with cream or yogurt only at the last minute, and it cannot be used fresh in jellied desserts; cooked or canned pineapple is not a problem as heat kills the enzyme. Pineapple slices, chunks and juice are available canned; the fruit is useful for cakes and the juice is good mixed with fresh juices such as orange. Pineapples are available all year, different varieties having different seasons.

PREPARATION The skin of a pineapple can be removed by cutting off the top and base, standing the fruit up and simply cutting down between the flesh and the skin, cutting off a thick enough layer to remove the eyes embedded in the flesh. This is rather wasteful; an attractive and less wasteful but more laborious way is to hold the knife at an angle to the skin and cut downward, following the curved line between one row of eyes and the next and going deep enough to cut below the eyes, until you reach the bottom, then repeat, holding the knife at the opposite slant, to cut out a wedge-shaped strip containing the eyes. Continued right around the fruit, this will give a handsome pattern of curving channels giving notched slices. Cut out the woody core as you come to it.

CHOOSING Skin colour is not a reliable indicator of ripeness, nor is the often-recommended test of checking whether a leaf will pull out easily from the top. The best judge is your nose — a ripe pineapple has a strong, sweet aroma. Avoid any that are damaged or have soft spots or that smell beery, indicating over-ripeness. In summer, you may find small roughy or golden-rough pineapples, which are sweeter than most large ones and identifiable by their dumpy shape and sawtooth-edged leaves. In winter, you may

Pineapples were among the first fruits brought back to Europe by Christopher Columbus, and when, after many attempts, they were grown in hothouses, they were such a rare and expensive delicacy that they became a symbol of hospitality. Pineapples were often carved in stone on top of gateposts as a sign of welcome and the fruit, with its patterning and crown of leaves, became a fashionable decorative motif for buildings and furniture which is still used for lamp bases, bookends and finials on banisters.

❦ OTHER RECIPES USING PINEAPPLE
Kiwifruit and pineapple salad with basil lemon syrup, p280
Pickled green papaya salad, p387
Sweet and sour pork, p446

see large pineapples with yellow stickers and no leafy tops, which are the bethonga gold variety, bred by a large Queensland grower; they are exceptionally well flavoured and are hard-shelled so that they can be harvested ripe and still be transported without damage.

STORING A pineapple can be stored at room temperature for a day or so or in the refrigerator, with the body enclosed in a paper bag and then a plastic one, tied under the crown which remains exposed, for 2–3 days. Peeled slices or chunks can be stored in a closed container in the refrigerator for several days.

Once the pineapple is prepared, this gorgeous drink takes only a minute to make, and you can get the preparation over up to a day ahead and refrigerate the pieces in a covered container until they are needed.

For information on oranges, see Oranges, pages 380–382.

Pineapple orange frappé

PREP TIME 10 MINUTES **MAKES** 1 LITRE (4 CUPS)

1 medium pineapple (1.25kg), chopped coarsely
½ cup (125ml) orange juice
3 cups crushed ice
1 tablespoon finely grated orange rind

1 Blend pineapple and juice, in batches, until smooth.
2 Pour into large jug with crushed ice and rind; stir to combine. Serve immediately.

NUTRITIONAL COUNT PER 250ML 0.2g total fat (0g saturated fat); 339kJ (81 cal); 16g carbohydrate; 1.9g protein; 3.6g fibre

A sugar syrup like the one in this recipe is a handy thing to have in the fridge during the hot weather when cooling drinks are the order of the day. It will keep for months in a screw-top jar.

Pineapple ice

PREP + COOK TIME 40 MINUTES (PLUS COOLING AND FREEZING TIME) **SERVES** 6

1 large pineapple (2kg), chopped coarsely
¾ cup (165g) caster sugar
2 cups (500ml) water
¼ cup finely chopped fresh mint leaves
4 egg whites

1 Blend or process pineapple until pureed; push through sieve into medium bowl. Discard pulp.
2 Stir sugar and the water in medium saucepan over low heat until sugar dissolves; bring to the boil. Reduce heat; simmer, uncovered, without stirring, about 10 minutes or until syrup thickens slightly. Cool then stir in mint.
3 Stir syrup into pineapple juice, cover with foil; freeze about 3 hours or until just set.
4 Remove mixture from freezer. Using fork, scrape mixture to break up then place in large bowl with egg whites; beat with electric mixer until smooth. Pour into 19cm x 29cm lamington pan, cover with foil; freeze overnight (stir occasionally to distribute evenly).

NUTRITIONAL COUNT PER SERVING 0.2g total fat (0g saturated fat); 811kJ (194 cal); 41.5g carbohydrate; 4g protein; 3.8g fibre

1

2

1 PINEAPPLE ICE
2 GRILLED PINEAPPLE WITH
COCONUT ICE-CREAM

Grilled pineapple with coconut ice-cream

PREP + COOK TIME 20 MINUTES (PLUS FREEZING TIME) **SERVES** 6

1 cup (50g) shredded coconut, toasted

¼ cup (60ml) Malibu liquour

1 litre vanilla ice-cream

1 tablespoon Malibu, extra

2 tablespoons brown sugar

1 large pineapple (2kg), peeled, sliced thickly

This super-easy coconut ice-cream goes really well with mango too.

1 Fold coconut and Malibu into ice-cream in tub; freeze, covered, overnight.

2 Combine extra Malibu and sugar in large bowl; add pineapple, toss to coat in mixture.

3 Cook pineapple on heated oiled grill plate until browned both sides.

4 Serve pineapple slices with coconut ice-cream.

NUTRITIONAL COUNT PER SERVING 26g total fat (19.8g saturated fat); 2128kJ (509 cal); 49.4g carbohydrate; 7.7g protein; 7.3g fibre

Plums

Plums are the stayers of the stone-fruit family, their many varieties coming into season successively from around midsummer until well into autumn, long after the rest of the family have departed until next year.

1 BLOOD PLUM
2 AMBER JEWEL PLUM
3 PLUM

They divide into those with soft, sweet, yellow or rosy flesh and those with firm, dark, sharp-sweet flesh, the best known of these being the dark crimson blood-plum varieties. Plums can be clingstone or freestone, defined by whether the flesh separates cleanly from the stone. Some dark varieties are good for cooking, especially jam, but too tough-skinned or dry to be good for eating raw, but in general both soft-fleshed and firm-fleshed plums can make good eating out of hand and both kinds are used for cooking. They can be pureed raw or cooked and folded through sweetened whipped cream for a fruit fool, poached in a wine or plain sugar syrup with lemon or orange rind and spices, used for cakes or crumbles, or made into jams, chutneys or sauces to serve with roasted and grilled meats. Plums are among the relatively few fruits that can continue to ripen properly after harvesting, though they must be fully mature when picked.

PREPARATION The thin skins are usually left on plums for cooking, especially for poaching as the skins are softened by the cooking and can be easily pulled off, leaving a perfect, glossy surface behind; if the skin is red-blushed it will also give a pretty rosy flush to the flesh. For peeled plums, the skins can be easily removed by dipping the fruit briefly into boiling water, then into cold, and slipping them off.

CHOOSING Plums should have taut, well-coloured, unblemished skins. When ripe, they will yield when gently pressed — soft types more than firm types.

STORING Perfectly ripe plums can be kept at room temperature for a day, but should be refrigerated and used within a few days as they deteriorate quickly. Slightly unripe plums should be stored at room temperature until fully ripe, which may take up to a week, then refrigerated and used within a few days.

Poached plums with almond milk ice-cream

PREP + COOK TIME 1 HOUR (PLUS STANDING AND FREEZING TIME) **SERVES** 4

2 cups (500ml) water

½ cup (70g) roasted slivered almonds

1 vanilla bean

300ml cream

¾ cup (165g) caster sugar

6 egg yolks

POACHED PLUMS

2 cups (500ml) water

1 cup (250ml) port

½ cup (110g) caster sugar

1 cinnamon stick

4 plums (450g), halved, seeded

1 Blend or process the water and nuts until fine. Strain almond milk through a muslin-lined strainer into medium saucepan; discard solids.

2 Halve vanilla bean lengthways, scrape seeds into pan with almond milk. Add pod with cream and ¼ cup of the sugar to pan; bring to the boil. Remove from heat; stand 30 minutes. Discard pod.

3 Line 14cm x 21cm loaf pan with baking paper.

4 Beat egg yolks and remaining sugar in medium bowl with electric mixer until thick and creamy. Gradually stir in almond milk mixture; return to same pan. Cook, stirring over low heat, until mixture thickens slightly. Remove from heat; cool to room temperature. Pour ice-cream mixture into loaf pan, cover with foil; freeze until firm.

5 Remove ice-cream from freezer, turn into large bowl; chop ice-cream coarsely then beat with electric mixer until smooth. Return to loaf pan, cover; freeze until firm.

6 Meanwhile, make poached plums.

7 Slice ice-cream into four pieces; divide among serving plates. Top with plums and syrup.

POACHED PLUMS Stir the water, port, sugar and cinnamon in medium saucepan, without boiling, until sugar dissolves. Add plums; cook, uncovered, over low heat, about 30 minutes or until just tender. Remove plums from syrup; discard skins. Bring syrup to the boil; boil, uncovered, about 10 minutes or until syrup is reduced to about 1 cup. Remove from heat, discard cinnamon; cool 10 minutes. Refrigerate, covered, until cold.

NUTRITIONAL COUNT PER SERVING 50.6g total fat (24.6g saturated fat); 3787kJ (906 cal); 85.8g carbohydrate; 10.3g protein; 3.5g fibre

You can use peaches or apricots instead of plums in this recipe.

For information on cream, see Cream, pages 142 & 143; and for almonds, see Nuts, page 344.

Plum clafoutis

PREP + COOK TIME 1 HOUR 10 MINUTES (PLUS COOLING TIME) **SERVES** 6

Clafoutis is a rustic dessert from the Limousin region of central France; in the local dialect it translates as "brimming over". It is usually made in the cherry season, when a baking dish is filled with the ripe fruit and a sweet batter is poured over and baked. Other stone fruits or plumped prunes can be used instead of cherries. We have used plums in this recipe but you could use apricots, peeled peaches or caramelised apple instead. Serve clafoutis warm with whipped cream.

10 small plums (750g), halved, seeded

1 cinnamon stick, halved

¼ cup (60ml) water

¼ cup (55g) brown sugar

⅔ cup (160ml) milk

⅔ cup (160ml) cream

1 teaspoon vanilla extract

4 eggs

½ cup (110g) caster sugar

¼ cup (35g) plain flour

1 Preheat oven to 200°C/180°C fan-forced. Grease shallow 2.5-litre (10-cup) ovenproof dish.

2 Place plums in medium baking dish with cinnamon and the water; sprinkle with brown sugar. Cook about 15 minutes or until plums soften.

3 Remove cinnamon from dish and add to medium saucepan with milk, cream and extract; bring to the boil. Cool; remove cinnamon stick.

4 Whisk eggs and caster sugar in medium bowl until light and frothy; whisk in flour then whisk mixture into cream mixture.

5 Place drained plums in shallow ovenproof dish; pour cream mixture over plums. Bake about 30 minutes or until browned lightly. Serve dusted with icing sugar.

NUTRITIONAL COUNT PER SERVING 16.1g total fat (9.3g saturated fat); 1417kJ (339 cal); 46.2g carbohydrate; 7.1g protein; 2.4g fibre

Plum and amaretti trifle

PREP + COOK TIME 15 MINUTES **SERVES** 6

If you keep UHT cream, amaretti biscuits and a can of plums in the store cupboard, you can make this impressive dessert at short notice. If you haven't got Tia Maria, use a tablespoon of black coffee and ½ teaspoon vanilla extract.

825g can whole plums, drained

300ml thickened cream

¼ cup (40g) sifted icing sugar

1 tablespoon Tia Maria

125g amaretti biscuits, chopped coarsely

1 Halve plums, remove seeds; cut each half into 4 wedges.

2 Beat cream, sugar and Tia Maria in small bowl with electric mixer until soft peaks form. Crush biscuits coarsely.

3 Divide half the plums among serving glasses; spoon half the cream mixture then half the crushed biscuits over plums. Repeat with remaining plum halves, cream and biscuits. Serve dusted with icing sugar.

NUTRITIONAL COUNT PER SERVING 25.5g total fat (14.5g saturated fat); 1555kJ (372 cal); 31.1g carbohydrate; 3.1g protein; 1.5g fibre

Pomegranate

The pomegranate, with its burnished red skin and calyx like a crown, looks what it is — a precious fruit of ancient Persia. Cut it across into halves (a job for a sharp serrated knife as the skin is leathery) and it is like a jewel-box, with myriad seeds, each in a sac of translucent carmine flesh set in cream-coloured pith.

The pomegranate spread eastwards from Persia to India and China, and was taken by Spanish sailors from the Mediterranean region, where it had long been cultivated, to America. It was a useful fruit for long sea voyages because its hard skin kept it in better condition than other fruits; those sailors didn't realise it, but pomegranates were also good to take to sea because they have useful amounts of Vitamin C, which prevents scurvy.

Sweet-sour and refreshing, the seeds can be scattered across salads, desserts, chicken, fish and rice dishes, or rubbed through a sieve to obtain the crimson juice, or the halved fruit can be juiced on a lemon-squeezer. Take care when doing this as the juice stains; it was used as a red dye for Persian rugs. A large pomegranate will give about ½ cup juice. It makes a cool, sharp-flavoured drink, good by itself or with vodka or gin, and is valued for its flavour in sauces, soups, stews and marinades, especially for duck to be grilled or roasted. It also makes a sharply fruity jelly to serve with poultry or ham or spread on croissants or brioche. Pomegranate juice is the basis of grenadine syrup which is used in cocktails such as tequila sunrise.

Pomegranate molasses, made with the boiled-down juice, is thick and brown with a sharp/sweet balance a little reminiscent of balsamic vinegar. It is a staple in Middle Eastern kitchens, used for salad dressings and sauces and for brushing on meat, seafood or poultry to be grilled or roasted. It is available at Middle Eastern food stores and some speciality food shops. Pomegranates are in season from autumn into winter.

PREPARATION To obtain the seeds, hold a pomegranate half over a bowl, cut-side down, and hit it with a wooden spoon to make them drop out.

CHOOSING Pomegranates should feel heavy for their size, show no signs of deterioration at the calyx end and have unmarked skin that gives slightly when gently pressed.

STORING Pomegranates will keep for a few days at room temperature, making a beautiful display. They can be refrigerated whole for a couple of weeks and the seeds can be frozen in an airtight container for a few months.

Pomegranate and orange juice

PREP TIME 10 MINUTES **MAKES** 1 CUP (250ML)

⅔ cup (160ml) pomegranate pulp

2 medium oranges (480g), peeled, quartered

1 Push ingredients through juice extractor into glass; stir to combine.

NUTRITIONAL COUNT PER 250ML 0.7g total fat (0g saturated fat); 1112kJ (266 cal); 49.2g carbohydrate; 6.8g protein; 17.1g fibre

---

Pomegranate, raspberry and cranberry punch

PREP + COOK TIME 25 MINUTES **SERVES** 8

120g fresh or frozen raspberries

750ml bottle chilled champagne

1 litre (4 cups) chilled unsweetened cranberry juice

1 cup firmly packed mint leaves

POMEGRANATE SYRUP

1 kg (4½ cups) caster sugar

2 cups (500ml) water

2 cups pomegranate pulp

2 tablespoons lemon juice

1 Place about three raspberries in each hole of a 16-hole (1-tablespoon/20ml) ice cube tray. Pour water over raspberries to fill holes. Freeze about 3 hours or until set.
2 Make pomegranate syrup.
3 Place 1 cup (250ml) of the pomegranate syrup in a large serving bowl (reserve remaining syrup for another use). Stir in champagne and cranberry juice. Add mint and raspberry ice cubes; serve immediately.

POMEGRANATE SYRUP Stir sugar and the water in medium saucepan over heat until sugar dissolves. Bring to the boil; simmer, without stirring, about 10 minutes or until thickened slightly. Add pomegranate pulp and juice; bring to the boil. Reduce heat, simmer 2 minutes. Remove pan from heat; stand 10 minutes. Strain into hot sterilised bottle; seal immediately. Store in refrigerator for up to 3 months.

NUTRITIONAL COUNT PER SERVING 0.3g total fat (0g saturated fat); 2918kJ (698 cal); 153.3g carbohydrate; 2g protein; 5.3g fibre

POMEGRANATE AND ORANGE JUICE

You will need 2 large pomegranates to get 1 cup of pulp. Chill the ingredients well or serve it over ice. For information on oranges, see Oranges, pages 380–382.

Depending on the size, you need 4–6 pomegranates to get 2 cups of pulp. You can use sparkling water instead of champagne for a non-alcoholic punch.

For information on raspberries and cranberries, see Berries, pages 58 & 59.

You will need 2 large pomegranates to get 1 cup of pulp. For notes on pomegranate molasses, see page 436.

For information on chicken, see Poultry, pages 456 & 457; and for burghul, see Grains, page 228.

Pomegranate and burghul chicken salad

PREP + COOK TIME 45 MINUTES (PLUS REFRIGERATION TIME) **SERVES** 6

¼ cup (60ml) olive oil

¼ cup (60ml) pomegranate molasses

1 tablespoon ground cumin

2 cloves garlic, crushed

1kg chicken breast fillets

1½ cups (375ml) chicken stock

1½ cups (240g) burghul

1 cup (250ml) pomegranate pulp

1 medium red onion (170g), sliced thinly

350g watercress, trimmed

2 cups firmly packed fresh flat-leaf parsley leaves

1 cup (110g) coarsely chopped roasted walnuts

150g piece fetta cheese, crumbled

POMEGRANATE DRESSING

¼ cup (60ml) olive oil

¼ cup (60ml) lemon juice

3 teaspoons honey

3 teaspoons pomegranate molasses

1 Combine oil, molasses, cumin and garlic in large bowl with chicken. Cover; refrigerate 3 hours or overnight.

2 Bring stock to the boil in medium saucepan. Remove from heat, add burghul; cover, stand 5 minutes.

3 Meanwhile, make pomegranate dressing.

4 Drain chicken, discard marinade. Cook chicken on heated oiled grill plate (or grill or barbecue), until browned both sides and cooked through. Cover chicken; stand 10 minutes then slice thickly.

5 Place chicken and burghul in large bowl with dressing and remaining ingredients; toss gently to combine. Divide salad among serving plates.

POMEGRANATE DRESSING Place ingredients in screw-top jar; shake well.

NUTRITIONAL COUNT PER SERVING 47.1g total fat (10.3g saturated fat); 3503kJ (838 cal); 47.6g carbohydrate; 50.2g protein; 13.1g fibre

Pork

Porkers, the breeds of pigs raised for eating as fresh meat, are nowadays slaughtered at less than six months, so the pork we buy is basically tender. It is the only meat sold with its skin still on because the gelatinous rind is a delicacy in itself, whether crisped by roasting or grilling or luxuriously rich from long, moist cooking.

If you have trimmed off excess fat from the pork before cooking it, render it (melt it down) to use as lard for making pie pastry or cooking lovely fried or roasted potatoes and other root vegetables. Dice the pieces, put them into a heavy saucepan, just cover with water and heat slowly to simmering point, then simmer uncovered until the pieces have melted and the water has evaporated. Strain into a container and refrigerate. It will keep in good condition for months provided that, each time you use some, you heat the remainder in the microwave until its top is melted and level, then return it to the refrigerator. Any lard that has been used for frying should not be returned to this container, but strained into another one, or discarded if it has darkened.

Pork is perhaps the supreme meat for cooking with spicy flavours, whether in the aromatic stir-fries and dumplings of Asia or the pork and beans or barbecued spareribs of America. It is also the supreme meat for dishes to be eaten cold, from large pieces such as pickled (salt) hand of pork to brawn, which consists of diced pickled pork cooked with aromatics and set in its own jelly; or rillettes, which consists of shredded fresh, fatty pork cooked with aromatics and set in its own fat. Lean pork has a tendency to dryness so it needs either its natural fat covering or, if it has been removed, a sauce, stuffing or ingredient like sour cream or fruit to provide moisture. It used to be necessary to cook pork thoroughly to ensure that any parasites which might have been picked up, because pigs eat anything and everything, would be destroyed. This is no longer necessary for commercially raised pork, which is hygienically fed, but is still a wise precaution for wild pig. Small cuts will be more tender if they are still pink in the centre, but most people enjoy roast pork best if it is cooked through (when juice runs clear when a fine skewer is inserted in the thickest part).

PORK CUTS

ROASTING cuts are the loin, bone-in or boned and sometimes rolled, which serves 8–10 and is often cut into two smaller roasts; the leg, also very large and often divided into the fillet end and the shank end, which is often boned and rolled; rump; fillet; individual leg muscles seamed out for small, boneless roasts; shoulder, either on the bone or boned and rolled; and rack or rib on the bone, consisting of 6–8 cutlets in one piece. For a spectacular presentation, two racks can be bent round and tied together to make a circular crown roast with the meat, trimmed of skin and excess fat, inside and the bones outside. Ask the butcher to chine it, which means chopping through the backbone between the cutlets or removing it altogether to make carving easy. You may see cheaper cuts than these marked "roasting", but they are often tough.

Suckling pig is the supreme roast pork for a special celebration. A 6–7kg one will serve 12 to 15 people. It must be ordered well ahead — ensure you measure your oven before ordering, to make sure the pig will fit. If it will be too big, the butcher can saw it in half across the middle and one half can be cooked in another oven. Ask the butcher to score the sides diagonally at 3cm intervals from behind the head to the tail. If the pig is in two halves, the join can be hidden by a wreath of watercress or other leaves round its middle for serving.

To judge when a roast is done to your taste, use a meat thermometer or run a fine skewer into the centre and check the juice that comes out. Red juice means rare, pink medium and clear well done.

All roasts should be rested in a warm place, loosely covered with foil, for 15 minutes before serving to allow the juices to settle and the meat to become more succulent.

GRILLING, CHAR-GRILLING AND PAN-FRYING cuts are loin chops and cutlets with their natural fat covering, and fatless fillet, chops and steaks. Cuts with fat covering are also suitable for barbecuing, but very lean cuts are not. Pork schnitzel, a leg steak cut thin and beaten out to be even thinner, is good for pan-frying but not for grilling. Cheaper cuts than these marked "grilling" or "barbecuing" may disappoint.

To judge when meat is grilled or pan-fried to your taste, press the surface with a finger or the back of the tongs. Rare meat feels soft and spongy, medium-rare soft but springy, and well-done quite firm.

All grilled meat should be rested in a warm place, loosely covered in foil, for 5 minutes to allow the juices to settle and the meat to become more succulent.

POT-ROASTING cuts (to be braised in one piece) are topside, silverside, boned and rolled shoulder and boned and rolled foreloin (neck). Shoulder and neck can also be slow-roasted, but will be tough if roasted at high temperatures.

CASSEROLING cuts (to be cut up and braised) are all the pot-roasting cuts, and the meat from belly or forequarter, usually sold already cut up.

PORK BELLY, also called spring of pork, which consists of layers of lean and fat, may be "twice-cooked" by simmering in a flavoursome liquid until tender, then roasting or grilling to crisp the outer layer, or may be preserved as a confit by cooking slowly and setting in its own fat, from

which slices can be taken to be used in bean or lentil dishes.

PICKLED (SALT) PORK, usually a piece of belly or a hand, consisting of the upper foreleg and adjoining belly, is simmered in water with aromatic vegetables and a little vinegar and served cold.

MINCED PORK is used for meatballs, especially in Chinese cooking where it is mixed with spices and aromatics for fragrance, and for pâtés and terrines. It is also used in pork and veal mince (see also minced veal, Veal page 620).

CHOOSING
As always when buying meat, your best bet is a supplier you can trust. In general, pork should have fine-grained, pale pink flesh, white fat and thin, smooth skin. Avoid any that has waxy fat or is wet, meaning it has been badly handled and may be from an animal in poor condition.

STORING
Transfer meat from its shop wrappings to a container with the bottom lined with two thicknesses of absorbent paper, cover loosely with foil and refrigerate. The more meat has been cut and handled, the less time it will keep. Mince and sausages should be stored for a maximum of 2 days, diced or cubed meat for 3 days, steaks, chops or cutlets for 3–5 days, boned and rolled roasting joints for 2–3 days, bone-in roasts for 3–5 days and pickled pork for 1 week. Pork freezes well though it will lose some juices as it thaws. Freeze in a freezer bag enclosed in a second bag; thaw in the refrigerator. Small cuts may take 24 hours or more, larger ones may need 36 hours or more.

Also see pig's trotters, Offal page 355.

❦ OTHER RECIPES USING PORK
Cashew-crumbed pork schnitzel, p348
Chipotle pork ribs with chorizo and smoked paprika, p123
Five-spice pork and nashi salad, p419
Hoisin pork with watercress salad, p512
Pork and lychee salad, p304
Pork cabbage rolls, p80
Pork kway teow, p343
Pork larb with broccolini, p76
Pork steaks with radish and beetroot salad, p489
Pork with celeriac and apple, p11
Pork with maple syrup, bourbon and pear sauce, p581
Prosciutto-wrapped veal and pork meatloaf, p621
Sticky pork with kaffir lime leaves, p276
Stir-fried pork, water chestnuts and buk choy, p630
Tamarind and citrus pork curry, p597
Terrine de campagne, p359

1 PORK SANG CHOY BOW
2 ROAST PORK RACK WITH
APPLE SAGE SAUCE

Pork sang choy bow

PREP + COOK TIME 40 MINUTES **SERVES** 4

Sang choy bow is eaten with the fingers, with the lettuce wrapped round the savoury mince filling. You can use chicken mince or a pork and veal mix instead; you can also serve the pork mixture in small witlof or betel leaves for impressive cocktail food.

1 tablespoon peanut oil

600g pork mince

2cm piece fresh ginger (10g), grated

2 cloves garlic, crushed

50g fresh shiitake mushrooms, chopped finely

227g can water chestnuts, rinsed, drained, chopped finely

2 tablespoons char siu sauce

1 tablespoon oyster sauce

1 tablespoon light soy sauce

1 tablespoon lime juice

1 cup (80g) bean sprouts

8 large iceberg lettuce leaves

2 green onions, sliced thinly

1 Heat oil in wok; stir-fry mince, ginger and garlic until mince browns.

2 Add mushrooms and water chestnut; stir-fry until vegetables are tender. Add sauces and juice; stir-fry until hot. Remove from heat; stir in sprouts.

3 Divide mince mixture among lettuce leaves; sprinkle with onion.

NUTRITIONAL COUNT PER SERVING 16.1g total fat (5g saturated fat); 1363kJ (326 cal); 9.6g carbohydrate; 33.7g protein; 4.1g fibre

Roast pork rack with apple sage sauce

PREP + COOK TIME 1 HOUR 10 MINUTES **SERVES** 6

1kg rack of pork (6 cutlets), rind on

1 tablespoon olive oil

1 tablespoon sea salt flakes

1.25kg kipfler potatoes

750g pumpkin, chopped coarsely

APPLE SAGE SAUCE

3 large green apples (600g)

¼ cup (60ml) water

4 fresh sage leaves

1 teaspoon white sugar

1 Preheat oven to 220°C/200°C fan-forced.

2 Rub pork rind with half the oil then the salt. Stand pork in medium baking dish; roast, uncovered, about 35 minutes or until rind is blistered.

3 Place vegetables in oven tray with pork, drizzle with remaining oil. Reduce oven to 180°C/160°C fan-forced; roast pork and vegetables, uncovered, about 40 minutes or until pork is cooked through. Remove pork from dish; cover with foil to keep warm.

4 Meanwhile, make apple sage sauce.

5 Increase oven to 220°C/200°C fan-forced; roast vegetables for further 15 minutes. Serve pork with vegetables and apple sage sauce.

APPLE SAGE SAUCE Peel and core apples; slice thickly. Place apple, the water and sage in medium saucepan; simmer, uncovered, about 10 minutes or until apple is soft. Remove from heat, stir in sugar.

NUTRITIONAL COUNT PER SERVING 19.5g total fat (6.7g saturated fat); 1914kJ (458 cal); 41.6g carbohydrate; 25.8g protein; 6.6g fibre

Kipfler potatoes are small finger-shaped ones. You can use quartered desirées or pontiacs if you like.

For information on green apples, see Apples, pages 8–10.

Pork cutlets with fennel apple relish

PREP + COOK TIME 35 MINUTES **SERVES** 4

2 tablespoons cider vinegar

¼ cup (60ml) olive oil

1 tablespoon dijon mustard

2 teaspoons caster sugar

4 x 235g pork cutlets

1 large unpeeled green apple (200g), chopped finely

1 small red onion (100g), chopped finely

1 medium fennel (300g), trimmed, chopped finely

1 Whisk vinegar, oil, mustard and sugar in medium bowl; transfer 2 tablespoons of dressing to large bowl. Place pork in large bowl; turn to coat cutlets in dressing.

2 To make relish, combine apple, onion and fennel in bowl with remaining dressing.

3 Meanwhile, cook drained pork on heated oiled grill plate (or grill or barbecue) until browned both sides and cooked as desired, brushing with dressing occasionally.

4 Serve pork with relish and crushed potato, or with roasted potato chips.

NUTRITIONAL COUNT PER SERVING 31.2g total fat (7.9g saturated fat); 1877kJ (449 cal); 9.6g carbohydrate; 32g protein; 2.3g fibre

For crushed potatoes: boil, steam or microwave 1kg unpeeled baby new potatoes, drain. Mash half the potatoes with ½ cup sour cream and 40g butter in a large bowl until smooth and stir in ¼ cup coarsely chopped flat-leaf parsley and 2 tablespoons chopped fresh dill. Roughly crush the remaining potatoes with the back of a fork until the skins burst and the flesh is just crushed; stir into herbed mash.

For information on green apples, see Apples, pages 8–10; and for fennel, see Fennel, page 174.

This recipe can be prepared up to step 5 the day before serving.

For information on wombok, see Cabbage, page 78.

Crisp pork belly with wombok salad

PREP + COOK TIME 2 HOURS 50 MINUTES (PLUS REFRIGERATION TIME) **SERVES** 4

2 cups (500ml) salt-reduced chicken stock

⅓ cup (80ml) chinese cooking wine

½ cup (125ml) lime juice

¼ cup (60ml) japanese soy sauce

2 dried red chillies

2 star anise

1 tablespoon coarsely chopped fresh coriander root and stem mixture

2cm piece fresh ginger (10g), sliced thinly

2 cloves garlic, halved

2 fresh kaffir lime leaves, torn

800g piece pork belly

¼ cup (60ml) oyster sauce

⅓ cup (90g) firmly packed grated palm sugar

2 tablespoons fish sauce

1 tablespoon peanut oil

2 fresh long red chillies, chopped finely

2cm piece fresh ginger (10g), grated

1 clove garlic, crushed

½ medium wombok (500g), shredded finely

1 medium red capsicum (200g), sliced thinly

1 large carrot (180g), sliced thinly

1 cup (80g) bean sprouts

2 green onions, sliced thinly

½ cup loosely packed fresh coriander leaves

½ cup loosely packed vietnamese mint leaves

½ cup (70g) roasted unsalted peanuts, chopped coarsely

¼ cup (20g) fried shallots

1 Place stock, wine, half the juice, soy sauce, dried chillies, star anise, coriander root and stem mixture, sliced ginger, halved garlic, lime leaves and pork in large deep flameproof dish; bring to the boil. Reduce heat; simmer, covered tightly, about 1½ hours or until pork is tender.

2 Remove pork from dish. Strain broth through muslin-lined sieve into medium saucepan; discard solids. Bring broth to the boil; boil, uncovered, 10 minutes.

3 Slice pork lengthways into 1cm-thick slices. Combine pork with half the broth and oyster sauce in large bowl. Cover; refrigerate 2 hours.

4 Meanwhile, to make dressing, stir sugar into remaining broth; bring to the boil, stirring until sugar dissolves. Reduce heat; simmer, uncovered, about 5 minutes or until thickened slightly. Remove from heat; stir in remaining juice, fish sauce, oil, fresh chilli, grated ginger and crushed garlic. Cool dressing.

5 Preheat oven to 240°C/220°C fan-forced. Oil two oven trays, line with baking paper.

6 Drain pork; discard marinade. Place pork, in single layer, on trays; cook, uncovered, turning occasionally, about 20 minutes or until crisp. Cut pork slices into 2cm pieces.

7 Place pork in large bowl with wombok, capsicum, carrot, sprouts, onion, coriander leaves, mint, nuts and dressing; toss gently to combine.

8 Divide salad among serving bowls, sprinkle with shallots.

NUTRITIONAL COUNT PER SERVING 58.7g total fat (17.6g saturated fat); 4009kJ (959 cal); 37.7g carbohydrate; 64.8g protein; 16.8g fibre

You will need half a pineapple (900g) to get the amount needed for this recipe. In a pinch, you can use a small can of pineapple pieces, drained, instead. Steamed white rice is a perfect accompaniment to this dish.

Sweet and sour pork

PREP + COOK TIME 40 MINUTES **SERVES** 4

800g pork fillet, sliced thinly

1 tablespoon sweet sherry

½ cup (125ml) light soy sauce

¾ cup (110g) plain flour

vegetable oil, for deep-frying

1 tablespoon vegetable oil, extra

1 medium red onion (170g), chopped coarsely

2 cloves garlic, crushed

1 medium red capsicum (200g), chopped coarsely

1 medium green capsicum (200g), chopped coarsely

1 medium carrot (120g), sliced thinly

500g fresh pineapple, chopped coarsely

150g sugar snap peas, trimmed

⅓ cup (80ml) chicken stock

¼ cup (70g) tomato sauce

¼ cup (60ml) white vinegar

¼ cup (55g) white sugar

½ cup loosely packed fresh coriander leaves

1 Combine pork with sherry and 2 tablespoons of the soy sauce in medium bowl. Coat pork in flour; shake off excess.

2 Heat oil in wok; deep-fry pork, in batches, until browned and crisp. Drain on absorbent paper. (Strain oil, save for another use.)

3 Heat extra oil in wok; stir-fry onion and garlic until onion softens. Add capsicums and carrot; stir-fry until tender. Return pork to wok with pineapple, peas, remaining soy sauce, stock, tomato sauce, vinegar and sugar; stir-fry until hot. Remove from heat; stir in coriander.

NUTRITIONAL COUNT PER SERVING 20.2g total fat (3.6g saturated fat); 2717kJ (650 cal); 57.7g carbohydrate; 53.7g protein; 7.5g fibre

Ask your butcher to cut pork spareribs American-style for this recipe. They will be cut in "slabs" of 8 to 10 ribs from the mid-loin, with almost all the fat removed.

Chinese barbecued spareribs

PREP + COOK TIME 1 HOUR 15 MINUTES (PLUS REFRIGERATION TIME) **SERVES** 4

¾ cup (180ml) barbecue sauce

2 tablespoons dark soy sauce

1 tablespoon honey

¼ cup (60ml) orange juice

2 tablespoons brown sugar

1 clove garlic, crushed

2cm piece fresh ginger (10g), grated

2kg slabs american-style pork spareribs

1 Combine sauces, honey, juice, sugar, garlic and ginger in large shallow dish; add ribs, turn to coat in marinade. Cover; refrigerate 3 hours or overnight.

2 Preheat oven to 180°C/160°C fan-forced.

3 Brush ribs both sides with marinade; place, in single layer, in large shallow baking dish. Roast, covered, 45 minutes. Uncover; roast about 15 minutes or until ribs are browned. Serve with fried rice.

NUTRITIONAL COUNT PER SERVING 26.4g total fat (10.2g saturated fat); 2675kJ (640 cal); 35.2g carbohydrate; 64.7g protein; 0.8g fibre

SLOW-ROASTED HONEY AND
SOY PORK NECK

Slow-roasted honey and soy pork neck

PREP + COOK TIME 1 HOUR 35 MINUTES **SERVES** 4

1 tablespoon peanut oil

1kg piece pork neck

1 large brown onion (200g), sliced thinly

2 cloves garlic, sliced thinly

4cm piece fresh ginger (20g), sliced thinly

1 cinnamon stick

2 star anise

½ cup (125ml) salt-reduced soy sauce

½ cup (125ml) chinese cooking wine

¼ cup (90g) honey

1 cup (250ml) water

450g baby buk choy, trimmed, leaves separated

It is worth making this recipe for only 2 people just for the pleasure of the leftovers – serve cold with a salad of wombok, finely sliced red onion and coriander tossed in a dressing of 2 tablespoons rice vinegar, 1 tablespoon lemon juice and 1 teaspoon brown sugar.

For information on honey, see Sugar, page 578.

1 Preheat oven to 160°C/140°C fan-forced.

2 Heat oil in large flameproof casserole dish; cook pork, turning occasionally, until brown. Remove from dish. Cook onion, garlic and ginger in same dish, uncovered, until onion softens.

3 Remove dish from heat; stir in spices, sauce, cooking wine, honey and the water. Return pork to dish, turning to coat in spice mixture. Cook, covered, in oven 1 hour. Uncover; cook 1 hour or until sauce thickens slightly. Remove pork, cover; stand 10 minutes before slicing.

4 Add buk choy to dish; cook, stirring, 5 minutes or until just tender. Serve with pork.

NUTRITIONAL COUNT PER SERVING 30.6g total fat (9.8g saturated fat); 2621kJ (627 cal); 5.9g carbohydrate; 76.4g protein; 2.5g fibre

Potatoes

A potato that is low in moisture, low in sugar and high in starch will bake to floury perfection with a crisp outside and make golden, rather than dark chips. It will also perform well when cooked in fat around a roast, through its low sugar content means it will take longer to brown than some others. However, it will tend to fall apart if boiled.

A waxy potato, lower in starch and higher in moisture, will boil beautifully and cut into clean slices for salad, but will not have that lovely mealy texture and crisp outside when baked or fried. Experts classify potatoes as floury or waxy by their specific gravity (weight for size compared to a given standard); the higher the specific gravity, the higher the starch level and the more floury the potato. The sugar/starch/moisture balance changes as the potato matures — sugar is gradually changed to starch as the tuber grows, and the final levels reached vary considerably from one variety to another. The way a potato is grown also makes a difference: one grown to full maturity on the plant, in the right soil, will taste better and keep better than one that was harvested earlier or grown in sandy soil which doesn't suit potatoes so well but makes machine harvesting easier.

BAKING AND FRYING varieties include russet burbank, idaho, coliban, king edward, spunta and kennebec.

MASHING varieties include the all-rounders desiree, dutch cream which is particularly smooth and creamy, nicola and pontiac which both give a firm-bodied mash, and the floury types king edward and spunta which give fluffy mash — you may prefer to steam, rather than boil these before mashing, in case they break down in the boiling water.

BOILING varieties include new potatoes of any variety, pinkeye, bintje, pink fir apple, nadine, jersey royal, nadine, red lasoda, petrone and purple congo, which has with purple skin and flesh.

ALL-ROUNDER varieties, which will perform satisfactorily with any cooking method, include nicola, dutch cream and kipfler, which have particularly good flavour, desiree, pontiac, sebago and royal blue, a blue/purple-skinned, yellow-fleshed potato with a buttery flavour.

CHOOSING

Potatoes should be very firm, dry and undamaged with no greening of the skin or sprouting eyes. Dirty potatoes store better as the dirt protects them from exposure to light and therefore, greening. Washed potatoes are more susceptible to greening and will not keep as well because their skins have been battered by the high-pressure hoses used to clean them. Green-tinged potatoes taste bitter and contain mildly toxic alkaloids which can cause stomach upsets and can be especially harmful to pregnant women, small children and the elderly.

STORING

Store potatoes in a cool, dark, dry place with air round them. Potatoes with thin, white skins will store for several days, others for several weeks.

Baby new

Coliban

Idaho

Pinkeye

Pontiac

Purple congo

Russet burbank

Sebago

Spunta

Kipfler

Royal blue

Desiree

This recipe demonstrates just how rich and satisfying an inexpensive soup without meat or stock can be.

For information on leeks, see Leeks, page 290.

Potato and leek soup

PREP + COOK TIME 1 HOUR 25 MINUTES (PLUS COOLING TIME) **SERVES** 4

2 medium potatoes (400g), chopped coarsely

2 medium carrots (240g), chopped coarsely

1 large brown onion (200g), chopped coarsely

1 medium tomato (150g), chopped coarsely

1 stalk celery (150g), trimmed, chopped coarsely

1.5 litres (6 cups) water

1 tablespoon olive oil

50g butter

4 medium potatoes (800g), chopped coarsely, extra

1 large leek (500g), sliced thickly

300ml cream

2 tablespoons finely chopped fresh chives

1 tablespoon finely chopped fresh basil

1 tablespoon finely chopped fresh dill

1 Bring potato, carrot, onion, tomato, celery and the water to the boil in large saucepan. Reduce heat; simmer, uncovered, 20 minutes. Strain broth through muslin-lined sieve or colander into large heatproof bowl; discard solids.

2 Heat oil and butter in same cleaned pan; cook extra potato and leek, covered, 15 minutes, stirring occasionally. Add broth; bring to the boil. Reduce heat; simmer, covered, 15 minutes. Cool 15 minutes.

3 Blend or process soup, in batches, until smooth. Return soup to same cleaned pan, add cream; stir over medium heat until hot.

4 Serve bowls of soup sprinkled with combined herbs and, if you like, croûtons.

NUTRITIONAL COUNT PER SERVING 47.9g total fat (28.8g saturated fat); 2822kJ (675 cal); 46.3g carbohydrate; 11g protein; 9.8g fibre

---

The best way to mash potato is with a potato ricer — a kitchen tool which resembles a giant garlic crusher. The potatoes go into the container and, as the flat side is pressed down, the potato falls through the perforated base in fine, soft flakes, back into the saucepan. If you make mashed potato often, it might be a worthwhile investment to purchase one.

Perfect mashed potato

PREP + COOK TIME 30 MINUTES **SERVES** 4

1kg spunta potatoes, chopped coarsely

40g butter

¾ cup (180ml) hot milk

1 Boil, steam or microwave potatoes until tender; drain.

2 Using the back of a wooden spoon; push potato through fine sieve into large bowl. Stir in butter and milk.

NUTRITIONAL COUNT PER SERVING 10.2g total fat (6.6g saturated fat); 1028kJ (246 cal); 30.1g carbohydrate; 6.7g protein; 3.4g fibre

Hasselback potatoes

PREP + COOK TIME 1 HOUR 30 MINUTES **SERVES** 4

HASSELBACK POTATOES

These crusty, cheesy treats are good with cold roast beef, ham steaks and just about any kind of grilled chop or cutlet.

4 medium desiree potatoes (800g), halved horizontally

40g butter, melted

2 tablespoons olive oil

¼ cup (25g) packaged breadcrumbs

½ cup (60g) finely grated cheddar cheese

1 Preheat oven to 180°C/160°C fan-forced.

2 Place one potato half, cut-side down, on chopping board; place a chopstick on board along each side of potato. Slice potato thinly, cutting through to chopsticks to prevent cutting all the way through. Repeat with remaining potato halves.

3 Coat potatoes in combined butter and oil in medium baking dish; place, rounded-side up, in single layer. Roast 1 hour, brushing frequently with oil mixture.

4 Sprinkle combined breadcrumbs and cheese over potatoes; roast about 10 minutes or until browned.

NUTRITIONAL COUNT PER SERVING 22.8g total fat (10g saturated fat); 1463kJ (350 cal); 24.5g carbohydrate; 8.8g protein; 3g fibre

Potato bake

PREP + COOK TIME 45 MINUTES **SERVES** 6

Serve this gloriously rich creation with grilled tomatoes and sausages for brunch or leftover roast chicken and a crisp salad for dinner.

1kg sebago potatoes, cut into 5mm-thick slices

2 teaspoons olive oil

1 medium brown onion (150g), sliced thinly

6 slices pancetta (90g), chopped coarsely

1 cup (250ml) cream

½ cup (120g) sour cream

2 tablespoons finely chopped fresh chives

1 cup (120g) coarsely grated cheddar cheese

1 Preheat oven to 200°C/180°C fan-forced. Grease 2 litre (8 cup) ovenproof dish.

2 Boil, steam or microwave potato until tender; drain.

3 Meanwhile, heat oil in medium frying pan; cook onion and pancetta, stirring, until onion softens and pancetta is crisp.

4 Combine cream, sour cream and chives in medium jug.

5 Layer a third of the potato slices over base of dish; sprinkle with half the pancetta mixture. Pour a third of the cream mixture over pancetta mixture; sprinkle with a third of the cheese. Repeat layering, finishing with cheese.

6 Bake, uncovered, about 30 minutes or until browned. Stand 10 minutes before serving.

NUTRITIONAL COUNT PER SERVING 36.5g total fat (22.4g saturated fat); 1956kJ (468 cal); 21.8g carbohydrate; 13g protein; 2.6g fibre

Classic potato salad

PREP + COOK TIME 45 MINUTES (PLUS REFRIGERATION TIME) **SERVES** 8

2kg waxy potatoes, peeled

2 tablespoons cider vinegar

4 green onions, sliced thinly

¼ cup finely chopped fresh flat-leaf parsley

MAYONNAISE

2 egg yolks

2 teaspoons lemon juice

1 teaspoon dijon mustard

1 cup (250ml) vegetable oil

2 tablespoons warm water, approximately

1 Cover potatoes with cold water in large saucepan; bring to the boil. Reduce heat; simmer, covered, until tender. Drain; cut into 3cm pieces. Spread potato on a tray, sprinkle with vinegar; refrigerate until cold.

2 Make mayonnaise.

3 Combine potato in large bowl with mayonnaise, onion and parsley.

MAYONNAISE Blend or process egg yolks, juice and mustard until smooth. With motor operating, gradually add oil in a thin, steady stream; process until mixture thickens. Add as much of the warm water as required to thin mayonnaise.

NUTRITIONAL COUNT PER SERVING 30.4g total fat (4.1g saturated fat); 1764kJ (422 cal); 29g carbohydrate; 6.2g protein; 3.7g fibre

Any of the potatoes listed as varieties for boiling or all-rounders on page 448 will hold their shape in a salad if properly cooked — that is, just until tender right through. Cover the saucepan while they are cooking, but lift the lid once or twice and give them a gentle stir to move them around. The best tools for mixing a potato salad gently but thoroughly are your clean hands.

Potato and anchovy gratin

PREP + COOK TIME 55 MINUTES **MAKES** 6

700g potatoes

1 small brown onion (80g)

12 undrained anchovy fillets in oil

300ml cream

½ cup (125ml) milk

½ teaspoon freshly ground black pepper

2 tablespoons finely chopped fresh dill

1 Preheat oven to 200°C/180°C fan-forced. Grease six-hole (¾-cup/180ml) texas muffin pan; line each hole with two criss-crossed 5cm x 20cm strips of baking paper.

2 Using sharp knife, mandoline or V-slicer, cut potatoes and onion into very thin slices.

3 Drain and reserve oil from anchovies (you need 2 teaspoons oil); chop anchovies coarsely. Layer potato, onion and anchovy in pan holes, starting and finishing with potato.

4 Heat reserved anchovy oil, cream, milk and pepper in small saucepan; pour over potato mixture. Bake about 35 minutes or until potato is tender. Stand in pan 10 minutes. Using baking-paper strips as lifters, gently remove gratin from pan holes. Serve sprinkled with dill.

NUTRITIONAL COUNT PER GRATIN 22.9g total fat (14.9g saturated fat); 1241kJ (297 cal); 16.1g carbohydrate; 6.3g protein; 1.8g fibre

These individual gratins could start a meal on a high note or be the centrepiece of an elegant light lunch.

For information on anchovies, see Seafood, pages 520, 522 & 523.

*These cakes are brilliant
to hand round at a party,
serve as a vegetable with
lamb or chicken, or serve
as part of a vegetarian
banquet with samosas or
other pastries, a platter of
roasted and blanched
vegetables with a yogurt
dip, curries and flatbreads
for scooping them up,
dhals, pappadums,
salads and so on.*

*For information on peanuts,
see Nuts, page 346.*

Crisp potato and peanut cakes

PREP + COOK TIME 1 HOUR 10 MINUTES **MAKES** 36

250g tapioca

1 tablespoon sunflower oil

1 teaspoon cumin seeds

¼ teaspoon ground turmeric

3 medium potatoes (600g),
peeled, chopped coarsely

2 tablespoons finely chopped
roasted unsalted peanuts

½ cup finely chopped fresh
coriander leaves

2 long green chillies,
chopped finely

4cm piece fresh ginger (20g),
grated

sunflower oil, for shallow-frying,
extra

TOMATO ONION RAITA

1 teaspoon black mustard seeds

500g yogurt

2 medium tomatoes (300g),
seeded, chopped finely

2 green onions, chopped finely

½ cup finely chopped fresh
coriander leaves

1 Make tomato onion raita.

2 Place tapioca in large heatproof bowl; cover with boiling water. Stand 10 minutes; drain.

3 Meanwhile, heat oil in small frying pan; cook cumin and turmeric, stirring, until fragrant.

4 Boil, steam or microwave potato until tender; drain. Mash potato in large bowl then stir
in tapioca, cumin, turmeric, nuts, coriander, chilli and ginger. Shape heaped tablespoons of
potato mixture into patty-size cakes. Heat extra oil in large frying pan; shallow-fry potato
cakes, in batches, until browned. Drain on absorbent paper; serve with raita.

TOMATO ONION RAITA Cook mustard seeds in heated small frying pan until seeds begin
to pop. Combine seeds in medium bowl with remaining ingredients.

NUTRITIONAL COUNT PER CAKE 2g total fat (0.2g saturated fat); 221kJ (53 cal); 7.9g carbohydrate;
0.5g protein; 0.4g fibre
NUTRITIONAL COUNT PER TABLESPOON RAITA 0.4g total fat (0.3g saturated fat); 42kJ (10 cal);
0.7g carbohydrate; 0.7g protein; 0.1g fibre

*Kipflers have outstanding
flavour and texture,
especially when cooked
in their skins.*

Warm kipfler potato salad

PREP + COOK TIME 30 MINUTES **SERVES** 4

1kg kipfler potatoes,
halved lengthways

¼ cup (60ml) olive oil

1 teaspoon finely grated
lemon rind

1 tablespoon lemon juice

2 teaspoons wholegrain mustard

1 small red onion (100g),
sliced thinly

1 cup loosely packed fresh
flat-leaf parsley

1 Boil, steam or microwave potato until tender; drain.

2 Whisk oil, rind, juice and mustard in large bowl; mix in potatoes, onion and parsley.

NUTRITIONAL COUNT PER SERVING 14g total fat (1.9g saturated fat); 1267kJ (303 cal); 34.4g carbohydrate;
6.8g protein; 6.2g fibre

CRISP POTATO AND PEANUT CAKES

Poultry

Chicken is one of the most convenient and adaptable meats, ready for a dinner party or a child's meal, an easy weekend lunch or sandwiches fit for wedding guests, a summery salad or cold-weather casserole, and at the end of it all, a good soup.

Duck and goose fat are kitchen treasures. They not only give wonderful flavour to fried and roasted vegetables, but they are healthier than other animal fats because they include less saturated fat and more of the healthy mono-unsaturated and poly-unsaturated types. Render any solid fat that you have removed before cooking, as described for lard (see Pork, pages 440 & 441) and also save the fat that these birds give up while they are being cooked. Follow the same directions as given for lard for keeping these great fats in good condition.

Duck, goose and turkey are birds for a celebration, and duck and turkey are also available in convenient portions to cook an easy weeknight dinner or weekend meal.

Whole birds and portions are marketed under various descriptions indicating how the birds have been grown. These are not always as clear-cut as they might be, but in general, free-range means that they have had access to open pasture, with the implication that they have had a varied diet and enough exercise to put on muscle rather than just fat. Free-range birds should be labelled to show where they came from and certify they are genuinely free-range. Organic means that the birds were free-range, have also been fed on a diet obtained without the use of pesticides, herbicides or artificial fertilisers, and have been grown more slowly and for longer than intensively produced birds. Organic birds should be labelled with the grower's name and certification number from a recognised organic growers' association. Grain-fed or corn-fed means that the birds have received a high proportion of grain/corn in their feed, implying that this has improved the flavour of the flesh; corn-feeding tends to give a yellow cast to the skin, though this is sometimes imitated by including yellow pigments in the feed of non-corn-fed birds. Grain-fed/corn-fed does not necessarily imply that that the feed or the way the bird was grown was organic or open-range.

CHICKEN

Chicken sold in butchers' shops, supermarkets and delicatessens is young meat — intensively produced chicken about 40 days old, organic chicken about 70 days old. An older and larger bird, called a boiler, may be a hen reared for egg-laying which has ceased to be productive. It will be tough but more flavoursome than its younger counterparts and is usually used for stock- and soup-making, though it may be successfully casseroled if not too old and carefully cooked. Boilers usually have to be ordered especially.

Chickens are sold whole or in portions:

BREAST Whole or halved with skin and bone intact.

BREAST FILLET Skinless, boneless half-breast; a double fillet is a full breast.

THIGH CUTLET (CHICKEN CHOP) Skin-on thigh with one bone.

THIGH FILLET Skinless, boneless thigh.

DRUMSTICK Skin-on, bone-in leg.

WING Skin-on, bone-in wing.

DRUMETTE Main wing joint trimmed to resemble a miniature drumstick.

MARYLAND Thigh and leg still joined, skin-on and bone-in.

CHICKEN LIVERS are readily obtainable.

GIBLETS The edible internal organs of a bird, usually supplied as a mixture of hearts and gizzards as the livers are sold separately. Added to stock or soup to give rich flavour, but are removed before serving.

SPATCHCOCKS OR POUSSINS are young, small chickens weighing between 300g and 600g. In European cookbooks, spatchcock refers to a technique — a full-size chicken or game bird split and opened out for grilling.

DUCK

Ducks are sold whole or in portions:

BONELESS BREAST Skin-on, boneless whole or half breast

BREAST FILLET Skinless, boneless whole or half-breast

MARYLAND Thigh and leg still joined, skin-on and bone-in

DUCK LIVERS are available but may have to be ordered ahead

GOOSE AND TURKEY

Goose is available only as a whole bird and usually has to to be ordered ahead. Turkeys are sold whole or in portions:

TURKEY BUFFE A whole, skin-on breast on the bone

BREAST FILLET A skinless, boneless half-breast

CHOOSING
Fresh birds and portions are preferable to frozen as frozen ones will lose juices as they thaw. If you do have to buy frozen, take an insulated bag with an ice-pack to the shop and take the bird home in that as quickly as you can. As always, a supplier you can trust is your best bet for buying good quality poultry, or if you are buying in a supermarket, a brand claiming at least free-range or, better, organic rearing of its birds is a better bet than anonymous offerings. Price is a guide too — genuine free-range/ organic poultry is more expensive than the intensively produced kind. If you can buy at a grower's market, that is usually an excellent way to buy poultry as the stallholders are, in general, enthusiasts who strive to produce the best.

QUANTITIES

The amounts given here are a general guide only and will vary with appetites and what else is being served.

CHICKEN 375g per person for roast or fried chicken; 500g per person of chicken on the bone for grilling or barbecuing; 250g to 500g per person of chicken on the bone for casseroling; 150g to 200g of boneless chicken, skin-on or skinless.

One **SPATCHCOCK** serves one.

DUCK has a larger frame and thinner meat covering than chicken. A 1.4kg duck will serve 2 or 3, a 1.6kg one 2 or 4, a 2kg one 4, and a 2.5kg one 5 or 6.

One **DUCK MARYLAND** serves one.

One skin-on or skinless **DUCK FILLET** (half-breast) serves one.

GOOSE, like duck, appears large but yields little meat for its size. Allow 750g per person.

TURKEY a 3 to 4kg turkey serves 8 to 10, a 4 to 6 kg turkey serves 10 to 14, a 6 to 8kg turkey serves 14 to 16. Allow 375g of turkey buffe per person, 150g to 200g of turkey breast fillet per person.

STORING
Remove poultry from its shop wrappings as soon as you get it home; transfer to a clean plate and cover generously with foil. Transfer frozen poultry immediately to the freezer or, to thaw it, remove its packaging, place it on several layers of absorbent paper on a plate and place, uncovered, in the refrigerator. It may take 24 hours or more to thaw properly; do not cook it partially frozen as this can be dangerous because the inside does not get hot enough to kill any potentially dangerous organisms such as salmonella. Before using a thawed frozen bird, dry it thoroughly inside and out. A whole fresh bird should be used within 3 days, a thawed one within 2 days, fresh or thawed portions within 2 days, and minced poultry or livers within 2 days.

✤ **OTHER RECIPES USING POULTRY**

Honey-glazed turkey with orange-pecan stuffing

PREP + COOK TIME 3 HOURS 15 MINUTES (PLUS STANDING TIME) **SERVES** 8

To carve a turkey, you need a carving knife with a blade at least 20cm long and a carving fork. Holding the turkey steady with the fork, push one leg outwards and find the joint, then cut through the joint between leg and body, removing leg and thigh in one piece. Cut through the joint between leg and thigh and, if the turkey is over 6kg, slice the meat from leg and thigh parallel to the bone. Remove the wing from the breast on that side by cutting through the joint, then carve the breast into thin slices at a parallel angle to the breast bone. Repeat on the other side and remove the seasoning with a spoon.

For information on honey, see Sugar, page 578; and for pecans, see Nuts, page 346.

4.5kg turkey

2 medium oranges (480g), unpeeled, chopped coarsely

1 cup (250ml) water

2 cups (500ml) chicken stock

½ cup (125ml) bourbon

50g butter, melted

2 tablespoons orange juice

½ cup (175g) honey

2 tablespoons plain flour

ORANGE-PECAN STUFFING

20g butter

1 large brown onion (200g), chopped finely

4 cups (280g) stale breadcrumbs

1 cup (120g) coarsely chopped roasted pecans

1 tablespoon finely grated orange rind

2 tablespoons orange juice

½ cup (125ml) water

40g butter, melted

2 eggs, beaten lightly

1 Preheat oven to 180°C/160°C fan-forced.

2 Discard neck from turkey. Rinse turkey under cold water; pat dry inside and out with absorbent paper. Tuck wings under turkey; fill large cavity with orange, tie legs together with kitchen string.

3 Place the water, stock and bourbon into large flameproof baking dish; place turkey on oiled wire rack over dish. Brush turkey all over with butter; cover dish tightly with two layers of oiled foil. Roast 2 hours 10 minutes. Uncover turkey; brush with half of the combined orange juice and honey. Roast, uncovered, about 50 minutes or until browned all over and cooked through, brushing frequently with remaining honey mixture. Remove turkey from dish; cover, stand 20 minutes.

4 Meanwhile, make orange-pecan stuffing.

5 Strain turkey juices from dish into large jug. Skim 2 tablespoons of the oil from juices; return oil to dish. Add flour to dish; cook, stirring, until mixture bubbles and browns. Add juices; cook, stirring, until gravy boils and thickens. Strain gravy into same jug.

6 Serve turkey with stuffing, accompany with a kumara mash and steamed green beans.

ORANGE-PECAN STUFFING Melt butter in medium frying pan; cook onion, stirring, until soft. Combine onion in medium bowl with breadcrumbs, nuts, rind, juice, water, melted butter and egg. Roll 2 tablespoons of the mixture into balls; place on oiled tray. Bake, uncovered, in oven about 20 minutes or until browned lightly.

NUTRITIONAL COUNT PER SERVING 59.7g total fat (19.1g saturated fat); 4874kJ (1166 cal); 51.4g carbohydrate; 95.8g protein; 4.5g fibre

You could also make this recipe with double lamb cutlets or butterflied quail instead of the chicken. To 'spatchcock' quail or small chickens, rinse the whole bird under cold water; pat dry inside and out with absorbent paper. Using kitchen scissors, cut along each side of each backbone; discard backbone. Place quail or chicken, skin-side up, on board; using heel of hand, press down on breastbone to flatten.

For information on goats cheese, see Cheese, pages 100 & 104; and for smoked salmon, see Seafood, pages 523 & 524.

Chicken breast stuffed with smoked salmon and goats cheese

PREP + COOK TIME 1 HOUR 35 MINUTES **SERVES** 4

4 medium potatoes (800g), sliced thinly

¼ cup coarsely chopped fresh flat-leaf parsley

2 cloves garlic, crushed

1 tablespoon olive oil

⅔ cup (160ml) milk, warmed

2 tablespoons finely chopped fresh chives

100g soft goats cheese

4 chicken breast fillets (800g)

4 slices smoked salmon (120g)

50g baby spinach leaves

1 Preheat oven to 200°C/180°C fan-forced.

2 Combine potato, parsley, garlic and oil in medium bowl. Layer potato mixture in 2.5-litre (10-cup) ceramic baking dish; pour over milk. Roast, uncovered, about 40 minutes or until potato is just tender.

3 Meanwhile, combine chives and cheese in small bowl. Cut fillets in half horizontally almost all the way through; open out each fillet. Spread each fillet with a quarter of the cheese mixture; top with one slice of salmon and a quarter of the spinach. Roll each fillet tightly to enclose filling; secure with toothpicks.

4 Cook chicken in large oiled frying pan, uncovered, until browned.

5 Place chicken on cooked potato; roast, uncovered, in oven about 15 minutes or until chicken is cooked through. Stand 5 minutes; remove toothpicks, slice chicken thickly.

6 Serve chicken with potato and accompanied with a spinach salad.

NUTRITIONAL COUNT PER SERVING 16.3g total fat (5.8g saturated fat); 2103kJ (503 cal); 25.3g carbohydrate; 61.4g protein; 3.6g fibre

Keep shantung sauce in mind as an easy way to add a sweet/hot/sour hit to fish, chicken, or stir-fried vegetables, noodles or tofu. Shantung chicken goes well with crisp fried noodles (see Noodles, pages 334 & 335).

Shantung chicken

PREP + COOK TIME 1 HOUR 30 MINUTES (PLUS REFRIGERATION TIME) **SERVES** 4

1 clove garlic, crushed

2cm piece fresh ginger (10g), grated

1 tablespoon dark soy sauce

1 tablespoon dry sherry

2 teaspoons sichuan peppercorns, crushed

2 teaspoons peanut oil

1.6kg whole chicken

SHANTUNG SAUCE

⅓ cup (75g) caster sugar

½ cup (125ml) water

2 tablespoons white wine vinegar

1 fresh small red thai chilli, chopped finely

1 Combine garlic, ginger, sauce, sherry, pepper and oil in large bowl; add chicken, coat in marinade. Cover; refrigerate overnight.

2 Preheat oven to 220°C/200°C fan-forced.

3 Half-fill a large baking dish with water; place chicken on oiled wire rack set over dish. Roast, uncovered, about 1 hour 20 minutes or until cooked through.

4 Meanwhile, make shantung sauce.

5 Remove chicken from oven; when cool enough to handle, remove bones. Chop meat coarsely; serve drizzled with sauce.

SHANTUNG SAUCE Stir sugar and the water in small saucepan over low heat until sugar dissolves. Bring to the boil; boil, uncovered, without stirring, about 5 minutes or until sauce thickens slightly. Remove from heat; stir in vinegar and chilli.

NUTRITIONAL COUNT PER SERVING 28.3g total fat (8.6g saturated); 2107kJ (504 cal); 19.2g carbohydrate; 42.1g protein; 0.2g fibre

CHICKEN GREEN CURRY

Green curry paste is one of the hottest of the traditional Thai pastes. Make your own as directed here, or purchase it ready-made from most supermarkets. Pea eggplants are available in Asian food stores and some specialist greengrocers.

For more information on green curry paste, see Curry pastes, page 152.

Chicken green curry

PREP + COOK TIME 50 MINUTES **SERVES** 4

1 tablespoon peanut oil

¼ cup (75g) green curry paste (page 153)

3 long green chillies, chopped finely

1kg chicken thigh fillets, cut into 3cm pieces

2 x 400ml cans coconut milk

2 tablespoons fish sauce

2 tablespoons lime juice

1 tablespoon grated palm sugar

150g pea eggplants

1 large zucchini (150g), sliced thinly

⅓ cup loosely packed fresh thai basil leaves

¼ cup loosely packed fresh coriander leaves

2 green onions, chopped coarsely

1 Heat oil in large saucepan; cook paste and about two-thirds of the chilli, stirring, about 2 minutes or until fragrant. Add chicken; cook, stirring, until browned.

2 Add coconut milk, sauce, juice, sugar and eggplants; simmer, uncovered, about 10 minutes or until eggplants are just tender.

3 Add zucchini, basil and coriander; simmer, uncovered, until zucchini is just tender.

4 Serve curry sprinkled with remaining chilli and green onion.

NUTRITIONAL COUNT PER SERVING 67.3g total fat (43.2g saturated fat); 3716kJ (889 cal); 17g carbohydrate; 52.9g protein; 6g fibre

Roast goose with fruit and nut seasoning

PREP + COOK TIME 3 HOURS **SERVES** 8

This roast goose is good with a rice pilaf or roasted kipfler potatoes.

20g butter, melted

1 tablespoon honey

1 teaspoon light soy sauce

3.5kg goose

plain flour

FRUIT AND NUT SEASONING

2 tablespoons vegetable oil

200g chicken giblets, chopped finely

1 medium brown onion (150g), chopped finely

1 stalk celery (150g), trimmed, chopped

1 medium apple (150g), chopped

½ cup (80g) coarsely chopped brazil nuts

½ cup (70g) slivered almonds

½ cup (75g) coarsely chopped dried apricots

½ cup (85g) finely chopped raisins

1 tablespoon chopped fresh mint

1½ cups (100g) stale breadcrumbs

1 Preheat oven to 200°C/180°C fan-forced.

2 Make fruit and nut seasoning.

3 Combine butter, honey and sauce in small bowl, brush mixture over inside and outside of goose. Fill goose with seasoning, secure opening with skewers. Tie legs together, tuck wings under goose. Prick skin to release fat during roasting.

4 Lightly flour large oven bag; place goose in bag, secure with tie provided. Make holes in bag as advised on package. Place goose breast-side-up in baking dish, cover dish with foil; roast 1 hour. Remove foil, roast goose further 1 hour.

FRUIT AND NUT SEASONING Heat half the oil in medium saucepan; cook giblets, stirring, until browned. Drain. Add remaining oil to pan; cook onion and celery, stirring, until onion is soft. Add apple and nuts; cook, stirring, until nuts are browned lightly. Remove from heat, stir in giblets, apricots, raisins, mint and breadcrumbs; cool.

NUTRITIONAL COUNT PER SERVING 113g total fat (32.2g saturated fat); 5405kJ (1293 cal); 27g carbohydrate; 43.4g protein; 4.3g fibre

Preserves

Pickles, chutneys and relishes are invaluable to keep on hand for adding piquant, complex flavours and juicy texture to hot and cold meats, poultry and fish, sandwiches, appetisers, curries, cheese and rice dishes. Jams, marmalades and conserves are, traditionally, variations on the theme of sweet spreads for bread, scones or the breakfast toast, but the family has been enlarged in recent years to include deep-flavoured savoury jams such as onion or chilli which can go with anything from meats and seafood to grilled or steamed vegetables.

Some preserves can be used as ingredients: for example, a spoonful of chutney or relish can balance the flavour of a curry; onion jam can deepen the colour and flavour of a casserole or soup; and marmalade can be brushed over chicken pieces as they bake to give the skin delicious caramelised flavour and a golden glaze.

❦ OTHER RECIPES
USING PRESERVES
*Duck liver parfait with red
   onion jam, p358
Fresh apricot jam, p16
Kangaroo fillet with beetroot
   relish, p211
Lentil and bean burger with
   chilli tomato relish, p474-5
Pork cutlets with fennel apple
   relish, p443
Prawn and scallop chilli jam
   stir-fry, p573
Quince jelly, p486
Tamarillo apple chutney, p594
Thai cucumber pickle, p148*

The classic Italian olive oil, garlic and herb sauce, pesto, also appears now in commercial versions which store well and are so versatile as spreads, dips, bruschetta toppings and relishes that they have joined the range of preserves for the pantry.

PICKLES are vegetables, and occasionally fruits, preserved in vinegar, brine or a mixture of the two, usually with additional flavourings such as herbs or spices and often with sugar or mustard added. The pickling process is one of preservation by acid and/or salt, often with the addition of sugar or mustard which are also preservatives. Fermentation can also play a part. Some of the best-known pickles are pickled onions in various sizes; pickled cucumbers called bread-and-butter pickles, dill pickles, gherkins or cornichons; clear single-vegetable pickles such as cauliflower or zucchini; and mixed mustard pickles. Some pickles such as piccalilli, a mixed mustard pickle, are thickened to give a rich sauce-like consistency. Pickles have usually been matured for weeks or months though a few, such as kosher-style dill pickles, are eaten at different stages from one day old to fully matured.

CHUTNEYS AND RELISHES Chutneys were originally relishes or pickles that originated in India and were adopted by the British in their colonial days, but the word now overlaps with relishes as names for spicy, sweet-sharp fruit and/or vegetable mixtures which have been cooked to a soft and thickened texture. Some of the best known are mango chutney, bengal chutney which was named for its cayenne heat, chow-chow, a mixed-vegetable relish with a mustardy tang, and many versions of tomato or capsicum relish.

PESTO is, traditionally, an Italian sauce made by beating olive oil into a finely pounded mixture of basil, garlic, pine nuts and parmesan or pecorino cheese, and used on pasta and as the garnish for the hearty vegetable and pasta soup, minestrone. It is now often made with other herbs such as mint or coriander and other nuts such as almonds or walnuts, and is available commercially, treated to store well. It goes well with chicken or spooned on to hot potatoes baked in their skins, and the basil version is excellent with any tomato dish while the mint version is good with lamb and the coriander version good with fish.

JAMS are cooked fruit preserves of a spreadable but set consistency, achieved by the action of pectin, a substance in the cell walls of fruit, when it is cooked with the right balance of sugar and acid. Fruits vary greatly in their pectin content, high-pectin ones include apples, citrus fruits, plums, quinces and black or red currants. Low-pectin fruits such as cherries, figs, peaches, pears, pineapples and rhubarb, and also strawberries and raspberries which have pectin of an inferior setting quality, can be mixed with high-pectin ones to make jam that sets well, or a bag of lemon pips and peel, including the high-pectin white pith, can be added. Commercial pectin is also available. As noted above, savoury jams such as onion or chilli are available, though these are not usually set but achieve their consistency by careful simmering down until they reach the required thickness.

MARMALADES are bittersweet jams nearly always made from one or more citrus fruits and deriving their bitterness from the pieces of peel that are included with the fruit and, in the case of seville orange marmalade, from the bitterness of the juice itself. Bittersweet jams made from other fruits, such as apple and ginger, may also be called marmalades. The name comes from the Portuguese marmelada and originally meant a sweet, solid Portuguese quince paste which was imported into medieval and Tudor England and eaten as a confection; the thick fruit pastes that are now popular items on the cheeseboard are still sometimes referred to as marmeladas.

CONSERVES are jams with whole fruits such as cherries or strawberries, or large pieces of such fruits as peaches or apricots.

STORING Preserves of all kinds made by large manufacturers can be stored, opened or unopened, at room temperature away from heat and light. Home-made preserves or home-style ones from small-scale producers selling at growers' markets can be stored in the same way until opened but should then be refrigerated and used within a month or two.

To test when jam is ready, remove pan from heat, allow bubbles to subside and drop a teaspoon of mixture on a freezer-chilled plate. Return plate to freezer briefly to cool jam to room temperature; smooth jam should be of a spreadable consistency, jam with pieces of fruit should form a skin and wrinkle when pushed with a finger. If not set, boil for a few minutes more and test again.

There are three methods of sterilising jars: run them through the hottest dishwasher cycle without detergent; cover with cold water in a large saucepan and boil, with the lid on for 20 minutes; stand right way up, not touching each other, on an oven tray in a cold oven, heat to 120°C/100°C fan-forced and leave 30 minutes.

For information on cherries, see Cherries, page 114.

Brandied cherry jam

PREP + COOK TIME 1 HOUR **MAKES** 1 LITRE (4 CUPS)

900g fresh or frozen seeded cherries

¾ cup (180ml) water

¼ cup (60ml) lemon juice

½ cup (125ml) cherry brandy

4 cups (880g) white sugar, approximately

1 Bring cherries, the water and juice to the boil in large saucepan. Reduce heat; simmer, covered, about 10 minutes or until cherries are soft. Stir in brandy.

2 Measure fruit mixture; allow ¾ cup (165g) sugar for each cup of mixture. Return mixture and sugar to pan; stir over heat, without boiling, until sugar dissolves. Boil, uncovered, about 40 minutes or until jam sets when tested on a cold saucer.

3 Pour into hot sterilised jars; seal immediately.

NUTRITIONAL COUNT PER TABLESPOON 0.1g total fat (0g saturated fat); 502kJ (120 cal); 27.6g carbohydrate; 0.4g protein; 0.4g fibre

Grate the rind from the oranges before juicing them. Use this gently spiced jam as a spread and, warmed and sieved, as a glaze to brush on skin-on chicken breasts before baking them. For instructions on testing when jam is set and how to sterilise jars, see page 465.

For information on granny smith apples, see Apples, pages 8–10; and for fresh figs, see Figs, page 178.

Spiced fig and apple jam

PREP + COOK TIME 1 HOUR 30 MINUTES **MAKES** 2 LITRES (8 CUPS)

2 large granny smith apples (500g), peeled, chopped finely

2 cups (500ml) water

16 medium fresh figs (1 kg), chopped coarsely

½ cup (125ml) orange juice

1.1kg (5 cups) caster sugar, approximately

2 tablespoons finely grated orange rind

3 star anise

1 cinnamon stick, halved

2 vanilla beans, halved lengthways

1 Combine apple and the water in large saucepan; bring to the boil. Reduce heat; simmer, covered, about 20 minutes or until apples are soft. Add figs and juice; simmer, covered, 10 minutes.

2 Measure fruit mixture; allow ¾ cup (165g) sugar for each cup of mixture. Return mixture and sugar to pan with remaining ingredients; stir over heat, without boiling, until sugar dissolves. Boil, uncovered, about 45 minutes or until jam sets when tested on a cold saucer.

3 Pour into hot sterilised jars; seal immediately.

NUTRITIONAL COUNT PER TABLESPOON 0g total fat (0g saturated fat); 226kJ (54 cal); 12.9g carbohydrate; 0.2g protein; 0.3g fibre

This chutney is quick and easy to make, and will keep in a cool place for up to 3 months providing that the jars were properly sterilised. Once opened, store it in the refrigerator.

For information on eggplant, see Eggplant, page 160.

Eggplant chutney

PREP + COOK TIME 1 HOUR (PLUS STANDING TIME) **MAKES** 3 CUPS

1 medium eggplant (300g), peeled, chopped coarsely

¼ cup (70g) coarse cooking salt

1 medium brown onion (150g), chopped coarsely

2 medium tomatoes (300g), seeded, chopped coarsely

1 small green capsicum (150g), chopped coarsely

2 cloves garlic, crushed

½ cup (125ml) cider vinegar

½ cup (125ml) white vinegar

1 teaspoon chilli powder

1 teaspoon ground turmeric

½ cup (110g) firmly packed brown sugar

1 Place eggplant in colander, sprinkle with salt; stand 30 minutes. Rinse eggplant, pat dry.

2 Place eggplant, onion, tomato, capsicum, garlic, vinegars, chilli and turmeric in large saucepan; simmer, uncovered, stirring occasionally, about 45 minutes or until vegetables are pulpy.

3 Stir in sugar; cook, stirring, over low heat, until sugar dissolves.

NUTRITIONAL COUNT PER TABLESPOON 0g total fat (0g saturated fat); 67kJ (16 cal); 3.5g carbohydrate; 0.3g protein; 0.3g fibre

1

2

1 EGGPLANT CHUTNEY
2 DATE AND TAMARIND
CHUTNEY

Date and tamarind chutney

PREP + COOK TIME 55 MINUTES **MAKES** 2½ CUPS

2 cinnamon sticks

5 cardamom pods, bruised

2 teaspoons cloves

3½ cups (500g) seeded
dried dates

1½ cups (375ml) white vinegar

½ cup (110g) firmly packed
brown sugar

2 teaspoons coarse cooking salt

¼ cup (60ml) vegetable oil

2 tablespoons tamarind
concentrate

2 teaspoons chilli powder

*This is a delicious, tangy
Indian relish that goes
well with meat curries,
or spread on cheese or
meat sandwiches for a
burst of flavour.*

*For information on dried
dates, see Dates, page
156; and for tamarind
concentrate, see Tamarind,
page 595.*

1 Place cinnamon, cardamom and cloves in centre of 20cm muslin square; tie tightly
with kitchen string.

2 Combine muslin bag with remaining ingredients in large saucepan; bring to the boil,
stirring constantly, then reduce heat.

3 Simmer, partially covered, stirring occasionally, about 40 minutes or until dates are
soft. Remove and discard spice bag before using.

NUTRITIONAL COUNT PER TABLESPOON 1.9g total fat (0.2g saturated fat); 343kJ (82 cal); 15g carbohydrate;
0.4g protein; 1.7g fibre

Chutney will keep for at
least 6 months if the jars
have been sterilised
properly. Store the jars
in a cool, dark place.
Once opened, store in
the refrigerator.

For information on peaches,
see Peaches, page 412;
and for allspice, cardamom
and cinnamon, see Spices,
pages 556 & 559.

Peach and cardamom chutney

PREP + COOK TIME 1 HOUR 15 MINUTES **MAKES** 2 LITRES (8 CUPS)

7 large peaches (1.5kg)

1 large brown onion (200g), chopped finely

¾ cup (120g) coarsely chopped raisins

1½ cups (330g) firmly packed brown sugar

¾ cup (180ml) cider vinegar

1 cinnamon stick

4 cardamom pods, bruised

1 teaspoon whole allspice

2 teaspoons finely grated lemon rind

1 Cut small cross in bottom of each peach. Lower peaches gently into large saucepan of boiling water, boil for 1 minute, then place in large bowl of cold water. Peel peaches, remove stones; chop flesh coarsely.

2 Place peaches with remaining ingredients in large saucepan; stir over heat until sugar dissolves. Bring to the boil; reduce heat. Simmer, uncovered, stirring occasionally, about 45 minutes or until thick.

3 Pour chutney into hot sterilised jars; seal immediately.

NUTRITIONAL COUNT PER TABLESPOON 0g total fat (0g saturated fat); 92kJ (22 cal); 5.2g carbohydrate; 0.2g protein; 0.3g fibre

Store the jars in a cool,
dark place. Once opened,
it will keep for several
weeks in the refrigerator.

For information on red
onions, see Onions, page
375; for cranberries, see
Berries, page 60; and for
balsamic and brown (malt)
vinegars, see Vinegar,
pages 633 & 634.

Cranberry and balsamic red onion relish

PREP + COOK TIME 1 HOUR 20 MINUTES **MAKES** 1.5 LITRES (6 CUPS)

50g butter

3 large red onions (900g), sliced thinly

1kg frozen cranberries

2 cups (440g) firmly packed brown sugar

1 cup (250ml) brown vinegar

½ cup (125ml) balsamic vinegar

1 teaspoon coarse cooking salt

4 whole cloves

½ teaspoon dried chilli flakes

1 Melt butter in large saucepan; cook onion, stirring, until soft.

2 Add remaining ingredients; stir over heat until sugar dissolves. Bring to the boil; reduce heat. Simmer, uncovered, stirring occasionally, for about 1 hour or until thick.

3 Pour relish into hot sterilised jars; seal immediately.

NUTRITIONAL COUNT PER TABLESPOON 0.6g total fat (0.4g saturated fat); 150kJ (36 cal); 7.1g carbohydrate; 0.3g protein; 0.4g fibre

Spicy mustard pickles

PREP + COOK TIME 50 MINUTES (PLUS STANDING AND COOLING TIME) **MAKES** 1 LITRE (4 CUPS)

¼ medium cauliflower (400g), chopped coarsely

250g green beans, trimmed, chopped coarsely

3 medium brown onions (450g), sliced thickly

1 medium red capsicum (200g), sliced thickly

¼ cup (70g) coarse cooking salt

2 teaspoons mustard powder

2 tablespoons wholegrain mustard

3 teaspoons curry powder

¼ teaspoon ground turmeric

2 cups (500ml) white vinegar

1 cup (220g) firmly packed brown sugar

2 tablespoons plain flour

1 Combine vegetables and salt in large bowl. Cover; stand overnight.

2 Rinse vegetables; drain. Stir vegetables, mustards, curry powder, turmeric, 1¾ cups of the vinegar and the sugar in large saucepan over heat, without boiling, until sugar dissolves. Bring to the boil; simmer, uncovered, about 10 minutes or until vegetables are just tender.

3 Stir in blended flour and remaining vinegar; stir over heat until mixture boils and thickens.

4 Pour into hot sterilised jars; seal immediately.

NUTRITIONAL COUNT PER TABLESPOON 0.1g total fat (0g saturated); 113kJ (27 cal); 5.7g carbohydrate; 0.6g protein; 0.5g fibre

An old-fashioned pickle that is splendid with cold roast lamb or cheddar cheese, or mix it with grated cheese, pile it on toast and grill.

For information on mustard powder and wholegrain mustard, see Mustard, pages 328 & 329.

Citrus marmalade

PREP + COOK TIME 1 HOUR 50 MINUTES (PLUS STANDING TIME) **MAKES** 1.75 LITRES (7 CUPS)

4 large oranges (1.2kg)

3 medium lemons (420g)

4 large limes (400g)

1.25 litres (5 cups) water

1.6kg (7 cups) white sugar, approximately

1 Peel all fruit thinly; cut rind into thin strips. Remove pith from all fruit; reserve half, discard remaining pith. Chop flesh coarsely, reserve seeds.

2 Combine flesh and rind in large bowl with the water. Tie reserved pith and seeds in a piece of muslin tied with kitchen string; add to bowl. Stand at room temperature overnight.

3 Place fruit mixture and muslin bag in large saucepan; bring to the boil. Simmer, covered, 25 minutes or until rind is soft. Discard bag.

4 Measure fruit mixture; allow 1 cup (220g) sugar for each cup of mixture. Return mixture and sugar to pan; stir over heat, without boiling, until sugar dissolves. Boil, uncovered, about 40 minutes or until marmalade sets when tested on a cold saucer.

5 Pour into hot sterilised jars; seal immediately.

NUTRITIONAL COUNT PER TABLESPOON 0g total fat (0g saturated fat); 326kJ (78 cal); 18.8g carbohydrate; 0.2g protein; 0.5g fibre

Lime rind will take the longest to cook, so it is the one to check for softness. For instructions on testing when jam is set and how to sterilise jars, see page 465.

Pulses

Dried beans, peas and lentils (collectively called pulses) have always been "poor man's meats" because they are cheap, filling and nourishing: pulses are high in the "good" carbohydrates, dietary fibre, vitamins and minerals, while they are cholesterol-free and have little or no fat.

1 YELLOW SPLIT PEAS
2 GREEN SPLIT PEAS
3 BLACK TURTLE BEANS
4 SOY BEANS
5 HARICOT/NAVY BEANS
6 ADZUKI BEANS
7 AUSTRALIAN GREEN LENTILS
8 RED LENTILS
9 BROWN LENTILS
10 SALTED BLACK BEANS
11 BORLOTTI BEANS
12 CHICKPEAS
13 BLACK-EYED BEANS
14 RED KIDNEY BEANS
15 LIMA BEANS
16 BROAD BEANS

Pulses are simmered rather than boiled because the turbulence of boiling water could damage their skins or outer layers and cause them to disintegrate.

They are also high in protein, though (except for soy beans) this is incomplete protein and you need to eat a grain product such as rice, bread or corn with them to make them comparable to animal protein. Their only drawback is that they tend to cause flatulence, though this can be minimised by pre-soaking, then thorough cooking in fresh water.

The reason why these humble foods are popular with both rich and poor today is that, over many years, generations of cooks transformed them into some of the great dishes of the world: India's dhals, heady with spices and aromatics, Italy's meal-in-a-pot soup, minestrone, and Provence's garlic-scented pistou soup, the Middle East's bean salads with lemon, herbs and olives and its garlicky chickpea dip, hummus bi tahina, Tex-Mex chilli con carne and Mexico's spicy refried beans, France's rich and savoury cassoulets, Tuscany's lemony bean and tuna salad, and Boston baked beans which became the ancestors of countless cans. Modern chefs, too, have taken to these great staples, pairing them with seafood, cured and fresh meats, grilled and roasted vegetables or fresh salad ingredients, pasta, rice and aromatics of every kind.

PREPARATION Most pulses need soaking in cold water to cover for 6–8 hours before they are cooked. Chickpeas need up to 12 hours and broad beans up to 24, and should be refrigerated during this time so that they won't begin to ferment. Soaking draws out indigestible substances so the soaking water should be discarded and fresh water used for cooking. A faster way to pre-soak is to cover the pulses generously with cold, unsalted water, bring slowly to the boil, simmer 2 minutes then remove from heat and stand, covered, for 1 hour. Lentils do not need pre-soaking.

Do not add salt, sugar or acid ingredients such as tomato to the cooking water until after the beans or peas are tender, as these will toughen them if added earlier.

Quite a few kinds of dried beans are available ready-cooked in cans, and these can be a satisfactory substitute for home-cooked, though they are sometimes a little mushy. It is usually best to drain and rinse them before using.

HARICOT BEANS The large family of haricot beans includes the French varieties soissons and flageolets, the white haricots called butter beans or haricots in Europe and known in America as navy beans or great northern beans, and the fat little Italian beans called cannellini. All are smooth, oval beans and all are white except flageolet, which are pale green. They differ slightly in texture and flavour but can be substituted for each other in recipes.

1 YELLOW SPLIT PEAS
2 GREEN SPLIT PEAS

SOY BEANS Round yellow, pale brown, green or black beans which are highly nutritious, being the only pulse providing complete protein They can be cooked like any other bean but many people dislike their toughness and distinctive flavour. They are more widely used to make soy sauce, bean curd (tofu) and many other soya products.

CHICKPEAS Also known as garbanzos, these are really a bean. They need long soaking and cooking.

KIDNEY BEANS A huge group that includes the haricot family, but the name is now usually used only for those that are kidney-shaped. They can be red, brown or white.

BROAD BEANS Also known as fava or field beans, these are large, flat, green or pale brown beans with tough skins that may be removed after soaking or cooking.

LIMA BEANS Also known as butter beans, small and pale green if picked young or large, flat and white if picked when fully grown.

BORLOTTI BEANS Also known as roman beans, these are a mottled pink, brown or fawn streaked Italian variety. Their markings disappear with cooking.

PINTO BEANS Speckled beans used in Central and South American cooking.

BLACK-EYED BEANS Also called black-eyed peas, these are named for the black spot at one end.

BLACK TURTLE BEANS Shiny black kidney beans with a big, meaty flavour, used in Caribbean and South American cooking.

ADZUKI BEANS Also known as hong tou, a small, red-brown sweet bean used in Japanese and Chinese cakes and puddings. They are also sold powdered.

SALTED BLACK BEANS Fermented soy beans, heavily salted, used in Chinese cooking. They are soft and are sold in bags, cans or jars.

MUNG BEANS Also know as green gram, these are tiny, sweetish green beans that cook quickly and are said to be easily digested and not to cause wind. They are used in Indian and other Asian cooking but are best known in the West in their sprouted form.

DRIED PEAS Green or yellow skinned split peas or whole blue peas. Split peas are usually pre-soaked but may be cooked without soaking. Whole peas need soaking to soften the skins so that they will not burst as the flesh swells with cooking.

LENTILS May be whole or skinned and split. Whole brown and green lentils may be briefly soaked but can be cooked without soaking. French-style dark-green lentils, cultivated in Australia to be similar to French puy lentils, which are considered the aristocrats of their kind, are sold under the name of Australian green lentils. Tiny, split red or orange lentils should not be soaked; they cook quickly to tenderness and break up into a mush if left for more than 15–20 minutes. Depending on the dish, this may be desirable, but if it is not, it can be discouraged by breaking the usual rule of cooking pulses and adding salt at the start of cooking — though even then, they should be carefully watched.

CHOOSING
Pulses should be clean, free of stones and reasonably uniform in size; most of those sold in the West meet these criteria. The older they are, the harder they are and the longer they will take to cook, so it is best to buy from a shop with a quick turnover and in quantities you will use within a month or two.

STORING
Keep pulses in airtight containers in a cool, dry place. Salted black beans should be stored in an airtight container in the refrigerator.

❧ **OTHER RECIPES USING PULSES**
Braised veal shoulder with white beans, p622
Cajun kingfish, p564
Char-grilled radicchio parcels, p251
Ham and black-eyed bean soup, p258
Italian-style bean salad with fresh mozzarella, p108
Merguez and bean soup, p518
Mexican sausages with beans, p517
Moroccan couscous salad with preserved lemon dressing, p232
Warm chorizo and lentil salad, p518

Dhal with pumpkin and eggplant

PREP + COOK TIME 1 HOUR 30 MINUTES **SERVES** 4

2 tablespoons olive oil

1 medium brown onion (150g), sliced thinly

2 cloves garlic, crushed

4cm piece fresh ginger (20g), grated

2 teaspoons ground cumin

2 teaspoons ground coriander

1 teaspoon ground turmeric

⅓ cup (65g) red lentils

⅓ cup (85g) yellow split peas

⅓ cup (85g) green split peas

410g can crushed tomatoes

1½ cups (375ml) vegetable stock

2 cups (500ml) water

300g piece pumpkin, chopped coarsely

1 medium eggplant (300g), chopped coarsely

400g can chickpeas, rinsed, drained

This vegetarian casserole is not only delicious and satisfying but, served with rice and/or chapatis, provides complete, low-fat nutrition.

For information on pumpkin, see Pumpkins, page 480; and for eggplant, see Eggplant, page 160.

1 Heat oil in large saucepan; cook onion, garlic and ginger, stirring, until onion softens. Add spices; cook, stirring, until fragrant.

2 Add lentils and peas to pan. Stir in undrained tomatoes, stock and the water; simmer, covered, stirring occasionally, 30 minutes. Add pumpkin and eggplant; bring to the boil. Reduce heat; simmer, covered, about 20 minutes or until pumpkin is tender. Add chickpeas, simmer 10 minutes.

NUTRITIONAL COUNT PER SERVING 12.9g total fat (2g saturated fat); 1793kJ (429 cal); 48.1g carbohydrate; 22.8g protein; 14.4g fibre

Green and yellow split pea salad

PREP + COOK TIME 30 MINUTES (PLUS STANDING TIME) **SERVES** 6

½ cup (100g) green split peas

½ cup (100g) yellow split peas

4 green onions, sliced thinly

250g cherry tomatoes, halved

½ cup coarsely chopped fresh flat-leaf parsley

WHOLEGRAIN MUSTARD DRESSING

¼ cup (60ml) lemon juice

¼ cup (60ml) olive oil

1 tablespoon wholegrain mustard

2 cloves garlic, crushed

1 Place split peas in medium bowl, cover with cold water; stand overnight, drain. Rinse under cold water; drain.

2 Place peas in medium saucepan, cover with boiling water. Simmer, covered, about 10 minutes or until split peas are tender; rinse under cold water, drain.

3 Whisk ingredients for wholegrain mustard dressing in small bowl.

4 Place split peas in large bowl with remaining ingredients and dressing; mix gently.

NUTRITIONAL COUNT PER SERVING 9.9g total fat (1.4g saturated fat); 836kJ (200 cal); 17.3g carbohydrate; 8.3g protein; 4.7g fibre

GREEN AND YELLOW
SPLIT PEA SALAD

1 LENTIL AND BEAN BURGER
WITH CHILLI TOMATO RELISH
2 FELAFEL

Lentil and bean burger with chilli tomato relish

PREP + COOK TIME 45 MINUTES (PLUS REFRIGERATION AND COOLING TIME) **SERVES** 4

*The relish is best made a
day or two ahead and
stored, covered, in the
refrigerator to allow the
flavours to blend. You can
add a finely chopped, fresh
red chilli to the mixture if
you want it hotter.*

1 cup (200g) red lentils

420g can four-bean mix, rinsed, drained

1 egg

4 green onions, chopped coarsely

2 tablespoons coarsely chopped fresh coriander

4 hamburger buns

8 butter lettuce leaves

40g bean sprouts

40g snow pea sprouts, trimmed

1 lebanese cucumber (130g), sliced thinly

CHILLI TOMATO RELISH

2 medium tomatoes (300g), chopped coarsely

1 small brown onion (80g), chopped finely

1 clove garlic, crushed

⅓ cup (80ml) sweet chilli sauce

2 tablespoons malt vinegar

1 Make chilli tomato relish.

2 Meanwhile, cook lentils in medium saucepan of boiling water until tender; drain. Cool 10 minutes.

3 Blend or process lentils, beans and egg until mixture forms a smooth paste. Combine in medium bowl with onion and coriander; cover, refrigerate 1 hour.

4 Using floured hands, shape lentil mixture into four patties; cook patties in large heated lightly oiled non-stick frying pan until browned both sides and heated through. Remove from pan; cover to keep warm.

5 Split buns in half; toast cut-sides of buns. Spread buns with relish; sandwich lettuce, sprouts, cucumber, patties and remaining relish between buns.

CHILLI TOMATO RELISH Cook tomato, onion and garlic in small saucepan, stirring, about 10 minutes or until tomato has softened. Add sauce and vinegar; bring to the boil. Reduce heat; simmer, uncovered, stirring occasionally, about 10 minutes or until relish thickens. Cool 15 minutes.

NUTRITIONAL COUNT PER SERVING 6.2g total fat (1.1g saturated fat); 1981kJ (474 cal); 76.6g carbohydrate; 28.3g protein; 18.9g fibre

---

Felafel

PREP + COOK TIME 1 HOUR (PLUS STANDING TIME) **MAKES** 50

2 cups (400g) dried chickpeas

1 medium brown onion (150g), chopped coarsely

2 cloves garlic, quartered

½ cup fresh flat-leaf parsley, chopped coarsely

2 teaspoons ground coriander

1 teaspoon ground cumin

1 teaspoon bicarbonate of soda

2 tablespoons plain flour

1 teaspoon salt

vegetable oil, for deep frying

1 Place chickpeas in large bowl, cover with cold water; stand overnight, drain.

2 Combine chickpeas, onion, garlic, parsley and spices in large bowl. Blend or process, in two batches, until almost smooth; return mixture to large bowl.

3 Add soda, flour and salt to chickpea mixture; knead on floured surface for 2 minutes. Stand 30 minutes.

4 Roll level tablespoons of mixture into balls; stand 10 minutes.

5 Deep-fry balls in hot oil, in batches, until golden brown. Serve with separate bowls of dukkah and yogurt for dipping.

NUTRITIONAL COUNT PER FELAFEL 0.9g total fat (0.1g saturated fat); 79kJ (19 cal); 1.8g carbohydrate; 0.7g protein; 0.6g fibre

These savoury chickpea balls are a popular snack and street food in many parts of the Middle East, whether dipped in spices and yogurt, as in this recipe, or wrapped in pitta bread with hummus, tahini (sesame seed paste) and salad. See page 566 for information on dukkah.

Cuban black bean soup stands beside French onion soup and bouillabaisse as one of the great soups of the world. Splendid in itself, it is traditionally served with bowls of sour cream, lime wedges, coriander leaves, chopped chilli, paper-thin slices of red onion and chopped hard-boiled egg for diners to add as they wish. The black beans for this recipe are the dried ones also known as turtle beans — not the salty black beans of Chinese cooking.

Cuban black bean soup

PREP + COOK TIME 2 HOURS 45 MINUTES (PLUS STANDING TIME) **SERVES** 8

2½ cups (500g) dried black beans

1kg ham bone

¼ cup (60ml) olive oil

2 medium brown onions (300g), chopped finely

1 medium red capsicum (200g), chopped finely

4 cloves garlic, crushed

1 tablespoon ground cumin

1 teaspoon dried chilli flakes

400g can chopped tomatoes

2.5 litres (10 cups) water

1 tablespoon dried oregano

2 teaspoons ground black pepper

¼ cup (60ml) lime juice

2 medium tomatoes (300g), chopped finely

¼ cup coarsely chopped fresh coriander

2 limes, quartered

1 Place beans in medium bowl, cover with water, stand overnight; drain. Rinse under cold water; drain.

2 Preheat oven to 220°C/200°C fan-forced.

3 Roast ham bone on oven tray, uncovered, 30 minutes.

4 Meanwhile, heat oil in large saucepan; cook onion, capsicum and garlic, stirring, until vegetables soften. Add cumin and chilli; cook, stirring, 1 minute. Add beans and ham bone to pan with undrained canned tomatoes, the water, oregano and pepper; bring to the boil. Reduce heat; simmer, uncovered, 1½ hours.

5 Remove ham bone from soup. When cool enough to handle, remove ham from bone, shred coarsely. Discard bone.

6 Return ham to soup; bring to the boil. Reduce heat, simmer, uncovered, until soup is hot. Remove from heat; stir in juice, fresh tomato and coriander. Serve with lime wedges.

NUTRITIONAL COUNT PER SERVING 9.4g total fat (1.6g saturated fat); 1279kJ (306 cal); 29.2g carbohydrate; 20.4g protein; 10.9g fibre

---

To reduce time, you can use two 400g cans white beans instead of the dried beans here. Rinse and drain well before placing in the processor.

White bean dip

PREP + COOK TIME 1 HOUR 10 MINUTES (PLUS STANDING AND COOLING TIME) **MAKES** 2 CUPS

2½ cups (300g) dried cannellini beans

2 cloves garlic, crushed

2 tablespoons lemon juice

⅓ cup (80ml) olive oil

1 tablespoon fresh basil leaves

1 Place beans in medium bowl, cover with water; stand overnight. Rinse and drain beans. Cook beans in medium saucepan of boiling water for 1 hour or until tender; drain. Cool.

2 Blend or process drained beans with garlic, juice and oil until almost smooth.

3 Sprinkle dip with basil.

NUTRITIONAL COUNT PER TABLESPOON 3.1g total fat (0.4g saturated fat); 125kJ (30 cal); 0.3g carbohydrate; 0.3g protein; 0.3g fibre

CUBAN BLACK BEAN SOUP

Creamy chickpea and garlic soup

PREP + COOK TIME 2 HOURS 30 MINUTES (PLUS STANDING TIME) **SERVES** 4

2 cups (400g) dried chickpeas

1 tablespoon olive oil

1 large brown onion (200g), chopped coarsely

4 cloves garlic, crushed

1.75 litres (7 cups) water

2 bay leaves

1 sprig fresh rosemary

300ml cream

1 Place chickpeas in large bowl, cover with water; stand overnight, drain. Rinse under cold water, drain.

2 Heat oil in large saucepan; cook onion and garlic, stirring, until onion softens. Add chickpeas, the water, bay leaves and rosemary; bring to the boil. Reduce heat; simmer, covered, about 2 hours or until chickpeas are tender. Remove from heat; cool 5 minutes.

3 Discard bay leaves and rosemary. Using hand-held blender, process soup in pan until smooth. Add cream; stir over medium heat until hot.

NUTRITIONAL COUNT PER SERVING 39.9g total fat (22.5g saturated fat); 2048kJ (490 cal); 21.1g carbohydrate; 10g protein; 6.9g fibre

Without the cream, this soup can be frozen. Reheat from frozen in a covered bowl in the microwave, stir in cream and heat again, lifting cover and stirring once or twice (being careful to avoid the steam) until hot.

For information on garlic, see Garlic, pages 214 & 215.

Baked lima beans

PREP + COOK TIME 1 HOUR 20 MINUTES (PLUS STANDING AND REFRIGERATION TIME) **SERVES** 4

1½ cups (285g) dried lima beans

2 teaspoons olive oil

1 large brown onion (200g), chopped finely

2 cloves garlic, crushed

400g can crushed tomatoes

1 tablespoon tomato paste

2 tablespoons brown sugar

1½ cups (375g) vegetable stock

1 Place beans in medium bowl, cover with water; soak overnight, drain. Rinse under cold water; drain. Place beans in medium saucepan of boiling water; return to the boil. Reduce heat; simmer, covered, about 15 minutes or until beans are just tender. Drain.

2 Preheat oven to 200°C/180°C fan-forced.

3 Heat oil in large flameproof dish; cook onion and garlic, stirring, until onion softens. Add beans, undrained tomatoes, paste, sugar and stock; bring to the boil. Cook, uncovered, in oven about 40 minutes or until sauce thickens. Serve with grilled polenta.

NUTRITIONAL COUNT PER SERVING 4.2g total fat (0.7g saturated fat); 1250kJ (299 cal); 39.5g carbohydrate; 18.1g protein; 14.9g fibre

You could double the amount of lima beans and prepare them as described in step 1, and refrigerate, covered, for a day or two before serving them as an accompaniment to roasted mushrooms or as a dip. Puree the beans with lemon juice, olive oil, chopped flat-leaf parsley and salt and pepper and heat, covered, in the microwave then serve with mushrooms. If serving as a dip, sprinkle with smoked paprika. These baked beans are even better if made a day in advance, as this allows the flavours to develop.

1 CREAMY CHICKPEA AND
GARLIC SOUP
2 BAKED LIMA BEANS

Hummus

PREP + COOK TIME 25 MINUTES **MAKES** 2 CUPS

2 cups (500ml) water

2 x 300g cans chickpeas, rinsed, drained

¼ cup (60ml) lemon juice

¼ cup (60ml) olive oil

⅓ cup (80ml) tahini

3 cloves garlic, crushed

1 tablespoon olive oil, extra

1 Place the water and chickpeas in medium saucepan; bring to the boil. Boil, uncovered, about 10 minutes or until tender. Strain chickpeas over medium bowl; reserve 1 cup cooking liquid.

2 Blend or process chickpeas and reserved cooking liquid with juice, oil, tahini and garlic until just smooth.

3 Serve hummus drizzled with extra oil.

NUTRITIONAL COUNT PER ¼ CUP 13.9g total fat (1.9g saturated fat); 752kJ (180 cal); 7.2g carbohydrate; 5.2g protein; 3.8g fibre

Hummus can be served as a sauce with kebabs or meatballs or as a dip with pitta bread. It is classically served in a shallow dish, drizzled with extra oil and sometimes sprinkled with paprika. It is a staple throughout the Middle East; the Egyptian version includes a little cumin and may be decorated with sumac (see Spices, pages 562 & 563) or pomegranate seeds (see Pomegranate, page 436). Tahini is a sesame seed paste (see also Eggplant, page 161).

Pumpkins

Pumpkin is an obliging vegetable, ready to be baked with the roast or mashed to go with the sausages or chops, lend its warm sweetness to spicy Middle Eastern soups, meat or rice dishes, go in vegetable or meat curries, team with strong herbs such as sage or rosemary for stuffing ravioli or serving with gnocchi, or blend with other good ingredients for healthy cakes or traditional pumpkin scones. Pumpkins are available all year round.

1 JARRAHDALE
2 GOLDEN NUGGET
3 QUEENSLAND BLUE
4 JAP OR JAPANESE
5 BUTTERNUT

Pumpkin not only provides lots of plant fibre but the warm orange colour of the flesh shows that it is rich in alpha and beta carotene, substances that make Vitamin A, important for vision and bone growth, and are potent antioxidants and disease fighters.

JARRAHDALE is a large pumpkin with ribbed, firm but not hard skin and sweet orange flesh.

GOLDEN NUGGET is a small, round pumpkin whose easily cut skin, many seeds and mild-flavoured flesh make it ideal for hollowing out, stuffing and baking.

QUEENSLAND BLUE is a large variety with hard, deeply indented skin and dry, full-flavoured flesh.

JAP OR JAPANESE PUMPKIN, also known as the kent variety, is small with easily peeled, mottled green and yellow skin and sweeter flesh than most other varieties.

BUTTERNUT is a small, creamy beige pumpkin with thin, tender skin and nutty-sweet flesh.

HUBBARD is a full-flavoured, pear-shaped pumpkin recognisable by its hard, bumpy, dark-green skin.

BUTTER PUMPKIN has easily cut orange-pink skin and well-flavoured yellow flesh.

CROWN PRINCE is a large, hard-skinned blue-grey pumpkin with full-flavoured, deep orange flesh.

WINDSOR BLACK is large and flattish with almost-black green skin and well-flavoured flesh.

PREPARATION Tender-skinned pumpkins can be baked or roasted skin and all and served that way as the cooked skin has pleasant texture and flavour. Hard-shelled pumpkin such as queensland blue, hubbard and crown prince can also be cooked with the skin on and then the skin can be cut away more easily than when it was raw.

CHOOSING Whole pumpkins should be unblemished, heavy for their size and still have some stem attached as a seal against disease and insect invasion. Cut pumpkin should be bright-coloured, look moist but not wet and be free of soft spots or discolouration.

STORING Whole pumpkins store well in a well-ventilated place away from heat and sunlight for up to 2 months. Hard-skinned ones will often store for much longer than this; some old-timers say that storing in the open through winter improves pumpkins, making them sweeter. Once cut, remove the seeds, cover with plastic wrap and store in the refrigerator for up to a week.

✿ OTHER RECIPES USING PUMPKIN
Dhal with pumpkin and eggplant, p473

You may like to fry the capers and scatter them over as a garnish instead of adding them to the dressing. Rinse them and dry well by patting between sheets of absorbent paper; heat 1cm of oil in a small frying pan until it shimmers, then fry capers for about 2 minutes or until crisp but not too darkened. Drain on crumpled absorbent paper. You can do this an hour or so ahead of the salad.

For information on radicchio, see Greens, Salad, page 248; and for haloumi cheese, see Cheese, pages 104 & 105.

Pumpkin, radicchio and haloumi salad

PREP + COOK TIME 30 MINUTES **SERVES** 4

1kg piece pumpkin, cut into 12 wedges

180g haloumi cheese

¼ cup (60ml) lemon juice

2 tablespoons olive oil

1 tablespoon drained baby capers, rinsed

1 medium radicchio (200g), trimmed, leaves separated

½ cup firmly packed fresh flat-leaf parsley leaves

¼ cup (50g) roasted pepitas

1 Boil, steam or microwave pumpkin until tender; drain.

2 Cut cheese horizontally into four slices, cut each slice into four triangles.

3 Cook pumpkin and cheese, in batches, on heated oiled grill plate (or grill or barbecue) until browned.

4 Meanwhile, place juice, oil and capers in screw-top jar; shake well.

5 Place radicchio in large bowl with dressing and parsley; toss gently to combine. Divide salad among serving plates; top with pumpkin, cheese and pepitas.

NUTRITIONAL COUNT PER SERVING 22g total fat (6.8g saturated fat); 1363kJ (326 cal); 15.2g carbohydrate; 14.8g protein; 5.2g fibre

Spiced pumpkin soup with cinnamon cream

PREP + COOK TIME 30 MINUTES **SERVES** 4

1 tablespoon olive oil

1 medium brown onion (150g), chopped coarsely

1 clove garlic, crushed

2 teaspoons ground cumin

½ teaspoon ground coriander

1kg butternut pumpkin, chopped coarsely

2 medium potatoes (400g), chopped coarsely

2 cups (500ml) water

1½ cups (375ml) vegetable stock

5cm strip orange rind

CINNAMON CREAM

⅔ cup (160ml) cream

½ teaspoon ground cinnamon

1 Heat oil in large saucepan; cook onion and garlic, stirring, until onion softens. Add spices; cook, stirring, until fragrant. Add pumpkin, potato, the water, stock and rind; bring to the boil. Reduce heat; simmer, covered, 20 minutes or until vegetables are tender.

2 Meanwhile, make cinnamon cream.

3 Blend or process soup, in batches, until smooth. Return soup to same pan; stir over heat until heated through. Serve bowls of soup topped with cinnamon cream.

CINNAMON CREAM Beat ingredients in small bowl with electric mixer until soft peaks form.

NUTRITIONAL COUNT PER SERVING 23.2g total fat (12.9g saturated fat); 1530kJ (366 cal); 28.6g carbohydrate; 8.8g protein; 4.5g fibre

1 SPICED PUMPKIN SOUP
WITH CINNAMON CREAM
2 PUMPKIN AND SAGE RAVIOLI

Pumpkin and sage ravioli

PREP + COOK TIME 25 MINUTES **SERVES** 4

¼ cup (40g) pine nuts

2 teaspoons olive oil

3 cloves garlic, crushed

600g piece pumpkin,
cut into 1cm cubes

625g ricotta ravioli

300ml cream

¼ cup (20g) finely grated
parmesan cheese

2 tablespoons coarsely chopped
fresh sage

2 tablespoons lemon juice

*Look in the refrigerated
section or freezer cabinets
at the supermarket for
ricotta ravioli; if you can't
find them, use any other
mild-flavoured variety.*

*For information on sage,
see Herbs, page 266;
and for ravioli, see Pasta,
page 396.*

1 Cook nuts in large frying pan, stirring, until browned lightly; remove from pan.

2 Heat oil in same pan; cook garlic and pumpkin, covered, stirring occasionally,
about 10 minutes or until pumpkin is almost tender.

3 Meanwhile, cook ravioli in large saucepan of boiling water, uncovered, until
just tender; drain.

4 Add nuts, cream, cheese and sage to pumpkin mixture; bring to the boil.
Reduce heat; simmer, uncovered, 5 minutes. Add ravioli and juice; stir until hot.

NUTRITIONAL COUNT PER SERVING 51.7g total fat (26.7g saturated fat); 2826kJ (676 cal); 32.5g carbohydrate;
19.2g protein; 4.7g fibre

Quince

This cousin to the apple is always eaten cooked as it is too hard and acidic to be enjoyable raw. It takes long cooking, but its glorious scent and lovely musky flavour are worth it. Its flesh is cream when raw, but turns deep pink as it is cooked.

For quince snow to serve 4, peel, core and slice 2 large quinces and cook gently, covered, in ¼ cup water until very soft. This may take 20–30 minutes so check from time to time and add more water if necessary to keep a little moisture in the bottom of the saucepan so the fruit will not stick. When soft, drain off any remaining liquid and puree fruit with a stick blender or by rubbing it through a sieve. Beat 2 egg whites in a metal, glass or china bowl until soft peaks form, then gradually fold in ¼ cup caster sugar and the quince puree alternately. Taste and add more sugar if needed. Transfer to a serving bowl, cover and chill. Serve with cream or custard. You could use tart-flavoured apples instead of quinces.

Quinces are excellent simply sliced, poached and served with cream, or the slices can be used as a tart filling, served beside a panacotta or crème caramel, folded through a plain buttercake batter or pureed for the delicious old-fashioned dessert called a snow (recipe at left). They are also good served with pork, duck, or roasted quail or chicken. Middle Eastern cooks often pair quince with meat in a casserole and use it in stuffings and rice dishes. Quince's other great gift is that it is high in pectin (see Preserves, pages 464 & 465) so it makes excellent jam or jelly and is the best of all fruits to use for the stiff fruit paste that is a popular addition to cheeseboards. Quinces' season is from early autumn until midwinter and cold-stored fruit are often available for a further month or two.

PREPARATION Quinces are covered with rather sticky down so this should be rubbed off under running water. Cutting the hard fruit takes a heavy knife and great care to keep your fingers out of harm's way. The skin can be removed with a vegetable peeler or small serrated knife. Drop each piece into water with a little lemon juice added as the flesh discolours quickly in contact with air.

CHOOSING Quinces should be undamaged and hard. When ripe, they are golden, but if you are buying them for jam, jelly or quince paste, those which are still slightly unripe, indicated by sharp-yellow or greenish-yellow skins, are ideal as they are at their highest in pectin at this stage.

STORING Quinces will keep well at room temperature, in a single layer not touching each other, for weeks. Refrigerate only if you want to keep them for much longer, and only in a lidded plastic box or other airtight container or they will perfume other food.

QUINCE AND CHICKEN TAGINE [P 486]

Quince and chicken tagine

PREP + COOK TIME 2 HOURS 20 MINUTES **SERVES** 4

You can prepare this recipe up the point where the zucchini is added the day before serving.

For information on chicken, see Poultry, pages 456 & 457.

2 medium quinces (700g), peeled, cored, cut into wedges

40g butter

⅓ cup (115g) honey

3 cups (750ml) water

2 teaspoons orange flower water

2 teaspoons olive oil

4 chicken drumsticks (600g)

4 chicken thigh cutlets (800g), skin removed

1 large brown onion (200g), chopped coarsely

3 cloves garlic, crushed

1 teaspoon ground cumin

1 teaspoon ground ginger

pinch saffron threads

2 cups (500ml) chicken stock

2 large zucchini (300g), chopped coarsely

¼ cup coarsely chopped fresh coriander

1 Place quinces, butter, honey, the water and orange flower water in medium saucepan; bring to the boil. Reduce heat; simmer, covered, 1 hour, stirring occasionally. Uncover, cook, stirring occasionally, about 45 minutes or until quinces are red in colour.

2 Meanwhile, heat oil in large frying pan; cook chicken, in batches, until browned. Cook onion, garlic and spices in same pan, stirring, until onion softens. Add stock and chicken; bring to the boil. Reduce heat; simmer, covered, 20 minutes. Uncover; simmer, about 20 minutes or until chicken is cooked though. Add zucchini; cook, uncovered, about 10 minutes or until zucchini is tender. Stir in quinces and ½ cup of the quince syrup.

3 Serve tagine sprinkled with coriander, accompany with couscous.

NUTRITIONAL COUNT PER SERVING 32.1g total fat (12.2g saturated fat); 2763kJ (661 cal); 41.2g carbohydrate; 46.7g protein; 11.4g fibre

---

Quince jelly

PREP + COOK TIME 1 HOUR 40 MINUTES (PLUS STANDING TIME) **MAKES** ABOUT 5 CUPS

Scented and sharp-sweet, this is heaven on bread, toast or brioche, and is also a delicious condiment with rich meats, soft cheeses and a traditional accompaniment to game birds. For instructions on testing when jam is set and how to sterilise jars, see Preserves, page 465.

6 large quinces (2kg)

1.75 litres (7 cups) water

5 cups (1.1kg) white sugar

½ cup (125ml) lemon juice, strained

1 Chop unpeeled, uncored quinces coarsely. Place quince and the water in large saucepan, bring to the boil. Reduce heat; simmer, covered, 1 hour or until quince is soft.

2 Strain mixture through fine cloth; stand overnight. Allow liquid to drip through cloth slowly, do not squeeze cloth; discard pulp.

3 Measure quince liquid. Allow 1 cup of sugar for each cup of quince liquid.

4 Stir quince liquid and sugar in large saucepan over heat, without boiling, until sugar is dissolved. Stir in juice, bring to the boil; boil, uncovered, without stirring, about 25 minutes or until jelly sets when tested on a cold saucer. Pour into hot sterilised jars; seal while hot.

NUTRITIONAL COUNT PER TABLESPOON 0g total fat (0g saturated fat); 343kJ (82 cal); 20.9g carbohydrate; 0.1g protein; 1.7g fibre

Quince tarte tatin

PREP + COOK TIME 3 HOURS 20 MINUTES (PLUS REFRIGERATION TIME) **SERVES** 6

4 medium quinces (1.2kg)

1 cup (220g) caster sugar

1 litre (4 cups) water

¼ cup (60ml) orange juice

1 teaspoon finely grated orange rind

40g butter

PASTRY

1 cup (150g) plain flour

¼ cup (40g) icing sugar

100g butter, chopped

1 egg yolk

1 tablespoon cold water, approximately

1 Peel and core quinces; quarter lengthways.

2 Place quince in large saucepan with sugar, the water, juice and rind; bring to the boil. Reduce heat; simmer, covered, about 2½ hours or until quince is rosy in colour. Using slotted spoon, remove quinces from syrup; bring syrup to the boil. Boil, uncovered, until syrup reduces to ¾ cup. Stir in butter.

3 Meanwhile, make pastry.

4 Preheat oven to 200°C/180°C fan-forced. Line base of deep 22cm-round cake pan with baking paper.

5 Place quince, rounded-sides down, in pan; pour syrup over quince.

6 Roll pastry between sheets of baking paper until large enough to line base of pan. Lift pastry into pan, tucking pastry down side of pan.

7 Bake tart about 30 minutes or until pastry is browned lightly. Cool 5 minutes; turn tart onto serving plate, serve with vanilla ice-cream, if you like.

PASTRY Blend or process flour, sugar and butter until crumbly. Add egg yolk and enough of the water to make the ingredients just come together. Shape dough into ball, enclose in plastic wrap; refrigerate 30 minutes.

NUTRITIONAL COUNT PER SERVING 20.7g total fat (12.9g saturated fat); 2098kJ (502 cal); 77.5g carbohydrate; 4.1g protein; 11.3g fibre

Some people draw breath at the long cooking time for quinces, but the result is worth the wait, and you can always time-shift that part of the recipe — steps 1 and 2 in this one — to the day before if it suits you.

For information on pastry, see Pastry, pages 404 & 405.

Radishes

The pretty little red radish is the root of a plant related to horseradish, and its crisp and juicy white flesh has a touch of the pepperiness that is a family characteristic. It is best when young, with bulbs the size of a cherry tomato or smaller; more mature ones are hotter and may be tough.

For maximum crispness, soak either red radish or daikon in ice-water for an hour or two before using.

⚜ OTHER RECIPES
USING RADISHES
Age-dashi tofu, p603
Asian greens salad with
  sesame ginger dressing, p245
Fattoush, p70
Soba and daikon salad, p339

The simplest and, for many people, the best way to enjoy radishes is to hold them by their green tops and eat them whole with bread, butter and good cheddar. They also make an attractive addition to an antipasto tray or platter of crudités (raw vegetables) to be dipped into mayonnaise or another sauce, and a fresh, bright garnish for potato salad or cold meats.

RED RADISHES are at their best in spring but are available all year.

DAIKON or japanese radish, is the shape of a carrot but larger. It can be eaten raw or cooked like turnip in soups and stews. It is most frequently used, shredded, as an accompaniment to sashimi (thinly sliced raw fish). Ribbons and slices of daikon are used for garnishing and slices are often included in stir-fries.

PREPARATION For red radishes, remove the outside leaves from the green tops, leaving two or three inside ones for decoration and as a handle, and nip off the long tails. Wash radishes, drain on a clean cloth or teatowel, fill loosely into lidded plastic boxes and refrigerate.

For daikon, remove the green top, peel thinly with a vegetable peeler and shred or slice as recipe directs.

CHOOSING Radishes should have undamaged, fresh green tops. Red radish should have bulbs no bigger than a cherry tomato, daikon should have a sheen and be firm, smooth and evenly coloured.

STORING If red radishes are to be stored untrimmed, remove the coarsest outside leaves and enclose radishes loosely in a paper bag, then in a plastic bag, and refrigerate for up to 2 days before trimming as described above, then refrigerate in a closed container for up to 1 day. To store daikon, remove the whole top, wrap unpeeled vegetable tightly in plastic wrap and refrigerate for up to 3 days if it is to be eaten raw or up to 6 days if it is to be cooked.

Red radish

Radish and orange salad

PREP TIME 20 MINUTES (PLUS REFRIGERATION TIME) **SERVES** 4

10 trimmed medium red radishes (150g), sliced thinly

4 large oranges (1.2kg), segmented

1 small red onion (100g), sliced thinly

2 tablespoons coarsely chopped fresh flat-leaf parsley

2 tablespoons coarsely chopped fresh coriander

¼ cup (60ml) orange juice

1 Assemble radish, orange and onion on serving platter; sprinkle with parsley and coriander, drizzle with juice.

2 Cover salad; refrigerate 1 hour before serving.

NUTRITIONAL COUNT PER SERVING 0.3g total fat (0g saturated fat); 447kJ (107 cal); 20.1g carbohydrate; 3g protein; 5.2g fibre

This salad goes well with a lamb casserole or kebabs.

For information on oranges and segmenting oranges, see Oranges, page 382.

Pork steaks with radish and beetroot salad

PREP + COOK TIME 1 HOUR **SERVES** 4

300g baby beetroot

1 tablespoon caraway seeds

2 teaspoons olive oil

4 x 175g butterflied pork steaks

150g firm goats cheese, crumbled

5 red radishes (175g), trimmed, sliced thinly

125g baby rocket leaves

DIJON VINAIGRETTE

2 teaspoons dijon mustard

2 teaspoons olive oil

2 tablespoons red wine vinegar

1 Preheat oven to 200°C/180°C fan-forced.

2 Discard beetroot stems and leaves; place unpeeled beetroot in small shallow baking dish. Roast about 45 minutes or until beetroot is tender. Cool 10 minutes; peel, cut into quarters.

3 Meanwhile, place ingredients for dijon vinaigrette in screw-top jar; shake well.

4 Using mortar and pestle, crush seeds and oil into smooth paste; rub into pork. Cook pork on heated oiled grill plate (or grill or barbecue) until cooked as desired.

5 Place beetroot in large bowl with remaining ingredients and vinaigrette; toss gently to combine. Serve pork with salad.

NUTRITIONAL COUNT PER SERVING 23.5g total fat (8.7g saturated fat); 1804kJ (431 cal); 7.4g carbohydrate; 47.4g protein; 3.3g fibre

Kumara, potato or parsnip crisps would be great with this dish. Make them as for jerusalem artichoke crisps (page 272), but cut them about 5mm thick, bake 30 minutes or until crisp on the outside but tender in the centre; serve them hot.

For information on beetroot, see Beetroot, page 54; and for pork, see Pork, pages 440 & 441.

Daikon

Rhubarb

Rhubarb belongs to the same family as sorrel. Its ribbed pink or red stalks are always eaten cooked, which changes their tart and earthy flavour to refreshing sharpness and their crispness to tenderness. It is available all year but its true season is later winter into spring.

If you want rhubarb to fall to a puree, cook it without sugar until soft, then sweeten to taste with white or brown sugar — process for a completely smooth texture. For rhubarb that holds its shape, cover the pieces with sugar syrup in a microwave dish and microwave in short bursts, checking after each burst until tender but still shapely.

Very slender stems which have been forced (grown through a tube placed over the plant) are sometimes to be seen in late autumn/winter. Rhubarb contains a lot of moisture and will give much of this out as it cooks, so only a spoonful of water should be added with the sugar for cooking.

It has a special affinity with orange and ginger and is usually eaten in a sweet context — pies, tarts, muffins, strudels, cakes, ice-cream or a fool, but it can also be used for the savoury part of the meal, for example with sliced orange and watercress to serve with ham, pork or poultry, or combined with apple and ginger in a sweet/sharp jelly to serve with turkey, pork or duck.

PREPARATION Remove and discard all leaves as they are poisonous. Trim the root ends, wash stalks and, unless they are very young and tender, string them by running a vegetable peeler or small, sharp knife firmly from top to bottom down each rib. Cut into slices or lengths as directed.

CHOOSING Rhubarb stalks should be undamaged, firm and well coloured; the leaves should be fresh and firm or only slightly wilted.

STORING Remove leaves, halve stalks if necessary and enclose in a paper bag, then in a plastic bag and store in the refrigerator for up to a week. Cooked rhubarb can be stored in a covered container in the refrigerator for a week.

Persian lamb and rhubarb stew

PREP + COOK TIME 2 HOURS 30 MINUTES **SERVES** 4

40g butter

1kg diced lamb

1 medium brown onion (150g), sliced thinly

¼ teaspoon saffron threads

½ teaspoon ground cinnamon

¼ teaspoon ground turmeric

1 cup (250ml) water

2 cups (500ml) chicken stock

2 tablespoons tomato paste

2¾ cups (300g) coarsely chopped rhubarb

¼ cup finely chopped fresh mint

Be sure to buy ripe rhubarb that is a rich red — greenish stems will make the stew too tart. If you can't find fresh rhubarb, you can use frozen instead.

For information on lamb, see Lamb, pages 282 & 283.

1 Melt half of the butter in large deep saucepan; cook lamb, in batches, until browned.
2 Melt remaining butter in same pan; cook onion, stirring, until soft. Add spices; cook, stirring, until fragrant. Add the water, stock and paste; bring to the boil. Return lamb to pan, reduce heat; simmer, covered, 1 hour 20 minutes, stirring occasionally.
3 Uncover; simmer about 20 minutes or until lamb is tender. Add rhubarb to lamb mixture; simmer, uncovered, about 10 minutes or until rhubarb has softened.
4 Stir mint into stew off the heat; serve stew over couscous.

NUTRITIONAL COUNT PER SERVING 17.8g total fat (9.7g saturated fat); 1705kJ (408 cal); 5g carbohydrate; 55.2g protein; 3g fibre

Rhubarb, white chocolate and ginger trifles

PREP + COOK TIME 30 MINUTES (PLUS REFRIGERATION TIME) **SERVES** 6

2 cups (220g) coarsely chopped rhubarb

2 tablespoons caster sugar

1 teaspoon finely grated orange rind

1 tablespoon orange juice

1 tablespoon finely chopped glacé ginger

12 gingernut biscuits (125g), chopped coarsely

1 cup (250ml) orange juice, extra

1 medium orange (240g), segmented

WHITE CHOCOLATE CREAM

½ cup (125ml) cream

180g white eating chocolate, chopped coarsely

You will need about 4 large stems of rhubarb for this recipe. For details on segmenting oranges, see Oranges page 382.

For information on glacé ginger see Fruit, Glacé, pages 198 & 199; and for white eating chocolate, see Chocolate, page 125.

1 Make white chocolate cream.
2 Bring rhubarb, sugar, rind and juice to the boil in small saucepan. Reduce heat; simmer, uncovered, stirring occasionally, about 5 minutes or until rhubarb softens. Cool; stir in ginger.
3 Divide rhubarb mixture among six ⅔ cup (160ml) glasses; top with combined biscuits and extra juice, then white chocolate cream and orange segments.

WHITE CHOCOLATE CREAM Stir cream and chocolate in small heatproof bowl over small saucepan of simmering water until smooth. Refrigerate 30 minutes or until spreadable. Beat chocolate mixture with electric mixer until firm peaks form.

NUTRITIONAL COUNT PER SERVING 21.9g total fat (13.5g saturated fat); 1693kJ (405 cal); 46.4g carbohydrate; 4.6g protein; 2.3g fibre

You will need 5 large stems of rhubarb for this recipe. The muffins can be stored in an airtight container for up to 2 days.

Rhubarb and custard muffins

PREP + COOK TIME 50 MINUTES **MAKES** 12

2 cups (300g) self-raising flour
½ cup (75g) plain flour
¾ cup (165g) caster sugar
100g butter, melted
1 cup (250ml) milk
1 egg
3 cups (330g) finely chopped rhubarb
1 tablespoon demerara sugar

CUSTARD
2 tablespoons custard powder
¼ cup (55g) caster sugar
1 cup (250ml) milk
1 teaspoon vanilla extract

1 Make custard.

2 Preheat oven to 200°C/180°C fan-forced. Line 12-hole (⅓-cup/80ml) muffin pan with paper cases.

3 Sift flours and caster sugar into large bowl. Stir in the combined butter, milk and egg. Do not over-mix; mixture should be lumpy. Stir in half the rhubarb.

4 Divide half the mixture between paper cases; top with custard. Divide remaining mixture over custard. Sprinkle with remaining rhubarb and demerara sugar.

5 Bake about 25 minutes. Stand muffins 5 minutes before turning, top-side up, onto wire rack to cool. Serve lightly dusted with sifted icing sugar.

CUSTARD Combine custard powder and sugar in small saucepan; gradually stir in milk. Stir mixture over medium heat until custard boils and thickens. Stir in extract; cool.

NUTRITIONAL COUNT PER MUFFIN 9.3g total fat (5.8g saturated fat); 1233kJ (295 cal); 45.7g carbohydrate; 5.7g protein; 1.9g fibre

For orange-flavoured mascarpone, stir together 1 cup of room-temperature mascarpone cheese, 2 teaspoons finely grated orange rind, 2 teaspoons orange juice, 2 teaspoons orange-flavoured liqueur and 1 tablespoon icing sugar. Dollop on to the warm fruit.

For information on dried cranberries, see Fruit, Dried, page 192.

Roasted rhubarb and cranberries

PREP + COOK TIME 25 MINUTES **SERVES** 4

1kg rhubarb, trimmed, chopped coarsely
¼ cup (35g) dried cranberries
¼ cup (55g) brown sugar
1 tablespoon orange juice

1 Preheat oven to 180°C/160°C fan-forced.

2 Combine ingredients in medium shallow baking dish. Roast, uncovered, 20 minutes or until rhubarb is just tender.

3 Serve rhubarb topped with orange-flavoured mascarpone.

NUTRITIONAL COUNT PER SERVING 0.6g total fat (0g saturated fat); 568kJ (136 cal); 24.2g carbohydrate; 4g protein; 8.4g fibre

RHUBARB AND CUSTARD MUFFINS

Rice

Rice is not a single ingredient but a family of ingredients that differ from each other in appearance and in how they perform when cooked. The rice that makes a good rice pudding won't make a good pilaf, and pilaf rice won't make a good risotto, and so on. There are some versatile varieties that can give satisfactory results for more than one kind of dish, see below.

1 BROWN
2 SUSHI
3 SHORT-GRAIN
4 BLACK
5 CALASPARRA
6 MEDIUM-GRAIN
7 GLUTINOUS
8 JASMINE
9 WILD
10 BASMATI
11 CARNAROLI
12 ARBORIO
13 LONG-GRAIN

Most of the rice eaten round the world is white (polished) rice, which has been hulled and had its outer bran layer removed. It is tender and easily digested. Rice that has been hulled but still has the bran layer intact is brown rice. It has a nutty taste and a chewy texture; brown rice takes longer to cook than white, is rather more filling and is more nutritious because the bran layer is rich in B vitamins and dietary fibre.

All rice is short-grain, medium-grain or long-grain, and within these three types there are many variations.

SHORT-GRAIN RICE has round, fat grains which cook to a soft, moist texture and cling together, perfect for puddings and a good food for babies before they get teeth.

MEDIUM-GRAIN RICE has rounded grains that are a little longer than they are fat. It is slightly clingy and is ideal for rice croquettes and moulds, and also for eating with chopsticks.

LONG-GRAIN RICE has long, thin grains and cooks to give the separate, fluffy grains required for rice as an accompaniment and for pilafs, salads, stuffings and most savoury dishes.

Some rices are borderline medium/short types and may be labelled by either description. If you want short but can't find it, used medium. If you need medium but can't find it, use long for croquettes and moulds, and short for puddings.

SPECIFIC VARIETIES

BASMATI is a fragrant long-grain white rice with a warm, nutty aroma, which cooks to firm, separate, dry grains.

JASMINE is a fragrant long-grain white rice with a delicate floral aroma; it is softer than basmati and, when cooked, its grains are slightly sticky.

CALROSE is the brand-name of an Australian medium-grain white rice that has been developed to serve as an all-purpose rice, as it gives different results according to how it is cooked — separate and fluffy after short cooking and rinsing, moist and easily compacted after longer cooking without rinsing. Calrose brown rice is also available.

ARBORIO, **CARNAROLI** and **VIALONE NANO** are risotto rices: medium-grain varieties whose special quality is that they can absorb liquid and stand up to long cooking and stirring without becoming soft and mushy, while at the same time they release just enough starch to give creaminess. Arborio, which is the best known and the least expensive, has large, plump grains which are classified as superfino (a classification according to size and shape, not quality). Carnaroli also has large, plump grains and is superfino, and is the aristocrat of risotto rices because of its especially fine flavour and texture. Vialone nano is a stubbier grain classified

Leftover long-grain rice that has been stored in the refrigerator is perfect for fried rice. Spread it on paper towels, cover with others and pat gently to make sure it is quite dry. If making fried rice from scratch, cook the rice a day ahead, drain it if necessary, spread it on a tray lined with baking paper or greaseproof paper, cover with paper towels and refrigerate overnight.

as semifino and is especially good for making Venetian-style risotto which should be loose enough to be all'onda or like a wave. Risotto rices are also good for paella.

CALASPARRA is a short-grain Spanish rice suited to making paella as it can absorb 2½ to 3 times its own volume of liquid.

GLUTINOUS RICE, also called sticky rice, is short-grain Asian rice which cooks to a very sticky, clinging consistency. It is used mainly for desserts and rice cakes.

BLACK RICE is a variety of glutinous rice, black-brown when raw and deep purple when cooked.

KOSHIHIKARI and **NISHIKI** are sushi rices: short-grain varieties that are moist and tender when cooked, but still firm and clingy enough to be picked up with chopsticks.

WILD RICE is not a true rice but the seed of an aquatic grass. Dark and elegantly long, it is often mixed with white rice to add a distinctive nutty taste, chewy texture and colour contrast. It takes longer to cook than white rice, so must be par-cooked before the white rice is added.

PARBOILED RICE Also called converted rice, this is made by steeping rice, still in the husk, in water, then steaming it in huge pressure-cookers. This drives the B-group vitamins and the golden-brown pigments from the outer bran layers into the interior of the grain. When it is milled to remove the husks and bran, the rice is pale gold and retains its nutritional value. It is firmer and less clingy than white rice when cooked.

CHOOSING
Buy rice in quantities that you expect to use within a month or two.

STORING
Store all rice airtight in a cool, dry place. Store cooked rice in a covered container in the refrigerator and use within a week.

TO COOK RICE

There are three methods of cooking rice on the stovetop. One is to boil it in lots of water, which makes it very easy to keep the grains separate but does mean you throw away some of the rice flavour with the cooking water. The second and third methods cook by absorption and give rice with all the flavour retained; some people prefer one of these methods, some the other — try both, using the same saucepan, and see which you like better. Rice can also be cooked in automatic rice cookers; they make it very easy and most Asian cooks and some Western ones swear by them, but some cooks find the results a little clumpy (the way Asians like it for eating with chopsticks).

BOILED RICE

Bring a large saucepan of lightly salted water to a rolling boil, slowly sprinkle in the rice through your fingers, then cook, uncovered, keeping the water at a brisk boil. Start testing after 10 minutes by lifting out a few grains on a fork and biting. The rice should be tender but firm in the centre, not mushy. Drain and run hot water through to separate the grains.

ABSORPTION METHODS

1 Rinse the rice in a sieve in several changes of cold water, rubbing it with your fingers to help dislodge surface starch. Measure into a wide saucepan with a really tight-fitting lid twice as much water, by volume, as the amount of rice you want to cook, salt lightly, cover and bring to a brisk boil over high heat. Uncover and slowly sprinkle in the rice, keeping the heat high so that the water does not go off the boil. Stir once, then cover again and turn the heat very low, using a heat-spreading mat if necessary. Cook for 10 minutes without lifting the lid, then remove from heat, stand with the lid on for at least 10 minutes, then uncover and fluff up with a fork.

2 Rinse the rice as above, place in a wide saucepan with a really tight-fitting lid, add a pinch of salt and cold water to cover, and shake the pan gently from side to side to level the surface. Place the tip of your forefinger in the surface of the rice and add more cold water until it comes up to your first finger joint (this applies no matter what quantity you are cooking). Bring to the boil, uncovered, and cook until the water evaporates, leaving steam holes in the rice, then cover and turn the heat very low, using a heat-spreading mat if necessary. Cook for 10 minutes; don't lift the lid until the last minute or two of cooking, then quickly remove a few grains of rice to test and replace the lid immediately. The rice should be tender but firm in the centre, not mushy; leave a few minutes more if it is not ready, and test again. When cooked, remove from the heat, stand for 10 minutes without lifting the lid, then uncover and fluff up with a fork.

⚜ OTHER RECIPES USING RICE
Avocado and wasabi rice salad, p642
Black grape, chicken and wild rice salad, p240
California handrolls, p543
Capsicums stuffed with pilaf, p86–7
Pork and cabbage rolls, p80
Thai salmon broth with sesame sticky rice patties, p628
Tofu zucchini patties, p603
Tuna cucumber mini-maki, p543
Wild mushroom risotto, p326

Chicken, pea and broad bean risotto

PREP + COOK TIME 55 MINUTES **SERVES** 4

1 litre (4 cups) chicken stock

1 cup (250ml) water

50g butter

600g chicken tenderloins, sliced thickly

4 green onions, sliced thinly

1 clove garlic, crushed

1½ cups (300g) arborio rice

1 cup (150g) frozen broad beans, thawed

1 cup (120g) frozen peas, thawed

1 cup (80g) finely grated parmesan cheese

1 tablespoon finely chopped fresh mint

You can use fresh broad beans in season, but shell them first, blanch in boiling water until just tender, and pop the bright green beans from their leathery overcoats while they are still warm.

For information on chicken, see Poultry, pages 456 & 457; for broad beans, see Beans, Fresh, page 40 & 41; and for fresh and frozen peas, see Peas, pages 422 & 424.

1 Place stock and the water in medium saucepan; bring to the boil. Reduce heat; simmer, covered.

2 Heat half of the butter in large saucepan; cook chicken, in batches, until just browned.

3 Heat remaining butter in same pan; cook onion and garlic, stirring, until soft. Add rice; stir to coat in onion mixture. Add ½ cup of the simmering stock mixture; cook, stirring, over low heat until stock is absorbed. Continue adding stock, in ½-cup batches, stirring, until stock is absorbed after each addition. Return chicken to pan halfway through cooking time. Total cooking time should be about 35 minutes or until rice is tender.

4 Meanwhile, pour boiling water over beans; stand 2 minutes. Drain; peel away grey-coloured outer shells.

5 Add peas and beans to risotto, stir gently until hot. Remove from heat; stir in cheese and mint. Serve immediately.

NUTRITIONAL COUNT PER SERVING 24.7g total fat (13.3g saturated fat); 2951 kJ (706 cal); 67.3g carbohydrate; 50.5g protein; 5.9g fibre

Nasi goreng

PREP + COOK TIME 40 MINUTES **SERVES** 4

720g cooked medium king prawns

1 tablespoon peanut oil

175g dried chinese sausages, sliced thickly

1 medium brown onion (150g), sliced thinly

1 medium red capsicum (200g), sliced thinly

2 fresh long red chillies, sliced

2 cloves garlic, crushed

2cm piece fresh ginger (10g), grated

1 teaspoon shrimp paste

4 cups (600g) cold cooked white long-grain rice

2 tablespoons kecap manis

1 tablespoon light soy sauce

4 green onions, sliced thinly

1 tablespoon peanut oil, extra

4 eggs

1 Shell and devein prawns.

2 Heat half the oil in wok; stir-fry sausage, in batches, until browned.

3 Heat remaining oil in wok; stir-fry onion, capsicum, chilli, garlic, ginger and paste, until vegetables soften. Add prawns and rice; stir-fry 2 minutes. Return sausage to wok with sauces and half the green onion; stir-fry until combined.

4 Heat extra oil in large frying pan; fry eggs, one side only, until just set. Divide nasi goreng among serving plates, top each with an egg; sprinkle with remaining green onion.

NUTRITIONAL COUNT PER SERVING 25.7g total fat (7.4g saturated fat); 2730kJ (653 cal); 48.5g carbohydrate; 54.7g protein; 3.3g fibre

Nasi goreng translates simply as "fried rice" and was first created as a way to use up leftovers. You need to cook 2 cups (400g) of raw rice to obtain the amount of cooked rice needed. Spread it on to an oiled tray and refrigerate, covered, overnight.

For information on dried chinese sausages (lap cheong), see Sausages, page 516.

Sushi rice

PREP + COOK TIME 25 MINUTES (PLUS STANDING TIME) **MAKES** 2 CUPS

1 cup (200g) koshihikari rice

1 cup (250ml) water

SUSHI VINEGAR

2 tablespoons rice vinegar

1 tablespoon sugar

¼ teaspoon salt

1 Place rice in large bowl, fill with cold water. Stir; drain. Repeat process until water is almost clear. Drain rice in strainer 30 minutes.

2 Meanwhile, stir ingredients for sushi vinegar in small bowl until sugar dissolves.

3 Place rice and the water in medium saucepan, cover; bring to the boil. Reduce heat; simmer, covered tightly, on low heat 12 minutes or until water is absorbed. Remove from heat; stand rice, covered, 10 minutes.

4 Place rice in large non-metallic bowl. Using large flat wooden spoon, slice through rice at sharp angles to break up lumps and separate grains. Gradually add sushi vinegar; lift and turn rice with spoon, from outside to centre of bowl, 5 minutes or until rice is almost cool.

NUTRITIONAL COUNT PER 1 CUP 0.5g total fat (0.1g saturated fat); 1622kJ (388 cal); 87.5g carbohydrate; 6.6g protein; 0.8g fibre

*Not all the sushi vinegar may be required in this recipe; the rice should not be wet. Sushi rice can be made up to 4 hours ahead. Cover; refrigerate until required.
When making sushi, cover the unused portion of rice with a damp cloth until needed. For sushi recipes, see page 543.*

NASI GORENG

The word paella, like the word casserole, means both the food and the vessel in which it is cooked. A paella pan is a large, heavy, wide and shallow steel pan with two handles, but paella can be made successfully in any frying pan large enough to hold all the ingredients. It can be made with seafood, as in this recipe, or meat such as chicken or game; the Valencian version uses rabbit and snails. Paella is served in the cooking pan with the seafood or meat arranged decoratively on top of the rice.

For information on blue swimmer crab, mussels, prawns and squid, see Seafood, pages 524, 526 & 527.

Seafood paella

PREP + COOK TIME 1 HOUR 45 MINUTES **SERVES** 4

8 uncooked large king prawns (560g)

500g small black mussels

600g squid hoods, cleaned

1 uncooked blue swimmer crab (325g)

1 tablespoon olive oil

6 green onions, chopped coarsely

2 cloves garlic, crushed

1 fresh long red chilli, chopped finely

1 medium yellow capsicum (200g), chopped coarsely

2 cups (400g) brown rice

pinch saffron threads

1 cup (250ml) dry white wine

4 medium tomatoes (600g), chopped coarsely

1 tablespoon tomato paste

1 litre (4 cups) chicken stock

1 Shell and devein prawns, leaving tails intact. Scrub mussels; remove beards. Cut squid down centre to open out; score inside in diagonal pattern then cut into thick strips.

2 To prepare crab, lift tail flap then, with a peeling motion, lift off the back shell. Remove and discard whitish gills, liver and brain matter. Rinse crab well; cut crab body in quarters.

3 Heat oil in large deep frying pan; cook onion, garlic, chilli and capsicum, stirring, until onion softens. Add rice and saffron; stir to coat in onion mixture. Stir in wine, tomato and paste. Cook, stirring, until wine has almost evaporated.

4 Add 1 cup of stock; cook, stirring, until absorbed. Add remaining stock; cook, covered, stirring occasionally, about 1 hour or until rice is tender.

5 Uncover rice; place seafood on top of the rice (do not stir to combine). Cover pan; simmer about 5 minutes or until seafood has changed in colour and mussels have opened (discard any that do not).

NUTRITIONAL COUNT PER SERVING 10g total fat (2.1g saturated fat); 2759kJ (660 cal); 85.4g carbohydrate; 43.2g protein; 5.4g fibre

For information on lamb, see Lamb, pages 282 & 283.

Lamb biryani

PREP + COOK TIME 2 HOURS 35 MINUTES (PLUS REFRIGERATION TIME) **SERVES** 4

1kg lamb shoulder, cut into 3cm pieces

3cm piece fresh ginger (15g), grated

2 cloves garlic, crushed

2 fresh small red thai chillies, chopped finely

2 teaspoons garam masala

1 tablespoon finely chopped fresh coriander

¼ teaspoon ground turmeric

½ cup (140g) yogurt

2 tablespoons ghee

½ cup (40g) flaked almonds

¼ cup (40g) sultanas

2 medium brown onions (300g), sliced thickly

½ cup (125ml) water

pinch saffron threads

1 tablespoon hot milk

1 ½ cups (300g) basmati rice

¼ cup firmly packed fresh coriander leaves

SEAFOOD PAELLA

1   Combine lamb, ginger, garlic, chilli, garam masala, chopped coriander, turmeric and yogurt in medium bowl, cover; refrigerate overnight.

2   Heat half the ghee in large saucepan; cook nuts and sultanas, stirring, until nuts brown lightly. Remove from pan.

3   Heat remaining ghee in same pan; cook onion, covered, 5 minutes. Uncover; cook, stirring occasionally, about 5 minutes or until browned lightly. Reserve half of the onion.

4   Add lamb mixture to pan; cook, stirring, until browned. Add the water; bring to the boil. Reduce heat; simmer, covered, 1 hour. Uncover; simmer about 30 minutes or until lamb is tender and sauce is thickened.

5   Meanwhile, combine saffron and milk in small bowl; stand 15 minutes. Cook rice in medium saucepan of boiling water, uncovered, 5 minutes; drain.

6   Preheat oven to 180°C/160°C fan-forced.

7   Spread half the lamb mixture into oiled deep 2-litre (8-cup) ovenproof dish. Layer with half the rice; top with remaining lamb mixture then remaining rice. Drizzle milk mixture over rice; cover tightly with greased foil and lid. Bake 30 minutes or until rice is tender.

8   Serve biryani topped with reserved onion, nut and sultana mixture and coriander leaves.

NUTRITIONAL COUNT PER SERVING 38.6g total fat (17.4g saturated fat); 3703kJ (886 cal); 73.8g carbohydrate; 58.7g protein; 3.4g fibre

Biryani can be prepared up to two days ahead, except for final reheating and garnishing, and stored in its presentation dish, covered, in the refrigerator. Serve it with raita, if you wish, and with chutneys, sambals and pappadums.

Smoked ocean trout kedgeree

PREP + COOK TIME 30 MINUTES **SERVES** 4

2 tablespoons olive oil

1 large brown onion (200g), sliced thinly

1 tablespoon brown sugar

2 tablespoons malt vinegar

4 green onions, cut into 3cm lengths

2 cloves garlic, crushed

2 teaspoons mild curry powder

4 cups (600g) cooked white medium-grain rice

600g smoked ocean trout fillets, skinned, flaked

1 cup (120g) frozen peas

1 tablespoon lemon juice

¼ cup finely chopped fresh flat-leaf parsley

4 hard-boiled eggs, quartered

This is a luxury version of an Anglo-Indian dish from the days of the Raj. The British make it with smoked haddock and without the peas and garlic and eat it for breakfast, but with smoked trout it can be happily served for lunch or dinner.

For information on trout, see Seafood, page 523.

1 Heat half the oil in large frying pan; cook brown onion, stirring, until soft. Add sugar and vinegar; cook, stirring, about 5 minutes or until onion is browned and caramelised. Transfer to small bowl.

2 Heat remaining oil in same pan; cook green onion, garlic and curry powder, stirring, about 3 minutes or until fragrant.

3 Return caramelised onion to pan with rice, fish, peas and juice; stir until heated through. Remove from heat; stir in parsley. Serve kedgeree topped with boiled egg.

NUTRITIONAL COUNT PER SERVING 20.7g total fat (4.3g saturated fat); 2391kJ (572 cal); 51.3g carbohydrate; 42.1g protein; 4.6g fibre

---

Creamed rice

PREP + COOK TIME 55 MINUTES **SERVES** 4

1 litre (4 cups) milk

⅓ cup (75g) caster sugar

1 teaspoon vanilla extract

½ cup (100g) uncooked white medium-grain rice

For sultana rice, add ½ cup sultanas after adding the rice. Rice desserts will keep, covered, in the refrigerator for 2 days.

1 Bring milk, sugar and extract in large saucepan to the boil. Gradually add rice to boiling milk. Reduce heat; simmer, covered, stirring occasionally, about 50 minutes or until rice is tender and milk is almost absorbed.

2 Serve creamed rice warm or cold, with fresh berries, if you like.

NUTRITIONAL COUNT PER SERVING 9.9g total fat (6.5g saturated fat); 1400kJ (335 cal); 50.6g carbohydrate; 10.1g protein; 0.2g fibre

SMOKED OCEAN TROUT KEDGEREE

Salt

Invaluable as it is for seasoning food to make it taste good, that is only the beginning of salt's usefulness to the human race. Its great role as a preservative was a necessity before we had refrigerators and freezers and is still appreciated when we enjoy ham, bacon, cheese, salami, smoked salmon and other fish, pickles, corned beef, olives, sauerkraut or the breakfast sausages.

The degree to which saltiness can be tasted varies greatly from person to person and also according to age in the same person. Most young adults can detect saltiness in a solution of 1 teaspoon salt in 10 litres of water, while people over 60 can generally detect it only at double that amount of salt.

❧ OTHER RECIPES USING SALT
Salt and pepper squid, p536
Salt and pepper tofu with chilli lime dressing, p604
Sweet potato crisps with chilli salt, p590

Pink sea salt

Saltiness is a basic taste that we are equipped to detect by some of the taste buds in our mouth (mostly on the front of the tongue). Although how much salt is too much is clearly a matter for concern in relation to blood pressure and heart disease, some is essential for the functioning of our bodies. Pure salt is sodium chloride. All salt came, originally, from the sea; depending on how and where it was procured, it may have varying impurities, some of which are undesirable, but others desirable because they make subtle flavour differences which are prized by interested palates. From the cook's point of view, the question is which salt to use.

ROCK SALT is mined from underground salt seams left from seawater which was trapped in the earth's ancient upheavals. Most is now mined by pumping water into the salt deposits to dissolve them, then pumping it out again and evaporating it to leave the salt behind. Rock salt may be whitish, black, grey, pink, yellow or blue, depending on what other mineral traces were in the water or the surrounding rock. Much of it is refined and ground to make table and cooking salt, but some is left in large, hard crystals for industrial use and de-icing roads in cold regions. At retail level, the term rock salt has come to denote the size of the crystals rather than their origin — as often as not, the large-

crystal sold as rock salt for packing round ice-cream freezers, using as a bed on which to bake potatoes or serve oysters, or filling salt grinders to use at the table, is sea salt. There is no inherent flavour benefit in grinding salt freshly as it is not like pepper in having volatile aromatics which are best fresh, but large crystals do indicate that the salt has not been over-refined nor had additives introduced.

SEA SALT is obtained by evaporating seawater, either gradually by drawing it into large, shallow pans and leaving it to be evaporated by the sun, or quickly in vacuum chambers. Sun-evaporated salt forms in flakes, vacuum-evaporated salt in fine grains. Both kinds can be rolled or crushed to make various particle sizes and shapes. Unrefined sea salt is the choice of most chefs because its complex composition gives it fuller flavour without the underlying bitterness that some palates detect in pure, refined sodium chloride.

KITCHEN or **COMMON SALT** has, traditionally, been refined to suit the popular demand that salt should look pure. It is usually coarser than table salt. Today, some sea salt is marketed as cooking or kitchen salt, though inspection of the package may show that it has undergone some processing to make it "brilliant white" and that it contains anti-caking agent. Common salt is useful for cleaning — for instance, to scrub and deodorise cutting boards.

TABLE SALT has also been refined to make it pure white and has been ground to very fine grains so that it will dissolve more or less instantly when sprinkled on food. Standard table salt also contains additives such as aluminium, magnesium and silicone compounds to ensure that it is free-running even in humid conditions. Iodised table salt has had potassium iodide added to prevent iodine deficiency, which causes physical and mental impairment, especially in children, and can occur in regions where the soil, and therefore crops and animals grown in or on it, has insufficient iodine to provide the necessary level in people who live there.

COLOURED SALTS Unrefined salts may be white or various other colours because of the other minerals or sediments in the water from which they came. Some of the most prized are French gris tradition, a coarse, dark, damp salt; salt from Trapani in Sicily, which is white and slightly damp, with grains about the same size as ordinary sugar; and English Maldon sea salt which is in brittle white flakes. Australia's pink Murray River salt, in small flakes, is not only admired by chefs but its harvesting is assisting in the control of the country's serious inland salinity problem. One of the most expensive salts is French fleur de sel (flower of salt), which consists of the delicate white crystals that accumulate on the surface of the sea-salt pans of west-central France when the humidity and breezes are right; they are gently raked off before they can fall down to where the ordinary grey salt is formed.

FLAVOURED SALTS such as garlic, onion and celery are made by adding dried and ground seeds (celery) or dehydrated granules of flesh (garlic and onion) to plain salt.

COARSE SEA SALT is preferred by many chefs because it is easy to dispense by hand; it also resists caking and is the right consistency for salt crusts on meat or fish. Kosher salt, used for the preparation of meat according to Jewish dietary laws, comes in coarse particles or flakes. It is sprinkled on the freshly butchered meat to draw out blood; because it is meant to draw out impurities, it must itself be free of additives. Many cooks use kosher salt for this reason and because it is easy to dispense by hand. Coarse salt is also required for curing meat or fish by dry-salting (rubbing and covering it repeatedly with salt over a period of days or weeks) because it is important that the exchange of salt and moisture from the meat be gradual, and fine salt would mop up the moisture too fast.

STORING
All salt should be stored in airtight containers. Even so, it may cake in humid conditions; an envelope of moisture-absorbing granules such as is often packed in bottles of pills or a little raw rice may help.

Sea salt

Rock salt

Pink sea salt

Whole fish in a salt crust

PREP + COOK TIME 45 MINUTES **SERVES** 8

2 x 1kg whole snapper, cleaned, scales left on

3kg coarse cooking salt, approximately

GREMOLATA

½ cup finely chopped fresh flat-leaf parsley

2 cloves garlic, crushed

1 tablespoon finely grated lemon rind

2 tablespoons extra virgin olive oil

1 Preheat oven to 240°C/220°C fan-forced.

2 Combine ingredients for gremolata in small bowl.

3 Wash fish, pat dry inside and out. Fill cavities of fish with half the gremolata.

4 Divide half the salt between two ovenproof trays large enough to hold fish. Place fish on salt. Place remaining salt in large sieve or colander and run quickly under cold water until salt is damp. Press salt firmly over fish to completely cover fish.

5 Bake fish 35 minutes. Remove fish from oven; stand 5 minutes.

6 Using a hammer or meat mallet and old knife, break open the crust then lift away with the scales and skin. Serve fish with remaining gremolata.

NUTRITIONAL COUNT PER SERVING 5.8g total fat (1.2g saturated fat); 531kJ (127 cal); 0.1g carbohydrate; 18.4g protein; 0.3g fibre

This great show-off dish delivers perfectly cooked, moist and fragrant flesh. The scales and skin come away with the crust. Measure your oven and baking tray before you buy the fish to make sure they will fit. You can use any whole fish weighing about 1kg each. Coarse sea salt is available from health food stores or supermarkets. Rock salt will not work as it will not meld into a crust.

For information on snapper, see Seafood, page 522.

Salt-cured gravlax

PREP TIME 10 MINUTES (PLUS REFRIGERATION TIME) **MAKES** 24

1 tablespoon sea salt

1 teaspoon finely ground black pepper

1 tablespoon sugar

1 tablespoon vodka

300g salmon fillet, skin on

24 mini toasts

SOUR CREAM SAUCE

⅓ cup (80g) sour cream

2 teaspoons drained baby capers, rinsed

2 teaspoons lemon juice

2 teaspoons finely chopped drained cornichons

½ small red onion (50g), chopped finely

1 Combine salt, pepper, sugar and vodka in small bowl.

2 Remove bones from fish; place fish, skin-side down, on piece of plastic wrap. Spread salt mixture over flesh side of fish; enclose securely in plastic wrap. Refrigerate overnight, turning parcel several times.

3 Combine ingredients for sour cream sauce in small bowl.

4 Slice fish thinly; spread sauce on toasts, top with fish.

NUTRITIONAL COUNT PER PIECE 9.2g total fat (4.3g saturated fat); 886kJ (212 cal); 17.8g carbohydrate; 12.3g protein; 1g fibre

Gravlax, meaning buried salmon, is a traditional Scandinavian way of preserving fish by covering with salt and, usually, fresh dill and burying it in the snow-covered ground for days or weeks to cure. Modern refrigeration has largely replaced this practice and the flavourings may vary and curing time be as little as 12 hours, so that the flesh is still firm and the taste given only a slightly soured edge by fermentation.

For information on salmon, see Seafood, page 523.

1 WHOLE FISH IN A SALT
CRUST
2 SALT-CURED GRAVLAX

Deep-fried potato crisps with smoky paprika salt

PREP + COOK TIME 30 MINUTES (PLUS STANDING TIME) **SERVES** 8

1kg potatoes, peeled

vegetable oil, for deep-frying

SMOKY PAPRIKA SALT

½ teaspoon smoked paprika

2 teaspoons sea salt flakes

½ teaspoon freshly ground black pepper

pinch cayenne pepper

Your own flavoursome, crunchy potato crisps are better than bought ones. You can use bintje, spunta or russet burbank potatoes.

For information on potatoes, see Potatoes, page 448.

1 Using sharp knife, mandoline or V-slicer, cut potatoes into 2mm slices. Stand potato pieces in large bowl of cold water for 30 minutes to prevent discolouration. Drain; pat dry with absorbent paper.

2 Meanwhile, combine ingredients for smoky paprika salt in small bowl.

3 Heat oil in wok; deep-fry potato, in batches, turning occasionally with slotted spoon, until browned lightly. Drain potato, in single layer, on absorbent paper; sprinkle with paprika salt.

NUTRITIONAL COUNT PER SERVING 5.5g total fat (0.7g saturated fat); 497kJ (119 cal); 13.9g carbohydrate; 2.6g protein; 1.7g fibre

Sauces, Asian

Certain classic sauces, once made by individual cooks but now commercially available, are an intrinsic part of the cuisines of China, Japan and South-East Asia. They are used not only as condiments but in marinades, stir-fries, salad dressings and dipping sauces and are added to dishes during cooking to balance the flavours. They should be used sparingly as they are strong and salty and too much can overwhelm other flavours and spoil the dish.

The idea of fermenting fish or other seafood to make strong-smelling flavourings such as South-East Asian fish sauce and shrimp paste is not confined to that region. Both the ancient Greeks and Romans made such products and used them, in the same way, as a "universal" flavour enhancer.

1 OYSTER SAUCE
2 SATAY SAUCE
2 SHRIMP PASTE

SOY SAUCE is to Asian cooks what salt is to Western ones. Good soy sauce is made by mixing soybeans and roasted grain (usually wheat), inoculating them with a yeast culture, salting and allowing them to ferment and mature for up to six months, then draining off and filtering the liquid that has formed. There are also soy sauces on sale that have been made in a few days via chemicals, with various additives to make up for their lack of flavour or colour, but these do not compare with the real thing. Good soy sauce can be identified by "naturally brewed" or similar wording on the label, and by an ingredient list consisting only of water, soy beans, wheat and salt. **Dark soy sauce** is used as a table condiment, in dipping sauces and for "red-cooked" dishes. **Light soy sauce** is lighter-coloured, thinner and saltier than dark soy but has a light, delicate flavour. **Mushroom soy sauce** is between dark and light soy and is flavoured with straw mushrooms added during the last stage of processing. It is delicately flavoured but very salty. **Shoyu** is a Japanese soy sauce, naturally brewed and left to mature for up to two years. It comes in light and dark versions and has a different flavour from other soy sauces, so others should not be substituted for it in recipes. **Tamari** is a thick Japanese soy sauce made with soy beans and rice. It

is often believed to be wheat-free but may contain a small amount of wheat, so the label should be carefully checked by those with wheat intolerance. Tamari is used as a dipping sauce, as a base for basting sauces such as yakitori sauce, and as an ingredient in sushi dipping sauces. **Kecap manis** is a thick, dark Indonesian soy sauce with the saltiness balanced by a definite sweetness from the palm sugar which is included in the brew. **Kecap asin** is a heavy, salty, dark Indonesian soy sauce.

TERIYAKI SAUCE is, traditionally, a blend of soy sauce, sugar and mirin (sweet sake). There are also teriyakis produced by respected Japanese manufacturers which include flavourings such as spices and garlic. Teriyaki is used as a marinade for food to be grilled and as a dipping sauce.

OYSTER SAUCE is made from oysters and their brine, cooked with salt and soy sauce and thickened with starches. Its flavour is not fishy but rich and savoury with a caramel note. As with soy sauce, there are good and poor oyster sauces: good ones include "oyster extract" in the ingredients list on the bottle, poor ones taste mostly of the caramel used in their manufacture. Good oyster sauce pulls together and enhances other flavours, whether in Asian or Western cooking. It is compatible with both meats and vegetables: a spoonful can make all the difference for a soup or stew that needs more depth of flavour. It is used as a dressing on steamed asian vegetables, as a flavouring ingredient in braises and stir-fries and as a thickener for other sauces.

FISH SAUCE, called nam pla in Thailand and nuoc nam in Vietnam, is a salty, smelly brown liquid which is a wonderful seasoning and flavour enhancer, its rankness magically disappearing when it meets other flavours. It is used by South-East Asian cooks as a universal seasoning, in the same way as soy sauce is used by Chinese and Japanese cooks, and like Chinese oyster sauce, it pulls together and brings out the flavours of other ingredients. It works as well with chicken and meats as with seafood and vegetables. It is made from fish or seafood (prawns, anchovies or squid), layered with salt in barrels and left to ferment for about three months, after which the liquid that has formed is drained off and filtered. It is used for dipping sauces, marinades and in almost every cooked savoury South-East Asian dish.

HOISIN SAUCE, made from red beans, garlic, sugar and spices, is often called chinese barbecue sauce and can be used instead of western-style barbecue sauces. Brushed over meat as it cooks, it gives sweet/savoury flavour and a rosy glow to the surface. It is often served with Peking duck instead of the traditional sweet bean sauce.

CHAR SIU SAUCE is used for making chinese barbecued pork or char siu. It is thick, more like a paste than a sauce, and is based on fermented soybean paste, honey and hoisin sauce, with spices. It can be diluted and used as a marinade or brushed directly onto the pork as it grills to give it sweet/ spicy flavour and a shiny dark-red surface. It is also good for grilling duck or chicken.

PLUM SAUCE is made from sugar, spices, vinegar, salt and special tart plums. It is dark and sweet/sour/spicy/salty. It is used

as a dip and sometimes served with Peking duck; it is also good brushed over chicken or spareribs as they grill.

SHRIMP PASTE, called terasi or trasi in Indonesia, blachan in Malaysia and mam tom in Vietnam, is made from dried shrimps that are ground and fermented; like fish sauce, its smell is stronger than its taste. It is often fried or roasted before use, which brings out the anchovy paste-like flavour for which it is loved. It is used sparingly in many South-East Asian dishes.

SATAY SAUCE, also spelt saté, is a thick, spicy peanut sauce from Indonesia, served with satay (grilled skewered meat, poultry or fish).

CHOOSING
The best places to shop for Asian ingredients are Asian food stores; the most expensive is usually the best. Also read labels carefully to check that soy sauce is naturally brewed and oyster sauce has oyster extract. If buying at the supermarket, look for Asian-produced sauces and again read labels carefully.

STORING
Asian sauces, being very salty, will store well at room temperature provided the necks of the bottles are clean.

❧ **OTHER RECIPES USING ASIAN SAUCES**
Cantonese beef patties with grilled gai lan, p52
Char siu lamb and noodle stir-fry, p340
Chilli beef stir-fry, p122
Chilli beef with snake beans, p45
Chilli chicken with broccoli and cashews, p74
Chinese barbecued spareribs, p446
Crisp pork belly with wombok salad, p444
Five-spice pork and nashi salad, p419
Ginger miso dressing, p553
Green nam jim, p120
Nasi goreng, p498
Peanut sambal, p348
Pork larb with broccolini, p76
Pork sang choy bow, p442
Singapore noodles, p339
Slow-roasted honey and soy pork neck, p447
Spicy tamarind chicken, p596–7
Stir-fried asian greens in black bean sauce, p245
Stir-fried choy sum, p244
Stir-fried pork, water chestnuts and buk choy, p630
Sticky pork with kaffir lime leaves, p276
Sweet and sour pork, p446
Tamarind and soy sauce, p595
Thai cucumber pickle, p148
Vegetable dumplings in asian broth, p336

4 HOISIN SAUCE
5 PLUM SAUCE
6 CHAR SIU SAUCE
7 FISH SAUCE
8 DARK SOY SAUCE
9 SOY SAUCE
10 LIGHT SOY SAUCE

Hoisin and peanut dipping sauce

PREP + COOK TIME 15 MINUTES **MAKES** 1 CUP

This is a good dipping sauce for dim sum, as well as a cooking sauce for marinating and basting spareribs and chicken wings. This quantity of sauce is enough for 1.5kg american-style spareribs or 16 chicken wings.

For information on peanuts, see Nuts, page 346.

1 tablespoon caster sugar

2 tablespoons rice vinegar

½ cup (125ml) water

½ cup (125ml) hoisin sauce

2 tablespoons crushed unsalted peanuts, roasted

1 Stir sugar, vinegar and the water in small saucepan over heat until sugar dissolves.

2 Add sauce; bring to the boil then reduce heat. Simmer, uncovered, about 5 minutes or until thickened slightly. Stir nuts into sauce off the heat.

3 Serve dipping sauce with barbecued pork spareribs or chicken wings.

NUTRITIONAL COUNT PER TABLESPOON 1.5g total fat (0.2g saturated fat); 171kJ (41 cal); 5.7g carbohydrate; 0.7g protein; 1.3g fibre

Satay sauce

PREP + COOK TIME 10 MINUTES **MAKES** 1 CUP

Serve this sauce with chicken, meat, vegetable or tofu satays (skewers). This quantity is enough for 16 satay sticks. It also goes well with grilled chicken breasts and cold mixed steamed vegetables.

For information on peanuts, see Nuts, page 346.

⅓ cup (95g) crunchy peanut butter

1 fresh long red chilli, chopped finely

140ml can coconut milk

2 teaspoons fish sauce

2 teaspoons kecap manis

1 tablespoon lime juice

1 Place ingredients in small saucepan; cook, stirring, over low heat until heated through.

2 Serve sauce with pork or chicken skewers.

NUTRITIONAL COUNT PER TABLESPOON 6.4g total fat (2.8g saturated fat); 309kJ (74 cal); 1.3g carbohydrate; 2.5g protein; 1.1g fibre

1 TERIYAKI SAUCE
2 TAMARI
3 MUSHROOM OYSTER SAUCE

Rice wine and soy sauce

PREP + COOK TIME 15 MINUTES **MAKES** 1 CUP

1 tablespoon peanut oil

2 teaspoons sesame oil

2 cloves garlic, crushed

5cm piece fresh ginger (25g), grated

1 green onion, sliced thinly

¼ cup (60ml) rice wine

2 tablespoons soy sauce

2 teaspoons caster sugar

1 teaspoon cornflour

½ cup (125ml) water

1 Heat oils in wok; stir-fry garlic, ginger and onion until fragrant. Add wine, sauce and sugar; bring to the boil then reduce heat. Simmer, uncovered, 2 minutes.

2 Add blended cornflour and the water; cook, stirring, until mixture comes to the boil and thickens slightly.

3 Serve sauce with steamed asian greens.

NUTRITIONAL COUNT PER TABLESPOON 2.3g total fat (0.4g saturated fat); 134kJ (32 cal); 1.4g carbohydrate; 0.3g protein; 0.2g fibre

Serve this sauce with stir-fried beef strips or steamed or grilled vegetables. This quantity is enough for 500g grilled baby buk choy.

Thai cucumber sauce

PREP + COOK TIME 15 MINUTES (PLUS REFRIGERATION TIME) **MAKES** 1 CUP

1 lebanese cucumber (130g), seeded, sliced thinly

¼ cup (55g) white sugar

¼ cup (60ml) white wine vinegar

4cm piece fresh ginger (20g), grated

1 teaspoon salt

½ cup (125ml) boiling water

1 fresh small red thai chilli, sliced thinly

3 green onions, sliced thinly

1 tablespoon coarsely chopped fresh coriander

1 Place cucumber in small heatproof bowl.

2 Combine sugar, vinegar, ginger, salt and the water in small saucepan; stir over low heat until sugar dissolves. Remove from heat; stand 5 minutes. Pour sauce over cucumber.

3 Sprinkle with chilli, onion and coriander; cover, refrigerate until chilled.

4 Serve sauce with thai fish cakes.

NUTRITIONAL COUNT PER TABLESPOON 0g total fat (0g saturated fat); 88kJ (21 cal); 4.9g carbohydrate; 0.1g protein; 0.2g fibre

Use this sauce as a marinade for chicken thighs and drumsticks, serve with sashimi, tempura, crudités, barbecued chicken breasts or whole baked fish, or add a little peanut oil and use as a dressing on Asian salads.

For information on lebanese cucumbers, see Cucumbers, page 146.

Lamb teriyaki with broccolini

PREP + COOK TIME 25 MINUTES **SERVES** 4

The teriyaki sauce to use here is the traditional kind, flavoured only with soy sauce and sugar, rather than one of the modern variations with other flavourings. This stir-fry goes well with steamed rice or noodles.

For information on lamb, see Lamb, pages 282 & 283; and for broccolini, see Broccolini, page 76.

1 tablespoon vegetable oil

800g lamb strips

4 green onions, chopped coarsely

3cm piece fresh ginger (15g), grated

175g broccolini, chopped coarsely

150g green beans, trimmed, halved crossways

⅓ cup (80ml) teriyaki sauce

2 tablespoons honey

2 teaspoons sesame oil

1 tablespoon toasted sesame seeds

1 Heat half the vegetable oil in wok; stir-fry lamb, in batches, until browned.

2 Heat remaining vegetable oil in wok; stir-fry onion and ginger until onion softens. Add broccolini and beans; stir-fry until vegetables are tender. Remove from wok.

3 Add sauce, honey and sesame oil to wok; bring to the boil. Boil, uncovered, 3 minutes or until sauce thickens slightly. Return lamb and vegetables to wok; stir-fry until hot. Sprinkle with seeds.

NUTRITIONAL COUNT PER SERVING 15.9g total fat (4.3g saturated fat); 1626kJ (389 cal); 14.1g carbohydrate; 45.7g protein; 3.4g fibre

---

Hoisin pork with watercress salad

PREP + COOK TIME 25 MINUTES (PLUS STANDING TIME) **SERVES** 2

If watercress is not available, use baby spinach leaves instead.

For information on pork, see Pork, pages 440 & 441; and for watercress, see Greens, Salad, page 250.

250g pork fillet

2 tablespoons hoisin sauce

cooking-oil spray

350g watercress, trimmed

⅓ cup coarsely chopped fresh mint

1 small green apple (130g), sliced thinly

½ small red onion (50g), sliced thinly

2 tablespoons lime juice

1 tablespoon light soy sauce

2cm piece fresh ginger (10g), grated

1 fresh small red thai chilli, chopped finely

1 Spread pork with hoisin sauce. Spray medium frying pan with cooking oil; heat pan, cook pork. Cover pork; stand 5 minutes.

2 Meanwhile, combine watercress, mint, apple and onion in medium bowl.

3 Combine juice, soy sauce, ginger and chilli in small jug. Add to salad; toss to combine.

4 Serve salad topped with sliced pork.

NUTRITIONAL COUNT PER SERVING 4.7g total fat (1.2g saturated fat); 1066kJ (255 cal); 16.7g carbohydrate; 32.3g protein; 8.1g fibre

1 | 2

1 HOISIN PORK WITH
WATERCRESS SALAD
2 MUSSELS IN BLACK
BEAN SAUCE

Mussels in black bean sauce

PREP + COOK TIME 20 MINUTES **SERVES** 4

2kg medium black mussels

1 tablespoon peanut oil

6cm piece fresh ginger (30g),
sliced thinly

4 cloves garlic, sliced thinly

8 green onions, sliced thinly

4 fresh small red thai chillies,
chopped finely

⅓ cup (100g) black bean sauce

¼ cup (60ml) fish stock

¼ cup (60ml) water

1 cup firmly packed fresh
coriander leaves

*The black bean sauce
to use here is the Asian
kind made from soybeans.
Serve these mussels with
steamed rice.*

*For information on mussels,
see Seafood, page 526.*

1 Scrub mussels under cold water; remove beards.
2 Heat oil in wok; stir-fry ginger, garlic, onion and chilli until fragrant. Add sauce, stock
and the water; bring to the boil.
3 Add mussels; simmer, covered, about 5 minutes or until mussels open (discard any
that do not). Remove pan from heat; sprinkle with coriander.

NUTRITIONAL COUNT PER SERVING 8.4g total fat (1g saturated fat); 882kJ (211 cal); 9.4g carbohydrate;
23.2g protein; 2.1g fibre

Sausages

From the point of view of the shopper or cook, the important thing is to know which of all the sausages hanging in the delicatessen are ready to eat just as they are and which need to be cooked before eating — and if so, how to cook them.

1 CONTINENTAL FRANKFURTS
2 LAMB SAUSAGES
3 ENGLISH SAUSAGES
4 CHIPOLATAS
5 BLUTWURST
6 KRANSKY
7 BLACK PUDDING
8 CABANOSSI
9 LAP CHEUNG
10 COCKTAIL FRANKFURTS
11 BEEF SAUSAGES
12 MERGUEZ
13 SOPRESSA SALAMI
14 CHILLI SALAMI
15 DANISH SALAMI
16 HUNGARIAN SALAMI
17 CHORIZO
18 CONTINENTAL PORK SAUSAGES

Fresh sausages, whether at the butcher or the delicatessen, are easy — we know them by their softness and slightly saggy shapes and we're fairly familiar with cooking them; but you can't tell just by looking how best to use a firm sausage. Luckily, they virtually all come from long sausage-making traditions and have traditional identifying names, and the name is the clue.

Many sausages are uncooked but are ready to eat and wholesome because they have been cured (of their tendency to spoil) by salting, sometimes smoking, and air-drying in a breezy place for weeks or months, naturally and slowly losing weight and becoming firm and concentrated in flavour in the process. They remain wholesome because salt, smoke and moving air all work to kill bacteria that might cause spoilage by drying them out. Sausages made this way are collectively called by the Italian name, salami (the singular form is salame, but almost no one outside Italy uses it), though there are fine Danish, French, German and Eastern European varieties. A few salami are lightly cured and then cooked, but the great majority are not.

FRESH SAUSAGES

These may be made of any meat; pork and beef are the most common but lamb and chicken sausages are also widely available. They may be grilled, fried or baked, with an occasional European type, such as

strasbourg sausage, meant to be poached. Sausage-makers implore us not to prick sausages and let the flavoursome juices out, so it is a good idea to par-cook them by gentle poaching to firm them and help skin and filling to expand together before grilling etc. With or without pre-poaching, fresh sausages should be cooked slowly, turning often, so that they don't burst. The pan should be barely greased as the sausages will soon provide their own fat. A skewer run end to end through sausages to be fried will help to keep them straight so that they can be browned all over. Bratwurst is one of the few fresh sausages sold by name; it is of German origin, made from pork and sometimes veal and subtly spiced. It is traditionally fried and served with potatoes and sauerkraut.

SAUSAGES EATEN COLD WITHOUT FURTHER COOKING

SALAMI are sometimes called by a specific name such as cabanossi or mortadella but many are simply called Danish, Hungarian and so on, and these names have come to be recognised as indicating a certain style, for instance mild and fairly fine for Danish, coarser and flavoured with paprika for Hungarian and so on. Salami are sold sliced, cut as a piece of a requested size, or whole.
MORTADELLA is the largest of all sausages. It is a fine- textured, smoked and cooked salami which originated in Bologna. It may

❦ **OTHER RECIPES USING SAUSAGES**

Beetroot, merguez and lentil salad, p56
Chipotle pork ribs with chorizo and smoked paprika, p123
Coppa and ricotta panini, p71
Nasi goreng, p498
Spanish tortilla, p169

be made with pure pork, including large flecks of fat, or with a mixture of pork, veal and beef. It is studded with pepper, mildly spiced and smoked before cooking. It is used for sandwiches or as part of an antipasto tray.

CABANOSSI MILANESE, usually called just cabanossi, is a long, thin, mild, smoked salami. It is usually cut across into chunks and served as a snack, often in the company of cheese and pickled cucumbers or onions. It is also good thickly sliced, fried and served with a fried egg, or folded through warm potato and egg salad.

PEPERONI is a spicy, chilli-hot Italian- or Spanish-style pork and beef salami. It is cold-smoked and air-dried and needs no cooking. Usually served as a snack with drinks or as a pizza topping.

SAUSAGES EATEN HOT OR COLD

BLACK PUDDING is a British blood sausage, its filling being made of pig's blood mixed with cereal, fat and flavourings. It is cooked when purchased and may be eaten cold, but is usually sliced, fried and served with bacon as a breakfast dish or with mashed potato, onion and fried apple rings for dinner.

BLUTWURST is a fine-textured, cooked German blood sausage made from beef, pork and beef blood. It is salty and spicy and may be eaten cold, but is usually heated. It is eaten as a snack, traditionally with beer, pretzels and radishes, or as a main dish with sauerkraut.

CHORIZOS are small, coarse-textured pork and beef Spanish sausages. They are deeply smoked, very spicy and dry-cured so that they do not need cooking. They are served cold with bread, pickled vegetables and a glass of sherry as a tapa (snack), or may be grilled or fried.

SAUSAGES EATEN HOT

MERGUEZ are small Algerian or Tunisian lamb sausages flavoured with garlic and hot spices. They are often used in couscous dishes, and have recently become fashionable in a restaurant starter of chilled oysters and hot, grilled merguez.

LAP CHEONG are small cured and dried chinese sausages made from pork meat or from pig or duck liver. They are sweet and mildly spicy and must be cooked, usually by steaming, before they are eaten. They are used in chicken and rice dishes.

KRANSKY are mildly spiced, red-skinned German sausages which are heavily smoked and already cooked, but are always poached or slashed and grilled and eaten with mustard.

FRANKFURTS are mild pork and beef sausages (kosher ones are all beef) which are fully cooked when purchased but are always poached, sometimes in soup, or slashed and grilled and served with tomato sauce or mustard. When place in mustard-smeared bread rolls, they become hot dogs. "Continental" frankfurts are spicier than ordinary ones.

CHOOSING
It is best to buy sausages of any kind from a busy shop with a fast turnover. Avoid any with sticky skins and try to shop where sliced or cut sausage is cut to order, not already cut and in a display cabinet.

STORING
Fresh sausages should be stored in a covered container in the refrigerator and used within 2 days. Most other sausages should be well wrapped in aluminium foil and refrigerated for 1–2 days if sliced, 4–5 days for a cut piece and up to a week if whole.

Mexican sausages with beans

PREP + COOK TIME 2 HOURS 35 MINUTES (PLUS STANDING TIME) **SERVES** 4

1 cup (200g) dried kidney beans

800g beef sausages, chopped coarsely

1 tablespoon olive oil

1 large white onion (200g), chopped coarsely

3 cloves garlic, crushed

1 large red capsicum (350g), chopped coarsely

½ teaspoon ground cumin

2 teaspoons sweet smoked paprika

1 teaspoon dried chilli flakes

2 x 400g cans crushed tomatoes

2 tablespoons coarsely chopped fresh oregano

Tortillas, the flatbreads of Mexico, come in wheat and corn varieties and are available fresh, frozen or vacuum-packed in tins.

For information on dried kidney beans, see Pulses, page 472.

1 Place beans in medium bowl, cover with cold water; stand overnight, drain. Rinse under cold water; drain. Place beans in medium saucepan of boiling water; return to the boil. Reduce heat; simmer, uncovered, about 30 minutes or until beans are almost tender. Drain.

2 Cook sausages, in batches, in large deep saucepan until browned; drain.

3 Heat oil in same pan; cook onion, garlic and capsicum, stirring, until onion softens. Add cumin, paprika and chilli; cook, stirring, about 2 minutes or until fragrant. Add beans and undrained tomatoes; bring to the boil. Reduce heat; simmer, covered, about 1 hour or until beans are tender.

4 Return sausages to pan; simmer, covered, about 10 minutes or until sausages are cooked through. Remove from heat; stir in oregano. Serve with tortillas.

NUTRITIONAL COUNT PER SERVING 56.9g total fat (25.2g saturated fat); 3323kJ (795 cal); 33.5g carbohydrate; 38.1g protein; 20.2g fibre

---

Salami, bocconcini and pasta salad

PREP + COOK TIME 25 MINUTES **SERVES** 6

500g mini penne pasta

½ cup (75g) seeded black olives, halved

250g cherry tomatoes, halved

180g bocconcini cheese, halved

100g spicy salami, chopped coarsely

1 cup firmly packed fresh basil leaves

RED WINE VINAIGRETTE

⅓ cup (80ml) olive oil

¼ cup (60ml) red wine vinegar

2 teaspoons dijon mustard

1 clove garlic, crushed

This salad is great for a summer weekend lunch or easy midweek dinner.

For information on penne, see Pasta, page 398; and for bocconcini cheese, see Cheese, page 102.

1 Cook pasta in large saucepan of boiling water, uncovered, until just tender; drain. Rinse under cold water; drain.

2 Meanwhile, place ingredients for red wine vinaigrette in screw-top jar; shake well.

3 Place pasta in large bowl with remaining ingredients and vinaigrette; toss to combine.

NUTRITIONAL COUNT PER SERVING 24.1g total fat (4.9g saturated fat); 2274kJ (544 cal); 61g carbohydrate; 18.6g protein; 3.9g fibre

For information
on canned beans,
see Pulses, page 470.

Merguez and bean soup

PREP + COOK TIME 50 MINUTES **SERVES** 4

1 medium red onion (170g),
chopped coarsely

2 rindless bacon rashers (130g),
chopped coarsely

2 cloves garlic, crushed

400g can diced tomatoes

1.5 litres (6 cups) chicken stock

6 merguez sausages (480g)

2 x 400g cans white beans,
rinsed, drained

GREMOLATA

⅓ cup finely chopped fresh
flat-leaf parsley

2 teaspoons finely grated
lemon rind

2 cloves garlic, crushed

1 Cook onion, bacon and garlic in heated oiled large saucepan, stirring, until onion softens and bacon crisps. Add undrained tomatoes and stock; bring to the boil. Reduce heat; simmer, uncovered, 20 minutes, stirring occasionally.
2 Meanwhile, cook sausages in heated oiled medium frying pan until browned and cooked through; slice thinly.
3 Add sausage to soup with beans; stir until soup is hot. Serve sprinkled with gremolata.

GREMOLATA Combine ingredients in small bowl.

NUTRITIONAL COUNT PER SERVING 42.4g total fat (15.6g saturated fat); 2504kJ (599 cal); 14.6g carbohydrate; 38.4g protein; 5.5g fibre

French green lentils, here,
refers to the Australian-
grown lentils of the French
puy variety.

For more information
on lentils, see Pulses,
page 472.

Warm chorizo and lentil salad

PREP + COOK TIME 40 MINUTES **SERVES** 6

1¼ cups (250g) french
green lentils

1 small brown onion (80g),
quartered

1 bay leaf

2 chorizo sausages (340g),
sliced thinly

3 shallots (75g), sliced thinly

2 stalks celery (300g), trimmed,
sliced diagonally

1 cup coarsely chopped fresh
flat-leaf parsley

MACADAMIA DRESSING

½ cup (125ml) red wine vinegar

⅓ cup (80ml) macadamia oil

1 Cook lentils, onion and bay leaf in large saucepan of boiling water, uncovered, about 15 minutes or until lentils are tender; drain. Discard onion and bay leaf.
2 Cook chorizo in large frying pan, stirring occasionally, until browned. Drain on absorbent paper; cool 10 minutes.
3 Meanwhile, place ingredients for macadamia dressing in screw-top jar; shake well.
4 Place lentils and chorizo in large bowl with remaining ingredients and dressing; toss gently to combine.

NUTRITIONAL COUNT PER SERVING 30.2g total fat (8.1g saturated fat); 1860kJ (445 cal); 19.1g carbohydrate; 21.8g protein; 7.3g fibre

MERGUEZ AND BEAN SOUP

Seafood

To experience seafood at its best, you must eat it truly fresh. It is worth the effort to make a special trip, if necessary, to buy it on the day you will eat it. Tomorrow it will still be perfectly edible, but the best of its pure and delicate flavour will have disappeared.

1 WHOLE BABY BREAM
2 WHOLE FLOUNDER
3 WHOLE JOHN DORY
4 WHOLE WHITING
5 WHOLE SALMON
6 WHOLE OCEAN TROUT
7 WHOLE GARFISH
8 WHOLE RAINBOW TROUT
9 WHOLE FLATHEAD
10 WHOLE SARDINES
11 WHOLE BABY SNAPPER
12 CAVIAR
13 SALMON ROE
14 SWORDFISH STEAK
15 TUNA STEAK
16 BLUE-EYE CUTLETS
17 OCEAN TROUT FILLETS
18 SALMON FILLET
19 KINGFISH FILLET

Buy from a busy shop with a fast turnover so that you get today's, not yesterday's fish or shellfish. It is also important for flavour that seafood stays chilled without a break until you are ready to use it, so take an insulated bag with an ice-pack to carry your purchase home and when you get there, transfer the seafood, loosely wrapped in aluminium foil, to the refrigerator. If you do have to store seafood overnight, refer to notes on STORING.

The following listings cover only the best-known Australian fish — it would take a separate book to describe the 600-odd species that are sold in the region — but it pays to ask the fishmonger about those with unfamiliar names, which are often cheaper than the well-known "stars". Like butchers, fishmongers like to show off their expertise and will be pleased to tell you how to cook them.

Fish

OILY AND NON-OILY FISH

Fish are classified as oily or non-oily, though even the "oily" ones are still a low-fat food, and their oils provide good-for-you omega-3 fatty acids which help to guard against high blood pressure, heart disease, diabetes and cancer. Fish classified as oily come in many variations of texture and fat content from undoubtedly oily mullet to succulent and delicate salmon and trout.

All fish that are commercially canned, smoked, cured or dried, such as tuna, sardines, mackerel, anchovies, herring, haddock, bacalao (dried salt cod), gravlax (see CURED, SMOKED AND DRIED FISH, page 523), sardines and so on, belong to the oily group. Non-oily fish, especially fillets, dry out easily and need to be protected when they are grilled or fried by basting them as they cook or coating them with flour or breadcrumbs.

SALTWATER FISH

BLUE-EYE (New Zealand blue-nose or bream) have succulent, full-flavoured white flesh which is easy to cook without drying out. They have few bones and can be steamed, grilled, barbecued, poached, pan-fried or baked whole. Blue-eye are large fish usually sold as fillets or steaks.

BREAM have white, fine-textured, sweet flesh. They are available in various sizes and are perfect for steaming, baking or barbecuing whole, while fillets can be deep-fried, steamed, grilled, pan-fried or poached.

FLAKE is the retail name for shark, which is a firm, white, mild-flavoured meat, completely boneless because sharks don't have bones but cartilage instead. For this reason (and because it is relatively inexpensive), it is widely used for fish and chips by the trade; it is also suitable for serving to children and others who don't like their fish too fishy.

Many people think that buying fish fillets means there should be no bones, but that is not so. Filleting means detaching the meat (the fillet) in one piece from the backbone. In many fish, a further procedure is needed to get boneless fish as there will still be small pin-bones under the cut surface of the fillet. To remove them, run your finger firmly along the surface from tail to head and, when you feel a bone, pick it out with tweezers.

To carve a whole, large fish, use a sharp, flexible knife and, holding the fish steady with the back of a fork, cut the full length beside the backbone, then across at 6–8cm intervals; slip a spatula under each block of flesh, steady it with the back of the fork and lift it off. When one side has been served, either turn the fish over and repeat with other side or, use kitchen scissors to snip through the backbone just behind the head and before the tail, lift off and cut portions from the other side. For salmon and trout, which have two fillets on each side, make an additional lengthwise cut along the centre and lift off flesh from each side. Practise this for the family before attempting it for a dinner party.

FLAT FISH Most flat fish on the Australian market are imported from New Zealand (NZ) as the Australian catch is small. Like many other Australasian fish, the different varieties of flat fish have been named for their similarity to northern hemisphere species but actually belong to different families. Officially, they should be called NZ sole, NZ turbot, NZ brill or NZ or Australian flounder, though outside of officialdom they are simply called sole, flounder and so on. Flat fish make excellent eating, especially if cooked whole; their flesh is slightly moist and of exquisite flavour.

FLATHEAD have firm flesh and outstanding flavour. They can be a little dry if not well protected during cooking, so they are perfectly suited to crumbing or coating with batter for fish and chips, and also good for moist cooking methods such as casseroling or cooking in a curry. They are usually sold filleted.

JOHN DORY, **SILVER DORY**, **MIRROR DORY** John dory, with its exquisite flavour, firm but moist and delicate white flesh, little fat and few bones, is one of the most prized of all fish. Its qualities are best brought out by brief cooking — pan-frying, grilling or poaching. Mirror dory and silver dory are related to john dory and are also choice fish, though not quite equal to their more famous relation, and can be cooked in the same ways.

KINGFISH are large fish with firm, meaty, full-flavoured flesh, good for baking, grilling, barbecuing or smoking and outstanding for sashimi (serving raw with a Japanese dipping sauce). Both wild-caught and farmed kingfish is available; the farmed fish is known as hiramasa, its Japanese name, and has a little more fat than wild ones. Kingfish are sold whole or as fillets or cutlets.

LING (NZ rock cod) are long, thick fish whose meaty, mild-flavoured white fillets have only a few bones which are easy to see and remove, making it good for serving to children and others who don't want their fish too fishy. Ling can be cooked in any way.

MAHI MAHI, also known as dolphin fish, are large, meaty fish with a mild flavour that is sometimes described as being almost like chicken. They are fished in Australian waters but their home ground is the Hawaii region and they are particularly good marinated Polynesian-style and served raw, but can be cooked by any method or used in curries and stews. They are sold as skinless steaks or fillet portions.

SMALL FISH Southern-hemisphere waters are rich in small fish that are similar to Europe's anchovies, sardines and pilchards — sometimes part of the same family, sometimes not — and are used in the same ways. Sardines are usually fried or grilled and are popular for barbecuing in a hinged wire griller. They are also canned. Pilchards are larger sardines and are used, fresh or canned, in the same ways. Anchovy can also be eaten as fresh fish but are best known as salty cured fish in small cans or jars. Whitebait may be the 4–5cm-long fry (young) of several kinds of fish, which are fried and eaten whole, or New Zealand whitebait which are the larval stage of a minnow. Tiny and transparent, they can be shaken with flour in a plastic bag and deep-fried until crisp, or mixed with beaten egg or a light batter to make fritters.

SNAPPER are great all-rounders with succulent flesh and delicate flavour, equally good grilled, barbecued. poached, pan-fried or baked whole. They come in sizes from plate-size to large enough to serve 4 and are available whole or as fillets or cutlets.

SWORDFISH are large fish with meaty, well-flavoured pale pink flesh that responds well to char-grilling, roasting, pan-searing or serving raw as carpaccio (thin slices topped with a flavoursome dressing). Swordfish should be served rare at the centre. They are sold whole or as boneless fillets or cutlets.

TUNA are big fish with firm, red, flesh and are sold as steaks or fillet portions. Their distinctive flavour has been described as "chicken of the sea". The fattiest part, the belly section, is greatly sought after for sashimi (see Kingfish, opposite). Tuna is also very good char-grilled, roasted or pan-seared; it should be served rare at the centre.

WHITING are small, long and slender fish with fine texture and exquisite flavour. They are available whole or as fillets and can be grilled, pan-fried, steamed or poached. Their small, thin fillets need to be protected when grilling or pan-frying (see OILY AND NON-OILY FISH, page 520).

FRESHWATER FISH

BARRAMUNDI are fished from rivers and estuaries in northern Australia and are also farmed. They vary in size from plate-size to more than a metre long. They are a popular sporting fish, though today many anglers practise catch and release. They are considered one of Australia's finest fish: their meat is white, firm and fine-grained, and deliciously flavoured if they have spent their lives in clear water, though it can disappoint if they have lived in muddy water.

MURRAY COD, which is really a freshwater perch, grows to great sizes. It is one of Australia's best table fish, with delicious mild flavour and meaty, succulent flesh. Its season extends from mid-summer to the end of winter, but it is considered endangered so fishing for it in the wild is now restricted and may soon be forbidden. It is also farmed.

GOLDEN, SILVER and **REDFIN PERCH** are found in inland and some coastal Australian rivers. The golden perch is much sought after and makes superb eating; silver and redfin perch, while not rated quite so high, are also very good eating.

SALMON spend part of their lives in the sea, but they are considered freshwater fish because they are caught in fresh rivers. Atlantic salmon are farmed in Tasmania and New Zealand and are sold whole or in steaks, cutlets or whole fillets (about 1 kg and called a side of salmon). Pacific salmon are also a good table fish but are not rated so high as the Atlantic salmon. The "Australian salmon" (kahawai in New Zealand) is not related to true salmon but is a member of the perch family with rather dark, coarse flesh.

TROUT Rainbow, brown and golden trout have been introduced into New Zealand and Australian rivers and lakes and are also farmed in both countries. They are considered among the choicest of fish. Sea-run trout, which are much bigger than river trout, are farmed in the same way as Atlantic salmon, spending part of their lives in fresh water and part in sea pens.

CURED, SMOKED AND DRIED FISH

Most cured (salted) fish is also smoked. The exceptions are Spain and Portugal's bacalao, which is cod, salted and dried until stiff as a board (it is soaked before using), anchovies, which are salt-cured before packing in oil and Scandinavia's gravlax, which is salmon covered with salt, sugar and other flavourings, then tightly wrapped and, traditionally, buried in snow or frost-bound earth until cured. Smoked fish may be salted and cold-smoked (with the fish in a separate chamber from the fire) so that it is uncooked but cured, and is sold thinly sliced; or it can be

❦ OTHER RECIPES USING FISH

hot-smoked above the fire, which wholly or partly cooks it, and is sold in serving portions. Salmon and trout are available both cold- and hot-smoked; mackerel, cod and haddock are hot-smoked. True caviar is the salted eggs of the Caspian Sea sturgeon, and there are also cheap imitation "caviars" in the shape of lumpfish eggs dyed red or black. Not caviar, but a luxurious delicacy in their own right, are salted golden salmon eggs, which are available in jars at large seafood outlets and speciality food shops and are used in the same ways as caviar.

CHOOSING FISH
Fish should smell fishy but fresh. Whole fish should have full, bright eyes, red gills and shiny, slippery skin, and should feel springy when prodded. Inspect fillets, steaks and cutlets especially carefully as stale fish is sometimes cut up for these. If they have skin, it should be shiny and slippery. The flesh should have a sheen, not a dull or tacky surface, should feel springy when prodded and the indentation should quickly disappear; if it stays and oozes moisture, the fish has probably been frozen and thawed and should not be sold as fresh fish. Fresh fish is always preferable to frozen, but if you do want frozen, it is better to buy commercially frozen then to freeze your own, because commercial "snap-freezing" is much faster than home freezing so it doesn't damage the texture so much.

Shellfish

ABALONE is a single-shelled deep-water shellfish which is harvested by divers. It is considered a great luxury by Asian chefs and much of the catch goes to China and Japan so it is rather scarce in Australian seafood outlets. It has a reputation for toughness and is usually sliced and pounded before cooking, but if bought live and used the same day by shelling, slicing and immediately dropping it into hot oil for seconds only, it tastes like lobster and is not tough.

BALMAIN and **MORETON BAY BUGS**
These small sand lobsters can be bought cooked or alive. Their flesh, which is mostly in the tail, resembles lobster in taste and texture. Allow 1 large or 2 small bugs per serving.

CRAB There are many crab varieties that are caught and cooked by locals, but the main commercial varieties are the small blue swimmer and the slightly larger spanner crab. Both give about the same amount of meat. Blue swimmers are sold both raw (but not live) and cooked and spanner crabs are almost always sold cooked (you may see uncooked ones, but they will probably have been frozen for transport and be watery). A medium blue swimmer or spanner crab will serve 1 person. Mud crabs range from big to very big and are sold alive. A medium to large mud crab will serve 2–3 people. Tiny sand crabs have so little flesh it is not worth digging out, but, cut in half and added to a stock or soup, they contribute rich flavour. Crabs have a hard shell which they moult (shed) when they grow too large for it, and for a short time they have only a soft covering; during this time they are soft-shell crabs which can be eaten in their entirety and are considered a great delicacy.

The dark vein that runs down the back of prawns, just under the surface, is the gut, which may or may not have some grit in it. Some people always devein, some don't, and some devein large prawns but not small ones. A simple way to remove the vein is to place a piece of absorbent paper on the kitchen bench then hold the peeled prawn with the vein side slightly tilted towards the paper and insert the tip of a small knife under the vein at the head end and simply turn the knife to touch the paper, and the vein will easily and immediately lift from the prawn and stick to the paper.

CRAYFISH The Australian "lobster" is, correctly, a crayfish, as are yabbies and marron; see those entries, below.

CLAMS This is a name given to bivalves of various sizes and families in many parts of the world. It is not much used in Australia, as the small edible bivalves to be found around its shores are called pipis and cockles. They may also be found at fish markets and large seafood outlets. They can be eaten raw from the shell with a squeeze of lemon juice, shelled and added to soup or made into fritters, or used, opened but still in shell, to top a bowl of pasta or a risotto. They are opened in the same way as oysters, below.

CUTTLEFISH are closely related to squid and are cooked in the same way (see Squid, opposite). Small cuttlefish are tender but large ones can be tough.

LOBSTER is sold alive or cooked. The flesh is mostly in the tail though the small amount in the legs is especially sweet and well worth picking out.

MUSSELS are bivalves that are found clustered on rocks or under jetties and are also farmed. The main Australasian ones are the New Zealand greenlip mussel and the black Australian mussel. Both are excellent in flavour. The greenlip is the larger and more decorative, but it cannot be imported live into Australia so it is first steamed to kill it, which puts it at a disadvantage there as mussels are best when cooked alive and eaten immediately. Mussels should be scrubbed all over with a stiff brush and rinsed in clean water, then the beards (hairy strands that protrude from the closed shell) removed by pulling sharply downward, and the mussels rinsed again. As noted in CHOOSING SHELLFISH, it is important to check that fresh mussels are alive when you buy them; it is equally important to be sure that they were still alive when cooked, this time by discarding any that have not opened, as live ones open when heated.

OCTOPUS belongs to the same family as cuttlefish and squid, and can be cooked in the same ways (below). Baby octopus are tender but larger ones are tough and must be tenderised by pounding — this will usually have been done by the fishmonger. Octopus is particularly good gently stewed with onions, garlic and tomatoes, and is a favourite snack in Greece when pickled in garlic, oil and vinegar.

OYSTERS One of the world's finest oysters is the Sydney rock oyster which is farmed in estuaries along Australia's New South Wales coast and in northern New Zealand. Another is the Bluff oyster which grows in one of the world's few remaining productive oyster beds in Foveaux Strait at the south end of New Zealand's South Island. Australia also has the native flat oyster, a relation of France's prized belon oyster, and both countries also grow the Pacific oyster.

Ideally, oysters should be bought alive in their closed shells and opened just before they are eaten, but most people jib at opening them themselves. The next-best way is to order oysters a day or two ahead and ask the fishmonger to open them for you on the day and to leave them in their natural juice. Fresh oysters can also be bought shelled and bottled and these are useful for soups, stews or fritters.

PRAWNS Fresh prawns come in sizes from the length of a child's finger to the 30cm that the Eastern king prawn can attain, and in varieties from the showy striped tiger prawn to the pale-grey school prawn. The flavour and texture differences between varieties are slight but apparent to prawn-fanciers, smaller prawns often considered sweeter and more tender than larger ones. King prawn is the name given to certain large varieties and, in common

usage, to all large prawns. Calculate 4–6 medium prawns or 3–4 medium king prawns per person for a main course with accompaniments such as rice or potato salad. Prawns are sold green (raw) or cooked. When shelled, they yield half their original weight in prawn meat. In the wild, their peak seasons are spring and summer; farmed prawns are available in good condition all year.

SCALLOPS You can buy these luscious bivalves on the beautiful fan-shaped half-shell, or shelled ones. They are also available frozen; these are not as good as fresh for eating separately, but they work well in a sauce. Southern Australian and New Zealand scallops are sold with the orange roe or "coral" still attached to the white meat, but Northern Australian saucer scallops, which are large and thin-shelled, are sold with the white meat only. Scallops are often eaten raw or barely seared, and should never be cooked for more than about 30 seconds as they will lose their juicy tenderness and be tough. Cooked scallops are often served on the natural half-shells (which can be washed and used again) or on porcelain shell-shaped dishes.

SCAMPI are also known as Norway lobsters, Dublin Bay prawns and langoustines. They are fished in deep water off the continental shelf of Western Australia. They look like a tiny crayfish and have meat that is similar in flavour but much softer, and care must be taken in cooking as overcooking will make it mushy.

SQUID, also known as calamari, are shellfish without an external shell but with a long, bony "quill" inside. Their sac-like body can be cut into rings or strips or left whole for stuffing. Like their close relation the cuttlefish, they have an ink sac which is often used in cooking them. Squid and cuttlefish can be cooked in the same ways. They must be cooked either very briefly —

a few minutes only, after which they become tough — or else gently cooked for long enough to become tender again. Small squid are tender and are used for the batter-dipped or crumbed and quickly deep-fried calamari rings that children and many others love. Squid and cuttlefish can also be barbecued and served with a dipping sauce, stuffed and baked, stir-fried or used cold in salads. They are available all year.

YABBIES and **MARRON** are closely related freshwater crayfish that live in creeks and dams and are also farmed. Marron, which are larger than yabbies, are native to the south of Western Australia, while yabbies are widely distributed. The Queensland redclaw is also part of the family. The peak seasons for all three are spring and autumn, but they are available all year. They are usually sold cooked though live ones may be found at fish markets or large seafood outlets.

PROCESSED SHELLFISH

Crab and lobster meat are available canned; though not as good as fresh, they can be satisfactory used as an ingredient in a cooked dish. Oysters and mussels are available canned, either plain or smoked; plain canned ones can be satisfactory in a soup or other cooked dish and smoked ones on bread or croûtes are a popular appetiser. Abalone is available canned and works well in Chinese recipes, and the liquid in which it was cooked is a good stock to use in sauces or dressings. Tiny dried prawns are available in Asian food stores and are used in various Asian dishes.

CHOOSING SHELLFISH All

shellfish should smell sweet and fresh — reject any with the slightest suggestion of an off odour — and be whole and undamaged. Live ones should be lively.

Bugs, crab, crayfish and scampi should feel heavy for their size. The tails of bugs and lobsters should be curled tightly against their bodies and should snap back if straightened.

A 1–1.5kg lobster is the best size — larger ones can be tough — and will serve 2. Don't buy dead but uncooked lobster, crab or crayfish as their flesh deteriorates quickly after death. Mussels should be alive and tightly closed; tap any opened ones on the counter and reject any that do not close. Select Australian fresh prawns rather than imports as they will be fresher. Cooked or green frozen prawns, both local and imported from Asia, are available; cooked ones are usually tasteless when thawed, but green ones can be an acceptable second-best to fresh. Any shellfish, especially prawns, may have been frozen but be offered as fresh. If they feel light or spongy, look discoloured or are oozing juice, reject them as they will be mushy. Fresh shellfish is always preferable to frozen, but if you do want frozen, it is better to buy a commercial product than to freeze your own, because commercial "snap-freezing" is much faster than home freezing so it doesn't damage the texture so much.

STORING As mentioned earlier, the ideal is not to have to store seafood but to eat it the day you buy it. If you have to store it overnight, it should be kept colder than refrigerator temperature by storing it in an ice slurry: either buy ice or make and store plenty ahead of time, break it into small pieces by hammering and put a layer into a waterproof refrigerator container or, if there is too much seafood for this, in a container with drainage holes. Lay the seafood on the ice, cover it with another layer of ice and then with the lid or several layers of wet newspaper or wet towels. Store in the refrigerator or in a cool place, and use within 48 hours, checking often and replacing ice as needed.

For juicy, flavoursome fish, cook only until a toothpick pushed into the thickest part meets just slight resistance. Remove from the heat the moment it reaches this stage as it will cook a little more as it is served.

For information on frozen and fresh peas, see Peas, pages 422–424; and for mint, see Herbs, page 264.

Seared ocean trout with pea and mint salsa

PREP + COOK TIME 45 MINUTES **SERVES** 4

¾ cup (90g) frozen peas

⅓ cup coarsely chopped fresh mint

2 tablespoons coarsely chopped fresh basil

2 tablespoons olive oil

2 tablespoons lemon juice

700g baby new potatoes, halved

40g butter

1 tablespoon olive oil, extra

4 x 200g ocean trout fillets

1 Boil, steam or microwave peas until just tender; rinse under cold water, drain. Combine peas in medium bowl with mint, basil, oil and juice.

2 Boil, steam or microwave potato until tender; drain. Using masher, roughly smash potato with butter in large bowl. Cover to keep warm.

3 Meanwhile, heat extra oil in large frying pan; cook fish, uncovered, until browned both sides and cooked as desired. Serve fish with smash and salsa.

NUTRITIONAL COUNT PER SERVING 29.8g total fat (9.1g saturated fat); 2324kJ (556 cal); 24.7g carbohydrate; 44.4g protein; 4.6g fibre

1 SEARED OCEAN TROUT WITH PEA AND MINT SALSA
2 CLASSIC FISH AND CHIPS

Classic fish and chips

PREP + COOK TIME 50 MINUTES **SERVES** 4

1 cup (150g) self-raising flour

1 cup (250ml) dry ale

1 tablespoon sea salt

1kg potatoes, peeled

peanut oil, for deep-frying

4 x 150g blue-eye fillets, halved lengthways

1 Sift flour into medium bowl; whisk in beer and salt until smooth.

2 Cut potatoes lengthways into 1cm slices; cut each slice lengthways into 1cm-chips; dry with absorbent paper.

3 Heat oil in large saucepan. Cook chips, in three batches, about 2 minutes or until tender but not brown. Drain on absorbent paper.

4 Dip fish in batter; drain away excess. Deep-fry fish, in batches, until cooked. Drain.

5 Deep-fry chips, in three batches, until crisp and golden brown; drain. Serve fish and chips with tartare sauce and lemon wedges.

NUTRITIONAL COUNT PER SERVING 14.6g total fat (3.1g saturated fat); 2261kJ (541 cal); 55.1g carbohydrate; 39.6g protein; 4.8g fibre

This dish is traditionally served with tartare sauce. Combine ⅔ cup whole-egg mayonnaise, ½ finely chopped small brown onion, 2 tablespoons finely chopped cornichons, 1 tablespoon finely chopped drained and rinsed capers, 1 tablespoon finely chopped fresh flat-leaf parsley and 1 tablespoon lemon juice in a medium bowl.

For information on all-round potatoes and other varieties suitable for frying, see Potatoes, page 448.

Banana-leaf steamed fish

PREP + COOK TIME 50 MINUTES **SERVES** 4

3 large banana leaves

3cm piece fresh galangal (15g), quartered

2 shallots (50g), quartered

2 cloves garlic

1 tablespoon fish sauce

¼ cup (60ml) lime juice

2 tablespoons peanut oil

2 x 10cm sticks fresh lemon grass (40g)

4 x 240g whole bream

⅓ cup firmly packed fresh coriander leaves

¼ cup coarsely chopped vietnamese mint

1 fresh long red chilli, sliced thinly

4 green onions, sliced thinly

1 lime, quartered

1 Trim two banana leaves into four 30cm x 40cm rectangles. Using metal tongs, dip one piece at a time into large saucepan of boiling water; remove immediately. Rinse under cold water; pat dry with absorbent paper. Trim remaining leaf to fit grill plate (or grill or barbecue).

2 Blend or process galangal, shallot, garlic, sauce, juice and oil. Strain dressing into small bowl; discard solids.

3 Place banana leaves on bench. Halve lemon grass lengthways then crossways.

4 Score fish both sides through thickest part of flesh. Place two pieces of cut lemon grass on each leaf; place one fish on top of lemon grass, top with equal amounts of dressing. Fold opposite corners of each leaf into centre to enclose fish; secure parcel at 5cm intervals with kitchen string.

5 Place remaining leaf pieces onto heated grill plate (or grill or barbecue); place parcels on leaf. Cook, turning halfway through cooking time, about 20 minutes or until fish is cooked as desired.

6 Meanwhile, combine herbs, chilli and onion in small bowl.

7 Open parcels; serve fish sprinkled with herb mixture and lime.

NUTRITIONAL COUNT PER SERVING 16.4g total fat (4.1g saturated fat); 1150kJ (275 cal); 3.2g carbohydrate; 28.2g protein; 1.7g fibre

Fish curry in lime and coconut

PREP + COOK TIME 55 MINUTES **SERVES** 4

6 fresh small red thai chillies, chopped coarsely

2 cloves garlic, quartered

10 shallots (250g), chopped

10cm stick fresh lemon grass (20g), chopped coarsely

5cm piece fresh galangal (25g), quartered

¼ cup coarsely chopped coriander root and stem mixture

¼ teaspoon ground turmeric

1 tablespoon peanut oil

2 x 400ml cans coconut milk

2 tablespoons fish sauce

4 fresh kaffir lime leaves, shredded

1 tablespoon lime juice

4 x 200g kingfish fillets

½ cup loosely packed fresh coriander leaves

1 Blend or process chilli, garlic, shallot, lemon grass, galangal, coriander root and stem mixture, turmeric and oil until mixture forms a smooth paste.

2 Cook paste in large frying pan, stirring, over medium heat, about 3 minutes or until fragrant. Add coconut milk, sauce and lime leaves; bring to the boil. Reduce heat; simmer, uncovered, about 15 minutes or until thickened slightly. Stir in juice.

3 Add fish to pan; simmer, uncovered, about 10 minutes or until cooked. Serve curry sprinkled with coriander leaves.

NUTRITIONAL COUNT PER SERVING 50.6g total fat (38.5g saturated fat); 2867kJ (686 cal); 10.6g carbohydrate; 45.9g protein; 4.9g fibre

ANCHOVY AND GARLIC TUNA WITH TOMATO AND OREGANO

Anchovy and garlic tuna with tomato and oregano

PREP + COOK TIME 45 MINUTES **SERVES** 4

1kg tuna fillet, trimmed, skinned

3 cloves garlic, sliced thinly

¼ cup firmly packed fresh oregano leaves

8 drained anchovy fillets, halved

¼ cup (60ml) olive oil

1 large brown onion (200g), sliced thinly

4 large egg tomatoes (360g), seeded, chopped coarsely

¼ cup (60ml) balsamic vinegar

2 tablespoons dry white wine

¼ cup (60ml) fish stock

1 tablespoon drained baby capers, rinsed

¼ cup coarsely chopped fresh basil

1 Preheat oven to 220°C/200°C fan-forced.

2 Using sharp knife, make 16 cuts in tuna; press 16 slices of the garlic, 16 oregano leaves and anchovy halves into cuts.

3 Heat 2 tablespoons of the oil in medium deep flameproof baking dish; cook tuna, uncovered, until browned. Remove from dish.

4 Heat remaining oil in same dish; cook onion, stirring, until soft. Combine tomato, vinegar, wine, stock, remaining garlic and remaining oregano in dish then add tuna; bring to the boil. Cook in oven about 10 minutes or until tuna is cooked as desired. Remove tuna from dish; slice thinly. Stir capers and basil into sauce in dish.

5 Serve with mashed potato.

NUTRITIONAL COUNT PER SERVING 28.7g total fat (7.8g saturated fat); 2286kJ (547 cal); 4.1g carbohydrate; 65.8g protein; 1.6g fibre

Serve this robust fish stew with fetta and black-olive mash: boil, steam or microwave 1kg coarsely chopped potato, mash in a large bowl with 1 tablespoon olive oil and stir in ⅔ cup warmed buttermilk, 200g finely chopped fetta cheese and ½ cup thinly sliced black olives. Drizzle another tablespoon of olive oil over to serve.

For information on garlic, see Garlic, page 214 & 215; and for egg tomatoes, see Tomatoes, page 607.

When using kaffir lime leaves whole, rub them first between your fingers to break open the cells in the leaf tissue and release their vivid flavour.

For more information on kaffir lime leaves, see Kaffir Lime Leaves, page 275; and for chillies, see Chillies, pages 118–120.

Lime and chilli roasted snapper

PREP + COOK TIME 20 MINUTES **SERVES** 4

4 x 500g plate-size snapper, cleaned

2cm piece fresh ginger (10g), sliced thinly

2 cloves garlic, sliced thinly

8 fresh kaffir lime leaves

1 fresh long red chilli, sliced thinly

2 tablespoons peanut oil

1 cup loosely packed fresh coriander leaves

CHILLI LIME DRESSING

⅓ cup (80ml) sweet chilli sauce

¼ cup (60ml) fish sauce

¼ cup (60ml) lime juice

2 teaspoons peanut oil

1 Preheat oven to 240°C/220°C fan-forced.

2 Rinse fish inside and out under cold water; pat dry with absorbent paper.

3 Divide ginger, garlic, lime leaves and chilli among fish cavities; rub fish all over with oil.

4 Place fish in two shallow oiled baking dishes; roast, uncovered, about 15 minutes or until cooked through.

5 Meanwhile, place ingredients for chilli lime dressing in screw-top jar; shake well.

6 Drizzle fish with dressing, sprinkle with coriander. Serve with asian greens.

NUTRITIONAL COUNT PER SERVING 15.1g total fat (3.5g saturated fat); 1354kJ (324 cal); 55g carbohydrate; 40.6g protein; 1.8g fibre

This is a curry for those who like it hot. It's all about the way the clean flavours of the fish and vegetables play against the chilli blast. To make your own green curry paste, see page 153.

For information on snow peas, see Peas, page 422.

Ling and snow pea green curry

PREP + COOK TIME 45 MINUTES **SERVES** 4

1¼ cups (250g) jasmine rice

2 teaspoons peanut oil

1 medium brown onion (150g), chopped finely

3 fresh small green chillies, seeded, sliced thinly

¼ cup (75g) green curry paste

1⅔ cups (400ml) coconut milk

4 x 200g ling fillets, skinned, chopped coarsely

200g snow peas, halved

4 green onions, sliced thinly

¼ cup coarsely chopped fresh coriander

1 Cook rice in large saucepan of boiling water, uncovered, until tender; drain. Cover to keep warm.

2 Meanwhile, heat oil in large saucepan; cook brown onion, chilli and curry paste, stirring, until onion softens. Stir in coconut milk; bring to the boil. Add fish, reduce heat; simmer, uncovered, 5 minutes. Add snow peas and green onion; stir gently until vegetables are just tender. Remove from heat; stir in half of the coriander. Serve curry with rice; sprinkle with remaining coriander.

NUTRITIONAL COUNT PER SERVING 16.4g total fat (4.1g saturated fat); 1150kJ (275 cal); 3.2g carbohydrate; 28.2g protein; 1.7g fibre

1 LIME AND CHILLI ROASTED SNAPPER **2** LING AND SNOW PEA GREEN CURRY
3 SEAFOOD CHOWDER [P 534] **4** SPICY SARDINES WITH ORANGE AND OLIVE SALAD [P 534]

1

2

3

4

Seafood chowder

PREP + COOK TIME 50 MINUTES **SERVES** 4

Chowder is the American name for a hearty soup, usually of seafood. It often has potatoes, too, and you could add some here, if you like: cut them, peeled or unpeeled, into chunks and add with the leek, garlic and bacon. Fish or chicken stock can be used instead of vegetable stock.

300g small mussels

500g uncooked medium prawns

40g butter

1 small leek (200g), sliced thinly

2 cloves garlic, crushed

2 rindless bacon rashers (130g), chopped finely

2 tablespoons plain flour

3 cups (750ml) milk

1 cup (250ml) vegetable stock

200g baby squid hoods, sliced thinly

300g firm white fish fillets, chopped coarsely

2 tablespoons finely chopped fresh chives

1 Scrub mussels; remove beards. Shell and devein prawns, leaving tails intact.

2 Melt butter in large saucepan; cook leek, garlic and bacon, stirring, until leek softens.

3 Add flour to pan; cook, stirring 1 minute. Stir in milk and stock; bring to the boil. Reduce heat; simmer, uncovered, 10 minutes.

4 Add seafood; simmer, uncovered, about 4 minutes or until prawns change colour and mussels open (discard any that do not). Serve chowder sprinkled with chives.

NUTRITIONAL COUNT PER SERVING 23.7g total fat (13.1g saturated fat); 2061kJ (493 cal); 15.8g carbohydrate; 53.3g protein; 1.4g fibre

Spicy sardines with orange and olive salad

PREP + COOK TIME 35 MINUTES **SERVES** 4

Sardines are among the best foods for your heart and bones. Their omega 3-rich oil is good for your arteries and their soft, edible bones provide high levels of calcium and significant amounts of Vitamin D. Most fishmongers have sardines already butterflied or will prepare them this way if you ask.

For information on oranges, see Oranges, pages 380-382; and for black olives, see Olives, page 370.

24 butterflied sardines (1kg)

1 clove garlic, crushed

1 tablespoon olive oil

2 tablespoons orange juice

1 teaspoon hot paprika

1 teaspoon finely chopped fresh oregano

ORANGE AND OLIVE SALAD

2 medium oranges (480g)

1/3 cup (40g) seeded black olives, chopped coarsely

50g baby rocket leaves

1 fresh long red chilli, sliced thinly

1 tablespoon orange juice

1/2 teaspoon finely chopped fresh oregano

1 tablespoon olive oil

1 Place sardines in medium bowl with remaining ingredients; mix gently.

2 Make orange and olive salad.

3 Cook sardines, in batches, on heated oiled grill plate (or grill or barbecue) until browned both sides and cooked through. Divide sardines among plates; serve with salad.

ORANGE AND OLIVE SALAD Peel then segment oranges over medium bowl, add remaining ingredients; toss gently to combine.

NUTRITIONAL COUNT PER SERVING 36.2g total fat (8.3g saturated fat); 2500kJ (598 cal); 11.5g carbohydrate; 56g protein; 2.2g fibre

Panang seafood curry

PREP + COOK TIME 45 MINUTES **SERVES** 4

2 x 400ml cans coconut milk

¼ cup (60g) panang curry paste
(page 154)

¼ cup (60ml) fish sauce

2 tablespoons grated palm sugar

4 fresh kaffir lime leaves, torn

2 tablespoons peanut oil

500g ling fillets,
cut into 3cm pieces

500g uncooked medium
king prawns

250g scallops

200g snake beans,
chopped coarsely

½ cup loosely packed fresh
thai basil leaves

½ cup (70g) coarsely chopped
roasted unsalted peanuts

2 fresh long red chillies,
sliced thinly

Panang curries are complex and relatively mild, with sweet underlying flavours.

For more information on panang and other curry pastes, see Curry pastes, page 152.

1 Place coconut milk, paste, sauce, sugar and lime leaves in wok; simmer, stirring, about 15 minutes or until mixture reduces by a third.
2 Meanwhile, heat oil in large frying pan; cook seafood, in batches, until just changed in colour. Drain on absorbent paper.
3 Add beans and seafood to curry mixture; cook, uncovered, stirring occasionally, about 5 minutes or until beans are just tender and seafood is cooked as desired.
4 Serve curry sprinkled with basil, nuts and chilli.

NUTRITIONAL COUNT PER SERVING 64.3g total fat (39.8g saturated fat); 3716kJ (889 cal); 18.3g carbohydrate; 57.1g protein; 7.2g fibre

---

Steamed mussels in tomato garlic broth

PREP + COOK TIME 55 MINUTES **SERVES** 4

1 tablespoon olive oil

2 shallots (50g), chopped finely

4 cloves garlic, crushed

410g can crushed tomatoes

1 cup (250ml) dry white wine

1 teaspoon caster sugar

2kg small black mussels

½ cup coarsely chopped fresh
flat-leaf parsley

Mussels must be cooked alive, as they may be unsafe to eat because their flesh deteriorates rapidly after death. For notes on how to check that they are alive when you buy them and again when you start to cook, see page 526.

1 Heat oil in large saucepan; cook shallot and garlic, stirring, until shallot softens.
2 Add undrained tomatoes, wine and sugar; bring to the boil. Reduce heat; simmer, uncovered, about 10 minutes or until sauce thickens slightly.
3 Meanwhile, scrub mussels; remove beards. Add mussels to pan; simmer, covered, about 5 minutes, shaking pan occasionally, until mussels open (discard any that do not). Remove mussels from pan, divide among serving bowls; cover with foil to keep warm.
4 Bring tomato mixture to the boil; boil, uncovered, about 5 minutes or until sauce thickens slightly. Pour tomato mixture over mussels; sprinkle with parsley.

NUTRITIONAL COUNT PER SERVING 6.7g total fat (1.2g saturated fat); 828kJ (198 cal); 9.9g carbohydrate; 13.3g protein; 2.2g fibre

Salt and pepper squid

PREP + COOK TIME 35 MINUTES **SERVES** 4

600g squid hoods, cleaned

¼ cup (35g) plain flour

1½ teaspoons sea salt flakes

1½ teaspoons cracked black pepper

1 teaspoon dried chilli flakes

vegetable oil, for deep-frying

40g baby rocket leaves

1 large tomato (220g), seeded, chopped finely

1 Cut squid down centre to open out; score the inside in a diagonal pattern. Halve squid lengthways; slice halves crossways into thick strips.

2 Combine flour, salt, pepper and chilli in medium bowl; add squid, toss to coat in flour mixture. Shake off excess.

3 Heat oil in wok; deep-fry squid, in batches, until tender, drain.

4 Serve squid with rocket and tomato, and lemon aïoli (see page 366).

NUTRITIONAL COUNT PER SERVING 9.6g total fat (1.6g saturated fat); 953kJ (228 cal); 7.7g carbohydrate; 26.9g protein; 1.3g fibre

Salt and pepper prawns are delicious, too. Shell and devein them, leaving tails intact, dip into the salt and pepper mixture and fry in the same way as squid. Serve either squid or prawns with aïoli as appetisers, or with a rocket and tomato or a greek salad as a lunch dish.

Prawn, crab and avocado salad

PREP + COOK TIME 25 MINUTES **SERVES** 4

16 cooked medium king prawns (800g)

4 large butter lettuce leaves

250g crab meat, shredded coarsely

1 large avocado (320g), sliced thinly

THOUSAND ISLAND DRESSING

½ cup (150g) mayonnaise

1 tablespoon tomato sauce

½ small red capsicum (75g), chopped finely

½ small white onion (40g), grated finely

8 pimiento-stuffed green olives, chopped finely

1 teaspoon lemon juice

1 Make thousand island dressing.

2 Shell and devein prawns, leaving tails intact.

3 Divide lettuce leaves among serving plates; divide prawns, crab and avocado among lettuce leaves. Drizzle with dressing.

THOUSAND ISLAND DRESSING Combine ingredients in small bowl.

NUTRITIONAL COUNT PER SERVING 26.5g total fat (4.4g saturated fat); 1718kJ (411 cal); 11.5g carbohydrate; 30.7g protein; 2.8g fibre

You can buy ready-made thousand island dressing, but your own is best. Use it also on coleslaw to go with corned beef and on the famous New York deli sandwich, the Reuben, made with toasted rye bread and filled with sliced corned beef, swiss cheese, sauerkraut and thousand island dressing.

For information on avocado, see Avocado, pages 24–26.

SALT AND PEPPER SQUID

Cook bug meat only briefly or it will be dry and tough. If uncooked bugs are not available, you can used cooked bugs and warm the meat briefly under the grill or in the microwave. You can also substitute prawns or lobster for the bugs.

For information on saffron, see Spices, page 559.

Warm balmain bug salad with saffron dressing

PREP + COOK TIME 40 MINUTES **SERVES** 4

24 uncooked balmain bugs (4.8kg)

500g cherry tomatoes

2 large avocados (640g), sliced thinly

1 medium red onion (170g), sliced thinly

80g snow pea tendrils

½ cup firmly packed fresh basil leaves

SAFFRON DRESSING

8 saffron threads

¼ cup (60ml) boiling water

1 egg yolk

1 clove garlic, crushed

1 teaspoon english mustard

2 tablespoons lemon juice

½ cup (125ml) light olive oil

1 Make saffron dressing.

2 Meanwhile, place each bug, upside down, on chopping board; cut tail from body. Discard body; cut through tail lengthways, remove and discard vein. Remove meat from both tail halves.

3 Cook bug meat and tomatoes, in batches, on heated oiled grill plate (or grill or barbecue) until browned all over.

4 Just before serving, combine tomatoes, avocado, onion, tendrils and basil in large bowl with one-third of the saffron dressing. Divide salad mixture among serving plates; top with bug meat, drizzle with remaining dressing.

SAFFRON DRESSING Combine saffron and the water in small heatproof bowl; stand 10 minutes. Strain through fine strainer into small bowl; discard threads. Whisk egg yolk, garlic, mustard and juice in small bowl; gradually add oil, in thin stream, whisking continuously. Whisk in saffron liquid.

NUTRITIONAL COUNT PER SERVING 58.8g total fat (10.7g saturated fat); 3804kJ (910 cal); 10.5g carbohydrate; 85.3g protein; 5.4g fibre

Mud crabs are sold alive and must be killed only just before cooking. The most humane way is to place them head down in fresh water and ice: the cold quickly stuns them and they drown painlessly. To make your own laksa paste, see page 155.

Chilli crab laksa

PREP + COOK TIME 1 HOUR 10 MINUTES (PLUS STANDING TIME) **SERVES** 4

2 uncooked whole mud crabs (1.5kg)

2 tablespoons peanut oil

3 fresh long red chillies, chopped finely

2 cloves garlic, crushed

2cm piece fresh ginger (10g), grated

½ cup (125ml) fish stock

⅔ cup (180g) laksa paste

3¼ cups (800ml) coconut milk

1 litre (4 cups) chicken stock

3 fresh kaffir lime leaves, shredded finely

1 fresh long red chilli, chopped finely, extra

1 tablespoon lime juice

1 tablespoon fish sauce

1 tablespoon grated palm sugar

250g rice stick noodles

3 green onions, sliced thinly

3 cups (240g) bean sprouts

½ cup loosely packed fresh coriander leaves

1 Place crabs in large container filled with ice and water; stand 1 hour. Leaving flesh in claws and legs, prepare crab by lifting tail flap and, with a peeling motion, lift off back shell. Remove and discard whitish gills, liver and brain matter; crack claws with back of knife. Rinse crabs well. Using cleaver or heavy knife, chop each body into quarters; crack large claws lightly with back of knife.

2 Heat oil in wok; stir-fry chilli, garlic and ginger until fragrant. Add crab and fish stock to wok; bring to the boil. Reduce heat; simmer, covered, about 20 minutes or until crab is changed in colour. Discard liquid in wok.

3 Meanwhile, cook paste in large saucepan, stirring, until fragrant. Stir in coconut milk, chicken stock, lime leaf and extra chilli; bring to the boil. Reduce heat; simmer, covered, 20 minutes. Stir in juice, sauce and sugar.

4 Meanwhile, place noodles in large heatproof bowl; cover with boiling water. Stand until tender; drain.

5 Divide noodles and crab among serving bowls; ladle laksa into bowls, top with onion, sprouts and coriander.

NUTRITIONAL COUNT PER SERVING 68.2g total fat (40g saturated fat); 4088kJ (978 cal); 31.6g carbohydrate; 55.9g protein; 10.8g fibre

VONGOLE AND
CHORIZO LINGUINE

Vongole and chorizo linguine

PREP + COOK TIME 30 MINUTES (PLUS STANDING TIME) **SERVES** 4

750g vongole (clams)

375g linguine pasta

1 tablespoon extra virgin olive oil

1 chorizo sausage (170g), sliced thinly

2 cloves garlic, crushed

2 long red chillies, sliced thinly

250g cherry tomatoes, halved

¾ cup loosely packed small fresh basil leaves

¼ cup (60ml) extra virgin olive oil, extra

1 Rinse vongole; place in bowl of cold water for 1 hour; drain.

2 Cook pasta in large saucepan of boiling until just tender; drain. Return to pan.

3 Meanwhile, heat oil in large frying pan; cook chorizo until crisp. Remove chorizo from pan; add vongole to same pan, cook, covered, about 3 minutes or until vongole open (discard any that do not open). Push the vongole to one side of pan.

4 Add garlic, chilli and tomatoes; cook, uncovered, about 2 minutes or until fragrant and softened.

5 Add chorizo and vongole mixture to hot pasta with basil and extra oil; toss gently to combine.

NUTRITIONAL COUNT PER SERVING 32.2g total fat (7.4g saturated fat); 2805kJ (671 cal); 67.1g carbohydrate; 25.8g protein; 4.6g fibre

The sweet flavour of vongole (clams/pipis/ sand cockles) and the hot spiciness of chorizo are wonderful together. Discard any vongole that do not open when heated as this shows they are dead and may be dangerous to eat as their flesh deteriorates quickly after death.

For information on linguine and other pasta, see Pasta, pages 396–398.

Thai coconut scallops

PREP + COOK TIME 45 MINUTES **SERVES** 4

2 tablespoons peanut oil

24 scallops without roe (600g)

1 shallot (25g), chopped finely

2cm piece fresh ginger (10g), grated

2 cloves garlic, crushed

2 tablespoons red curry paste

400ml can coconut milk

1 tablespoon fish sauce

1 tablespoon lime juice

1 tablespoon grated palm sugar

1 fresh kaffir lime leaf, torn

HERB SALAD

½ cup loosely packed fresh mint leaves

½ cup loosely packed thai basil leaves

½ cup (40g) shaved fresh coconut

2 fresh long red chillies, shredded finely

1 green onion, sliced thinly

1 Combine ingredients for herb salad in large bowl.

2 Heat half the oil in medium frying pan; cook scallops, in batches, until browned.

3 Heat remaining oil in same pan; cook shallot, ginger and garlic, stirring, until shallot softens. Add paste; cook, stirring, until fragrant. Add coconut milk, sauce, juice, sugar and lime leaf; bring to the boil. Reduce heat; simmer, uncovered, about 5 minutes or until sauce thickens slightly. Add scallops; reheat gently.

4 Divide scallops among serving plates, pour sauce around scallops; serve with salad.

NUTRITIONAL COUNT PER SERVING 37.8g total fat (22.9g saturated fat); 1956kJ (468 cal); 10.3g carbohydrate; 21.2g protein; 4.8g fibre

You will need a small fresh coconut for this recipe. To open it, preheat oven to 240°C/220°C fan-forced. Pierce one of the coconut's eyes with a sharp knife, place on an oven tray and bake 10 minutes or until cracks appear. Remove from oven and, when cool enough to handle, pull coconut apart and use the firm white flesh inside. If you can't get fresh coconut, substitute half a small mango, thinly sliced. To make your own red curry paste, see page 153.

Oysters with two dressings

PREP TIME 10 MINUTES **MAKES** 24

24 oysters, on the half shell

RED WINE VINEGAR DRESSING

1 ½ teaspoons finely chopped shallots

1 tablespoon red wine vinegar

1 teaspoon extra virgin olive oil

SPICY LIME DRESSING

1 ½ tablespoons lime juice

½ teaspoon hot chilli sauce

1 teaspoon finely chopped fresh coriander

1 Place ingredients for red wine vinegar dressing in screw-top jar; shake well.

2 Place ingredients for spicy lime dressing in screw-top jar; shake well.

3 Just before serving, drizzle half of the oysters with each dressing.

NUTRITIONAL COUNT PER OYSTER [12] WITH RED WINE VINEGAR DRESSING 1g total fat (0.3g saturated fat); 92kJ (22 cal); 0.2g carbohydrate; 3.1g protein; 0g fibre
NUTRITIONAL COUNT PER OYSTER [12] WITH SPICY LIME DRESSING 0.6g total fat (0.2g saturated fat); 79kJ (19 cal); 0.3g carbohydrate; 3.1g protein; 0g fibre

To prevent oysters from sliding around on the plate, serve them on a bed of rock salt or crushed ice. Another way to serve them is to take them out of the shells and put them on Chinese porcelain soup spoons, then top them with a little combined lime juice and Asian fish sauce plus a sprinkle of finely shredded lime rind and fresh coriander. They are often served this way at cocktail parties; guests pick up the spoons from the offered tray and tip the oysters straight into their mouths.

THAI COCONUT SCALLOPS

Seaweed

Coast-dwellers in various parts of the world have been using seaweed as a healthy part of their diet for centuries, but it is Japanese cuisine, especially sushi that has become hugely popular round the world, that has everyone eating seaweed. Sea vegetables would be a better name for these nourishing "greens."

Nori sheets

Kombu

Wakame

They are high in iodine and calcium and often in protein and Vitamins A and B, and contain valuable trace minerals. The Japanese consider them rejuvenative to the nervous system and effective against arthritis and the effects of animal food. Their kilojoule content is negligible. Their taste varies slightly from one kind to another, but is, in general, briny/fishy. The most pronounced differences between the types are those of texture, from the firm crunch of uncooked kombu to the delicate softness of wakame and crispness of dried nori, the form in which it is always used.

NORI is a fine seaweed related to the laver that the Welsh gather from the rocks, cook, roll in oatmeal and fry for breakfast. Nori is pressed into thin sheets and dried. The best grades are lustrous, deep, rich green or purple-black. It should be lightly toasted on one side over a flame or under a griller before using; ready-toasted nori is available, but benefits from quick crisping. It is used for wrapping sushi, rice balls, vegetable patties or seafood; chopped or crumbled, it is used as a garnish or added to soup, breads, seafood, rice or vegetables.

KOMBU is a thick, deep-sea kelp dried in long, flat strips. The best grades are blackish green, streaked with a white surface powder from natural glutamates. Don't wipe it off, it adds to the flavour. Kombu is essential for preparing dashi, the light fish stock that is basic to many Japanese soups, vegetable dishes and sauces. The dried strips should be soaked in water so that they swell to three to four times their previous volume. At this stage, it is edible though still firm to the bite. It can be further softened by boiling or can be cut into bite-size pieces, dried and deep-fried to serve with a dipping sauce. Kombu has natural tenderising properties and is useful for speeding the cooking of dried beans: add a strip to the beans as they soak and cook it with them.

WAKAME is a dried ocean-floor seaweed transformed by soaking from a blackish, papery substance to a fresh-looking, soft green leaf; it also expands to five to seven times its previous volume. It is good added to soups, batters, doughs and sauces, or in salads. It is very decorative. Unsoaked wakame, toasted and crumbled, adds flavour and crunch to salads, cooked vegetables and rice or other grain dishes. Like kombu, it has tenderising properties and a small piece is often added to root vegetables as they cook.

STORING

Keep dried seaweeds in airtight containers in a cool place. Refrigerate fresh seaweed, after washing well, in a covered container and use as soon as possible. If it has to be kept longer than a day or two, store, refrigerated, covered in brine. Dried seaweeds can be kept for 24 hours in their soaking water, but may become slimy if left for longer.

California handrolls

PREP + COOK TIME 45 MINUTES **MAKES** 40

⅓ cup (100g) mayonnaise

1 teaspoon wasabi paste

10 sheets toasted nori, each cut into four squares

2 cups sushi rice (recipe page 498)

60g cooked crab, shredded

1 lebanese cucumber (130g), seeded, sliced thinly

1 small avocado (200g), sliced thinly

1 small red capsicum (150g), sliced thinly

1 Combine mayonnaise and wasabi in small bowl.

2 Place nori, shiny-side down, diagonally across palm of hand. Using damp fingers, mould rounded teaspoons of rice into oblong shape; place across centre of seaweed. Make a slight groove down the middle of the rice for filling. Dab some of the wasabi mayonnaise along groove; top with a little crab, cucumber, avocado and capsicum.

3 Fold one side of seaweed over; fold other side of seaweed over the first to form a cone shape. Tip of cone can be folded inwards to hold shape securely.

NUTRITIONAL COUNT PER PIECE 1.6g total fat (0.3g saturated fat); 163kJ (39 cal); 5.1g carbohydrate; 0.8g protein; 0.5g fibre

Like all sushi, california handrolls should be eaten as soon as possible after making.

For information on crab, see Seafood, page 524.

Tuna cucumber mini-maki

PREP + COOK TIME 30 MINUTES **MAKES** 48

4 sheets toasted nori, cut in half widthways

2 cups sushi rice (recipe page 498)

2 teaspoons wasabi paste

120g piece sashimi tuna, cut into 5mm strips

1 lebanese cucumber (130g), halved lengthways, seeded, cut into thin strips

¼ cup (60ml) japanese soy sauce

1 Place one nori sheet shiny-side down on sushi mat. Using damp fingers, spread ¼ cup rice over nori, leaving 2cm strip at end.

2 Dab some of the wasabi across centre of rice; layer tuna and cucumber over wasabi. Using mat, roll firmly to form sushi roll. Place roll, seam-side down, on board; using sharp knife, cut roll into six mini-maki pieces. Repeat with remaining nori, rice, tuna and cucumber.

3 Serve mini-maki immediately with soy sauce, and more wasabi.

NUTRITIONAL COUNT PER PIECE 0.2g total fat (0.1g saturated fat); 88kJ (21 cal); 3.7g carbohydrate; 1g protein; 0.2g fibre

TUNA CUCUMBER MINI-MAKI

Sushi mats are available from Asian food stores and many supermarkets.

For information on tuna, see Seafood, page 523.

Seeds

The crisp textures and good, nutty flavours of seeds work especially well on or in breads, cakes, pastries and biscuits, whether plain, sweet or savoury.

In Turkey and the Middle East, taratoor is served with roasted vegetables (especially eggplant), roasted or barbecued whole fish and falafel, and is added to salad rolls or pitta pockets of meat and salad. You can vary it by adding chopped parsley, chilli or cumin. To make taratoor sauce at home, combine ½ cup (140g) tahini, 2 crushed garlic cloves, ½ cup (125ml) hot water and ⅓ cup (80ml) lemon juice in small bowl.

Always stir tahini well before using it as it tends to settle in layers.

❦ OTHER RECIPES USING SEEDS
Age-dashi tofu, p603
Apple cider and poppy seed vinaigrette, p635
Baba ghanoush, p161
Boxty, p186
Dukkah-crusted lamb cutlets with roasted garlic yogurt, p566
Hummus, p479
Lamb korma, p289
Lamb teriyaki with broccolini, p512
Roasted duck and stir-fried greens salad, p246
Thai salmon broth with sesame sticky rice patties, p628
Thai-style green mango salad with seared tuna, p309

SESAME SEEDS come from a plant which has been cultivated since the days of ancient Egypt, mainly for the oil which can be crushed from the seeds but also for the seeds themselves. which are used in the ways mentioned above and also in confectionery, toasted and sprinkled on salads and desserts, or fried in butter or oil and tossed with cooked carrot sticks or chunks of roasted pumpkin or sweet potato. Unhulled sesame seeds are black or golden brown. The white (actually cream) seeds used in cooking have been hulled. Unless they are to be baked, white sesame seeds are usually toasted before using to bring out their flavour and aroma. Black sesame seeds are not toasted as it makes them bitter; they are used in Asian cooking and, in Japan, mixed with salt and MSG and sprinkled on food. Both hulled and unhulled seeds are used for tahini, the sesame paste which is used with chickpeas and garlic for the Middle Eastern dip, hummus.

PEPITAS (PUMPKIN SEEDS) Be sure to buy pumpkin seed kernels, as the outer husk is difficult to remove once the seed is dried. Pepitas, which are highly nutritious, are mostly eaten salted as a snack and are also used commercially in breakfast cereals. In the kitchen, they are used in the ways mentioned above and also in salads and rice dishes.

POPPY SEEDS come from the opium poppy and contain narcotic substances when immature but, when the seed ripens, these change to harmless forms. Poppy seeds are especially valued by Central and Eastern European cooks for their breads and cakes, whether sprinkled on top or ground and mixed with sugar, raisins, almonds and such as a filling for sweet pastries. They are also used in some egg, potato and pasta dishes. European poppy seeds are dark, but Indian ones are cream and are roasted and used in spice mixtures or ground to thicken curries and sauces.

SUNFLOWER SEEDS A single sunflower may contain hundreds of seeds. Dried and hulled, the highly nutritious kernels are salted and eaten as a popular snack and used in confectionery and breakfast cereals; unhulled seeds are sold as bird food. In the kitchen, kernels are used in the ways mentioned above and in salads and rice dishes.

CHOOSING
Buy seeds in quantities that you will use within a month or so as they are high in oil and will become rancid if stored for too long. Buy from busy stores with a fast turnover and, if the seeds are packaged, be sure to check the use-by date.

STORING
Store seeds in airtight containers in the refrigerator.

Sesame tofu salad

PREP + COOK TIME 35 MINUTES **SERVES** 4

For information on firm silken tofu, see Tofu, page 602; and for kalonji seeds, see Spices, page 558.

2 x 300g blocks firm silken tofu

2 tablespoons toasted sesame seeds

2 tablespoons kalonji seeds

2 teaspoons dried chilli flakes

2 tablespoons cornflour

vegetable oil, for deep-frying

5 green onions, sliced thinly

1 large avocado (320g), chopped coarsely

100g red oak lettuce leaves, torn

100g mizuna

1 fresh long red chilli, seeded, sliced thinly

SESAME DRESSING

2 shallots (50g), chopped finely

2 tablespoons toasted sesame seeds

1 tablespoon sesame oil

1 tablespoon kecap manis

1cm piece fresh ginger (5g), grated

¼ cup (60ml) lemon juice

1 Place ingredients for sesame dressing in screw-top jar; shake well.

2 Cut each tofu block lengthways into four slices; dry with absorbent paper. Combine seeds, chilli and cornflour in large shallow bowl; press mixture onto both sides of tofu slices.

3 Heat oil in wok; deep-fry tofu, in batches, until browned. Drain on absorbent paper.

4 Combine remaining ingredients in large bowl; top with tofu, drizzle with dressing.

NUTRITIONAL COUNT PER SERVING 59.7g total fat (9.9g saturated fat); 2796kJ (669 cal); 9.2g carbohydrate; 22.8g protein; 6.2g fibre

Salmon and tuna sold as sashimi-grade have to meet stringent standards of freshness and hygiene regarding their handling and treatment after leaving the water. However, it is best to seek local advice from knowledgeable authorities before eating any raw fish.

For more information on tuna and salmon, see Seafood, page 523.

Sesame-crusted sashimi

PREP + COOK TIME 30 MINUTES (PLUS REFRIGERATION TIME) **SERVES** 4

2 tablespoons sesame seeds

1 tablespoon black sesame seeds

2 teaspoons coriander seeds

1 teaspoon sea salt

½ teaspoon cracked black pepper

2 tablespoons finely chopped fresh chives

300g piece sashimi tuna

300g piece sashimi salmon

GINGER DRESSING

2cm piece fresh ginger (10g), grated

1 tablespoon rice vinegar

1 tablespoon vegetable oil

1 teaspoon sesame oil

2 teaspoons mirin

2 teaspoons soy sauce

1 Dry-fry seeds in small frying pan, stirring, until fragrant; cool. Using mortar and pestle, crush seeds; combine in large bowl with salt, pepper and chives.

2 Cut each piece of fish into three 5cm-thick pieces. Roll each piece in seed mixture; enclose tightly, individually, in plastic wrap. Refrigerate 20 minutes

3 Place ingredients for ginger dressing in screw-top jar; shake well.

4 Unwrap fish; slice thinly. Serve fish drizzled with dressing.

NUTRITIONAL COUNT PER SERVING 18.9g total fat (4.1g saturated fat); 1313kJ (314 cal); 0.4g carbohydrate; 35.1g protein; 0.8g fibre

Have the lime at room temperature and roll it, pressing down hard, before using it, in order to obtain the maximum amount of juice. You can use the same weight of other citrus fruit — lemons, mandarins, blood oranges, oranges etc — instead of limes if you wish.

For information on lime, see Limes, page 300.

Lime and poppy seed syrup cake

PREP + COOK TIME 1 HOUR 20 MINUTES **SERVES** 12

¼ cup (40g) poppy seeds

½ cup (125ml) milk

250g butter, softened

1 tablespoon finely grated lime rind

1¼ cups (275g) caster sugar

4 eggs

2¼ cups (335g) self-raising flour

¾ cup (110g) plain flour

1 cup (240g) sour cream

LIME SYRUP

½ cup (125ml) lime juice

1 cup (250ml) water

1 cup (220g) caster sugar

1 Preheat oven to 180°C/160°C fan-forced. Grease base and sides of deep 23cm-square cake pan. Combine poppy seeds and milk in small jug; soak 10 minutes.

2 Beat butter, rind and sugar in small bowl with electric mixer until light and fluffy. Beat in eggs, one at a time; transfer mixture to large bowl. Stir in sifted flours, cream and poppy seed mixture, in two batches. Spread mixture into pan; bake about 1 hour.

3 Meanwhile, stir ingredients for lime syrup in small saucepan over heat, without boiling, until sugar dissolves. Simmer, uncovered, without stirring, 5 minutes.

4 Stand cake 5 minutes, turn onto wire rack over tray. Pour hot lime syrup over hot cake.

NUTRITIONAL COUNT PER SERVING 29.1g total fat (17.5g saturated fat); 2395kJ (573 cal); 69.1g carbohydrate; 7.6g protein; 2.1g fibre

LIME AND POPPY SEED SYRUP CAKE

Silver Beet

Also known as chard, swiss chard or, incorrectly, spinach, silver beet's large, fleshy-stemmed dark-green leaves do taste rather like spinach but more assertive, and the two are not related.

1 SILVER BEET
2 RAINBOW SILVER BEET
3 RED (RUBY) SILVER BEET

Silver beet usually has white stems, but red silver beet (also known as ruby silver beet), a variety with decorative red stems, and rainbow silver beet, with stems in various pastel colours, are available; these are picked young and sweet so that they can be used for salads or, if cooked, the stems can be cooked with the leaves. Usually, silver beet stems are removed but should not be discarded as they are good stringed, sliced, boiled and served with cheese sauce as a vegetable in their own right. The leaves can be blanched by dropping them into boiling water for a minute or so, or they can be washed, sliced and steamed with a grinding of nutmeg in a non-reactive saucepan just until they wilt, then tossed with butter or cream and seasonings. If using young stems to be served with the leaves, slice them and steam with a little butter or cream for a few minutes before adding the leaves. Cooked leaves can be served with meats, poultry and seafood, used in a frittata or pureed, mixed with ricotta and used as a filling for ravioli or the Greek fillo pastries called spanakopita. Uncooked leaves can be shredded and added to a clear meat and vegetable soup a few minutes before serving, or sliced and added to a rice and onion pilaff for the last 5 minutes of cooking. In southern Europe, where silver beet is popular, it is often used with other vegetables for a savoury pie filling or with apple, nuts, raisins, eggs and sugar for a dessert tart.

CHOOSING Silver beet should be undamaged and fresh with stiff stems and crisp leaves.

STORING Cut off the stems if necessary to fit them into the refrigerator and store leaves and stems together enclosed in a paper bag, then in a plastic bag, refrigerated, for up to 3 days.

❦ **OTHER RECIPES USING SILVER BEET**
Ham and black-eyed bean soup, p258
Zesty beetroot juice, p56

For a great, inexpensive and sustaining Turkish soup to serve 4–6, gently fry 2 finely chopped onions and 1 teaspoon each of paprika and cumin in 80g butter, then add 2 tablespoons tomato paste, 1 cup red lentils and 8 cups vegetable or beef stock. Bring to the boil, salt lightly if necessary, add cayenne pepper or chilli flakes to taste and simmer, half-covered, about 1 hour. Add 1 cup shredded silver beet leaves and 1 tablespoon lemon juice and cook a further 5 minutes. Check seasoning and serve with a spoonful of yogurt on each bowl and a lemon wedge alongside.

This recipe is best made just before serving.

For information on raisins, see Fruit, Dried, page 192; and for pine nuts, see Nuts, page 344.

Rainbow silver beet with pine nuts, garlic and raisins

PREP + COOK TIME 20 MINUTES **SERVES** 6

1 bunch rainbow silver beet (750g)

2 tablespoons olive oil

1 medium brown onion (150g), chopped finely

2 cloves garlic, crushed

½ cup (85g) raisins

⅓ cup (50g) pine nuts, roasted

1 tablespoon lemon juice

1 Separate leaves and stems of silver beet; chop coarsely.

2 Heat half the oil in large saucepan; cook onion and garlic, stirring, until softened. Add silver beet stems, cook, stirring, until just tender. Add leaves, cook, stirring, until wilted.

3 Remove pan from heat, stir in raisins and half the pine nuts. Season to taste with salt and pepper. Drizzle with the remaining oil and lemon juice; sprinkle with the remaining pine nuts.

NUTRITIONAL COUNT PER SERVING 12.3g total fat (1.3g saturated fat); 782kJ (187 cal); 13.2g carbohydrate; 3.7g protein; 5g fibre

Fillo pastry dries very quickly, so spread a tea towel on the work surface, cover with a sheet of baking paper and lay the pastry on that when you take it from the package. Cover with another sheet of baking paper and then a damp tea towel, and, after removing each sheet of pastry, cover the stack again while you work.

For information on fillo pastry, see Pastry, page 405.

Silver beet, cheese and fillo stacks

PREP + COOK TIME 30 MINUTES **SERVES** 6

4 sheets fillo pastry

40g butter, melted

1 tablespoon olive oil

1 medium brown onion (150g), chopped finely

1 clove garlic, crushed

2 rindless bacon rashers (130g), chopped finely

1kg silver beet, trimmed, shredded finely

2 tablespoons lemon juice

200g ricotta cheese

100g fetta cheese, crumbled

1 Preheat oven to 200°C/180°C fan-forced. Oil oven trays.

2 Place one sheet of pastry on board; brush with butter, top with another pastry sheet. Repeat layering with pastry and butter. Cut pastry stack in half widthways; place on tray. Grease base of another similar-sized oven tray; place on top of pastry stack (this is to stop the pastry from puffing up too much). Bake about 12 minutes or until browned. Cut each fillo stack into 9 rectangles (you will have 18 rectangles).

3 Meanwhile, heat oil in large deep saucepan; cook onion, garlic and bacon, stirring, until onion softens and bacon is crisp. Add silver beet and juice; cook, covered, stirring occasionally, until silver beet is wilted and tender. Remove from heat; stir in cheeses.

4 Place one fillo rectangle on each serving plate; top equally with half the silver beet mixture then another fillo rectangle. Top with remaining silver beet mixture and remaining fillo rectangles.

NUTRITIONAL COUNT PER SERVING 19.6g total fat (10.1g saturated fat); 1162kJ (278 cal); 8.9g carbohydrate; 14.5g protein; 5.1g fibre

RAINBOW SILVER BEET WITH PINE NUTS, GARLIC AND RAISINS

Soya

The remarkable soya bean (or soybean) is one of the world's most important foods. Its high protein content, comparable with that of red meat, provides vital sustenance to the peoples of China, Japan and South-East Asia, more than a quarter of humankind, most of whose diets are largely or entirely vegetarian. In addition, soybeans are rich in oil — they are the world's main source of cooking oil.

Fermentation means changes brought about in food and drink by the living micro-organisms yeasts, moulds or bacteria. The changes may be intended and desirable or unintended and undesirable. The term fermentation is usually reserved for the good changes, while the bad changes are called spoilage. Soya products, bread, cheese, chocolate, vanilla, yogurt, vinegar, wine and beer are some of the foods and drinks in whose production fermentation plays an essential part.

Vegans are those who choose not to eat flesh or animal products such as milk and eggs.

For an explanation of lactose intolerance, see Milk, page 316.

They have, however, two drawbacks: dried, then boiled like other beans, they are tough, indigestible and gas-producing, and they have a strong, bitter "beany" flavour that most people dislike. Immature fresh soybeans, eaten raw or briefly cooked, are more palatable and digestible, but these do not offer the non-perishable, portable, year-round source of nourishment that dried beans represent. These problems have long since been overcome by human ingenuity in developing soy products so palatable, as well as healthy, that they are becoming more and more popular in the affluent, meat-eating West.

SOY MILK at its simplest is made by soaking, grinding, cooking and sieving soybeans. The resulting liquid is nutritious, digestible and enjoyable to the Chinese, who have drunk it for millennia, but smells and tastes awful to Westerners and is also disagreeable to the Japanese. A careful process of soaking and brief cooking at specific temperatures to minimise the enzyme action that develops the unwanted smell and taste, and sometimes the addition of sugar or other flavourings, make it acceptable to non-Chinese palates and a useful health food for people who are lactose-intolerant or who wish to avoid animal fats, and for vegans. Soy milk compares with cow's milk for protein and fat content and soy milk's fat is less

saturated. However, it must be fortified with calcium to compare with cow's milk in that respect. It can be used for puddings, custards and sauces. Soy milk skin, the coagulated layer that forms on the top after heating, is valued as a delicacy in China and Japan and layered together with flavourings to make a variety of sweet and savoury products. Coagulating the milk itself by adding mineral salts separates it into soft curds and "whey", creating bean curd or tofu (see Tofu, page 602).

MISO is the Japanese name for fermented soybean paste, important in both Japanese and Chinese cuisines. It is the equivalent of the Chinese bean pastes called dou jiang in China and simply bean paste in English (see Bean Pastes, page 38). In both cuisines, these essential flavour bases are made in many different styles. They are made from soybeans and usually a grain — nearly always rice but sometimes barley or rye in Japan, and wheat in China. The traditional process starts with inoculating the steamed grain with a mould which is allowed to grow to form the starter culture, then the soaked, steamed and chopped soybeans are mixed in together with water which has been inoculated with yeast and bacteria cultures. The mixture is then allowed to ferment and ripen for months or years, depending on the style of miso/bean paste being made.

The result is a product with rich, deep, complex flavour. There are also misos/bean pastes on sale that have been made in a few days via chemicals, with various additives to make up for their lack of flavour or colour, but these do not compare with the real thing, which can be identified (if the labelling is in English) by such statements as "traditionally made" and by the ingredients list which should include soybeans, rice (or another grain), salt, koji seed (the starter mould) and nothing else. Japanese cooks use miso in many ways, principally as an ingredient in soup, simmered dishes, sauces and pickles and as a seasoning for salads and grilled food. It is sold in tubes and plastic packs and can be stored in the refrigerator for months.

Some of the best-known types of miso are:

Hatcho-miso, which is made from soybeans only and matured for up to two years. Usually used as a soup base, it is dark, strong and salty.

Shinshu-miso, perhaps the best known miso in Western countries. It is a versatile type, smooth, yellow and salty, which can be used in most recipes calling for miso.

Inaka-miso, which is red and can be sweet or salty. Used in soups and simmered dishes.

Shiro-miso, which is sweet-salty and mild. Used for soups or dressings.

Also see Sauces, Asian pages 508 & 509; Tofu, page 602 and Yogurt, pages 652–653.

Ginger miso dressing

PREP + COOK TIME 20 MINUTES **MAKES** ½ CUP

For information on ginger, see Ginger, page 222.

¼ cup (60ml) rice vinegar

2 tablespoons white miso

1 tablespoon mirin

2 teaspoons caster sugar

2cm piece fresh ginger (10g), grated

1 clove garlic, crushed

1 teaspoon soy sauce

1 teaspoon sesame oil

1 tablespoon water

1 Combine ingredients in small saucepan; stir, over low heat, until sugar dissolves.

2 Remove pan from heat; strain over small jug and discard solids.

3 Serve dressing with steamed buns or dumplings, stir-fried asian greens, or barbecued chicken, if you like.

NUTRITIONAL COUNT PER TABLESPOON 1.3g total fat (0.2g saturated fat); 125kJ (30 cal); 3.3g carbohydrate; 1.0g protein; 0.6g fibre

GINGER MISO DRESSING

Soy yogurt, available at supermarkets, is mild but readily takes up other flavours.

For information on baby new potatoes, see Potatoes, pages 448–449; and for asparagus, see Asparagus, page 20.

Potato and asparagus salad with yogurt and mint dressing

PREP + COOK TIME 40 MINUTES **SERVES** 2

300g baby new potatoes, unpeeled

250g asparagus, trimmed, cut into 3cm lengths

1 lebanese cucumber (130g), sliced thinly

50g watercress, trimmed

½ cup (80g) toasted pepitas

YOGURT AND MINT DRESSING

¼ cup (60g) soy yogurt

1 teaspoon finely grated lime rind

1 tablespoon fresh lime juice

¼ cup finely chopped fresh mint

1 Boil, steam or microwave potatoes until tender; drain. When cool enough to handle, quarter potatoes.

2 Meanwhile, boil, steam or microwave asparagus until tender; drain. Rinse under cold water; drain.

3 Combine ingredients for yogurt and mint dressing in small bowl.

4 Place potato and asparagus in medium bowl with cucumber, watercress, pepitas and dressing; toss gently to combine.

NUTRITIONAL COUNT PER SERVING 19.4g total fat (3.6g saturated fat); 1584kJ (379 cal); 34.2g carbohydrate; 17.7g protein; 7.6g fibre

You need about six passionfruit for this recipe.

For information on passionfruit, see Passionfruit, page 392; and for bananas, see Bananas, pages 32–34.

Banana passionfruit soy smoothie

PREP TIME 10 MINUTES **MAKES** 1 LITRE (4 CUPS)

½ cup (125ml) passionfruit pulp

2 cups (500ml) soy milk

2 medium ripe bananas (400g), chopped coarsely

1 Strain passionfruit pulp through sieve into small bowl; reserve liquid and seeds.

2 Blend passionfruit liquid, milk and banana, in batches, until smooth.

3 Pour smoothie into large jug; stir in reserved seeds.

NUTRITIONAL COUNT PER 250ML 4.7g total fat (0.5g saturated fat); 702kJ (168 cal); 21.5g carbohydrate; 6.6g protein; 6.5g fibre

POTATO AND ASPARAGUS SALAD WITH YOGURT AND MINT DRESSING

Spices

Spices add greatly to the pleasures of cooking and eating. Like herbs, they come from plants, but from different parts such as seeds and fruits. Most spices are dried — in fact, many must be dried in order to develop the taste and aroma for which they are valued. Some spices are always used whole, but many are sold and used both whole and ground.

1 CARAWAY SEEDS
2 WHOLE ALLSPICE
3 WHOLE CLOVES
4 CARDAMOM PODS
5 CUMIN SEEDS
6 CORIANDER SEEDS
7 KALONJI (NIGELLA) SEEDS
8 FENUGREEK SEEDS
9 GARAM MASALA
10 WHOLE NUTMEG
11 JUNIPER BERRIES
12 HARISSA
13 CINNAMON QUILLS
14 CASSIA BARK
15 CASSIA QUILLS

CARAWAY SEEDS comes from a plant which grows wild in many parts of Europe and Asia. Its flavour is freshly anise — oil extracted from the seeds is used to flavour mouth-washes and toothpaste as well as liqueurs such as aquavit and schnapps. Caraway is included in many spice blends and is used in cheeses, rye bread and old-fashioned seed cake. It is popular in German and Austrian cooking, being used in pastries and desserts, sauerkraut, sausages and other meat dishes, and cooked with cabbage and apples, especially if these are to be served with pork.

ALLSPICE, also called pimento or jamaican pepper, is the dried berry of a tree native to Central America. During sun-drying and curing, enzyme reactions cause the berries and the tiny seeds they contain to develop the characteristic aroma of mixed cloves, cinnamon and nutmeg for which the spice is named. Ground allspice is used in cakes and biscuits and in sausages, pork pies, curry powders, marinades for curing fish and Jamaica's famous jerk mixture for marinating meat or chicken to be barbecued. Whole berries may be used with other whole spices for a poaching syrup for fruit or in a pickling spice mixture, or be added to the pepper mill for fragrant spiced pepper.

CLOVES are the unopened flower buds of a tropical tree. Once dried, they look like little brown nails. They should be used with restraint because their strong, clean, pungent smell can overwhelm other flavours. Whole cloves are used for cooking apples and decorating and flavouring the Christmas ham, and in spice mixtures for pickles and spiced hot drinks. Ground cloves are included in garam masala, chinese five-spice, mixed spice for puddings and cakes, curry powders and various Middle Eastern and North African spice mixtures.

CARDAMOM is the dried seed-pod of a lily-like plant; the best is pale green. The pods are used both whole when a recipe calls for cardomom pods, and without the husk, ie seeds only, when a recipe calls for cardomom seeds. Recipes often call for bruised cardamom, obtained by laying the flat of a knife over pods or seeds and pressing down hard. Cardamom's aroma is warm and slightly pungent, with a refreshing eucalyptus note. It is used for sweet fruit dishes, cakes and biscuits, milk puddings and also for savoury dishes such as pilaffs and curries. In the Middle East, it is used to flavour coffee.

CUMIN looks like a seed but is actually the tiny fruit of an Eastern Mediterranean annual plant. Its pungent, warm, earthy aroma brings curry to mind and it is indeed a basic curry spice. It is also used, whole or ground, in rice dishes, breads, pickles,

Although coriander, the spice, comes from the same plant as coriander, the herb, they cannot be substituted for one another.

Enzymes are proteins which are present in all living things from animals and plants to algae and bacteria. They are catalysts — that is, substances which cause chemical reactions without themselves being part of the reaction. Enzyme action regulates innumerable changes in food, both desirable and undesirable, including the way some spices change colour and develop flavour as they dry, the cut surface of a peach goes brown when exposed to air, beef becomes more flavoursome and tender when it is aged, fats go rancid and dry mustard becomes hot when it is moistened. Enzymes can be destroyed by heat and rendered inactive by acid, lack of moisture or oxygen, or the presence of some chemicals including salt and sugar; all these ways of controlling enzyme action are used in food preparation and preserving.

barbecue spice mixes, Indian spice blends such as panch phora, Moroccan ones such as harissa and Mexican chilli powder. The cumin discussed here, and the one that is always meant when "cumin" is mentioned without any further description, is white (actually pale brown) cumin. There is also black cumin, which is darker brown, with a more piny aroma and piny, astringent, bitter flavour. It is often confused with kalonji (nigella) seed, though they are not related, and is of limited interest in spice cookery.

CORIANDER is the seed of the same green herb whose leaves, leaves, stems and roots are an essential part of Asian and South American cooking, but tastes and smells quite different: drying brings out clean, spicy aromas with a pleasant lemon note. Coriander seed is included in many Indian, Middle Eastern and North African spice mixtures because it has the gift of balancing sweet and pungent flavours and aromas. It is used alone in chicken and seafood dishes, cakes, breads, biscuits and fruit desserts, having a special affinity for apples and pears.

KALONJI SEEDS, also called nigella seeds, come from a bush related to love-in-a-mist and native to southern Europe and western Asia. Black, nutty and slightly peppery, they are used in spice mixtures, baked on breads and in savoury pastries and are good sprinkled on fried or roasted root vegetables. Lightly frying before use improves the flavour.

FENUGREEK is the hard, golden-brown seed of an annual herb native to western Asia. Its aroma brings curries to mind but has a sharp edge and its flavour is reminiscent of lentils with an added bitter note. It is an important curry spice and also used in other spice blends. It goes well with potato, spinach and mixed-vegetable dishes.

GARAM MASALA is an Indian ground-spice blend which varies from maker to maker but may include fennel, cardamom, cumin, cinnamon, clove and pepper. It is meant to be a basic aromatic ingredient that can be used for many different dishes without dominating. It is usually added towards the end of cooking.

NUTMEG AND MACE Nutmeg is the hard kernel of the seed of a tropical tree native to Indonesia and mace is the nut's frond-like outer covering. Nutmeg's distinctive clean, spicy aroma and flavour are best when it is grated directly on to the food, though it can also be bought ground. It is used in apple pies, on milk puddings and eggnog, in biscuits, cakes and tea breads, and a little added to spinach as it cooks will balance that vegetable's metallic flavour note. Nutmeg should be used with restraint as too much can be strident.

Mace is available in its frond-like form, when it is called blade mace, or ground. Its taste is like that of nutmeg but milder, warmer and sweeter. Its gentle flavour notes are excellent in cakes and puddings, sausages, pork pies and simple sauces: it is one of the flavourings used to infuse the milk for bechamel sauce.

JUNIPER BERRIES come from a spiky bush found in various cold parts of the world. The berries are blue-black with clean, resinous aroma and flavour. Their great characteristic is that they "freshen" rich meat dishes by cutting their gaminess or fattiness. Their oil is used to flavour gin; whole berries, which should still be soft enough to crush between the fingers, are used in pâtés and terrines and crushed or ground to go in game, pork, fish and lamb dishes.

HARISSA is a fiery Tunisian paste made from dried chillies, with other flavours from such ingredients as garlic, caraway seed, coriander and cumin. It is the basic

Tunisian condiment, always on the table for diners to help themselves. Harissa is commercially available in tubes.

CINNAMON AND CASSIA are the dried barks of two different but related trees. They are both sold in the form of furled quills or "sticks" which can be told apart by colour — cinnamon bark is light brown to tan and cassia bark is reddish brown — and the thickness of the layers: cinnamon quills have paper-thin layers and cassia quills have layers about 2mm thick. Cassia bark is also sold in flat strips. Both spices can be bought ground, and it is best to buy them that way if needed, as it is hard to grind the bark to an even-textured powder. Both are sweet spices: the aroma of cinnamon is perfumed, warm and woody with no trace of pungency or bitterness, while cassia is more strongly sweet and perfumed and its taste has an agreeable bitter note. Cinnamon and cassia quills are used whole or broken to the required length in curries, rice dishes such as pilaf or biryani and spiced drinks such as glühwein. Ground cinnamon is used in curry powders, garam masala, mixed spice and other spice blends, and also for home cooking such as poaching syrups for fruit, milk puddings, cakes, muffins and pies. Ground cassia is used by commercial bakers for its strong scent in "cinnamon" doughnuts, apple strudel, fruit muffins and biscuits.

TURMERIC is the juicy, orange-fleshed rhizome (root-like stem) of a tropical plant of the ginger family believed to be native to India or South-East Asia, though, like saffron, it has been known for so long that its origin is uncertain. Fresh turmeric can sometimes be bought in Asian food shops. Dried, ground turmeric is made by boiling, then oven-drying the rhizomes and finally crushing and grinding them. It is bright yellow with an earthy aroma and warm/

earthy/bitter/peppery flavour. It is an important curry spice, providing both flavour and colour, and is used with other spices and aromatics in fish, chicken and vegetable dishes. As well as being a spice, turmeric is used as a dye and care should be taken not to get it on one's clothes.

SAFFRON is the stigmas — three per flower — of the saffron crocus, a small blue flower which is believed to be native to Greece or Asia Minor, though knowledge and appreciation of it go so far back into antiquity that this cannot be certain. Saffron is valued as both a dye and a spice. It is, famously, the most expensive of all spices because it is impossible to harvest the flowers by mechanical means without damaging them, and hand-harvesting is extremely labour-intensive. The bright orange-red stigmas are dark red when dried; their aroma is woody/sweet, their flavour is pungent and reminiscent of bitter almond and the colour they impart to the food is golden. They are sold whole and ground. Saffron should be used with restraint — too much can overwhelm other flavours and it only takes a little to colour a pilaff for eight or 10 people. One must be sure of one's supplier when buying saffron, especially ground saffron, as imitations abound: even whole stigmas may be counterfeited with dyed cornsilk, coconut fibre and such. The fact to bear in mind is that there is no such thing as cheap saffron.

"TRUE" OR VINE PEPPER The name pepper is given to several different spices, some from the same plant but treated in different ways, and some from other families which are called pepper for their hot, biting flavour. "True" or vine pepper is the berry of a tropical climber, is green when unripe and turns yellow, then pink to red as it ripens. By picking at different stages, it is processed to become the

Vine pepper

peppercorns that are ground for familiar black or white pepper, and also green and "true" pink peppercorns. **Black peppercorns** are produced by fermenting and sun-drying whole, just-ripe berries, which makes them shrivel and activates an enzyme which turns them black. They are ground, either commercially or in domestic pepper-grinders, to become the most-used form of pepper as a seasoning. Black pepper has a stronger flavour but less hot bite than white. **White peppercorns** are produced by picking the berries at a riper stage, soaking to soften them and removing the skin and flesh to leave the white seed which is then dried. The flavour of white pepper is both different from and hotter than that of black. White pepper has traditionally been used by European cooks when they didn't want black-pepper specks in a pale sauce, but is also used for its specific flavour. **Green peppercorns** are produced by picking the berries green and either preserving them in brine, which keeps them soft and does not activate the enzyme, or boiling them briefly to kill the enzyme, then drying. They are also freeze-dried, a process which retains their fresh colour and plumpness, and are easily reconstituted by contact with moisture. Brined or reconstituted freeze-dried green peppercorns are used as a whole spice in pâtés and terrines, served with other foods as a decorative seasoning or crushed to go in dressings, stuffings and sauces; dried ones may be included in a blend for peppermills. Their flavour is different from but compatible with both black and white pepper; it is especially good with rich meats such as pork, duck and game. **Pink peppercorns** are produced by picking the berries fully ripe and preserving them in brine. They cannot be produced as dried pink peppercorns because, if dried without pre-boiling as for green ones, they would

turn black, and they cannot be pre-boiled because their softer flesh would collapse. They are also too fragile for freeze-drying. Their flavour is different again from black, white and green peppercorns. Pink peppercorns are used in the same ways as brined green peppercorns.

PINK "SCHINUS" PEPPERCORNS are the berries of a tree of the schinus family, which is native to South America. One member of the family is the pepper tree that gives shade in many Australian school playgrounds and paddocks. That tree does bear pink berries, but it is another member of the family that bears the berries sold for culinary purposes. These berries are larger and more brightly coloured than those of the common pepper tree. They are packed in brine, freeze-dried or sun-dried (retaining their colour), and are marketed as pink peppercorns. Their flavour is warm, piny and astringent with a faint black pepper-like note. They became fashionable in the 1970s-1980s, then controversial when it was disclosed that they could cause intestinal irritation, then acceptable again when studies showed that they were no more dangerous in this respect than black pepper or chilli. It is difficult for the non-expert to distinguish these berries, merely from appearance, from true pink peppercorns. One can be fairly certain that dried pink peppercorns are "schinus" as there are no dried true pink peppercorns.

SICHUAN (SZECHWAN) PEPPER is the dried, ripe berries of the prickly ash, a small tree native to Szechwan, the south-west province of China bordering Tibet. Its flavour and aroma are woody/spicy/peppery/tangy and it briefly numbs the tongue. The leaves of the same tree, dried and powdered, are the Japanese pepper sansho. The berries split open when ripe, revealing a black seed; when dried, they resemble one seed section of star anise

and this likeness is thought to be why sichuan pepper is also called anise pepper. Sichuan pepper is available whole or ground: the flavour is better if the whole berries are crushed or ground just before using, but care must be taken to remove any seeds as they are gritty when ground, and also to pick over the berries and remove any pieces of prickly stem or thorns as these are so difficult to remove by machinery that they often remain in even good-quality whole-berry pepper. Sichuan pepper is used in Chinese and Japanese cooking and as a condiment, especially with rich meats such as pork and duck; it contributes to the flavour of Peking duck. It is also used in spice mixtures including chinese five-spice.

STAR ANISE is the dried seed pod of a tree native to southern China and northern Vietnam. It grows in the form of eight separate segments round a central stem, forming a star shape. Each segment holds a seed. When dried, it is brown and woody looking; drying develops its strong spicy/anise aroma and flavour. It is sold whole and ground and is widely used in Chinese cooking, both alone and as one of the spices in five-spice mixture, in which it is the strongest flavour. It is especially good with pork or duck. Star anise should be used with restraint — it takes only a pinch of powder or one whole star to flavour a wokful or average potful of food.

AUSTRALIAN MOUNTAIN PEPPER comes in two forms, one made from the leaves and the other from the berries of a shrub native to Australia. Leaves and berries are dried, ground and sold separately. The leaf pepper smells woody and slightly peppery and tastes woody and camphor-like followed by a sharp pepper taste and lingering heat. The berries have an oily, mineral and turpentine aroma and taste momentarily sweet and fruity followed

by intense, biting, mouth-numbing heat that increases for some minutes. This experience with both leaves and berries is caused by an enzyme reaction when the powder is moistened in the mouth. Mountain leaf pepper can be used like ordinary black or white pepper but in much smaller quantities. Mountain berry pepper is too hot to use as a condiment but using a small amount in long-cooked dishes or marinades dissipates its fire and lets its flavour come through.

PAPRIKA is made from the dried and ground fruits of several members of the capsicum/chilli family. It may be sweet or hot, depending on the fruit variety from which it was made, and smoked paprika is also available. Both Hungary and Spain produce particularly fine paprika and it is an important ingredient in many of their dishes, notably Hungarian goulash and Spanish romesco sauce which is served with grilled meats and vegetables. Paprika is used both as an ingredient and as a sprinkle, for instance on bread and cream cheese. It is an essential ingredient in many spice mixtures both for flavouring and colouring — most commercial barbecue seasonings include it and commercial barbecued and roasted chicken gets its rich colour from seasoning, including paprika, rubbed on before cooking.

ZA'ATAR is a Middle Eastern herb and spice mixture which varies slightly from one maker to another but always includes thyme, from which it gets its Arabic name, with ground sumac and, usually, toasted sesame seeds. It is sprinkled on yogurt and flatbreads and can be used as a rub on lamb or chicken to be grilled or roasted.

SUMAC is the dried and ground berries of a tree of the rhus family which grows wild in the Middle East and eastern Mediterranean region. It is a purplish, moist-feeling powder with a fruity aroma

Star anise

and a tangy, pleasantly sour taste. It is used in Middle Eastern cooking, especially Turkish and Lebanese, in much the same way as lemon juice or vinegar are used in Western kitchens, to season meat, chicken or fish before grilling or roasting, or to sprinkle on them, often mixed with other spices or herbs, afterwards. It has an affinity with tomatoes and onions and is often cooked with them or sprinkled on them raw. The sumac tree is not poisonous but as many trees of the rhus family are, it is important to be sure it came from the right trees by buying ground sumac only from a reputable spice shop or Middle Eastern food shop.

CHOOSING Spices should be of a reputable brand or bought from a reputable spice shop or specialist food shop, preferably one with a fast turnover. Properly packaged spices, that is, packaged in glass, preferably with metal, not plastic lids, or in thick plastic or foil packs that can be resealed airtight, are better than loose spices or spices packed in cardboard or cellophane as these admit air and allow aroma to dissipate so that the spice has been deteriorating in them. One should always check the use-by date, and buy in small quantities that you expect to use within a year at most.

STORING Spices should be stored away from heat or light in airtight packages or containers. They should not be stored in the refrigerator because being removed from the cold to warmth to be used, and then returned to the cold, may cause condensation to form in the pack and spoil the contents. All spices deteriorate over time so they should be checked at least once a year and those that are past their use-by dates should be thrown away.

Also see Chillies, pages 118–120 and Vanilla, page 616.

Saffron velouté

PREP + COOK TIME 35 MINUTES **MAKES** 2 CUPS

2¼ cups (560ml) chicken stock

40g butter

2 tablespoons plain flour

2 egg yolks

1 tablespoon lemon juice

¼ teaspoon saffron threads

¼ cup (60ml) cream

Tangier and more free-flowing than a basic velouté, this rich pouring sauce goes beautifully with seafood or vegetables such as beans, broccoli and asparagus.

1 Place stock in small saucepan; bring to the boil then remove from heat.

2 Melt butter in medium saucepan, add flour; cook, stirring, about 2 minutes or until mixture bubbles and thickens. Stir in hot stock gradually; bring to the boil. Cook, stirring, until sauce boils and thickens. Reduce heat; simmer, uncovered, about 20 minutes or until reduced by half. Strain velouté into small bowl.

3 Place velouté in small saucepan; bring to the boil, remove from heat. Combine egg yolks, juice, saffron and cream in small bowl; gradually whisk into hot velouté. Stir, over low heat, until heated through. Serve with grilled chicken, fish or steamed greens.

NUTRITIONAL COUNT PER TABLESPOON 3g total fat (1.8g saturated fat); 138kJ (33 cal); 0.9g carbohydrate; 0.7g protein; 0g fibre

Sichuan duck

There are many classic Chinese dishes that marry duck and sichuan pepper. In this recipe, the fresh-flavoured salad sets off the spicy union to perfection.

For information on duck, see Poultry, pages 456–457.

PREP + COOK TIME 55 MINUTES (PLUS REFRIGERATION TIME) **SERVES** 4

½ cup (125ml) chinese cooking wine

2 tablespoons light soy sauce

2 cloves garlic, crushed

4cm piece fresh ginger (20g), sliced thinly

1 teaspoon sesame oil

4 duck marylands (1.2kg)

2 teaspoons sichuan peppercorns

1 teaspoon sea salt

1 Combine wine, sauce, garlic, ginger and sesame oil in large bowl with duck. Cover; refrigerate 3 hours or overnight.

2 Drain duck; discard marinade. Dry-fry peppercorns in small frying pan until fragrant. Crush peppercorns and salt using mortar and pestle; press mixture onto duck skin.

3 Cook duck on heated oiled flat plate, turning midway through cooking time, about 40 minutes or until cooked. Serve with a salad.

NUTRITIONAL COUNT PER SERVING 79.8g total fat (23.8g saturated fat); 3586kJ (858 cal); 1.4g carbohydrate; 28.4g protein; 0.4g fibre

Cajun kingfish

"Cajun" in the name of a dish means spicy and cayenne-hot.

For information on kingfish, see Seafood, page 522.

PREP + COOK TIME 30 MINUTES **SERVES** 4

2 teaspoons sweet paprika

2 teaspoons ground cumin

2 teaspoons ground coriander

2 teaspoons mustard powder

2 teaspoons fennel seeds

¼ teaspoon cayenne pepper

4 x 200g kingfish fillets

2 teaspoons olive oil

1 small red onion (100g), sliced thinly

1 large tomato (220g), chopped coarsely

420g can kidney beans, rinsed, drained

1 Combine spices in small bowl. Rub mixture into fish fillets.

2 Cook fish in heated oiled large frying pan until cooked as desired, remove from pan.

3 Heat oil in same cleaned pan; cook onion and tomato, until soft. Add beans; stir until hot, serve with fish. The fish also goes well with coleslaw.

NUTRITIONAL COUNT PER SERVING 7.4g total fat (2g saturated fat); 1321kJ (316 cal); 12.5g carbohydrate; 46.7g protein; 5.6g fibre

1 SICHUAN DUCK **2** CAJUN KINGFISH **3** ZA'ATAR-CRUMBED LAMB BACKSTRAP [P 566] **4** DUKKAH-CRUSTED CUTLETS WITH ROASTED GARLIC YOGURT [P 566]

1

2

3

4

Za'atar-crumbed lamb backstrap

PREP + COOK TIME 35 MINUTES **SERVES** 4

2 tablespoons za'atar

½ cup (75g) roasted unsalted cashews, coarsely chopped

800g lamb backstraps

2 tablespoons olive oil

1 Blend or process za'atar and nuts until mixture resembles coarse breadcrumbs.

2 Combine lamb with 2 tablespoons olive oil in large bowl; add za'atar mixture, turn lamb to coat all over.

3 Cook lamb in heated oiled large frying pan, in batches, until cooked as desired. Cover; stand 5 minutes then slice thickly.

4 Serve lamb with couscous with lemon and parsley, if you like.

NUTRITIONAL COUNT PER SERVING 28.2g total fat (6.3g saturated fat); 1877kJ (449 cal); 3.4g carbohydrate; 45.2g protein; 1.6g fibre

The backstrap is the eye of loin, a quickly cooked strip of tender meat. Couscous with some chopped parsley and grated lemon rind through it takes only minutes to make and would be excellent with this spicy backstrap.

For more information on lamb, see Lamb, pages 282 & 283.

Dukkah-crusted lamb cutlets with roasted garlic yogurt

PREP + COOK TIME 30 MINUTES **SERVES** 4

6 cloves garlic, unpeeled

1 teaspoon vegetable oil

1 cup (280g) yogurt

2 tablespoons roasted hazelnuts

2 tablespoons roasted pistachios

2 tablespoons sesame seeds

2 tablespoons ground coriander

1 tablespoon ground cumin

12 french-trimmed lamb cutlets (600g)

1 Preheat oven to 180°C/160°C fan-forced.

2 Place garlic on oven tray; drizzle with oil. Roast 10 minutes. Peel garlic then crush in small bowl with yogurt. Cover; refrigerate.

3 To make dukkah, blend or process nuts until chopped finely. Dry-fry seeds and spices in small frying pan until fragrant; combine with nuts in medium bowl, add lamb, turn to coat in dukkah mixture.

4 Cook lamb, both sides, in heated oiled grill pan until cooked.

5 Serve lamb with roasted garlic yogurt.

NUTRITIONAL COUNT PER SERVING 27.8g total fat (8.7g saturated fat); 1547kJ (370 cal); 5.7g carbohydrate; 22.9g protein; 2.9g fibre

An Egyptian blend of nuts, spices and seeds, dukkah is mixed with oil or mayonnaise for a dip and sprinkled over meats, salads and vegetables as a flavouring. If you don't want to make your own, you can buy it ready-made from speciality spice shops and delicatessens.

For information on yogurt, see Yogurt, pages 652 & 653; and for lamb, see Lamb, pages 282 & 283.

Sugar and spice snaps

PREP + COOK TIME 35 MINUTES (PLUS REFRIGERATION TIME) **MAKES** 30

1½ cups (225g) plain flour

¾ cup (165g) firmly packed dark muscovado sugar

2 teaspoons ground ginger

1 teaspoon mixed spice

¼ teaspoon ground clove

150g butter, chopped coarsely

1 egg yolk

¼ cup (55g) raw sugar

1 Process flour, muscovado sugar, spices and butter until crumbly. Add egg yolk; process until combined. Knead dough on floured surface until smooth. Cover; refrigerate 30 minutes.

2 Divide dough in half; roll each half between sheets of baking paper to 3mm thickness. Refrigerate 30 minutes.

3 Preheat oven to 180°C/160°C fan-forced. Line three oven trays with baking paper.

4 Cut thirty 7cm rounds from dough. Place rounds on trays; sprinkle with raw sugar. Bake snaps about 10 minutes; cool on trays.

NUTRITIONAL COUNT PER BISCUIT 4.3g total fat (2.7g saturated fat); 393kJ (94 cal); 12.8g carbohydrate; 0.9g protein; 0.3g fibre

Once completely cold, these will store in an airtight container for a week or more. If they should soften and lose their snap, heat them, in a single layer on an oven tray, in a preheated 170°C/150°C fan-forced oven for 3 minutes, turn the oven off and leave them there with the door closed for 10 minutes, then remove and cool completely.

Gingernuts

PREP + COOK TIME 25 MINUTES (PLUS COOLING TIME) **MAKES** 32

90g butter

⅓ cup (75g) firmly packed brown sugar

⅓ cup (115g) golden syrup

1⅓ cups (200g) plain flour

¾ teaspoon bicarbonate of soda

1 tablespoon ground ginger

1 teaspoon ground cinnamon

¼ teaspoon ground clove

1 Preheat oven to 180°C/160°C fan-forced. Grease oven trays.

2 Combine butter, sugar and syrup in medium saucepan; stir over low heat until smooth. Remove from heat; stir in sifted dry ingredients. Cool 10 minutes.

3 Roll rounded teaspoons of mixture into balls. Place about 3cm apart on trays; flatten slightly. Bake about 10 minutes; cool on trays.

NUTRITIONAL COUNT PER BISCUIT 2.4g total fat (1.5g saturated fat); 263kJ (63 cal); 9.5g carbohydrate; 0.7g protein; 0.2g fibre

It is an old tradition to dip these dense, crunchy biscuits into one's tea or coffee for a moment to soften them slightly before biting into them.

Spinach

Spinach is prized both for its own tenderness and delicate earthy/"green"/slightly tart flavour, and for the way it complements other ingredients from cream, eggs and cheese to pastry, pasta, rice, herbs, Middle Eastern and Indian spices, garlic, lemon, other vegetables and almost any meat or fish.

Spinach is one of the most nutritious vegetables, being an excellent source of fibre, vitamins A, C and E and the B vitamin folate (especially important for women planning pregnancies as it helps to guard against birth defects). It also has good levels of the antioxidant lutein, which has been linked with a lower risk of macular degeneration, a leading cause of blindness.

Full-size spinach is sold by the bunch of 3 or 4 plants; baby spinach — little round leaves about 4–5cm long, used mainly for salads — is sold by weight (see also Greens, Salad, pages 248 & 249).

Spinach is nutritious but claims that it provides high levels of iron and calcium are not true. It does contain plenty of these minerals but the oxalic acid also present in spinach prevents the body from absorbing them.

PREPARATION Spinach needs thorough washing as dirt can hide in its crevices, but do so just before using. Holding the bunch upside down with both hands, plunge it into a sinkful of cold water and swish it vigorously several times, then lift it out. This works better than washing it under running water.

CHOOSING Spinach should be undamaged and have bright, firm leaves and crisp stems. Be sure to buy enough — as spinach cooks down to about a third of its raw volume, an average bunch will serve only two as a side dish.

STORING Enclose full-size spinach or baby leaves, untrimmed and unwashed, in a paper bag and then in a plastic bag. Store in the refrigerator for up to 3 days for a bunch, 2 days for baby leaves.

Luxuriously simple, spinach cooked like this is the perfect complement to delicate fish, chicken or veal, rack of lamb or a filet mignon. A large frying pan is used here to take the spinach in a shallow layer and help evaporate any water from it before the cream is added.

Creamed spinach

PREP + COOK TIME 15 MINUTES **SERVES** 4

20g butter
600g spinach, trimmed
½ cup (125ml) cream

1 Melt butter in large frying pan; cook spinach, stirring, until wilted.
2 Add cream; bring to the boil. Reduce heat; simmer, uncovered, until liquid reduces by half.

NUTRITIONAL COUNT PER SERVING 38.7g total fat (25.4g saturated fat); 1555kJ (372 cal); 2.8g carbohydrate; 3.5g protein; 2.1g fibre

Hand these round at a party or serve them as an accompaniment to grilled lamb, fish or chicken.

For information on fillo pastry, see Pastry, page 405.

Spinach fillo triangles

PREP + COOK TIME 1 HOUR **MAKES** 16

400g spinach, trimmed, shredded finely

2 teaspoons sumac

2 green onions, chopped finely

1 tablespoon lemon juice

4 sheets fillo pastry

olive-oil spray

1 Preheat oven to 220°C/200°C fan-forced. Oil oven tray.

2 Boil, steam or microwave spinach until wilted; drain, squeeze out as much excess liquid as possible. Combine spinach in small bowl with sumac, onion and juice.

3 Cut each pastry sheet lengthways into four strips. Place one strip on board; cover remaining strips with baking paper, then with damp tea towel.

4 Spray strip with oil; place 1 rounded teaspoon of spinach filling on one corner, 5mm from edge, flatten slightly. Fold opposite corner of strip diagonally across filling to form triangle; continue folding to end of strip, retaining triangular shape. Place fillo triangle on tray, seam-side down; repeat process with remaining strips and filling.

5 Spray tops of fillo triangles lightly with oil; bake about 10 minutes or until just crisp and browned lightly.

NUTRITIONAL COUNT PER TRIANGLE 0.8g total fat (0.1g saturated fat); 88kJ (21 cal); 2.1g carbohydrate; 1g protein; 0.8g fibre

Steamed spinach dumplings
with fresh tomato and herb sauce

PREP + COOK TIME 50 MINUTES (PLUS STANDING TIME) **SERVES** 4

2 x 250g packets frozen spinach, thawed

200g ricotta cheese

1 clove garlic, crushed

1 egg white

1 tablespoon plain flour

¼ cup (20g) finely grated parmesan cheese

1½ cups (110g) stale breadcrumbs

¼ teaspoon ground nutmeg

1 tablespoon finely chopped fresh chives

2 tablespoons finely grated parmesan cheese, extra

FRESH TOMATO AND HERB SAUCE

½ cup (125ml) dry white wine

4 medium tomatoes (600g), chopped finely

2 tablespoons finely chopped fresh flat-leaf parsley

1 teaspoon white sugar

A superb vegetarian lunch dish, or you could make it into dinner for 4 by doubling the quantities for the tomato and herb sauce and serving it, with the dumplings, on 500g spaghetti. Alternatively, you could make just the dumplings and team them with any purchased pasta sauce to serve on the spaghetti.

For information on tomatoes, see Tomatoes, pages 606 & 607.

1 Squeeze excess liquid from spinach. Combine spinach in large bowl with ricotta, garlic, egg white, flour, parmesan, breadcrumbs, nutmeg and chives; roll level tablespoons of the mixture into balls.

2 Place balls, in single layer, about 2cm apart in baking-paper-lined bamboo steamer fitted over large saucepan of boiling water. Steam, covered, about 10 minutes or until dumplings are hot.

3 Meanwhile, make fresh tomato and herb sauce.

4 Serve dumplings with sauce and extra parmesan.

FRESH TOMATO AND HERB SAUCE Bring wine to the boil in medium saucepan. Reduce heat; simmer, uncovered, until reduced by half. Add tomato; return to the boil. Boil, uncovered, about 10 minutes or until thickened slightly. Stir in parsley and sugar.

NUTRITIONAL COUNT PER SERVING 10.2g total fat (5.5g saturated fat); 1233kJ (295 cal); 25.7g carbohydrate; 19.4g protein; 9.3g fibre

Sprouts

Crunchy, nutritious sprouted seeds, part of the Asian kitchen for many centuries, are now routinely available at Western greengrocers and are not only good for Asian dishes but for adding to a chicken, seafood or rice salad, garnishing hot or cold meats, mixing with sliced, fried mushroom for an omelette filling, or using in cheese, egg, chicken, seafood or roast beef sandwiches.

The greengrocer's sprouts are usually limited to alfalfa, mung bean and perhaps mustard and cress, and Asian food stores may have soybean sprouts, but it is easy to grow your own. Besides those mentioned, broccoli, lentil, fenugreek, sesame, sunflower, mustard, celery and pumpkin are popular sprouts for home growers.

❦ OTHER RECIPES USING SPROUTS

Chilli crab laksa, p538–9
Crisp pork belly with wombok salad, p444
Pear, walnut and fetta salad with walnut dressing, p418
Pork sang choy bow, p442
Roasted duck and stir-fried greens salad, p246
Singapore noodles, p339
Thai-style green mango salad with seared tuna, p309

SPROUTING SEEDS

You can use any fresh seeds you have, such as pumpkin seeds, but dried seeds can't be used. You can buy suitable seeds at health-food shops — be sure to ask for sprouting seeds. Soak about a tablespoon of seed in water for about 2 hours for large seeds, 1 hour for small ones, then drain, put the seeds into a jar and cover the top with a piece of muslin held in place with a rubber band. Put the jar somewhere with good natural light but out of direct sunlight (which could cook the seeds) and rinse the seeds twice a day in warm weather, once a day in cold weather, pouring the water through the muslin, swishing it round and pouring it out slowly, then shaking the seeds back to the bottom. Different seeds take from a few days to a week or two to produce sprouts worth harvesting. If you don't want to use the whole harvest at once, take what you want, replace the muslin and put the jar into the refrigerator. Continue to rinse once a day; the seeds will stop growing but keep in good condition for about 5 days to a week.

CHOOSING When buying sprouts at the greengrocers, check that they have clean, pale stems and that any leaves are fresh and unwilted.

STORING Sprouts sold in a punnet should be refrigerated the in punnet and used within a day or two. Mustard and cress still growing should be placed in the shade, kept moist but not wet and used within a few days. Mung bean or other fleshy sprouts should be refrigerated in a container of salt water (about 1 part salt to 20 parts water) and used within a week or so, changing the water every day. Sprouts cannot be frozen.

Alfalfa sprouts

Mung bean sprouts

Mustard sprouts

Snow pea sprouts

Turkey, cranberry and sprout salad

PREP + COOK TIME 50 MINUTES (PLUS COOLING TIME) **SERVES** 6

1.5kg boneless turkey breast

1.5 litres (6 cups) water

½ cup (125ml) red wine vinegar

1 teaspoon dijon mustard

¼ cup (60ml) light olive oil

⅔ cup (90g) dried cranberries

3 stalks celery (450g), trimmed, sliced thinly

1 ¼ cups (100g) bean sprouts

1 cup (50g) snow pea sprouts

½ cup (70g) roasted unsalted peanuts

½ cup firmly packed fresh mint leaves, torn

1 butter lettuce, leaves separated

Turn down the heat under the turkey as soon as you add it to the boiling water and then take care that the liquid never goes above a gentle simmer with single bubbles rising, or the meat will be dry and tough.

For information on turkey, see Poultry, pages 456 & 457; and for dried cranberries, see Fruit, Dried, page 192.

1 Cut turkey into three equal-sized pieces. Bring the water to the boil in large saucepan; add turkey. Simmer, covered, about 35 minutes or until turkey is cooked. Cool turkey in poaching liquid 15 minutes. Drain turkey; shred coarsely.

2 Combine vinegar, mustard and oil in large bowl. Add turkey, dried cranberries, celery, sprouts, nuts and mint; toss gently. Serve salad with lettuce leaves.

NUTRITIONAL COUNT PER SERVING 23.1g total fat (4.1g saturated fat); 2019kJ (483 cal); 6.7g carbohydrate; 59.7g protein; 4.2g fibre

Prawn and scallop chilli jam stir-fry

PREP + COOK TIME 40 MINUTES **SERVES** 4

1kg uncooked medium king prawns

2 tablespoons peanut oil

300g scallops, roe removed

2 cloves garlic, crushed

2cm piece fresh ginger (10g), grated

200g green beans, cut into 5cm lengths

350g gai lan, trimmed, chopped coarsely

⅔ cup (190g) prepared thai chilli jam

1 ½ cups (120g) bean sprouts

½ cup firmly packed thai basil leaves

For information on prawns and scallops, see Seafood, pages 526 & 527.

1 Shell and devein prawns leaving tails intact.

2 Heat half the oil in wok; stir-fry prawns and scallops, in batches, until cooked as desired. Drain on absorbent paper.

3 Heat remaining oil in wok; stir-fry garlic and ginger until fragrant. Add beans and gai lan; stir-fry until gai lan is wilted. Return prawns and scallops to wok with chilli jam; stir-fry 2 minutes.

4 Stir in sprouts and basil off the heat; serve with steamed jasmine rice, if you like.

NUTRITIONAL COUNT PER SERVING 14.6g total fat (2.9g saturated fat); 1513kJ (362 cal); 16.8g carbohydrate; 38.6g protein; 3.9g fibre

Glazed-chicken tortilla with sprout and herb salad

PREP + COOK TIME 35 MINUTES **SERVES** 4

You could set out a platter of sliced chicken, bowl of salad with serving tongs and stack of tortillas for everyone to assemble their own great food-to-go.

For information on chicken, see Poultry, pages 456 & 457.

¼ cup (80g) cranberry sauce

1 tablespoon wholegrain mustard

1 tablespoon lemon juice

5cm piece fresh ginger (25g), grated

1 clove garlic, crushed

500g chicken breast fillets

1 small red onion (100g), sliced thinly

60g snow pea sprouts

¼ cup finely sliced fresh coriander leaves

¼ cup finely sliced fresh mint leaves

1 tablespoon white wine vinegar

4 large flour tortillas

1 Heat combined sauce, mustard, juice, ginger and garlic in small saucepan, stirring, until glaze comes to the boil.

2 Cook chicken, in batches, in heated lightly oiled large frying pan, brushing frequently with glaze, until cooked through. Cover chicken; stand 5 minutes before slicing thickly.

3 Meanwhile, place onion, sprouts, herbs and vinegar in medium bowl; toss salad gently to combine. Heat tortillas according to manufacturer's instructions.

4 Divide chicken and salad among centres of tortillas; roll tortillas around filling to form cone shapes.

NUTRITIONAL COUNT PER SERVING 5.6g total fat (1.2g saturated fat); 1296kJ (310 cal); 31g carbohydrate; 33.4g protein; 2.9g fibre

Chicken, cabbage and mixed sprout salad

PREP + COOK TIME 10 MINUTES **SERVES** 4

This salad recipe is perfect for a lunchbox. Pack the dressing in a separate little bottle for adding at lunchtime. Combo sprouts are a commercially available mix of sprouts containing alfalfa, snow pea, mung bean, lentil, garden and caloona sprouts.

For information on chicken, see Poultry, pages 456 & 457; and for wombok, see Cabbages, page 78.

3 cups (480g) shredded cooked chicken

1 small wombok (700g), sliced thinly

2 green onions, sliced thinly

100g combo sprouts

½ cup firmly packed fresh coriander leaves

½ cup (75g) salted cashews

2 tablespoons toasted pepitas

SOY DRESSING

¼ cup (60ml) soy sauce

⅓ cup (80ml) rice vinegar

2 tablespoons peanut oil

2 teaspoons brown sugar

1 teaspoon sesame oil

1 Place ingredients for soy dressing in screw-top jar; shake well.

2 Place all salad ingredients in large bowl with dressing; toss gently to combine.

NUTRITIONAL COUNT PER SERVING 30.2g total fat (6.3g saturated fat); 1935kJ (463 cal); 9.5g carbohydrate; 37g protein; 4g fibre

GLAZED-CHICKEN TORTILLA WITH SPROUT AND HERB SALAD

Sugar

Sweetness comes in many forms, each with its own characteristics to suit a cook's purpose. In general, it is best to use the kind of sugar specified in any kind of baking — cake, pastry, biscuits, meringue etc — as other kinds may behave differently and affect the appearance, texture, taste or keeping quality of the finished product. For serious confectionery making or pâtisserie where correct temperatures of sugar syrups are important, kitchen equipment should include a sugar thermometer.

1 CASTER SUGAR
2 ICING SUGAR
3 BROWN SUGAR
4 DARK MUSCOVADO SUGAR
5 DEMERARA SUGAR
6 PALM SUGAR
7 HONEY WITH HONEYCOMB
8 LIQUID GLUCOSE
9 GOLDEN SYRUP

WHITE (GRANULATED) SUGAR The word sugar in a recipe without further description means the everyday white sugar used for sweetening tea, sprinkling on cornflakes and in many kinds of cooking. Its scientific name is sucrose and it is refined to more than 99% purity; most of the world's supply comes from sugar cane and about a third comes from sugarbeet, a common European root vegetable.

CASTER SUGAR is white sugar that has been ground a little finer. It is mainly used in baking as its smaller crystals dissolve more readily in pastry, cake and biscuit mixtures and meringue. It is also good for sprinkling over fruit as it dissolves quickly.

ICING SUGAR is white sugar ground to a fine powder. Two types are sold: pure icing sugar, which is inclined to cake in storage and is mostly used for cake decorating, and icing sugar mixture, which has some cornflour added to prevent caking. Icing sugar dissolves instantly so it is the best kind for icings and for sweetening whipped cream; it is also sieved over baked cakes or over a dessert and its plate as decoration.

BROWN SUGAR is made in light or dark types. In the past, it was partly refined sugar whose crystals were still coated with a film of molasses. Today, it is made by adding some molasses syrup, browned to the required colour, back into white sugar

— a lighter grade of molasses for light brown sugar, a darker grade for dark brown sugar. Brown sugar is soft and clingy and has a flavour with caramel notes because of the molasses coating. "Brown sugar" without further description in a recipe means light brown sugar. Both light and dark are used in baking, on hot or cold breakfast cereal and in fruit crumble toppings.

RAW SUGAR is granulated sugar that has not been through the final stage of refining that makes white sugar. It is golden with larger crystals than white sugar, and has a slightly richer flavour. It is used in certain cakes and biscuits. It is often used instead of white as a basic household sugar.

MUSCOVADO SUGAR is a fine-grained, moist brown sugar made in two types, light or dark. Like other brown sugars, it is now made by adding molasses syrup back into white sugar instead of by the traditional method of partial refining. As with other brown sugars, some flavour nuances have been lost with the modern method. Muscovado is used in sweet and spicy sauces and is good for sticky toffee sauce and caramel ice-cream.

DEMERARA SUGAR is a large-crystal, light brown sugar named after the Demerara district in Guyana. Like brown sugar, it was once produced as a partly refined sugar but is now made by adding molasses syrup

back into refined, large-crystal white sugar; this modern kind is sometimes called london demerara. The traditional kind is still made and is still preferred by connoisseurs as its flavour is richer and more complex, but is not widely available. Demerara is used for crunchy toppings on sticky buns, streusels and such and to give caramelised flavour to the glaze for baked ham. It is the traditional sweetener for coffee because it dissolves slowly so it gives the traditionally correct experience of the last mouthful being the sweetest.

PALM SUGAR is made by boiling down the sweet sap of various types of palm tree to concentrate it into a thick syrup, which sets as it dries. The blocks are then chipped or grated for use. Palm sugar is used in Indonesian and Malaysian cooking and also in India, where it is called gur or jaggery; these same words are also used in India for sugar made in the same way from sugar cane, which is sweet with a bitter undertone. The complex flavours of these unrefined sugars are important in the flavouring of certain curries, especially vegetable ones.

YELLOW ROCK SUGAR, also called yellow rock candy, is sugar in the form of solid, clear, irregular yellowish chunks that have been called "rock sugar" in China for centuries. It produces a clear syrup and helps make sauces translucent. It is available from Chinese supermarkets in flat, round or square cakes.

BLACK SUGAR is a Japanese sugar made from whole boiled sugar cane. It is high in minerals and tastes rather like muscovado with added smoky and salty flavours. Nuggets of black sugar are a popular treat in Japan, and it is made into hard candies.

LIQUID GLUCOSE, also known as glucose syrup, is a form of sugar that is chemically different from ordinary sugar and will not crystallise, making it useful for preventing crystallisation in confectionery cooking.

White sugar cubes

CORN SYRUP is a sweet syrup made by heating cornstarch with water under pressure. It comes in light and dark types, the darker being the more strongly flavoured. It is used in baking and in confectionery, where it prevents other sugars from crystallising and making the texture grainy.

HONEY Some honey is sold in its beeswax honeycomb, but producers usually extract it and treat it to extend its shelf life. It is then sold in the form of a clear, thick syrup, or "creamed", meaning it is set to a semi-solid, spreadable paste that does not run and drip as clear honey does. Creamed honey is actually crystallised into crystals so small that the mouth does not feel them. It is made by "seeding" liquid honey with a small amount of already crystallised honey, which starts a crystallising reaction that travels thoughout the honey. Because it is hydroscopic (water-attracting), honey used as an ingredient in breads and cakes keeps them moist.

GOLDEN SYRUP is a clear, sweet, deep-flavoured syrup of the same consistency as honey. It is a combination of by-products of the cane sugar-refining process at the crystallisation stage. It is used as a spread, in tarts, on steamed or boiled puddings and dumplings and as an ingredient in brandy snaps.

MOLASSES is the thick, sticky substance that remains after sugar has been refined. It comes in three grades, "first", "second" and "third" or "blackstrap", denoting the number of times it has been boiled and spun in a centrifuge to separate out the sugar. First molasses still contains some sugar, second rather less and blackstrap less again. The molasses becomes darker and more bitter with each boiling and spinning as the remaining sugar becomes more caramelised. The edible molasses available to consumers today is usually made by blending clarified cane syrups with first or second molasses. It ranges from mild to strong and bitter and from golden brown to very dark; the darker the colour, the less sweet and more bitter it is. Molasses is made from sugarbeet as well as sugar cane but the sugarbeet product is bitter and has a strong, unpleasant odour so it is used as animal food and industrially.

TREACLE is a dark syrup refined from molasses. It is sweet with a bitter edge and is used as a spread, in old-fashioned puddings and in gingerbread.

MAPLE SYRUP is the boiled-down sap of the rock or sugar maple and the black maple, both of which are native to north-eastern America. It is used on the table to pour over pancakes and in cooking. There are many imitations so it is important to check that it is labelled "pure maple syrup".

SUGAR SUBSTITUTES are usually made from substances that are many times sweeter than sugar and are used in tiny quantities. Among the best known are saccharin and aspartame. Intensive

sweeteners often have some shortcoming compared to sugar: for example, saccharin fell out of favour because it has a metallic aftertaste, while aspartame is broken down by heat and by acidity so cannot be used in cooking. Others are slower than sugar to give the sensation of sweetness, or their taste lingers long after swallowing. Fructose, a natural sugar that is much sweeter than ordinary sugar and has a glycaemic index (GI) rating of only 20 compared to ordinary sugar's 90, has replaced it in some soft drinks that are said to be suitable for diabetics, though this is disputed. Fructose is also available in crystal form.

STORING

Sugars should be stored in airtight containers away from sunlight. If brown sugar hardens, this is because its molasses coating contains moisture that makes it clingy so that it sticks together, then hardens as it dries. Putting a slice of apple in with it to gradually make it moist again should help.

✤ OTHER RECIPES USING SUGAR
Apricot and honey soufflés, p16
Carrot cupcakes with maple frosting, p90
Chilli and honey barbecued steak, p47
Honey-glazed turkey with orange-pecan stuffing, p458
Lamb racks with mustard maple glaze, p289
Orange and honey nut mix, p353
Orange and maple-glazed baby carrots with hazelnuts, p89
Pistachio, honey and cardamom kulfi, p318
Pork larb with broccolini, p76
Slow-roasted honey and soy pork neck, p447

Duck with spiced honey and coriander sauce

PREP + COOK TIME 30 MINUTES **SERVES** 4

4 x 150g duck breast fillets

20g butter

2cm piece fresh ginger (10g), grated

2 teaspoons finely grated orange rind

pinch ground clove

2 cardamom pods, bruised

½ teaspoon caraway seeds

⅓ cup (80ml) orange juice

¼ cup (90g) honey

¼ cup (60ml) chicken stock

2 teaspoons coarsely chopped fresh coriander leaves

This fragrant sauce is also good with grilled pork fillets, barbecued spareribs and pan-fried chicken-breast fillets.

For information on duck, see Poultry, pages 456 & 457; and for coriander, see Herbs, page 262.

1 Cook duck, skin-side down, in heated large frying pan 5 minutes or until brown and crisp. Turn duck; cook 5 minutes or until cooked as desired. Remove from pan; cover to keep warm.

2 Drain duck fat from pan. Melt butter in same uncleaned pan; cook ginger, rind, clove, cardamom and seeds, stirring, until fragrant. Stir in juice, honey and stock; bring to the boil. Reduce heat; simmer, uncovered, 2 minutes or until thickened slightly. Discard cardamom; stir in coriander off the heat. Serve duck drizzled with sauce.

NUTRITIONAL COUNT PER SERVING 59.5g total fat (19.4g saturated fat); 2888kJ (691 cal); 20.5g carbohydrate; 19.9g protein; 0.2g fibre

Pork with maple syrup, bourbon and pear sauce

PREP + COOK TIME 25 MINUTES **SERVES** 4

20g butter

2 teaspoons olive oil

4 pork cutlets (950g)

1 large pear (330g), sliced thinly

¼ cup (60ml) bourbon

2 tablespoons maple syrup

½ cup (125ml) chicken stock

1 teaspoon lemon juice

½ cup (50g) coarsely chopped walnuts, roasted

1 Heat butter and oil in large frying pan; cook pork, in batches, until browned both sides and cooked as desired. Cover to keep warm.

2 Cook pear in same pan, turning gently, until browned and softened. Deglaze pan with bourbon. Simmer 1 minute.

3 Add remaining ingredients; bring to the boil. Boil, uncovered, about 3 minutes or until sauce thickens slightly. Serve pork drizzled with sauce.

NUTRITIONAL COUNT PER SERVING 31.9g total fat (9.3g saturated fat); 2174kJ (520 cal); 20.4g carbohydrate; 30.7g protein; 2.3g fibre

Use any very firm pear (or nashi) that will slice cleanly. For notes on deglazing, see page 223.

For information on pork, see Pork, pages 440 & 441; and for pears, see Pears, page 416–418.

Maple syrup-glazed lamb shanks

PREP + COOK TIME 2 HOURS 10 MINUTES **SERVES** 4

⅓ cup (80ml) pure maple syrup

1 cup (250ml) chicken stock

1 tablespoon dijon mustard

1½ cups (375ml) orange juice

8 french-trimmed lamb shanks (2kg)

1 Combine syrup, stock, mustard and juice in large deep flameproof casserole dish, add lamb; toss lamb to coat in syrup mixture. Bring to the boil then cover tightly. Reduce heat; cook lamb, turning every 20 minutes, about 2 hours or until lamb is tender.

2 Serve lamb with roasted potatoes.

NUTRITIONAL COUNT PER SERVING 5.2g total fat (2.4g saturated fat); 1668kJ (399 cal); 25.7g carbohydrate; 61.1g protein; 0.3g fibre

Serve lamb with roast potatoes: boil, steam or microwave 6 halved, medium potatoes until half-cooked. Drain, pat dry with absorbent paper and place in a single layer, cut-side down, on an oiled oven tray. Brush with 2 tablespoons olive oil and roast, uncovered, in a preheated 220°C/200°C fan-forced oven for about 50 minutes or until lightly browned and crisp.

PORK WITH MAPLE SYRUP, BOURBON AND PEAR SAUCE

Matzo is the biscuit-like unleavened "bread" eaten by Jews at Passover. Matzo meal can be found at some supermarkets and delicatessens in areas with a Jewish community and boxes of whole matzo crackers are available at most supermarkets. If you can't find matzo meal, make your own by processing 180g matzo crackers to fine crumbs. It is important to use regular honey in this cake, not the liquefied easy-to-pour kind.

Matzo honey cake

PREP + COOK TIME 55 MINUTES **SERVES** 12

3 eggs, separated

1 ½ cups (180g) matzo meal

2 teaspoons finely grated orange rind

¼ teaspoon ground clove

1 teaspoon ground cinnamon

⅔ cup (160ml) orange juice

¾ cup (270g) honey

½ cup (110g) firmly packed brown sugar

1 tablespoon icing sugar

1 Preheat oven to 180°C/160°C fan-forced. Grease base of deep 22cm-round cake pan; line base with baking paper.

2 Combine egg yolks, matzo, rind, spices, juice, honey and brown sugar in large bowl.

3 Beat egg whites in small bowl with electric mixer until soft peaks form; fold into matzo mixture, in two batches. Pour mixture into pan.

4 Bake cake about 40 minutes. Stand 5 minutes; turn, top-side up, onto wire rack to cool.

5 Serve dusted with sifted icing sugar.

NUTRITIONAL COUNT PER SERVING 1.6g total fat (0.4g saturated fat); 819kJ (196 cal); 41.1g carbohydrate; 3.4g protein; 0.6g fibre

---

For coconut and lime icing, stir in ½ teaspoon coconut essence and 1 teaspoon finely grated lime rind.
For orange icing, stir in 1 teaspoon finely grated orange rind and replace 1 tablespoon hot water with orange juice.
For passionfruit icing, stir in 1 tablespoon passionfruit pulp.

This icing is suitable for Patty cakes on page 191.

Glacé icing

PREP + COOK TIME 10 MINUTES **MAKES** 12

2 cups (320g) icing sugar

20g butter, melted

2 tablespoons hot water, approximately

1 Sift icing sugar into small bowl; stir in butter and enough of the water to make a firm paste.

2 Stir over small saucepan of simmering water until icing is spreadable.

NUTRITIONAL COUNT PER SERVING 1.5g total fat (1g saturated fat); 510kJ (122 cal); 26.7g carbohydrate; 0.1g protein; 0g fibre

1 MATZO HONEY CAKE **2** GLACE ICING
3 BABY TOFFEE FIGS [P 584] **4** ORANGE CARAMELS [P 584]

1

2

3

4

Other fruit such as baby apples, baby pears, small clusters of grapes, cherries on their stems or strawberries still with their green calyxes can be used instead of figs. The molten toffee is very hot, so take care when dipping.

Baby toffee figs

PREP + COOK TIME 20 MINUTES **MAKES** 24

2 cups (240g) caster sugar

⅔ cup (160ml) water

24 baby figs (440g)

2 tablespoons mascarpone cheese

1 Stir sugar and the water in medium heavy-based saucepan over heat until sugar dissolves. Bring to the boil; boil about 10 minutes or until toffee turns golden brown.

2 Remove pan from heat, allow bubbles to subside. Stand toffee about 2 minutes or until thickened slightly.

3 Holding figs by their stem, very carefully dip them, one at a time, into toffee, leaving half of the fig toffee-free. Repeat this process to double toffee-coat figs; hold figs over toffee for a few seconds to drain. Place on baking-paper-lined tray to set.

4 Pour any remaining toffee onto baking-paper-lined tray, set at room temperature; chop finely.

5 Cut a small cross in tops of figs; gently open figs. Pipe or spoon mascarpone into figs, sprinkle with a little chopped toffee.

NUTRITIONAL COUNT PER SERVING 0.8g total fat (0.5g saturated fat); 234kJ (56 cal); 14.5g carbohydrate; 0.3g protein; 0.5g fibre

These caramels are easy to make for a school fête and gorgeous to serve with after-dinner coffee.

Orange caramels

PREP + COOK TIME 25 MINUTES (PLUS STANDING TIME) **MAKES** 24

1 cup (220g) caster sugar

90g unsalted butter

2 tablespoons golden syrup

⅓ cup (115g) glucose syrup

½ cup (125ml) sweetened condensed milk

¼ cup (60ml) cream

2 teaspoons finely grated orange rind

¼ cup (30g) finely chopped roasted, unsalted pistachios

1 Grease two 12-hole (1-tablespoon/20ml) mini muffin pans.

2 Combine sugar, butter, syrups, condensed milk and cream in medium heavy-based saucepan; stir over heat, without boiling, until sugar dissolves. Bring to the boil; boil, stirring, about 8 minutes or until mixture is caramel in colour. Stir in rind. Remove pan from heat; allow bubbles to subside.

3 Divide mixture between pan holes; sprinkle with nuts. Stand 20 minutes before removing from pan with greased palette knife.

NUTRITIONAL COUNT PER SERVING 5.5g total fat (3.3g saturated fat); 535kJ (128 cal); 18.6g carbohydrate; 0.9g protein; 0.1g fibre

Palm sugar and lime cheesecakes

PREP TIME 40 MINUTES (PLUS REFRIGERATION TIME) **SERVES** 12

250g butternut snap biscuits

50g butter, melted

1 teaspoon gelatine

2 tablespoons lime juice

¼ cup (65g) grated palm sugar

250g cream cheese, softened

2 teaspoons finely grated lime rind

1 cup (250ml) cream

PALM SUGAR SYRUP

1 lime

½ cup (125ml) water

⅓ cup (90g) grated palm sugar

1 Grease 12-hole (¼ cup/60ml) mini cheesecake pan with removable bases.

2 Process biscuits until fine. Add butter; process until combined. Divide mixture between holes; press firmly. Refrigerate 30 minutes.

3 Sprinkle gelatine over juice in small heatproof jug; stand jug in small saucepan of simmering water. Stir until gelatine dissolves. Cool 5 minutes. Stir in sugar.

4 Beat cheese and rind in small bowl with electric mixer until smooth; beat in cream. Stir in gelatine mixture. Divide filling mixture among holes; refrigerate overnight.

5 Make palm sugar syrup. Serve cheesecakes with palm sugar syrup.

PALM SUGAR SYRUP Remove rind from lime; cut into thin strips. Stir the water and sugar in small saucepan over low heat until sugar dissolves. Boil, uncovered, without stirring, about 5 minutes or until syrup thickens slightly. Remove from heat; add rind. Cool.

NUTRITIONAL COUNT PER SERVING 24.4g total fat (15.9g saturated fat); 1404kJ (336 cal); 25.6g carbohydrate; 3.8g protein; 0.9g fibre

If you can't get palm sugar, use light or dark brown sugar instead.

For information on limes, see Limes, page 300; and for cream cheese, see Cheese, pages 100–102.

Caramel fondue with fresh fruit

PREP + COOK TIME 10 MINUTES **SERVES** 4

½ cup (110g) firmly packed brown sugar

⅔ cup (160ml) cream

50g butter

250g strawberries, halved

2 medium bananas (400g), sliced thickly

2 small pears (360g), sliced thinly

1 Place sugar, cream and butter in small saucepan; cook, stirring, until sugar dissolves and butter melts. Bring to the boil. Reduce heat; simmer, uncovered, 3 minutes.

2 Remove from heat; cool 10 minutes before serving with fruit.

NUTRITIONAL COUNT PER SERVING 27.7g total fat (18.2g saturated fat); 2002kJ (479 cal); 52.8g carbohydrate; 3.3g protein; 4.6g fibre

This recipe makes 1 ½ cups of fondue sauce. You can put the platter of fruit and pot of sauce in the middle of the table and let diners choose their own fruit and dip it, or serve individual plates of fruit, each with its own small pot of sauce.

Swedes

Also called neeps in Scotland and rutabaga in America, swedes are not true root vegetables, being the rhizomes (root-like stems) of a member of the cabbage family, but their earthy flavour and firm, dense texture rank them with root vegetables in the kitchen.

They can be dull if simply boiled, but are at their best with robust meats and rich gravies, in soups or stews, mashed with butter or cream and herbs, or roasted round a joint, which makes them melting and juicy, or by themselves with oil or duck fat, which makes them crisp and tender. In Scotland, bashed neeps or mashed swedes and champit tatties or mashed potatoes are a traditional accompaniment to the haggis at a Burns Night (January 25, poet Robert Burns' birthday) supper. Alternatively, a dish with the wonderful name of clapshot, made by boiling swedes, potatoes and onion together and mashing them with chives and butter, may be served.

PREPARATION Swedes should be peeled before cooking, large ones thickly peeled as the skin and outer layer may be bitter.

CHOOSING Swedes should be firm and heavy for their size. Choose small ones if you prefer mild flavour, larger ones if you prefer robust, but avoid giant specimens or any that smell unpleasant.

STORING Store swedes in the refrigerator crisper, where they will keep for two weeks or more.

The swede is thought to be a hybrid (cross) of the cabbage and the turnip. It is a relatively "modern" vegetable, having been known only since the 17th Century, unlike its parents which have both been cultivated for thousands of years.

Chilli and herb swede crush

PREP + COOK TIME 30 MINUTES **SERVES** 4

1kg swedes, chopped coarsely
40g butter
¼ cup (60ml) cream
1 fresh long red chilli, chopped finely
1 tablespoon finely chopped fresh flat-leaf parsley
2 teaspoons finely grated lemon rind

1 Boil, steam or microwave swede until tender; drain.
2 Coarsely crush swede with butter and cream in medium bowl. Stir in remaining ingredients. Serve with a chicken or lamb casserole and a green vegetable.

NUTRITIONAL COUNT PER SERVING 14.7g total fat (9.7g saturated fat); 773kJ (185 cal); 8.6g carbohydrate; 2.3g protein; 5.8g fibre

Sweet potatoes

Sweet potatoes are not really potatoes at all — they belong to a different family of plants — but they can be cooked in the same ways: boil and mash, slice and fry, bake in their skins, roast, turn into soup or a salad, take off thin strips with a vegetable-peeler and deep-fry for crisps.

1 KUMARA (ORANGE SWEET POTATO)
2 PURPLE-SKINNED SWEET POTATO
3 WHITE-SKINNED SWEET POTATO

Their earthy sweetness has an affinity with spices and strong or smoky flavours so they are good mashed with cumin or garlic, used in a vegetable curry with cauliflower, peas and onion, or thinly sliced, brushed with oil and barbecued. They don't get crisp outside when roasted but break down and become deliciously caramelised, and they don't take as long to cook as potato so be careful not overcook them as they can become mushy.

KUMARA OR ORANGE SWEET POTATOES have dry, dense, nutty-sweet flesh, which holds together well for a salad or curry. Good for boiling, baking in their skins and serving with sour cream and chives, and for frying.

PURPLE-SKINNED SWEET POTATOES have white flesh which discolours quickly when cut, so drop pieces into icy water as you go. Good for any of the cooking methods mentioned previously.

WHITE-SKINNED SWEET POTATOES have purple, earthy-tasting flesh which is only slightly sweet. Best for baking.

CHOOSING
Sweet potatoes should be undamaged, firm, evenly coloured and heavy for their size.

STORING
Do not refrigerate sweet potatoes — store in a well-ventilated place away from heat and light; use within a week.

✤ **OTHER RECIPES USING SWEET POTATOES**
Massaman beef curry, p51
Roasted vegetable lasagne, p402–3

Serve this soup with rosemary sourdough: combine 2 tablespoons olive oil and 2 teaspoons finely chopped fresh rosemary in a large bowl and cut a sourdough loaf into 3cm-thick slices. Add the bread to the bowl, turning the slices to coat well in the mixture. Bake on oven tray in preheated 180°C/160°C fan-forced oven about 15 minutes, turning once, until golden and crisp on the outside.

Cream of kumara soup

PREP + COOK TIME 40 MINUTES (PLUS COOLING TIME) **SERVES** 6

1 tablespoon olive oil
2 medium kumara (800g), chopped coarsely
1 medium brown onion (150g), chopped coarsely
2 cloves garlic, quartered
2 teaspoons coarsely chopped fresh rosemary

1 teaspoon finely grated lemon rind
2 cups (500ml) vegetable stock
2 cups (500ml) water
1 tablespoon lemon juice
½ cup (125ml) cream

1 Heat oil in large frying pan; cook kumara, onion and garlic, stirring, 10 minutes. Add rosemary, rind, stock and the water; bring to the boil. Reduce heat; simmer, covered, about 15 minutes or until kumara is soft. Cool 15 minutes.

2 Blend or process soup, in batches, until smooth. Return soup to same cleaned pan, add juice; stir over medium heat until hot. Serve drizzled with cream and toasted sourdough.

NUTRITIONAL COUNT PER SERVING 12.3g total fat (6.4g saturated fat); 890kJ (213 cal); 20.4g carbohydrate; 3.5g protein; 3.6g fibre

Kumara takes longer to
brown and crisp than white
or purple sweet potato,
so fry the kumara crisps
separately before the
others. The crisps will keep
well if, once quite cold, they
are stored in an airtight
container. If they should
soften, re-crisp them, on an
oven tray, in a single layer,
in a preheated 170°C/
150°C fan-forced oven for
3 minutes, turn the oven
off and leave them there
with the door closed for
10 minutes, then remove
and cool completely.

Sweet potato crisps with chilli salt

PREP + COOK TIME 25 MINUTES **SERVES** 4

1 medium kumara (400g)

1 medium white-skinned sweet potato (400g)

1 medium purple-skinned sweet potato (400g)

vegetable oil, for deep-frying

2 teaspoons sea salt flakes

½ teaspoon dried chilli flakes

½ teaspoon sweet paprika

1 Using vegetable peeler, slice vegetables into long, thin strips.

2 Heat oil in wok; deep-fry kumara and sweet potato strips, in batches, until browned lightly and crisp. Drain on wire rack over paper-lined tray.

3 Combine salt, chilli and paprika in small bowl. Sprinkle hot sweet potato crisps with chilli salt mixture.

NUTRITIONAL COUNT PER SERVING 13.2g total fat (1.6g saturated fat); 1254kJ (300 cal); 38.7g carbohydrate; 4.4g protein; 4.8g fibre

For tomato and bean
salad: place the torn leaves
of 1 small oakleaf lettuce,
250g halved cherry
tomatoes, ½ cup loosely
packed basil leaves, a
425g can of drained
and rinsed white beans,
100g crumbled fetta
cheese in a large bowl
with 1 tablespoon olive oil,
1 tablespoon white wine
vinegar and 1 teaspoon
dijon mustard, and toss
gently to combine.

Basil-butter kumara patties

PREP + COOK TIME 45 MINUTES **SERVES** 4

2 medium kumara (800g), chopped coarsely

40g butter, softened

⅓ cup finely chopped fresh basil

¼ cup (40g) roasted pine nuts

1 clove garlic, crushed

2 tablespoons coarsely grated parmesan cheese

½ cup (35g) stale wholemeal breadcrumbs

2 tablespoons olive oil

1 Boil, steam or microwave kumara until tender; drain.

2 Mash kumara with butter in medium bowl; stir in basil, nuts, garlic, cheese and breadcrumbs. When cool enough to handle, shape kumara mixture into 8 patties.

3 Heat oil in large frying pan; cook patties, in two batches, until browned both sides and heated through. Serve patties with a tomato and bean salad.

NUTRITIONAL COUNT PER SERVING 25.9g total fat (7.9g saturated fat); 1634kJ (391 cal); 30.9g carbohydrate; 7.2g protein; 4.2g fibre

SWEET POTATO CRISPS WITH CHILLI SALT

1 KUMARA RAVIOLI WITH
TOMATO AND BASIL SAUCE
2 KUMARA AND PECAN LOAF

Kumara ravioli with tomato and basil sauce

PREP + COOK TIME 45 MINUTES **SERVES** 4

*Any leftover ravioli can
be frozen on a baking-
paper-lined oven tray,
then transferred to a
freezer bag. They will
keep in the freezer for a
month or two and can
be cooked from frozen.
Wonton wrappers are thin
pasta squares, available
from Asian food stores
and most supermarkets.*

*For information on egg
tomatoes, see Tomatoes,
page 607; and for basil,
see Herbs, page 262.*

1 large kumara (500g), chopped coarsely

2 tablespoons finely grated romano cheese

1 tablespoon dried currants

40 wonton wrappers

1 egg white, beaten lightly

TOMATO AND BASIL SAUCE

2 teaspoons olive oil

1 medium brown onion (150g), sliced thinly

½ cup (125ml) dry white wine

3 large egg tomatoes (270g), seeded, chopped finely

¼ cup (60ml) vegetable stock

1 tablespoon finely chopped fresh basil

1 Boil, steam or microwave kumara until tender; drain. Mash in medium bowl until smooth. Stir in cheese and currants.

2 Meanwhile, make tomato and basil sauce.

3 Place 1 tablespoon of the kumara mixture in centre of each of 20 wonton wrappers; brush around edge with egg white. Top each with a remaining wrapper, press around edges firmly to seal.

4 Cook ravioli, in batches, in large saucepan of boiling water, uncovered, about 4 minutes or until ravioli float to the surface.

5 Serve ravioli topped with tomato and basil sauce, sprinkled with fresh basil leaves and served with a baby rocket and parmesan salad.

TOMATO AND BASIL SAUCE Heat oil in medium frying pan; cook onion, stirring, until onion softens. Add wine; bring to the boil. Reduce heat; simmer, uncovered, until wine has almost evaporated. Add tomato and stock; stir until heated through. Stir in basil.

NUTRITIONAL COUNT PER SERVING 4.5g total fat (1.2g saturated fat); 1580kJ (374 cal); 64.6g carbohydrate; 14g protein; 3.1g fibre

Kumara and pecan loaf

PREP + COOK TIME 2 HOURS **SERVES** 10

200g butter, softened

¾ cup (165g) firmly packed brown sugar

2 eggs

¾ cup (90g) pecans, chopped coarsely

½ cup (40g) desiccated coconut

1 cup mashed kumara

1½ cups (225g) self-raising flour

½ cup (125ml) milk

Serve the loaf sliced and buttered; it is good for school lunches.

For information on pecans, see Nuts, page 346.

1 Preheat oven to 170°C/150°C fan-forced. Grease 14cm x 21cm loaf pan; line base and long sides with baking paper, extending paper 2cm over sides.

2 Beat butter, sugar and eggs in small bowl with electric mixer until just combined; transfer mixture to large bowl. Fold in nuts, coconut and kumara. Stir in sifted flour and milk, in two batches. Spread mixture into pan.

3 Bake loaf about 1 hour 40 minutes. Stand in pan 10 minutes; turn, top-side up, onto wire rack to cool.

NUTRITIONAL COUNT PER SERVING 27.3g total fat (14.2g saturated fat); 1797kJ (430 cal); 39g carbohydrate; 6g protein; 3.1g fibre

Tamarillo

A glossy, egg-shaped fruit of South American origin whose smooth, tough, bitter, red or orange skin encloses tart/sweet pink-gold flesh decoratively set with black seeds.

The peeled fruit can be eaten raw, poached in a sugar or wine syrup with cinnamon, halved, seasoned with salt and pepper and baked round roast pork towards the end of cooking, made in a refreshing sorbet, or pureed with sugar and folded through cream for a sauce that is brilliant with a chocolate dessert or cake. Tamarillos' season is late autumn to early spring.

PREPARATION Immerse tamarillos in boiling water for 2–3 minutes, then remove to icewater for a minute or two, drain and peel by slitting skins with a sharp knife and slipping them off.

CHOOSING Select well-coloured fruit that yields when cradled in the hands and gently pressed. Stems should be firmly attached.

STORING Keep at room temperature until as soft as a ripe but firm tomato, then refrigerate for up to three days.

For a great presentation, cut peeled tamarillos, still attached to the stem, lengthwise into quarters or slices, poach for about 3–5 minutes in any of the syrups mentioned here and serve opened like a flower (quarters) or fanned (slices) with the reduced syrup and cream or crème anglaise.

Tamarillo apple chutney

COOK + PREP TIME 2 HOURS 25 MINUTES **MAKES** 5 CUPS

20 medium tamarillos (1.5kg)
6 large apples (1.25kg), peeled, chopped
4 medium onions (500g), chopped finely
¾ cup (120g) sultanas
1kg (4 cups) firmly packed brown sugar
2 cups (500ml) brown vinegar
1 teaspoon ground allspice
1 teaspoon ground cinnamon

1 Cut small cross in bottom of each tamarillo. Lower tamarillos gently into large saucepan of boiling water, boil for 1 minute, then place in large bowl of cold water. Peel tamarillos; chop flesh finely.

2 Combine tamarillos with remaining ingredients in large saucepan; stir over heat, without boiling, until sugar dissolves. Bring to the boil; reduce heat. Simmer, uncovered, stirring occasionally, about 2 hours or until thick.

3 Pour chutney into hot sterilised jars; seal immediately.

NUTRITIONAL COUNT PER TABLESPOON 0.8g total fat (0.1g saturated fat); 71kJ (17 cal); 1.8g carbohydrate; 0.5g protein; 0.3g fibre

Tamarind

The tropical tamarind tree is valued for its seed pods, which contain a pleasantly acid/fruity-tasting pulp which is used by South-East Asian and Indian cooks as a souring ingredient in curries and chutneys, in the same way as Western cooks might use lemon juice or vinegar. Tamarind is also an ingredient in worcestershire sauce.

The sticky, fibrous, semi-dried pulp is sold in blocks which still contain the seeds, and is also processed into a seedless, semi-liquid concentrate which is sold in jars. The concentrate is salty, so bear this in mind when adding salt or other salty ingredients such as soy sauce. Both forms are available from spice shops and Asian and Indian food stores, and concentrate can be found in many supermarkets.

PREPARATION Tamarind is used in the form of tamarind water, made by soaking block tamarind or diluting tamarind concentrate. Recipes will call for a certain quantity of tamarind water.

If using block tamarind, cut off a walnut-size piece, put it into ½ cup hot water and stir it around with a spoon, then soak for about 15 minutes before stirring and pressing the solids against the side of the bowl to extract all the flavour. Strain the liquid off, pressing the pulp as dry as possible; discard pulp. If using concentrate, dissolve 2 teaspoons in ½ cup of warm water. Any leftover tamarind water can be frozen in ice-cube trays.

STORING Block tamarind should be wrapped in plastic wrap and stored in an airtight pack to prevent drying out. It does not require refrigeration. Store tamarind concentrate at room temperature.

Fresh tamarind

The tamarind is a large, beautiful, slow-growing and long-lived tree. Tamarinds in certain places on the north coast of Australia were planted by Indonesian traders and fishermen who called there regularly for many centuries before Europeans arrived to settle the continent.

Tamarind and soy sauce

PREP + COOK TIME 15 MINUTES **MAKES** ½ CUP

1 teaspoon peanut oil

1 clove garlic, crushed

2 tablespoons tamarind concentrate

2 tablespoons soy sauce

1 teaspoon brown sugar

2cm piece fresh ginger (10g), grated

⅓ cup (80ml) water

1 green onion, sliced thinly

This recipe makes enough sauce for 4 duck marylands or grilled chicken breast fillets, or for a dipping sauce for 12 barbecued chicken wings.

1 Heat oil in small saucepan; cook garlic, stirring, until fragrant.
2 Add tamarind, sauce, sugar, ginger and the water; bring to the boil then reduce heat. Simmer, uncovered, about 2 minutes or until sauce thickens. Stir in onion off the heat. Serve with pan-fried duck or chicken.

NUTRITIONAL COUNT PER TABLESPOON 0.8g total fat (0.1g saturated fat); 71kJ (17 cal); 1.8g carbohydrate; 0.5g protein; 0.3g fibre

❦ **OTHER RECIPES USING TAMARIND**
Date and tamarind chutney, p467
Massaman beef curry, p51
Okra and tomato in coconut sauce, p369
Peanut sambal, p348

Spicy tamarind chicken

PREP + COOK TIME 1 HOUR 10 MINUTES **SERVES** 4

*Serve each maryland
on a bed of thin rice
noodles to absorb the
flavoursome juices.*

*For information on
chicken, see Poultry,
pages 456 & 457.*

4 chicken marylands (1.5kg)

1 cup (250ml) water

¼ cup (85g) tamarind concentrate

¼ cup (60ml) japanese soy sauce

⅓ cup (90g) firmly packed grated palm sugar

CHILLI, GINGER AND LIME PASTE

2 fresh small red thai chillies

5cm piece fresh ginger (25g), chopped coarsely

6 shallots (150g), chopped coarsely

2 cloves garlic

3 fresh kaffir lime leaves

1 tablespoon vegetable oil

1 tablespoon water

1 Make chilli, ginger and lime paste.

2 Preheat oven to 180°C/160°C fan-forced.

3 Heat oiled large shallow flameproof dish; cook chicken, uncovered, until browned, turning occasionally. Remove chicken from dish.

4 Cook paste, stirring, in same heated dish until fragrant. Stir in remaining ingredients then return chicken to dish, turning to coat in paste mixture.

5 Cook chicken, uncovered, in oven about 30 minutes or until cooked through, brushing frequently with paste mixture. Serve with lime wedges.

CHILLI, GINGER AND LIME PASTE Blend or process ingredients until mixture forms a smooth paste.

NUTRITIONAL COUNT PER SERVING 39.6g total fat (11.8g saturated fat); 2713kJ (649 cal); 26.5g carbohydrate; 46.9g protein; 1.1g fibre

Tamarind and citrus pork curry

PREP + COOK TIME 1 HOUR 10 MINUTES (PLUS STANDING TIME) **SERVES** 4

70g dried tamarind, chopped coarsely

¾ cup (180ml) boiling water

1 tablespoon peanut oil

1 large red onion (300g), chopped finely

1 fresh long red chilli, sliced thinly

5cm piece fresh ginger (25g), grated

2 cloves garlic, crushed

10 fresh curry leaves

2 teaspoons fenugreek seeds

½ teaspoon ground turmeric

1 teaspoon ground coriander

1 teaspoon finely grated lime rind

1 tablespoon lime juice

400ml can coconut cream

6 baby eggplants (360g), chopped coarsely

1kg pork fillet, cut into 2cm dice

This is a Cambodian dish, typical of that country's distillation of Indian, Chinese and Thai cooking influences, with the Cambodians' liking for sharp tastes coming through in the tamarind and lime juice. Serve it with rice.

For information on pork, see Pork, pages 440 & 441.

1 Soak tamarind in the boiling water 30 minutes. Place fine sieve over small bowl; push tamarind through sieve. Discard solids in sieve; reserve pulp in bowl.

2 Heat oil in large saucepan; cook onion, chilli, ginger, garlic, curry leaves, seeds and spices, stirring, until onion softens.

3 Add pulp, rind, juice, coconut cream and eggplant; simmer, covered, 20 minutes. Add pork; simmer, uncovered, about 20 minutes or until pork is cooked.

NUTRITIONAL COUNT PER SERVING 45.8g total fat (25.7g saturated fat); 3060kJ (732 cal); 19.7g carbohydrate; 57.7g protein; 6.8g fibre

Tea

Although many kinds of infusions are called teas, the name should really be reserved for the beverage made from *Camellia sinenis* or the tea bush (the others are, correctly, tisanes, though this is a pedantic point and the name tea for herb and other infusions is here to stay).

Traditionally, different tea blends are designed for different times of the day: breakfast teas are strong "wake-up" blends and afternoon teas such as darjeeling, earl grey and orange pekoe or broken orange pekoe (the difference is in the size of the leaf and therefore the brewing time) are brisk and refreshing but more delicate. Lapsang souchong, also called russian caravan, is a smoked black tea from China's Fujian province and is meant for the adventurous tea-drinker at any time of day.

☙ OTHER RECIPES USING TEA
Mixed berry punch, p61

The fresh leaves of the bush taste nothing like tea but are transformed by the processes which have been developed over many years to give the tastes and aromas that tea-drinkers prize. The three main tea styles, which account for most of the tea drunk in the world, are green, oolong and black. They are all made from the same plant but the way they are processed gives three quite different results. The fundamental variations are in whether the leaves are fermented, and for how long. The term "fermenting" in tea production does not mean the kind of changes that happen in bread- or wine-making, but is the traditional term in the industry for the process of pressing the leaves to break open their cells and then leaving them to stand, which allows their own enzymes to cause changes leading to flavour development. Within these major types there are many different blends, arrived at by the highly skilled selection and blending of leaves from different varieties of *Camellia sinensis*, different places and different grades according to leaf size, how much of the tip was plucked, whether the leaves are whole or broken and many other factors.

GREEN TEA is unfermented tea, meaning that it is dried straight after picking. It retains some of the fresh leaf's flavour and acquires new flavours from enzyme reactions which start when it is picked.

Green tea makes pale tea with a distinctive, slightly grassy aroma and taste.

OOLONG TEA is partly fermented, meaning that it is left to ferment for a short time before being dried. It makes light amber tea with a fruity aroma.

BLACK TEA is fermented for much longer, causing the leaves to develop strong aroma and flavour and turn copper-brown; drying turns them black. Its aroma is rich and its taste is full with a slight acid edge.

FLAVOURED TEAS such as jasmine are made with a mixture of dried flowers and green tea. Earl grey is black tea which has been scented with oil of bergamot from bergamot oranges.

WHITE TEA is made from buds plucked from the tea bush while they are still covered with fine white hairs. Many health benefits are claimed for it. Once reserved for Chinese emperors, it is now available at larger supermarkets.

TEA MAKING

Tea made with loose tea tastes fresher and "brisker" than the same blend made with tea bags. A hinged infuser is useful for making one cup of tea and a teapot with a supplementary pot of hot water is best when catering for several people. Both pots should be pre-heated by filling with near-boiling water, standing a few minutes and emptying just before the tea is made. The usual measure of tea is one teaspoon per person plus one teaspoon extra. The water should be added immediately it boils, the lids put on both pots and the teapot swirled gently to mix the leaves through, then stood a few minutes before pouring, using a strainer. The strength can be adjusted to individual preferences with the hot water. Milk is usually added after the tea so that people can see when it looks the way they like it. Connoisseurs use a teapot with a removable infuser so that brewing will not continue as the pot stands. For crystal-clear iced tea, brew the initial tea with cold water (this needs planning ahead, as it will take several hours to get up to strength) rather than hot water. The reason that iced tea often clouds when the ice cubes are added is that substances which were extracted from the leaves by boiling water suddenly precipitate and become visible when the water is chilled; low-temperature infusing doesn't extract these substances in the first place.

STORING Tea should be stored in an airtight container away from heat and light. It will remain in good condition for several months, but will eventually lose aroma and briskness if stored too long.

Ginseng and star anise tea

PREP + COOK TIME 5 MINUTES (PLUS STANDING TIME) **SERVES** 4

2 teaspoons ginseng

2 star anise

3 x 10cm strips orange rind

1 tablespoon honey

1 litre (4 cups) boiling water

1 Combine ingredients in large heatproof jug. Stand, uncovered, 5 minutes.

2 Strain mixture into teapot or large heatproof jug.

NUTRITIONAL COUNT PER SERVING 0g total fat (0g saturated fat); 113kJ (27 cal); 6.9g carbohydrate; 0.1g protein; 0.2g fibre

Ginseng is available at Asian food stores. It is the aromatic dried root of an Asian plant, believed to be invigorating.

Spiced rosehip and hibiscus tea

PREP + COOK TIME 5 MINUTES (PLUS STANDING TIME) **SERVES** 4

2 rosehip and hibiscus teabags

2 x 10cm strips orange rind

1 cinnamon stick

1 litre (4 cups) boiling water

1 Combine ingredients in large heatproof jug; stand, uncovered, 2 minutes.

2 Strain mixture into teapot or large heatproof jug.

NUTRITIONAL COUNT PER SERVING 0g total fat (0g saturated fat); 13kJ (3 cal); 0.7g carbohydrate; 0.1g protein; 0.2g fibre

1

2

1 INDIAN CHAI
2 GREEN TEA ICE-CREAM
WITH FRUIT SALSA

Indian chai

PREP + COOK TIME 10 MINUTES (PLUS STANDING TIME) **MAKES** 1 LITRE (4 CUPS)

5 cardamom pods, bruised

10 cloves

1 cinnamon stick

1cm piece fresh ginger (5g),
sliced thickly

2 teaspoons fennel seeds

1 teaspoon vanilla extract

3 cups (750ml) water

4 darjeeling teabags

2 cups (500ml) milk

⅓ cup (90g) grated palm sugar

*India's smooth, spicy
comfort drink is now a
fashionable offering at
smart cafés in the West.*

1 Combine cardamom, cloves, cinnamon, ginger, fennel, extract and the water in
medium saucepan; bring to the boil. Cover; simmer 5 minutes. Remove from heat;
stand, covered, 10 minutes.

2 Return spice mixture to the boil, add teabags; remove from heat. Stand 5 minutes.

3 Meanwhile, heat milk in medium saucepan without boiling. Add milk to tea mixture;
add sugar, stir until dissolved.

NUTRITIONAL COUNT PER 250ML 4.9g total fat (3.2g saturated fat); 727kJ (174 cal); 27.9g carbohydrate;
4.3g protein; 0g fibre

Green tea ice-cream with fruit salsa

PREP + COOK TIME 25 MINUTES (PLUS REFRIGERATION AND FREEZING TIME) **SERVES** 4

Home-made ice-cream is more dense than the commercial kind, so transfer it from the freezer to the refrigerator 20 minutes before serving.

2 tablespoons green tea powder

2 tablespoons boiling water

1 tablespoon caster sugar

1 vanilla bean

1 cup (250ml) milk

2 egg yolks

¼ cup (55g) caster sugar, extra

300ml thickened cream, whipped

10 fresh lychees (250g), chopped finely

2 medium kiwifruits (170g), chopped finely

½ small papaya (325g), chopped finely

1 tablespoon finely chopped fresh mint

1 Combine tea, the water and sugar in small bowl; stand 10 minutes.

2 Split vanilla bean lengthways; scrape out seeds. Combine pod, seeds and milk in small saucepan; bring to the boil. Stir in tea mixture; stand 5 minutes.

3 Meanwhile, whisk egg yolks and extra sugar in small bowl until creamy; gradually whisk into hot milk mixture. Stir over low heat, without boiling, until mixture thickens slightly.

4 Strain mixture into medium heatproof bowl; discard pod. Cover surface of custard with plastic wrap; cool. Refrigerate about 1 hour or until cold.

5 Fold whipped cream into cold custard. Pour mixture into ice-cream maker; churn according to manufacturer's instructions. (Or place custard in shallow container, cover with foil; freeze until almost firm. Place ice-cream in large bowl, chop coarsely then beat with electric mixer until smooth. Cover; freeze until firm. Repeat process twice more.)

6 Combine fruit and mint in small bowl. Serve ice-cream with salsa.

NUTRITIONAL COUNT PER SERVING 33.5g total fat (20.9g saturated fat); 2123kJ (508 cal); 43.7g carbohydrate; 6.9g protein; 3.3g fibre

---

Raspberry mint iced tea

PREP TIME 10 MINUTES (PLUS REFRIGERATION TIME) **MAKES** 1 LITRE (4 CUPS)

For information on raspberries, see Berries, page 58.

2 tablespoons caster sugar

2 cups (500ml) hot water

6 raspberry teabags

100g fresh raspberries

1 cup coarsely chopped fresh mint leaves

2 cups (500ml) chilled water

crushed ice

1 Combine sugar and the hot water in large heatproof jug; stir until sugar dissolves. Add tea bags; stand 10 minutes.

2 Add raspberries, mint and the chilled water. Cover, refrigerate 20 minutes; remove teabags. Serve over crushed ice.

NUTRITIONAL COUNT PER 250ML 0.2g total fat (0g saturated fat); 180kJ (43 cal); 9.5g carbohydrate; 0.5g protein; 1.4g fibre

Tofu

Also known as bean curd, tofu is made by adding mineral salts to soy milk (see Soya, page 552) so that it separates into curds, which are tofu, and "whey", which is drained off. Tofu is bland, but has the gift of absorbing other flavours. It is low-joule, provides protein with no cholesterol and has beneficial amounts of iron and, depending on the coagulant used in manufacturing, may be high in calcium and magnesium.

Firm tofu

Silken tofu

Tofu comes in many forms — the refrigerated cabinets in supermarkets and Asian food stores have such convenience foods as marinated tofu, sweet chilli tofu cubes, pickled tofu, deep-fried tofu puffs, sweetened dessert tofu and more. Fresh tofu comes in two main types, firm and silken.

FIRM TOFU is made by pressing the curds to remove more moisture, giving a consistency that can be cut into blocks. It may be firm or extra firm and is used in stir-fries, added to stews, curries and soups, or dusted with rice flour and fried to make it crisp and served with dips or with flavoursome accompaniments such as green onions, grated ginger and soy sauce. It can also be served with sweet sauces. Firm tofu is sold fresh, vacuum-packed or packed in water in sealed packages.

SOFT OR SILKEN TOFU is not pressed, only drained of whey. It is too soft to be cut and is usually scooped into a bowl and eaten with savoury additions such as pickled vegetables and garlic teriyaki sauce, or sweet ones such as mango or lychees. People who want to avoid dairy products use silken tofu for making ice-cream, cheesecake and creamy tart fillings and sauces. It is sold fresh, vacuum-packed or in the packages in which it was made by filling the pack with soy milk and then coagulating it, so that the curd fills the package and remains intact and moist. The package is then sealed.

DEEP-FRIED TOFU PUFFS are cubes of firm tofu that have been deep-fried so that they puff up. They are sold in packages and are used in stir-fries, or can be crisped in an oiled pan and served as snacks with pickles, green onions, sesame oil and other savoury additions.

STORING Firm tofu packed in water should be stored in the refrigerator. Packaged silken tofu does not require refrigeration and has a shelf life of up to a year, though it is usually chilled before serving. Once opened, both types of tofu should be stored in the refrigerator in a container of water to cover them completely, and used within a few days, changing the water daily. Fresh tofu bought loose should also be stored like this, once opened.

❧ **OTHER RECIPES USING TOFU**
Sesame tofu salad, p545

Age-dashi tofu

PREP + COOK TIME 45 MINUTES (PLUS STANDING TIME) **SERVES** 4

300g firm tofu

1 teaspoon instant dashi

1 cup (250ml) hot water

1 tablespoon sake

1 tablespoon mirin

1½ tablespoons light soy sauce

1 tablespoon toasted
sesame seeds

2 tablespoons cornflour

vegetable oil, for deep-frying

2 tablespoons coarsely
grated daikon

1cm piece fresh ginger (5g),
grated

2 green onions, chopped finely

2 teaspoons dried bonito flakes

1 Press tofu between chopping boards with weight on top, raise one end; stand 25 minutes.

2 Meanwhile, combine dashi and the water in small saucepan. Add sake, mirin and sauce; bring to the boil. Remove from heat.

3 Cut tofu into eight even-sized pieces; pat dry between layers of absorbent paper then toss in combined sesame seeds and cornflour. Heat oil in wok; deep-fry tofu, in batches, until browned lightly. Drain on absorbent paper.

4 Place two pieces of tofu in each serving bowl. Divide daikon, ginger and onion among bowls; pour dashi dressing over tofu then sprinkle with bonito flakes.

NUTRITIONAL COUNT PER SERVING 10.5g total fat (1.4g saturated fat); 715kJ (171 cal); 6.4g carbohydrate; 10.2g protein; 1.8g fibre

AGE-DASHI TOFU

Dashi, made from dried bonito (mackerel) flakes and kombu (kelp), is the basic stock for hundreds of Japanese dishes. Bonito flakes can be found in Asian food stores and instant dashi, called dashi-no-moto, is available in concentrated or granule form: in this recipe, we have used granules.

Tofu zucchini patties

PREP + COOK TIME 30 MINUTES **SERVES** 4

300g firm silken tofu,
chopped coarsely

1½ cups cooked brown rice

3 medium zucchini (360g),
grated coarsely

1 medium brown onion (150g),
chopped finely

1 cup (100g) packaged
breadcrumbs

2 eggs

2 tablespoons finely chopped
fresh flat-leaf parsley

1 clove garlic, crushed

2 tablespoons olive oil

2 lemons, cut into wedges

1 Blend or process tofu until smooth; transfer to large bowl. Add rice, zucchini, onion, breadcrumbs, eggs, parsley and garlic; mix well. Shape mixture into 12 patties.

2 Heat oil in large frying pan; cook patties, in batches, about 3 minutes each side or until browned and heated through. Drain on absorbent paper.

3 Serve patties with lemon wedges.

NUTRITIONAL COUNT PER SERVING 18.8g total fat (3.2g saturated fat); 1831kJ (438 cal); 43.2g carbohydrate; 19.8g protein; 6.6g fibre

You need to cook ⅔ cup brown rice to obtain the quantity of cooked rice needed for this recipe.

For information on zucchini, see Zucchini, page 656.

Salt and pepper tofu with chilli lime dressing

PREP + COOK TIME 35 MINUTES (PLUS STANDING TIME) **SERVES** 4

2 x 300g packets fresh firm tofu

1 small red capsicum (150g), sliced thinly

1 small yellow capsicum (150g), sliced thinly

100g snow peas, sliced thinly

1 small carrot (70g), sliced thinly

1 cup (80g) bean sprouts

½ cup loosely packed fresh coriander leaves

1 teaspoon coarsely ground black pepper

1 tablespoon sea salt

¼ teaspoon five-spice powder

⅓ cup (50g) plain flour

peanut oil, for deep-frying

CHILLI LIME DRESSING

2 tablespoons peanut oil

¼ cup (60ml) lime juice

2 tablespoons sweet chilli sauce

1 Dry tofu with absorbent paper. Cut each piece in half horizontally; cut each half into quarters (you will have 16 pieces). Place tofu pieces, in single layer, on absorbent paper. Cover with more absorbent paper; stand 15 minutes.

2 Meanwhile, combine capsicums, snow peas, carrot, sprouts and coriander in large bowl.

3 Make chilli lime dressing by whisking ingredients together in small bowl.

4 Combine pepper, salt, five-spice and flour in medium bowl; coat tofu in mixture, shake away excess. Heat oil in wok; deep-fry tofu, in batches, until browned lightly. Drain on absorbent paper.

5 Serve tofu with salad; drizzle with dressing.

NUTRITIONAL COUNT PER SERVING 28.2g total fat (4.7g saturated fat); 1772kJ (424 cal); 17.8g carbohydrate; 22g protein; 6.1g fibre

Chicken and water chestnut tofu pouches

PREP + COOK TIME 45 MINUTES **SERVES** 4

500g chicken mince

⅓ cup (65g) water chestnuts, rinsed, drained, chopped finely

¼ teaspoon five-spice powder

1 tablespoon finely chopped fresh coriander

1 clove garlic, crushed

2cm piece fresh ginger (10g), grated

1 fresh long red chilli, chopped finely

12 seasoned fried bean curd pouches

⅓ cup (80ml) tonkatsu sauce

1 Combine mince, chestnut, five-spice, coriander, garlic, ginger and chilli in medium bowl.

2 Carefully open pouches on one side, gently pushing fingers into each corner.

3 Spoon one rounded tablespoon of chicken mixture into pouch, pushing mixture into corners (be careful not to overfill or tear pouch). Fold one side of pouch down over chicken mixture; fold other side over top of first side. Turn pouch over so fold is underneath. Repeat with remaining pouches and mixture.

4 Place pouches, in single layer, in baking-paper-lined bamboo steamer. Steam, covered, over wok of simmering water, about 15 minutes or until cooked through.

5 Cook pouches in heated lightly oiled large frying pan, uncovered, about 5 minutes or until browned. Serve pouches with tonkatsu sauce.

NUTRITIONAL COUNT PER SERVING 15.4g total fat (4.2g saturated fat); 1233kJ (295 cal); 8.4g carbohydrate; 29.2g protein; 3.6g fibre

Tomatoes

The tomato is a cook's hero, always ready to be whizzed into a hot or chilled soup, chopped for a cooked or instant pasta sauce, grilled as an accompaniment, stuffed for a main course, fried for breakfast, piled on bruschetta or arranged on a pizza, used for a tart filling, a salsa, a salad, and in autumn, when tomatoes are at their best, made into a year's supply of relishes, sweet or savoury jams and the proper home-made tomato sauce that is the foundation of much good cooking.

To peel fresh tomatoes, cut a cross in the skins at the base, drop each one into simmering water for 30 seconds, then into a bowl or sink of cold water; hold tomato and strip off the skin, starting from the cross. To seed them, halve horizontally and squeeze each half into a sieve set over a bowl. Return the juice in the bowl to the dish you are making.

The key question when buying tomatoes is whether they were picked ripe or unripe. Like many fruits and vegetables, they can become softer and brighter-coloured after they leave the parent plant, but they cannot continue to be nourished and it is nourishment that produces optimum flavour, so if they were picked unripe they will never taste truly ripe. Truly vine-ripened tomatoes taste wonderful, but there are many impostors — you have to trust your greengrocer. Truss tomatoes (those still attached to a stem) look convincing, but buy only if they have a good tomato aroma and are slightly soft. Tomatoes are available all year, but are best in their natural season, which is summer and early autumn. In winter, canned, packaged or bottled tomato products, which are among the most

successful processed vegetables, may be more satisfactory than flavourless fresh ones.

ROUND TOMATOES are the kind seen most often at the greengrocer's. They have been developed as the perfect tomato from the trade's point of view: brightly coloured, uniform in shape, thick-skinned so that they can be transported without damage. From the customer's point of view, they are a mixed lot, sometimes good if they have truly been, as the sign may proudly say, vine-ripened, but often disappointing.

OXHEART TOMATOES are an old-fashioned tomato that has appeared at some greengrocers in the past few years. They are thin-skinned and don't keep well, and they don't look thrilling, being pink rather than red and often misshapen, but, in their natural season, they are juicy and

Round tomatoes

Vine-ripened truss tomatoes

Oxheart tomatoes

Egg tomatoes

flavoursome. Out of season, they may disappoint though they may still be better than others.

EGG OR PLUM TOMATOES are less juicy and more fleshy than others so they are best for cooking and drying. Roma is the best-known variety and is available either full-size or miniature.

CHERRY TOMATOES are miniature varieties sold in punnets. They are decorative and usually well-flavoured, and are used both raw and lightly grilled, fried or roasted. Teardrop-shaped miniatures, usually yellow teardrop, are delicately sweet and sharp, and red or yellow grape tomatoes are smaller again than cherry ones.

GREEN TOMATOES are considered a separate vegetable from ripe ones and are valued for their tartness and crunchy texture. They are grilled, baked, used in Indian and Mediterranean vegetable dishes and relishes and, for the famous dish of the American south, dipped in cornmeal and fried in bacon fat.

KUMATOES are a "black" tomato variety, originally from the Galapagos Islands, with striking nearly-black skin and dark-patched pink flesh.

DRIED TOMATOES may be completely dried to make them shrivelled, dark and chewy with a strong, savoury, different taste from fresh tomatoes, or semi-dried to make them shrivelled but still tender, red

and tasting like fresh tomatoes but more concentrated. Drying can be done in the sun over two or three days (bringing them in each evening) or in a low oven over eight to ten hours.

CHOOSING The best test for a truly ripe tomato is its aroma, which should be reminiscent of tomato leaves and stems. Choose fruit that is heavy for its size, preferably with the calyx on as it helps to maintain freshness and flavour, though its presence does not guarantee a good tomato. Tomatoes to be eaten raw should be slightly soft, those to be cooked may be softer or, if they are to be stuffed, a little firmer. They should be undamaged, though a dry crack or scar on an otherwise good tomato doesn't matter. Bright colour is important but is not, of itself, a guarantee of good flavour. Buy only as many tomatoes as you plan to use in the next few days.

STORING Do not refrigerate tomatoes. They are sub-tropical in origin and chilling destroys some of their flavour. Store them at room temperature, away from sunlight and not touching each other.

❀ **OTHER RECIPES USING TOMATOES**
Anchovy and garlic tuna with tomato and oregano, p531
Avocado, cos and tomato salad, p27
Baked mushrooms with tomato and basil, p327
Braised borlotti beans with tomato and garlic, p42
Cheese gnocchi with fresh tomato sauce and pancetta, p109
Chilli tomato relish, p474–5
Fresh tomato and herb sauce, p571
Kumara ravioli with tomato and basil sauce, p592–3
Lamb and okra in rich tomato sauce with garlic confit, p369
Okra and tomato in coconut sauce, p369
Roasted tomato salad, p87
Seared scallops with pea puree and tomato, p631
Steamed mussels in tomato garlic broth, p535
Tomato braised lamb shanks, p285
Tomato, fetta and pancetta frittatas, p166
Tomato mustard beef with baby fennel, p48
Veal and tomato dolmades, p639

Baby egg & grape tomatoes

Cherry tomatoes

Green tomatoes

Kumatoes

Insalata caprese, meaning
"salad in the style of
Capri", is a marvellously
simple, arrangement of
tomatoes, cheese and basil
which relies for its effect on
top-quality ingredients. It
is usually served as a first
course but could be part
of a summer buffet.

For information on
bocconcini cheese, see
Cheese, page 102.

Mixed tomato caprese salad

PREP TIME 20 MINUTES **SERVES** 4

4 small green tomatoes (360g), sliced thinly
4 small black tomatoes (360g), sliced thinly
4 small vine-ripened tomatoes (360g), sliced thinly
4 bocconcini cheese (240g), sliced thinly
⅓ cup coarsely chopped fresh basil
2 tablespoons olive oil
1 tablespoon balsamic vinegar

1 Layer tomato, cheese and basil on serving plate; drizzle with combined oil and vinegar.

NUTRITIONAL COUNT PER SERVING 18.5g total fat (7.3g saturated fat); 1020kJ (244 cal); 5.2g carbohydrate; 13.1g protein; 3.3g fibre

You could also serve this
soup chilled, with grilled
cheese toasts: grill the
bread on one side, cover
the other side with grated
gruyère or cheddar, grill
until cheese melts and
browns a little, then cut
into fingers.

For information on fennel,
see Fennel, page 174.

Tomato and fennel soup

PREP + COOK TIME 1 HOUR **SERVES** 4

2 teaspoons olive oil
1 medium fennel bulb (300g), chopped coarsely
2 medium brown onions (300g), chopped coarsely
2 cloves garlic, quartered
1kg tomatoes, quartered
3 cups (750ml) vegetable stock
4 slices white bread, crusts removed
cooking-oil spray

1 Preheat oven to 180°C/160°C fan-forced.
2 Heat oil in large saucepan; cook fennel, onion and garlic, stirring, until onion softens. Add tomato and stock; bring to the boil. Reduce heat; simmer, covered, stirring occasionally, 15 minutes. Uncover; simmer, stirring occasionally, about 15 minutes or until tomato is soft and pulpy.
3 Meanwhile, cut bread into 2cm cubes. Place on oven tray; spray lightly with oil. Toast about 10 minutes or until croûtons are crisp.
4 Blend or process soup, in batches, until smooth. Pass soup through food mill or fine sieve; reheat soup in same pan. Serve soup topped with croûtons.

NUTRITIONAL COUNT PER SERVING 4.3g total fat (0.8g saturated fat); 589kJ (141 cal); 17.3g carbohydrate; 7.5g protein; 5.9g fibre

1 MIXED TOMATO
CAPRESE SALAD
2 TOMATO AND FENNEL SOUP

Basic tomato pasta sauce

PREP + COOK TIME 1 HOUR **MAKES** 2 CUPS

2 tablespoons olive oil

1 small brown onion (80g), chopped finely

1 clove garlic, crushed

2kg ripe tomatoes, peeled, seeded, chopped coarsely

⅓ cup loosely packed fresh basil leaves

1 Heat oil in large saucepan; cook onion and garlic, stirring, until onion softens.
2 Add tomato and basil; cook, stirring, 5 minutes or until tomato begins to soften.
Bring to the boil. Reduce heat; simmer, uncovered, stirring occasionally, 40 minutes or
until sauce thickens. Serve over cooked pasta.

NUTRITIONAL COUNT PER ¼ CUP 4.8g total fat (0.6g saturated fat); 343kJ (82 cal); 5.4g carbohydrate;
2.7g protein; 3.3g fibre

*It is good strategy to make
this endlessly useful sauce
in quantity in late summer
when tomatoes are cheap
and good. Ladled, hot, into
hot sterilised jars, it will
keep through winter.*

The pizzaiola sauce can be made up to 3 days ahead and refrigerated until required. It can also be used as a pasta sauce — the quantity in this recipe is enough for 375g of pasta.

For information on veal, see Veal, pages 620 & 621.

Spicy veal pizzaiola

PREP + COOK TIME 30 MINUTES **SERVES** 4

2 tablespoons olive oil

2 cloves garlic, crushed

4 slices pancetta (60g), chopped finely

¼ cup (60ml) dry white wine

700g bottled tomato pasta sauce

1 teaspoon dried chilli flakes

4 x 170g veal cutlets

75g baby spinach leaves

1 Heat 2 teaspoons of the oil in large saucepan; cook garlic and pancetta, stirring, about 5 minutes. Add wine; cook, stirring, until wine is reduced by half. Add sauce and chilli; simmer, uncovered, about 15 minutes or until sauce thickens.

2 Meanwhile, heat remaining oil in large frying pan. Cook veal, uncovered, until cooked as desired.

3 Remove sauce from heat; stir in spinach. Top veal with sauce.

NUTRITIONAL COUNT PER SERVING 14.6g total fat (2.8g saturated fat); 1555kJ (372 cal); 18.8g carbohydrate; 36.3g protein; 4.3g fibre

The ultimate hot-weather cooler, often ladled over a couple of ice-cubes in each bowl and served with bowls of the vegetables for garnishing so that diners can help themselves.

Gazpacho

PREP TIME 25 MINUTES (PLUS REFRIGERATION TIME) **SERVES** 6

1kg ripe tomatoes, peeled, chopped coarsely

2 lebanese cucumbers (260g), seeded, chopped coarsely

2 large red capsicums (700g), chopped coarsely

1 large green capsicum (350g), chopped coarsely

1 large red onion (200g), chopped coarsely

2 cloves garlic, chopped coarsely

415ml can tomato juice

2 tablespoons red wine vinegar

1 tablespoon olive oil

2 teaspoons Tabasco

1 medium avocado (250g), chopped finely

1 small yellow capsicum (150g), chopped finely

¼ cup finely chopped fresh coriander

1 Blend or process tomatoes, cucumber, capsicums, onion, garlic, juice, vinegar, oil and Tabasco, in batches, until smooth. Pour into large jug. Cover; refrigerate 3 hours.

2 Stir soup; pour into serving bowls, top with remaining ingredients. Serve gazpacho sprinkled with extra Tabasco, if you like.

NUTRITIONAL COUNT PER SERVING 10.4g total fat (1.9g saturated fat); 786kJ (188 cal); 14.5g carbohydrate; 6.2g protein; 6.3g fibre

Sun-dried tomato mayonnaise

PREP TIME 20 MINUTES **MAKES** 1 CUP

2 egg yolks

½ teaspoon salt

¾ teaspoon dry mustard

⅔ cup (160ml) extra light olive oil

2 tablespoons olive oil

2 tablespoons sun-dried tomato oil

1 tablespoon finely chopped drained sun-dried tomatoes

2 tablespoons hot water

1 tablespoon white vinegar

1 Combine egg yolks, salt and mustard in medium bowl. Gradually add combined oils, in thin, steady stream, whisking constantly until mixture thickens.

2 Add tomato and the water; whisk until combined. Stir in vinegar.

NUTRITIONAL COUNT PER TABLESPOON 19.2g total fat (2.8g saturated fat); 723kJ (173 cal); 0.3g carbohydrate; 0.6g protein; 0.1g fibre

Serve this mayonnaise with potato wedges or fresh vegetables for dipping, on a chicken burger or alongside corn fritters, or in a sandwich filling. Be sure to add the oil slowly, whisking constantly, so that the mayonnaise won't separate. If it does show signs of separating, whisk in 1–2 tablespoons of boiling water.

Roasted truss tomatoes with crispy basil leaves

PREP + COOK TIME 20 MINUTES **SERVES** 8

500g baby vine-ripened truss tomatoes

2 cloves garlic, sliced thinly

1 tablespoon olive oil

2 teaspoons balsamic vinegar

vegetable oil, for deep-frying

⅓ cup loosely packed fresh basil leaves

1 Preheat oven to 180°C/160°C fan-forced.

2 Place tomatoes on oven tray; pour over combined garlic, oil and vinegar. Roast about 10 minutes or until tomatoes soften.

3 Meanwhile, heat vegetable oil in small saucepan; deep-fry basil, in batches, until crisp.

4 Serve tomatoes sprinkled with basil.

NUTRITIONAL COUNT PER SERVING 2.5g total fat (0.3g saturated fat); 134kJ (32 cal); 1.5g carbohydrate; 0.4g protein; 1.2g fibre

Use a small, deep saucepan with only about 3cm of oil to deep-fry the basil; the water content of the fresh leaves will make the oil bubble up and spit.

For information on basil, see Herbs, page 262.

1 ROASTED TRUSS TOMATOES
WITH CRISPY BASIL LEAVES
2 ROASTED MIXED TOMATO
SALAD

Roasted mixed tomato salad

PREP + COOK TIME 20 MINUTES (PLUS COOLING TIME) **SERVES** 10

4 small red tomatoes (360g), halved

4 small green tomatoes (360g), halved

250g cherry tomatoes

200g red teardrop tomatoes

200g yellow teardrop tomatoes

2 tablespoons olive oil

2 tablespoons balsamic vinegar

2 tablespoons small fresh basil leaves

1 tablespoon fresh oregano leaves

1 tablespoon fresh thyme leaves

This salad will travel well — it would make a great picnic lunch with cold meats, or the prosciutto-wrapped veal and pork meatloaf on page 621.

1 Preheat oven to 240°C/220°C fan-forced.

2 Combine tomatoes and oil in large shallow baking dish. Roast, uncovered, 10 minutes. Remove from oven; cool 30 minutes.

3 Place tomato mixture in large bowl with remaining ingredients; toss gently to combine.

NUTRITIONAL COUNT PER SERVING 3.8g total fat (0.5g saturated fat); 209kJ (50 cal); 2.4g carbohydrate; 1g protein; 1.6g fibre

Turnips

As members of the cabbage family, turnips have pungent and bitter flavour notes. They also have sweet ones and an agreeable earthiness. Mature ones are best used in a stew with meat and other vegetables, mashed with potatoes and garlic, roasted round a joint, which makes them sweeter, or cooked with such spices as cumin, coriander and paprika, whose flavours go well with pungency.

Pickled turnips, coloured a wonderful pink by beetroot juice, are wrapped in flatbread for a street snack in the Middle East and are also used as part of a mezze platter or to accompany main dishes. The turnips are peeled and cut into quarters or chunks, depending on size, and layered in a jar or crock (which must have a tight-fitting lid) with garlic, small chunks or slices of peeled raw beetroot and a few celery leaves, then covered in a vinegar brine, sealed with the lid and kept in a warm place but out of the sun for about 10 days, when they are ready to eat; the jar is swirled gently once a day during this time to blend the flavours. The pickles should then be stored in a cool place and eaten within a month. A brine of 2 cups water, 2 tablespoons salt and 150ml white-wine vinegar is enough for 500g turnips.

Young turnips are much sweeter and more delicate and can be braised in meat stock, or quartered, boiled and lightly browned in butter, or baby ones can be cooked whole with small onions, glazed with the onions in sugar and butter or duck fat and served with roast duck for the classic French dish caneton aux navets. Young turnips cooked like this are also good with baked ham. Turnip tops, if young and fresh, can be cooked in the same ways as spinach.

PREPARATION Turnip skin can be bitter, so all sizes should be peeled, mature ones thickly as the outside layer may also be bitter.

CHOOSING Turnips should be firm, heavy for their size and undamaged, with no soft spots and no rank odour. Avoid huge specimens which may be stringy.

STORING Turnips should be stored without wrappings in the refrigerator crisper for up to 4–5 days. Turnip tops should be enclosed in a paper bag, then a plastic one, refrigerated and used within 24 hours.

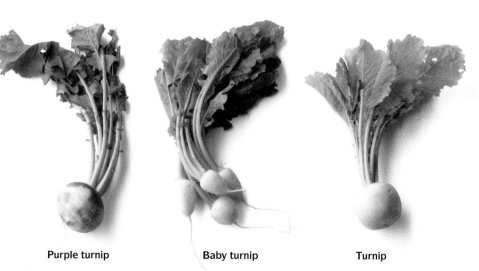

Purple turnip　　　**Baby turnip**　　　**Turnip**

Moroccan turnip soup

PREP + COOK TIME 50 MINUTES **SERVES** 4

Turnip has an affinity with warm-flavoured spices. This is a great winter soup.

1 tablespoon olive oil

1 large brown onion (200g), chopped coarsely

2 cloves garlic, crushed

2 teaspoons cumin seeds

2 teaspoons ground coriander

½ teaspoon hot paprika

1.5kg turnips, trimmed, chopped coarsely

1.5 litres (6 cups) chicken stock

½ cup (125ml) cream

⅓ cup coarsely chopped fresh flat-leaf parsley

1 Heat oil in large saucepan; cook onion and garlic, stirring, until onion softens. Add spices; cook, stirring, until fragrant. Add turnip and stock; bring to the boil. Reduce heat; simmer, uncovered, until turnips are tender.

2 Blend or process soup, in batches, until smooth. Return soup to same pan with cream; stir until hot.

3 Serve bowls of soup sprinkled with parsley.

NUTRITIONAL COUNT PER SERVING 19.7g total fat (10.3g saturated fat); 1267kJ (303 cal); 17.5g carbohydrate; 9.9g protein; 10g fibre

Vanilla

The fragrance and flavour of vanilla are available to the cook in the form of vanilla beans, vanilla extract, which is made by soaking finely chopped beans in alcohol to extract the substances that give that wonderful scent and taste, or vanilla bean paste, a sweetened and concentrated extract containing vanilla bean seeds. There are also vanilla essence, which may be extract diluted with water or may have other ingredients, and imitation vanilla essence, which is made with chemicals and fails completely to capture the complexity and delicate nuances of the real thing. It is advisable to read the label carefully.

Vanilla beans

Vanilla beans have little or no flavour or smell when fresh, and it is only during the drying and curing process that their natural enzymes react to transform them into what we know as vanilla.

Vanilla beans are the dried and cured seed-pods of an orchid native to Central America and Mexico. They are now grown mainly in Mexico, Madagascar and the neighbouring Comoro and Réunion islands, and Tahiti. They are added whole to cooking liquids, or may be slit open and the microscopic black seeds added to the mixture for custard, ice-cream etc; it is considered that the black specks in the dish give it cachet as they show that the real thing has been used. Each bean can be washed, dried and re-used several times, and then be put into a jar of sugar to scent it for using in cakes and desserts. Vanilla is essential to the flavours of cakes, biscuits and pastries, ice-creams, milk drinks and creamy desserts, fruit poaching syrups, confectionery and liqueurs. It also contributes to the fragrance of some perfumes and has been successfully used by a few creative chefs to scent chicken and lobster dishes, as without sugar it is not sweet.

CHOOSING Check the ingredient list on the label when buying vanilla extract or essence. True *vanilla extract* will list vanilla bean extractives, a stated percentage of alcohol, water and sugars, and only these ingredients. The label may also say Mexican or Bourbon vanilla, which indicate both the country of origin (Bourbon means Madagascar, the Comoros and Réunion, which was once called Île de Bourbon) and the grade of vanilla, as Mexican and Bourbon are considered the best. If the label says "2 folds", that means the extract is twice as concentrated as the industry standard. Good *vanilla bean paste* will list vanilla extract, sugar, water, vanilla seeds and perhaps a natural thickener such as gum tragacanth. *Vanilla essence* will list vanilla extract, water and perhaps other ingredients such as glycerin, corn syrup, propylene glycol and dextrose. Imitation vanilla essence will list chemicals and may list vanilla extract too, as a little of the real thing is sometimes added to improve the flavour.

STORING Store vanilla extract, essence or paste in their tightly closed bottles or containers, away from heat, light and humidity. Store vanilla beans, also away from heat, light and humidity, in an airtight pack or in a tightly closed jar of sugar.

✤ **OTHER RECIPES USING VANILLA**
Creamed rice, p503
Crème anglaise, p318
Crème brûlée, p144
Poached plums with almond milk ice-cream, p433
Vanilla bean ice-cream, p144

Mixed berry cake with vanilla bean syrup

PREP + COOK TIME 1 HOUR **SERVES** 8

125g butter, chopped

1 cup (220g) caster sugar

3 eggs

½ cup (75g) plain flour

¼ cup (35g) self-raising flour

½ cup (60g) almond meal

1½ cups (225g) frozen mixed berries

½ cup (100g) drained canned seeded black cherries

⅓ cup (80g) sour cream

VANILLA BEAN SYRUP

½ cup (125ml) water

½ cup (110g) caster sugar

2 vanilla beans

1 Preheat oven to 180°C/160°C fan-forced. Grease 20cm baba pan thoroughly.

2 Beat butter and sugar in small bowl with electric mixer until light and fluffy. Beat in eggs. Transfer mixture to large bowl; stir in sifted flours, almond meal, berries, cherries and sour cream. Pour mixture into pan.

3 Bake cake about 40 minutes. Stand cake in pan 5 minutes; turn onto wire rack, over a large tray.

4 Meanwhile, make vanilla bean syrup; pour hot syrup over hot cake.

VANILLA BEAN SYRUP Place the water and sugar in small saucepan. Split vanilla beans in half lengthways; scrape seeds into pan then add pods. Stir over heat, without boiling, until sugar dissolves. Simmer, uncovered, without stirring, 5 minutes. Using tongs, remove pods from syrup.

NUTRITIONAL COUNT PER SERVING 23.1g total fat (12g saturated fat); 1906kJ (456 cal); 54.8g carbohydrate; 6.4g protein; 2g fibre

MIXED BERRY CAKE WITH VANILLA BEAN SYRUP

A baba pan is a tall, cylindrical one with a fluted top, resembling a turban. If you don't have one, you can use a kugelhopf or bundt pan instead.

For information on various berries, see Berries, pages 58–60.

Vanilla bean thins

PREP + COOK TIME 25 MINUTES **MAKES** 24

1 vanilla bean

30g butter, softened

¼ cup (55g) caster sugar

1 egg white, beaten lightly

¼ cup (35g) plain flour

1 Preheat oven to 200°C/180°C fan-forced. Grease oven trays; line with baking paper.

2 Halve vanilla bean lengthways; scrape seeds into medium bowl with butter and sugar, discard vanilla pod. Stir until combined, stir in egg white and flour. Spoon mixture into piping bag fitted with 5mm plain tube.

3 Pipe 6cm-long strips (making them slightly wider at both ends) 5cm apart on trays. Bake about 5 minutes or until edges are browned lightly; cool biscuits on trays.

NUTRITIONAL COUNT PER BISCUIT 1g total fat (0.7g saturated fat); 100kJ (24 cal); 3.4g carbohydrate; 0.3g protein; 0.1g fibre

When a dessert or ice-cream recipe says "serve with a crisp biscuit", these elegant thins are the perfect ones to use.

Vanilla spice cheesecake

PREP + COOK TIME 1 HOUR 20 MINUTES (PLUS COOLING AND REFRIGERATION TIME) **SERVES** 12

¾ cup (110g) plain flour

¼ teaspoon ground cinnamon

pinch ground nutmeg

⅓ cup (75g) caster sugar

80g butter, melted

½ teaspoon vanilla extract

⅓ cup (45g) roasted hazelnuts, chopped coarsely

¼ cup (80g) apricot jam, warmed, strained

FILLING

1 vanilla bean

250g cream cheese, softened

500g ricotta cheese

2 tablespoons lemon juice

⅔ cup (150g) caster sugar

2 eggs

1 Grease 24cm springform tin.

2 Sift flour, spices and sugar into medium bowl; stir in butter, extract and nuts. Press mixture over base of tin. Place tin on oven tray; refrigerate 30 minutes.

3 Preheat oven to 180°C/160°C fan-forced.

4 Bake base about 20 minutes or until browned lightly. Spread with jam. Reduce oven temperature to 150°C/130°C fan-forced.

5 Make filling by splitting vanilla bean in half lengthways; scrape seeds into medium bowl. Add cheeses, juice and half the sugar; beat, with electric mixer until combined. Beat remaining sugar and eggs in small bowl with electric mixer about 5 minutes or until thick and creamy; fold into cheese mixture.

6 Pour filling into tin; bake about 35 minutes. Cool cheesecake in oven with door ajar. Refrigerate cheesecake 3 hours or overnight.

NUTRITIONAL COUNT PER SERVING 20.4g total fat (11.4g saturated fat); 1438kJ (344 cal); 31.1g carbohydrate; 8.9g protein; 0.8g fibre

To prepare the roasted hazelnuts, first blanch (skin) them by heating on an oven tray in a 180°C/160°C fan-forced oven, stirring once or twice, about 5 minutes or until skins are crisp, then rubbing skins off in a cloth. To roast, increase oven to 200°C/180°C fan-forced and roast nuts on an oven-tray, stirring once or twice, until just changed in colour, about 7 minutes. You can skin and roast them in a heavy-based frying pan on the stovetop, if you prefer: work on low heat, stir the nuts often and watch to ensure that they don't scorch.

For information on nutmeg and cinnamon, see Spices, pages 558 & 559; and for cream cheese and ricotta cheese, see Cheese, pages 100–102.

Veal

Veal comes from calves and may be milk-fed, meaning that the animal never ate grass, or grass-fed, meaning that the animal spent some time on pasture before slaughter. Milk-fed veal is very pale and delicate in flavour and grass-fed is pink and fuller-flavoured.

Perhaps the most famous veal dish is Wiener (Vienna) schnitzel, a steak pounded very thin, coated with egg and breadcrumbs, browned in butter and oil and garnished with a slice of lemon topped with 2 crossed anchovy fillets and a few capers. To make the egg and crumb coating set firmly, arrange the schnitzels in a single layer on an oven tray and refrigerate for 20 minutes before cooking.

Italy is the home of many great veal dishes, including osso buco ("bone with a hole"), which is a braise of slices of veal shin, each with a central marrow-bone. The marrow, which becomes very soft and luscious as it cooks, is the final treat; to ensure that it doesn't drop out when it softens, stand the slices upright, on their sides, to cook. This works best if you cook them in a saucepan into which they will fit with just a little room to spare.

In some countries, calves bred for milk-fed veal are confined in small spaces to keep the meat tender and white, but this is forbidden in Australia, where the calves move freely in an open barn and have access to fresh air and to milk, first from their mothers and then on demand. Veal has little or no fat so it has a tendency to dryness and needs to be cooked at low or moderate heat, either by moist methods (stewing, pot-roasting or casseroling) or, if roasted, by frequent basting and/or protecting it with a fatty covering such as streaky bacon. The exceptions to moderate-heat cooking are the thinly beaten-out steaks called schnitzel, scaloppine or escalope, which are sauteed briefly at high heat, and pan-fried chops, steaks and cutlets, which are browned at high heat and then cooked gently until done. Most people prefer veal to be cooked through but not overdone, as underdone veal is indigestible and tastes unpleasant, while overcooked veal is dry.

VEAL CUTS

ROASTING cuts are loin on the bone or boned and rolled, rib, rump, silverside, topside, round and boned and rolled rib.

To judge when a roast is done to your taste, use a meat thermometer or run a fine skewer into the centre and check the juice that comes out. Red juice means rare, pink medium and clear well done.

All roasts should be rested in a warm place, loosely covered with foil, for 15 minutes before serving to allow the juices to settle and the meat to become more succulent.

GRILLING, CHAR-GRILLING AND PAN-FRYING cuts are chops, cutlets and leg or fillet steaks. Schnitzel (scalloppine) is suitable for pan-frying but does not suit grilling.

To judge when meat is grilled or pan-fried to your taste, press the surface with a finger or the back of the tongs. Rare meat feels soft and spongy, medium-rare soft but springy, and well-done quite firm.

All grilled meat should be rested in a warm place, loosely covered in foil, for 5 minutes to allow the juices to settle and the meat to become more succulent.

POT-ROASTING Cuts for pot-roasting (braising in one piece) are shoulder on the bone or boned and rolled, stuffed and rolled breast (brisket) or any of the roasting cuts.

CASSEROLING OR STEWING Cuts for cutting up for casseroles and stews are boneless shoulder, neck, breast, shin (shank) or any of the pot-roasting cuts.

VEAL SWEETBREADS (thymus glands), veal kidneys and calf's liver are prized for their delicacy.

MINCED VEAL is close-textured and mild-flavoured so it is an excellent base for highly flavoured stuffings. It is often sold mixed with pork mince to incorporate some fat and give richer flavour, and is used for meatballs, meatloaves, pâtés and terrines.

VEAL BONES make the best stock as they are very gelatinous.

CHOOSING
In general, veal should be fine-grained and smooth, with little or no visible fat; if there is any fat, it should be white and satiny. The bones should be bluish-white and look large for the cut, compared to beef. As always, your best bet for good meat is a trustworthy supplier.

STORING
Transfer meat from its shop wrappings to a container with the bottom lined with 2 thicknesses of absorbent paper towels, cover loosely with foil and refrigerate. The more meat has been cut and handled, the less time it will keep. Mince and offal (liver etc) should be used within 24 hours, diced and cubed meat within 48 hours and larger cuts within 3 days.

❦ OTHER RECIPES USING VEAL
Balsamic rosemary grilled veal steaks, p635
Spicy veal pizzaiola, p610
Veal and tomato dolmades, p639
Veal sweetbreads with duxelles, p359

Prosciutto-wrapped veal and pork meatloaf

PREP + COOK TIME 1 HOUR 20 MINUTES **SERVES** 4

4 slices white bread (180g)

½ cup (125ml) milk

550g veal mince

200g pork mince

1 small leek (200g), chopped finely

2 cloves garlic, crushed

2 teaspoons fresh thyme leaves

½ cup finely chopped fresh flat-leaf parsley

½ cup (40g) finely grated parmesan cheese

2 eggs

8 slices prosciutto (120g)

1 tablespoon dijon mustard

This rather grand meatloaf is superb both hot and cold. For a perfect picnic or outdoor lunch, team it with the Roasted mixed tomato salad on page 613.

For information on pork, see Pork, pages 440 & 441; and for prosciutto, see Ham page 256.

1 Preheat oven to 200°C/180°C fan-forced.

2 Remove crusts from bread; tear bread into pieces. Pour milk over bread in large bowl; stand 2 minutes. Add minces, leek, garlic, herbs, cheese and eggs to bowl; mix well. Roughly shape mixture into a mound.

3 Lay 6 slices of prosciutto on board, overlapping slightly; brush with mustard. Place mince mound onto prosciutto slices; using wet hands, pat mixture into loaf shape. Lay remaining 2 slices prosciutto lengthways on top of meatloaf. Wrap bottom prosciutto slices around sides of meatloaf to meet slices on top. Turn meatloaf over carefully; place on wire rack set in large shallow baking dish.

4 Cook meatloaf, uncovered, about 1 hour or until juices run clear. Cover meatloaf; stand 10 minutes before serving.

NUTRITIONAL COUNT PER SERVING 23.4g total fat (9.5g saturated fat); 2249kJ (538 cal); 23.4g carbohydrate; 56.8g protein; 2.9g fibre

Braised veal shoulder with white beans

PREP + COOK TIME 1 HOUR 40 MINUTES **SERVES** 6

Order the veal shoulder a few days ahead and ask your butcher to bone, roll and tie it for you. Any kind of canned white bean can be used for this recipe. Drain them and rinse well under cold water before using them.

For information on canned and dried white beans, see Pulses, page 470.

¼ cup (60ml) olive oil

1.2kg boned veal shoulder, rolled, tied

2 medium brown onions (300g), sliced thickly

3 cloves garlic, crushed

½ cup (125ml) dry red wine

1 cinnamon stick

2 bay leaves

2 sprigs rosemary

2 x 410g cans crushed tomatoes

½ cup (60g) seeded green olives

2 medium carrots (240g), chopped coarsely

½ cup (60g) frozen peas

400g can white beans, rinsed, drained

1 Preheat oven to 200°C/180°C fan-forced.

2 Heat 2 tablespoons of the oil in large flameproof dish; cook veal, turning frequently, until browned.

3 Heat remaining oil in same dish; cook onion and garlic, stirring, until onion softens. Add wine, cinnamon, bay leaves, rosemary, undrained tomatoes and olives; bring to the boil.

4 Return veal to dish; cover. Transfer to oven; cook, 30 minutes. Turn veal and stir tomato mixture. Add carrots; cook, covered, 30 minutes.

5 Remove veal from dish; cover to keep warm. Add peas and beans to dish; cook, covered, 10 minutes. Serve roasted vegetables with sliced veal.

NUTRITIONAL COUNT PER SERVING 14.7g total fat (2.8g saturated fat); 1697kJ (406 cal); 12.7g carbohydrate; 49.2g protein; 5.4g fibre

Veal saltimbocca

PREP + COOK TIME 35 MINUTES **SERVES** 4

It's easy to understand why these luscious veal "sandwiches" are called saltimbocca ("jump in the mouth"). You can assemble them a day ahead and refrigerate, covered, until required. Serve them on a bed of plain noodles to soak up the savoury juices.

8 veal schnitzels (800g)

8 slices prosciutto (120g)

4 bocconcini cheese (240g), sliced thinly

⅔ cup (100g) drained semi-dried tomatoes

16 fresh sage leaves

40g butter

1 cup (250ml) dry white wine

1 tablespoon lemon juice

2 tablespoons coarsely chopped fresh sage

1 Top each piece of veal with prosciutto, cheese, tomatoes and sage leaves. Fold in half to secure filling; secure with toothpicks or small skewers.

2 Melt half the butter in medium frying pan; cook veal, in batches, until cooked as desired. Cover to keep warm.

3 Add wine to same pan; bring to the boil. Boil, uncovered, until wine reduces by half. Stir in remaining butter, juice and sage. Serve saltimbocca drizzled with sauce.

NUTRITIONAL COUNT PER SERVING 24g total fat (13.1g saturated fat); 2312kJ (553 cal); 9g carbohydrate; 63.3g protein; 3.6g fibre

BRAISED VEAL SHOULDER WITH WHITE BEANS

A ragoût usually means a dish of meat and vegetables cooked slowly together, but it can also mean a dish of vegetables only, as in this recipe. You could serve this luxurious mushroom and capsicum combination as a bed for lamb chops or a fine steak.

For information on flat, swiss brown and shiitake mushrooms, see Mushrooms, pages 320 & 321.

Veal shin on mushroom ragoût

PREP + COOK TIME 2 HOURS 30 MINUTES **SERVES** 4

40g butter

4 pieces veal shin (osso buco) (1kg)

2 cloves garlic, crushed

1 tablespoon fresh rosemary leaves

½ cup (125ml) port

1 cup (250ml) beef stock

MUSHROOM RAGOUT

40g butter

2 cloves garlic, crushed

1 large flat mushroom (100g), sliced thickly

200g swiss brown mushrooms, trimmed

200g shiitake mushrooms, sliced thickly

1 medium red capsicum (200g), sliced thickly

1 medium green capsicum (200g), sliced thickly

½ cup (125ml) beef stock

2 tablespoons port

1 Preheat oven to 180°C/160°C fan-forced.

2 Melt butter in medium flameproof casserole dish; cook veal, uncovered, until browned both sides. Add garlic, rosemary, port and stock; cook, covered, in oven 2¼ hours.

3 Meanwhile, make mushroom ragoût.

4 Divide veal and ragoût among serving dishes; serve with soft polenta.

MUSHROOM RAGOUT Heat butter in large frying pan; cook garlic, mushrooms and capsicums, stirring, until vegetables are browned lightly and tender. Stir in stock and port; cook, covered, 30 minutes.

NUTRITIONAL COUNT PER SERVING 17.8g total fat (11.1g saturated fat); 1735kJ (415 cal); 10.4g carbohydrate; 41.1g protein; 4.3g fibre

For information on haloumi cheese, see Cheese, pages 104 & 105.

Haloumi-crumbed veal cutlets

PREP + COOK TIME 25 MINUTES **SERVES** 4

2 eggs

¼ cup (60ml) water

1½ cups (100g) stale breadcrumbs

125g haloumi cheese, grated

¼ cup finely chopped fresh flat-leaf parsley

4 x 150g veal cutlets

vegetable oil, for shallow-frying

1 Whisk eggs and the water in medium bowl. Combine breadcrumbs, cheese and parsley on plate. Dip veal cutlets in egg mixture; press in breadcrumb mixture to coat. Refrigerate 10 minutes.

2 Shallow-fry veal in heated oil in large frying pan until browned and cooked as desired.

3 Serve veal with lemon wedges.

NUTRITIONAL COUNT PER SERVING 20.4g total fat (6.1g saturated fat); 1751kJ (418 cal); 17.7g carbohydrate; 40.3g protein; 1.3g fibre

1 VEAL SHIN ON
MUSHROOM RAGOUT
2 HALOUMI-CRUMBED
VEAL CUTLETS

Fennel-flavoured veal chops with garlic mustard butter

PREP + COOK TIME 25 MINUTES **SERVES** 4

2 teaspoons fennel seeds

1 teaspoon sea salt

½ teaspoon cracked black pepper

2 tablespoons olive oil

4 x 200g veal chops

4 flat mushrooms (320g)

80g butter, softened

1 tablespoon coarsely chopped fresh flat-leaf parsley

1 clove garlic, crushed

1 tablespoon wholegrain mustard

80g baby rocket leaves

Serve these chops with a green leafy salad and/or the roasted truss tomatoes with crisp basil leaves on page 612.

For information on butter, see Oils & Fats, pages 360 & 361.

1 Using mortar and pestle, crush combined seeds, salt and pepper coarsely; stir in oil. Rub mixture all over veal.

2 Cook veal and mushrooms on heated oiled grill plate (or grill or barbecue) until browned both sides and cooked as desired.

3 Meanwhile, combine butter, parsley, garlic and mustard in small bowl.

4 Divide rocket among serving plates; top each with mushroom, veal then butter.

NUTRITIONAL COUNT PER SERVING 29.7g total fat (13.2g saturated fat); 1831kJ (438 cal); 2.1g carbohydrate; 39.9g protein; 2.7g fibre

Vegetables, Asian

Asian vegetables sometimes call for considerable preparation ahead, but once prepared, they are usually cooked quickly to preserve their textures, which are as important as flavours in Asian cooking.

Some vegetables are considered medicinal: bitter melon, besides being stuffed and fried or used in soups, is dried and prescribed as a diuretic, and lotus root, used in salads and stir-fries, is said to cool the blood. Bamboo shoots are used in soups and stir-fries. Palm hearts are sliced and added to curries in India, used in salads, and coated with batter and deep-fried like tempura. Water chestnuts are prized for the way they retain their crisp texture through cooking and even reheating. They are chopped to go in minced-meat dishes and wontons, sliced for stir-fries and boiled whole, sometimes peeled and cooked with rock sugar, as a street snack.

BAMBOO SHOOTS are tender, mild-flavoured shoots that appear at the base of bamboo in spring and winter. Spring shoots are large, winter shoots are smaller,

more tender and more delicate in flavour. They are available canned and, occasionally, fresh in Asian food shops. Canned shoots are very much like fresh ones because they stay crunchy even through cooking or canning. Rinse canned ones before using. To prepare fresh bamboo shoots, strip off the leaves, trim off the hard bases and boil the central cores for at least 5 minutes to remove their toxins and bitterness. The shoots are then ready to be used as the recipe directs.

LOTUS ROOT is the crisp, delicately flavoured root of a waterlily. Crosswise slices are decoratively patterned with holes arranged like a flower. To prepare it, simply peel and slice as the recipe directs, dropping the slices into water with a little lemon juice added to prevent them from browning. Lotus root can be bought canned or frozen and sometimes fresh.

⚜ **OTHER RECIPES**
ASIAN VEGETABLES
Asian crispy noodle salad, p338
Mushroom and duck broth, p324
Pork sang choy bow, p442
Vegetable dumplings in
*   asian broth, p336*

Bamboo shoots

Lotus root

Water chestnuts

WATER CHESTNUTS are the corms (solid bulbs) of an aquatic plant native to South-East Asia. They are about the size of a walnut and have been eaten in China for centuries, especially in the south where they are sometimes grown in paddies between rice plants. They are prepared by peeling off the dark skin to reveal crunchy white flesh. They are sometimes available fresh in Asian food shops and are also available canned and still crunchy but lacking the delicate flavour of the fresh vegetable.

PALM HEARTS are the terminal shoots of several types of palm, usually the central shoot whose removal kills the tree. There are, however, some palms which produce multiple shoots, some of which can be harvested without damaging the tree as a whole. Palm hearts are firm, with a mild flavour reminiscent of artichoke. They are available canned.

BITTER MELON looks like a large, dark or light green cucumber covered in blisters. The more intensely green the melon, the more bitter the taste, and many cooks look for yellow-green melons as they are milder. To prepare one, cut lengthwise in half and scoop out the seeds and membrane, then, to lessen its bitterness, salt it and leave for 30 minutes. Rinse off the salt, place melon in a saucepan, cover with cold water and bring slowly to the boil, then drain and taste and, if the melon is still too bitter for your taste, repeat the process. The melon is then ready to be used as the recipe directs.

CHOOSING

All fresh vegetables should be firm and undamaged. Choose small, light-coloured bitter melon; lotus root should have no dark or soft spots; water chestnuts should be hard, with no soft spots.

STORING

Any leftover canned vegetables can be kept in a container of water in the refrigerator, changing the water daily, for two or three days. Bitter melon and fresh water chestnuts can be stored unpeeled and uncut in the refrigerator crisper for up to 3 days. Fresh bamboo shoots and lotus root should be enclosed in a paper bag, then a plastic one, and refrigerated for up to 3 days.

Aside from its role in Asian cooking, lotus root makes delectable and lovely-looking baked chips: peel root, slice 2–3mm thick, drop into boiling water for 4 minutes, drain and dry thoroughly between two tea towels. Preheat the oven to 250°C/230°C fan-forced. Mix 2 tablespoons vegetable oil with garlic salt, seasoned salt or chilli powder and plain salt to taste in a shallow dish, add the lotus root and turn the slices in the oil to coat them, then arrange them in one layer on a baking tray and bake for about 20 minutes or until brown and crisp, turning the slices over halfway through cooking.

Palm hearts

Bitter melon

For information on salmon, see Seafood, page 523; and for glutinous rice, see Rice, page 496.

Thai salmon broth with sesame sticky rice patties

PREP + COOK TIME 50 MINUTES (PLUS STANDING TIME) **SERVES** 4

2 cups (500ml) water

3 cups (750ml) fish stock

3 x 10cm sticks fresh lemon grass (60g), bruised

3 fresh kaffir lime leaves, torn

1 fresh long red chilli, sliced thinly

2cm piece fresh ginger (10g), grated

440g skinless salmon fillets

1 tablespoon fish sauce

2 tablespoons lime juice

150g snow peas, halved crossways

230g can sliced bamboo shoots, rinsed, drained

3 green onions, sliced thinly

SESAME STICKY RICE PATTIES

1 cup (200g) glutinous rice

1 tablespoon toasted black sesame seeds

1½ tablespoons rice wine vinegar

1 Cover rice for sesame sticky rice patties with water; stand overnight.

2 Make sesame sticky rice patties.

3 Meanwhile, place the water and stock in large saucepan with lemon grass, lime leaf, chilli and ginger; bring to the boil. Reduce heat; simmer, uncovered, 10 minutes.

4 Add fish to pan; simmer, uncovered, about 10 minutes or until cooked as desired. Transfer fish to medium bowl; using fork, flake into small pieces. Stir sauce, juice, snow peas and bamboo shoots into soup; simmer, uncovered, about 2 minutes or until snow peas are just tender. Discard lemon grass.

5 Divide fish and rice patties among serving bowls; ladle soup into bowls, sprinkle with onion.

SESAME STICKY RICE PATTIES Drain rice; rinse well under cold water, drain. Place rice in steamer lined with muslin or cloth. Place steamer over saucepan of boiling water, cover tightly; steam about 20 minutes or until rice is tender. Combine rice in medium bowl with seeds and vinegar; roll level tablespoons of rice mixture into balls. Gently flatten balls, place on tray; cover with damp tea towel until required.

NUTRITIONAL COUNT PER SERVING 10.3g total fat (2.2g saturated fat); 402kJ (176 cal); 44.7g carbohydrate; 30.4g protein; 2.9g fibre

For information on pork, see Pork, pages 440 & 441; and for baby buk choy, see Greens, Asian, page 242.

Stir-fried pork, water chestnuts and buk choy

PREP + COOK TIME 30 MINUTES (PLUS REFRIGERATION TIME) **SERVES** 4

¼ cup (60ml) light soy sauce

2 tablespoons oyster sauce

1 tablespoon honey

1 tablespoon chinese cooking wine

1 teaspoon five-spice powder

½ teaspoon sesame oil

1 clove garlic, crushed

600g pork fillets, sliced thinly

2 tablespoons peanut oil

600g baby buk choy, chopped coarsely

227g can water chestnuts, rinsed, drained, sliced thickly

½ cup (75g) roasted unsalted cashews

2 long green chillies, sliced thinly

1 tablespoon water

1 Combine 2 tablespoons of the soy sauce, 1 tablespoon of the oyster sauce, honey, wine, five-spice, sesame oil, garlic and pork in large bowl. Cover; refrigerate 3 hours or overnight.

2 Stir-fry pork in oiled wok, in batches, until browned. Heat peanut oil in same wok; stir-fry buk choy, water chestnuts, nuts and chilli until tender.

3 Return pork to wok with remaining soy and oyster sauces and the water; stir-fry until hot.

NUTRITIONAL COUNT PER SERVING 23g total fat (4.5g saturated fat); 1827kJ (437 cal); 15.8g carbohydrate; 39.1g protein; 4.1g fibre

---

For information on swordfish and scallops, see Seafood, pages 522, 523 & 527.

Swordfish and scallops with water chestnuts

PREP + COOK TIME 30 MINUTES **SERVES** 4

2 tablespoons peanut oil

350g swordfish steak, cut into strips

300g scallops, without roe

2 cloves garlic, crushed

4cm piece fresh ginger (20g), grated

2 medium carrots (240g), cut into matchsticks

2 shallots (50g), sliced thinly

227g can water chestnuts, rinsed, halved

1 small red capsicum (150g), sliced thinly

2 tablespoons water

1 tablespoon oyster sauce

1 tablespoon light soy sauce

1 tablespoon sweet chilli sauce

2 teaspoons golden syrup

150g snow peas, trimmed, sliced diagonally

1 Heat half the oil in wok; stir-fry swordfish until browned. Remove from wok. Add scallops, garlic and ginger to wok; stir-fry until scallops change in colour. Remove from wok.

2 Heat remaining oil in wok; stir-fry carrot and shallot until browned. Add chestnuts, capsicum, the water, sauces and syrup; stir-fry until mixture thickens slightly.

3 Return seafood to wok with snow peas; stir-fry until just tender.

NUTRITIONAL COUNT PER SERVING 12.3g total fat (2.5g saturated fat); 1258kJ (301 cal); 15.6g carbohydrate; 29.7g protein; 4.6g fibre

Verjuice

Verjuice is the juice of grapes picked green, usually when a vineyard is thinned ahead of the harvest.

It has a refreshing, complex sweet/sour taste and is used as an alternative to lemon juice, vinegar or wine for marinades, dressings and sauces, deglazing roasting and frying pans, poaching fruit or fish, braising rabbit or game, reconstituting dried fruits or sundried tomatoes and more. It is also pleasant to drink, mixed half and half with tonic, soda or lemonade. Verjuice is available from delicatessens, speciality food shops and some supermarkets, and is also sold at some vineyard cellar doors. Refrigerate after opening and, if stabilised as virtually all commercial verjuice is, it will remain in good condition for a year or more.

When dressing a salad that will be served with wine, use verjuice rather than lemon juice or vinegar as its mellow flavour is more compatible with wine.

Seared scallops with pea puree and tomato

PREP + COOK TIME 30 MINUTES **MAKES** 24

2 medium tomatoes (300g), peeled, seeded, chopped finely

1 tablespoon olive oil

1 tablespoon verjuice

2 tablespoons fresh chervil leaves

2 teaspoons finely grated lemon rind

24 scallops on the half shell

PEA PUREE

1½ cups (180g) frozen peas

¼ cup (60ml) cream

2 tablespoons hot water, approximately

1 Make pea puree.

2 Combine tomato, oil, verjuice, chervil and rind in medium bowl.

3 Remove scallops from shells; wash and dry shells. Divide pea puree between shells.

4 Heat large oiled frying pan; cook scallops about 30 seconds each side or until browned lightly but still soft in the centre.

5 Place scallops on pea puree; top scallops with tomato mixture. Serve immediately.

PEA PUREE Boil, steam or microwave peas until tender; drain. Blend peas with cream and enough of the water to give a thick pouring consistency.

NUTRITIONAL COUNT PER SCALLOP 2.1g total fat (0.9g saturated fat); 159kJ (38 cal); 0.9g carbohydrate; 3.5g protein; 0.6g fibre

Vinegar

The word vinegar comes from the French for sour wine or vin aigre, though vinegar can be made from other bases than wine, such as apple cider for cider vinegar, sake or rice wine for Japanese and Chinese rice vinegar, a type of beer made from malted (sprouted) barley for malt vinegar and distilled grain alcohol for distilled white vinegar. All have been made by fermentation of the base liquid by a bacterial culture, transforming it into acetic acid or vinegar.

For tarragon or other herb vinegar, pack ½ cup of trimmed and washed herb sprigs into a 500ml jar and fill with red or white wine vinegar. Cover tightly and leave at room temperature for 3 weeks, shaking jar daily. Strain vinegar into a sterilised bottle, add a few herb sprigs, put top on and store at room temperature.

In the past, a partly filled barrel of wine or other liquid would be left out in the sun and, after some months, it would usually have turned into vinegar because naturally occurring airborne bacteria had settled on it and clumped together to form a fermentation culture. Later batches could be made by collecting the culture, which looked like a grey skin, and introducing it into more barrels, and so on. The culture was called a vinegar plant or vinegar mother and those that produced especially fine vinegar became heirlooms passed down through families.

The best vinegar is still made by the old Orléans process, named for the French city that was once the capital of vinegar-making. The process begins with good-quality wine which is mixed with vinegar in wooden barrels, inoculated with vinegar mother and left in well ventilated oak casks for months or years to allow the wine to ferment slowly and then the vinegar to age, gradually mellowing and acquiring further aroma and flavour, just as wine does, from the wood. Today, many vinegars are made quickly by spraying the base liquid over wood or other porous materials that have been impregnated with the required bacteria, while everything is kept warm and well oxygenated to speed up the process. These vinegars are matured for a few weeks in stainless-steel vats and are then ready for sale. As the heat involved in their production drives off the more volatile flavours and aromas and ageing has been minimal, the end product lacks the complexity and subtlety of vinegars made in the old, slow way. There is a place for cheap vinegars such as malt and distilled white (below), but their simple sharpness doesn't marry with food in the way that the complex flavour of traditionally made vinegar does. The cost implications of slow versus fast help to explain the sometimes startling price differences among vinegars. Another major cost component is the quality of the base liquid: fine vinegars are made from fine wines or ciders, while lesser vinegars start with poorer ones.

WINE VINEGAR Any red, rosé or white wine, including champagne, can be used for making vinegar. Red wine vinegar usually has a full and mellow flavour, reflecting the wine type from which it was made, and white wine vinegar is more delicate but sometimes more acid, reflecting its wine type. Champagne vinegar is the result of a process that starts when the second, in-bottle fermentation of champagne (the one that produces the bubbles) is complete. The spent yeast is collected in the bottle neck, then the neck is frozen and uncapped, and the yeast is expelled in a plug of frozen wine. This wine, filtered, is used as the base for delicate champagne vinegar. If wine vinegar is stored for six months or more it may be called aged wine vinegar. Some vinegars are named for the wine variety from which they were made, for example chardonnay or cabernet sauvignon vinegars. The implication is that the base wine was a quality one so the vinegar possesses the same fine characters.

SHERRY VINEGAR is made in oak sherry casks from oloroso (medium-sweet) sherries. The best is made in Jerez, on Spain's Atlantic coast, where it is matured by the same solera system as the sherries, a complex system in which younger vinegar is gradually blended with more and more aged ones. By the time they are ready for sale, the vinegars have been maturing for an average of six years and have extraordinary depth and complexity. Other good sherry vinegars are blended and aged, though not necessarily by the solera system.

BALSAMIC VINEGAR is made from the concentrated must (unfermented juice) of Trebbiano grapes. It is classified as tradizionale (traditional) or commercial. Traditional balsamic is aged by being moved gradually through a sort of solera system — a series of casks of different woods and decreasing size. When ready for sale, it has been aged for at least 12 years and the price of a small bottle is breathtaking. Tradizionale aceto balsamico di Modena is always identified thus on the label. Commercial balsamic is made from the same base as traditional and is aged with no transfer from one barrel to another and for shorter periods, though still at least a year; the addition of caramel and other ingredients is permitted. If it was made in Modena, the label will say

balsamic vinegar of Modena, aceto balsamico di Modena, or possibly both, and may also say barrel-matured. This vinegar is a superb, complex, sharp/sweet condiment or ingredient in its own right. It is expensive but not frighteningly so, and worth it. Cheaper vinegars labelled balsamic in other countries than Italy are often locally made from imported must; they may still be good, but in general, the price reflects the quality.

WHITE BALSAMIC VINEGAR, also called white balsamic condiment, is not a true balsamic but a combination of white wine vinegar and grape juice. It is sometimes used in place of true balsamic vinegar so as not to discolour the dish as dark balsamic would.

CIDER VINEGAR The best is aged in wood and has a delicate, underlying apple note. It is sharper than wine vinegar but not as sharp as malt vinegar. It is used for pickling fruit and is especially good in a dressing for a salad including apples or pears. Cider vinegar is widely believed to have health-giving properties and many people take some every day, usually with honey.

RICE VINEGAR Chinese and Japanese rice vinegars come in black, the strongest, red, which is sweeter and milder, and white which is the mildest. They are less acid than western vinegars, and Thai vinegar is milder still. All have a subtle tangy/sweet taste.

MALT VINEGAR is quickly made and inexpensive. It is usually darkened and deepened in flavour by the addition of caramel. Its strong, rather harsh flavour limits its uses in cookery, but countless fish-and-chip fanciers consider a sprinkle of the pungent liquid an essential seasoning. It is used in pickling and making old-fashioned toffee and is one of the ingredients that give worcestershire sauce its distinctive flavour. It is also useful for

1 AGED RICE VINEGAR
2 SHERRY VINEGAR
3 BALSAMIC VINEGAR
4 WHITE BALSAMIC VINEGAR
5 MALT VINEGAR
6 WHITE VINEGAR

kitchen tasks such as deodorising and removing stains from saucepans, cleaning copper and, together with salt, scrubbing and deodorising cutting boards.

DISTILLED WHITE VINEGAR, like malt vinegar, is quickly made, inexpensive and useful for such tasks as making windows sparkle and hair squeaky clean when added to the rinsing water. It is valued for pickling because it preserves the colours of fruit and vegetables, and is added to the cooking water for cauliflower to keep it white and to egg whites for a more tender meringue.

FLAVOURED VINEGARS such as raspberry or herb vinegar are made by steeping the flavouring ingredient or ingredients in white or red wine vinegar for 24 hours or more, then filtering. They can be made at home:

squash berries slightly and bruise herbs before adding them so that their flavours will be released into the vinegar.

CHOOSING Reading the label may reveal how a vinegar was made by such words as "barrel-aged", but not all makers give such information. One can be reasonably sure that French-made wine vinegar and Jerez-made sherry vinegar are quality products, and price is usually a good indicator, but vinegar in fancy bottles is often overpriced compared to the same thing in an ordinary bottle.

STORING Store vinegar, tightly capped, away from heat and light and it should keep more or less indefinitely.

The balsamic and garlic flavours go well with steamed asparagus or broccolini and with roasted or steamed potatoes or potato salad.

Balsamic and garlic vinaigrette

PREP TIME 5 MINUTES **MAKES** 1¼ CUPS

2 tablespoons balsamic vinegar
¼ cup (60ml) lemon juice
1 clove garlic, crushed
¾ cup (180ml) olive oil

1 Whisk ingredients in small bowl until combined.

NUTRITIONAL COUNT PER TABLESPOON 10.9g total fat (1.5g saturated fat); 406kJ (97 cal); 0.1g carbohydrate; 0g protein; 0g fibre

You'll use this basic dressing again and again for salads and cooked vegetables.

French dressing

PREP TIME 5 MINUTES **MAKES** 1 CUP

⅓ cup (80ml) white wine vinegar
2 teaspoons dijon mustard
1 teaspoon caster sugar
⅔ cup (160ml) olive oil

1 Whisk vinegar, mustard and sugar in small jug until smooth.
2 Gradually whisk in oil, in a thin steady stream, until thickened.

NUTRITIONAL COUNT PER TABLESPOON 12.1g total fat (1.7g saturated fat); 456kJ (109 cal); 0.4g carbohydrate; 0g protein; 0g fibre

Balsamic rosemary grilled veal steaks

PREP + COOK TIME 25 MINUTES **SERVES** 4

2 tablespoons olive oil

2 tablespoons balsamic vinegar

1 tablespoon fresh rosemary leaves

2 cloves garlic, crushed

4 x 125g veal steaks

4 medium egg tomatoes (300g), halved

4 flat mushrooms (320g)

1 Combine oil, vinegar, rosemary, garlic and veal in medium bowl.

2 Cook veal on heated oiled grill plate (or grill or barbecue), brushing occasionally with vinegar mixture, until cooked as desired. Remove from heat; cover to keep warm.

3 Cook tomato and mushrooms on heated oiled grill plate until tender. Serve veal with grilled vegetables.

NUTRITIONAL COUNT PER SERVING 11.3g total fat (1.8g saturated fat); 1016kJ (243 cal); 2.1g carbohydrate; 31.6g protein; 3.3g fibre

Balsamic vinegar gives the basting mixture rich but smooth acidity with an underlying sweet edge. You could also use this mixture as a marinade for pork chops.

For information on veal, see Veal, pages 620 & 621.

Apple cider and poppy seed vinaigrette

PREP TIME 10 MINUTES **MAKES** 1 CUP

2 teaspoons finely grated orange rind

¼ cup (60ml) orange juice

2 tablespoons apple cider vinegar

1 tablespoon poppy seeds

⅓ cup (80g) sour cream

2 teaspoons honey mustard

¼ cup (60ml) water

1 Whisk rind, juice, vinegar, seeds, sour cream and mustard in small bowl. Add water; whisk until combined.

NUTRITIONAL COUNT PER TABLESPOON 3.1g total fat (1.8g saturated fat); 138kJ (33 cal); 0.7g carbohydrate; 0.4g protein; 0.2g fibre

This vinaigrette goes well with seafood, coleslaw, steamed asparagus or a green leafy salad.

For information on poppy seeds, see Seeds, page 544.

Apple cider vinegar

Balsamic strawberries with mascarpone

PREP TIME 10 MINUTES (PLUS REFRIGERATION TIME) **SERVES** 4

Standing the strawberries with the vinegar and sugar brings out their flavour.

For information on strawberries, see Berries, page 58; and for mascarpone, see Cheese, page 100.

500g strawberries, halved
¼ cup (55g) caster sugar
2 tablespoons balsamic vinegar
1 cup (250g) mascarpone cheese
1 tablespoon icing sugar
1 teaspoon vanilla extract
¼ cup coarsely chopped fresh mint leaves

1 Combine strawberries, sugar and vinegar in medium bowl, cover; refrigerate 20 minutes.

2 Meanwhile, combine mascarpone, icing sugar and extract in small bowl.

3 Stir mint into strawberry mixture; divide among serving dishes. Serve with mascarpone.

NUTRITIONAL COUNT PER SERVING 29.8g total fat (20.3g saturated fat); 1572kJ (376 cal); 21.2g carbohydrate; 5.2g protein; 3g fibre

Red wine vinegar and raspberry dressing

PREP TIME 5 MINUTES **MAKES** 1 CUP

For an extra-fruity flavour, use raspberry vinegar in place of red wine vinegar. If the dressing is too thick, thin with a little cold water. If fresh raspberries are not available, use thawed frozen ones. These flavours go well with goats cheese, radicchio and crumbed, fried camembert.

For information on raspberries, see Berries, page 58.

¼ cup (60ml) red wine vinegar
½ cup (125ml) olive oil
150g fresh raspberries
¼ cup (80g) whole-berry cranberry sauce

1 Blend or process ingredients until smooth.

2 Push dressing through fine sieve into small bowl.

NUTRITIONAL COUNT PER TABLESPOON 9.5g total fat (1.3g saturated fat); 418kJ (100 cal); 3.4g carbohydrate; 0.2g protein; 0.7g fibre

Vine Leaves

Fresh or preserved grapevine leaves can be used as wrappers for small foods to be braised or baked. The best-known stuffings are a savoury rice or meat mixture for dolmades, but the idea works well with a piece of cheese with herbs or other flavourings and for small birds such as quail or for small fish.

Leaves of either type can also be used to line individual dishes in which savoury mixtures will be cooked and then turned out for serving, and a fresh leaf makes a good "plate" for a runny cheese on the cheeseboard. Preserved leaves, available at delicatessens, are packed in brine which should be rinsed off and the leaves dried before using. Fresh leaves should be from an unsprayed vine that bears edible grapes, and they should be large, medium light green and not too young. They need to be softened by dropping them into boiling water for a minute or so to make them pliable, then dried, before they are used. Vine leaves give a slightly lemony taste to food cooked in them.

For information on ocean trout, see Seafood, page 523.

Vine leaf-wrapped ocean trout

PREP + COOK TIME 1 HOUR 10 MINUTES **SERVES** 4

2 medium fennel bulbs (600g), untrimmed

1 large brown onion (200g), sliced thinly

2 cloves garlic, sliced thinly

1 tablespoon olive oil

¼ cup (60ml) orange juice

½ cup (125ml) chicken stock

¼ cup (60ml) dry white wine

8 large fresh grapevine leaves

4 x 200g ocean trout fillets

1 tablespoon finely grated orange rind

180g seedless white grapes

1 Preheat oven to 180°C/160°C fan-forced.

2 Reserve enough of the fennel leaves to make ¼ cup before trimming fennel bulbs. Slice fennel thinly then combine in large shallow baking dish with onion, garlic, oil, juice, stock and wine. Cook, covered, in oven 30 minutes. Uncover, stir; cook a further 20 minutes or until vegetables soften, stirring occasionally.

3 Meanwhile, dip vine leaves in medium saucepan of boiling water for 10 seconds; transfer immediately to medium bowl of iced water. Drain on absorbent paper. Slightly overlap two vine leaves, vein-sides up, on board; centre one fish fillet on leaves, top with a quarter of the rind and a quarter of the reserved fennel leaves. Fold vine leaves over to enclose fish. Repeat with remaining leaves, fish, rind and fennel leaves. Place vine-leaf parcels on oiled oven tray; bake about 15 minutes or until fish is cooked as desired.

4 Stir grapes into hot fennel mixture; stand, covered, 2 minutes before serving with fish.

NUTRITIONAL COUNT PER SERVING 12.5g total fat (2.5g saturated fat); 1433kJ (342 cal); 13.6g carbohydrate; 41g protein; 4.3g fibre

Veal and tomato dolmades

PREP + COOK TIME 1 HOUR 10 MINUTES (PLUS COOLING TIME) **MAKES** 36

200g packet grapevine leaves in brine

1 tablespoon olive oil

1 large red onion (300g), chopped finely

4 cloves garlic, crushed

500g veal mince

400g can crushed tomatoes

¼ cup (30g) seeded green olives, chopped finely

¼ cup (35g) drained sun-dried tomatoes, chopped finely

1 tablespoon tomato paste

VEAL AND TOMATO
DOLMADES

1 Place leaves in large heatproof bowl, cover with boiling water; stand 10 minutes, drain. Rinse under cold water; drain. Pat 36 similar-size, well-shaped leaves dry with absorbent paper; reserve remaining leaves for another use.

2 Heat oil in large frying pan; cook onion and garlic, stirring, until onion softens. Add mince; cook, stirring, until just changed in colour.

3 Add remaining ingredients; bring to the boil. Reduce heat; simmer, uncovered, about 5 minutes or until liquid is almost evaporated; cool 15 minutes.

4 Place leaves, vein-side up, on board. Spoon 1 tablespoon of the filling near stem in centre of 1 leaf; roll once toward tip of leaf to cover filling then fold in two sides. Continue rolling toward tip of leaf; place, seam-side down, in baking-paper-lined steamer. Repeat process with remaining leaves and filling mixture, placing rolls about 1cm apart in steamer.

5 Place steamer over large saucepan of boiling water. Steam, covered, about 15 minutes or until dolmades are heated through.

6 Serve hot or cold, drizzled with lemon juice, if you like.

Fresh vine leaves can be used instead of purchased ones if you like.

For information on veal, see Veal, pages 620 & 621.

NUTRITIONAL COUNT PER DOLMADES 1.6g total fat (0.6g saturated fat); 150kJ (36 cal); 1.4g carbohydrate; 3.6g protein; 0.7g fibre

Fresh vine leaves   **Preserved vine leaves**

Fresh vine leaves can be used instead of purchased ones. Hand these round at a party or serve them as part of a selection of appetisers.

For information on burghul, see Grains, page 228.

Burghul-stuffed vine leaves with yogurt dip

PREP + COOK TIME 40 MINUTES (PLUS STANDING TIME) **SERVES** 6

1 cup (160g) burghul

1 cup (250ml) boiling water

1 tablespoon olive oil

1 green onion, chopped finely

¼ cup (35g) roasted slivered almonds

2 tablespoons finely chopped raisins

2 tablespoons finely chopped fresh mint

1 tablespoon finely chopped fresh coriander

1 tablespoon finely chopped fresh flat-leaf parsley

2 teaspoons ground cinnamon

2 teaspoons finely grated lemon rind

1 tablespoon lemon juice

40 grapevine leaves in brine (200g), rinsed, drained

YOGURT DIP

¾ cup (200g) low-fat yogurt

1 tablespoon finely chopped fresh mint

1 tablespoon finely chopped fresh coriander

1 teaspoon lemon juice

5cm piece fresh ginger (25g), grated

1 Combine burghul and the boiling water in medium heatproof bowl. Cover; stand 5 minutes. Stir in oil, onion, nuts, raisins, herbs, cinnamon, rind and juice.

2 Line base of large bamboo steamer with about 10 vine leaves.

3 Place one of the remaining leaves, vein-side up, on board; place 1 tablespoon of the burghul mixture in centre of leaf. Fold in two opposing sides; roll to enclose filling. Repeat with remaining leaves and burghul mixture.

4 Place rolls, in single layer, on leaves in steamer. Steam, covered, over wok of simmering water about 15 minutes or until rolls are heated through.

5 Meanwhile, combine ingredients for yogurt dip in small bowl.

6 Serve rolls with yogurt dip.

NUTRITIONAL COUNT PER SERVING 7g total fat (0.8g saturated fat); 757kJ (181 cal); 21.7g carbohydrate; 7.5g protein; 7g fibre

Wasabi

Wasabi is often called japanese horseradish though it comes from a different plant family altogether. It is the knobbly, greenish root of a plant native to Japan and eastern Siberia, which grows wild and is also cultivated.

Wasabi paste

The fresh, peeled root is grated and served as the essential seasoning with sushi and sashimi, delivering a taste and pungency like that of horseradish but much hotter and more nose-stinging; it is often mixed with light soy sauce to soften the impact, but connoisseurs use it straight. Fresh wasabi is seldom available outside Japan, but it is sold, dried and ground, in cans and also as a paste in tubes. In these forms, it is often adulterated with or even entirely composed of dried and green-dyed horseradish. True wasabi is expensive so price may be an indication of the real thing, and asking for hon (real) wasabi may also help.

Serve with cold chicken or cold fish, or fold through good-quality canned salmon, drained and with skin and bones removed, for a lunch dish.

For information on jasmine rice, see Rice, page 494; and for avocado, see Avocado, pages 24–26.

Avocado and wasabi rice salad

PREP + COOK TIME 25 MINUTES **SERVES** 8

2 cups (400g) jasmine rice

2 medium avocados (500g), halved, chopped coarsely

2 tablespoons lime juice

1 cup (50g) snow pea tendrils, chopped coarsely

1 sheet nori, shredded finely

WASABI DRESSING

¾ cup (225g) mayonnaise

2 tablespoons lime juice

2 tablespoons rice wine vinegar

3 teaspoons wasabi

1 Cook rice in large saucepan of boiling water, uncovered, until tender; drain. Rinse under cold water; drain.

2 Meanwhile, combine ingredients for wasabi dressing in small bowl.

3 Place avocado and juice in large bowl with rice, tendrils, nori and dressing; toss gently to combine.

NUTRITIONAL COUNT PER SERVING 19.5g total fat (3.3g saturated fat); 1622kJ (388 cal); 47.2g carbohydrate; 5.1g protein; 1.7g fibre

1 AVOCADO AND WASABI
RICE SALAD
2 WASABI AND LIME
MAYONNAISE

Wasabi and lime mayonnaise

PREP TIME 10 MINUTES **SERVES** 4

½ cup (150g) mayonnaise

2 teaspoons wasabi paste

1 teaspoon finely chopped fresh coriander

1 teaspoon lime juice

1 Combine mayonnaise, wasabi, coriander and juice in small bowl.

2 Serve mayonnaise with grilled salmon or chicken.

NUTRITIONAL COUNT PER SERVING 12.1g total fat (1.4g saturated fat); 581kJ (139 cal); 7.5g carbohydrate; 0.4g protein; 0.2g fibre

This piquant mayonnaise can be served with any fish, hot or cold. A cooling cucumber salad would be a good accompaniment.

For information on limes, see Limes, page 300.

Yeast

Yeasts are a large family of microscopic plants that are, invisibly, all around us in the air, on the skins of fruits and vegetables, on leaves and bark and in the soil. When they are provided with warmth, moisture and food, they multiply.

Fresh yeast

Once a yeast dough has risen, it is turned on to a floured work surface, deflated by punching it a couple of times, kneaded lightly, then shaped as required and placed on a baking tray or in a bread tin and left to partially rise again. This allows for the "oven spring" or expansion that takes place when the dough is put in the oven, as the yeast becomes more active and the gas in the myriad pockets expands before the yeast is killed by the heat.

Some yeasts cause infections and spoilage in foods, but many are useful. The one that interests cooks is one of the saccharomyces ("sugar yeasts"), the family that makes not only bread-making but brewing and wine-making possible. Its effect has been known for thousands of years: cooks knew that something made bread dough rise and that they could make it happen in a new batch by adding a piece of dough from the last batch (see Bread/Sourdough, page 66), but it was not understood how this happens until Louis Pasteur (1822–95) showed that the agent was a growing mass of single-celled fungi which fed on starch and sugar and gave off alcohol and a gas, carbon dioxide, in the process. The gas, dispersed in many pockets, inflated the dough. Today, selected strains of saccharomyces, which produce relatively little alcohol but a lot of carbon dioxide, are produced for baking, and bakers' yeast is available fresh, dried or in the form of yeast compounds made from yeast and other ingredients.

COMPRESSED (FRESH) YEAST is partially dried and compressed into softish, easily crumbled, putty-coloured cakes. It is highly perishable, see STORING, opposite. This form of yeast is becoming hard to find as dried yeast has largely displaced it at retail level, but some cooks feel that it mixes better. It is reactivated and liquefied before using, either by mixing it with some of the liquid in the recipe, or by mixing it with a little of the sugar in the recipe, on which it will feed and become liquid. Fresh yeast must be used at lukewarm temperature, 37–38°C, which can be tested with the inner wrist in the same way as for a baby's bath. It will not become active at lower temperatures, and higher temperatures may kill it. Compressed yeast may be available in the refrigerated cabinets of health food shops and delicatessens.

DRY YEAST is in tiny granules and is sold in packages of a dozen or so small, sealed sachets usually containing 7g (1½ teaspoons). It can be added directly to the flour in most recipes without prior mixing with sugar or liquid, but if preferred it can be mixed with the liquid to be used in the recipe and stirred until dissolved before adding to the dry ingredients. Dry yeast needs a warmer temperature than compressed to reactivate it — the liquid needs to be comfortably hand-warm, 41–43°C, rather than lukewarm. The yeast will not become active at lower temperatures, and higher temperatures may kill it. Dry yeast keeps much longer than fresh, see Storage, below, and can be substituted for it in recipes: proportions are on the packet, or as a guide, use half the weight of dry yeast to fresh, ie one sachet per 15g of fresh yeast. Dry yeast is available at virtually all supermarkets, delicatessens and health food shops.

YEAST COMPOUNDS are designed for people who make bread regularly, being packed, usually, in 500g cans. They are formulated to promote yeast activity and good flavour with such ingredients as sugar, malt flour and enzymes as well as yeast. The best known are Fermipan and Dribarm, both of which perform well so long as the can is well shaken to distribute the yeast granules evenly before measuring. The cans carry instructions for usage; both are used at about half the quantity you would use for ordinary dry yeast.

USING YEAST

Because yeast produces carbon dioxide relatively slowly, the dough for a yeast-raised bread or pastry must be strong and elastic enough to be stretched for a considerable time without breaking and letting the gas escape. Yeast-raised products are meant to be somewhat chewy, quite differently from baking-powder raised cakes, scones and quickbreads which are considered failures if they are chewy. If you added yeast to a typical cake mixture, most of the gas would simply bubble to the surface and escape (baking powder produces only a little gas during mixing and does most of its work in the oven when the outside of the mixture is set enough to retain the gas produced).

When working with yeast, the fermentation process must be given its own unforced time, not only to inflate the dough but to develop its flavour and texture, while at the same time the gluten (see Flour, page 182) goes through a ripening process that also contributes to the final effect. Although a yeast dough needs to be in a warm place for rising, this means only up to about 27°C; the rise will be faster if it is warmer than that, but the final product will be drier and less flavoursome. On the other hand, no harm

is done by leaving the dough in a colder place for a slow rise to suit your convenience: many cooks say that slow rising actually improves quality. Dough can even be left in the refrigerator overnight without harm, provided that it is guarded against drying by enclosing it in a plastic bag greased on the inside and large enough to allow for rising; this works best if the dough has started to rise, showing that the yeast has been activated, and if it is allowed to return to room temperature before proceeding with the recipe.

STORING Compressed yeast must

be stored airtight and cold. It should be refrigerated in its wrapping or, if this is inadequate, tightly wrapped in plastic film and then enclosed in a plastic bag, and used within a few days. If it must be kept for longer, it should be frozen and used within a few weeks, being allowed to return to room temperature first. Dry yeast and yeast compounds can be kept, away from heat, light and humidity, for much longer; check use-by dates on the packages.

Also see Bread, pages 64–68 and Flour, pages 182–185.

Dried yeast

Hot cross buns

PREP + COOK TIME 1 HOUR 25 MINUTES (PLUS STANDING TIME) **MAKES** 16

2 x 7g sachets granulated yeast

¼ cup (55g) caster sugar

1½ cups (375ml) warm milk

4 cups (600g) plain flour

1 teaspoon mixed spice

½ teaspoon ground cinnamon

60g butter

1 egg

¾ cup (120g) sultanas

FLOUR PASTE FOR CROSSES

½ cup (75g) plain flour

2 teaspoons caster sugar

⅓ cup (80ml) water, approximately

GLAZE

1 tablespoon caster sugar

1 teaspoon gelatine

1 tablespoon water

1 Combine yeast, sugar and milk in small bowl or jug; cover, stand in warm place about 10 minutes or until mixture is frothy.

2 Sift flour and spices into large bowl, rub in butter. Stir in yeast mixture, egg and sultanas; mix to a soft sticky dough. Cover; stand in warm place about 45 minutes or until dough has doubled in size.

3 Grease 23cm-square slab cake pan.

4 Turn dough onto floured surface, knead about 5 minutes or until smooth. Divide dough into 16 pieces, knead into balls. Place balls into prepared pan; cover, stand in warm place about 10 minutes or until buns have risen to top of pan.

5 Meanwhile, preheat oven to 220°C/200°C fan-forced.

6 Place flour paste for crosses in piping bag fitted with small plain tube, pipe crosses on buns.

7 Bake buns about 20 minutes or until well browned. Turn buns onto wire rack, brush tops with hot glaze; cool on wire rack.

FLOUR PASTE FOR CROSSES Combine flour and sugar in bowl. Gradually blend in enough of the water to form a smooth paste.

GLAZE Stir ingredients in small saucepan over heat, without boiling, until sugar and gelatine are dissolved.

NUTRITIONAL COUNT PER BUN 4.9g total fat (2.8g saturated fat); 1016kJ (243 cal); 41.6g carbohydrate; 6.5g protein; 2.2g fibre

Brioche

PREP + COOK TIME 55 MINUTES (PLUS STANDING TIME) **MAKES** 12

2½ cups (375g) plain flour

1½ teaspoons (5g) dried yeast

¼ teaspoon salt

¼ cup (55g) caster sugar

¾ cup (180ml) warm milk

5 egg yolks

125g butter

1 egg yolk, extra

2 teaspoons sugar

1 Combine flour, yeast and salt in large bowl. Combine caster sugar and milk in small jug; stir until sugar dissolves. Add milk mixture to flour mixture, then stir in egg yolks. Using wooden spoon, stir until mixture stiffens, then, using hand, mix until a firm dough forms.

2 Divide butter into 10 portions. Turn dough onto lightly floured surface; work each portion of butter into dough, kneading well after each addition, until all of the butter is incorporated and the dough is smooth and glossy. Place dough in lightly oiled large bowl, cover; stand in warm place about 2 hours or until dough doubles in size. (Can be refrigerated overnight at this stage.)

3 Grease 12 (⅓-cup/80ml) fluted ovenproof moulds or 12-hole (⅓-cup/80ml) muffin pan. Divide dough into 12 portions; remove about a quarter of each portion. Roll both the small and the large portions into balls. Place large balls in prepared moulds; make small indentation in top of each with fingertip, sit small round in each indentation. Brush each brioche with extra egg yolk; sprinkle with sugar. Stand, uncovered, in warm place about 1 hour or until dough doubles in size.

4 Meanwhile, preheat oven to 180°C/160°C fan-forced.

5 Bake brioche about 15 minutes. Serve warm.

NUTRITIONAL COUNT PER BRIOCHE 12.8g total fat (7.1g saturated fat); 1070kJ (256 cal); 28.7g carbohydrate; 5.9g protein; 1.3g fibre

Brioche à tête or "brioche with a head", a roll with a small ball on top of a larger one, is the shape in which sweet, butter and egg-rich brioche is most widely available, but some bakeries also make square brioche loaves or plain roll shapes. All are wonderful, slathered with jam, for breakfast, and are also great to use instead of plain bread for desserts such as bread-and-butter pudding and summer pudding. Like most breads, brioche rolls and loaves freeze well.

Piroshki

PREP + COOK TIME 55 MINUTES (PLUS STANDING TIME) **MAKES** 16

6 cups plain flour (900g)

1 tablespoon dry yeast (12g)

1 tablespoon salt

⅓ cup (75g) caster sugar

2 egg yolks

2 cups (500ml) milk, warmed

250g butter, melted

1 egg, beaten lightly

FILLING

1 tablespoon olive oil

1 medium brown onion (150g), chopped finely

1 clove garlic, crushed

250g sebago potatoes, peeled, chopped finely

2 bacon rashers (140g), rind removed, chopped finely

400g beef mince

⅓ cup (90g) tomato paste

2 teaspoons fresh thyme leaves

Piroshki or "little pies" are a Russian invention for serving as appetisers with drinks before the meal, or to accompany soups, especially the beetroot soup called borscht.

1 Combine flour, yeast, salt and sugar in large bowl. Make a well in the centre; using hand, mix in egg yolks, milk and butter until mixture is soft and elastic. Scrape down sides of bowl, cover; stand in warm place about 1 hour or until dough doubles in size.

2 Meanwhile, make the filling.

3 Turn dough onto floured surface; knead until smooth. Divide dough into 16 pieces; press each piece into 12cm round.

4 Preheat oven to 220°C/200°C fan-forced. Lightly oil two oven trays.

5 Place rounded tablespoon of the filling in centre of each round; gather edges, pinch firmly to enclose filling. Place piroshki, pinched-side down, on trays; brush with egg. Stand, uncovered, in warm place 15 minutes. Bake about 15 minutes or until golden brown.

FILLING Heat oil in large frying pan; cook onion, garlic, potato and bacon, stirring, until potato softens. Add beef; cook, stirring, until changed in colour. Stir in paste and thyme. Cool 10 minutes.

NUTRITIONAL COUNT PER PIROSHKI 20.4g total fat (11.3g saturated fat); 1881kJ (450 cal); 49.8g carbohydrate; 15.3g protein; 2.9g fibre

BREAD ROLLS

Bread rolls

PREP + COOK TIME 45 MINUTES (PLUS STANDING TIME) **MAKES** 20

2 cups (500ml) warm water

1 teaspoon sugar

2 teaspoons (7g) dried yeast

4 cups (640g) bakers' flour

2 teaspoons salt

cooking-oil spray

1 Whisk the water, sugar and yeast in medium jug until yeast dissolves, cover; stand in warm place about 15 minutes or until mixture is frothy.

2 Combine flour and salt in large bowl; stir in yeast mixture. Turn dough onto floured surface; knead about 15 minutes or until dough is smooth and elastic. Place dough in large oiled bowl, turning dough once to coat in oil. Cover; stand in warm place 1 hour or until dough doubles in size.

3 Preheat oven to 200°C/180°C fan-forced.

4 Turn dough onto lightly floured surface; knead about 1 minute or until smooth. Divide dough into quarters; divide each quarter into five pieces.

5 Shape each piece into ball; place balls 5cm apart on two oiled oven trays. Cut small cross in top of each ball; spray lightly with oil. Cover loosely with plastic wrap; stand in warm place about 20 minutes or until dough doubles in size.

6 Bake rolls about 15 minutes. Transfer to wire rack to cool.

NUTRITIONAL COUNT PER ROLL 0.5g total fat (0.1g saturated fat); 485kJ (116 cal); 23.3g carbohydrate; 3.6g protein; 1.3g fibre

These are like the crisp-crusted warm rolls served in restaurants.

For information on bakers' flour, see Flour, page 182.

Ricotta and herb calzones

PREP + COOK TIME 55 MINUTES (PLUS STANDING AND COOLING TIME) **SERVES** 4

2 cups (300g) plain flour

1 ¼ teaspoons dry yeast (5g)

½ teaspoon salt

2 teaspoons olive oil

¾ cup (180ml) warm water

8 sun-dried tomatoes (50g)

1 clove garlic, crushed

¼ teaspoon dried chilli flakes

1 medium green capsicum (200g), sliced thinly

1 cup (200g) low-fat ricotta cheese

⅓ cup (35g) coarsely grated low-fat mozzarella cheese

⅓ cup (25g) finely grated parmesan cheese

1 tablespoon coarsely chopped fresh oregano

1 tablespoon coarsely chopped fresh flat-leaf parsley

1 egg white, beaten lightly

1 Place flour, yeast and salt in large bowl; gradually stir in oil and the water, mix to a soft dough. Knead dough on floured surface about 5 minutes or until smooth and elastic. Place dough in large oiled bowl, turning dough once to coat in oil. Cover; stand in warm place about 1 hour or until dough doubles in size.

2 Meanwhile, place tomatoes in small heatproof bowl, cover with boiling water; stand 20 minutes, drain. Chop tomatoes coarsely.

3 Cook garlic, chilli and capsicum in medium heated, lightly oiled frying pan 5 minutes or until capsicum has softened. Remove from heat; stir in tomato. Cool to room temperature. Combine capsicum mixture in medium bowl with cheeses and herbs.

4 Preheat oven to 240°C/220°C fan-forced. Lightly oil two oven trays.

5 Turn dough onto floured surface; knead until smooth. Divide dough into quarters; using rolling pin, flatten dough and roll each quarter out to an 18cm round. Place a quarter of the cheese mixture in centre of dough; brush edge of dough with a little of the egg white; fold over to enclose filling, press edge to seal. Repeat with remaining dough, cheese mixture and egg white.

6 Place calzones onto trays; brush with egg white and sprinkle with a little extra salt, if you like. Cut two slits in top of each calzone. Bake calzone about 15 minutes or until browned lightly.

NUTRITIONAL COUNT PER SERVING 13.1g total fat (6.1g saturated fat); 1898kJ (454 cal); 60.6g carbohydrate; 22.6g protein; 5.5g fibre

Yogurt

Yogurt has been used as a staple food for centuries in Balkan, Middle Eastern, central Asian and Indian kitchens. Cooks in those countries use it daily as a dressing or ingredient in countless soups, dips, meat and vegetable dishes, desserts, cakes and pastries, as well as making it into a cheese or a refreshing drink. The West has taken to it with enthusiasm but, as yet, most of us eat it mainly on its own as a portable snack which is available in many flavours.

The Indian yogurt drink called lassi is a perfect hot-day refresher and accompaniment to curries and other spicy foods. For a sweet saffron lassi, combine pinch saffron threads and 1 tablespoon boiling water in small heatproof cup and stand 5 minutes. Whisk 2 cups yogurt, 1 cup iced water, 2 tablespoons caster sugar and ½ teaspoon ground cardamom in large jug then stir in saffron mixture. Serve lassi over ice cubes.

To make yogurt, milk is fermented by a bacterial culture which sets it into a semi-solid. Part of the process is that the bacteria convert most of the lactose (milk sugar) in the milk to lactic acid, giving the new product its typical sharp taste; this also makes it a suitable food for people who are lactose intolerant. Yogurt is easy to make at home. The milk may be cow, sheep, goat or buffalo (or, in some countries, reindeer, mare, camel or yak), and may be full-cream or skimmed. Commercial yogurt usually contains added powdered milk to boost the protein level and give smoothness and thickness, and may also contain stabilisers such as gelatine or starch to help prevent it from separating from physical shocks during transport and handling. Some brands contain live bacterial cultures that are believed to confer health benefits, including re-establishing flora needed for a healthy gut if these have been depleted, for example by antibiotics. All yogurt is easily digested and nourishing, being an excellent source of calcium and protein, though flavoured ones may also have high sugar levels. Commercial yoghurt is available in set or stirred forms.

SET YOGURT is made in the tub or jar in which it will be sold, so that the smooth, unbroken curd is not disturbed and retains the whey in its delicate structure. For flavoured or fruit yogurt, the appropriate ingredients are added to the milk before it is fermented.

STIRRED YOGURT is made in a large vat; once the degree of setting reaches the desired level it is pumped through a cooler to stop the process. For flavoured or fruit yogurt, the appropriate ingredients are mixed through before it is filled into tubs, or may be placed in the tubs before they are filled. Stirred yogurt gradually leaks whey because its structure has been disturbed; the whey is easily stirred back into the curd or can be poured off. Greek-style yogurt is full-cream, stirred, natural (unflavoured) yogurt which is especially thick as it has been drained of whey.

COW'S MILK YOGURT is a good all-round yogurt because it suits sweet as well as savoury flavours.

SHEEP'S MILK YOGURT, if full-cream, has higher protein and fat levels than cow's milk yogurt. It is white and satiny with the distinctive earthy aftertaste of sheep's milk, which marries well with spicy and savoury flavours.

GOAT'S MILK YOGURT has comparable protein and fat levels to cow's milk. It is white and silky and has the distinctive earthy flavour of goat's milk, which is well suited to spicy and savoury flavours.

BUFFALO'S MILK YOGURT is mild and naturally sweet, with a smooth and silky/creamy texture. It suits sweet as well as savoury flavours.

LABNE is a soft cheese made by salting plain (natural) yogurt and draining it of whey for up to 2 days until it becomes thick enough to roll into small balls, which may be scattered with or rolled in chopped herbs or spices. Stored in a flat container and covered with olive oil, they keep for weeks and are served with flatbread as a snack or as part of a mezze table (small dishes served before the meal in Greece and the Middle East in the same way as Italian antipasto).

SOY YOGURT is not a dairy product but is made from soy milk (see Soya, page 552). It contains added thickener and tastes like sharper-flavoured soy milk.

CHOOSING
Yogurt keeps well but its flavour does become more acid over time, so it is best to check the use-by dates and buy those with the longest time to go. If you want natural yogurt, check the label carefully, as sweetened but otherwise unflavoured ones don't always show this clearly.

STORING
Store yogurt in airtight containers in the refrigerator for up to 3 weeks; store labne in oil, in a covered container, for up to 4 weeks.

❦ OTHER RECIPES USING YOGURT
Bircher muesli, p234
Burghul-stuffed vine leaves with yogurt dip, p640
Crisp potato and peanut cakes, p454
Dukkah-crusted lamb cutlets with roasted garlic yogurt, p566
Grilled nectarines with passionfruit yogurt, p332
Lamb korma, p289
Moroccan carrot dip, p90
Onion and spinach pakoras with cucumber raita, p377
Potato and asparagus salad with yogurt and mint dressing, p554
Turkish beetroot dip, p57

Chilled yogurt, cucumber and mint soup

PREP TIME 10 MINUTES (PLUS REFRIGERATION TIME) **SERVES** 4

3 medium green cucumbers (510g), peeled, grated coarsely

1 clove garlic, quartered

1 tablespoon lemon juice

1 tablespoon coarsely chopped fresh mint

500g greek-style yogurt

1 Place cucumber in sieve over bowl, cover; refrigerate 3 hours or overnight. Reserve cucumber liquid in bowl. Squeeze excess liquid from cucumber.

2 Blend or process cucumber, garlic, juice and mint until mixture is smooth; transfer to large bowl. Stir yogurt into cucumber mixture then add reserved cucumber liquid, a little at a time, stirring, until soup is of desired consistency.

3 Serve bowls of soup topped with extra mint and toasted turkish bread.

NUTRITIONAL COUNT PER SERVING 8.9g total fat (5.7g saturated fat); 715kJ (171 cal); 13.9g carbohydrate; 7.6g protein; 0.8g fibre

Make this refreshing soup no more than 20 minutes before serving time as chopped mint goes black if left to stand too long.

For information on green cucumber, see Cucumbers, page 146.

Spicy yogurt dipping sauce

PREP + COOK TIME 10 MINUTES **MAKES** 1½ CUPS

1 teaspoon sweet paprika

1 teaspoon ground cinnamon

1 teaspoon ground coriander

1 teaspoon ground cumin

2 teaspoons fennel seeds

4cm piece fresh ginger (20g) grated

1 tablespoon sambal oelek

1¼ cups (350g) yogurt

1 tablespoon lemon juice

1 Dry-fry paprika, cinnamon, coriander, cumin and seeds in small frying pan, stirring over low heat until fragrant.

2 Combine roasted spices with ginger, sambal, yogurt and juice in small bowl.

NUTRITIONAL COUNT PER TABLESPOON 0.7g total fat (0.4g saturated fat); 67kJ (16 cal); 1.3g carbohydrate; 0.9g protein; 0g fibre

This quantity is enough to go with 6 servings of fried chicken drumettes, grilled pork fillets or cutlets or roasted potato wedges. The sauce can be made up to 2 days ahead and refrigerated until needed.

Cucumber raita

PREP + COOK TIME 10 MINUTES **SERVES** 6

2 teaspoons vegetable oil

¼ teaspoon black mustard seeds

¼ teaspoon cumin seeds

2 lebanese cucumbers (260g), seeded, chopped finely

500g yogurt

1 Heat oil in small frying pan; cook seeds, stirring, over low heat, 2 minutes or until seeds pop. Combine seeds and remaining ingredients in medium bowl; mix well.

NUTRITIONAL COUNT PER SERVE 4.4g total fat (2g saturated fat); 314kJ (75 cal); 4.5g carbohydrate; 4.1g protein; 0.4g fibre

Raita or yogurt sauce can be served as a cooling accompaniment for curry or pilaf. Stand raita for 30 minutes after making to allow the flavours to blend.

For information on lebanese cucumbers, see Cucumbers, page 146.

Labne

PREP TIME 20 MINUTES (PLUS REFRIGERATION TIME) **MAKES** 24

3 cups (840g) greek-style yogurt

3 teaspoons salt

¼ cup (60ml) olive oil

1 Combine yogurt and salt in medium bowl; pour into muslin-lined large sieve or colander set over large bowl. Gather corners of muslin together, twist, then tie with kitchen string. Place heavy can on muslin to weight yogurt mixture; refrigerate 24 to 36 hours until yogurt thickens (yogurt will lose about half its weight in water; discard water in bowl).

2 Place thickened yogurt in small bowl; discard muslin. Roll level tablespoons of yogurt into balls; place balls on platter, drizzle with oil.

NUTRITIONAL COUNT PER BALL 3.6g total fat (1.1g saturated fat); 188kJ (45 cal); 1.6g carbohydrate; 1.6g protein; 0g fibre

Labne will keep for up to 2 months in the fridge: pack the balls into a clean glass jar with a tight-fitting lid, pour in olive oil to cover them completely and seal tightly before refrigerating.

1 LABNE
2 GREEK YOGURT CAKE

Greek yogurt cake

PREP + COOK TIME 55 MINUTES (PLUS COOLING TIME) **SERVES** 12

125g butter, softened
1 cup (220g) caster sugar
3 eggs, separated
2 cups (300g) self-raising flour

½ teaspoon bicarbonate of soda
¼ cup (40g) finely chopped blanched almonds
1 cup (280g) yogurt

Serve this delicate cake, cut into squares, with coffee, fruit or both.

1 Preheat oven to 180°C/160°C fan-forced. Grease 20cm x 30cm lamington pan; line base and sides with baking paper.

2 Beat butter and sugar in small bowl with electric mixer until light and fluffy. Add egg yolks, beat well. Transfer mixture to large bowl; stir in sifted flour and soda in two batches, then nuts and yogurt.

3 Beat egg whites in small bowl with electric mixer until soft peaks form. Gently fold egg whites into yogurt mixture in two batches. Spread mixture into pan.

4 Bake cake about 35 minutes. Turn cake onto wire rack to cool; dust with sifted icing sugar, if you like.

NUTRITIONAL COUNT PER SERVING 12.8g total fat (6.7g saturated fat); 1216kJ (291 cal); 37.3g carbohydrate; 5.9g protein; 1.2g fibre

Zucchini

Zucchini (courgettes in France and Britain) are delicate and delicious when treated properly, watery and flavourless when boiled too long. In fact, these smallest members (with patty pan squash) of the squash family are best if not boiled at all but steamed, fried, or baked with or without a stuffing such as minced meat or cheese sauce.

1 LEBANESE OR
GREY ZUCCHINI
2 GREEN ZUCCHINI
3 YELLOW ZUCCHINI
4 PATTY PAN SQUASH
5 ZUCCHINI FLOWERS

They are also excellent coarsely grated and mixed with herbs for a salad to go with a grill, or grated and tossed in foaming butter with a touch of nutmeg just until hot. They go beautifully with spices and rich flavours and are happy sliced into curry, ratatouille or risotto so long as they are added late in the cooking so that the slices will be just softened. Zucchini flowers are a summer treat to dip into batter and deep-fry or stuff with a savoury mixture, coat with egg and breadcrumbs and pan-fry.

Cooks debate whether zucchini should be disgorged (salted and drained of any bitter juices) before using, but you only need to find once that your beautifully cooked zucchini are bitter to come down on the side of disgorging, except for definitely young and tender babies. Zucchini are available in green or yellow and are available all year round. Patty pan squash are also available all year and can be treated in the same ways as zucchini.

CHOOSING The smaller, the better is a good rule for buying zucchini and small squash, unless a certain size is required for stuffing. Whatever the size, they should be brightly coloured with a sheen on the skin, and firm with no soft spots.

STORING Enclose zucchini or squash in a paper bag, then in a plastic one; store in the refrigerator. Use within a few days.

These delectable little fritters are great served with a tomato and herb salad.

Zucchini and sumac fritters

PREP + COOK TIME 25 MINUTES   **SERVES** 4

6 medium zucchini (700g), grated coarsely

1 medium brown onion (150g), chopped finely

1¼ cups (85g) stale breadcrumbs

3 eggs

2 tablespoons finely chopped fresh oregano

1 teaspoon sumac

2 tablespoons olive oil

1 Squeeze excess liquid from zucchini using absorbent paper until as dry as possible. Combine zucchini in medium bowl with onion, breadcrumbs, eggs, oregano and sumac.
2 Heat oil in large frying pan; drop rounded tablespoons of zucchini mixture, in batches, into pan. Cook until browned both sides and cooked through.

NUTRITIONAL COUNT PER SERVING 14.4g total fat (2.6g saturated fat); 1066kJ (255 cal); 18.9g carbohydrate; 10.6g protein; 4.3g fibre

**⚜ OTHER RECIPES
USING ZUCCHINI**
Chicken green curry, p462–3
*Grilled corn and zucchini salsa,
   p140*
Ham and zucchini quiche, p259
*Rigatoni with zucchini,
   lemon and mint, p398*
*Roasted vegetable lasagne,
   p402–3*
Tofu zucchini patties, p603

Oven-roasted ratatouille

PREP + COOK TIME 1 HOUR 25 MINUTES **SERVES** 4

1 medium eggplant (300g), chopped coarsely

6 small tomatoes (540g), peeled, chopped coarsely

4 cloves garlic, sliced thinly

1 tablespoon olive oil

2 tablespoons tomato paste

1 large red onion (300g), chopped coarsely

1 small red capsicum (150g), chopped coarsely

1 small green capsicum (150g), chopped coarsely

2 medium zucchini (240g), chopped coarsely

1 Preheat oven to 200°C/180°C fan-forced.

2 Combine eggplant, tomato, garlic, oil, paste, onion, capsicum and zucchini in large baking dish. Roast, covered, 40 minutes. Uncover; roast about 20 minutes or until vegetables are tender.

3 Serve ratatouille with couscous.

NUTRITIONAL COUNT PER SERVING 5.4g total fat (0.7g saturated fat); 564kJ (135 cal); 12.9g carbohydrate; 5.4g protein; 6.9g fibre

---

Summer squash salad

PREP + COOK TIME 30 MINUTES **SERVES** 4

A salad like this, chunky and flavoursome, is the right kind for a barbecue or pool party. Serve it while the squash and potatoes are still warm, if possible, but it will also be good cold.

500g yellow patty-pan squash, halved

500g green patty-pan squash, halved

200g baby new potatoes, halved

⅓ cup (80ml) olive oil

2 tablespoons lemon juice

1 clove garlic, crushed

1 tablespoon finely chopped fresh dill

250g cherry tomatoes, halved

1 cup loosely packed fresh flat-leaf parsley leaves

1 Boil, steam or microwave squash and potatoes, separately, until tender; drain.

2 Combine warm squash and potatoes with remaining ingredients in large bowl.

NUTRITIONAL COUNT PER SERVING 18.9g total fat (2.6g saturated fat); 1191 kJ (285 cal); 16.6g carbohydrate; 8.4g protein; 8.6g fibre

1 SUMMER SQUASH SALAD
2 LEMON AND RICOTTA-FILLED
ZUCCHINI FLOWERS

Lemon and ricotta-filled zucchini flowers

PREP + COOK TIME 45 MINUTES **SERVES** 4

250g ricotta cheese

2 tablespoons finely grated parmesan cheese

1 teaspoon finely grated lemon rind

1 tablespoon lemon juice

1 tablespoon finely chopped fresh mint

2 tablespoons roasted pine nuts

12 zucchini flowers with stem attached (240g)

1 Combine cheeses, rind, juice, mint and nuts in small bowl.

2 Discard stamens from inside zucchini flowers; fill flowers with cheese mixture, twist petal tops to enclose filling.

3 Place zucchini flowers, in single layer, in large bamboo steamer, over large saucepan of boiling water. Steam, covered, about 20 minutes or until zucchini are tender.

NUTRITIONAL COUNT PER SERVING 13.4g total fat (5.5g saturated fat); 711kJ (170 cal); 2.2g carbohydrate; 9.6g protein; 1.4g fibre

Four people could eat these very happily as a stand-alone first course or lunch dish, or 6 could enjoy them as a superb vegetable accompaniment to veal or chicken schnitzel.

For information on ricotta and parmesan cheeses, see Cheese, pages 100 & 104.

Conversion Charts

One Australian metric measuring cup or jug holds approximately 250ml; one Australian metric tablespoon holds 20ml; one Australian metric teaspoon holds 5ml.

The difference between one country's measuring cups and another's is within a two- or three-teaspoon variance, which is only 10 or 15ml and will not affect your cooking results. Most countries, including the US, the UK and New Zealand, use a 15ml tablespoon.

All cup and spoon measurements are level. The most accurate way of measuring dry ingredients is to weigh them. When measuring liquids, use a clear glass or plastic jug with metric markings at eye level.

In this book we used large eggs with an average weight of 60g each. Please note that those who might be at risk from the effects of salmonella poisoning (such as pregnant women, the elderly or young children) should consult their doctor before eating raw eggs.

OVEN TEMPERATURES

These oven temperatures are only a guide for conventional ovens. For fan-forced ovens, check the manufacturer's manual.

	°C (CELSIUS)	°F (FAHRENHEIT)	GAS MARK
Very slow	120	250	½
Slow	150	275-300	1-2
Moderately slow	160	325	3
Moderate	180	350-375	4-5
Moderately hot	200	400	6
Hot	220	425-450	7-8
Very hot	240	475	9

DRY MEASURES

METRIC	IMPERIAL
15g	½oz
30g	1oz
60g	2oz
90g	3oz
125g	4oz (¼lb)
155g	5oz
185g	6oz
220g	7oz
250g	8oz (½lb)
280g	9oz
315g	10oz
345g	11oz
375g	12oz (¾lb)
410g	13oz
440g	14oz
470g	15oz
500g	16oz (1lb)
750g	24oz (1½lb)
1kg	32oz (2lb)

LIQUID MEASURES

METRIC	IMPERIAL
30ml	1 fluid oz
60ml	2 fluid oz
100ml	3 fluid oz
125ml	4 fluid oz
150ml	5 fluid oz (¼ pint/1 gill)
190ml	6 fluid oz
250ml	8 fluid oz
300ml	10 fluid oz (½ pint)
500ml	16 fluid oz
600ml	20 fluid oz (1 pint)
1000ml (1 litre)	1¾ pints

LENGTH MEASURES

METRIC	IMPERIAL
3mm	⅛in
6mm	¼in
1cm	½in
2cm	¾in
2.5cm	1in
5cm	2in
6cm	2½in
8cm	3in
10cm	4in
13cm	5in
15cm	6in
18cm	7in
20cm	8in
23cm	9in
25cm	10in
28cm	11in
30cm	12in (1ft)

Glossary

APPLE CIDER, SPARKLING unfermented non-alcoholic type of apple juice with sugar added to make it effervescent.

BAKING POWDER a raising agent consisting mainly of two parts cream of tartar to one part bicarbonate of soda. Gluten-free baking powder is also available; suitable for people with an allergic response to glutens or seeking an alternative to everyday baking powder.

BICARBONATE OF SODA also known as baking soda.

BISCUITS

butternut snap biscuits made from sugar, flour, rolled oats, butter, coconut and golden syrup.

plain chocolate crunchy biscuits made from cocoa; uniced.

plain sweet crisp, sweet and vanilla flavoured; any plain sweet biscuit can be used.

BONITO FLAKES fish from the mackerel family. It is available in dried flaked form, and is an ingredient of Japanese dashi.

BRAN FLAKES a breakfast cereal based on processed wheat bran enriched with vitamins.

BRANDY short for brandywine, the translation of the Dutch "brandwijn", burnt wine. A general term for a liqueur distilled from wine grapes (usually white), it is used as the basis for many sweet-to-dry spirits made with fruits. Cognac and Armagnac are two of the finest aged brandies available.

BREADCRUMBS

fresh bread, usually white, processed into crumbs. *see also BREAD page 67 on making fresh breadcrumbs*

packaged fine-textured, crunchy, purchased, white breadcrumbs.

stale one- or two-day-old bread made into crumbs by grating, blending or processing.

CHAMPAGNE we used a sweet sparkling wine in this book.

CHERRY RIPE BARS dark chocolate bar made with coconut and cherries; standard size bar weighs 55g.

CHINESE COOKING WINE made from rice, wheat, sugar and salt, with 13.5% alcohol; available from Asian food stores. Mirin or sherry can be substituted.

COCOA POWDER also known as unsweetened cocoa; cocoa beans (cacao seeds) that have been fermented, roasted, shelled, ground into powder then cleared of most of the fat content. Unsweetened cocoa is used in hot chocolate drink mixtures; milk powder and sugar are added to the ground product.

CORNICHON is the French word for gherkin, a very small variety of cucumber. Pickled, they are traditionally served with pâté; the Swiss always serve them with fondue or raclette.

CREAM OF TARTAR the acid ingredient in baking powder; added to confectionery mixtures to help prevent sugar crystallising. Keeps frostings creamy and improves volume when beating egg whites.

CUSTARD POWDER instant mixture used to make pouring custard; similar to North American instant pudding mixes.

FOOD COLOURING vegetable-based substances; available as liquid, paste or gel.

GINGER WINE beverage 14% alcohol by volume, has the taste of fresh ginger. In cooking, you can use dry vermouth instead.

ICE-CREAM we use a good quality ice-cream having 5g of fat per 100ml for the recipes in this book.

LIQUEUR *see also brandy, champagne, marsala, rum, sherry, vermouth, wine*

coconut-flavoured we use malibu.

coffee-flavoured we use kahlua, but you could also use crème de cacao or tia maria.

cointreau citrus-flavoured liqueur.

crème de cacao chocolate-flavoured liqueur.

curaçao orange-flavoured liqueur.

frangelico hazelnut-flavoured liqueur.

grand marnier orange-flavoured liqueur based on Cognac-brandy.

kahlua coffee-flavoured liqueur.

malibu coconut-flavoured rum.

orange-flavoured we use cointreau, but you could also use curaçao or Grand Marnier.

pernod an aniseed-flavoured liqueur.

tia maria coffee-flavoured liqueur.

vodka clear, colourless, flavourless spirit.

MARSALA a fortified Italian wine produced in the region surrounding the Sicilian city of Marsala; recognisable by its intense amber colour and complex aroma. Often used in cooking.

MAYONNAISE we use whole-egg mayonnaise; a commercial mayonnaise of high quality made with whole eggs and labelled as such. Some prepared mayonnaises substitute emulsifiers such as food starch, cellulose gel or other thickeners to achieve the same thick and creamy consistency but never achieve the same rich flavour. Must be refrigerated once opened.

MIRIN a sweet low-alcohol rice wine used in Japanese cooking; sometimes referred to simply as rice wine but should not be confused with sake, the Japanese rice wine made for drinking.

ORANGE FLOWER WATER distilled from orange blossoms.

RICE WINE *see mirin*

ROSEWATER extract made from crushed rose petals.

RUM we use a dark underproof rum (not overproof) for a more subtle flavour in cooking. White rum is almost colourless, sweet and used mostly in mixed drinks.

SASHIMI fish sold as sashimi has to meet stringent guidelines regarding its handling. We suggest you seek local advice from authorities before easting any raw seafood. *see also page 546*

SAMBAL OELEK also ulek or olek; Indonesian in origin, this is a salty paste made from ground chillies and vinegar.

SAUCE

barbecue spicy, tomato-based sauce used to marinate, baste or as an accompaniment.

hot chilli we use a hot Asian variety made from bird's-eye chillies, salt and vinegar. Use sparingly, increasing the quantity to suit your taste.

sweet chilli comparatively mild, fairly sticky and runny bottled sauce made from red chillies, sugar, garlic and white vinegar; used in Thai cooking.

tabasco brand-name of an extremely fiery sauce made from vinegar, hot red peppers and salt.

tomato also known as ketchup or catsup; a flavoured condiment made from tomatoes, vinegar and spices.

tonkatsu a Japanese dipping sauce traditionally served with the crumbed pork cutlet dish called tonkatsu. The sauce consists of tomato sauce (ketchup), japanese soy sauce, worcestershire sauce, mustard and sake in varying proportions.

vegetarian mushroom oyster a "vegetarian" oyster sauce made from blended mushrooms and soy sauce.

worcestershire thin, dark-brown spicy sauce developed by the British when in India; used as a seasoning for meat, gravies and cocktails, and as a condiment.

SHERRY fortified wine consumed as an aperitif or used in cooking. Sold as fino (light, dry), amontillado (medium sweet, dark) and oloroso (full-bodied, very dark).

STOCK available in cans or tetra packs; stock cubes or powder can also be used. As a guide, 1 teaspoon of stock powder or 1 small crumbled stock cube mixed with 1 cup (250ml) water will give a fairly strong stock. Be aware of the salt and fat content of stock cubes and powders and prepared stocks.

TOMATO

bottled pasta sauce a prepared sauce made of a blend of tomatoes, herbs and spices.

canned whole peeled tomatoes in natural juices; available crushed, chopped or diced, sometimes unsalted or reduced salt. Use in recipes undrained.

paste triple-concentrated tomato puree used to flavour soups, stews, sauces and casseroles.

TOP 'N' FILL CARAMEL a canned milk product made of condensed milk that has been boiled to a caramel.

TORTILLA thin, round unleavened bread originating in Mexico; can be made at home or purchased frozen, fresh or vacuum-packed. Wheat and corn flour varieties are available.

VERMOUTH a wine flavoured with a number of different herbs, mostly used as an aperitif and for cocktails.

WINE the adage is that you should never cook with wine you wouldn't drink; we use good-quality dry white and red wines in our recipes.

Index

Entries and/or page numbers in italics refer to the sidebar text.

T

tabbouleh 232
tagine 288
  lamb, apricot and almond 288
  quince and chicken 486
tahini 161
  taratoor sauce 544
tamarillo 594
  choosing 594
  preparation 594
  storing 594
  tamarillo apple chutney 594
tamarind 595
  date and tamarind chutney 467
  preparation 595
  spicy tamarind chicken 596–7
  storing 595
  tamarind and citrus pork curry 597
  tamarind and soy sauce 595
tandoori curry paste 152
tangelos 380–1
tapenade, black olive 373
tapioca 230
taratoor sauce 544
tarragon 266
  dressing 240
tartare sauce 529
tarts
  caramel cashew 349
  caramelised fennel 176
  gruyère, leek and bacon 406
  lime curd 301
  onion and anchovy tartlets 378
  peach and apricot 414
  portuguese custard 409
  quince tarte tatin 487
  sweet cherry and almond tarts 116
tat soi 242
tayberries 58–9
tea 598–9
  blends 598
  ginseng and star anise tea 599
  green tea ice-cream with
    fruit salsa 601
  indian chai 600
  making 598–9
  raspberry mint iced tea 601
  spiced rosehip and hibiscus tea 599
  storing 599
tea cakes
  caramelised apple 12
teriyaki sauce 508
  lamb teriyaki with broccolini 512
terrine de campagne 359
thai apple eggplant 160
thai coconut scallops 541
thai cucumber pickle 148
thai cucumber sauce 511
thai green curry paste 152
thai pea eggplant 160
thai red curry paste 152

thai salmon broth with sesame
  sticky rice patties 628
thai-style green mango salad with
  seared tuna 309
thousand island dressing 536
thyme 266
  dressing 56
tikka paste 152–3
tiramisu, individual 113
toasts
  anchovy 391
  grilled cheese 608
toffee banana and date upside-down
  cake 37
toffee figs, baby 584
tofu 602
  age-dashi tofu 603
  chicken and water chestnut
    tofu pouches 604–5
  salt and pepper tofu with
    chilli lime dressing 604
  sesame tofu salad 545
  storing 602
  tofu zucchini patties 603
  types 602
tom ka gai 206–7
tomatoes 606–7
  anchovy and garlic tuna with
    tomato and oregano 531
  avocado, cos and tomato salad 27
  baked mushrooms with tomato
    and basil 327
  basic tomato pasta sauce 609
  bottled pasta sauce 663
  braised borlotti beans with
    tomato and garlic 42
  canned 663
  cheese gnocchi with fresh tomato
    sauce and pancetta 109
  chilli tomato relish 474–5
  choosing 607
  fresh tomato and herb sauce 571
  gazpacho 610
  lamb and okra in rich tomato sauce
    with garlic confit 369
  mixed tomato caprese salad 608
  okra and tomato in coconut sauce 369
  paste 663
  peeling 606
  roasted mixed tomato salad 613
  roasted tomato salad 87
  roasted truss tomatoes with
    crispy basil leaves 612
  seared scallops with pea puree
    and tomato 631
  spicy veal pizzaiola 610
  steamed mussels in tomato
    garlic broth 535
  storing 607
  sun-dried tomato mayonnaise 612
  tomato and basil sauce 592–3
  tomato and bean salad 590

(*tomatoes* continued)
  tomato and fennel soup 608
  tomato braised lamb shanks 285
  tomato, fetta and pancetta
    frittatas 166
  tomato mustard beef with
    baby fennel 48
  tomato onion raita 454
  varieties 606–7
  veal and tomato dolmades 639
tongue 354–5
tortilla *517*, 663
  spanish 169
trail mix, dried fruit and coconut 195
treacle 579
trifle
  plum and amaretti 434
  rhubarb, white chocolate and
    ginger trifles 491
tripe *354*, 355
trout
  smoked ocean trout kedgeree 503
truffles 323
  white chocolate, lemon and
    thyme truffles 128
tuna
  anchovy and garlic tuna with
    tomato and oregano 531
  salade niçoise with caperberries 83
  sashimi-grade 546
  sesame-crusted sashimi 546
  thai-style green mango salad
    with seared tuna 309
  tuna cucumber mini-maki 543
turkey
  carving 458
  honey-glazed, with orange-pecan
    stuffing 458
  mixed pea and turkey salad 426
  turkey, cranberry and sprout salad 573
turkish beetroot dip 57
turkish bread 67
turmeric 559
turnips 614
  choosing 614
  moroccan turnip soup 615
  pickled 614
  preparation 614
  storing 614
tzatziki 161

V

vanilla 616
  choosing 616
  mixed berry cake with vanilla
    bean syrup 617
  storing 616
  vanilla bean ice-cream 144
  vanilla bean thins 617
  vanilla spice cheesecake 618
vanilla bean paste *421*, 616

General manager *Christine Whiston*
Editor-in-chief *Susan Tomnay*
Creative director & designer *Hieu Chi Nguyen*
Senior editor *Stephanie Kistner*
Writer *Meg Thomason*
Food director *Pamela Clark*
Food editor *Cathie Lonnie*
Sales & rights director *Brian Cearnes*
Marketing manager *Bridget Cody*
Senior business analyst *Rebecca Varela*
Circulation manager *Jarna Mclean*
Operations manager *David Scotto*
Production manager *Victoria Jefferys*

ACP Books are published by ACP Magazines
a division of PBL Media Pty Limited
PBL Media, Chief Executive Officer *Ian Law*
Publishing & sales director, Women's lifestyle *Lynette Phillips*
Editor at large, Women's lifestyle *Pat Ingram*
Marketing director, Women's lifestyle *Matthew Dominello*
Commercial manager, Women's lifestyle *Seymour Cohen*
Research Director, Women's lifestyle *Justin Stone*

Photographers *Stuart Scott, Andre Martin*
Stylist *Vicki Liley*
Home economists *Rebecca Squadrito, Dominique Gekas*

The publishers would like to thank the following
for props used in photography
*Afghan Interiors; Ici et la; Leung Tim Choppers Company;
Michael's Shoppe; That Vintage Shop; Venucci.*

Produced by ACP Books, Sydney. Published by ACP Books, a division of ACP Magazines Ltd.
54 Park St, Sydney NSW Australia 2000. GPO Box 4088, Sydney, NSW 2001.
Phone +61 2 9282 8618 Fax +61 2 9267 9438
acpbooks@acpmagazines.com.au www.acpbooks.com.au
Printed by C&C Offset Printing, China.

Australia Distributed by Network Services, GPO Box 4088, Sydney, NSW 2001.
Phone +61 2 9282 8777 Fax +61 2 9264 3278 networkweb@networkservicescompany.com.au
United Kingdom Distributed by Australian Consolidated Press (UK),
10 Scirocco Close, Moulton Park Office Village, Northampton, NN3 6AP.
Phone +44 1604 642 200 Fax +44 1604 642 300 books@acpuk.com www.acpuk.com
Canada Distributed by Publishers Group Canada, Unit 402, 559 College Street, Toronto, Ontario
M6G 1A9. Phone (416) 934 9900 or (800) 747 8147 Fax (416) 9341410 www.pgcbooks.ca
Order Desk & Customer Service, 9050 Shaughnessy Street, Vancouver, BC V6P 6E5
Phone (800) 663 5714 Fax (800) 565 3770 service@raincoast.com
New Zealand Distributed by Southern Publishers Group, 21 Newton Road, Auckland, NZ.
Phone +64 9 360 0692 Fax +64 9 360 0695 hub@spg.co.nz
South Africa Distributed by PSD Promotions, 30 Diesel Road Isando, Gauteng Johannesburg.
PO Box 1175, Isando 1600, Gauteng Johannesburg.
Phone +27 11 392 6065/6/7 Fax +27 11 392 6079/80 orders@psdprom.co.za

Title: The complete cook / food director Pamela Clark.
ISBN: 978-1-86396-877-5
Notes: Includes index.
Subjects: Cookery; Health.
Other authors/contributors: Clark, Pamela
Also titled: Australian women's weekly.
Dewey number: 641.5

© ACP Magazines Ltd 2009
ABN 18 053 273 546
This publication is copyright. No part of it may be reproduced or transmitted
in any form without the written permission of the publishers.

To order books, phone 136 116 (within Australia) or online at www.acpbooks.com.au
Send recipe enquiries to: recipeenquiries@acpmagazines.com.au